Mike Meyers

CompTIA A+®
Guide to 802: Managing and Troubleshooting PCs

Fourth Edition
(Exam 220-802)

Mike Meyers'

CompTIA A+®
Guide to 802: Managing and Troubleshooting PCs

Fourth Edition
(Exam 220-802)

Mike Meyers

New York Chicago San Francisco
Lisbon London Madrid Mexico City Milan
New Delhi San Juan Seoul Singapore Sydney Toronto

The **McGraw·Hill** Companies

Cataloging-in-Publication Data is on file with the Library of Congress

Mike Meyers' CompTIA A+® Guide to 802: Managing and Troubleshooting PCs, Fourth Edition (Exam 220-802)

1234567890 QDB QDB 1098765432

ISBN: Book p/n 978-0-07-179594-4 and CD p/n 978-0-07-179596-8 of set 978-0-07-179597-5

MHID: Book p/n 0-07-179594-4 and CD p/n 0-07-179596-0 of set 0-07-179597-9

Sponsoring Editor
TIMOTHY GREEN

Editorial Supervisor
JANET WALDEN

Project Manager
YASHMITA HOTA,
CENVEO PUBLISHER SERVICES

Acquisitions Coordinator
STEPHANIE EVANS

Technical Editor
CHRISTOPHER A. CRAYTON

Copy Editor
BILL MCMANUS

Proofreaders
EMILIA THIURI AND PAUL TYLER

Indexer
JACK LEWIS

Production Supervisor
JAMES KUSSOW

Composition
CENVEO PUBLISHER SERVICES

Illustration
FORD PIERSON AND
CENVEO PUBLISHER SERVICES

Art Director, Cover
JEFF WEEKS

■ About the Author

Mike Meyers, lovingly called the "AlphaGeek" by those who know him, is the industry's leading authority on CompTIA A+ certification. He is the president and co-founder of Total Seminars, LLC, a provider of PC and network repair seminars, books, videos, and courseware for thousands of organizations throughout the world. Mike has been involved in the computer and network repair industry since 1977 as a technician, instructor, author, consultant, and speaker.

Author of numerous popular PC books and videos, including the best-selling *CompTIA A+ Certification All-in-One Exam Guide*, Mike is also the series editor for the highly successful *Mike Meyers' Certification Passport* series, the *Mike Meyers' Computer Skills* series, and the *Mike Meyers' Guide to* series, all published by McGraw-Hill.

As well as writing, Mike has personally taught (and continues to teach) thousands of students, including U.S. senators, U.S. Supreme Court justices, the United Nations, every branch of the U.S. Armed Forces, most branches of the Department of Justice, hundreds of corporate clients, academic students at every level, prisoners, and pensioners.

> E-mail: michaelm@totalsem.com
> Facebook: Mike Meyers (Houston, TX)
> Twitter/Skype/most instant messaging clients: desweds
> Web forums: www.totalsem.com/forums

About the Editor in Chief

Scott Jernigan wields a mighty red pen as Editor in Chief for Total Seminars. With a Master of Arts degree in Medieval History, Scott feels as much at home in the musty archives of London as he does in the warm CRT glow of Total Seminars' Houston headquarters. After fleeing a purely academic life, he dove headfirst into IT, working as an instructor, editor, and writer.

Scott has written, edited, and contributed to dozens of books on computer literacy, hardware, operating systems, networking, and certification, including *Computer Literacy—Your Ticket to IC³ Certification*, and co-authoring with Mike Meyers the *All-in-One CompTIA Strata® IT Fundamentals Exam Guide*.

Scott has taught computer classes all over the United States, including stints at the United Nations in New York and the FBI Academy in Quantico. Practicing what he preaches, Scott is a CompTIA A+ and CompTIA Network+ certified technician, a Microsoft Certified Professional, a Microsoft Office User Specialist, and Certiport Internet and Computing Core Certified.

About the Technical Editor

Chris Crayton (CompTIA A+, CompTIA Network+, MCSE) is an author, editor, technical consultant, and trainer. Mr. Crayton has worked as a computer and networking instructor at Keiser University, as network administrator for Protocol, an eCRM company, and as a computer and network

specialist at Eastman Kodak. Mr. Crayton has authored several print and online books on PC Repair, CompTIA A+, CompTIA Security+, and Microsoft Windows. Mr. Crayton has served as technical editor on numerous professional technical titles for leading publishing companies, including the *CompTIA A+ All-in-One Exam Guide*, the *CompTIA A+ Certification Study Guide*, and the *Mike Meyers' CompTIA A+ Certification Passport*.

Peer Reviewers

Thank you to the reviewers, past and present, who contributed insightful reviews, criticisms, and helpful suggestions that continue to shape this textbook.

Donat Forrest
Broward County Community College
Pembroke Pines, FL

Brian Ives
Finger Lakes Community College
Canadaigua, NY

Farbod Karimi
Heald College
San Francisco, CA

Tamie Knaebel
Jefferson Community College
Louisville, KY

Keith Lyons
Cuyahoga Community College
Parma, OH

Winston Maddox
Mercer County Community College
West Windsor, NJ

Rajiv Malkan
Montgomery College
Conroe, Texas

Scott Sweitzer
Indiana Business College
Indianapolis, IN

Randall Stratton
DeVry University
Irving, TX

Thomas Trevethan
CPI College of Technology
Virginia Beach, VA

■ Acknowledgments

Scott Jernigan, my Editor in Chief at Total Seminars and boon companion on many an evening, worked his *usual* magic *again* pulling together this latest edition. My thanks, amigo!

My acquisitions editor, Tim Green, and his trusty assistant, Stephanie Evans, had this book schedule dialed in from day one and never let up. I mean, *never* let up. Better still, they browbeat me into working with their incessantly chirpy voices. I long for the mean Tim of old who just yelled at me.

Chris Crayton, my technical editor, did a great job once again. Thank you for helping make this book happen.

Aaron Verber stepped up in a big way for this edition, with stellar editing, writing, and research. You did a great job with every chapter thrown at you (and managed to pull together the lab manual at the same time). Let's do this again!

Michael Smyer devoted his superb skills in photography and tech to making this book the best edition ever. He kept me on my toes on the tech and helped greatly with the research. Excellent work, Michael.

Ford Pierson, my in-house editor and illustrator, worked very hard to upgrade the line art in this book, including turning man in the box into Mini Me, a touch that displays his wit, cleverness, and complete lack of fear. Great job, Ford.

Scott Strubberg, Doug Jones, and Dave Rush, instructors at Total Seminars, were my sounding boards and research partners for this book, helping me turn the complicated into the understandable on many subjects. Thank you all very much!

On the McGraw-Hill side, the crew once again demonstrated why McGraw-Hill is the best in show as a publisher. With excellent work and even better attitude, this book came together smoothly.

■ *To my daughter Emily: Beautiful, happy, healthy, and successful—with a clear path ahead. I am content.*

—Dad

ABOUT THIS BOOK

◼ Important Technology Skills

Information technology (IT) offers many career paths, leading to occupations in such fields as PC repair, network administration, telecommunications, Web development, graphic design, and desktop support. To become competent in any IT field, however, you need certain basic computer skills. Mike Meyers' CompTIA A+ Guide to 802: Managing and Troubleshooting PCs builds a foundation for success in the IT field by introducing you to fundamental technology concepts and giving you essential computer skills.

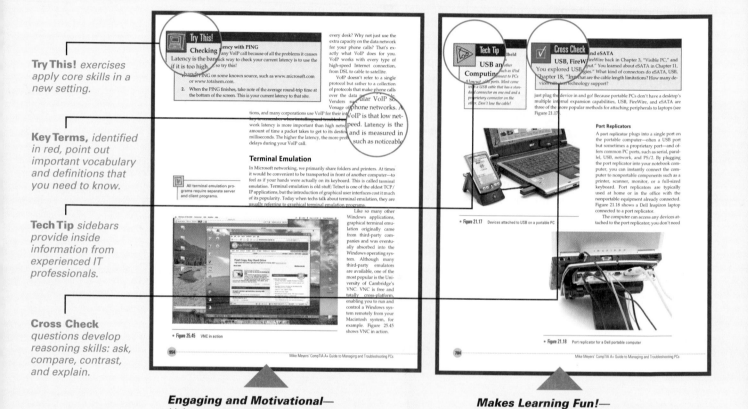

Try This! exercises apply core skills in a new setting.

Key Terms, identified in red, point out important vocabulary and definitions that you need to know.

Tech Tip sidebars provide inside information from experienced IT professionals.

Cross Check questions develop reasoning skills: ask, compare, contrast, and explain.

Engaging and Motivational—
Using a conversational style and proven instructional approach, the author explains technical concepts in a clear, interesting way using real-world examples.

Makes Learning Fun!—
Rich, colorful text and enhanced illustrations bring technical subjects to life.

Proven Learning Method Keeps You on Track

Mike Meyers' CompTIA A+ Guide to 802: Managing and Troubleshooting PCs is structured to give you comprehensive knowledge of computer skills and technologies. The textbook's active learning methodology guides you beyond mere recall and, through thought-provoking activities, labs, and sidebars, helps you develop critical-thinking, diagnostic, and communication skills.

Effective Learning Tools

This pedagogically rich book is designed to make learning easy and enjoyable and to help you develop the skills and critical-thinking abilities that will enable you to adapt to different job situations and troubleshoot problems.

Mike Meyers' proven ability to explain concepts in a clear, direct, even humorous way makes these books interesting, motivational, and fun.

Chapter Review *sections provide concept summaries, key terms lists, and lots of questions and projects.*

Notes, Tips, *and* **Warnings** *create a road map for success.*

Full-color photographs *help you identify and recognize key PC components.*

Offers Practical Experience—
Tutorials and lab assignments develop essential hands-on skills and put concepts in real-world contexts.

Robust Learning Tools—
Summaries, key terms lists, quizzes, essay questions, and lab projects help you practice skills and measure progress.

Each chapter includes

- **Learning objectives** that set measurable goals for chapter-by-chapter progress
- **Try This!**, **Cross Check**, and **Tech Tip** sidebars that encourage you to practice and apply concepts in real-world settings
- **Notes, Tips,** and **Warnings** that guide you through difficult areas
- **Exam-driven organization** that divides chapters into Historical/Conceptual, 802, and Beyond A+ sections, making it easy to focus study time on the core and specialization areas of the exams

- Plenty of full-color **photographs** and **illustrations** that provide clear, up-close pictures of the technology, making difficult concepts easy to visualize and understand
- **Highlighted Key Terms**, **Key Terms lists**, and **Chapter Summaries** that provide you with an easy way to review important concepts and vocabulary
- **Challenging End-of-Chapter Quizzes** that include vocabulary-building exercises, multiple-choice questions, essay questions, and on-the-job lab projects

CONTENTS AT A GLANCE

CONTENTS

Chapter 8
■ Maintaining and Optimizing Windows 288

Chapter 9
■ Working with the Command-Line Interface 334

Chapter 10
■ Troubleshooting Windows 372

Chapter 11
■ Video 422

I started writing computer books for the simple reason that no one wrote the kind of books I wanted to read. The books were either too simple (Chapter 1, "Using Your Mouse") or too complex (Chapter 1, "TTL Logic and Transistors"), and none of them provided a motivation for me to learn the information. I believed that there were geeky readers just like me who wanted to know *why* they needed to know the information in a computer book.

Good books motivate readers to learn what they are reading. If a book discusses binary arithmetic but doesn't explain why I need to learn it, for example, that's not a good book. Tell me that understanding binary makes it easier to understand how a CPU works or why a megabyte is different from a million bytes—then I get excited, no matter how geeky the topic. If I don't have a good motivation to do something, then I'm simply not going to do it (which explains why I haven't jumped out of an airplane!).

In this book, I teach you why you need to understand the technology that runs almost every modern business. You'll learn to build and fix computers, exploring every nook and cranny, and master the art of the PC tech. In the process, you'll gain the knowledge you need to pass the CompTIA A+ certification exams.

Enjoy, my fellow geek.

Michael D. Myers

■ It Pays to Get Certified

In a digital world, digital literacy is an essential survival skill. Certification proves you have the knowledge and skill to solve business problems in virtually any business environment. Certifications are highly valued credentials that qualify you for jobs, increased compensation, and promotion.

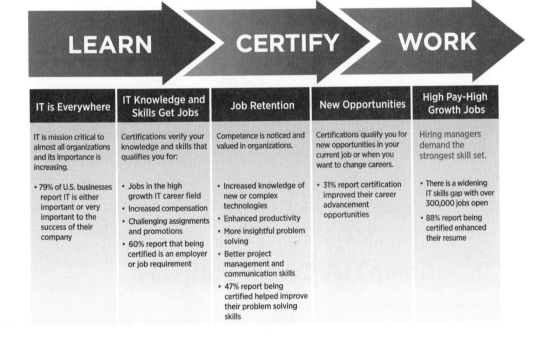

IT is Everywhere	IT Knowledge and Skills Get Jobs	Job Retention	New Opportunities	High Pay-High Growth Jobs
IT is mission critical to almost all organizations and its importance is increasing.	Certifications verify your knowledge and skills that qualifies you for:	Competence is noticed and valued in organizations.	Certifications qualify you for new opportunities in your current job or when you want to change careers.	Hiring managers demand the strongest skill set.
• 79% of U.S. businesses report IT is either important or very important to the success of their company	• Jobs in the high growth IT career field • Increased compensation • Challenging assignments and promotions • 60% report that being certified is an employer or job requirement	• Increased knowledge of new or complex technologies • Enhanced productivity • More insightful problem solving • Better project management and communication skills • 47% report being certified helped improve their problem solving skills	• 31% report certification improved their career advancement opportunities	• There is a widening IT skills gap with over 300,000 jobs open • 88% report being certified enhanced their resume

CompTIA A+ Certification Advances Your Career

- **The CompTIA A+ credential**—provides foundation-level knowledge and skills necessary for a career in PC repair and support.

- **Starting Salary**—CompTIA A+ Certified individuals can earn as much as $65,000 per year.

- **Career Pathway**—CompTIA A+ is a building block for other CompTIA certifications such as Network+, Security+ and vendor-specific technologies.

- **More than 850,000**—individuals worldwide are CompTIA A+ certified.

- **Mandated/Recommended by organizations worldwide**—such as Cisco and HP and Ricoh, the U.S. State Department, and U.S. government contractors such as EDS, General Dynamics, and Northrop Grumman.

- **Some of the primary benefits individuals report from becoming CompTIA A+ certified are**
 - More efficient troubleshooting
 - Improved career advancement
 - More insightful problem solving

CompTIA Career Pathway

CompTIA offers a number of credentials that form a foundation for your career in technology and that allow you to pursue specific areas of concentration. Depending on the path you choose to take, CompTIA certifications help you build upon your skills and knowledge, supporting learning throughout your entire career.

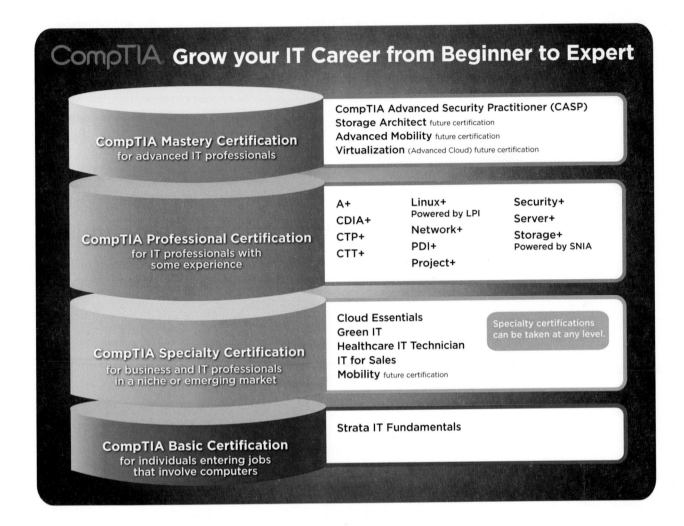

Steps to Getting Certified and Staying Certified

1. **Review exam objectives.** Review the certification objectives to make sure you know what is covered in the exam:
 www.comptia.org/certifications/testprep/examobjectives.aspx

2. **Practice for the exam.** After you have studied for the certification, take a free assessment and sample test to get an idea what type of questions might be on the exam:
 www.comptia.org/certifications/testprep/practicetests.aspx

3. **Purchase an exam voucher.** Purchase your exam voucher on the CompTIA Marketplace, which is located at: www.comptiastore.com

4. **Take the test!** Select a certification exam provider and schedule a time to take your exam. You can find exam providers at the following link:

www.comptia.org/certifications/testprep/testingcenters.aspx

5. **Stay Certified!** Continuing education is required. Effective January 1, 2011, CompTIA A+ certifications are valid for three years from the date of certification. There are a number of ways the certification can be renewed. For more information go to: http://certification .comptia.org/getCertified/steps_to_certification/stayCertified.aspx

■ Join the Professional Community

The free online IT Pro Community provides valuable content to students and professionals. Join the IT Pro Community:

http://itpro.comptia.org

Career IT job resources include

- Where to start in IT
- Career assessments
- Salary trends
- U.S. job board

Join the IT Pro Community and get access to:

- Forums on networking, security, computing, and cutting-edge technologies
- Access to blogs written by industry experts
- Current information on cutting edge technologies
- Access to various industry resource links and articles related to IT and IT careers

■ Content Seal of Quality

This courseware bears the seal of CompTIA Approved Quality Content. This seal signifies this content covers 100 percent of the exam objectives and implements important instructional design principles. CompTIA recommends multiple learning tools to help increase coverage of the learning objectives.

Why CompTIA?

- **Global recognition**—CompTIA is recognized globally as the leading IT nonprofit trade association and has enormous credibility. Plus, CompTIA's certifications are vendor-neutral and offer proof of foundational knowledge that translates across technologies.

- **Valued by hiring managers**—Hiring managers value CompTIA certification because it is vendor- and technology-independent validation of your technical skills.

- **Recommended or required by government and businesses**—Many government organizations and corporations (for example, Dell, Sharp, Ricoh, the U.S. Department of Defense, and many more) either recommend or require technical staff to be CompTIA certified.

- **Three CompTIA certifications ranked in the top 10**—In a study by DICE of 17,000 technology professionals, certifications helped command higher salaries at all experience levels.

How to Obtain More Information

- *Visit CompTIA online*
 Go to www.comptia.org to learn more about getting CompTIA certified.

- *Contact CompTIA*
 Please call 866-835-8020, ext. 5 or e-mail questions@comptia.org.

- *Join the IT Pro Community*
 Go to http://itpro.comptia.org to join the IT community to get relevant career information.

- *Connect with CompTIA*
 Find us on Facebook, LinkedIn, Twitter, and YouTube.

CAQC Disclaimer

The logo of the CompTIA Approved Quality Curriculum (CAQC) program and the status of this or other training material as "Approved" under the CompTIA Approved Quality Curriculum program signifies that, in CompTIA's opinion, such training material covers the content of CompTIA's related certification exam.

The contents of this training material were created for the CompTIA A+ exams covering CompTIA certification objectives that were current as of the date of publication.

CompTIA has not reviewed or approved the accuracy of the contents of this training material and specifically disclaims any warranties of merchantability or fitness for a particular purpose. CompTIA makes no guarantee concerning the success of persons using any such "Approved" or other training material in order to prepare for any CompTIA certification exam.

For instructor and student resources, please visit:

www.mhprofessional.com/certification802

Students will find the chapter quizzes from the end of each chapter, and teachers can access instructor support materials.

■ Additional Resources for Teachers

The Online Learning Center provides resources for teachers in a format that follows the organization of the textbook.

This site includes the following:

- Answer keys to the end-of-chapter activities in the textbook
- Answer keys to the Mike Meyers' Lab Manual activities (Lab Manual available separately)
- Access to test bank files and software that allows you to generate a wide array of paper- or network-based tests, and that features automatic grading. The test bank includes
 - Hundreds of practice questions and a wide variety of question types categorized by exam objective, enabling you to customize each test to maximize student progress
 - Blackboard cartridges and other formats may also be available upon request; contact your sales representative
- Engaging PowerPoint slides on the lecture topics that include full-color artwork from the book
- Instructor's Manual that contains learning objectives, classroom preparation notes, instructor tips, and a lecture outline for each chapter

Please contact your McGraw-Hill sales representative for details.

The Path of the PC Tech

"Never trust a computer you can't throw out a window."

—STEVE WOZNIAK

In this chapter, you will learn how to

■ **Explain the importance of skill in managing and troubleshooting PCs**

■ **Explain the importance of CompTIA A+ certification**

■ **Describe how to become CompTIA A+ certified**

Computers have taken over the world, or at least many professions. Everywhere you turn, a quick dig beneath the surface sawdust of construction, the grease of auto mechanics, and the hum of medical technology reveals one or more personal computers (PCs) working away, doing essential jobs. Because the PC evolved from novelty item to essential science tool to everyday object in a short period of time, there's a huge demand for a workforce that can build, maintain, troubleshoot, and repair PCs.

The Importance of Skill in Managing and Troubleshooting PCs

The people who work with computers, often lumped into a single group known as the **Information Technology (IT)** workforce, do an amazingly varied number of jobs. These include diverse pursuits such as designing hardware, writing computer programs, and creating **networks** (groups of computers connected together to share data or programs). IT people built the Internet and maintain the millions of computers that keep it running.

But for all this IT diversity, it's the computer technicians (or **PC techs**, as those of us in the field call each other) who make up the core of the IT workforce. Without us techs, none of the other stuff would work, so none of the other jobs could exist. Getting workers with skill in building, maintaining, troubleshooting, and fixing PCs is essential for the success of every modern business. We need more PC techs. We need you!

In the early days of the personal computer, anyone who used a PC had to have skills as a PC tech. The PC was new, buggy, and prone to problems. If you owned a PC back then, you didn't want to rely on others to fix your PC when the inevitable problems arose. Today's PCs are much more robust and have fewer problems, so *using* one no longer requires having PC tech skills, but they're also much more complex machines. Today's IT industry, therefore, needs specialized workers who know how to make the machines run well and fix them when they break for the millions of users who lack PC tech skills.

Every profession requires specialized skills. For the most part, if you want to *get* or *keep* a job that requires those specialized skills, you need some type of **certification** or license. If you want a job fixing automobiles in the United States, for example, you get the Automotive Service Excellence (ASE) certification. If you want to perform companies' financial audits in the United Kingdom, you get your Chartered Accountant certification.

Nearly every profession has some criteria that you must meet to show your competence and ability to perform at a certain level. Although the way this works varies widely from one profession to another, all of them will at some point make you take an exam or series of exams. Passing these exams proves that you have the necessary skills to work at a certain level in your profession, whether you're an aspiring plumber, teacher, barber, or lawyer.

If you successfully pass these exams, the organization that administers them grants you a certification. You receive some piece of paper or pin or membership card that you can show to potential clients or employers. This certification gives those potential clients or employers a level of confidence that you can do what you say you can do. Without this certification, either you will not find suitable work in that profession or no one will trust you to do the work. Until relatively recently, PC technicians have been the exception to this rule.

■ The Importance of CompTIA A+ Certification

Microcomputers were introduced in the late 1970s, and for many years PC technicians did not have a universally recognized way to show clients or employers that they know what to do under the hood of a personal computer. Sure, vendor-specific certifications existed, but the only way to get them was to get a job at an authorized warranty or repair facility first and then get the certification. There's nothing wrong with vendor-specific training, but no single manufacturer has taken enough market share to make IBM training, for example, something that works for any job. (Then there is always that little detail of getting the job first before you can be certified…)

The software and networking sides of our business have not suffered from the same lack of certifications. Due to the dominance of certain companies at one time or another (for example, Microsoft and Cisco), the vendor-specific certifications have provided a great way to get and keep a job. For example, Microsoft's Microsoft Certified IT Professional (MCITP) and Cisco's Cisco Certified Internetwork Expert (CCIE) certifications have opened the employment doors for many.

But what about the person who runs around all day repairing printers, repartitioning hard drives, upgrading device drivers, and assembling systems? What about the PC hobbyists who want to be paid for their skills? What about the folks who, because they had the audacity to show that they knew the difference between a homegroup and a workgroup, find themselves with a new title such as PC Support Technician or Electronic Services Specialist? On the other hand, how about the worst title of them all: "The Person Who Doesn't Get a Nickel Extra but Who Fixes the Computers"? CompTIA A+ certification gives these people a universally recognized way to prove their PC technical proficiency to employers or clients (and to seek due compensation for their skills).

What Is CompTIA A+ Certification?

CompTIA A+ certification is an industry-wide, vendor-neutral certification program developed and sponsored by the Computing Technology Industry Association (CompTIA). The CompTIA A+ certification shows that you have a basic competence in supporting microcomputers. You achieve this certification by taking two computer-based, multiple-choice exams. The tests cover what technicians should know after 12 months of hands-on work on PCs, either from a job or as a student in the lab. CompTIA A+ certification enjoys wide recognition throughout the computer industry. To date, more than 800,000 technicians have become CompTIA A+ certified, making it the most popular of all IT certifications.

Who Is CompTIA?

CompTIA is a nonprofit industry trade association based in Oakbrook Terrace, Illinois. It consists of over 20,000 members in 102 countries. You'll

find CompTIA offices in such diverse locales as Amsterdam, Dubai, Johannesburg, Tokyo, and São Paulo.

CompTIA provides a forum for people in these industries to network (as in meeting people), represents the interests of its members to the government, and provides certifications for many aspects of the computer industry. CompTIA sponsors CompTIA A+, CompTIA Network+, CompTIA Security+, and other certifications. CompTIA works hard to watch the IT industry and constantly looks to provide new certifications to meet the ongoing demand from its membership. Check out the CompTIA Web site at **www.comptia.org** for details on the other certifications you can obtain from CompTIA.

Virtually every company of consequence in the IT industry is a member of CompTIA. Here are a few of the biggies:

Adobe Systems	AMD	Best Buy	Brother International
Canon	Cisco Systems	CompUSA	Fujitsu
Gateway	Hewlett-Packard	IBM	Intel
Kyocera	McAfee	Microsoft	NCR
Novell	Panasonic	Sharp Electronics	Siemens
Symantec	Toshiba	Total Seminars, LLC (that's my company)	Plus many thousands more

CompTIA began offering CompTIA A+ certification back in 1993. When it debuted, the IT industry largely ignored CompTIA A+ certification. Since that initial stutter, however, the CompTIA A+ certification has grown to become the de facto requirement for entrance into the PC industry. Many companies require CompTIA A+ certification for all of their PC support technicians, and the CompTIA A+ certification is widely recognized both in the United States and internationally. Additionally, many other certifications recognize CompTIA A+ certification and use it as credit toward their certifications.

The Path to Other Certifications

Most IT companies—big and small—see CompTIA A+ certification as the entry point to IT. From CompTIA A+, you have a number of certification options, depending on whether you want to focus more on hardware and operating systems or move into network administration (although these aren't mutually exclusive goals). The following three certifications are worth serious consideration:

- CompTIA Network+ certification
- Microsoft technical certifications
- Cisco certifications

CompTIA Network+ Certification

If you haven't already achieved CompTIA Network+ certification, make it your next certification goal after CompTIA A+ certification. Just as CompTIA A+ certification shows that you have solid competency as a PC

CompTIA A+ is the entry point to IT, though definitely not the only route for learning about computers and having certifications to prove that knowledge. Several certifications cover computer literacy or digital literacy, the phrase that means "what every person needs to know about computers to survive in the 21st century." The most popular computer literacy certification is Certiport's IC³ certification that tests on general computer knowledge; office productivity applications, such as Word and PowerPoint; and Internet applications such as Web browsers and e-mail clients.

CompTIA has a pre–CompTIA A+ exam (*not* a certification), called the *CompTIA Strata IT Fundamentals exam*, that's geared a bit more to a user preparing to become a tech. It's designed to check basic knowledge levels for people getting into IT.

technician, **CompTIA Network+ certification** demonstrates your skills as a network technician, including your understanding of network hardware, installation, and troubleshooting. CompTIA's Network+ certification is a natural step for continuing toward your Microsoft or Cisco certifications. Take the CompTIA Network+: it's your obvious next certification.

Microsoft Technical Certifications

Microsoft operating systems control a huge portion of all installed networks, and those networks need qualified support people to make them run. Pursuing Microsoft's series of certifications for networking professionals is a natural next step after completing the CompTIA certifications. They offer a whole slew of tracks and exams, ranging from simple specializations in Windows 7 to numerous **Microsoft Certified IT Professional (MCITP)** certifications and beyond. You can find more details on the Microsoft Learning Web site at www.microsoft.com/learning/en/us/certification/cert-overview.aspx.

Cisco Certification

Let's face it: Cisco routers pretty much run the Internet and most intranets in the world. A *router* is a networking device that controls and directs the flow of information over networks, such as e-mail messages, Web browsing, and so on. Cisco provides five levels of IT certification for folks who want to show their skills at handling Cisco products, such as the **Cisco Certified Network Associate (CCNA)**, plus numerous specialty certifications. See the Cisco IT Certification Web site here for more details: www.cisco.com/web/learning/le3/learning_career_certifications_and_learning_paths_home.html.

■ How Do I Become CompTIA A+ Certified?

You become CompTIA A+ certified, in the simplest sense, by taking and passing two computer-based, multiple-choice exams. No prerequisites are required for taking the CompTIA A+ certification exams (although there's an assumption of computer literacy, whether or not you have one of the computer literacy certifications). There is no required training course and no training materials to buy. You *do* have to pay a testing fee for each of the two exams. You pay your testing fees, go to a local testing center, and take the tests. You immediately know whether you have passed or failed. By passing both exams, you become CompTIA A+ certified.

What's the Deal with "No More Lifetime Certification"?

In early 2010, CompTIA announced that, effective January 1, 2011, CompTIA A+, CompTIA Network+, and CompTIA Security+ certifications would no longer be considered "certified for life." If you passed any of these exams before the deadline, you're still certified for life for those exams. For any

exams that you pass on or after January 1, 2011, to stay certified, every three years you'll need to either retake the exam or perform sufficient continuing education as specified by CompTIA.

Retaking the exams isn't that hard to understand, but the continuing education requirement is a bit more complex. Instead of trying to explain it all here, please review CompTIA's documentation at http://certification .comptia.org/Libraries/Certification_Documents/ceu_faq.sflb.ashx.

Most importantly, if you pursue the continuing education path, you'll need to earn 20 continuing education units (CEUs) each three-year period to renew your CompTIA A+ certification. How do you earn these CEUs? You can participate in industry events and seminars, complete a presentation, participate in IT training, teach a course, or earn another higher-level certification. The number of CEUs that you earn by completing each of these requirements varies, and each requires that you submit documentation to CompTIA for their review.

Personally, I think this is a long-overdue feature. Someone who took the CompTIA A+ exam in 2010 had no way to distinguish himself from a person who took the exam in 1997, and that wasn't fair. By no longer awarding "certified for life" status, CompTIA's certifications are now in line with Microsoft, Cisco, and other industry certifications.

The Basic Exam Structure

The two exams introduced by CompTIA in 2012 are **CompTIA A+ 220-801** (Hardware) and **CompTIA A+ 220-802** (Operating Systems). The terms "Hardware" and "Operating Systems" are not officially part of the exam names, but I've included them here because they're commonly used to reference the exams. It's also common to refer to these two exams as the "2012" exams to differentiate them from older CompTIA exams. Although you may take either of the two exams first, I recommend taking 220-801 followed by 220-802. The 220-801 exam concentrates on understanding terminology and technology, how to do fundamental tasks such as upgrading RAM, and basic network and laptop support. The 220-802 exam builds on the first exam, concentrating on Windows support, advanced configuration, and troubleshooting scenarios.

Both of the exams are extremely practical, with little or no interest in history. All questions are multiple-choice, simulation, or "click on the right part of the picture" questions. The following is an example of the type of questions you will see on the exams:

Your laser printer is printing blank pages. Which item should you check first?

 A. Printer drivers

 B. Toner cartridge

 C. Printer settings

 D. Paper feed

The correct answer is B, the toner cartridge. You can make an argument for any of the others, but common sense (and skill as a PC technician) tells you to check the simplest possibility first.

The 2012 exams use a regular test format in which you answer a set number of questions and are scored based on how many correct answers you give. These exams have no more than 100 questions each. (Both exams have 100 questions each at the time of this writing.)

Be aware that CompTIA may add new questions to the exams at any time to keep the content fresh. The subject matter covered by the exams won't change, but new questions may be added periodically at random intervals. This policy puts strong emphasis on understanding concepts and having solid PC-tech knowledge rather than on trying to memorize specific questions and answers that may have been on the tests in the past. No book or Web resource will have all the "right answers" because those answers change constantly. Luckily for you, however, this book not only teaches you what steps to follow in a particular case, but also explains how to be a knowledgeable tech who understands *why* you're doing those steps. That way when you encounter a new problem (or test question), you can work out the answer. This will help you not only to pass the exams but also to be a better PC tech!

To keep up to date, we monitor the CompTIA A+ exams for new content and update the special Tech Files section of the Total Seminars Web site (www.totalsem.com) with new articles covering subjects we believe may appear on future versions of the exams.

Windows-Centric

The CompTIA A+ exams focus on the Microsoft Windows operating systems you would expect to find on a PC at a workstation or in a home. There are no Linux questions. There are no Mac OS X questions. The 802 exam will ask you about the common mobile device operating systems, iOS and Android, but the vast majority of operating system questions on both exams address Windows. Objectives in the exams cover the following operating systems:

- Windows XP Home, Windows XP Professional, Windows XP Media Center, Windows XP 64-bit Professional

- Windows Vista Home Basic, Windows Vista Home Premium, Windows Vista Business, Windows Vista Ultimate, Windows Vista Enterprise

- Windows 7 Starter, Windows 7 Home Premium, Windows 7 Professional, Windows 7 Ultimate, Windows 7 Enterprise

Windows 8

CompTIA has the darnedest luck when it comes to the timing of new CompTIA A+ exams compared to releases of new Windows versions. In 2006, CompTIA released an update to the CompTIA A+ exams about four months before Microsoft released Windows Vista. In 2009, CompTIA missed Windows 7 by about one month (though CompTIA released a Windows 7 update to the exams in late 2009).

It seems that CompTIA will once again run into what I'm going to call the "CompTIA Windows Curse." As the new 220-801 and 220-802 exams come out in late 2012, there's a good chance that Windows 8 will come out

a few month later. Assuming CompTIA stays true to form, there's a very good chance that you'll see a Windows 8 update on the exams within a year or two of the Windows 8 rollout. Be sure to check the CompTIA Web site or contact me directly at michaelm@totalsem.com to see if any Windows 8 updates have taken place.

Exam 220–801

The questions on the CompTIA A+ 220-801 exam fit into one of five domains. The number of questions for each domain is based on the percentages shown in Table 1.1.

Table 1.1	Exam 220-801 Domains and Percentages
Domain	**Percentage**
1.0 PC Hardware	40%
2.0 Networking	27%
3.0 Laptops	11%
4.0 Printers	11%
5.0 Operational Procedures	11%

The 220-801 exam tests your knowledge of computer components, expecting you to be able to identify just about every common device on PCs, including variations within device types. Here's a list:

- Floppy drives
- Hard drives
- Optical drives
- Solid state drives
- Motherboards
- Power supplies
- CPUs
- RAM
- Monitors
- Input devices, such as keyboards, mice, and touchscreens
- Video and multimedia cards
- Network and modem cards
- Cables and connectors
- Heat sinks, fans, and liquid cooling systems
- Laptops and portable devices
- Printers
- Scanners
- Network switches, cabling, and wireless adapters
- Biometric devices

The 220-801 exam tests your ability to install, configure, and maintain all the hardware technology involved in a personal computer. You need to be able to install and set up a hard drive, for example, and configure devices in Windows XP, Windows Vista, and Windows 7. You have to understand device drivers. Additionally, this exam puts a lot of emphasis on operational procedures, such as safety and environmental issues, communication, and professionalism. You need to understand how to avoid hazardous situations. The exam tests your ability to communicate effectively with customers and coworkers. You need to understand professional behavior and demonstrate that you have tact, discretion, and respect for others and their property.

Exam 220-802

The CompTIA A+ 220-802 exam (covered in this book) contains four domains. Table 1.2 lists the domains and the percentage of questions dedicated to each domain.

Table 1.2	Exam 220-802 Domains and Percentages
Domain	**Percentage**
1.0 Operating Systems	33%
2.0 Security	22%
3.0 Mobile Devices	9%
4.0 Troubleshooting	36%

The 220-802 exam covers the configuration, repair, and troubleshooting of the Windows operating system. You have to know your way around Windows and understand the tasks involved in updating, upgrading, and installing Windows XP, Windows Vista, and Windows 7. You need to know the standard diagnostic tools available in Windows so that you can fix problems and work with higher-level techs. Make sure you know Windows; 33% of the 220-802 questions are going to challenge you on this.

The biggest part of the 220-802 exam is dedicated to troubleshooting. Think in terms of a hands-on approach to determining the appropriate technology for a situation—running diagnostics and troubleshooting—rather than identification of hardware or operating system utilities. You need to understand how all the technology should work, know the proper steps to figure out why something doesn't work, and then know how to fix it.

The 220-802 exam adds mobile devices to the objectives, a new topic for 2012. While the smartphone and tablet market covers an impossibly wide array of hardware and software, the 220-802 exam focuses on Apple iOS and Google Android devices. You'll need to know how to interact with the hardware and software, as well as configure personal settings, such as those for e-mail clients and security.

Security is a big topic on the 220-802 exam. You need to know quite a bit about computer security, from physical security (door locks to retinal scanners), to knowledge of security threats (malware and viruses), to the ways in which to secure an individual computer. This also includes coverage of how to recycle and dispose of computer gear properly.

You'll also be tested on methods of securing networks. You'll need to know how to access a small office/home office (SOHO) router or wireless access point and configure that device to protect your network.

How Do I Take the Exams?

Pearson VUE administers the CompTIA A+ testing at over 5000 testing centers in 165 countries. You may take the exams at any testing center. You can select the closest training center and schedule your exams right from the comfort of your favorite Web browser by going to the Pearson VUE Web site:

www.vue.com

Alternatively, in the United States and Canada, call Pearson VUE at 877-551-PLUS (7587) to schedule the exams and to locate the nearest testing

center. International customers can find a list of Pearson VUE international contact numbers for various regions of the world on CompTIA's Web site at www.comptia.org.

You must pay for the exam when you call to schedule. Be prepared to sit on hold for a while. Have your Social Security number (or international equivalent) and a credit card ready when you call. Pearson VUE will be glad to invoice you, but you won't be able to take the exam until they receive full payment.

Pearson VUE will accommodate any special needs, although this may limit your selection of testing locations.

How Much Does the Exam Cost?

The cost of the exam depends on whether you work for a CompTIA member or not. At this writing, the cost for non-CompTIA members is $178 (U.S.) for each exam. International prices vary, but you can check the CompTIA Web site for international pricing. Of course, the prices are subject to change without notice, so always check the CompTIA Web site for current pricing.

Very few people pay full price for the exam. Virtually every organization that provides CompTIA A+ training and testing also offers discount vouchers. You buy a discount voucher and then use the voucher number instead of a credit card when you schedule the exam. Vouchers are sold per exam, so you'll need two vouchers to take the two CompTIA A+ exams. Total Seminars is one place to get discount vouchers. You can call Total Seminars at 800-446-6004 or 281-922-4166, or get vouchers via the Web site: www.totalsem.com. No one should ever pay full price for CompTIA A+ exams.

How to Pass the CompTIA A+ Exams

The single most important thing to remember about the CompTIA A+ certification exams is that CompTIA designed the exams to test the knowledge of a technician with only 12 months of experience, so keep it simple! The exams aren't interested in your ability to overclock DDR3 CAS timings in CMOS or whether you can explain the exact difference between the Intel ICH10 and the AMD 790 southbridges. Think in terms of practical knowledge and standards. Read this book, do whatever works for you to memorize the key concepts and procedures, take the practice exams on the media accompanying this book, review any topics you miss, and you should pass with no problem.

Some of you may be in or just out of school, so studying for exams is nothing novel. But if you haven't had to study for and take an exam in a while, or if you think maybe you could use some tips, you may find the next section valuable. It lays out a proven strategy for preparing to take and pass the CompTIA A+ exams. Try it. It works.

Those of you who just want more knowledge in managing and troubleshooting PCs can follow the same strategy as certification-seekers. Think in practical terms and work with the PC as you go through each chapter.

Obligate Yourself

The very first step you should take is to schedule yourself for the exams. Have you ever heard the old adage, "Heat and pressure make diamonds"? Well, if you don't give yourself a little "heat," you'll end up procrastinating

and delay taking the exams, possibly forever. Do yourself a favor. Using the following information, determine how much time you'll need to study for the exams, and then call Pearson VUE and schedule the exams accordingly. Knowing the exams are coming up makes it much easier to turn off the television and crack open the book. You can schedule an exam as little as a few weeks in advance, but if you schedule an exam and can't take it at the scheduled time, you must reschedule at least a day in advance or you'll lose your money.

Set Aside the Right Amount of Study Time

After helping thousands of techs get their CompTIA A+ certification, we at Total Seminars have developed a pretty good feel for the amount of study time needed to pass the CompTIA A+ certification exams. The following table provides an estimate to help you plan how much study time you must commit to the CompTIA A+ certification exams. Keep in mind that these are averages. If you're not a great student or if you're a little on the nervous side, add 10 percent; if you're a fast learner or have a good bit of computer experience, you may want to reduce the figures.

To use Table 1.3, just circle the values that are most accurate for you and add them up to get your estimated total hours of study time.

To that value, add hours based on the number of months of direct, professional experience you have had supporting PCs, as shown in Table 1.4.

A total neophyte often needs roughly 240 hours of study time. An experienced tech shouldn't need more than 60 hours.

Total hours for you to study: _____.

A Strategy for Study

Now that you have a feel for how long it's going to take to prepare for the exams, you're ready to develop a study strategy. I'd like to suggest a strategy that has worked for others who've come before you, whether they were experienced techs or total newbies.

This book is designed to accommodate the different study agendas of these two groups of students. The first group is experienced techs who already have strong PC experience but need to be sure they're ready to be tested on the specific subjects covered by the CompTIA A+ exams. The second group is those with little or no background in the computer field. These techs can benefit from a more detailed understanding of the history and concepts that underlie modern PC technology, to help them remember the specific subject matter information they must know for the exams. I'll use the shorthand terms Old Techs and New Techs for these two groups. If you're not sure which group you fall into, pick a few chapters and go through some end-of-chapter questions. If you score less than 70%, go the New Tech route.

I have broken some of the chapters into three distinct parts:

Not all chapters have all three parts.

- **Historical/Conceptual** Topics that are not on the CompTIA A+ exams but will help you understand more clearly what is on the CompTIA A+ exams

- **802** Topics that clearly fit under the CompTIA A+ 220-802 exam domains

Table 1.3	Analyzing Skill Levels			
		Amount of Experience		
Tech Task	**None**	**Once or Twice**	**Every Now and Then**	**Quite a Bit**
Installing an adapter card	6	4	2	1
Installing and configuring hard drives	12	10	8	2
Installing modems and NICs	8	6	6	3
Connecting a computer to the Internet	16	10	8	4
Installing printers and scanners	16	8	4	2
Installing RAM	8	6	4	2
Installing CPUs	8	7	5	3
Repairing printers	6	5	4	3
Repairing boot problems	8	7	7	5
Repairing portable computers	8	6	4	2
Configuring mobile devices	4	3	2	1
Building complete systems	12	10	8	6
Using the command line	8	8	6	4
Installing and optimizing Windows	10	8	6	4
Using Windows XP	6	6	4	2
Using Windows Vista	8	6	4	2
Using Windows 7	8	6	4	2
Configuring NTFS, Users, and Groups	6	4	3	2
Configuring a wireless network	6	5	3	2
Configuring a software firewall	6	4	2	1
Configuring sound	2	2	1	0
Removing malware	4	3	2	0
Using OS diagnostic tools	8	8	6	4
Using a multimeter	4	3	2	1

Table 1.4	Adding Up Your Study Time
Months of Direct, Professional Experience...	**Hours to Add to Your Study Time...**
0	50
Up to 6	30
6 to 12	10
Over 12	0

- **Beyond A+** More advanced issues that probably will not be on the CompTIA A+ exams—yet

The beginning of each of these parts is clearly marked with a purple-shaded banner, as you'll see next.

Historical/Conceptual

Those of you who fall into the Old Tech group may want to skip everything except the 802 parts in each chapter. After reading the sections in those parts, jump immediately to the questions at the end of the chapter. The end-of-chapter questions concentrate on information in the 802 sections. If you run into problems, review the Historical/Conceptual sections in that chapter. Note that you may need to skip back to previous chapters to get the Historical/Conceptual information you need for later chapters.

After going through every chapter as described, Old Techs can move directly to testing their knowledge by using the free practice exams on the media that accompanies the book. Once you start scoring above 90%, you're ready to take the exams. If you're a New Tech—or if you're an Old Tech who wants the full learning experience this book can offer—start by reading the book, *the whole book*, as though you were reading a novel, from page one to the end without skipping around. Because so many computer terms and concepts build on each other, skipping around greatly increases the odds that you will become confused and end up closing the book and firing up your favorite PC game. Not that I have anything against PC games, but unfortunately that skill is *not* useful for the CompTIA A+ exams!

Your goal on this first read is to understand concepts, the *whys* behind the *hows*. Having a PC nearby as you read is helpful so you can stop and inspect the PC to see a piece of hardware or how a particular concept manifests in the real world. As you read about hard drives, for example, inspect the cables. Do they look like the ones in the book? Is there a variation? Why? It is imperative that you understand why you are doing something, not just how to do it on one particular system under one specific set of conditions. Neither the exams nor real life as a PC tech works that way.

If you're reading this book as part of a managing and troubleshooting PCs class rather than a certification-prep course, I highly recommend going the New Tech route, even if you have a decent amount of experience. The book contains a lot of details that can trip you up if you focus only on the test-specific sections of the chapters. Plus, your program might stress historical and conceptual knowledge as well as practical, hands-on skills.

The CompTIA A+ certification exams assume that you have basic user skills. The exams really try to trick you with questions on processes that you may do every day and not think much about. Here's a classic: "To move a file from the C:\DATA folder to the D:\ drive using Windows Explorer, what key must you hold down while dragging the file?" If you can answer that without going to your keyboard and trying a few likely keys, you're better than most techs! In the real world, you can try a few wrong answers before you hit on the right one, but for the exams, you have to *know* it. Whether Old Tech or New Tech, make sure you are proficient at user-level Windows skills, including the following:

- Recognizing all the components of the standard Windows desktop (Start menu, notification area, etc.)
- Manipulating windows—resizing, moving, and so on

- Creating, deleting, renaming, moving, and copying files and folders within Windows
- Understanding file extensions and their relationship with program associations
- Using common keyboard shortcuts/hotkeys
- Installing, running, and closing a Windows application

Any PC technician who has been around a while will tell you that one of the great secrets in the computer business is that there's almost never anything completely new in the world of computer technology. Faster, cleverer, smaller, wider—absolutely—but the underlying technology, the core of what makes your PC and its various peripheral devices operate, has changed remarkably little since PCs came into widespread use a few decades ago. When you do your initial read-through, you may be tempted to skip the Historical/Conceptual sections—don't! Understanding the history and technological developments behind today's PCs helps you understand why they work—or don't work—the way they do. Basically, I'm passing on to you the kind of knowledge you might get by apprenticing yourself to an older, experienced PC tech.

After you've completed the first read-through, go through the book again, this time in textbook mode. If you're an Old Tech, start your studying here. Try to cover one chapter at a sitting. Concentrate on the 802 material. Get a highlighter and mark the phrases and sentences that bring out major points. Be sure you understand how the pictures and illustrations relate to the concepts being discussed.

Once you feel you have a good grasp of the material in the book, you can check your knowledge by using the practice exams included on the media accompanying this book. You can take these in Practice mode or Final mode. In Practice mode, you can use the Assistance window to get a helpful hint for the current questions, use the Reference feature to find the chapter that covers the question, check your answer for the question, and see an explanation of the correct answer. In Final mode, you answer all the questions and receive an exam score at the end, just like the real thing. You can also adjust the number of questions on a Practice or Final mode exam with the Customize option.

Both modes show you an overall grade, expressed as a percentage, as well as a breakdown of how well you did on each exam domain. The Review Questions feature lets you see which questions you missed and what the correct answers are. Use these results to guide further studying. Continue reviewing the topics you miss and taking additional exams until you are consistently scoring in the 90% range. When you get there, you are ready to pass the CompTIA A+ certification exams.

Study Tactics

Perhaps it's been a while since you had to study for a test. Or perhaps it hasn't, but you've done your best since then to block the whole experience from your mind. Either way, savvy test-takers know that certain techniques make studying for tests more efficient and effective.

Here's a trick used by students in law and medical schools who have to memorize reams of information: write it down. The act of writing something down (not typing, *writing*) in and of itself helps you to remember it, even if you never look at what you wrote again. Try taking separate notes on the material and re-creating diagrams by hand to help solidify the information in your mind.

Another oldie but goodie: Make yourself flash cards with questions and answers on topics you find difficult. A third trick: Take your notes to bed and read them just before you go to sleep. Many people find they really do learn while they sleep!

Contact

If you have any problems, any questions, or if you just want to argue about something, feel free to send an e-mail to the author—michaelm@totalsem.com— or to the editor—scottj@totalsem.com.

For any other information you might need, contact CompTIA directly at their Web site: www.comptia.org.

Chapter 1 Review

■ Chapter Summary

After reading this chapter and completing the exercises, you should understand the following about the path of the PC tech.

Explain the importance of skill in managing and troubleshooting PCs

■ The IT workforce designs, builds, and maintains computers, computer programs, and networks. PC techs take care of personal computers, thus representing an essential component in that workforce. As PCs become more complex, the IT workforce needs specialized PC techs.

■ Certifications prove to employers that you have the necessary skills to perform the job. If you want a job fixing automobiles in the United States, for example, you get the Automotive Service Excellence (ASE) certification. To become certified, you take and successfully pass exams. Then the organization that developed those exams grants you certification. Gaining certification is particularly important for IT workers.

Explain the importance of CompTIA A+ certification

■ In the early days of the personal computer, you could get vendor-specific certifications, such as IBM Technician, but nothing general for PC techs. Worse, you often had to have a job at an authorized warranty or repair facility to get the vendor-specific certification. The software and networking side of IT has not suffered from the same lack of certifications. To prove skill in working with Windows, for example, you could become a Microsoft Certified IT Professional (MCITP).

■ CompTIA A+ certification is an industry-wide, vendor-neutral certification program that shows that you have a basic competence in supporting microcomputers. You achieve this certification by taking two computer-based, multiple-choice exams. The tests cover what technicians should know after 12 months of hands-on work on PCs, either from a job or as a student in the lab. CompTIA A+ certification enjoys wide recognition throughout the computer industry.

■ CompTIA is a nonprofit, industry trade association based in Oakbrook Terrace, Illinois. It consists of over 20,000 members in 102 countries. CompTIA provides a forum for people in these industries to network, represents the interests of its members to the government, and provides certifications for many aspects of the computer industry. CompTIA sponsors CompTIA A+, CompTIA Network+, CompTIA Security+, and other certifications.

■ The CompTIA A+ certification is the de facto entry point to IT. From CompTIA A+, you have a number of certification options, depending on whether you want to focus more on hardware and operating systems or move into network administration. You can get CompTIA Network+ certification, for example, or go on to get Microsoft or Cisco certified. CompTIA Network+ certification is the most obvious certification to get after becoming CompTIA A+ certified.

Describe how to become CompTIA A+ certified

■ You become CompTIA A+ certified, in the simplest sense, by taking and passing two computer-based, multiple-choice exams. No prerequisites are required for taking the CompTIA A+ certification exams. There is no required training course and no training materials to buy. You *do* have to pay a testing fee for each of the two exams. To stay current, you need to retest every three years or gain continuing education credits.

■ The CompTIA exams introduced in 2012 are *220-801* and *220-802*. It's common to refer to these two exams as the 2012 exams to differentiate them from older CompTIA exams. Although you may take either of the two exams first, I recommend taking the 220-801 followed by the 220-802.

■ Both of the exams are extremely practical, with little or no interest in theory. All questions are multiple-choice, simulation, or "click on the right part of the picture" questions. CompTIA may add new questions to the exams at any time to keep the content fresh, although the subject matter covered by the exams won't change.

- The Pearson VUE company administers the CompTIA A+ exams. You can schedule the exam times and location via the Pearson VUE Web site at www.vue.com. Check CompTIA's Web site for international links.

- To achieve success with the CompTIA A+ certification exams, think in terms of practical knowledge. Read the book. Work through the problems. Work with computers. Take the practice exams. You should obligate yourself by scheduling your exams. This keeps you focused on study.

- Read the book all the way through once. Experienced techs ("Old Techs") should then concentrate on the test-specific sections to prepare for the exams. Less experienced techs ("New Techs") should read the book all the way through again until everything makes sense.

- If you're reading this book as part of a managing and troubleshooting PCs class rather than a certification-prep course, I highly recommend going the New Tech route, even if you have a decent amount of experience. The book contains a lot of details that can trip you up if you focus only on the test-specific sections of the chapters.

■ Key Terms

certification *(1)*
Cisco Certified Network Associate (CCNA) *(4)*
CompTIA A+ 220-801 *(5)*
CompTIA A+ 220-802 *(5)*
CompTIA A+ certification *(2)*
CompTIA Network+ certification *(4)*
Computing Technology Industry Association (CompTIA) *(2)*

Information Technology (IT) *(1)*
Microsoft Certified IT Professional (MCITP) *(4)*
network *(1)*
PC tech *(1)*
Pearson VUE *(8)*
voucher *(9)*
www.comptia.org *(3)*

■ Key Term Quiz

Use the Key Terms list to complete the sentences that follow. Not all terms will be used.

1. You can lump together all the folks who design, build, program, and fix computers into the _____ workforce.

2. You become CompTIA A+ certified by passing the _____ and CompTIA A+ 220-802 exams.

3. A(n) _____ gives clients and employers a level of confidence that you can do what you say you can do.

4. A casual term for a person who builds and maintains computers is _____.

5. The _____ company administers the CompTIA A+ certification exams.

6. You can use a(n) _____ when you schedule your exam to save some money.

7. Persons desiring to work in Windows-based networking should pursue _____ certification after completing their CompTIA certifications.

8. You can find the latest information about the CompTIA A+ certification exams here:

 _____.

9. Typically, techs who attain CompTIA A+ certification then pursue _____ to add to their computer credentials.

10. A grouping of computers that enables people to share resources is called a(n) _____.

■ Multiple-Choice Quiz

1. Which of the following is a vendor-specific certification? (Select all that apply.)

 A. Cisco Certified Network Associate

 B. CompTIA A+

 C. CompTIA Network+

 D. Microsoft Certified IT Professional

2. Which of the following certifications is the de facto requirement for entrance into the PC industry?

 A. Certified Cisco Network Associate

 B. CompTIA A+

 C. CompTIA Network+

 D. Microsoft Certified IT Professional

3. John loves the Internet and wants a career working on the machines that make the Internet work. He has completed both CompTIA A+ and CompTIA Network+ certifications. Which of the following certifications would make a good next step?

 A. Cisco Certified Network Associate

 B. Certified Cisco Network Professional

 C. CompTIA Security+

 D. Microsoft Certified IT Professional

4. Which of the following exams focuses on installing, configuring, and maintaining all the standard technology involved in a personal computer?

 A. Certified Cisco Network Associate

 B. CompTIA A+ 220-801

 C. CompTIA A+ 220-802

 D. Microsoft Certified IT Professional

5. At which of the following Web sites can you register to take the CompTIA A+ certification exams?

 A. www.comptia.org

 B. www.microsoft.com

 C. www.totalsem.com

 D. www.vue.com

6. How many exams must you pass to become CompTIA A+ certified?

 A. One

 B. Two

 C. Three

 D. Four

7. How much practical IT experience do you need to become CompTIA A+ certified?

 A. Six months

 B. One year

 C. Two years

 D. None

8. How many questions should you expect on the 220-802 exam?

 A. 25

 B. 50

 C. 100

 D. The number of questions varies because the exams are adaptive.

9. The CompTIA A+ certification covers which of the following operating systems? (Select two.)

 A. Linux

 B. Mac OS X

 C. Windows XP Media Center

 D. Windows 7

10. What percentage of questions should you expect on operating systems in the 220-802 exam?

 A. 15%

 B. 22%

 C. 30%

 D. 33%

11. What percentage of questions should you expect on mobile devices in the 220-802 exam?

 A. 15%

 B. 9%

 C. 25%

 D. 5%

12. How much does it cost to take each exam (at the time of this book's publication)?

 A. $100 each

 B. $138 each

 C. $178 each

 D. $150 each

13. What percentage of questions should you expect on Windows 8 in the 220-802 exam?

 A. 10%

 B. 13%

 C. 20%

 D. 0%

14. Which mobile OSs does the 220-802 exam *not* cover? (Select two.)

 A. Web OS

 B. iOS

 C. Android

 D. Windows Phone 7

15. If you skip the continuing education path to recertify, how often do you need to take the CompTIA A+ exams to retain your status as a CompTIA A+ certified technician?

 A. Every year

 B. Every three years

 C. Every ten years

 D. Never

■ Essay Quiz

1. Write a short essay on the benefits of certification in the field of computers. Include discussion on how the CompTIA certifications function within the broader category of computer certification. Why do you suppose people get certifications rather than (or in addition to) two- and four-year college degrees in IT?

Lab Project

• Lab Project 1.1

If you have access to the Internet, do some searching on computer certifications. Make a personal certification tree or pathway that maps out a series of certifications to pursue that might interest you.

Which certifications would be useful if you want to be a graphics designer, for example? What if you want to create computer games?

Visible Windows

"Hard-working, easy-going software <u>everyone</u> will use"
—Tagline for Microsoft Bob, an operating system interface

In this chapter, you will learn how to

- **Relate the history of Microsoft Windows**
- **Explain the Windows interface**
- **Identify the operating system folders of Windows XP, Windows Vista, and Windows 7**
- **Describe the utilities in Windows that are essential to techs**

As a PC tech, you need to understand Windows at a level beyond that of regular users. Not only must techs run through the standard Windows features that everyone uses every day (Start button, Recycle Bin, and so on), they must also be comfortable drilling down underneath that user-friendly surface to get their hands a little dirty.

This chapter begins by introducing and organizing the many variations of Windows on the market today and helping you appreciate the difference between, for example, Windows XP Professional and Windows 7 Ultimate. The chapter then takes you through the Windows interface in detail. The third section looks more closely at the techie aspects of Windows, including the structure of the operating system. The fourth section provides an overview of the many utilities for techs available in Windows. The chapter closes in the "Beyond A+" section with a discussion of the versions of Windows not on the current CompTIA A+ exams, such as Windows 8 and non-desktop versions of Windows. Let's get started!

Historical/Conceptual

A Brief History of Microsoft Windows

Many users think of Windows as a monolithic thing, as *the* operating system (OS) for the PC (as opposed to the Mac), but as a tech you need to understand that Microsoft produces many varieties of the OS, each with specific tools, utilities, file structures, and interfaces. And you need to be able to navigate through any modern version of Windows fluidly.

Microsoft currently supports many versions of Windows, of which three concern the CompTIA A+ certified technician: Windows XP, Windows Vista, and Windows 7. Within each of these versions, Windows comes in multiple editions. Table 2.1 presents a list for the three versions you need to know for the exams.

Table 2.1	Versions of Windows on the CompTIA A+ Exams	
Windows Version	**Editions (32-bit)**	**Editions (64-bit)**
Windows XP	■ Windows XP Home ■ Windows XP Professional ■ Windows Media Center	■ Windows XP 64-bit Edition ■ Windows XP Professional x64 Edition
Windows Vista[1]	■ Windows Vista Home Basic ■ Windows Vista Home Premium ■ Windows Vista Business ■ Windows Vista Ultimate ■ Windows Vista Enterprise	■ Windows Vista Home Basic ■ Windows Vista Home Premium ■ Windows Vista Business ■ Windows Vista Ultimate ■ Windows Vista Enterprise
Windows 7[1]	■ Windows 7 Starter ■ Windows 7 Home Premium ■ Windows 7 Professional ■ Windows 7 Ultimate ■ Windows 7 Enterprise	■ Windows 7 Home Premium ■ Windows 7 Professional ■ Windows 7 Ultimate ■ Windows 7 Enterprise

1 Microsoft has also released Windows Vista Starter Edition and Windows 7 Home Basic. These are simplified editions of the operating system designed for the developing world and are not sold in developed countries.

The problem of variety is compounded the minute you start working with older computers or talking with users or techs who've been working with computers for several years. You'll hear about old versions of Windows such as Windows 98 or Windows 2000. Huh? What are these versions (see Figure 2.1)? How do they fit in the picture?

This section outlines the history of Microsoft Windows and then takes an in-depth look at the differences among the many versions of Microsoft's flagship operating system. That way you can sort out the essentials for today's techs from the many varieties you'll hear about.

Microsoft entered the operating system game in the early 1980s with a command-line OS called Microsoft Disk Operating System, or MS-DOS. With a command-line OS, you interacted with the computer to run programs, save files, and perform all the other computing functions by typing and then pressing the ENTER key on your keyboard. This whole typing thing

worked for people who could memorize commands and such, but alternative operating systems, such as Apple's Mac OS, offered a visual interface, where you could interact with the computer by clicking on pictures. The time came for Microsoft to step up its game and produce a graphical user interface (GUI) where users could use a mouse to point and click.

Early Windows

• **Figure 2.1** Lots of Windows!

The earliest version of Windows, Microsoft Windows 1.0, arrived in 1985 and was little more than a graphical overlay of the DOS command-line operating system. This overlay version of Windows went through a number of updates, ending with the first truly popular version of Windows, Windows for Workgroups version 3.1 (see Figure 2.2).

Microsoft released several editions of Windows 3.1, with minor differences in name. Techs call the editions collectively Windows 3.*x*.

In 1989, Microsoft offered a completely separate version of Windows called Windows NT. Windows NT was a true graphical operating system and was dramatically more powerful than the Windows overlay versions. Windows NT went through a number of editions, culminating with Windows NT 4.0 in 1996 (see Figure 2.3).

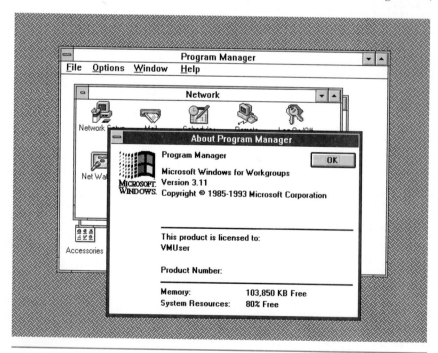

Windows NT had so many features that showing them all could take days, but one is important. NT came with a new way to organize hard drives and files, called the NT File System (NTFS). Before NTFS, all versions of Windows used an ancient file system called the file allocation table (FAT). NTFS took care of a number of problems, the biggest of which was security. FAT had no file security, meaning it had no user accounts, passwords, or permissions to enable people to control access to files. NTFS was built from the ground up with security in mind. We'll cover both FAT and NTFS later in the book; for now, just appreciate that NTFS began with Windows NT.

It wasn't until 1995 that Microsoft dumped the overlay concept and introduced Windows 95, the first

• **Figure 2.2** Windows for Workgroups

• **Figure 2.3** Windows NT 4.0

version of Windows for the standard user that was also a full-blown operating system (see Figure 2.4). Windows 95 offered many improvements over Windows 3.*x*, and eventually Microsoft released several upgraded versions as well, such as Windows 98, Windows 98 SE, and Windows Me.

The arrival of Windows 2000 in 2001 changed things. Throughout most of the 1990s, Windows was in a bit of a mess. Microsoft had two totally different operating systems—each called Windows—that it sold for two different markets. Microsoft sold the Windows 9*x* series for the home user and small office, and it sold the much more powerful Windows NT series for corporate environments.

Windows 2000 was the first step toward changing this mess. It was based on Windows NT (including support for NTFS), but it included a great interface, provided support for nearly any program, and was substantially easier to use than Windows NT. Microsoft originally presented Windows 2000 as a replacement for Windows NT, but its stability and ease of use motivated many knowledgeable Windows 9*x* users to upgrade to Windows 2000 as well. Windows 2000 started to appear as "the single Windows to replace all the other versions."

Modern Windows

The vast majority of computers in the field today run one of the three modern versions of Windows, so the CompTIA A+ certification focuses on those: Windows XP, Windows Vista, and Windows 7. But as you know from Table 2.1 at the beginning of this chapter, just saying the name of a Windows version doesn't do justice to the editions within that version. The trick is to organize these editions in a way that enables you to discover their

When we describe Windows 95, 98, 98 SE, and Me from a historical standpoint, we lump them all together, using the term "Windows 9*x*."

Windows 2000 was the last version of Windows to come in both Server and Professional editions. After the release of Windows XP, Microsoft introduced the next version of Windows Server as Server 2003. Windows Server 2008 R2 is the latest edition of Windows Server. As of this writing, Microsoft's newest server product, codenamed Windows Server 8 (WS8), is right around the corner, so keep your eyes peeled!

Windows 95—the Windows of your forefathers

similarities and differences. In this section, we'll look at editions of Windows XP, Vista and 7, as well as a few other versions of Windows, and see the differences in detail.

802

Windows XP

Windows XP came hot on the heels of Windows 2000. Under the hood, XP was basically the same as Windows 2000, but it added a dramatically improved interface and a number of new features, such as a built-in CD writer. Microsoft also broke with the beauty of 2000's "one OS for everyone" idea. Microsoft visualized three types of users—professionals, home users, and media junkies—so Windows XP came in three editions: Windows XP Professional, Windows XP Home, and Windows XP Media Center.

Windows XP Professional

Microsoft Windows XP Professional is, in many people's opinions, the most versatile and therefore the most mainstream edition of Windows XP. Microsoft tuned Windows XP Professional for office environments with many users sharing lots of data and multiple users sharing single computers. Windows XP Professional provides full-blown data security, and it is the only edition of Windows XP with the capability of logging onto a special Windows Server–controlled network called a *domain*.

• **Figure 2.5** Windows XP Professional

A Windows domain is a group of networked computers all under the control of a single computer running some edition of Windows Server. Users on a domain can use a single logon with their computer that defines everything they can do on every other computer on the domain. (See Chapter 14 for all the details of the amazing Windows domain.) Figure 2.5 shows a typical Windows XP Professional desktop.

Windows XP Home

As its name implies, Windows XP Home is designed for the home and small-office user. Windows XP Home is a stripped-down edition of Windows XP Professional. The best way to describe Windows XP Home is to list the Windows XP Professional features that Windows XP Home lacks. Windows XP Home does *not* have

- **The ability to log on to a Windows domain** A Windows Home PC may log on to any single Windows server, but you must have a user name and password on every single server. With a domain, you can have one user name and password that works on all computers that are members of the domain.

- **Encrypting file system** With Windows XP Professional, you can encrypt a file or a folder so that only you can read it. Windows XP Home lacks this feature.

- **Support for multiple processors** Windows XP Home does not support more than one physical CPU. Windows XP Professional supports two separate CPUs.

CPU support is based on physical CPUs, not the number of cores in a single CPU.

- **Support for Remote Desktop** A Windows XP Professional PC may be remotely accessed from another computer by using Remote Desktop (see Figure 2.6). You cannot access a Windows XP Home system in this fashion.

- **Support for NTFS Access Control** The NTFS file system is capable of powerful controls on what users may do to a file or folder. Windows XP Home doesn't give you the ability to control these NTFS permissions individually. When you look at the properties of a file or folder in Windows XP Home, you'll notice that there is no Security tab. Instead, Windows XP Home's Sharing tab (see Figure 2.7) shows that only one folder, the Shared Documents folder, is open for sharing—very different from XP Professional.

- **Support for group policies** Do you need to keep users from using a certain program? Do you want to prevent them from changing the screensaver? What do you want to do if they try to log in three times unsuccessfully? That's the job of group polices. Well, if you want this level of control on your system, get Windows XP Professional, because XP Home doesn't support them. Group policies are discussed in Chapter 18.

A few more differences exist between Windows XP Professional and XP Home, but the preceding are the ones you're most likely to run into. Basically, if you want serious control of the folders, files, users, and network, you need XP Professional.

• **Figure 2.6** Remote Desktop

Windows XP Media Center

Windows XP Media Center is a specialized XP edition that includes the very handy Windows Media Center program (see Figure 2.8). Media Center is a Personal Video Recorder (PVR) program that enables you to watch and record television (you'll need a TV tuner card) and organize all of your media, from photos to music.

Other than the Media Center program, Windows XP Media Center's capabilities are identical to those of Windows XP Home.

Windows Vista

In January of 2007, Microsoft announced Windows Vista. Vista introduced a new interface as well as some very different underpinnings, which we will discuss both in this chapter and later chapters. These changes created some serious teething problems that Microsoft fixed over time, though not fast enough to protect Vista from a nasty "bad operating system" opinion that lasts to this day. Love it or hate it, the CompTIA A+ 220-802 exam expects you to know Vista.

Microsoft carried on the concept of different editions of Windows for different markets. Let's look at the most common editions of Vista.

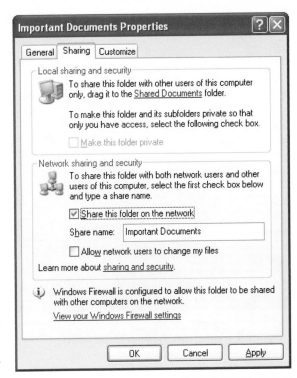

• **Figure 2.7** Windows XP Home Sharing tab

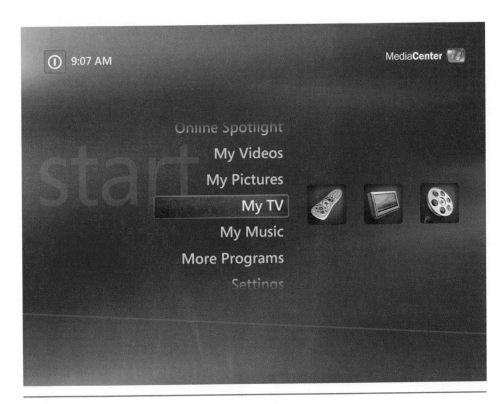

• **Figure 2.8** Windows XP Media Center

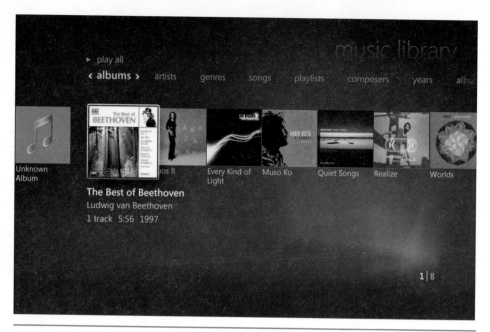

Windows Vista Home Basic

Windows Vista Home Basic is roughly equivalent to Windows XP Home. Microsoft gears it to home users not needing more advanced multimedia support.

Windows Vista Home Premium

Windows Vista Home Premium is the same as Windows Vista Home Basic, but it adds an upgraded Windows Media Center PVR application, similar to the one found in Windows XP Media Center (see Figure 2.9).

• **Figure 2.9** Vista Home Premium Media Center

 You can determine your Windows version by right-clicking My Computer in Windows XP, or Computer in Vista and Windows 7, and selecting Properties.

Windows Vista Business

Windows Vista Business is the basic business edition and has all the security, file-sharing, and access controls seen in Windows XP Professional.

Windows Vista Ultimate

Windows Vista Ultimate combines all of the features of every other Vista edition and includes some other features, such as a game performance tweaker and DVD ripping capability (see Figure 2.10).

Windows Vista Enterprise

Windows Vista Enterprise is an enhanced edition of Windows Vista Business and includes extra features like BitLocker Drive Encryption and support for two physical CPUs. This edition cannot be purchased through normal stores. You'll have to go through Microsoft directly to purchase it.

• **Figure 2.10** Vista Ultimate

Windows 7

Comparing the look and feel of Windows Vista to Windows 7 might make you think that the two operating systems are far more alike than different—and you'd be right. So if Windows Vista and Windows 7 look and act so much alike, why didn't Microsoft just call Windows 7 "Windows Vista: The Fixed Version"? By the time Microsoft "fixed" Windows Vista, nobody wanted anything to do with it—people were reinstalling Windows XP! Microsoft didn't have a choice; it had to call this "fixed" Vista something new. Enter Windows 7 (see Figure 2.11).

Microsoft created several editions of Windows 7, closely following Windows Vista's release model. Let's look at each edition of Windows 7 and see how they compare.

Windows 7 Starter

Around the time of Windows 7's release, netbooks (super-lightweight laptops, mostly used for Web browsing) were incredibly popular. Windows 7 Starter is a stripped-down edition of the OS designed to complement the limited role of the netbook. Windows 7 Starter lacks many of the advanced networking, media, and graphics capabilities of other versions of Windows, focusing instead on easy Internet access.

Windows 7 Home Premium

Windows 7 Home Premium is the most basic and most widely released edition of Windows 7. Roughly comparable to Windows Vista Home Premium, this edition of Windows 7 includes a lot of media functionality and some advanced network functions.

• **Figure 2.11**　The Windows 7 desktop

Chapter 2: Visible Windows

You should know which tools are available in the various editions of Windows for the CompTIA A+ 802 exam. For example, Windows XP Mode works only with Windows 7 Professional, Ultimate, and Enterprise. It comes as a separate download and requires virtualization software such as Windows Virtual PC.

Windows 7 Professional

Stepping up from Windows 7 Home Premium, Windows 7 Professional adds support for joining domains, as well as support for powerful features like Windows XP Mode (enabling you to run Windows XP programs inside Windows 7) and Remote Desktop Connection (enabling you to connect to another computer over a network and see that computer's desktop as if it were your own).

Windows 7 Ultimate

Windows 7 Ultimate includes, as the name implies, everything that Windows 7 has to offer. You'll find advanced networking, backup, and security tools to complete your ultimate OS experience.

Windows 7 Enterprise

Windows 7 Enterprise is very similar to Windows Vista Enterprise and can only be purchased directly from Microsoft. Based on Windows 7 Professional, Enterprise includes extra features designed for large businesses, such as enhanced network searches, increased application security, and data protection using BitLocker.

Enter 64-bit Windows

From roughly 1986 to around 2001, all CPUs were 32-bit. While it's possible to go into agonizing depth about the difference between 32- and 64-bit CPUs, for now let's keep it simple: a 32-bit CPU can only use a maximum of 4 gigabytes (2^{32} bytes = 4,294,967,296 bytes) of RAM. Starting in 2001, we began to see 64-bit CPUs that could accept more than 4 gigabytes. 64-bit-capable CPUs are now the norm, while 32-bit-only CPUs are mostly relegated to netbooks and smartphones.

The leap from 32-bit to 64-bit processing has a number of advantages. The really big compelling reason to go from 32- to 64-bit is that 64-bit CPUs support more than 4 GB of RAM. The more RAM you have, the more programs—and the bigger the programs—your system can run. Until fairly recently, not too many of us cared to go above 4 GB of RAM. We didn't need the extra RAM, and we didn't have a CPU that could run at 64 bits. My, how things have changed over the past few years!

The 64-bit CPUs first showed up with the Intel Itanium back in 2001. At that time the only folks interested in 64-bit processing were large data centers and a few organizations that needed to crunch big numbers. To run a computer with an Itanium, you needed an operating system that worked with a 64-bit processor. Up to that point, every version of Windows ran only at 32-bit. Microsoft answered the call by creating special 64-bit editions of Windows 2000 and XP, but these 64-bit editions were very rare and ran only on the Itanium.

In 2003, Advanced Micro Devices (AMD) started to ship the popular Athlon 64 CPU. This CPU could run in either 32-bit or 64-bit mode, making 64-bit a realistic option for most of us. Intel followed AMD around 2004 with Pentium 4 CPUs also capable of 32-bit or 64-bit processing. Since then, almost every CPU sold by Intel or AMD has the ability to run in either 32-bit or 64-bit mode. Moving from 32-bit to 64-bit is easy, but only if you

Remember for the exams that 32-bit CPUs can support up to 4 GB of RAM. In concept, 64-bit CPUs can support up to 16 *exabytes* of memory. No one has made a CPU that supports the full 64-bit amount, however, and you certainly won't find that much memory in the typical PC.

have an edition of Windows to support 64-bit. Microsoft has multiple editions of Windows designed to support 64-bit CPUs.

Windows XP 64-bit Edition

The 64-bit-only edition of Windows XP was called Windows XP 64-bit Edition (apparently Microsoft decided not to get cute when naming that one). Given that it worked only on Intel Itanium processors, the chance of your seeing this operating system is pretty small unless you decide to work in a place with powerful server needs. The Windows XP Professional x64 Edition is a little more common, as it runs on any AMD or Intel processor that supports both 32 and 64 bits (see Figure 2.12).

Windows XP 64-bit editions have had some impact, as they were the first stable Windows editions that truly supported 64-bit processing, but it was the introduction of Microsoft Vista that really started the move into 64-bit computing.

Windows Vista and Windows 7 64-bit Editions

Each of the previously listed Vista and Windows 7 editions comes in both 32-bit and 64-bit editions (except for Windows 7 Starter). As we move into PCs with more than 4 GB of RAM, it's important to make sure your edition of Windows is a 64-bit edition (see Figure 2.13).

Transitioning to 64-bit Windows

Techs use "x86" or "x64" to describe a particular computer architecture, implying that there is some compatibility within that architecture. This matters because people need to know that the software they purchase will work

Tech Tip

Four-Gigabyte Limit
All 32-bit editions of Windows support a maximum of 4 GB of RAM. If your PC has more than 4 GB and you're not running 64-bit Windows, you might as well remove any RAM above 4 GB—you're wasting it!

Every installation DVD of Windows 7 comes with both 32-bit and 64-bit editions on the same disc.

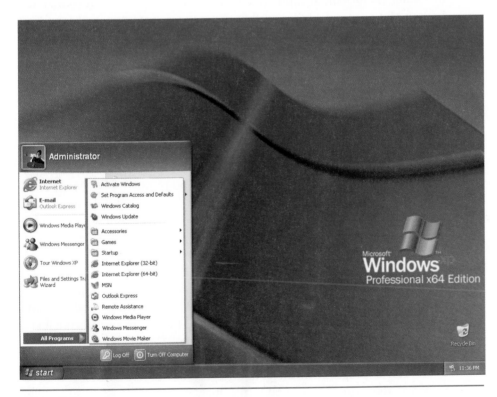

• **Figure 2.12** Windows XP Professional x64 Edition

properly with the computer they have. The transition from 32-bit editions of Windows to 64-bit editions of Windows requires a certain update in terminology.

x86 versus x64 Intel originally used numbers to name its CPUs, such as 8086, 80286, 80386, and so on. To talk about them collectively, the industry replaced the leading numbers with an *x* and kept the numbers that stayed consistent for all the processors, thus **x86** describes the Intel CPU architecture for PCs. All the 32-bit editions of Windows were designed to run on x86 architecture.

The move to 64-bit CPUs and, equally importantly, to 64-bit editions of Windows required some sort of change in terminology. Microsoft and others picked up the x86 terminology and changed it to market 64-bit-only

editions of their software, branding the 64-bit software as **x64**. A consumer, therefore, could look at a product such as Windows XP Professional x64 Edition and very quickly know that the software was designed for 64-bit CPUs rather than 32-bit CPUs.

Software Compatibility Transitions to updated architecture, such as the change from x86 to x64, create concern among users, because they fear that their old programs won't run or will run poorly, or that they'll have problems with compatibility down the road. Techs need to allay those fears by educating users properly. Here's the scoop.

Most of the 64-bit processors run either 32-bit or 64-bit editions of Windows without missing a beat. The 64-bit editions of Windows require a 64-bit CPU; they snicker at 32-bit processors and refuse to play. Many companies have produced 64-bit editions of applications that only work with 64-bit Windows running with a 64-bit CPU. Great, right? But what about all those 32-bit applications out there working for a living? It gets interesting.

Windows Vista and Windows 7 64-bit editions support most 32-bit applications, sometimes without any user intervention and sometimes through explicit use of the Windows compatibility mode options. (Just for the record, you sometimes need to use Windows compatibility mode options to run older programs on Windows 32-bit editions, so it's not just a function of 64-bit support for 32-bit applications.) Windows can try to emulate previous versions of Windows if an application balks at loading.

To run a program in an emulated version of Windows, you need to access the primary executable file that, when double-clicked, makes the program run. We'll go through where to find the program files in the

various versions of Windows later in this chapter, but a quick example should suffice here. A user has a custom program—called "Widgets for XP"—designed to take advantage of particular features in Windows XP Professional with Service Pack 2 installed and it doesn't work in Windows Vista or 7. Open Computer and go to C:\Program Files\Widgets for XP and look for a file with the type listed as Application, such as WidgetsXP.exe (see Figure 2.14). Right-click and select Properties.

On the Compatibility tab, you can select the checkbox next to *Run this program in compatibility mode for:* and select the OS of choice (see Figure 2.15). In this case, you would select Windows XP (Service Pack 2) to provide optimal compatibility for the application. Windows saves the configuration change and tries to open the program in compatibility mode each time the program loads.

• **Figure 2.14** Finding an executable file

Microsoft regularly patches Windows to fix problems. That's what the "with Service Pack 2" means in the example here. Chapter 8 covers updating Windows in detail.

• **Figure 2.15** Compatibility mode options

■ The Windows Interface

All versions of Windows share certain characteristics, configuration files, and general look and feel. Here's some good news: You'll find the same, or nearly the same, utilities in almost all versions of Windows, and once you master one version—both GUI and command-line interface—you'll pretty much have them all covered. This section covers the essentials: where to find things, how to maneuver, and what common utilities are available. Where versions of Windows differ in concept or detail, I'll point that out along the way. You'll get to the underlying structure of Windows in the subsequent two sections of this chapter. For now, let's look at the common user interface.

User Interface

Windows offers a set of utilities, or **interfaces**, that every user should know about—both how and why to access them. And since every user should know about them, certainly every CompTIA A+ certified tech should as well! Let's take a quick tour of the typical Windows GUI.

Logon

Logging onto a Windows computer is something we all do, but few of us take time to appreciate the process. Your user name and password define what you can do on your computer. Every version of Windows supports multiple users on a single machine, so the starting point for any tour of the Windows user interface starts with the **logon screen**. Figure 2.16 shows the Windows XP logon screen.

Windows XP introduced a new type of logon called the **Welcome screen** (see Figure 2.17). If you're using Windows XP Home or Media Center, this is the only logon screen you will see. Windows XP Professional also has the Welcome screen, but if you connect to a domain, you'll see a more classic logon screen harkening back to the days of Windows 2000 (see Figure 2.18).

• **Figure 2.16** Windows XP logon screen

All editions of Windows Vista and Windows 7 use an improved version of Windows XP's Welcome screen (see Figure 2.19).

Desktop

The Windows **desktop** is your primary interface to the computer. The desktop is always there, underneath whatever applications you have

• **Figure 2.17** Windows XP Welcome screen

• **Figure 2.18** Windows XP domain logon screen

open. The desktop analogy appeals to most people—we're used to sitting down at a desk to get work done. Figure 2.20 shows a nice, clean Windows XP desktop; note the icons on the left and the various graphical elements across the bottom. You can add folders and files to the desktop and customize the background to change its color or add a picture. Most people like to do so—certainly, I do! As an example, Figure 2.21 shows the desktop from my home system—a Windows 7 Ultimate PC.

Clearly the Windows Vista and Windows 7 desktops differ a lot compared to the Windows XP desktop. What you're seeing is something called the Aero desktop. The Aero desktop adds a number of impressive aesthetic features to your desktop that Microsoft claims makes the user experience more enjoyable and productive. I'm not going to get into an argument on the value of the Aero desktop, but it is an important part of the modern Windows interface. Most of the Aero features are more about looks than adding

Tech Tip

Your Desktop Is a Folder

Your desktop is actually a folder in your computer. Whatever is in that folder shows up on your desktop. It's critical that you know how to get to that folder in every version of Windows covered on the CompTIA A+ exam.

Windows Vista Home Basic and Windows 7 Starter do not support the Aero desktop.

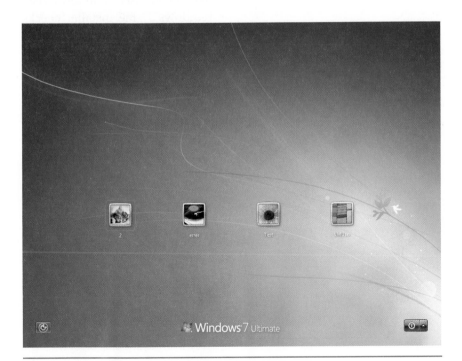

• **Figure 2.19** Windows 7 Welcome screen

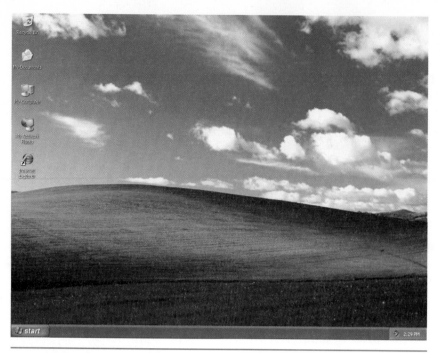

● **Figure 2.20** Windows XP desktop

functionality, but the end result is a smoother desktop with a few noteworthy features. **Transparency**, as the name implies, gives an adjustable amount of transparency to the edges of your windowed programs, as you can see in Figure 2.22.

Flip 3D enables you to view and select all of your open windows in a 3D format, as shown in Figure 2.23.

Flip 3D is fun to use. Press the WINDOWS KEY followed by the TAB key to start it. Keep pressing TAB to cycle through the windows. When the window you want is in the front, release both keys, and that window will become the active window. Try WINDOWS KEY-TAB-SHIFT to scroll through your windows in the opposite direction.

To use the Aero desktop, you must have a video card that supports it. Here's what Microsoft says you need:

- DirectX 9 capability or better
- At least 128 megabytes of video RAM
- Windows Display Driver Model (WDDM) driver
- Pixel Shader version 2.0

● **Figure 2.21** Mike's messy desktop

When you install Windows Vista or Windows 7, the installer checks your video to determine if it can support Aero. If your video card is capable, Aero turns on automatically. To check, press the WINDOWS KEY-TAB combination. If Flip 3D appears, you have Aero. If it doesn't, Aero is not active.

To turn on Aero in Windows Vista, right-click on your desktop and select the Personalize menu option. Next, select Window Color and Appearance. If you see a screen that looks like Figure 2.24, you already have Aero running. If you see a screen that looks like Figure 2.25, select the Windows Aero color scheme to activate the Aero desktop.

• **Figure 2.22** Transparency

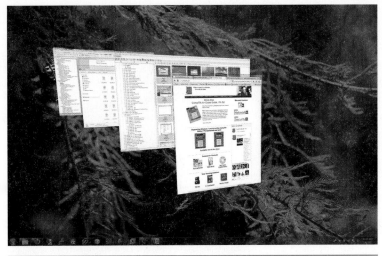

• **Figure 2.23** Flip 3D

If you're running Aero, note that the Window Color and Appearance screen shown in Figure 2.24 has a slider to adjust the transparency settings and a checkbox to turn transparency off completely.

Windows 7 makes activating Aero even easier. Right-click on your Desktop and select Personalize. If you see any Aero themes, as shown in Figure 2.26, you can select one to activate the Aero desktop.

There are a number of other features that, although not on the CompTIA A+ certification exams, you really should try. The WINDOWS KEY-T combination gives a preview of all minimized windows. ALT-TAB gives a preview of all running windows. Also, in Windows 7, pressing WINDOWS KEY-LEFT ARROW or WINDOWS KEY-RIGHT ARROW will fill the respective half of your screen with the active window. Try Aero. It may not be the productivity tool Microsoft promises it to be, but it sure is fun.

Tech Tip

Upgrade Time!

If your computer can't run the Aero desktop, you need to upgrade your system to meet the minimum requirements. This usually means a new video card or updated video card drivers. See Chapter 11 for details.

• **Figure 2.24** You've got Aero!

• **Figure 2.25** The lack of transparency and the flat window with no drop shadow show that Aero is not activated.

Taskbar and Start Menu

The **taskbar** runs along the bottom of all Windows desktops and includes up to four sections (depending on the version of Windows and your configuration). Starting at the left side, these are the Start button, the Quick Launch toolbar (in Windows XP and Windows Vista), the running programs area, and the notification area. Although the taskbar sits at the bottom of the desktop by default, you can move it to either side or to the top of the screen.

• **Figure 2.26** Select one of the Aero themes to activate the Aero Desktop in Windows 7.

The taskbar contains the **Start button**, probably the most clicked button on all Windows systems. You can find the Start button on the far left end of the taskbar. Figure 2.27 shows the Start buttons for Windows XP, Windows Vista, and Windows 7 (in order). Click the Start button to open the Start menu, where you can see the applications installed on the system and start them.

• **Figure 2.27** Three different Windows Start buttons

Try moving your cursor onto the All Programs menu item. When the All Programs menu appears, move the cursor to Accessories. Locate the Notepad program and click it. By default, Windows XP hides lesser-used menu options, so if you don't see Notepad, click the double down-arrows at the bottom of the Accessories menu to make Notepad appear.

Great! If you opened Notepad properly, you should see something like Figure 2.28, with Notepad displaying an untitled text page. Notice how Notepad shows up on the taskbar at the bottom of your screen. Most running programs appear on the taskbar in this way. Close the Notepad program by clicking on the button with the X in the upper-right corner of the Notepad window. Look again at the taskbar to see that Notepad no longer appears there.

• **Figure 2.28** Notepad application (note the buttons in the upper-right corner)

Now look all the way to the right end of the taskbar. This part of the taskbar is known officially as the **notification area**, though many techs and the CompTIA A+ 220-802 exam calls it the **system tray**. You will at a minimum see the current time displayed in the system tray, and on most Windows systems you'll also see a number of small icons there. Figure 2.29 shows the system tray on a Windows Vista PC.

These icons show programs running in the background. Most programs run in a window. Background programs function like any other program except they do not use a window, simply because the nature of their particular jobs makes a window unnecessary. Thousands of programs like to run in the system tray: network status, volume controls, battery state (on laptops), and removable device status are just a few examples. What shows up on yours depends on your version of Windows, what hardware you use, and what background programs you have installed. Some of the icons in Figure 2.29, for example, include virtual machine software, a monitor calibration program, and my e-mail program.

On Windows XP and Vista systems, you'll find the **Quick Launch toolbar** near the left end of the taskbar (see Figure 2.30). Here, you can place often-used programs and open them with a single click. On Windows XP systems, the Quick Launch toolbar is not displayed on the taskbar by default, so before you can use this convenient feature, you must right-click the taskbar, select Properties, and check Show Quick Launch. To change the contents of the Quick Launch toolbar, simply drag icons onto or off of it.

You have a lot of clicking to do in this chapter, so take a moment to reflect on what I call the General Rules of Clicking. With a few exceptions, these rules always apply, and they really help in manipulating the Windows interface to do whatever you need done:

- Click menu items once to use them.
- Click icons once to select them.
- Click icons twice to use them.
- Right-click anything and select Properties to see its properties.

Microsoft calls the area at the far right of the taskbar the *notification area*, but you might see it referred to on the CompTIA A+ 220-802 exam as the *system tray*.

• **Figure 2.29** System tray showing several icons and the time

• **Figure 2.30** Quick Launch toolbar

● **Figure 2.31** Pinned applications

Windows 7 takes the Quick Launch toolbar and marries it to the running program area thumbnails, creating **pinned applications** (see Figure 2.31). You can pin application icons directly onto the running application area. When you open one of these pinned applications, its icon changes to show that it is now open. If you open an application that isn't pinned to the task-bar, its icon still shows up, but will disappear when you close it. If you've ever used the Apple OS X dock (perish the thought!), then you've used this type of feature.

Microsoft introduced the **Jump List** with Windows 7 to show you context-sensitive information about whatever is on your taskbar (see Figure 2.32). If you look at the Jump List for Microsoft Word, for example, you'll see recently opened documents. The Jump List for iTunes enables you to skip forward and backward through the songs in your playlist. To open a Jump List, click and drag upward on the icon in the taskbar or right-click on the icon.

The Many Faces of Windows Explorer

Windows Explorer enables you to manipulate files and folders stored on all the drives in or connected to your computer. Microsoft presents the tool in a variety of ways to help you focus quickly on what you want to accomplish. If you want to see the contents of an optical disc, for example, you can open **My Computer** (Windows XP) or **Computer** (Windows Vista/7) by double-clicking the icon on the desktop or selecting the icon from the Start menu to have Windows Explorer open with the drives displayed (see Figure 2.33). To display the contents of a drive or folder, double-click it.

Windows Explorer in Windows XP offers a series of common tasks in a bar along the left side of the screen, as you can see in Figure 2.34. Windows Vista and Windows 7 also offer tasks, but the options display in a bar below the location bar, near the top of the window (see Figure 2.34).

● **Figure 2.32** A Jump List

When you access My Documents (Windows XP) or Documents (Windows Vista/7) by double-clicking the icon on the desktop or selecting it from the Start menu, Windows opens Windows Explorer with your user folders displayed. Because your My Documents/Documents folder is stored (by default) on the C: hard drive, Windows Explorer shows the contents of that drive, drilled down specifically to your folders.

The fact that one way to open Windows Explorer is to double-click My Computer or Computer, and another way to open Windows Explorer is to double-click My Documents or Documents—and the two methods show different contents initially—leads many users to assume that they have two distinct tools. That's simply not the case. Windows Explorer changes what's displayed to suit specific tasks preset by Microsoft, but it's a single tool that can point to different locations on your computer.

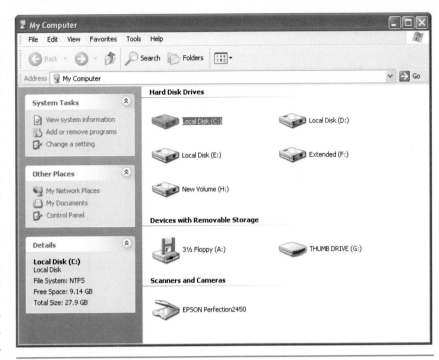

• **Figure 2.33** Windows Explorer in Windows XP displaying the drives installed, as well as common tasks on the left

Even better, you can change the look of Windows Explorer by clicking a button. The Folders button in Windows XP toggles the **Folders list** on or off on the left (see Figure 2.35). The Folders list is a tree menu that enables you to move the focus of Windows Explorer to different folders or drives. The Folders list replaces the common tasks bar in Windows XP. Note that

• **Figure 2.34** Windows Explorer in Windows 7 displaying the drives installed and showing tasks

• **Figure 2.35** Windows Explorer in Windows XP with the Folders list toggled on

the Folders list is enabled by default in Windows Vista and Windows 7 no matter whether you open the tool through Computer or Documents.

In Windows Vista and Windows 7, you can alter the view of Windows Explorer in several ways. On the taskbar, you can click the down arrow next to the *Change your view* button to change the size of the icons, the details displayed, and more. You can turn off the Folders list (known in Vista and 7 as the **Navigation pane**) if desired by clicking the down arrow next to Organize, selecting Layout from the menu options, and then deselecting Navigation pane.

The Folders list view makes copying and moving files and folders from one location to another very easy. The steps differ slightly when you copy to a folder on the same drive versus when you copy to a folder on a different drive, although the first step is the same: select a folder in the Folders list, and the contents of that folder appear in the main pane on the right.

To move or copy a file from one folder to another folder on the same drive, click and hold a file or folder in the main pane and then drag the cursor over to any folder in the Folders list. A → symbol will appear (in Windows Vista and 7, although not in Windows XP). Release the mouse button, and you move that file or folder to the new folder. If you want to copy a file or folder rather than move it, press the CTRL key on your keyboard and then click and drag into the desired folder. The → symbol (if any) changes to a +; release the mouse button to copy the file or folder.

To copy or move a file from one folder to another folder on a different drive, click and hold a file or folder in the main pane and then drag the cursor over to any folder on the other drive in the Folders list, and a + symbol will appear. Release the mouse button, and you'll make a copy of that file or folder in the new folder. If you want to move a file or folder rather than just copy it, press the SHIFT key on your keyboard and then click and drag into the desired folder. The + symbol changes to a → in Windows Vista/7 or just goes away in Windows XP; release the mouse button to move the file or folder.

Notice the differences in the icons displayed in Windows Explorer? Windows assigns different icons to different types of files, based on their **extensions**, the set of characters at the end of a filename, such as .EXE, .TXT, or .JPG. The oldest extensions, starting from back in the DOS era, are usually three characters, but current programs may use two-character extensions, such as .JS (JavaScript) or .AU (audio), or even four-character extensions, such as the ubiquitous .HTML for Web pages. In rare cases, a filename might actually have no extension.

As you look at these icons on your own screen, some of you might say, "But I don't see any extensions!" That's because Windows hides them by default. To see the extensions in Windows XP, select Tools | Folder Options to open the Folder Options dialog box. Click the View tab and uncheck *Hide*

 Try This!

Practice Moving and Copying

If the Folders list option is new to you and you haven't done a lot of moving or copying files or folders, try this.

1. Open My Computer or Computer and double-click on the C: drive.

2. Right-click in a blank spot and select New | Folder from the context menu. This will create a new folder named New Folder by default. The name of the New Folder is highlighted for changing when you first create it. If you click elsewhere, the folder keeps the default New Folder name.

3. Select the folder and press F2 or right-click and select Rename from the options. Change the name to something other than New Folder, such as temp, tmp, practice, etc. The rest of this exercise assumes you named the new folder "temp."

4. Click the Folders button in Windows XP or select Organize | Layout | Navigation Pane in Windows Vista/7 if necessary to display the Folders list on the left part of the Windows Explorer screen.

5. In the Folders list, select the temp folder. The contents of that folder should be blank in the main pane.

6. Select any other folder in the Folders list to change the focus of the main pane.

7. Hold down the CTRL key and then click and drag a file or folder from that new folder so that the cursor hovers over the temp folder and you see the + symbol. Release the mouse button and then select the temp folder to see the file or folder you just copied. Note that if you don't hold the CTRL key down, you'll move rather than copy the file.

8. Try this a few more times to increase your comfort level with copying.

9. Now move a file or folder from one folder to the temp folder and then back, verifying that you moved rather than just copied the file. Do *not* do this with any files or folders in the C:\Windows folder! When you move a file in Windows Vista/7, you'll see the + appear before you release the mouse button. In Windows XP you won't see any symbol at all.

extensions for known file types. In Windows Vista/7, select Organize | Folder and search options and then click the View tab to see the same dialog box, which has the same checkbox to uncheck (see Figure 2.36).

There are two other very handy settings under the View tab, but to see the results well, you need to be in the C: drive of Computer, as shown in Figure 2.37.

• **Figure 2.36** Folder Options dialog box

Go back into the View tab of the Folder Options dialog box, click the *Show hidden files and folders* radio button (named *Show hidden files, folders, and drives* in Windows Vista/7), and then uncheck *Hide protected operating system files.* Click the Apply to Folders button in Windows Vista/7 or the Apply to All Folders button in Windows XP. Your C: drive should look like Figure 2.38 when you are finished. As before, when you return to examining the folder contents, you will see the file extensions, and possibly some previously hidden files. You can tell which ones are hidden because they appear somewhat faded or ghostly compared to the non-hidden folders and files.

Now that those files are visible, you have the awesome responsibility of keeping them safe. In general, the less you handle your vital system files, the better. You'll learn some ways to do useful things with files that were previously hidden, but unless you really know what you're doing, it's best to leave them alone. Before you turn a PC over to someone who isn't a trained PC tech, you'll probably want to hide those system files again.

Microsoft has tried to help users organize their files and folders through various user folders and subfolders that you access through Windows Explorer. The different operating systems offer different choices, so let's look at My Documents (Windows XP), the User's Files (Windows Vista/7), and Windows 7's libraries.

There are many scenarios where you'd want to see hidden file extensions and hidden files as well. What if you need to run a program from its executable file, for example, and there are four files in the same folder all named "setup"? Which one do you double-click? Turn the file extensions visible, see which one is setup.exe, and double-click that one. Viewing hidden and system files, on the other hand, enables them to show up in a search. That's very handy for techs. The CompTIA A+ 220-802 exam quizzes you on these topics.

• **Figure 2.37** Default Computer view where many things are hidden

• **Figure 2.38** Computer displaying hidden files and folders

My Documents, My [*Whatever*] All versions of Windows provide a special folder structure for each user account so users have their own places to store personal data. This folder grouping is called **My Documents** in Windows XP. Many Windows programs take advantage of My Documents and by default store their files in the folder or in a subfolder.

Windows XP installations do not show My Documents on the desktop by default. On Windows XP, you can access it through the Start menu, or you can add it to your desktop. Right-click the desktop and select Properties to open the Display Properties dialog box. Select the Desktop tab, and then click on the Customize Desktop button to open the Desktop Items dialog box (see Figure 2.39). On the General tab, select the checkbox next to My Documents, My Computer, or both, and then click OK to close the dialog box and make any selected icons appear on the desktop.

Windows XP's My Documents folder includes several subfolders: My Pictures (which offers filmstrip and thumbnail views of pictures you store there), My Music (which will fire up Media Player to play any file), My Videos (which, again, starts Media Player), and more. Figure 2.40 shows My Pictures using the thumbnail view. Many applications have since jumped on the bandwagon and added their own My [*Whatever*] folders in My Documents. Before I retired my Windows XP machine, for example, I had My eBooks, My Web Sites, My Received Files, My Virtual Machines…My Goodness!

User's Files Windows Vista and Windows 7 take the equivalent of My Documents to a whole new level with the **User's Files**. (Although a Documents folder is available, it's designed literally for documents, such as text files.) Click on the Start menu and you'll see a folder option with the user name of the account that's currently logged into the computer. With that

As with most tools in Windows, Microsoft gives you more than one way to accomplish tasks. In Windows XP and Vista, try right-clicking the Start menu icon, selecting Properties, and choosing the Classic Start Menu radio button.

• **Figure 2.39** Windows XP Desktop Items dialog box

• **Figure 2.40** My Pictures subfolder in My Documents

option, not only do you get all of the folders you get in Windows XP, but Windows Vista/7 also add a number of other folders as well as interesting but important data such as your Internet Explorer favorites and copies of recent searches.

Just as with Windows XP, the user's folder does not appear on the desktop by default. To see this folder, right-click on the desktop, select Personalize, and then click *Change desktop icons* on the left of the Personalization window. You'll see a Desktop Icon Settings dialog box where you can select the User's Files option to display the personal files of the logged-in user account. Figure 2.41 shows the User's Files folder for my editor, with the Desktop Icon Settings dialog box in the background.

Windows 7 Libraries Windows 7 introduced only one new—but very useful—feature to Windows Explorer: libraries. The idea behind libraries is based on two fairly straightforward assumptions:

- People tend to need the same data over and over.
- The data you need for one job/project/function/whatever is rarely stored in a single folder.

• **Figure 2.41** Typical user accounts folder in Windows Vista

Libraries aggregate folders from multiple locations and place them in a single, easy-to-find spot in Windows Explorer. The files and folders don't actually move. The library just creates links to them (see Figure 2.42).

By default, every user has at least four libraries: Documents, Music, Pictures, and Videos. These libraries consist of two folders: the user's My *Whatever* folder for that type of data plus the Public *Whatever* folder under C:\Users\Public. (You'll learn more about these a little later in the chapter.) Let's clarify this subtle but critical concept.

Libraries are *not* folders, but collections of existing folders. Let's say you keep some digital photos in your My Photos folder, but you also have a separate stash of photos on an external hard drive in a folder called "Vacation Pictures." Instead of flipping back and forth between these folders to see all of your photos, you could use a library to link them.

When you open a library, you see the contents of every folder in the library together, as if they were all in the same folder (but they aren't). Your photos in My Photos and Vacation Pictures will appear side by side.

You can create a library from any instance of Windows Explorer. Right-click Libraries in the navigation pane, select New | Library, and give the library a name. Ta-da! You've just made your first library.

Now you need to add folders to your library. You can add folders from your system or from shares on other systems. To add a folder to a library, right-click the folder in Windows Explorer, select *Include in library*, and then click the library you want to use in the fly-out menu. You can also right-click a library, select Properties, and use the *Include a folder* button to add folders.

Remember two important items:

- Only folders can populate a library—no individual files, no printers, etc.

- Don't try to remove a folder from a library by deleting it. If you do, you will delete the actual folder. Instead, right-click the folder name under the library name on the Navigation pane and select *Remove location from library*.

 Make sure you can name the four default libraries in Windows 7.

• **Figure 2.42** Libraries in Windows Explorer

Recycle Bin

In Windows, a file is not erased when you delete it. Windows adds a level of protection in the form of a special folder called the **Recycle Bin**. When you delete a file in Windows, the file moves into the Recycle Bin. It stays there until you empty the Recycle Bin or restore the file, or until the Recycle Bin reaches a preset size and starts erasing its oldest contents.

To access the Recycle Bin's properties, right-click the icon on the desktop and select Properties. (You'll find the icon usually in the top left corner of the desktop.) The Recycle Bin's properties look different in different versions of Windows, but they all work basically the same. Figure 2.43 shows the properties of a typical Windows 7 Recycle Bin. Windows will set aside a certain percentage by default (it changes according the size of the drive), but you can specify the amount of drive space to use for the Recycle Bin as well. If a hard drive starts to run low on space, this is one of the first places to check.

• **Figure 2.43** Windows 7 Recycle Bin Properties

My Network Places/Network

Systems tied to a network, either via a network cable or by a modem, have a folder called **My Network Places** in Windows XP or simply **Network** in Windows Vista/7 (see Figure 2.44). This folder shows all the current network connections available to you. You'll learn about My Network Places/Network in Chapter 14.

Windows Sidebar

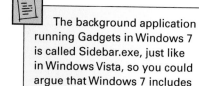

The background application running Gadgets in Windows 7 is called Sidebar.exe, just like in Windows Vista, so you could argue that Windows 7 includes Windows Sidebar.

Windows Vista comes with a GUI feature called the **Windows Sidebar**, a tool that sits on one side of the desktop and enables small helper applications—called Microsoft Gadgets—to run. You can display a clock, for example, or a dynamic weather update. Vista comes with a handful of Gadgets, but developers have gone crazy with them, enabling you to add all sorts of useful tools, such as the Twitter feed and *World of Warcraft* search and realm status Gadgets in Figure 2.45.

Windows 7 also includes Gadgets, but removes the Sidebar concept. You can place Windows 7 Gadgets anywhere on your desktop.

Hot Keys

In Windows, you can use key combinations to go directly to various programs and places. Here's a reasonably extensive list of general-purpose commands for Windows. Be aware that some applications may change the use of these commands.

Function Keys

- **F1** Help
- **F2** Rename

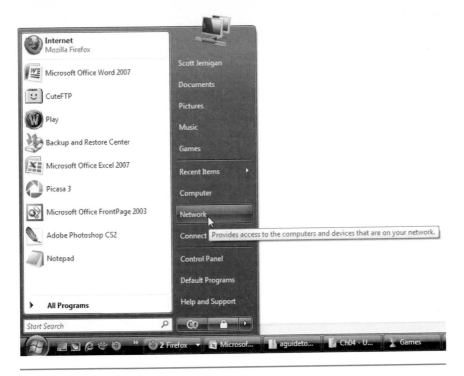

• **Figure 2.44** Network in Windows Vista

- ■ F3 Search menu
- ■ F5 Refresh the current window
- ■ F6 Move among selections in current windows

Popular Hot Keys

- ■ CTRL-ESC Open Start menu
- ■ ALT-TAB Switch between open programs
- ■ ALT-F4 Quit program
- ■ CTRL-Z Undo the last command
- ■ CTRL-A Select all the items in the current window
- ■ SHIFT-DELETE Delete item permanently
- ■ SHIFT-F10 Open a shortcut menu for the selected item (this is the same as right-clicking an object)
- ■ SHIFT Bypass the automatic-run feature for optical media (by pressing and holding down the SHIFT key while you insert optical media)
- ■ ALT-SPACE Display the main window's System menu (from this menu you can restore, move, resize, minimize, maximize, or close the window)
- ■ ALT-ENTER Open the properties for the selected object

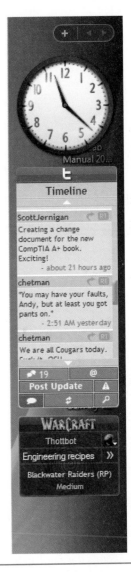

• **Figure 2.45** Windows Sidebar in action

Working with Text

- **CTRL-C** Copy
- **CTRL-X** Cut
- **CTRL-V** Paste
- **CTRL-Z** Undo

Windows Key Shortcuts

These shortcuts use the special Windows key:

- **WINDOWS KEY** Start menu
- **WINDOWS KEY-D** Show desktop
- **WINDOWS KEY-E** Windows Explorer
- **WINDOWS KEY-L** Lock the computer
- **WINDOWS KEY-TAB** Cycle through taskbar buttons (or Flip 3D with Windows Aero in Vista/7)
- **WINDOWS KEY-PAUSE/BREAK** Open the System Properties dialog box

I've covered only the most basic parts of the Windows desktop in this chapter. The typical Windows desktop includes many other parts, but for techs and for the CompTIA A+ 220-802 exam, what you've learned here about the desktop is more than enough.

The CompTIA A+ 802 exam loves to ask detailed questions about the locations of certain folders. Make sure you know this section!

■ Operating System Folders

The modern versions of Windows organize essential files and folders in a relatively similar fashion. All have a primary system folder for storing most Windows internal tools and files. All have a set of folders for programs and user files. Yet once you start to get into details, you'll find some very large differences. It's very important for you to know in some detail the location and function of many common folders and their contents.

System Folder

SystemRoot is the tech name given to the folder in which Windows has been installed. Windows XP, Vista, and 7 all use C:\Windows as the default SystemRoot. Be warned: this is the default folder, but you can change where Windows is installed during the installation process.

It's handy to know about SystemRoot. You'll find it cropping up in many other tech publications, and you can specify it when adjusting certain Windows settings to make sure they work under all circumstances. When used as part of a Windows configuration setting, add percent signs (%) to the beginning and end like so: %SystemRoot%, which means you'll almost never see it as just plain SystemRoot.

If you don't know where Windows is installed on a particular system, here's a handy trick. Get to a command prompt, type **cd %systemroot%**, and press ENTER. The prompt changes to the directory in which the Windows OS files are stored. Slick! See Chapter 9 for details on how to use the command prompt in Windows.

Windows Vista labels the Search bar as *Start Search*. Windows 7 labels it as *Search programs and files*. Techs just call it the *Search bar* because it functions the same in both versions of Windows.

Try This!

Getting to a Command Prompt

Each version of Windows gives you several ways to access a command prompt, so depending on your version, try the steps below.

1. In Windows XP, go to Start | Run to open the Run dialog box.

2. Type **cmd** and press ENTER to open a command prompt.

3. Alternatively, go to Start | All Programs | Accessories | System Tools and select Command Prompt.

1. In Windows Vista and Windows 7, go to Start and type **cmd** into the Search bar. Press ENTER to open a command prompt.

2. Alternatively, go to Start | All Programs | Accessories and select Command Prompt.

The system folder contains many subfolders, too numerous to mention here, but CompTIA wants you to know the names of a number of these subfolders as well as what goes in them. Let's run through the subfolders you should recognize and define (these folders are in all versions of Windows):

- **%SystemRoot%\Fonts** All of the fonts installed in Windows live here.

- **%SystemRoot%\Offline Files (Offline Web Pages in Windows 7)** When you tell your Web browser to save Web pages for offline viewing, they are stored in this folder. This is another folder that Windows automatically deletes if it needs the space.

- **%SystemRoot%\System32** This is the *real* Windows! All of the most critical programs that make Windows run are stored here. 64-bit editions of Windows also store critical files in %SystemRoot%\SysWOW64.

- **%SystemRoot%\Temp** Anytime Windows or an application running on Windows needs to create temporary files, they are placed here. Windows deletes these files automatically as needed, so never place an important file in this folder.

Program and Personal Document Folders

Windows has a number of important folders that help organize your programs and documents. They sit in the root directory at the same level as the system folder, and of course they have variations in name depending on the version of Windows. We'll assume that your computer is using a C: drive—a pretty safe assumption, although there actually is a way to install all of Windows on a second hard-drive partition.

C:\Program Files (All Versions)

By default, most programs install some or all of their essential files into a subfolder of the Program Files folder. If you installed a program, it should have its own folder in here. Individual companies decide how to label their subfolders. Installing Photoshop made by Adobe, for example, creates the Adobe subfolder and then an Adobe Photoshop subfolder within it. Installing Silverlight from Microsoft, on the other hand, only creates a Microsoft Silverlight folder with the program files within it. (Some programmers choose to create a folder at the root of the C: drive, bypassing Program Files altogether, but that's becoming increasingly rare.)

C:\Program Files (x86)

The 64-bit editions of Windows Vista and Windows 7 create two directory structures for program files. The 64-bit applications go into the C:\Program Files folder, whereas the 32-bit applications go into the C:\Program Files (x86) folder. The separation makes it easy to find the proper version of whatever application you seek.

Personal Documents

As you might expect, given the differences among the desktop names for personal document locations outlined earlier in the chapter, the personal folders for Windows XP, Windows Vista, and Windows 7 differ in location and name. Windows XP places personal folders in the Documents and Settings folder, whereas Windows Vista and Windows 7 use the Users folder. From there, they differ even more.

(4)C:\Documents and Settings (Windows XP)

All of the personal settings for each user are stored here. All users have their own subfolders in Documents and Settings. In each user folder, you'll find another level of folders with familiar names such as Desktop, My Documents, and Start Menu. These folders hold the actual contents of these items. Let's dive through these to see the ones you need to know for the CompTIA A+ 220-802 exam.

- **\Documents and Settings\Default User (hidden)** All of the default settings for a user. This folder is a template that Windows copies and customizes when a new user logs on for the first time.

- **\Documents and Settings\All Users** You can make settings for anyone who uses the computer. This is especially handy for applications: some applications are installed so that all users may use them and some applications might be restricted to certain users. This folder stores information for any setting or application that's defined for all users on the PC.

- **\Documents and Settings\Shared Documents** If you're using Windows XP's Simple File Sharing, this is the only folder on the computer that's shared.

- **\Documents and Settings\<User Name>** This folder stores all settings defined for a particular user (see Figure 2.46).

• **Figure 2.46** Contents of a typical \Documents and Settings folder in Windows XP

Opening any user's folder reveals a number of even lower folders. Each of these stores very specific information about the user.

- **\Documents and Settings\<User Name>\Desktop** This folder stores the files on the user's desktop. If you delete this folder, you delete all the files placed on the desktop.

- **\Documents and Settings\<User Name>\<User name's> Documents** This is the My Documents folder for that user.

- **\Documents and Settings\<User Name>\Application Data (hidden)** This folder stores information and settings used by various programs that the user has installed.

- **\Documents and Settings\<User Name>\Start Menu** This folder stores any customizations the user made to the Start menu.

C:\Users (Windows Vista/7) Windows Vista and Windows 7 dump the old Documents and Settings folder for the Users folder. Functionally similar to Documents and Settings, there are a number of subfolders here that you need to know to pass the CompTIA A+ 220-802 exam.

Let's repeat the process, locating the same functions in their new locations.

- **\Users\Default (hidden), \Users\All Users,** and **\Users\<User Name>** All of these folders retain the same functions as in Windows XP.

- **\Users\<User Name>** The big change takes place under each of the \Users\<User Name> folders. This folder still stores all settings defined for a particular user; however, this folder contains more subfolders in Vista/7 than in XP (see Figure 2.47). Luckily, you only need to know a few folders for the exams.

- **\Users\<User Name>\Desktop** Same as in Windows XP.

When you're looking at your own account folders, you'll see My Documents rather than <User name's> Documents in the \Documents and Settings\<User Name> folder.

Vista and 7 make a special hidden folder called "Default User" that points to the User folder to support older applications.

- **\Users\\<User Name>\Documents** This is the Documents folder for that user. Note that in Vista, it's simply known as "Documents," while in Windows 7, it is once again "My Documents."

- **\Users\\<User Name>\Downloads** Microsoft's preferred download folder for applications to use. Most applications do use this folder, but some do not.

- **\Users\\<User Name>\Start Menu** Same as in Windows XP.

Any good tech knows the name and function of all the folders just listed. As a tech, you will find yourself manually drilling into these folders for a number of reasons. Users rarely go directly into any of these folders with Windows Explorer. As a tech, you know that's a good thing, since you appreciate how dangerous it is for them to do so. Imagine a user going into a \Users\<User Name>\Desktop folder and wiping out someone's desktop folders. Luckily, Windows protects these folders by using NTFS permissions, making it very difficult for users to destroy anything other than their own work.

Be very careful here. Some of the folder name differences between XP and Vista/7 are subtle. Make sure you know the difference.

Tech Utilities

Windows offers a huge number of utilities that enable techs to configure the OS, optimize and tweak settings, install hardware, and more. The trick is to know where to go to find them. This section shows the most common locations in Windows where you can access utilities: right-click, Control Panel, Device Manager, System Tools, command line, Microsoft Management

• **Figure 2.47** Contents of a typical \Users\<User Name> folder in Vista

Console, Administrative Tools, and the Action Center. Note that these are locations for tools, not tools themselves, and you can access many tools from more than one of these locations. You'll see some of the same utilities in many of these locations. Stay sharp in this section, as you'll need to access utilities to understand the inner workings of Windows.

Right-Click

Windows, being a graphical user interface OS, covers your monitor with windows, menus, icons, file lists—all kinds of pretty things you click on to do work. Any single thing you see on your desktop is called an *object*. If you want to open any object in Windows, you double-click on it. If you want to change something about an object, you right-click on it.

Right-clicking on an object brings up a small menu called the **context menu**, and it works on everything in Windows. In fact, try to place your mouse somewhere in Windows where right-clicking does *not* bring up a menu (there are a few places, but they're not easy to find). What you see on the little menu when you right-click varies dramatically depending on the item you decide to right-click. If you right-click a running program in the running program area on the taskbar, you'll see items that relate to a window. Windows XP and Vista will present options such as Move, Size, and so on (see Figure 2.48). Windows 7 gives you the Jump List, as we discussed earlier. If you right-click on your desktop, you get options for changing the appearance of the desktop and more (see Figure 2.49). Even different types of files show different results when you right-click on them. Right-clicking is something techs do often.

One menu item you'll see almost anywhere you right-click is Properties. Every object in Windows has properties. When you right-click on something and can't find what you're looking for, select Properties. Figure 2.50 shows the results of right-clicking on Computer in the Start menu—not very exciting. But if you select Properties, you'll get a dialog box like the one shown in Figure 2.51.

Control Panel

The **Control Panel** handles most of the maintenance, upgrade, and configuration aspects of Windows. As such, the Control Panel is the first set of tools for every tech to explore. You can find the Control

• **Figure 2.48** Right-clicking on a running program in Windows XP

• **Figure 2.49** Right-clicking on the desktop in Windows 7 offers numerous settings.

• **Figure 2.50** Right-clicking on Computer

Figure 2.51 Computer properties

Panel by clicking the Start button and choosing Control Panel from the Start menu.

Windows XP, Vista, and 7 open in the Control Panel's Category view by default, which displays the icons in groups like "Printers and Other Hardware." The categories change between each edition of Windows. This view requires an additional click (and sometimes a guess about which category includes the icon you need), so many techs use a more classic view.

The CompTIA A+ 802 exam assumes you use classic view with large icons, so do what every tech does: switch from category view to classic view. In Windows XP, select Switch to Classic View. In Windows Vista, choose Classic View. In Windows 7, select Large icons or Small icons from the View by drop-down list for a similar effect. Figure 2.52 shows the Windows XP Control Panel in both Category and Classic views.

A large number of programs, called **applets**, populate the Control Panel. The names and selection of applets vary depending on the version of Windows and whether any installed programs have added applets. But all versions of Windows have applets that enable you to control specific aspects of Windows, such as the appearance, installed applications, and system settings. Windows XP has Display and Windows Vista/7 have Personalization which enable you to make changes to the look and feel of your Windows desktop and tweak your video settings. Add or Remove Programs (Windows XP) and Programs and Features (Windows Vista/7) enable you to add or remove programs. The System applet (all versions) gives you access to essential system information and tools, such as Device Manager, although Microsoft wisely added Device Manager right on the Control Panel starting with Vista.

Figure 2.52 Windows XP Control Panel in two views: Category (left) and Classic (right)

Every icon you see in the Control Panel is actually a file with the extension .CPL. Any time you get an error opening the Control Panel, you can bet you have a corrupted CPL file. These are a pain to fix. You have to rename all of your CPL files with another extension (I use .CPB) and then rename them back to .CPL one at a time, each time reopening the Control Panel, until you find the CPL file that's causing the lockup.

You can use the Control Panel applets to do an amazing array of things to a Windows system, and each applet displays text that helps explain its functions. The Add Hardware applet in Windows XP, for example, says quite clearly, "Installs and troubleshoots hardware" (see Figure 2.53). They are all like that. Figure 2.54 shows the User Accounts applet. Can you determine its use? (If not, don't sweat it. I'll cover users in Chapter 7.) Don't bother trying to memorize all these applets. Each Control Panel applet relevant to the CompTIA A+ 802 exam is discussed in detail in the relevant chapter throughout the rest of the book. For now, just make sure you can get to the Control Panel and appreciate why it exists.

Even these common applets vary slightly among Windows versions. The CompTIA A+ 220-802 exam does not test you on every little variance among the same applets in different versions—just know what each applet does.

Device Manager

With **Device Manager**, you can examine and configure all of the hardware and drivers in a Windows PC. As you might suspect from that description, every tech spends a lot of time with this tool! You'll work with Device Manager many more times during the course of this book and your career as a PC tech.

There are many ways to get to Device Manager—make sure you know all of them! The first way is to open the Control Panel and double-click the System applet icon. This brings up the System Properties dialog box in Windows XP and the System dialog box in Windows Vista/7. In Windows XP, you access Device Manager by selecting the Hardware tab and then clicking the Device Manager button. Figure 2.55 shows the Hardware tab of the System Properties dialog box in Windows XP. In Windows Vista/7, the System dialog box has a direct connection to Device Manager (see Figure 2.56).

You can also get to the System Properties/System dialog box in all versions of Windows by right-clicking My Computer/Computer and selecting

• **Figure 2.53** Add Hardware Wizard of the Add Hardware applet

Holding down the WINDOWS KEY and pressing PAUSE/BREAK is yet another way to get to the System Properties/System dialog box. Keyboard shortcuts are cool!

• **Figure 2.54** User Accounts window of the User Accounts applet

• **Figure 2.55** Windows XP System applet with the Hardware tab selected

Properties. From there, the path to Device Manager is the same as when you access this dialog box from the Control Panel.

The second (and more streamlined) method is to right-click My Computer/Computer and select Manage. This opens a window called Computer Management, where you'll see Device Manager listed on the left side of the screen, under System Tools. Just click on Device Manager and it opens. You can also access Computer Management by opening the Administrative Tools applet in the Control Panel and then selecting Computer Management (see Figure 2.57).

Why are there so many ways to open Device Manager? Well, remember that we're only looking at locations in Windows from which to open utilities, not at the actual utilities themselves. Microsoft wants you to get to the tools you need when you need them, and it's better to have multiple paths to a utility rather than just one.

Device Manager displays every device that Windows recognizes, organized in special groups called *types*. All devices of the same type are grouped under the same type heading. To see the devices of a particular type, you must open that type's group. Figure 2.57 shows a Windows Vista Device Manager screen with all installed devices in good order—which makes us techs happy. If

The CompTIA A+ 802 exam wants you to know multiple ways to open Device Manager.

• **Figure 2.56** Windows Vista System applet with the Device Manager menu option circled

There is one other "problem" icon you might see on a device in Device Manager—a blue *i* on a white field. According to Microsoft, this means you turned off automatic configuration for a device.

• **Figure 2.57** Device Manager in Computer Management

Windows detects a problem, the device has a down arrow, a red *X*, or a black exclamation point on a yellow field, as in the case of the Digital Still Camera device in Figure 2.58.

A down arrow in Windows Vista/7 or a red *X* in Windows XP means Windows (or you) disabled the device—right-click on the device to enable it (see Figure 2.59). With a black exclamation point, right-click on the device and select Properties. Read the error code and explanation in the Device Status pane (see Figure 2.60). If necessary, look up a Microsoft Knowledge Base article that matches the number to see what to do. There are around 40 different errors—nobody bothers to memorize them!

Device Manager isn't just for dealing with problems. It also enables you to update drivers with a simple click of the mouse (assuming you have a replacement driver on your

• **Figure 2.58** Problem device

• **Figure 2.59** Enabling a disabled device

• Figure 2.60 Problem device properties

computer). Right-click a device and select Update Driver Software from the menu to get the process started. Figure 2.61 shows the options in Windows Vista.

Make sure you can get to Device Manager! You will come back to it again and again in subsequent chapters, because it is the first tool you should access when you have a hardware problem.

System Tools

The Start menu offers a variety of tech utilities collected in one place: System Tools. In the **System Tools** menu, you'll find commonly accessed tools such as System Information and Disk Defragmenter (see Figure 2.62).

Many techs overlook memorizing how to find the appropriate Windows tool to diagnose problems, but nothing hurts your credibility with a client like fumbling around, clicking a variety of menus and applets, while mumbling, "I know it's around here somewhere."

• Figure 2.61 Selecting Update Driver Software in Windows Vista Device Manager

The CompTIA A+ 220-802 exam therefore tests you on a variety of paths to appropriate tools.

To access System Tools in all three versions of Windows, go to Start | All Programs | Accessories | System Tools. Each version of Windows shares many of the same tools, but each includes its own utilities as well. I'll note which version of Windows uses each particular system tool.

Activate Windows (All)

Windows XP unveiled a copy-protection scheme called **activation**. Activation is a process where your computer sends Microsoft a unique code generated on your machine based on the Install CD/DVD's product key and a number of hardware features, such as the amount of RAM, the CPU processor model, and other ones and zeros in your PC. Normally, activation is done at install time, but if you choose not to activate at install or if you make "substantial" changes to the hardware, you'll need to use the Activate Windows utility (see Figure 2.63). With the Activate Windows utility, you can activate over the Internet or over the telephone.

Backup (Windows XP)

The Backup utility enables you to back up selected files and folders to removable media such as tape drives. Backing up is an important function that's covered in detail in Chapter 18.

System Tools
- Character Map
- Computer
- Control Panel
- Disk Cleanup
- Disk Defragmenter
- Internet Explorer (No Add-ons)
- Private Character Editor
- Resource Monitor
- System Information
- System Restore
- Task Scheduler
- Windows Easy Transfer Reports
- Windows Easy Transfer

• **Figure 2.62** System Tools menu options

Once you've activated Windows, the Activate Windows applet goes away.

Neither Windows XP Home nor Windows XP Media Center includes Backup during installation. You must install the Backup program from the Windows installation CD by running the \Valueadd\MSFT\Ntbackup\NTbackup.msi program.

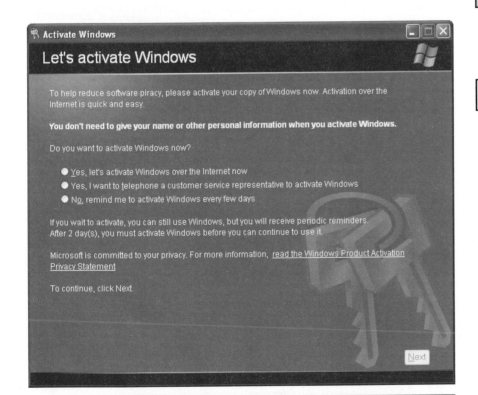

• **Figure 2.63** Activate Windows

Windows 7 has a more powerful backup utility than Windows Vista has, but you won't find it in the System Tools folder. Check out Chapter 18 for more information on Windows 7's backup tools.

Windows 7 includes the Private Character Editor tool, enabling you to create your own characters and symbols for use with the Character Map.

Backup Status and Configuration (Windows Vista)

Vista does not enable you to back up files on your computer selectively. You can only back up personal data with the Backup Status and Configuration Tool or, if you have Vista Business, Ultimate, or Enterprise, perform a complete PC backup by using Windows Complete PC Backup. If you want to pick and choose the file to back up, you need to buy a third-party tool. This tool allows you to back up to optical media, a hard drive, or a networked drive.

Character Map (All)

Ever been using a program only to discover you need to enter a strange character such as the euro character (€) but your word processor doesn't support it? That's when you need the Character Map. It enables you to copy any Unicode character into the Clipboard (see Figure 2.64).

Disk Cleanup (All)

Disk Cleanup looks for unneeded files on your computer, which is handy when your hard drive starts to get full and you need space. Every version of Windows since XP starts this program whenever your hard drive gets below 200 MB of free disk space.

Disk Defragmenter (XP and Vista)

You use Disk Defragmenter to make your hard drive run faster—you'll see more details on this handy tool in Chapter 4. You can access this utility in the same way you access Device Manager; you also find Disk Defragmenter in the Computer Management Console. A simpler method is to select Start | All Programs | Accessories | System Tools—you'll find Disk Defragmenter listed there. You can also right-click on any drive in My Computer

• **Figure 2.64** Character Map

or Computer, select Properties, and click the Tools tab, where you'll find a convenient Defragment Now button.

Files and Settings Transfer Wizard (Windows XP)

Suppose you have an old computer full of files and settings, and you just bought yourself a brand new computer. You want to copy everything from your old computer onto your new computer—what to do? Microsoft touts the Files and Settings Transfer Wizard as just the tool you need (see Figure 2.65). This utility copies your desktop files and folders and, most conveniently, your settings from Internet Explorer and Outlook Express; however, it won't copy over your programs, not even the Microsoft ones, and it won't copy settings for any programs other than Internet Explorer and Outlook Express. If you need to copy everything from an old computer to a new one, you'll probably want to use a disk-imaging tool such as Norton Ghost.

• **Figure 2.65** Files and Settings Transfer Wizard

Windows Easy Transfer (Windows Vista/7)

Windows Easy Transfer is an aggressively updated version of the Files and Settings Transfer Wizard. It does everything the older version does and adds the capability to copy user accounts and other settings (see Figure 2.66).

Microsoft provides a data transfer tool called the *User State Migration Tool* (*USMT*) for advanced users. It's functionally similar to Windows Easy Transfer, but it uses a scripting language to provide more power and flexibility. CompTIA also lists "User Data Migration Tool (UDMT)" on the objectives, but that tool hasn't existed since Windows NT and thus won't be covered on the exam.

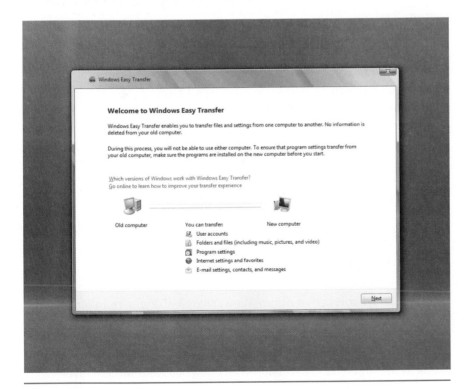

• **Figure 2.66** Windows Easy Transfer

Chapter 2: Visible Windows

Figure 2.67 Task Scheduler

Tech Tip

System Restore on a Non-Booting PC

If your system won't boot and you are unable to run System Restore from within Windows, you can access System Restore by booting from the Windows Installation CD or DVD and accessing System Restore from the System Recovery Options menu.

Windows Vista has a tool that offers features similar to Resource Monitor called Reliability and Performance Monitor. You can find it in the Control Panel applet called Administrative Tools. (More on the latter a little bit later in the chapter.)

Scheduled Tasks (All)

With the Scheduled Tasks utility, you can schedule any program to start and stop any time you wish. The only trick to this utility is that you must enter the program you want to run as a command on the command line, with all the proper switches. Figure 2.67 shows the configuration line for running the Disk Defragmenter program.

Security Center (Windows XP)

Security Center is a one-stop location for configuring many security features on your computer. This tool is also in the Control Panel. Windows Vista and Windows 7 remove Security Center from System Tools. Windows Vista retains the Control Panel applet, but Windows 7 has a beefed-up applet called the Action Center (discussed later in this chapter). All of these security features, and many more, are discussed in detail in their related chapters.

System Information (All)

System Information is one of those tools that everyone (including the CompTIA A+ 220-802 exam) likes to talk about, but it's uncommon to meet techs who say they actually use this tool. System Information shows tons of information about the hardware and software on your PC (see Figure 2.68).

System Restore (All)

System Restore is arguably the most important single utility you'll ever use in Windows when it comes to fixing a broken system. This handy tool enables you to take a "snapshot"—a copy of a number of critical files and settings—and return to that state later (see Figure 2.69). System Restore holds multiple snapshots, any of which you may restore to in the future.

Imagine you're installing some new device in your PC, or maybe a piece of software. Before you actually install, you take a snapshot and call it "Before Install." You install the device, and now something starts acting weird. You go back into System Restore and reload the previous Before Install snapshot, and the problem goes away.

System Restore isn't perfect, but it's usually the first thing to try when something goes wrong—assuming, of course, you made a snapshot!

Resource Monitor (Windows 7)

Resource Monitor tracks CPU, memory, disk, and network usage on your computer and displays that information across a dizzying number of charts and graphs. Resource Monitor can help you track down any pesky program or service that you think is hogging all of your system resources and slowing down your PC. If you've seen the Windows Task Manager before, think of this as the supercharged version with extra bells and more whistles.

• Figure 2.68 System Information

• Figure 2.69 System Restore

C:\>ver

MS-DOS Version 6.00

C:\>_

• **Figure 2.70** DOS command prompt

Command Line

The Windows command-line interface is a throwback to how Microsoft operating systems worked a long, long time ago when text commands were entered at a command prompt. Figure 2.70 shows the command prompt from DOS, the first operating system commonly used in PCs.

DOS is dead, but the command-line interface is alive and well in every version of Windows—including Windows 7. Every good tech knows how to access and use the command-line interface. It is a lifesaver when the graphical part of Windows doesn't work, and it is often faster than using a mouse if you're skilled at using it. An entire chapter (Chapter 9) is devoted to the command line, but let's look at one example of what the command line can do. First, you need to get there. In Windows XP, select Start | Run, and type **cmd** in the dialog box. Click OK and you get to a command prompt. In Windows Vista/7, you do the same thing in the Start | Search dialog box. Figure 2.71 shows a command prompt in Windows Vista.

Once at a command prompt, type **dir** and press ENTER on your keyboard. This command displays all the files and folders in a specific directory—probably your user folder for this exercise—and gives sizes and other information. DIR is just one of many useful command-line tools you'll learn about in this book.

Microsoft Management Console

One of the biggest complaints about earlier versions of Windows was the wide dispersal of the many utilities needed for administration and troubleshooting. Despite years of research, Microsoft could never find a place for all the utilities that would please even a small minority of support people. In a moment of sheer genius, Microsoft determined that the ultimate utility was one that the support people made for themselves! This brought on the creation of the amazing Microsoft Management Console.

The **Microsoft Management Console (MMC)** is simply a shell program in Windows that holds individual utilities called *snap-ins*. To start an MMC, select Start | Run in Windows XP, or select Start | Search bar in

• **Figure 2.71** Command prompt in Windows Vista

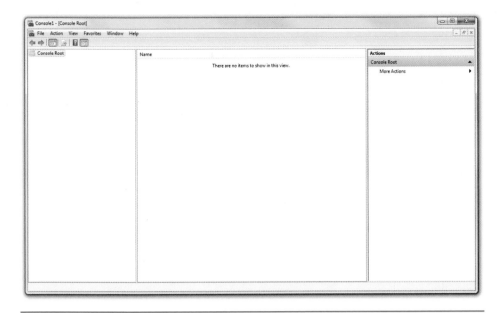

• **Figure 2.72** Blank MMC

Windows Vista/7. Type **mmc** and press ENTER to get a blank MMC. Blank MMCs aren't much to look at (see Figure 2.72).

You make a blank MMC console useful by adding snap-ins, which include most of the utilities you use in Windows. Even good old Device Manager is a snap-in. You can add as many snap-ins as you like, and you have many to choose from. Many companies sell third-party utilities as MMC snap-ins.

For example, to add the Device Manager snap-in, in the blank MMC, select File | Add/Remove Snap-ins. In the Add or Remove Snap-ins dia-

log box, you will see a list of available snap-ins in Windows Vista/7 (see Figure 2.73); click the Add button in Windows XP to open a similar screen. Select Device Manager in the list, and click the Add button to open a Device Manager dialog box that prompts you to choose the local or a remote PC for the snap-in to work with. Choose Local computer for this exercise, and click the Finish button. Click the Close button to close the Add Stand-alone Snap-in dialog box, and then click OK to close the Add or Remove Snap-ins dialog box.

You should see Device Manager listed in the console. Click it. Hey, that looks kind of familiar, doesn't it (see Figure 2.74)?

• **Figure 2.73** Available snap-ins

• **Figure 2.74** Device Manager as a snap-in

• **Figure 2.75** The Device Manager shortcut on the desktop

Once you've added the snap-ins you want, just save the console under any name, anywhere you want. I'll save this console as Device Manager MMC, for example, and drop it on my desktop (see Figure 2.75). I'm now just a double-click away from Device Manager.

Administrative Tools

Windows combines the most popular snap-ins into an applet in the Control Panel called **Administrative Tools**. Open the Control Panel and open Administrative Tools (see Figure 2.76).

• **Figure 2.76** Administrative Tools

Administrative Tools is really just a folder that stores a number of pre-made consoles. As you poke through these, notice that many of the consoles share some of the same snap-ins—nothing wrong with that. Of the consoles in a standard Administrative Tools collection, the ones you'll spend the most time with are Computer Management, Event Viewer, Performance Monitor (Reliability and Performance Monitor in Windows Vista), and Services.

The CompTIA A+ 220-802 exam has little interest in some of these snap-ins, so this book won't cover them all. If I don't mention it, it's almost certainly not on the test!

Computer Management

The **Computer Management** applet is a tech's best buddy, or at least a place where you'll spend a lot of time when building or maintaining a system (see Figure 2.77). You've already spent considerable time with one of its components: System Tools. Depending on the version of Windows, System Tools also offers Event Viewer, Performance, Device Manager, and more. Storage is where you'll find Disk Management.

Event Viewer

Event Viewer shows you at a glance what has happened in the last day, week, or more, including when people logged in and when the PC had problems (see Figure 2.78). You'll see more of Event Viewer in Chapters 18.

Performance (Windows XP)

The **Performance** console consists of two snap-ins: System Monitor and Performance Logs and Alerts. You can use these for reading *logs*—files that record information over time. System Monitor can also monitor real-time data (see Figure 2.79).

Suppose you are adding a new cable modem and you want to know just how fast you can download data. Click the plus sign (+) on the toolbar to add a counter. Click the *Use local computer counters* radio button, and then choose Network Interface from the Performance Object pull-down menu. In the Add Counters dialog box, make sure the *Select counters from list* radio button is selected. Last, select Bytes Received/sec. The dialog box should look like Figure 2.80.

Click Add, and then click Close; probably not much is happening. Go to a Web site, preferably one where

• **Figure 2.77** Computer Management applet

• **Figure 2.78** Event Viewer reporting system errors

• **Figure 2.79** System Monitor in action

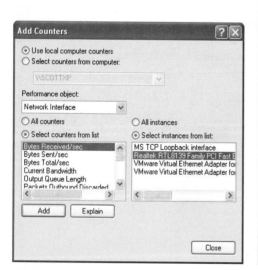

You'll learn more about the Performance console in Chapter 8.

You'll learn more about Reliability and Performance Monitor/Performance Monitor in Chapter 8.

you can download a huge file. Start downloading and watch the chart jump; that's the real throughput (see Figure 2.81).

Reliability and Performance Monitor/Performance Monitor (Windows Vista/7)

Reliability and Performance Monitor in Windows Vista offers just about everything you can find in the Performance applet of older versions of Windows—although everything is monitored by default, so there's no need to add anything. In addition, it includes Reliability Monitor. Reliability Monitor enables you to see at a glance what's been done to the computer over a period of time, including software installations and uninstallations, failures of hardware or applications, and general uptime (see Figure 2.82). It's a nice starting tool for checking a Vista machine that's new to you.

Windows 7 drops Reliability Monitor from this tool and calls it **Performance Monitor,** but everything else is the same. You can still find Reliability Monitor in Windows 7 by searching for it in the Search bar.

Services

Windows runs a large number of separate programs called **services.** The best way to visualize a service is to think of it as something that runs, yet is invisible. Windows comes with about 100 services by default, and they

• **Figure 2.80** Setting up a throughput test

• **Figure 2.81** Downloading with blazing speed

handle a huge number of tasks, from application support to network functions. You can use the Services applet to see the status of all services on the system, including services that are not running (see Figure 2.83).

Right-click a service and select Properties to modify its settings. Figure 2.84 shows the properties for the Bluetooth Support Service. See the Startup type pull-down menu? It shows four options: Automatic (Delayed Start), Automatic, Manual, and Disabled. Automatic means it starts when the system starts (Delayed Start services start two minutes after startup), Manual means you have to come to this tab to start it, and Disabled prevents anything from starting it. Also make sure you understand how to start, stop, pause, and resume services (note the four buttons below Startup Type).

• **Figure 2.82** Reliability and Performance Monitor open to the Reliability Monitor screen in Vista

Action Center (Unique to Windows 7)

Sometimes, you just want to glance at your system and know that nothing has gone terribly wrong. Previous versions of Windows lacked a single "peephole" to view the status of your computer. **Action Center** fills that gap, providing a one-page aggregation of event messages, warnings, and maintenance messages that, for many techs, might quickly replace Event Viewer as the first place to look for problems. Unlike Event Viewer, Action Center

> The CompTIA A+ 220-802 exam is not interested in having you memorize all of these services—just make sure you can manipulate them.

• **Figure 2.83** Services applet

● **Figure 2.84** Bluetooth Support Service properties

● **Figure 2.85** Action Center

separates issues into two sections, Security and Maintenance, making it easier to scan a system quickly (see Figure 2.85).

Action Center only compiles the information, taking data from well-known utilities such as Event Viewer, Windows Update, Windows Firewall, and User Account Control (UAC) and placing it into an easy-to-read format. If you wish, you can tell Action Center where to look for information by selecting *Change Action Center settings* (see Figure 2.86).

If you see a problem, Action Center includes plenty of links to get you to the utility you need. From the Action Center applet, you get direct links to

- UAC settings
- Performance Information and Tools
- Backup and Restore
- Windows Update
- Troubleshooting Wizard
- System Restore

Although Action Center does little more than reproduce information from other utilities, it makes finding problems quick and easy. Combined with quick links to most of the utilities you'll need, Action Center should become your base of operations when something goes wrong on a Windows 7 PC.

● **Figure 2.86** Change Action Center settings

Beyond A+

Windows 8

Windows 8 will launch sometime in 2012 (according to Microsoft), but it's not covered on the 220-801 and 220-802 exams. While the differences between Windows Vista and Windows 7 were minor enough that you could know a lot about 7 if you knew about Vista, Windows 8 looks to reimagine how we interface with our PCs.

The biggest idea behind Windows 8 is to unify Microsoft's multiple platforms: PCs, tablets, phones—even the Xbox 360 now has an interface very similar to Windows 8's "Modern" user interface (see Figure 2.87). You'll be able to use touch-enabled monitors to slide, drag, pinch, and zoom your way around apps specifically designed for the new look. Don't worry, though—your old desktop is safely hidden behind the Modern UI Start screen.

Beyond the interface, Microsoft has said they want to make it easier for developers to quickly program applications for multiple platforms. They've also previewed new tools and enhanced utilities from previous versions of Windows. The new Task Manager alone, as shown in Figure 2.88, should be enough to whet your appetite until the final release.

• **Figure 2.87** The Windows 8 Modern UI

Windows Embedded

The world is filled with PCs in the most unlikely places. Everything from cash registers to the F-22 Raptor fighter plane contains some number of tiny PCs. These aren't the PCs you're used to seeing, though. They almost never have mice, monitors, keyboards, and the usual I/O you'd expect to see, but they are truly PCs, with a CPU, RAM, BIOS, and storage.

These tiny PCs need operating systems just like any other PC, and a number of companies make specialized OSs for embedded PCs. Microsoft makes Windows Embedded just for these specialized embedded PCs.

• **Figure 2.88** Windows 8's upgraded Task Manager

Chapter 2 Review

■ Chapter Summary

After reading this chapter and completing the exercises, you should understand the following about Microsoft Windows.

Relate the history of Microsoft Windows

■ Microsoft entered the operating system game in the early 1980s with a command-line OS called Microsoft Disk Operating System, or MS-DOS. With a command-line OS, you interacted with the computer to run programs, save files, and do all the other computing functions by typing and pressing the ENTER key on your keyboard.

■ The earliest versions of Windows were little more than a graphical overlay of the DOS command-line operating system. This overlay version of Windows went through a number of updates, ending with the first truly popular version of Windows, Windows for Workgroups version 3.1. The last editions are collectively referred to as Windows 3.*x*.

■ In 1989, Microsoft offered a completely separate version of Windows called Windows NT, a true graphical operating system that was dramatically more powerful than the Windows overlay versions. It cost a lot more, unfortunately, so it did not see widespread adoption by regular users, only by business users. What set NT apart from other versions of Windows (including later, consumer-oriented products) was its very secure file system, NTFS.

■ From 1995 through 2000, Microsoft offered consumers an alternative version of Windows that went through several updates, such as Windows 95 and Windows 98. Collectively these versions of Windows are called Windows 9*x*. All of these versions of Windows used forms of FAT for file systems, not the more secure NTFS.

■ Three Windows versions concern the CompTIA A+ certified technician: Windows XP, Windows Vista, and Windows 7. All can use the NTFS file system.

■ Microsoft released several editions of Windows XP, including Windows XP Professional and Windows XP Home. Windows XP Professional provides full-blown data security, and it is the only edition of Windows XP with the capability of logging onto a special Windows Server–controlled domain. Windows XP Home is a stripped-down edition of XP Professional, without some of the important security features, such as no access to the Encrypting File System. Windows XP Media Center offers features for the media junkie, such as a personal video recorder to capture television shows for later viewing.

■ Windows Vista comes in many flavors, such as Windows Vista Home Premium and Windows Vista Business. Windows Vista Ultimate combines all of the features of every other Vista edition and includes some other features, such as a game performance tweaker and DVD ripping capability.

■ Microsoft also released several editions of Windows 7, including Windows 7 Home Premium, Windows 7 Professional, and Windows 7 Ultimate. Windows 7 introduced new features including a new taskbar and libraries.

■ Windows XP, Vista, and 7 come in 64-bit editions to take advantage of the extra computing power and memory capacity available with modern 64-bit processors. A 32-bit operating system is limited to a mere 4 GB of RAM, whereas a 64-bit OS can have gobs more. The 64-bit editions of Windows XP saw some use, but the 64-bit editions of Vista and 7 took the 64-bit OS into the mainstream.

Explain the Windows interface

■ Every version of Windows supports multiple users on a single machine, so the starting point for any tour of the Windows user interface starts with the logon screen. Windows XP offers the Welcome screen in addition to the standard logon, where users can click on an icon next to their user name to log in, although this feature is disabled in a domain environment. Windows Vista and 7 use a beefed-up Welcome screen that works in both workgroups and domains.

- The Windows desktop is the primary interface to the computer in every version of Windows. Windows Vista and Windows 7 differ from Windows XP with the use of transparencies and other nice features of the Windows Aero interface. Flip 3D enables users to quickly and visually cycle through open programs.

- Some of the important items on the desktop are the taskbar, Start button, Quick Launch toolbar (in Windows XP and Vista), and notification area, or system tray. The taskbar shows running programs. The Start button gives you access to the Start menu from which you can run installed applications. The Quick Launch toolbar enables you to select often-used programs with a single click, though it's not displayed by default in Windows XP. The notification area shows icons for applications running in the background, such as your antivirus software. Windows 7 merges the Quick Launch toolbar to the running program thumbnails, creating pinned applications.

- My Computer in Windows XP and Computer in Windows Vista and Windows 7 offer access to the files and folders on mass storage drives on the computer. To view the contents of any device, double-click its icon in My Computer/Computer. You can tell by a file's icon or extension—if you alter the default folder view to show file extensions—what type of file it is, such as a .JPG picture file.

- Windows Explorer is the main tool for observing and manipulating files on a system. The tool differs in some ways among the versions of Windows tested on the CompTIA A+ exams. Windows Explorer and My Computer/Computer are two facets of the same application.

- When you delete a file in Windows, it moves into the Recycle Bin. It stays there until you empty the Recycle Bin or restore the file, or until the Recycle Bin reaches a preset size and starts erasing its oldest contents.

- Windows offers many useful keyboard key combinations for accomplishing common tasks. Some combinations work specifically with the operating system utilities, such as pressing the WINDOWS KEY and the PAUSE/BREAK key to open the System Properties/System dialog box. Other combinations work throughout most applications, such as CTRL-C to copy something and CTRL-V to paste whatever was copied.

Identify the operating system folders of Windows XP, Windows Vista, and Windows 7

- SystemRoot is the tech name given to the folder in which Windows has been installed. The default SystemRoot in Windows XP, Vista, and 7 is C:\Windows. Mostly you'll see percent signs added, so: %SystemRoot%.

- Most programs install some or all of their essential files into a subfolder of the Program Files folder. This folder is found almost always in the root of the same drive where you find the Windows system folder. Windows Vista/7 64-bit versions have a separate Program Files (x86) folder for 32-bit applications.

- Personal documents are stored by default in the Documents and Settings folder (Windows XP) or the Users folder (Windows Vista/7). Within the folder structure, you'll find folders for each user account and, within those user account folders, folders such as Desktop, Start Menu, and so on. Just as with Program Files, the Documents and Settings/Users folder will be on the same drive as the Windows system folder.

- In Windows 7, you can link folders and create libraries, which show the contents of multiple folders in a single place.

Describe the utilities in Windows that are essential to techs

- Windows offers many utilities that enable techs to configure the operating system, optimize and tweak settings, install hardware, and more. Utilities that techs use frequently are right-click, Control Panel, Device Manager, System Tools, command line, Microsoft Management Console, Administrative Tools, and the Action Center.

- Right-clicking an object brings up the context menu for the object so you can act on it. One common right-click option is Properties.

- The Control Panel handles most of the maintenance, upgrade, and configuration aspects of Windows. The Control Panel contains many applets that are displayed in categories.

- Device Manager enables techs to examine and configure all the hardware and drivers in a Windows PC. Device Manager displays every device that Windows recognizes, organized in special groups called types. You can see resources used by devices and update drivers directly in

Device Manager. Device Manager places an icon on top of any hardware device that's not functioning properly or is manually disabled. Device Manager is the first tool you should access when you have a hardware problem.

■ The System Tools menu in the Start menu offers techs a one-stop shop for many handy utilities. You'll find Disk Defragmenter and Disk Cleanup here, for example. The Files and Settings Transfer Wizard in Windows XP or the Windows Easy Transfer tool in Windows Vista and Windows 7 appears in this menu as well.

■ The command-line interface enables you to type commands to the operating system. This can give you access to utilities and tools that often provide quicker results than graphical tools.

■ The Microsoft Management Console (MMC) is simply a shell program in Windows that holds individual utilities called snap-ins. These snap-ins enable you to accomplish varying tech tasks. You can create custom MMCs or use ones preconfigured by Microsoft.

■ The Administrative Tools applet in the Control Panel is a collection of preconfigured MMCs, such as Computer Management and Event Viewer. Users rarely need to access these MMCs, but good techs know their Administrative Tools.

■ Action Center in Windows 7 enables techs to see at a glance what issues need to be addressed on a PC.

■ Key Terms

Action Center *(71)*

activation *(61)*

Administrative Tools *(68)*

Aero *(35)*

applets *(56)*

Computer *(40)*

Computer Management *(69)*

context menu *(55)*

Control Panel *(55)*

desktop *(34)*

Device Manager *(57)*

extension *(42)*

Flip 3D *(36)*

Folders list *(41)*

interface *(34)*

Jump List *(40)*

library *(47)*

logon screen *(34)*

Microsoft Management Console (MMC) *(66)*

My Computer *(40)*

My Documents *(45)*

My Network Places *(48)*

Navigation pane *(42)*

Network *(48)*

notification area *(39)*

Performance *(69)*

Performance Monitor *(70)*

pinned application *(40)*

Quick Launch toolbar *(39)*

Recycle Bin *(48)*

Reliability and Performance Monitor *(70)*

service *(70)*

Start button *(39)*

SystemRoot *(50)*

System Tools *(60)*

system tray *(39)*

taskbar *(38)*

transparency *(36)*

User's Files *(45)*

Welcome screen *(34)*

Windows Explorer *(40)*

Windows Sidebar *(48)*

x64 *(32)*

x86 *(32)*

Key Term Quiz

Use the Key Terms list to complete the sentences that follow. Not all terms will be used.

1. You can readily see some of the programs running in the background by looking at the _____ (also known as the notification area).

2. A(n) _____ links folders and displays them together for quick and easy access to your files.

3. The first place you should look on a PC with malfunctioning hardware is _____.

4. Most tech tools in Windows can be found in _____.

5. The _____ in Windows XP offers a great spot for accessing favorite programs without resorting to the Start menu.

6. Jill accidentally deleted a critical file. Winona the tech assures her that the file is no doubt in the _____ and not lost forever.

7. You can place handy Gadgets that display useful information on the _____.

8. Windows 7 uses _____ to enable transparency and Flip 3D.

9. By default, Windows Vista uses the _____ for logon.

10. A file type is defined by its _____.

Multiple-Choice Quiz

1. Which of the following do you not need to use the Aero desktop in Windows 7?

 A. DirectX 9

 B. 128 MB of video RAM

 C. WDDM driver

 D. 64-bit version of Windows 7

2. Windows XP provides a number of ready-made MMC snap-ins stored in the _____ applet in the Control Panel.

 A. System

 B. Network

 C. Administrative Tools

 D. MMC

3. Which of the following are parts of the Windows desktop?

 A. Services, command line, applications

 B. Right-click, drag and drop, point and click

 C. Quick Launch toolbar, system tray, taskbar

 D. CPU, RAM, hard drive

4. The Microsoft Management Console holds individual utilities called what?

 A. Built-ins

 B. Snap-ins

 C. Applets

 D. MMCs

5. The folder in which Windows is installed is known generically as what?

 A. RootFolder

 B. WinRoot

 C. SystemRoot

 D. System32

6. Which version of Windows 7 must be purchased directly from Microsoft?

 A. Windows 7 Home Premium

 B. Windows 7 Professional

 C. Windows 7 Ultimate

 D. Windows 7 Enterprise

7. How do you access a command prompt in Windows 7?

 A. Start | Run, type **cmd**, and press ENTER

 B. Start | Run, type **dos**, and press ENTER

 C. Start | Search programs and files, type **cmd**, and press ENTER

 D. Start | Search programs and files, type **dos**, and press ENTER

8. What copy protection scheme is used in Windows 7?

 A. Activation

 B. BitLocker

 C. Event Viewer

 D. Services

9. Which of the following operating systems uses the Backup Status and Configuration Tool to back up files and folders?

 A. Windows 2000

 B. Windows XP Home

 C. Windows XP Professional

 D. Windows Vista

10. Which key combination enables you to switch between loaded programs?

 A. ALT-ESC

 B. ALT-TAB

 C. CTRL-C

 D. CTRL-X

11. What is the benefit of 64-bit Windows over 32-bit Windows?

 A. Supports more hard drives

 B. Fewer lockups

 C. Supports more memory

 D. Supports more monitors

12. Which version of Windows 7 was designed primarily for netbooks?

 A. Windows 7 Starter

 B. Windows 7 Home Basic

 C. Windows 7 Home Premium

 D. Windows 7 Professional

13. For a user account called "Ethan," where would you expect to find the personal documents folder in a Windows Vista computer?

 A. C:\Ethan

 B. C:\Users\Ethan

 C. C:\Documents and Settings\Ethan

 D. C:\Windows\Ethan

14. Which applet can you use to view the status of all services on a system?

 A. Character Map

 B. Performance Monitor

 C. Services

 D. System Information

15. What is the primary tool you use to observe and manipulate files on a computer?

 A. Flip 3D

 B. Windows Aero

 C. Windows desktop

 D. Windows Explorer

Essay Quiz

1. Your department just added four new interns who will share two PCs running Windows XP. Your boss has decided that you're the person who should take the newbies under your wing and teach them about Windows. Write a brief essay on some essential Windows folders and interfaces that every *user* should know.

2. Your boss just got off the phone with the corporate headquarters and is in somewhat of a panic. She doesn't know the first thing about the Microsoft Management Console, but now every tech is going to be issued a custom MMC. Write a brief essay explaining the function of the MMC to help allay her worries.

3. As part of your promotion, it is your responsibility to train the new techs your boss just hired. Write a brief essay describing the tools in the System Tools folder group.

Lab Projects

• Lab Project 2.1

Create your own MMC loaded with the snap-ins you use the most, or that you would like to experiment with. Add at least three snap-ins. Save the MMC on your desktop and give it an appropriate name.

• Lab Project 2.2

In a couple of places in the chapter, you got a taste of working with some of the more complex tools in Windows, such as Event Viewer and the Performance console. Go back through the text and reread those sections, and then do an Internet search for a how-to article. Then work with the tools.

Troubleshooting Essential Hardware

"A child of five could understand this. Send someone to fetch a child of five."

—Groucho Marx

In this chapter, you will learn how to

- ■ **Troubleshoot CPUs**
- ■ **Troubleshoot RAM**
- ■ **Troubleshoot the power-on self test (POST)**
- ■ **Maintain BIOS and CMOS properly**
- ■ **Troubleshoot motherboards**
- ■ **Troubleshoot power supplies**

Just about everyone these days can use a computer to some degree—until things start going wrong, that is. The difference between a tech and a regular user is what they do when things stop working correctly.

This chapter takes a look at the various methods used to troubleshoot your computer's essential hardware (the stuff it won't work without). You'll start off by looking at CPUs, which rarely go bad, then RAM, which sometimes does. After that you'll look at BIOS, CMOS, and motherboards. Finally, you'll look at one of the most error-prone components of your PC, the power supply.

■ Troubleshooting CPUs

Troubleshooting CPU issues falls into two categories: overheating and catastrophic failures, with overheating being far more common than the latter. Once a CPU is installed properly and functioning, it rarely causes problems. The only exception is when you ask a CPU to do too much too quickly. Then you'll get a sluggish PC. The Intel Atom processor in my netbook, for example, does a great job at surfing the Web, working on e-mail, and writing stellar chapters in your favorite textbook. But if you try to play a game more advanced than Half-Life (the original, circa 1998), the machine stutters and complains and refuses to play nice.

The vast majority of problems with CPUs come from faulty installation or environmental issues that cause overheating. Very rarely will you get a catastrophic failure, but we'll look at the signs of that, too.

Symptoms of Overheating

Failure to install a CPU properly results in either nothing—that is, you push the power button and nothing at all happens—or a system lock-up in a short period of time. Because of the nature of zero insertion force (ZIF) sockets, you're almost guaranteed that the issue isn't the CPU itself, but rather the installation of the heat-sink and fan assembly. Here's a checklist of possible problems that you need to address when faced with a CPU installation problem:

1. Too much thermal paste can impede the flow of heat from the CPU to the heat sink and cause the CPU to heat up rapidly. All modern CPUs have built-in fail-safes that tell them to shut down before getting damaged by heat.

2. Not enough thermal paste or thermal paste spread unevenly can cause the CPU to heat up and consequently shut itself down.

3. Failure to connect the fan power to the motherboard can cause the CPU to heat up and shut itself down.

The fan and heat-sink installation failures can be tricky the first few times you encounter them (and yes, even the Alpha Geek has failed to install these things correctly). You might see the text from the system setup. You might even get into an installation of Windows before the crash happens. The key is that as soon as you put the CPU under load—that is, make it work for a living—it heats up beyond where the faulty heat-sink connection can dissipate the heat and then shuts down.

With a system that's been running fine for a while, environmental factors can cause problems. An air conditioning failure in my office last summer, deep in the heart of very hot Texas, for example, caused machines throughout the office to run poorly. Some even shut down entirely. (At that point it was time to close the doors and send the staff to the beach,

but that's another story.) A client called the other day to complain about his computer continuously rebooting and running slowly. When I arrived on the scene, I found a house with seven cats. Opening up his computer case revealed the hairy truth: the CPU fan was so clogged with cat hair that it barely spun at all! A quick cleaning with a computer vacuum and a can of compressed air and he was a happily computing client.

The CPU needs adequate ventilation. The CPU fan is essential, of course, but the inside of the case also needs to get hot air out through one or more exhaust fans and cool air in through the front vent. If the intake vent is clogged or the exhaust fans stop working or are blocked somehow, the inside of the case can heat up and overwhelm the CPU cooling devices. This will result in a system running slowly or spontaneously rebooting.

Catastrophic Failure

You'll know when a catastrophic error occurs. The PC will suddenly get a **Blue Screen of Death (BSoD)**, technically called a Windows Stop error (see Figure 3.1). Or the entire PC will simply stop and go black, perhaps accompanied by a loud pop. The acrid smell of burnt electronics or ozone will grace your nasal passages. You might even see trails of smoke coming out of the case. You might not know immediately that the CPU has smoked, but follow your nose. Seriously. Sniff the inside of the case until you find the strongest smell. If it's the CPU, that's bad news. Whatever electrical short hit it probably caused damage to the motherboard too, and you're looking at a long day of replacement and rebuilding.

```
A problem has been detected and windows has been shut down to prevent damage
to your computer.

PAGE_FAULT_IN_NONPAGED_AREA

If this is the first time you've seen this stop error screen,
restart your computer. If this screen appears again, follow
these steps:

Check to make sure that any new hardware or software is properly installed.
If this is a new installation, ask your hardware or software manufacturer
for any windows updates you might need.

If problems continue, disable or remove any newly installed hardware
or software. Disable BIOS memory options such as caching or shadowing.
If you need to use Safe Mode to remove or disable components, restart
your computer, press F8 to select Advanced Startup Options, and then
select Safe Mode.

Technical information:

*** STOP: 0x00000050 (0x00000000,0xF866C51E,0x00000008,0xC00000000)

***      cdrom.sys - Address F866C51E base at F866A000, DateStamp 36B027B2
```

• **Figure 3.1** Blue Screen of Death

■ Troubleshooting RAM

"Memory" errors show up in a variety of ways on modern systems, including parity errors, ECC error messages, system lockups, page faults, and other error screens in Windows. These errors can indicate bad RAM, but often point to something completely unrelated. This is especially true with intermittent problems. Techs need to recognize these errors and determine which part of the system caused the memory error.

You can get two radically different types of parity errors: real and phantom. *Real parity errors* are simply errors that the memory controller chip (MCC) detects from the parity or error correction control (ECC) chips (if you have them). The operating system then reports the problem in an error message, such as "Parity error at *xxxx:xxxxxxxx*," where *xxxx:xxxxxxxx* is a hexadecimal value (a string of numbers and letters, such as A5F2:004EEAB9). If you get an error like this, write down the value (see Figure 3.2). A real parity/ECC error shows up at the same place in memory each time and almost always indicates that you have a bad RAM stick.

Phantom parity errors show up on systems that don't have parity or ECC memory. If Windows generates parity errors with different addresses, you most likely do *not* have a problem with RAM. These phantom errors can occur for a variety of reasons, including software problems, heat or dust, solar flares, fluctuations in the Force...you get the idea.

System lockups and page faults (they often go hand in hand) in Windows can indicate a problem with RAM. A system lockup is when the computer stops functioning. A **page fault** is a milder error that can be caused by memory issues but not necessarily system RAM problems. Certainly page faults *look* like RAM issues because Windows generates frightening error messages filled with long strings of hexadecimal digits, such as "KRNL386 caused a page fault at 03F2:25A003BC." Just because the error message contains a memory address, however, does not mean that you have a problem with your RAM. Write down the address. If it repeats in later error messages, you probably have a bad RAM stick. If Windows displays different memory locations, you need to look elsewhere for the culprit.

Every once in a while, something potentially catastrophic happens within the PC, some little electron hits the big red panic button, and the operating system has to shut down certain functions before it can save data. This panic button inside the PC is called a **non-maskable interrupt (NMI)**, more simply defined as an interruption the CPU cannot ignore. An NMI manifests to the user as our old friend, the Blue Screen of Death.

Bad RAM sometimes triggers an NMI, although often the culprit lies with buggy programming or clashing code. The BSoD varies according to

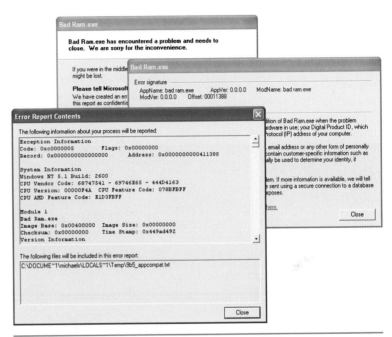

• **Figure 3.2** Windows error message

You can speed up your computer by changing the location of the page file, a file on your hard drive that acts as virtual memory. Open the System applet from the Control Panel, then click *Advanced system settings*. After that, click *Settings* under the Performance section, then click the Advanced tab. Clicking the Change button brings up a screen where you can move your page file to a non-system drive.

If you add a fast thumb drive to a Windows Vista/7 PC, you can use that thumb drive as extra program cache. This feature is called ReadyBoost.

the operating system, and it would require a much lengthier tome than this one to cover all the variations. Suffice it to say that RAM *could* be the problem when that delightful blue screen appears.

Finally, intermittent memory errors can come from a variety of sources, including a dying power supply, electrical interference, buggy applications, buggy hardware, and so on. These errors show up as lock-ups, general protection faults, page faults, and parity errors, but they never have the same address or happen with the same applications. I always check the power supply first.

Testing RAM

Once you discover that you may have a RAM problem, you have a couple of options. First, several companies manufacture hardware RAM-testing devices, but unless you have a lot of disposable income, they're probably priced way too high for the average tech ($1,500 and higher). Second, you can use the method I use—*replace and pray*. Open the system case and replace each stick, one at a time, with a known good replacement stick. (You have one of those lying around, don't you?) This method, although potentially time-consuming, certainly works. With PC prices as low as they are now, you could simply replace the whole system for less than the price of a dedicated RAM tester.

Third, you could run a software-based tester on the RAM. Because you have to load a software tester into the memory it's about to scan, there's always a small chance that simply starting the software RAM tester might cause an error. Still, you can find some pretty good free ones out there. Windows 7 includes the Memory Diagnostics Tool, which can automatically scan your computer's RAM when you encounter a problem. If you're using another OS, my favorite tool is the venerable Memtest86 written by Mr. Chris Brady (www.memtest86.com). Memtest86 exhaustively checks your RAM and reports bad RAM when it finds it (see Figure 3.3).

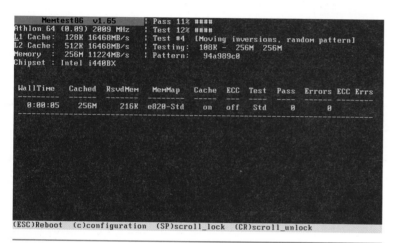

• **Figure 3.3** Memtest86 in action

A **general protection fault (GPF)** is an error that can cause an application to crash. Often GPFs are caused by programs stepping on each other's toes. Chapter 10 goes into more detail on GPFs and other Windows errors.

■ Troubleshooting the Power-On Self Test (POST)

When the computer is turned on or reset, it initiates a special program, stored on the system ROM chip, called the **power-on self test (POST)**. The POST program checks out the system every time the computer boots. To perform this check, the POST sends out a command that says to all of the devices, "Check yourselves out!" All of the standard devices in the computer then run their own internal diagnostic—the POST doesn't specify

what they must check. The quality of the diagnostic is up to the people who made that particular device.

Let's consider the POST for a moment. Suppose some device—let's say it's the keyboard controller chip—runs its diagnostic and determines that it is not working properly. What can the POST do about it? Only one thing really: tell the human in front of the PC! So how does the computer tell the human? PCs convey POST information to you in two ways: beep codes and text messages.

Before and During the Video Test: The Beep Codes

The computer tests the most basic parts of the computer first, up to and including the video card. In early PCs, you'd hear a series of beeps—called **beep codes**—if anything went wrong. By using beep codes before and during the video test, the computer could communicate with you. (If a POST error occurs before the video is available, obviously the error must manifest itself as beeps, because nothing can display on the screen.) The meaning of the beep code you'd hear varied among different BIOS manufacturers. You could find the beep codes for a specific motherboard in its motherboard manual.

Most modern PCs have only two beep codes: one for bad or missing video (one long beep followed by two or three short beeps), and one for bad or missing RAM (a single beep that repeats indefinitely).

You'll hear three other beep sequences on most PCs (although they're not officially beep codes). At the end of a successful POST, the PC produces one or two short beeps, simply to inform you that all is well. Most systems make a rather strange noise when the RAM is missing or very seriously damaged. Unlike traditional beep codes, this code repeats until you shut off the system. Finally, your speaker might make beeps for reasons that aren't POST or boot related. One of the more common is a series of short beeps after the system's been running for a while. That's a CPU alarm telling you the CPU is approaching its high heat limit.

 You'll find lots of online documentation about beep codes, but it's usually badly outdated.

Tech Tip

Talking BIOS
Some newer motherboards can also talk to you if there is a problem during POST. To use this feature, all that is normally required is to plug a pair of speakers or headphones into the audio output port on the back of the motherboard.

Text Errors

After the video has tested okay, any POST errors display on the screen as text errors. If you get a text error, the problem is usually, but not always, self-explanatory (see Figure 3.4). Text errors are far more useful than beep codes because you can simply read the screen to determine the bad device.

• **Figure 3.4** POST text error messages

POST Cards

Beep codes, numeric codes, and text error codes, although helpful, can sometimes be misleading. Worse than that, an inoperative device can sometimes disrupt the POST, forcing the machine into an endless loop. This causes the PC to act dead—no beeps and nothing on the screen. In this case,

• **Figure 3.5** POST card in action

you need a device, called a **POST card**, to monitor the POST and identify which piece of hardware is causing the trouble.

POST cards are simple cards that snap into expansion slots on your system. A small, two-character light-emitting diode (LED) readout on the card indicates which device the POST is currently testing (see Figure 3.5).

POST cards used to be essential tools for techs, but today I use them only when I have a "dead" PC to determine at which level it's dead. If the POST card shows no reading, I know the problem is before the POST and must be related to the power, the CPU, the RAM, or the motherboard. If the board posts, then I know to look at more issues, such as the drives and so on.

The Boot Process

All PCs need a process to begin their operations. Once you feed power to the PC, the tight interrelation of hardware, firmware, and software enables the PC to start itself, to "pull itself up by the bootstraps" or boot itself.

When you first power on the PC, the power supply circuitry tests for proper voltage and then sends a signal down a special wire called the **power good** wire to awaken the CPU. The moment the power good wire wakes it up, the CPU immediately sends a built-in memory address via its address bus. This special address is the same on every Intel and

```
▶ Hard Disk Book Priority      [Press Enter]
  First Boot Device            [CDROM]
  Second Boot Device           [Hard Disk]
  Third Boot Device            [CDROM]
```

• **Figure 3.6** CMOS boot order

clone CPU, from the oldest 8086 to the most recent microprocessor. This address is the first line of the POST program on the system ROM! That's how the system starts the POST. After the POST has finished, there must be a way for the computer to find the programs on the hard drive to start the operating system. The POST passes control to the last BIOS function: the bootstrap loader. The **bootstrap loader** is little more than a few dozen lines of BIOS code tacked to the end of the POST program. Its job is to find the operating system. The bootstrap loader reads CMOS information to tell it where to look first for an operating system. Your PC's CMOS setup utility has an option that you configure to tell the bootstrap loader which devices to check for an operating system and in which order (see Figure 3.6).

Almost all storage devices—floppy disks, hard disks, CDs, DVDs, and even USB thumb drives—can be configured to boot an operating system by setting aside a specific location called the *boot sector*. If the device is bootable, its boot sector contains special programming designed to tell the system where to locate the operating system. Any device with a functional operating system is called a **bootable disk** or a **system disk**. If the bootstrap loader locates a good boot sector, it passes control to the operating system and removes itself from memory. If it doesn't, it goes to the next device in the boot order you set in the CMOS setup utility. Boot order is an important tool for techs because you can set it to load in special bootable devices so you can run utilities to maintain PCs without using the primary operating system.

Some BIOS include a feature that enables a PC to use a **preboot execution environment (PXE)**. A PXE enables you to boot a PC without any local storage by retrieving an OS from a server over a network. You'll see more on PXE when we talk about installing Windows in Chapter 5.

■ Care and Feeding of BIOS and CMOS

BIOS and CMOS are areas in your PC that you don't go to very often. BIOS itself is invisible. The only real clue you have that it even exists is the POST. The CMOS setup utility, on the other hand, is very visible if you start it. Most CMOS setup utilities today work acceptably well without ever being touched. You're an aspiring tech, however, and all self-respecting techs start up the CMOS setup utility and make changes. That's when most CMOS setup utility problems take place.

If you mess with the CMOS setup utility, remember to make only as many changes at one time as you can remember. Document the original settings and the changes on a piece of paper so you can put things back if necessary. Don't make changes unless you know what they mean! It's easy to screw up a computer fairly seriously by playing with CMOS settings you don't understand.

Losing CMOS Settings

Your CMOS needs a continuous trickle charge to retain its data. Motherboards use some type of battery, usually a coin battery like those in wrist watches, to give the CMOS the charge it needs when the computer is turned off (see Figure 3.7). This battery also keeps track of the date and time when the PC is turned off.

If the battery runs out of charge, you lose all of your CMOS information. If some mishap suddenly erases the information on the CMOS chip, the computer might not boot or you'll get nasty-looking errors at boot. Any PC made after 2002 will boot to factory defaults if the CMOS clears, so the chances of not booting are slim—but you'll still get errors at boot. Here are a few examples of errors that point to lost CMOS information:

- CMOS configuration mismatch
- CMOS date/time not set
- No boot device available
- CMOS battery state low

• **Figure 3.7** A CMOS battery

Here are some of the more common reasons for losing CMOS data:

- Pulling and inserting cards
- Touching the motherboard
- Dropping something on the motherboard
- Dirt on the motherboard
- Faulty power supplies
- Electrical surges

If you encounter any of these errors, or if the clock in Windows resets itself to January 1st every time you reboot the system, the battery on the motherboard is losing its charge and needs to be replaced. To replace the battery, use a screwdriver to pry the battery's catch gently back. The battery should pop up for easy removal. Before you install the new battery, double-check that it has the same voltage and amperage as the old battery. To retain your CMOS settings while replacing the battery, simply leave your PC plugged into an AC outlet. The 5-volt soft power on all modern motherboards provides enough electricity to keep the CMOS charged and the data secure. Of course, I know you're going to be *extremely* careful about electrostatic discharge (ESD) while prying up the battery from a live system!

Flashing ROM

Flash ROM chips can be reprogrammed to update their contents. With flash ROM, when you need to update your system BIOS to add support for a new technology, you can simply run a small command-line program, combined with an update file, and voilà, you have a new, updated BIOS! Different BIOS makers use slightly different processes for *flashing the BIOS*, but, in general, you insert a removable disk of some sort (usually a USB thumb drive) containing an updated BIOS file and use the updating utility in CMOS setup.

Some motherboard makers provide Windows-based flash ROM update utilities that check the Internet for updates and download them for you to install (see Figure 3.8). Most of these utilities

• **Figure 3.8** ROM-updating program for an ASUS motherboard

While techs usually talk about "flashing the BIOS," the CompTIA A+ 220-802 exam refers to this process also as "installing firmware upgrades."

also enable you to back up your current BIOS so you can return to it if the updated version causes trouble. Without a good backup, you could end up throwing away your motherboard if a flash BIOS update goes wrong, so you should always make one.

Finally, don't update your BIOS unless you have some compelling reason to do so. As the old saying goes, "If it ain't broke, don't fix it!"

■ Troubleshooting Motherboards

It's typically pretty easy to fix BIOS and CMOS errors, but motherboards are a different story. Motherboards and motherboard components can die from many causes: time, dust, cat hair, or simply slight manufacturing defects made worse by the millions of amps of current sluicing through the motherboard traces. Installing cards, electrostatic discharge, flexing the motherboard one time too many when swapping out RAM or drives—any of these factors can cause a motherboard to fail. The motherboard is a hard-working, often abused component of the PC. Unfortunately for the common tech, troubleshooting a motherboard problem can be difficult and time-consuming. This section looks at symptoms of a failing motherboard, techniques for troubleshooting, and the options you have when you discover a motherboard problem.

If your PC's fans spin, but you get no power anywhere else, you could have several problems. The CPU, RAM, or video card might not be connected to the motherboard properly. The only way to determine the problem is to reseat all those devices. Do the RAM and video card before reseating the CPU, though.

Symptoms

Motherboard failures commonly fall into three types: catastrophic, component, and ethereal. With a **catastrophic failure**, the PC just won't boot. This sort of problem happens to brand-new systems because of manufacturing defects—often called a **burn-in failure**—and to any system that gets a shock of ESD. Burn-in failure is uncommon and usually happens in the first 30 days of use. Swap out the motherboard for a replacement and you should be fine. If you accidentally zap your motherboard when inserting a card or moving wires around, be chagrined. Change your daring ways and wear an anti-static wrist strap!

Component failure happens rarely and appears as flaky connections between a device and motherboard, or as intermittent problems. A hard drive plugged into a faulty controller on the motherboard, for example, might show up in CMOS autodetect but be inaccessible in Windows. Another example is a serial controller that worked fine for months until a big storm took out the external modem hooked to it, and doesn't work anymore, even with a replacement modem.

If your PC won't boot, check the power and hard drive activity indicator lights. If they worked before and are now dead, that points to power supply or motherboard failure.

The most difficult of the three types of symptoms to diagnose are those I call *ethereal* symptoms. Stuff just doesn't work all of the time. The PC reboots itself. You get a BSoD in the midst of heavy computing, such as right before you smack the villain and rescue the damsel. What can cause such symptoms? If you answered any of the following, you win the prize:

- Faulty component
- Buggy device driver
- Buggy application software

- Slight corruption of the operating system
- Power supply problems

Err…you get the picture.

What a nightmare scenario to troubleshoot! The Way of the Tech knows paths through such perils, though, so let's turn to troubleshooting techniques now.

Techniques

Troubleshooting a potential motherboard failure requires time, patience, and organization. Some problems will certainly be quicker to solve than others. If the hard drive doesn't work as expected, as in the previous example, check the settings on the drive. Try a different drive. Try the same drive with a different motherboard to verify that it's a good drive. Like every other troubleshooting technique, what you're trying to do with motherboard testing is to isolate the problem by eliminating potential factors.

This three-part system—check, replace, verify good component—works for both simple and more complicated motherboard problems. You can even apply the same technique to ethereal-type problems that might be anything, but you should add one more verb: *document*. Take notes on the individual components you test so you don't repeat efforts or waste time. Plus, taking notes can lead to the establishment of patterns. Being able to re-create a system crash by performing certain actions in a specific order can often lead you to the root of the problem. Document your actions. Motherboard testing is time-consuming enough without adding inefficiency.

Options

Once you determine that the motherboard has problems, you have several options for fixing the three types of failures. If you have a catastrophic failure, you must replace the motherboard. Even if it works somewhat, don't mess around. The motherboard should provide bedrock stability for the system. If it's even remotely buggy or problematic, get rid of it!

If you have a component failure, you can often replace the component with an add-on card that will be as good as or better than the failed device. Adaptec, for example, makes fine cards that can replace the built-in SATA ports on the motherboard (see Figure 3.9).

If your component failure is more a technology issue than physical damage, you can try upgrading the BIOS on the motherboard. As you'll recall from the earlier section on BIOS, every motherboard comes with a small set of code that enables the CPU to communicate properly with the devices built into the motherboard. You can quite readily upgrade this programming by *flashing the BIOS*: running a small command-line program to write new BIOS in the flash ROM chip. Refer to the BIOS section of this chapter for the details on flashing.

Finally, if you have an ethereal, ghost-in-the-machine type of problem that you have finally determined to be motherboard related, you have only a couple of options for fixing the problem. You can flash the BIOS in a desperate attempt to correct whatever it is, which sometimes does work and is less expensive than the other option, which is replacing the motherboard.

 If you've lost components because of ESD or a power surge, you would most likely be better off replacing the motherboard. The damage you can't see can definitely sneak up to bite you and create system instability.

 Tech Tip

Limits of BIOS Upgrades
Flashing the BIOS for a motherboard can fix a lot of system stability problems and provide better implementation of built-in technology. What it cannot do for your system is improve the hardware. If AMD comes out with a new, improved, lower-voltage Phenom, for example, and your motherboard cannot scale down the voltage properly, you cannot use that CPU—even if it fits in your motherboard's Socket AM3. No amount of BIOS flashing can change the hardware built into your motherboard.

• **Figure 3.9** Adaptec PCIe SATA card

■ Troubleshooting Power Supplies

Power supplies fail in two ways: sudden death and slowly over time. When they die suddenly, the computer will not start and the fan in the power supply will not turn. In this case, verify that electricity is getting to the power supply before you do anything. Avoid the embarrassment of trying to repair a power supply when the only problem is a bad outlet or an extension cord that is not plugged in. Assuming that the system has electricity, the best way to verify that a power supply is working or not working is to use a multimeter to check the voltages coming out of the power supply (see Figure 3.10).

Do not panic if your power supply puts out slightly more or less voltage than its nominal value. The voltages supplied by most PC power supplies can safely vary by as much as ±10 percent of their stated values. This means that the 12-V line can vary from roughly 10.5 to 12.9 V without exceeding the tolerance of the various systems in the PC. The 5.0- and 3.3-V lines offer similar tolerances.

Be sure to test every connection on the power supply—that means every connection

• **Figure 3.10** Testing one of the 5-V DC connections

on your main power as well as every Molex and mini. Because all voltages are between –20 and +20 VDC, simply set the voltmeter to the 20-V DC setting for everything. If the power supply fails to provide power, throw it into the recycling bin and get a new one—even if you're a component expert and a whiz with a soldering iron. Don't waste your or your company's time; the price of new power supplies makes replacement the obvious way to go.

 Many CMOS utilities and software programs monitor voltage, saving you the hassle of using a multimeter.

No Motherboard

Power supplies will not start unless they're connected to a motherboard, so what do you do if you don't have a motherboard you trust to test? First, try an ATX tester. Many companies make these devices. Look for one that supports both 20- and 24-pin motherboard connectors as well as all of the other connectors on your motherboard. Figure 3.11 shows a power supply tester.

Switches

Broken power switches form an occasional source of problems for power supplies that fail to start. The power switch is behind the on/off button on every PC. It is usually secured to the front cover or inside front frame on your PC, making it a rather challenging part to access. To test, try shorting the soft power jumpers. A key or screwdriver will do the trick.

• **Figure 3.11** ATX power supply tester

When Power Supplies Die Slowly

If all power supplies died suddenly, this would be a much shorter section. Unfortunately, the majority of PC problems occur when power supplies die slowly over time. This means that one of the internal electronics of the power supply has begun to fail. The failures are *always* intermittent and tend to cause some of the most difficult to diagnose problems in PC repair. The secret to discovering that a power supply is dying lies in one word: intermittent. Whenever you experience intermittent problems, your first guess should be that the power supply is bad. Here are some other clues you may hear from users:

- "Whenever I start my computer in the morning, it starts to boot, and then locks up. If I press CTRL-ALT-DEL two or three times, it will boot up fine."

- "Sometimes when I start my PC, I get an error code. If I reboot, it goes away. Sometimes I get different errors."

- "My computer will run fine for an hour or so. Then it locks up, sometimes once or twice an hour."

Sometimes something bad happens and sometimes it does not. That's the clue for replacing the power supply. And don't bother with the voltmeter; the voltages will show up within tolerances, but only *once in a while* they will spike and sag (far more quickly than your voltmeter can measure) and cause these intermittent errors. When in doubt, change the power supply. Power supplies break in computers more often than any other part of the PC except hard drives and floppy disk drives. You might choose to keep extra power supplies on hand for swapping and testing.

Fuses and Fire

Inside every power supply resides a simple fuse. If your power supply simply pops and stops working, you might be tempted to go inside the power supply and check the fuse. This is not a good idea. First off, the capacitors in most power supplies carry high-voltage charges that can hurt a lot if you touch them. Second, fuses blow for a reason. If a power supply is malfunctioning inside, you want that fuse to blow because the alternative is much less desirable.

Failure to respect the power of electricity will eventually result in the most catastrophic of all situations: an electrical fire. Don't think it won't happen to you! Keep a fire extinguisher handy. Every PC workbench needs a fire extinguisher, but make sure you have the right one. The fire prevention industry has divided fire extinguishers into four fire classes:

- **Class A** Ordinary free-burning combustible, such as wood or paper
- **Class B** Flammable liquids, such as gasoline, solvents, or paint
- **Class C** Live electrical equipment
- **Class D** Combustible metals such as titanium or magnesium

If your power supply is smoking or you smell something burning inside of it, stop using it now. Replace it with a new power supply.

As you might expect, you should only use a Class C fire extinguisher on your PC if it catches on fire. All fire extinguishers are required to have their type labeled prominently on them. Many fire extinguishers are multiclass in that they can handle more than one type of fire. The most common fire extinguisher is type ABC—it works on all common types of fires.

Chapter 3 Review

■ Chapter Summary

After reading this chapter and completing the exercises, you should understand the following facts about troubleshooting essential hardware.

Troubleshoot CPUs

- If your computer is continuously rebooting or won't start up, you may have a CPU cooling problem. Open your case up and make sure the heat sink is properly seated and all the fans are running.

- If you get a Blue Screen of Death or random shutdown, check for the smell of burnt electronics. If you smell something burning, you may have had a catastrophic CPU failure. The only thing to do to fix that is to replace the CPU.

Troubleshoot RAM

- Symptoms of bad RAM include parity errors, system lockups, page faults, and other error screens in Windows. However, other failing components can cause similar problems. Bad RAM usually results in error screens displaying messages such as "Parity error at *xxxx:xxxxxxxx*," where *xxxx:xxxxxxxx* is a hexadecimal value such as A5F2:004EEAB9. A real parity error shows up in the same place in memory each time—if that hexadecimal code is always the same, you probably have bad RAM.

- Page faults result in error screens such as "KRNL386 caused a page fault at 03F2:25A003BC." The process that caused the page fault (in this case, KRNL386) may change, but if the hexadecimal address is the same across numerous error screens, you probably have bad RAM.

- A non-maskable interrupt (NMI) results in a Blue Screen of Death (BSoD). Although BSoDs are often blamed on bad RAM, they are more often caused by buggy application code.

- If you suspect you have bad RAM and you don't have a hardware RAM-testing device, swap one of the sticks in your system with a known good stick. If the system works, you've found the bad stick.

If the system still has errors, replace the stick you removed and swap a different stick for the known good stick. Another option is to use a software RAM tester such as Memtest86.

Troubleshoot the power-on self test (POST)

- In addition to the BIOS routines and the CMOS setup program, the system ROM also includes a special program called the power-on self test (POST) that is executed every time the computer boots. POST first sends a command to basic devices, up to and including video, instructing them to run self-diagnostics. If a device detects an error, the computer alerts you with a series of beeps. Different ROM manufacturers have used different beep codes, but your motherboard book should explain them (particularly in older systems). After addressing the basic devices, POST tells the rest of the devices to run tests and displays a text error message on the screen if anything is wrong. Some manufacturers use numeric error codes or combine numeric and text messages.

- The computer may beep in two situations that are not related to POST beep codes. If the computer beeps constantly until you shut it off, it means RAM is missing or damaged. If the computer beeps after it is booted, it is probably warning you that the system is overheating.

- If the computer appears dead, with no beeps or screen response, you can place a POST card in an expansion slot to diagnose the problem by using the LED readout on the card. The documentation that comes with the POST card explains the LED codes for your particular BIOS.

- A beep code, text error message, or POST error may identify a problem, but it does not fix it. After you know which device is causing the problem, you should check the connection for the troublesome device and replace it if possible. If you cannot remove the bad part or if you cannot interpret the error message, you may need to replace the motherboard.

- When you first power on the PC, the power supply circuitry tests for proper voltage and then sends a signal down a special wire called the power good wire to awaken the CPU. The moment the power good wire wakes it up, the CPU sends a built-in memory address via its address bus. This address is the first line of the POST program on the system ROM, which is how the system starts the POST. After the POST has finished, it passes control to the bootstrap loader function on the system BIOS. This program looks for an operating system, checking the floppy drive, hard drives, or other bootable devices to find the boot sector that identifies the location of the OS. When the BIOS finds a bootable or system disk or device that has a functional operating system, it passes control to that disk or device.

- Some BIOS include a feature enabling your PC to use a preboot execution environment (PXE). PXE enables you to boot your PC from a network location.

Maintain BIOS and CMOS properly

- If you make changes to the CMOS settings, make only as many changes at one time as you can remember. Document the original settings and the changes on a piece of paper so you can reverse any changes that have the wrong effect.

- If you have CMOS settings that keep reverting to defaults or if the clock in Windows resets itself to January 1st every time you reboot the system, the battery on the motherboard is losing its charge and needs to be replaced.

- You can update the firmware in ROM by flashing the BIOS. Some motherboards enable you to update the BIOS through Windows programs; others come with drivers for USB devices and have a flashing utility built in.

Troubleshoot motherboards

- Motherboards and motherboard components can die for many reasons, including time, dust, pet hair, manufacturing defects, ESD, or physical damage. Motherboard failures usually fall into one of three main categories: catastrophic, component, or ethereal.

- Catastrophic failure is typically caused by manufacturing defects (burn-in failure) or ESD.

Burn-in failures are uncommon and usually manifest within the first 30 days of use. In the case of a catastrophic failure, replace the motherboard.

- Component failure appears as a flaky connection between a device and the motherboard or as intermittent problems. In the case of a component failure, replace the failed component with an expansion card or peripheral device. Sometimes a BIOS upgrade can fix component failures.

- Ethereal failure is the most difficult to diagnose. Symptoms vary from the PC rebooting itself to Blue Screens of Death and can be caused by a faulty component, buggy device driver, buggy application software, operating system corruption, or power supply problems.

- Use three steps to troubleshoot problems: check, replace, and verify. For example, first check the settings of the problem device. If the device still fails, replace the device. If the device continues to malfunction, try the device with a different motherboard. Remember to document your troubleshooting steps. Not only will it help you to become an efficient troubleshooter, but it also can lead to the establishment of patterns. Being able to re-create a system crash by performing certain actions in a specific order can often lead you to the root of the problem.

Troubleshoot power supplies

- If one of the internal electrical components in the power supply begins to fail, the result is usually intermittent problems, making diagnosis difficult. If you are experiencing intermittent problems, such as lockups or different error codes that disappear after rebooting, suspect the power supply. Unfortunately, the voltmeter is not good for diagnosing intermittent problems. Power supplies fail almost as often as floppy drives and hard drives, so it is a good idea to keep power supplies in stock for swapping and testing.

- Never open a power supply, even to check the fuse; the unit contains capacitors that carry high-voltage charges that can hurt you.

- Every PC workbench should have a Class C fire extinguisher handy in case of an electrical fire. Some fire extinguishers are multiclass and will work fine for a PC as well.

Key Terms

beep codes *(85)*
Blue Screen of Death (BSoD) *(82)*
bootable disk *(87)*
bootstrap loader *(87)*
burn-in failure *(90)*
catastrophic failure *(90)*
component failure *(90)*
general protection fault (GPF) *(84)*

non-maskable interrupt (NMI) *(83)*
page fault *(83)*
POST card *(86)*
power good *(86)*
power-on self test (POST) *(84)*
preboot execution environment (PXE) *(87)*
system disk *(87)*

Key Term Quiz

Use the Key Terms list to complete the sentences that follow. Not all terms will be used.

1. If the computer appears dead, with no beeps or screen responses, you can insert a _____ in an expansion slot to diagnose what is wrong.

2. The dreaded Windows stop error is also popularly called the _____.

3. When the computer starts, it runs a program on the system BIOS called _____ that checks the hardware.

4. You can use _____ to troubleshoot errors that happen before your video card starts.

5. Another name for the Blue Screen of Death is _____.

6. A disk containing an operating system is called a _____ or a _____.

7. A _____ is an error caused by memory problems, but not necessarily by bad system RAM.

8. The _____ is a short bit of code that looks for an installed operating system.

9. A device that dies shortly after purchasing it suffers from _____.

10. _____ happens rarely and appears as flaky connections between a device and motherboard, or as intermittent problems.

Multiple-Choice Quiz

1. Which kind of fire extinguisher should you use for computer equipment?
 A. Class A
 B. Class B
 C. Class C
 D. Class D

2. What should you check first if a computer will not start and the fan in the power supply will not turn?
 A. The voltages coming out of the power supply
 B. The motherboard power connector
 C. The power coming into the power supply
 D. The power switch

3. When you test voltage with a multimeter, you can assume the outlet or connector is functioning properly if the reading is within a certain percentage of the expected number. What is that maximum percentage by which the reading can vary?
 A. 5 percent
 B. 10 percent
 C. 20 percent
 D. 25 percent

4. When you turn on your computer, what is accessed first?

 A. The CPU

 B. The setup program

 C. The POST

 D. The CMOS chip

5. Which of the following problems points to a dying power supply?

 A. Intermittent lockups at bootup

 B. A power supply fan that does not turn

 C. A multimeter reading of 11 V for the 12-V power line

 D. A computer that won't start by shorting the soft power jumpers

6. Which statement is true?

 A. Removing the expansion slot covers on the back of your case will improve cooling by allowing hot air to escape.

 B. Shop around when purchasing a case; you will often find good deals that include a powerful PSU.

 C. Always keep the power supply plugged in to the wall outlet when working on the inside of a computer, as this helps to ground it.

 D. If your power supply fails, don't try to repair it; buy a new one.

7. A client calls to complain that his computer starts up, but crashes when Windows starts to load. After a brief set of questions, you find out that his nephew upgraded his RAM for him over the weekend and couldn't get the computer to work right afterward. What could be the problem?

 A. Thermal compound degradation

 B. Disconnected CPU fan

 C. Bad CPU cache

 D. There's nothing wrong. It usually takes a couple of days for RAM to acclimate to the new system.

8. Sam has installed a new CPU in a client's computer, but nothing happens when he pushes the power button on the case. The LED on the motherboard is lit up, so he knows the system has power. What could the problem be?

 A. He forgot to disconnect the CPU fan.

 B. He forgot to apply thermal compound between the CPU and the heat-sink and fan assembly.

 C. He used an AMD CPU in an Intel motherboard.

 D. He used an Intel CPU in an AMD motherboard.

9. Which of the following will most likely result in a POST beep code message?

 A. The system is overheating.

 B. The video card is not seated properly.

 C. The keyboard is unplugged.

 D. The hard drive has crashed.

10. After a sudden power outage, Morgan's PC rebooted, but nothing appeared on the screen. The PC just beeps at him, over and over and over. What's most likely the problem?

 A. The power outage toasted his RAM.

 B. The power outage toasted his video card.

 C. The power outage toasted his hard drive.

 D. The power outage toasted his CPU.

11. Amanda bought a new system that, right in the middle of an important presentation, gave her a Blue Screen of Death. Now her system won't boot at all, not even to CMOS. After extensive troubleshooting, she determined that the motherboard was at fault and replaced it. Now the system runs fine. What was the most likely cause of the problem?

 A. Burn-in failure

 B. Electrostatic discharge

 C. Component failure

 D. Power supply failure

12. Solon has a very buggy computer that keeps locking up at odd moments and rebooting spontaneously. He suspects the motherboard. How should he test it?

A. Check settings and verify good components.

B. Verify good components and document all testing.

C. Replace the motherboard first to see if the problems disappear.

D. Check settings, verify good components, replace components, and document all testing.

13. What does a non-maskable interrupt cause the CPU to produce?

A. The Blue Screen of Death

B. A parity error

C. Excessive heat

D. An incorrect memory count

■ Essay Quiz

1. Helene's computer worked fine last week. Although she has not changed anything since then, today her computer won't even boot. You suspect that the power supply died. You know she does not have a multimeter. What will you tell her to check to confirm this opinion? If she does need to replace the power supply, how can she be sure the new one will work with her PC?

2. What symptoms will your computer show if the CMOS battery is dying or dead? What happens to the information stored in CMOS when you replace the battery? What must you do if a built-in battery goes dead?

3. Your computer is acting funny. Sometimes you get an error message on the screen. Other times data seems to be corrupted. Sometimes the computer just locks up. You suspect that it may be bad memory. How can you find out whether a memory problem or something else is causing your trouble?

Lab Project

• Lab Project 3.1

Download Memtest86 (www.memtest86.com) and create a bootable Memtest86 optical disc. Boot your lab PC to the disc and run Memtest86 on your lab computer. When the tests are completed, do some research on the Web to help interpret the results. Write a paragraph interpreting the results of the scan.

Implementing Hard Drives

"Wisely and slow; they stumble that run fast."

—SHAKESPEARE, *ROMEO AND JULIET*, ACT 2, SCENE 3

In this chapter, you will learn how to

- ■ **Troubleshoot hard drive installation**
- ■ **Explain the partitions available in Windows**
- ■ **Discuss hard drive formatting options**
- ■ **Partition and format hard drives**
- ■ **Maintain and troubleshoot hard drives**

From the standpoint of your PC, a freshly installed hard drive is nothing more than a huge pile of sectors. Sure, CMOS recognizes it as a drive—always a step in the right direction—but your operating system is clueless without more information. Your operating system must organize those sectors so you can use the drive to store data. This chapter begins by looking at the process of troubleshooting physical hard drive installations. You'll then look at partitioning and formatting, eventually going through the process of partitioning and formatting hard drives. The chapter wraps with a discussion on hard drive maintenance and troubleshooting issues.

Historical/Conceptual

After you've successfully installed a hard drive, you must perform two more steps to translate the drive's geometry and circuits into something the system can use: partitioning and formatting. **Partitioning** is the process of electronically subdividing the physical hard drive into smaller units called **partitions**. A hard drive must have at least one partition, and you can create multiple partitions on a single hard drive if you wish. In Windows, each of these partitions typically is assigned a drive letter such as C: or D:. After partitioning, you must **format** the drive. Formatting installs a **file system** onto the drive that organizes each partition in such a way that the operating system can store files and folders on the drive. Several types of file systems are used by Windows. This chapter will go through them after covering partitioning.

Partitioning and formatting a drive is one of the few areas remaining on the software side of PC assembly that requires you to perform a series of fairly complex manual steps. The CompTIA A+ 220-802 exam tests your knowledge of *what* these processes do to make the drive work, as well as the steps needed to partition and format hard drives in Windows XP, Vista, and 7.

 This chapter uses the term "hard drive" as a generic term that covers all drive types. Once you get into Windows, the operating system doesn't particularly care if the drive is a platter-based hard disk drive (HDD), a flash-based solid-state drive (SSD), or some hybrid combination of the two. The tools and steps for preparing the drives for data are the same.

■ Hard Drive Partitions

Partitions provide tremendous flexibility in hard drive organization. With partitions, you can organize a drive to suit your personal taste. For example, I partitioned my 1.5-terabyte (TB) hard drive into a 250-GB partition where I store Windows 7 and all my programs, a second 250-GB partition for Windows Vista, and a 1-TB partition where I store all my personal data. This is a matter of personal choice; in my case, backups are simpler because the data is stored in one partition, and I can back up that partition without including the applications.

You can partition a hard drive to store more than one operating system: store one OS in one partition and create a second partition for another OS. Granted, most people use only one OS, but if you want the option to boot to Windows or Linux, partitions are the key.

802

■ Troubleshooting Hard Drive Installation

Before you can get on with formatting and partitioning your hard drives, you must first make sure the drive installation went smoothly. If you notice any errors, it's time to troubleshoot your installation.

The best friend a tech has when it comes to troubleshooting hard drive installation is the autodetection feature of the CMOS setup utility. When a drive doesn't work, the biggest question, especially during installation, is "Did I plug it in correctly?" With autodetection, the answer is simple: If the system doesn't see the drive, something is wrong with the hardware configuration. Either a device has physically failed or, more likely, you didn't give the hard drive power, you plugged a cable in backward, or you messed up some other connectivity issue.

Getting a drive installed and recognized by the system takes three or four things: jumpers (PATA only), data cable, power, and the CMOS setup recognizing the drive. If you miss or mess up any of these steps, you have a drive that doesn't exist according to the PC! To troubleshoot hard drives, simply work your way through each step to figure out what went wrong.

First, remember to set your PATA drive to master, slave, standalone, or cable select, depending on where you decide to install it. If a drive is alone on the cable, set it to master or standalone. With two drives, one must be master and the other slave. Alternatively, you can set both drives to cable select and use a cable-select cable.

Second, you must connect the data cable to both the drive and the controller, pin 1 to pin 1. Reversing the data cable at one end is remarkably easy to do, especially with rounded cables. They obviously don't have a big red stripe down the side to indicate the location of pin 1! If you can't autodetect the drive, check the cabling.

Third, be sure to give the hard drive power. PATA hard drives use a standard Molex connector, and SATA drives use the SATA power connector. If you don't hear the whirring of the drive, make certain you plugged in a Molex from the power supply rather than from another source such as an otherwise disconnected fan. You'd be surprised how often I've seen that.

Fourth, you need to make sure that BIOS recognizes your hard drive. Use the CMOS setup program to check. Most of the time, however, it's all automatic.

Once you've checked the physical connections, run through these issues in CMOS. Is the controller enabled? Is the storage technology—LBA, INT13, ATA/ATAPI-6—properly set up? Similarly, can the motherboard support the type of drive you're installing? If not, you have a couple of options. You can either flash the BIOS with an upgraded BIOS from the manufacturer or get a hard drive controller that goes into an expansion slot.

Finally, with nonintegrated hard drive controllers such as those that come with many SATA drives, make certain that you've installed the proper drivers for the controller. Driver issues can crop up with new, very large drives and with changes in technology. Always check the manufacturer's Web site for new drivers.

■ Windows Partitioning

Windows supports three different partitioning methods: the older but more universal master boot record (MBR) partitioning scheme, Windows' proprietary dynamic storage partitioning scheme, and the GUID partition table (GPT). Microsoft calls a hard drive that uses either the MBR partitioning

scheme or the GPT partitioning scheme a **basic disk** and calls a drive that uses the dynamic storage partitioning scheme a **dynamic disk**. A single Windows system with three hard drives may have one of the drives partitioned with MBR, another with GPT, and the third set up as a dynamic disk, and the system will run perfectly well. The bottom line? You get to learn about three totally different types of partitioning. I'll also cover a few other partition types, such as hidden partitions, tell you when you can and should make your partitions, and demystify some of Microsoft's partition-naming confusion.

Techs often refer to MBR-partitioned drives as "MBR drives." The same holds true for GPT-partitioned drives, which many techs refer to as "GPT drives."

Master Boot Record

The first sector of an MBR hard drive contains the **master boot record (MBR)**. To clarify, hard drives that use the MBR partitioning scheme have a tiny bit of data that is also called the "master boot record." While your computer boots up, BIOS looks at the first sector of your hard drive for instructions. At this point, it doesn't matter which OS you use or how many partitions you have. Without this bit of code, your OS will never load.

The master boot record also contains the **partition table**, which describes the number and size of partitions on the disk (see Figure 4.1). MBR partition tables support up to four partitions—the partition table is large enough to store entries for only four partitions. The instructions in the master boot record use this table to determine which partition contains the active operating system.

After the MBR locates the appropriate partition, the **partition boot sector** loads the OS on that partition. The partition boot sector stores information important to its partition, such as the location of the OS boot files (see Figure 4.2).

1. The master boot record looks for a partition with an operating system.

2. The partition table tells the master boot record where to look.

• **Figure 4.1** The master boot record

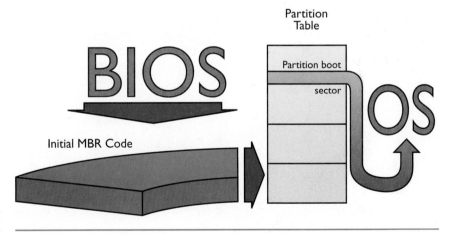

• **Figure 4.2** Using the master boot record to boot an OS

MBR partition tables support two types of partitions: primary partitions and extended partitions. **Primary partitions** are designed to support bootable operating systems. **Extended partitions** are not bootable. A single MBR disk may have up to four primary partitions or three primary partitions and one extended partition.

Only one master boot record and one partition table within that master boot record exist per MBR disk. Each partition has a partition boot sector.

Partition Table

• **Figure 4.3** The active partition containing Windows

Partitions don't always get drive letters. See the section "Mounting Partitions as Folders" later in this chapter for details.

Primary Partitions and Multiple Operating Systems

Primary partitions are usually assigned drive letters and appear in My Computer/Computer (once you format them). The first primary partition in Windows is always C:. After that, you can label the partitions D: through Z:.

Only primary partitions can boot operating systems. On an MBR disk, you can easily install four different operating systems, for example, each OS on its own primary partition, and boot to your choice each time you fire up the computer.

Every primary partition on a single drive has a special setting stored in the partition table called *active* that determines the **active partition**. The MBR finds the active partition and boots the operating system on that partition. Only one partition can be active at a time because you can run only one OS at a time (see Figure 4.3).

To control multiboot setups, many people use a free, Linux-based boot manager called Grand Unified Bootloader (GRUB), shown in Figure 4.4, although some people prefer Partition Commander by Avanquest Software to set up the partitions. When the computer boots, the boot manager software yanks control from the MBR and asks which OS you wish to boot. Once a partition is set as active, the partition boot sector loads the operating system.

Extended Partitions

With a four-partition limit, an MBR disk would be limited to only four drive letters if using only primary partitions. An extended partition overcomes this limit. An extended partition can contain multiple **logical drives**, each of which can get a drive letter (see Figure 4.5).

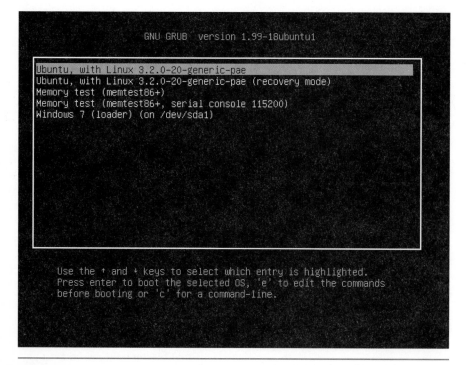

• **Figure 4.4** GRUB in action

• **Figure 4.5** An extended partition containing multiple logical drives

A logical drive works like a primary partition—it usually gets a drive letter such as D: or E:—but you can't boot an OS from it. You format it just like you would a primary partition. The only difference is that each logical drive is actually in the same extended partition.

Extended partitions do not receive drive letters, but the logical drives within an extended partition do.

Dynamic Disks

With the introduction of Windows 2000, Microsoft defined an entirely new type of partitioning called *dynamic storage partitioning*, better known as *dynamic disks*. Microsoft calls a drive structure created with dynamic disk a **volume**. There is no dynamic disk equivalent to primary versus extended partitions. A dynamic disk volume is still technically a partition, but it can do things a regular partition cannot do.

First off, when you turn a hard drive into a dynamic disk, you can create as many volumes on it as you want. You're not limited to four partitions.

Second, you can create—in software—new drive structures that you can't do with MBR drives. Specifically, you can implement RAID, span volumes over multiple drives, and extend volumes on one or more drives. Table 4.1 shows you which version of Windows supports which volume type.

The terms "volume" and "partition" refer to the same thing: a defined chunk of your hard drive.

Table 4.1	Dynamic Disk Compatibility			
Volume	Windows XP Professional	Windows Vista Business/ Ultimate/Enterprise	Windows 7 Professional/ Ultimate/Enterprise	Windows Server 2008/ Server 2008 R2
Simple	X	X	X	X
Spanned	X	X	X	X
Striped	X	X	X	X
Mirrored			X	X
RAID 5				X

Simple volumes work a lot like primary partitions. If you have a hard drive and you want to make half of it E: and the other half F:, for example, you create two volumes on a dynamic disk. That's it.

Spanned volumes use unallocated space on multiple drives to create a single volume. Spanned volumes are a bit risky: if any of the spanned drives fails, the entire volume is lost.

Striped volumes are RAID 0 volumes. You may take any two unallocated spaces on two separate hard drives and stripe them. But again, if either drive fails, you lose all of your data.

Mirrored volumes are RAID 1 volumes. You may take any two unallocated spaces on two separate hard drives and mirror them. If one of the two mirrored drives fails, the other keeps running.

RAID 5 volumes, as the name implies, are for RAID 5 arrays. A RAID 5 volume requires three or more dynamic disks with equal-sized unallocated spaces.

Only the high-end editions of each version of Windows support dynamic disks. This includes Windows XP Professional; Windows Vista Business, Ultimate, and Enterprise; and Windows 7 Professional, Ultimate, and Enterprise.

GUID Partition Table

MBR partitioning came out a long time ago, in an age where 32-MB hard drives were more than you would ever need. While it's lasted a long time as the partitioning standard for bootable drives, there's a newer kid in town with the power to outshine the aging partitioning scheme and assume all the functions of the older partition style.

The **globally unique identifier partition table (GPT)** shares a lot with the MBR partitioning scheme, but most of the MBR scheme's limitations have been fixed. Here are the big improvements:

- While MBR drives are limited to four partitions, a GPT drive can have an almost unlimited number of primary partitions. Microsoft has limited Windows to 128 partitions.

- MBR partitions can be no larger than 2.2 TB, but GPT partitions have no such restrictions. Well, there is a maximum size limit, but it's so large, we measure it in zettabytes. A zettabyte, by the way, is a million terabytes.

- Remember all the lies that MBR drives had to tell BIOS so that the logical block addressing (LBA) looked like cylinder-head-sector (CHS) values? With GPT disks, the lies are over. GPT partitioning supports LBA right out of the box.

On paper, a GPT drive looks a lot like an MBR drive, except it's arranged by LBA instead of sectors (see Figure 4.6). LBA 0, for instance, is the *protective MBR*. This is a re-creation of the master boot record from MBR drives so that disk utilities know it is a GPT drive and don't mistakenly overwrite any partition data.

Instead of the old master boot record and partition table, GPT drives use a GPT header and partition entry array. Both are located at the beginning and end of the drive so there is a protected backup copy. The partitions on a GPT drive go between the primary and backup headers and arrays, as shown in Figure 4.6.

You can configure only the 64-bit versions of Windows Vista and Windows 7 to boot from GPT if you use a UEFI motherboard. All other operating systems are out of luck when it comes to booting, but every current version of Windows can use GPT on additional, non-boot drives.

• **Figure 4.6** GUID partition table

Other Partition Types

The partition types supported by Windows are not the only partition types you may encounter; other types exist. One of the most common is called the *hidden partition*. A hidden partition is really just a primary partition that

is hidden from your operating system. Only special BIOS tools may access a hidden partition. Hidden partitions are used by some PC makers to hide a backup copy of an installed OS that you can use to restore your system if you accidentally trash it—by, for example, learning about partitions and using a partitioning program incorrectly.

A *swap partition* is another special type of partition, but swap partitions are found only on Linux and BSD systems. A swap partition's only job is to act like RAM when your system needs more RAM than you have installed. Windows has a similar function with a *page file* that uses a special file instead of a partition.

CompTIA refers to a hidden partition that contains a restorable copy of an installed OS as a *factory recovery partition*.

When to Partition

Partitioning is not a common task. The two most common situations likely to require partitioning are when you're installing an OS on a new system, and when you're adding an additional drive to an existing system. When you install a new OS, the installation disc asks you how you would like to partition the drive. When you're adding a new hard drive to an existing system, every OS has a built-in tool to help you partition it.

Each version of Windows offers a different tool for partitioning hard drives. For more than 20 years, through the days of DOS and early Windows (up to Windows Me), we used a command-line program called **FDISK** to partition drives. Figure 4.7 shows the FDISK program. Modern versions of Windows use a graphical partitioning program called **Disk Management**, shown in Figure 4.8.

Linux uses a number of different tools for partitioning. The oldest is called FDISK—yes, the same name as the DOS/Windows version. That's where the similarities end, however, as Linux FDISK has a totally different command set. Even though every copy of Linux comes with the Linux FDISK,

• **Figure 4.7** FDISK

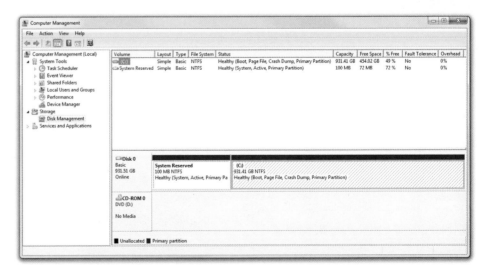

• **Figure 4.8** Windows 7 Disk Management tool in Computer Management

it's rarely used because so many better partitioning tools are available. One of the newer Linux partitioning tools is called GParted. See the "Beyond A+" section for more discussion on third-party partitioning tools.

In the early days of PCs, you couldn't change a partition's size or type (other than by erasing it) once you'd made it with any Microsoft tools. A few third-party tools, led by PartitionMagic, gave techs the tools to resize partitions without losing the data they held.

Current Microsoft tools have more flexibility than the older tools that came with DOS and Windows. Windows XP can nondestructively resize a partition to be larger, but not smaller. In Windows Vista and Windows 7, you can nondestructively resize partitions by shrinking or expanding existing partitions with available free space.

Partition Naming Problems

So far, you've learned that MBR and GPT disks use partitions and dynamic disks use volumes. Unfortunately, Windows Vista and Windows 7 foul up this perfectly clear distinction when you use the Disk Management utility. Here's the scoop.

When you create a drive structure on an MBR or GPT disk, you create a *partition*, regardless of which operating system you use. Figure 4.9 shows the partitioning tool in Windows XP with the properly named partitions—primary and extended—and the logical drives in the extended partition. They're color coded so you can readily see the different structures.

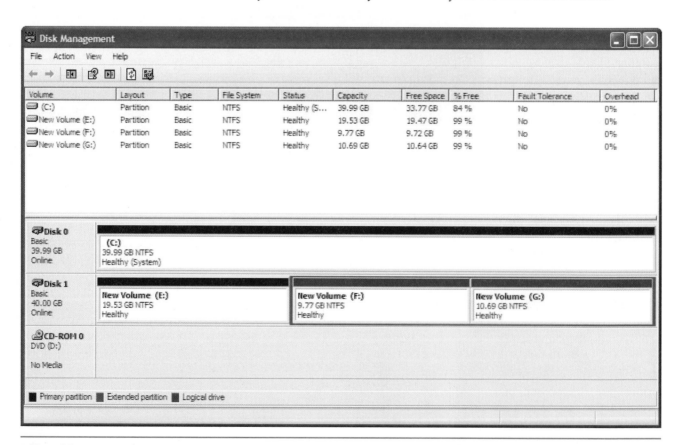

• **Figure 4.9** Windows XP very clearly showing primary and extended partitions and logical drives in the extended partition

• **Figure 4.10** New volume option

If you create a dynamic disk drive structure, Windows makes a *volume*. A dynamic disk volume is proprietary to Microsoft, so no other tool enables you to create them.

Both during installation and in Disk Management, the names of the partitions stay the same. It's not that way in Windows Vista and Windows 7. During installation, everything is a partition, just like with Windows XP.

Here's the really bad punch line. For some reason only fathomable to Microsoft marketing folks, Microsoft decided to describe the process of creating every drive structure in Windows Vista and Windows 7 in Disk Management as *creating a volume* (see Figure 4.10). As you'll discover when we get to the partitioning process, you can create primary partitions, extended partitions, and logical drives in Disk Management, but you'll create them as volumes.

▉ Hard Drive Formatting

Once you've partitioned a hard drive, you must perform one more step before your OS can use that drive: formatting. *Formatting* does two things: it creates a file system—like a library's card catalog—and makes the root directory in that file system. You must format every partition and volume you create so it can hold data that you can easily retrieve. The various versions of Windows you're likely to encounter today can use several different file systems, so we'll look at those in detail next. The *root directory* provides the foundation upon which the OS builds files and folders.

If you've ever been to a library and walked past all of the computers connected to the Internet, down the stairs into a dark basement, you might have seen a dusty set of drawers full of cards with information about every book in the library. This is a "card catalog" system, invented over 2000 years ago. These days, you probably won't encounter this phrase anywhere outside of explanations for formatting.

File Systems in Windows

Every version of Windows comes with a built-in formatting utility with which to create one or more file systems on a partition or volume. The versions of Windows in current use support three separate Microsoft file systems: FAT16, FAT32, and NTFS.

The simplest hard drive file system, called FAT or FAT16, provides a good introduction to how file systems work. More complex file systems fix many of the problems inherent in FAT and add extra features as well.

FAT

The base storage area for hard drives is a sector; each sector stores up to 512 bytes of data. If an OS stores a file smaller than 512 bytes in a sector, the rest of the sector goes to waste. We accept this waste because most files are far larger than 512 bytes. So what happens when an OS stores a file larger than 512 bytes? The OS needs a method to fill one sector, find another that's unused, and fill it, continuing to fill sectors until the file is completely stored. Once the OS stores a file, it must remember which sectors hold the file, so it can be retrieved later.

MS-DOS version 2.1 first supported hard drives using a special data structure to keep track of stored data on the hard drive, and Microsoft called this structure the **file allocation table (FAT)**. Think of the FAT as nothing more than a card catalog that keeps track of which sectors store the various parts of a file. The official jargon term for a FAT is **data structure**, but it is more like a two-column spreadsheet.

The left column (see Figure 4.11) gives each sector a hexadecimal number from 0000 to FFFF. Each hexadecimal character represents four binary numbers or four bits. Four hex characters, therefore, represent 16 bits. If you do the math (2^{16}), you'll find that there are 65,536 (64 K) sectors.

We call this type of FAT a *16-bit FAT* or *FAT16*. Not just hard drives have FATs. Many USB thumb drives use FAT16. Floppy disks use FATs, but their FATs are only 12 bits because they store much less data.

The right column of the FAT contains information on the status of sectors. All hard drives, even brand-new drives fresh from the factory, contain faulty sectors that cannot store data because of imperfections in the construction of the drives. The OS must locate these bad sectors, mark them as unusable, and then prevent any files from being written to them. This mapping of bad sectors is one of the functions of **high-level formatting**. After the format program creates the FAT, it proceeds through the entire partition, writing and attempting to read from each sector sequentially. If it finds a bad sector, it places a special status code (FFF7) in the sector's FAT location, indicating that the sector is unavailable for use. Formatting also marks the good sectors as 0000.

Using the FAT to track sectors, however, creates a problem. The 16-bit FAT addresses a maximum of 64 K (2^{16}) locations. Therefore, the size of a hard drive partition should be limited to 64 K × 512 bytes per sector, or 32 MB. When Microsoft first unveiled FAT16, this 32-MB limit presented no problem because most hard drives were only 5 to 10 MB. As hard drives grew in size, you could use FDISK to break them up into multiple partitions. You could divide a 40-MB hard drive into two partitions, for example,

0000	
0001	
0002	
0003	
0004	
0005	
0006	
FFF9	
FFFA	
FFFB	
FFFC	
FFFD	
FFFF	
FFFF	

• **Figure 4.11** 16-bit FAT

making each partition smaller than 32 MB. But as hard drives started to become much larger, Microsoft realized that the 32-MB limit for drives was unacceptable. We needed an improvement to the 16-bit FAT, a new and improved FAT16 that would support larger drives while still maintaining backward compatibility with the old-style 16-bit FAT. This need led to the development of a dramatic improvement in FAT16, called *clustering*, that enabled you to format partitions larger than 32 MB (see Figure 4.12). This new FAT16 appeared way back in the DOS-4 days.

Clustering simply refers to combining a set of contiguous sectors and treating them as a single unit in the FAT. These units are called **file allocation units** or **clusters**. Each row of the FAT addressed a cluster instead of a sector. Unlike sectors, the size of a cluster is not fixed. Clusters improved FAT16, but it still only supported a maximum of 64 K storage units, so the formatting program set the number of sectors in each cluster according to the size of the partition. The larger the partition, the more sec-

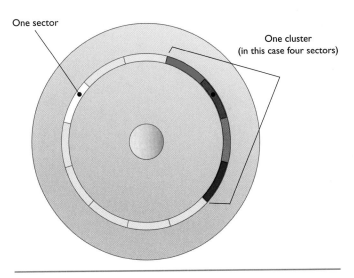

• **Figure 4.12** Cluster versus sector

tors per cluster. This method kept clustering completely compatible with the 64 K locations in the old 16-bit FAT. The new FAT16 could support partitions up to 2 GB. (The old 16-bit FAT is so old it doesn't really even have a name—if someone says "FAT16," they mean the newer FAT16 that supports clustering.) Table 4.2 shows the number of sectors per cluster for FAT16.

Table 4.2	FAT16 Cluster Sizes
If FDISK makes a partition this big:	**You'll get this many sectors/cluster:**
16 to 127.9 MB	4
128 to 255.9 MB	8
256 to 511.9 MB	16
512 to 1023.9 MB	32
1024 to 2048 MB	64

FAT16 in Action

Assume you have a copy of Windows using FAT16. When an application such as Microsoft Word tells the OS to save a file, Windows starts at the beginning of the FAT, looking for the first space marked "open for use" (0000), and begins to write to that cluster. If the entire file fits within that one cluster, Windows places the code *FFFF* (last cluster) into the cluster's status area in the FAT. That's called the *end-of-file marker*. Windows then goes to the folder storing the file and adds the filename and the cluster's number to the folder list. If the file requires more than one cluster, Windows searches for the next open cluster and places the number of the next cluster in the status area, filling and adding clusters until the entire file is saved. The last cluster then receives the end-of-file marker (FFFF).

Let's run through an example of this process, and start by selecting an arbitrary part of the FAT: from 3ABB to 3AC7. Assume you want to save a file called mom.txt. Before saving the file, the FAT looks like Figure 4.13.

Cluster	Status
3ABB	0000
3ABC	0000
3ABD	FFF7
3ABE	0000
3ABF	0000
3AC0	0000
3AC1	0000
3AC2	0000
3AC3	0000
3AC4	0000
3AC5	0000
3AC6	0000
3AC7	0000

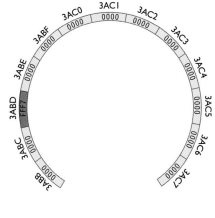

• **Figure 4.13** The initial FAT

Cluster	Status
3ABB	**3ABC**
3ABC	0000
3ABD	FFF7
3ABE	0000
3ABF	0000
3AC0	0000
3AC1	0000
3AC2	0000
3AC3	0000
3AC4	0000
3AC5	0000
3AC6	0000
3AC7	0000

• **Figure 4.14** The first cluster used

Cluster	Status
3ABB	3ABC
3ABC	**3ABE**
3ABD	FFF7
3ABE	0000
3ABF	0000
3AC0	0000
3AC1	0000
3AC2	0000
3AC3	0000
3AC4	0000
3AC5	0000
3AC6	0000
3AC7	0000

• **Figure 4.15** The second cluster used

Windows finds the first open cluster, 3ABB, and fills it. But the entire mom.txt file won't fit into that cluster. Needing more space, the OS goes through the FAT to find the next open cluster. It finds cluster 3ABC. Before filling 3ABC, the value *3ABC* is placed in 3ABB's status (see Figure 4.14).

Even after filling two clusters, more of the mom.txt file remains, so Windows must find one more cluster. The 3ABD cluster has been marked FFF7 (bad cluster or *bad-sector marker*), so Windows skips over 3ABD, finding 3ABE (see Figure 4.15).

Before filling 3ABE, Windows enters the value *3ABE* in 3ABC's status. Windows does not completely fill 3ABE, signifying that the entire mom .txt file has been stored. Windows enters the value *FFFF* in 3ABE's status, indicating the end of file (see Figure 4.16).

After saving all of the clusters, Windows locates the file's folder (yes, folders also are stored on clusters, but they get a different set of clusters, somewhere else on the disk) and records the filename, size, date/time, and starting cluster, like this:

> mom.txt 19234 05-19-09 2:04p 3ABB

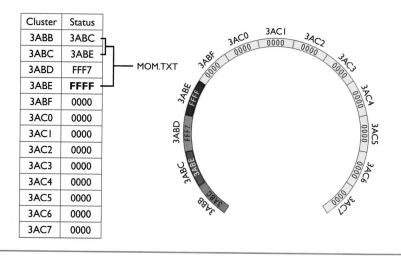

Cluster	Status
3ABB	3ABC
3ABC	3ABE
3ABD	FFF7
3ABE	**FFFF**
3ABF	0000
3AC0	0000
3AC1	0000
3AC2	0000
3AC3	0000
3AC4	0000
3AC5	0000
3AC6	0000
3AC7	0000

• **Figure 4.16** End of file reached

If a program requests that file, the process is reversed. Windows locates the folder containing the file to determine the starting cluster and then pulls a piece of the file from each cluster until it sees the end-of-file cluster. Windows then hands the reassembled file to the requesting application.

Clearly, without the FAT, Windows cannot locate files. FAT16 automatically makes two copies of the FAT. One FAT backs up the other to provide special utilities a way to recover a FAT that gets corrupted—a painfully common occurrence.

Even when FAT works perfectly, over time the files begin to separate in a process called **fragmentation**.

Fragmentation

Continuing with the example, let's use Microsoft Word to save two more files: a letter to the IRS (irsrob.doc) and a letter to IBM (ibmhelp.doc). The irsrob.doc file takes the next three clusters—3ABF, 3AC0, and 3AC1—and ibmhelp.doc takes two clusters—3AC2 and 3AC3 (see Figure 4.17).

Now suppose you erase mom.txt. Windows does not delete the cluster entries for mom.txt when it erases a file. Windows only alters the information in the folder, simply changing the first letter of mom.txt to the Greek letter Σ (sigma). This causes the file to "disappear" as far as the OS knows. It won't show up, for example, in Windows Explorer, even though the data still resides on the hard drive for the moment (see Figure 4.18).

Cluster	Status
3ABB	3ABC
3ABC	3ABE
3ABD	FFF7
3ABE	FFFF
3ABF	3AC0
3AC0	3AC1
3AC1	FFFF
3AC2	3AC3
3AC3	FFFF
3AC4	0000
3AC5	0000
3AC6	0000
3AC7	0000

MOM.TXT (3ABB, 3ABC, 3ABD, 3ABE)
IRSROB.DOC (3ABF, 3AC0, 3AC1)
IBMHELP.DOC (3AC2, 3AC3)

• **Figure 4.17** Three files saved

Note that under normal circumstances, Windows does not actually delete files when you press the DELETE key. Instead, Windows moves the files to a special hidden directory that you can access via the Recycle Bin. The files themselves are not actually deleted until you empty the Recycle Bin. (You can skip the Recycle Bin entirely if you wish, by highlighting a file and then holding down the SHIFT key when you press DELETE.)

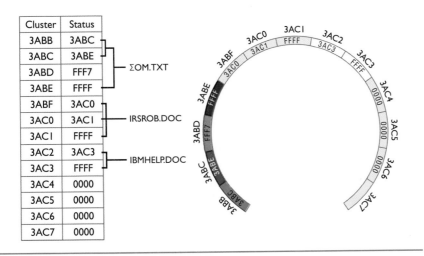

Cluster	Status
3ABB	3ABC
3ABC	3ABE
3ABD	FFF7
3ABE	FFFF
3ABF	3AC0
3AC0	3AC1
3AC1	FFFF
3AC2	3AC3
3AC3	FFFF
3AC4	0000
3AC5	0000
3AC6	0000
3AC7	0000

ΣOM.TXT (3ABB, 3ABC, 3ABD, 3ABE)
IRSROB.DOC (3ABF, 3AC0, 3AC1)
IBMHELP.DOC (3AC2, 3AC3)

• **Figure 4.18** The mom.txt file erased

Figure 4.19 WinUndelete in action

Because all of the data for mom.txt is intact, you could use some program to change the Σ back into another letter and thus get the document back. A number of third-party undelete tools are available. Figure 4.19 shows one such program at work. Just remember that if you want to use an undelete tool, you must use it quickly. The space allocated to your deleted file may soon be overwritten by a new file.

Let's say you just emptied your Recycle Bin. You now save one more file, taxrec.xls, a big spreadsheet that will take six clusters, into the same folder that once held mom.txt. As Windows writes the file to the drive, it overwrites the space that mom.txt used, but it needs three more clusters. The next three available clusters are 3AC4, 3AC5, and 3AC6 (see Figure 4.20).

Notice that taxrec.xls is in two pieces, thus *fragmented*. Fragmentation takes place all of the time on FAT16 systems. Although the system easily negotiates a tiny fragmented file split into only two parts, excess fragmentation slows down the system during hard drive reads and writes. This example is fragmented into two pieces; in the real world, a file might fragment into hundreds of pieces, forcing the read/write heads to

Cluster	Status
3ABB	3ABC
3ABC	3ABE
3ABD	FFF7
3ABE	3AC4
3ABF	3AC0
3AC0	3AC1
3AC1	FFFF
3AC2	3AC3
3AC3	FFFF
3AC4	3AC5
3AC5	3AC6
3AC6	FFFF
3AC7	0000

TAXREC.XLS

Figure 4.20 The taxrec.xls file fragmented

travel all over the hard drive to retrieve a single file. You can dramatically improve the speed at which the hard drive reads and writes files by eliminating this fragmentation.

Windows comes with a program called Disk Defragmenter, which can rearrange the files into neat contiguous chunks (see Figure 4.21). Defragmentation is crucial for ensuring the top performance of a hard drive. The "Maintaining and Troubleshooting Hard Drives" section of this chapter gives the details on working with the various Disk Defragmenters in Windows.

FAT32

When Microsoft introduced Windows 95 OSR2 (OEM Service Release 2), it also

• **Figure 4.21** Windows Disk Defragmenter

unveiled a totally new file format called **FAT32** that brought a couple of dramatic improvements. First, FAT32 supports partitions up to 2 TB (more than 2 trillion bytes). Second, as its name implies, FAT32 uses 32 bits to describe each cluster, which means clusters can drop to more reasonable sizes. FAT32's use of so many FAT entries gives it the power to use small clusters, making the old "keep your partitions small" rule obsolete. A 2-GB partition using FAT16 would use 32-KB clusters, while the same 2-GB partition using FAT32 would use 4-KB clusters. You get far more efficient use of disk space with FAT32, without the need to make multiple small partitions. FAT32 partitions still need defragmentation, however, just as often as FAT16 partitions.

Table 4.3 shows cluster sizes for FAT32 partitions.

Table 4.3	FAT32 Cluster Sizes
Drive Size	**Cluster Size**
512 MB or 1023 MB	4 KB
1024 MB to 2 GB	4 KB
2 GB to 8 GB	4 KB
8 GB to 16 GB	8 KB
16 GB to 32 GB	16 KB
>32 GB	32 KB

If you have a geeky interest in what version of NTFS you are running, open a prompt and type this command: **fsutil fsinfo ntfsinfo c:**

Microsoft has never released the exact workings of NTFS to the public.

NTFS

The Windows format of choice these days is the **New Technology File System (NTFS)**. NTFS came out a long time ago with the first version of Windows NT, thus the name. Over the years, NTFS has undergone a number of improvements. The version used in modern Windows is called NTFS 3.1, although you'll see it referred to as NTFS 5.0/5.1. NTFS uses clusters and file allocation tables but in a much more complex and powerful way compared to FAT or FAT32. NTFS offers six major improvements and refinements: redundancy, security, compression, encryption, disk quotas, and cluster sizing.

NTFS Structure

NTFS utilizes an enhanced file allocation table called the **master file table (MFT)**. An NTFS partition keeps a backup copy of the most critical parts of the MFT in the middle of the disk, reducing the chance that a serious drive error can wipe out both the MFT and the MFT copy. Whenever you defragment an NTFS partition, you'll see a small, immovable chunk somewhere on the drive, often near the front; that's the MFT (see Figure 4.22).

Security

NTFS views individual files and folders as objects and provides security for those objects through a feature called the *Access Control List (ACL)*. Future chapters go into this in much more detail.

Compression

NTFS enables you to compress individual files and folders to save space on a hard drive. Compression makes access time to the data slower because the OS has to uncompress files every time you use them, but in a space-limited environment, sometimes that's what you have to do. Explorer displays filenames for compressed files in blue.

Encryption

One of the big draws with NTFS is file encryption, the black art of making files unreadable to anybody who doesn't have the right key. You can encrypt a single file, a folder, or a folder full of files. Microsoft calls the encryption utility in NTFS the **encrypting file system (EFS)**, but it's simply an aspect of NTFS, not a standalone file system. You'll learn more about encryption when you read Chapter 7.

Disk Quotas

NTFS supports **disk quotas**, enabling administrators to set limits on drive space usage for users. To set quotas, you must log on as an Administrator, right-click the hard drive name, and select Properties. In the Drive Properties dialog box, select the Quota tab and make changes. Figure 4.23 shows configured quotas for a hard drive. Although rarely used on single-user systems, setting disk quotas on multi-user systems prevents any individual user from monopolizing your hard disk space.

• **Figure 4.22** The NTFS MFT appears in a defragmenter program as the highlighted red blocks.

• **Figure 4.23** Hard drive quotas in Windows 7

Cluster Sizes

Unlike FAT16 or FAT32, you can adjust the cluster sizes in NTFS, although you'll probably rarely do so. Table 4.4 shows the default cluster sizes for NTFS.

Table 4.4	NTFS Cluster Sizes	
Drive Size	**Cluster Size**	**Number of Sectors**
512 MB or less	512 bytes	1
513 MB to 1024 MB (1 GB)	1024 bytes (1 KB)	2
1025 MB to 2048 MB (2 GB)	2048 bytes (2 KB)	4
2049 MB and larger	4096 bytes (4 KB)	8

By default, NTFS supports partitions up to ~16 TB on a dynamic disk (though only up to 2 TB on a basic disk). By tweaking the cluster sizes, you can get NTFS to support partitions up to 16 exabytes, or 18,446,744,073,709,551,616 bytes! That might support any and all upcoming hard drive capacities for the next 100 years or so.

With so many file systems, how do you know which one to use? In the case of internal hard drives, you should use the most feature-rich system your OS supports. For all modern versions of Windows, use NTFS. External hard drives still often use FAT32 because NTFS features such as the ACL and encryption can make access difficult when you move the drive between systems, but with that exception, NTFS is your best choice on a Windows-based system.

NTFS supports partitions up to 16 TB by default.

FAT32 only supports drives up to 2 TB and only supports files up to 4 GB.

An exabyte is 2^{60} bytes; a zettabyte is 2^{70} bytes. For comparison, a terabyte is 2^{40} bytes. Remember from your binary practice that each superscript number doubles the overall number, so $2^{41} = 2$ TB, $2^{42} = 4$ TB, and so on. That means a zettabyte is really, really big!

FAT64

Everyone loves USB thumb drives. Their ease of use and convenience make them indispensible for those of us who enjoy sharing a program, some photos, or a playlist. But people today want to share more than just a few small files, and they can do so with larger thumb drives. As thumb drives grow bigger in capacity, however, the file system becomes a problem.

The file system we have used for years on thumb drives, FAT32, does not work on drives larger than 2 TB. Worse, FAT32 limits *file* size to 4 GB. Now that you can find many thumb drives larger than 2 GB, Microsoft wisely developed a replacement for FAT32.

The newer file system, called *exFAT* or **FAT64**, breaks the 4-GB file-size barrier, supporting files up to 16 exabytes (EB) and a theoretical partition limit of 64 zettabytes (ZB). Microsoft recommends a partition size of up to 512 TB on today's USB flash drives, which should be enough for a while. The exFAT file system extends FAT32 from 32-bit cluster entries to 64-bit cluster entries in the file table. Like FAT32, on the other hand, exFAT still lacks all of NTFS's extra features such as permissions, compression, and encryption.

Now, if you're like me, you might be thinking, "Why don't we just use NTFS?" And I would say, "Good point!" Microsoft, however, sees NTFS

as too powerful for what most of us need from flash drives. For example, flash drives don't need NTFS permissions. However, if for some reason you *really* want to format large USB thumb drives with NTFS, Windows 7 will gladly allow you to do so, as shown in Figure 4.24.

◼ The Partitioning and Formatting Process

Now that you understand the concepts of formatting and partitioning, let's go through the process of setting up an installed hard drive by using different partitioning and formatting tools. If you have access to a system, try following along with these descriptions. Remember, don't make any changes to a drive you want to keep, because both partitioning and formatting are destructive processes.

Bootable Media

Imagine you've built a brand-new PC. The hard drive has no OS, so you need to boot up something to set up that hard drive. Any software that can boot up a system is by definition an operating system. You need an optical disc or USB thumb drive with a bootable OS installed. Any removable media that has a bootable OS is generically called a *boot device* or *boot disk*. Your system boots off of the boot device, which then loads some kind of OS that enables you to partition, format, and install an OS on your new hard drive. Boot devices come from many sources. All Windows OS installation discs are boot devices, as are Linux installation discs.

Every boot disk or device has some kind of partitioning tool and a way to format a new partition. A hard drive has to have a partition and has to be formatted to support an OS installation.

Partitioning and Formatting with the Installation Disc

When you boot up a Windows installation disc and the installation program detects a hard drive that is not yet partitioned, it prompts you through a sequence of steps to partition (and format) the hard drive. Chapter 5 covers the entire installation process, but we'll jump ahead and dive into the partitioning part of the installation here to see how this is done.

The partitioning and formatting tools differ between Windows XP and Windows Vista/7. Windows XP has a text-based installation tool. Windows Vista and Windows 7 use a graphical tool. But the process of setting up drives is nearly identical.

• **Figure 4.24** Formatting a thumb drive in Windows 7

Tech Tip

Backward Availability of exFAT
Microsoft introduced exFAT in Windows 7, but Windows Vista with SP1 also supports exFAT. Microsoft even enabled Windows XP support for exFAT with a special download (check Microsoft Knowledge Base article 955704).

• **Figure 4.25** Windows installation CD

Partitioning During Windows XP Installation

The most common partitioning scenario involves turning a new blank drive into a single bootable C: drive. To accomplish this goal, you need to make the entire drive a primary partition and then make it active. Let's go through the process of partitioning and formatting a single brand-new 1-TB hard drive.

The Windows XP installation begins by booting from a Windows installation CD-ROM like the one shown in Figure 4.25. The installation program starts automatically from the CD. The installation first loads some needed files but eventually prompts you with the screen shown in Figure 4.26. This is your clue that partitioning is about to start.

Press the ENTER key to start a new Windows installation and accept the license agreement to see the main partitioning screen (see Figure 4.27). The bar that says Unpartitioned space is the drive.

The Windows installer is pretty smart. If you press ENTER at this point, it partitions the hard drive as a single primary partition, makes it active, and installs Windows for you. That's the type of partitioning you will do on the vast majority of installations.

As you can see on the screen, the partitioning tool also gives you the option to press C to create a partition on the drive. You can also press D to delete an existing partition.

When you press C, the installer asks you how large a partition to make (see Figure 4.28). You may make the partition any size you want by erasing the current number (the whole unpartitioned space by default) and typing in a number, from a minimum of 8 MB up to the size of the entire drive. Once you have your number set, press ENTER to create the partition.

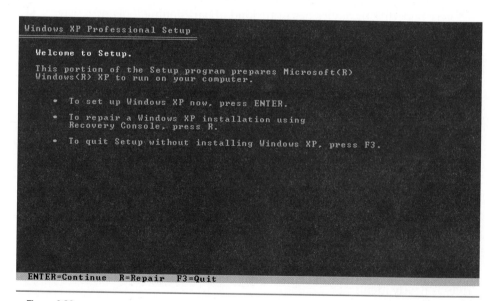

• **Figure 4.26** Welcome to Setup

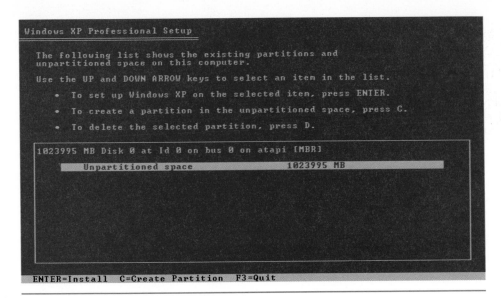

```
Windows XP Professional Setup

The following list shows the existing partitions and
unpartitioned space on this computer.

Use the UP and DOWN ARROW keys to select an item in the list.

   • To set up Windows XP on the selected item, press ENTER.

   • To create a partition in the unpartitioned space, press C.

   • To delete the selected partition, press D.

  ┌────────────────────────────────────────────────────────────┐
  │ 1023995 MB Disk 0 at Id 0 on bus 0 on atapi [MBR]           │
  │     Unpartitioned space                 1023995 MB          │
  │                                                              │
  │                                                              │
  └────────────────────────────────────────────────────────────┘

  ENTER=Install   C=Create Partition   F3=Quit
```

• **Figure 4.27** Partitioning screen

If you select a size smaller than the maximum and press ENTER, you'll see the newly created partition and the remaining drive as Unpartitioned space (see Figure 4.29). You can create more "partitions" by moving the selection bar onto the Unpartitioned space and pressing C to create a new partition. Repeat this for as many new "partitions" as you want to create.

The installer on the Windows XP disc calls all the drive structures you create at this time partitions, but what's happening is a little different. The first partition you create will be a primary partition. The second partition you create will be automatically an extended partition. Every "partition" you create after the second will be a logical drive in the extended partition.

```
Windows XP Professional Setup

   You asked Setup to create a new partition on
   1023995 MB Disk 0 at Id 0 on bus 0 on atapi [MBR].

     • To create the new partition, enter a size below and
       press ENTER.

     • To go back to the previous screen without creating
       the partition, press ESC.

   The minimum size for the new partition is       8 megabytes (MB).
   The maximum size for the new partition is 1023987 megabytes (MB).
   Create partition of size (in MB):   1023987_

  ENTER=Create   ESC=Cancel
```

• **Figure 4.28** Setting partition size

```
Windows XP Professional Setup

     The following list shows the existing partitions and
     unpartitioned space on this computer.

     Use the UP and DOWN ARROW keys to select an item in the list.

        •  To set up Windows XP on the selected item, press ENTER.

        •  To create a partition in the unpartitioned space, press C.

        •  To delete the selected partition, press D.

     ┌──────────────────────────────────────────────────────────────────┐
     │ 1023995 MB Disk 0 at Id 0 on bus 0 on atapi [MBR]                  │
     │                                                                    │
     │   C:  Partition1 [New (Raw)]          340989 MB ( 340989 MB free)  │
     │       Unpartitioned space             683006 MB                    │
     │                                                                    │
     │                                                                    │
     │                                                                    │
     │                                                                    │
     │                                                                    │
     │                                                                    │
     └──────────────────────────────────────────────────────────────────┘

   ENTER=Install   D=Delete Partition   F3=Quit
```

• **Figure 4.29** A newly created partition along with unpartitioned space

Once you finish partitioning, select the partition you want to use for the installation. Again, almost every time you should select C:. At that point, Windows asks you how you want to format that drive (see Figure 4.30).

So you might be asking, where's the basic versus dynamic option? Where do you tell Windows to make the partition primary instead of extended? Where do you set it as active?

The Windows installer makes a number of assumptions for you, such as always making the first partition primary and setting it as active. The installer also makes all hard drives basic disks. You'll have to convert a drive to dynamic later (if you even want to convert it at all).

Select NTFS for the format. Either option—quick or full—will do the job here. (Quick format is quicker, as the name would suggest, but the full option is more thorough and thus safer.) After Windows formats the drive, the installation continues, copying the new Windows installation to the C: drive.

```
Windows XP Professional Setup

     A new partition for Windows XP has been created on

     1023995 MB Disk 0 at Id 0 on bus 0 on atapi [MBR].

     This partition must now be formatted.

     From the list below, select a file system for the new partition.
     Use the UP and DOWN ARROW keys to select the file system you want,
     and then press ENTER.

     If you want to select a different partition for Windows XP,
     press ESC.

        Format the partition using the NTFS file system (Quick)
        Format the partition using the NTFS file system

   ENTER=Continue   ESC=Cancel
```

• **Figure 4.30** Format screen

```
Windows XP Professional Setup

You asked Setup to delete the partition
    E:  Partition3 [New (Raw)]            340989 MB ( 340989 MB free)
on 1023995 MB Disk 0 at Id 0 on bus 0 on atapi [MBR].

    •  To delete this partition, press L.
       CAUTION: All data on this partition will be lost.

    •  To return to the previous screen without
       deleting the partition, press ESC.

L=Delete   ESC=Cancel
```

● **Figure 4.31** Option to delete partition

The installation program can delete partitions just as easily as it makes
them. If you use a hard drive that already has partitions, for example, you
just select the partition you wish to delete and press D. This brings up a
dialog box where Windows gives you one last chance to change your mind
(see Figure 4.31). Press L to kill the partition.

Partitioning During Windows Vista/7 Installation

The process of partitioning and formatting with the Windows Vista or
Windows 7 installation differs from the Windows XP process primarily in

looks—it's graphical—and
not in function. You'll go
through a couple of instal-
lation screens (see Fig-
ure 4.32) where you select
things such as language
and get prompted for a
product key and acceptance
of the license agreement.
Eventually you'll get to the
*Where do you want to install
Windows?* dialog box (see
Figure 4.33).

Click Next to do the
most common partition-
ing and formatting action:
creating a single C: parti-
tion, making it active, and
formatting it as NTFS. Note
that Windows 7 creates two
partitions, a 100-MB System
Reserved partition and the
C: partition. This is normal,

● **Figure 4.32** Starting the Windows 7 installation

● **Figure 4.33** Where do you want to install Windows?

the way the system was designed to work. Figure 4.34 shows a typical Windows 7 installation in Disk Management.

If you want to do any custom partitioning or delete existing partitions, you click on *Drive options (advanced)* in the *Where do you want to install Windows?* dialog box. To create a new partition, click the New button. Type in an amount in gigabytes that you want to use for a new partition, then click Apply. In Windows 7, you will get a notice that Windows might create additional partitions for system files. When you click OK, Windows will create the 100-MB System Reserved partition as well as the partition you specified (see Figure 4.35). Any leftover drive space will be listed as Unallocated Space.

Once you create a new partition, click the Format button. The installer won't ask you what file system to use. Windows Vista and Windows 7 can read FAT and FAT32 drives, but they won't install to such a partition by default.

The example here has a 1-TB drive with a 499-GB

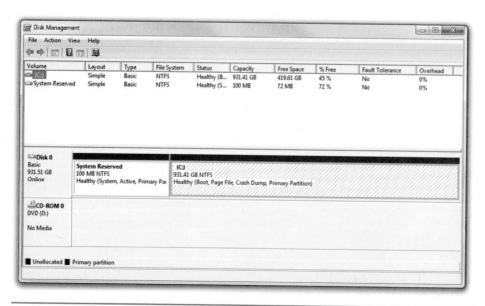

● **Figure 4.34** Disk Management showing the default partitions in Windows 7

• **Figure 4.35** New 499-GB partition with 100-MB System Reserved partition and
Unallocated Space

partition and 500 GB of unallocated space. If you've gone through this process
and have changed your mind, wanting to make the partition use the full tera-
byte, what do you have to do? In Windows XP, you would have to delete the
partition and start over, but not so
in Windows Vista or Windows 7.
You can simply click the Extend
button and then apply the rest of
the unallocated space to the cur-
rently formatted partition. The
extend function enables you to
tack unpartitioned space onto an
already partitioned drive with the
click of the mouse.

Disk Management

The primary tool for partition-
ing and formatting drives after
installation is the Disk Manage-
ment utility (see Figure 4.36).
You can use Disk Management
to do everything you want to
do to a hard drive in one handy
tool. You can access Disk Man-
agement by going to the Control
Panel and opening the Computer

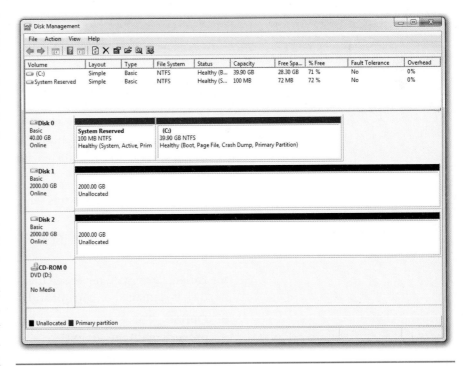

• **Figure 4.36** Disk Management

The CompTIA A+ 220-802 exam will test you on how to get into Disk Management. Know the ways.

Management applet. You can also click Start | Run in Windows XP and type **diskmgmt.msc**—or just type **diskmgmt.msc** in the Start menu Search bar in Windows Vista/7—and press ENTER.

Disk Initialization

Every hard drive in a Windows system has special information placed onto the drive through a process called **disk initialization**. This initialization information includes identifiers that say, "this drive belongs in this system" and other information that defines what this hard drive does in the system. If the hard drive is part of a software RAID array, for example, its RAID information is stored in the initialization. If it's part of a spanned volume, this is also stored there.

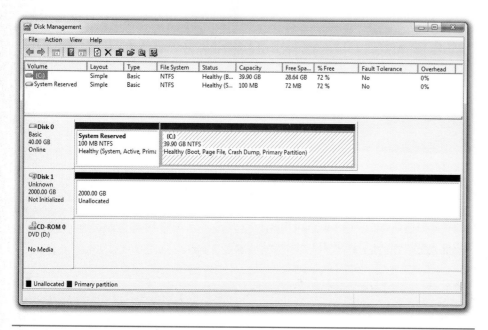

• **Figure 4.37** Unknown drive in Disk Management

All new drives must be initialized before you can use them. When you install an extra hard drive into a Windows system and start Disk Management, it notices the new drive and starts the Hard Drive Initialization Wizard. If you don't let the wizard run, the drive will be listed as unknown (see Figure 4.37).

To initialize a disk, right-click the disk icon and select Initialize. In Windows 7, you will get the option to select MBR or GPT as a partition style. Once a disk is initialized, you can see the status of the drive—a handy tool for troubleshooting.

Disk Management enables you to view the status of every drive in your system. Hopefully, you'll mostly see the drive listed as Healthy, meaning that nothing is happening to it and things are going along swimmingly. You're also already familiar with the Unallocated and Active statuses, but here are a few more to be familiar with for the CompTIA A+ 220-802 exam and real life as a tech:

- **Foreign drive** You see this when you move a dynamic disk from one computer to another.

- **Formatting** As you might have guessed, you see this when you're formatting a drive.

- **Failed** Pray you never see this status, because it means that the disk is damaged or corrupt and you've probably lost some data.

- **Online** This is what you see if a disk is healthy and communicating properly with the computer.

- **Offline** The disk is either corrupted or having communication problems.

A newly installed drive is always set as a basic disk. There's nothing wrong with using basic disks, other than that you miss out on some handy features.

Creating Partitions and Volumes in Disk Management

To create partitions or volumes, right-click the unallocated part of the drive and select New Partition in Windows XP or New Simple Volume in Windows Vista/7. Disk Management runs the New Partition Wizard or the New Simple Volume Wizard. In Windows XP, you'll be asked to select a primary partition or an extended partition (see Figure 4.38). Once you do that, you'll go to a screen where you specify the partition or volume size. Because Windows Vista and Windows 7 don't give you the option to specify whether you want primary or extended partitions, you'll go straight to the sizing screen (see Figure 4.39).

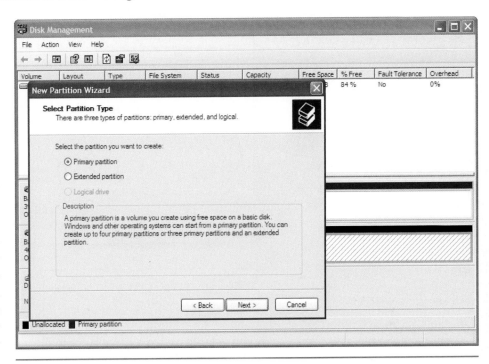

• **Figure 4.38** The New Partition Wizard in Windows XP at the Select Partition Type dialog box

• **Figure 4.39** Specifying the simple volume size in the New Simple Volume Wizard

● **Figure 4.40** Assigning a drive letter to a partition

Specify a partition or volume size and click Next. The wizard will ask if you want to assign a drive letter to the partition or volume, mount it as a folder to an existing partition or volume, or do neither (see Figure 4.40). In almost all cases, you'll want to give primary partitions and simple volumes a drive letter.

It's important to note here that Windows Vista and Windows 7 do not enable you to specify whether you want a primary or extended partition when you create a volume. The first three volumes you create will be primary partitions. Every volume thereafter will be a logical drive in an extended partition.

The last screen of the New Partition Wizard or New Simple Volume Wizard asks for the type of format you want to use for this partition (see Figure 4.41). If your partition is 4 GB or less, you may format it as FAT, FAT32, or NTFS. If your partition is greater than 4 GB but less than 32 GB, you can make the drive FAT32 or NTFS. Windows requires NTFS on any partition greater than 32 GB. Although FAT32 supports partitions

● **Figure 4.41** Choosing a file system type

Mike Meyer's CompTIA A+ Guide to 802: Managing and Troubleshooting PCs

up to 2 TB, Microsoft wants you to use NTFS on larger partitions and creates this limit. With today's big hard drives, there's no good reason to use anything other than NTFS.

You have a few more tasks to complete at this screen. You can add a volume label if you want. You can also choose the size of your clusters (*Allocation unit size*). There's no reason to change the default cluster size, so leave that alone—but you can sure speed up the format if you select the *Perform a quick format* checkbox. This will format your drive without checking every cluster. It's fast and a bit risky, but new hard drives almost always come from the factory in perfect shape—so you must decide whether to use it or not.

Last, if you chose NTFS, you may enable file and folder compression. If you select this option, you'll be able to right-click any file or folder on this partition and compress it. To compress a file or folder, choose the one you want to compress, right-click, and select Properties. Then click the Advanced button and turn compression on (see Figure 4.42). Compression is handy for opening up space on a hard drive that's filling up, but it also slows down disk access, so use it only when you need it.

Dynamic Disks

You create dynamic disks from basic disks in Disk Management. Once you convert a drive from a basic disk to a dynamic disk, primary and extended partitions no longer exist; dynamic disks are divided into volumes instead

• **Figure 4.42** Turning on compression

When you move a dynamic disk from one computer to another, it shows up in Disk Management as a foreign drive. You can import a foreign drive into the new system by right-clicking the disk icon and selecting Import Foreign Disks.

of partitions. This is obvious in Windows XP because the name changes. Because Window Vista and Windows 7 call partitions *volumes*, the change to dynamic disk isn't obvious at all.

To convert a basic disk to dynamic, just right-click the drive icon and select Convert to Dynamic Disk (see Figure 4.43). The process is very quick and safe, although the reverse is not true. The conversion from dynamic disk to basic disk first requires you to delete all volumes off of the hard drive.

Once you've converted the disk, you can make one of the five types of volumes on a dynamic disk: simple, spanned, striped, mirrored, or RAID 5. You'll next learn how to implement the three most common volume types. The final step involves assigning a drive letter or mounting the volume as a folder.

Simple Volumes A simple volume acts just like a primary partition. If you have only one dynamic disk in a system, it can have only a simple volume. It's important to note here that a simple volume may act like a traditional primary partition, but it is very different because you cannot install an operating system on it.

In Disk Management, right-click any unallocated space on the dynamic disk and choose New Simple Volume (see Figure 4.44) to run the New Simple Volume Wizard. You'll see a series of screens that prompt you on size and file system, and then you're finished. Figure 4.45 shows Disk Management with three simple volumes.

Spanning Volumes You can extend the size of a simple volume to any unallocated space on a dynamic disk. You can also extend the volume to grab extra space on completely different dynamic disks, creating a spanned

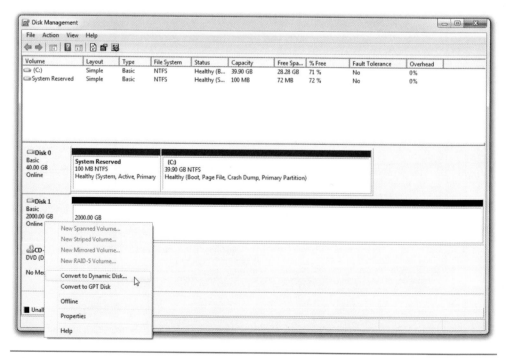

• **Figure 4.43** Converting to a dynamic disk

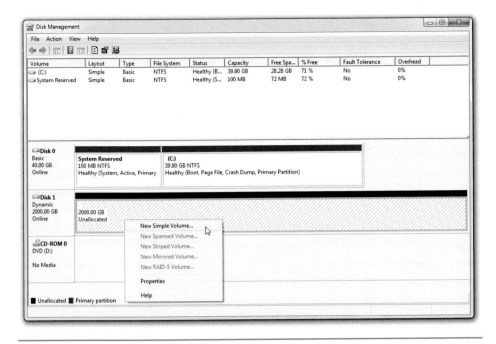

● **Figure 4.44** Selecting to open the New Simple Volume Wizard

volume. To extend or span, simply right-click the volume you want to make bigger, and choose Extend Volume from the options (see Figure 4.46). This opens the Extend Volume Wizard, which prompts you for the location of free space on a dynamic disk and the increased volume size you want to assign (see Figure 4.47). If you have multiple drives, you can span the volume just as easily to one of those drives.

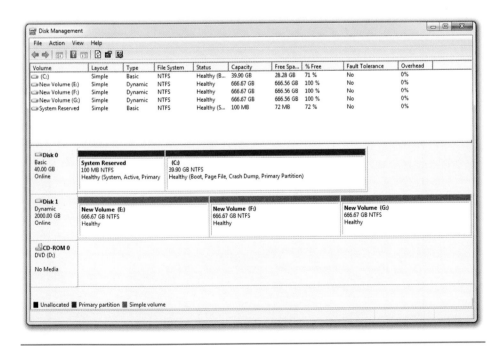

● **Figure 4.45** Simple volumes

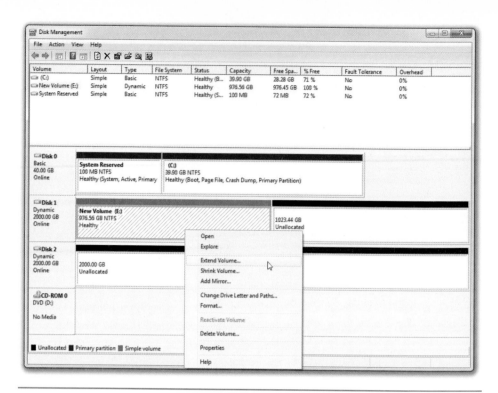

● **Figure 4.46** Selecting the Extend Volume option

Once you convert a drive to dynamic, you cannot revert it to a basic disk without losing all of the data on that drive. Be prepared to back up all data before you convert.

The capability to extend and span volumes makes dynamic disks worth their weight in gold. If you start running out of space on a volume, you can simply add another physical hard drive to the system and span the volume to the new drive. This keeps your drive letters consistent and unchanging so your programs don't get confused, yet enables you to expand drive space when needed.

● **Figure 4.47** The Extend Volume Wizard

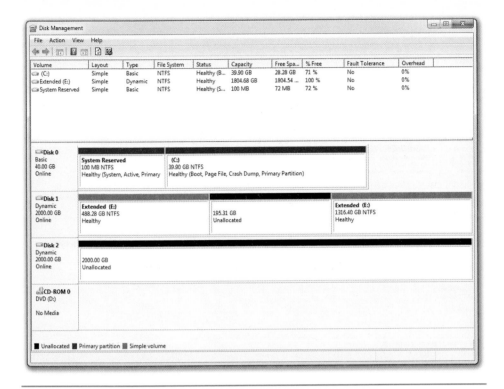

● **Figure 4.48** Extended volume

You can extend or span any simple volume on a dynamic disk, not just the "one on the end" in the Disk Management console. You simply select the volume to expand and the total volume increase you want. Figure 4.48 shows a simple 488.28-GB volume named Extended that has been enlarged an extra 1316.40 GB in a portion of the hard drive, skipping the 195.31-GB section of unallocated space contiguous to it. This created an 1804.68-GB volume. Windows has no problem skipping areas on a drive.

Striped Volumes If you have two or more dynamic disks in a PC, Disk Management enables you to combine them into a *striped* volume. Although Disk Management doesn't use the term, you know this as a RAID 0 array. A striped volume spreads out blocks of each file across multiple disks. Using two or more drives in a group called a **stripe set**, striping writes data first to a certain number of clusters on one drive, then to a certain number of clusters on the next drive, and so on. It speeds up data throughput because the system has to wait a much shorter time for a drive to read or write data. The drawback of striping is that if any single drive in the stripe set fails, all the data in the stripe set is lost.

To create a striped volume, right-click any unused space on a drive, choose New Volume, and then choose Striped. The wizard asks for the other drives you want to add to the stripe, and you need to select two unallocated spaces on other dynamic disks. Select the other unallocated spaces and go through the remaining screens on sizing and formatting until you've created a new striped volume (see Figure 4.49). The two stripes in Figure 4.49 appear to have different sizes, but if you look closely you'll see they are both 1000 GB. All stripes must be the same size on each drive.

> **Tech Tip**
>
> **Extending Hard Drives in Windows Vista and Windows 7**
> *You can extend and shrink volumes in Vista and 7 without using dynamic disks. You can shrink any volume with available free space (though you can't shrink the volume by the whole amount of free space, based on the location of unmovable sectors such as the MBR), and you can expand volumes with unallocated space on the drive.*
>
> *To shrink a volume, right-click it and select Shrink Volume. Disk Management will calculate how much you can shrink it, and then you can choose up to that amount. To extend, right-click and select Extend Volume. It's a pretty straightforward process.*

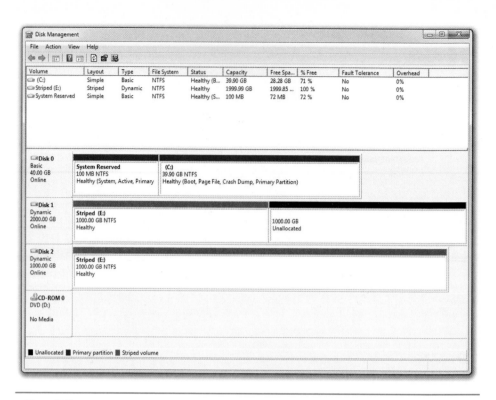

● **Figure 4.49** Two striped drives

Mirrored Volumes Windows 7 Professional, Enterprise, and Ultimate editions can create a **mirror set** with two drives for data redundancy. Mirrors are known as *RAID 1*. To create a mirror, right-click on unallocated space on a drive and select New Mirrored Volume (see Figure 4.50). This runs the New Mirrored Volume Wizard. Click Next to continue. Select an available disk in the Available box and click the Add button to move it to the Selected box (see Figure 4.51). Click Next to get to the by-now-familiar Assign Drive Letter or Path dialog box and select what is appropriate for the PC.

Other Levels of RAID Disk Management enables you to create a *RAID 5 array* that uses three or more disks to create a robust solution for storage. This applies to all the professional versions of Windows XP, Windows Vista, and Windows 7. Unfortunately for

● **Figure 4.50** Selecting a new mirror

Mike Meyer's CompTIA A+ Guide to 802: Managing and Troubleshooting PCs

New Mirrored Volume

Select Disks
You can select the disks and set the disk size for this volume.

Select the disks you want to use, and then click Add.

Available:

Disk 2 2047997 (null)

[Add >]
[< Remove]
[< Remove All]

Selected:

Disk 1 2047997 (null)

Total volume size in megabytes (MB): 0
Maximum available space in MB: 2047997
Select the amount of space in MB: 2047997

[< Back] [Next >] [Cancel]

• **Figure 4.51** Selecting drives for the array

users of those operating systems, you can only make the array on a Windows Server machine that you access remotely across a network.

Disk Management cannot do any nested RAID arrays. So if you want RAID 0+1 or RAID 1+0 (RAID 10), you need to use third-party software (or go with hardware RAID).

Mounting Partitions as Folders

While partitions and volumes can be assigned a drive letter, D: through Z:, they can also be mounted as a folder on another drive, also known as a **mount point**. This enables you to use your existing folders to store more data than can fit on a single drive or partition/volume (see Figure 4.52).

Imagine you use your My Documents folder on a Windows XP machine to store your digital photos. As your collection grows, you realize your current 500-GB hard drive is running out of space. You're willing to buy another hard drive, but you have a great organizational structure in your existing My Documents folder and you don't want to lose that. You don't have to move everything to the new hard drive, either.

After you install the new hard drive, you can *mount* the primary partition (or logical drive) as a folder within the existing My Documents folder on your C: drive (for example, C:\Users\Mike\My Photos). At this point, the drive doesn't have a letter (though you could add one later, if you wanted). To use

• **Figure 4.52** Mounting a drive as a folder

• **Figure 4.53** Adding photos to the mounted folder stores them on the second hard drive.

the new drive, just drop your files into the My Photos folder. They'll be stored on the second hard drive, not the original 500-GB drive (see Figure 4.53). Amazing!

To create a mount point, right-click an unallocated section of a disk and choose New Partition or New Simple Volume. This opens the appropriately named wizard. In the second screen, you can select a mount point rather

Try This!

Working with Dynamic Drives and Mount Points

You can't begin to appreciate the ease and elegant simplicity of Disk Management until you play with it, so Try This! Get a couple of spare drives and install them into a Windows PC. Fire up the Disk Management console and try the following setups.

1. Make a mirror set.

2. Make a stripe set.

3. Make them into a single volume spanned between both drives.

4. Make a single volume that takes up a portion of one drive, and then extend that volume onto another portion of that drive. Finally, span that volume to the other hard drive as well.

5. Create a volume of some sort—you decide—and then mount that volume to a folder on the C: drive.

You'll need to format the volumes after you create them so you can see how they manifest in My Computer/Computer. Also, you'll need to delete volumes to create a new setup. To delete a volume, simply right-click the volume and choose Delete Volume. It's almost too easy.

• **Figure 4.54** Choosing to create a mounted volume

than a drive letter (see Figure 4.54). Browse to a blank folder on an NTFS-formatted drive or create a new folder and you're in business.

The CompTIA A+ 802 exam objectives mention "splitting" partitions. To be clear, you never actually split a partition. If you want to turn one partition into two, you need to remove the existing partition and create two new ones, or shrink the existing partition and add a new one to the unallocated space. If you see it on the exam, know that this is what CompTIA means.

Formatting a Partition

You can format any Windows partition/volume in My Computer/Computer. Just right-click the drive name and choose Format (see Figure 4.55). You'll see a dialog box that asks for the type of file system you want to use, the cluster size, a place to put a volume label, and two other options. The Quick Format option tells Windows not to test the clusters and is a handy option when you're in a hurry—and feeling lucky. The Enable Compression option tells Windows to give users the capability to compress folders or files. It works well but slows down your hard drive.

Disk Management is today's preferred formatting tool for Windows. When you create a new partition or volume, the wizard also asks you what type

• **Figure 4.55** Choosing Format in Computer

of format you want to use. Always use NTFS unless you're that rare and strange person who wants to dual-boot some ancient version of Windows.

All OS installation discs partition and format as part of the OS installation. Windows simply prompts you to partition and then format the drive. Read the screens and you'll do great.

■ Maintaining and Troubleshooting Hard Drives

Hard drives are complex mechanical and electrical devices. With platters spinning at thousands of rotations per minute, they also generate heat and vibration. All of these factors make hard drives susceptible to failure. In this section, you will learn some basic maintenance tasks that will keep your hard drives healthy, and for those inevitable instances when a hard drive fails, you will also learn what you can do to repair them.

Maintenance

Hard drive maintenance can be broken down into two distinct functions: checking the disk occasionally for failed clusters, and keeping data organized on the drive so it can be accessed quickly.

Error-Checking

Individual clusters on hard drives sometimes go bad. There's nothing you can do to prevent this from happening, so it's important that you check occasionally for bad clusters on drives. The tools used to perform this checking are generically called error-checking utilities, although the terms for two older Microsoft tools—ScanDisk and **chkdsk** (pronounced "check-disk")—are often used. Microsoft calls the tool **Error-checking** in Windows XP/Vista/7. Whatever the name of the utility, each does the same job: when the tool finds bad clusters, it puts the electronic equivalent of orange cones around them so the system won't try to place data in those bad clusters.

Most error-checking tools do far more than just check for bad clusters. They go through all of the drive's filenames, looking for invalid names and attempting to fix them. They look for clusters that have no filenames associated with them (we call these *lost chains*) and erase them. From time to time, the underlying links between parent and child folders are lost, so a good error-checking tool checks every parent and child folder. With a folder such as C:\Test\Data, for example, a good error-checking tool makes sure that the Data folder is properly associated with its parent folder, C:\Test, and that C:\Test is properly associated with its child folder, C:\Test\Data.

To access Error-checking on a Windows system, open My Computer/Computer, right-click the drive you want to check, and choose Properties to open the drive's Properties dialog box. Select the Tools tab and click the Check now button (see Figure 4.56) to display the Check Disk dialog box, which has two options (see Figure 4.57). Check the box next to *Automatically fix file system errors*, but save the option to *Scan for and attempt recovery of bad sectors* for times when you actually suspect a problem, because it takes a while on bigger hard drives.

CompTIA A+ uses the terms CHKDSK and check disk rather than Error-checking.

Now that you know how to run Error-checking, your next question should be, "How often do I run it?" A reasonable maintenance plan would include running it about once a week. Error-checking is fast (unless you use the *Scan for and attempt recovery of bad sectors* option), and it's a great tool for keeping your system in top shape.

Defragmentation

Fragmentation of clusters can increase your drive access times dramatically. It's a good idea to **defragment**—or *defrag*—your drives as part of monthly maintenance. You access the defrag tool Disk Defragmenter the same way you access Error-checking—right-click a drive in My Computer/Computer and choose Properties—except you click the Defragment now button on the Tools tab to open Disk Defragmenter. In Windows Vista/7, Microsoft has given Disk Defragmenter a big visual makeover (see Figure 4.58), but both the old and new versions do the same job.

Defragmentation is interesting to watch—once. From then on, schedule Disk Defragmenter to run late at night. You should defragment your drives about once a month, although you could run Disk Defragmenter every week, and if you run it every night, it takes only a few minutes. The longer you go between defrags, the longer it takes.

• **Figure 4.56** The Tools tab in the Properties dialog box

• **Figure 4.57** Check Disk options

• **Figure 4.58** Disk Defragmenter in Windows 7 (left) and Windows XP

If you have Windows 7, Microsoft has made defragging even easier by automatically defragging disks once a week. You can adjust the schedule or even turn it off altogether, but remember that if you don't run Disk Defragmenter, your system will run slower. If you don't run Error-checking, you may lose data.

Disk Cleanup

Did you know that the average hard drive is full of trash? Not the junk you intentionally put in your hard drive such as the 23,000 e-mail messages that you refuse to delete from your e-mail program. This kind of trash is all of the files that you never see that Windows keeps for you. Here are a few examples:

- **Files in the Recycle Bin** When you delete a file, it isn't really deleted. It's placed in the Recycle Bin in case you decide you need the file later. I just checked my Recycle Bin and found around 3 GB worth of files (see Figure 4.59). That's a lot of trash!

• **Figure 4.59** Mike's Recycle Bin

■ **Temporary Internet files** When you go to a Web site, Windows keeps copies of the graphics and other items so the page will load more quickly the next time you access it. You can see these files by opening the Internet Options applet on the Control Panel. Click the Settings button under the Browsing history label and then click the View files button in the Temporary Internet Files and History Settings dialog box. Figure 4.60 shows temporary Internet files from Internet Explorer.

• **Figure 4.60** Lots of temporary Internet files

■ **Downloaded program files** Your system always keeps a copy of any Java or ActiveX applets it downloads. You can see these in the Internet Options applet by clicking the Settings button under the Browsing history label and then clicking the View objects button in the Temporary Internet Files and History Settings dialog box. You'll generally find only a few tiny files here.

■ **Temporary files** Many applications create temporary files that are supposed to be deleted when the application is closed. For one reason or another, these temporary files sometimes aren't deleted. The location of these files varies with the version of Windows, but they always reside in a folder called "Temp."

Every hard drive eventually becomes filled with lots of unnecessary trash. All versions of Windows tend to act erratically when the drives run out of unused space. Fortunately, all versions of Windows have a powerful tool called **Disk Cleanup** (see Figure 4.61). You can access Disk Cleanup in all versions of Windows by choosing Start | All Programs | Accessories | System Tools | Disk Cleanup.

• **Figure 4.61** Disk Cleanup

Disk Cleanup gets rid of the four types of files just described (and a few others). Run Disk Cleanup once a month or so to keep plenty of space available on your hard drive.

Troubleshooting Hard Drive Implementation

There's no scarier computer problem than an error that points to trouble with a hard drive. This section looks at some of the more common problems that occur with hard drives and how to fix them. These issues fall into four broad categories: installation errors, data corruption, dying hard drives, and RAID issues.

Installation Errors

Installing a drive and getting to the point where it can hold data requires four distinct steps: connectivity, CMOS, partitioning, and formatting. If you make a mistake at any point on any of these steps, the drive won't work. The beauty of this is that if you make an error, you can walk back through each step and check for problems. The "Troubleshooting Hard Drive Installation" section earlier in this chapter covered physical connections and CMOS, so this section concentrates on the latter two issues.

Partitioning Partitioning errors generally fall into two groups: failing to partition at all and making the wrong size or type of partition. You'll recognize the former type of error the first time you open My Computer/Computer after installing a drive. If you forgot to partition it, the drive won't even show up in My Computer/Computer, only in Disk Management. If you made the partition too small, that'll become painfully obvious when you start filling it up with files.

The fix for partitioning errors is simply to open Disk Management and do the partitioning correctly. If you've added files to the wrongly sized drive, don't forget to back them up before you repartition in Windows XP. Just right-click and select Extend Volume in Windows Vista/7 to correct the mistake.

Formatting Failing to format a drive makes the drive unable to hold data. Accessing the drive in Windows results in a drive "is not accessible" error, and from a C:\ prompt, you'll get the famous "Invalid media" type error. Format the drive unless you're certain that the drive has a format already. Corrupted files can create the invalid media error. Check the upcoming "Data Corruption" section for the fix.

Most of the time, formatting is a slow, boring process. But sometimes the drive makes "bad sounds" and you start seeing errors like the one shown in Figure 4.62 at the top of the screen.

An *allocation unit* is another term for a cluster. The drive has run across a bad cluster and is trying to fix it. For years, I've told techs that seeing this error a few (610) times

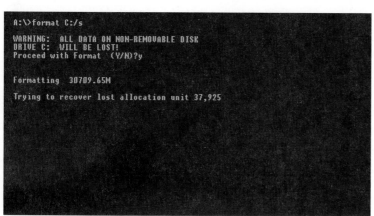

• **Figure 4.62** The "Trying to recover lost allocation unit" error

doesn't mean anything; every drive comes with a few bad spots. This is no longer true. Modern drives actually hide a significant number of extra sectors that they use to replace bad sectors automatically. If a new drive gets a lot of "Trying to recover lost allocation unit" errors, you can bet that the drive is dying and needs to be replaced. Get the hard drive maker's diagnostic tool to be sure. Bad clusters are reported by S.M.A.R.T.

Mental Reinstallation Focus on the fact that all of these errors share a common thread—you just installed a drive! Installation errors don't show up on a system that has been running correctly for three weeks; they show up the moment you try to do something with the drive you just installed. If a newly installed drive fails to work, do a "mental reinstallation." Does the drive show up in the CMOS? No? Then recheck the cables, master/slave settings on old PATA drives, and power. If it does show up, did you remember to partition and format the drive? Did it need to be set to active? These are commonsense questions that come to mind as you march through your mental reinstallation. Even if you've installed thousands of drives over the years, you'll be amazed at how often you do things such as forget to plug in power to a drive. Do the mental reinstallation—it really works!

Data Corruption

All hard drives occasionally get corrupted data in individual sectors. Power surges, accidental shutdowns, corrupted installation media, and viruses, along with hundreds of other problems, can cause this corruption. In most cases, this type of error shows up while Windows is running. Figure 4.63 shows a classic example.

• **Figure 4.63** A corrupted data error

You may also see Windows error messages saying one of the following:

- "The following file is missing or corrupt"
- "The download location information is damaged"
- "Unable to load file"

If core boot files become corrupted, you may see text errors at boot, such as the following:

- "Cannot find COMMAND.COM"
- "Error loading operating system"
- "Invalid BOOT.INI"
- "NTLDR is missing or corrupt"
- "An error occurred while attempting to read the boot configuration data"

On older programs, you may see a command prompt open with errors such as this one:

```
Sector not found reading drive C: Abort, Retry, Fail?
```

The first fix for any of these problems is to run the Error-checking utility. Error-checking will go through and mark bad clusters and, hopefully, move your data to a good cluster.

If the same errors continue to appear after you run the Error-checking utility, there's a chance that the drive has bad sectors.

Almost all drives today take advantage of built-in **error correction code (ECC)** that constantly checks the drive for bad sectors. If the ECC detects a bad sector, it marks the sector as bad in the drive's internal error map. Don't confuse this error map with a FAT. The partitioning program creates the FAT. The drive's internal error map was created at the factory on reserved drive heads and is invisible to the system. If the ECC finds a bad sector, you will get a corrupted data error as the computer attempts to read the bad sector. Disk-checking utilities fix this problem most of the time.

Many times, the ECC thinks a bad sector is good, however, and fails to update the internal error map. In this case, you need a program that goes back into the drive and marks the sectors as bad. That's where the powerful SpinRite utility from Gibson Research comes into play. SpinRite marks sectors as bad or good more accurately than ECC and does not disturb the data, enabling you to run SpinRite without fear of losing anything. And if it finds a bad sector with data in it, SpinRite has powerful algorithms that usually recover the data on all but the most badly damaged sectors (see Figure 4.64).

Without SpinRite, you must use a low-level format program supplied by the hard drive maker, assuming you can get one (not all are willing to distribute these). These programs work like SpinRite in that they aggressively check the hard drive's sectors and update the internal error map. Unfortunately, all of them wipe out all data on the drive. At least you can use the drive, even if it means repartitioning, formatting, and reinstalling everything.

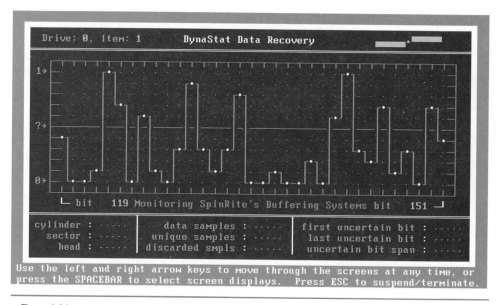

• **Figure 4.64** SpinRite at work

Dying Hard Drive

Physical problems are rare but devastating when they happen. If a hard drive is truly damaged physically, there is nothing that you or any service technician can do to fix it. Fortunately, hard drives are designed to take a phenomenal amount of punishment without failing. Physical problems manifest themselves in several ways: you start getting read/write failures, the drive works properly but makes a lot of noise, or the drive seems to disappear.

Windows will give you error messages with read/write failures. Good hard drives don't fail to read or write. Only dying ones have these problems.

All hard drives make noise—the hum as the platters spin and the occasional slight scratching noise as the read/write heads access sectors are normal. However, if your drive begins to make any of the following sounds, it is about to die:

- Continuous high-pitched squeal
- Series of loud clicks, a short pause, and then another series of clicks
- Continuous grinding or rumbling

Back up your critical data and replace the drive. Windows comes with great tools for backing up data.

You'll know when a drive simply dies. If it's the drive that contains your operating system, the system will lock up. When you try to restart the computer, you'll see this error message or something similar to it:

```
No Boot Device Present
```

If it's a second drive, it will simply stop showing up in My Computer/ Computer. The first thing to do in this case is to fire up the System Setup program and see if autodetect sees the drive. If it does, you do not have a physical problem with the drive. If autodetect fails, shut off the system and remove the data cable, but leave the power cable attached. Restart the system and listen to the drive. If the drive spins up, you know it is getting good power. This is usually a clue that the drive is probably good. In that case, you need to look for more mundane problems such as an unplugged data cord or jumpers incorrectly set. If the drive doesn't spin up, try another power connector. If it still doesn't spin up and you've triple-checked the jumpers (PATA only) and data cable, you have a problem with the onboard electronics, and the drive is dead.

Troubleshooting RAID

For the most part, drive problems in a RAID array are identical to those seen on individual drives. There are a couple of errors unique to RAID, however, that need their own separate discussion.

Drives Not Recognized If you're using hardware RAID and the configuration firmware doesn't recognize one of the drives, first check to make sure the drives are powered and that they are connected to the proper connections. This is especially true of motherboards with onboard RAID that require you to use only certain special RAID connectors.

Tech Tip

Long Warranties

Most hard drives have three-year warranties. Before you throw away a dead drive, check the hard drive maker's Web site or call them to see if the drive is still under warranty. Ask for a return material authorization (RMA). You'll be amazed how many times you get a newer, usually larger, hard drive for free. It never hurts to check!

Tech Tip

Data Rescue Specialists

If you ever lose a hard drive that contains absolutely critical information, you can turn to a company that specializes in hard drive data recovery. The job will be expensive—prices can go up to $1000 (U.S.)—but when you have to have the data, such companies are your only hope. Do a Web search for "data recovery" or check the Yellow Pages for companies in this line of business.

RAID Stops Working When one of the drives in a RAID array fails, several things can happen depending on the type of array and the RAID controller. With RAID 0, the effect is dramatic. Many enthusiasts use RAID 0 for their OS drive to make it snappier. If you're running such a rig that then loses a drive, you'll most likely get a critical stop error, a Blue Screen of Death (BSoD). On reboot, the computer will fail to boot or you'll get a message that the OS can't be found. You lose all your data because there's no redundancy on a stripe set.

All the other levels of RAID tend to do nothing extraordinary when one drive in the array fails. When you reboot the system, that's when the RAID controller—if hardware—or Windows—if you've used the built-in tools—will squeal and tell you that a drive has failed.

Often, the failure of a drive will cause access to the contents of the drive to slow to a crawl, and that *slow performance* is your clue to check Device Manager or the RAID controller firmware. Some drive failures will cause the computer to crash. Others will show no effects until you get the error messages at reboot.

Regardless of the reason, a RAID stops working or the effects, the fix is simple. Replace the failed drive and let the RAID rebuild itself. Life is good.

RAID Not Found The CompTIA A+ 220-802 exam objectives use the term "RAID not found," which doesn't really exist as an error but instead implies a series of errors where an existing RAID array suddenly fails to appear. The problem with these errors is that they vary greatly depending on the make and model of hardware RAID or (heaven forbid) if you used software RAID.

A properly functioning hardware RAID array will always show up in the configuration utility. If an existing array stops working and you enter the configuration utility only to find the array is gone, you have big trouble. This points to either dead drives or faulty controllers. In either case they must be replaced.

If the array is gone but you can still see the drives, then the controller may have broken the array on its own. This is a rare action that some controllers do to try to save data. You should at least try to rebuild the array using whatever tools the controllers provide.

<aside>
If you've got a dying hard drive, you can use a drive in an external enclosure (also called an external drive) to back up your files before they're lost.
</aside>

Beyond A+

Modern hard drives have many other features that are worth knowing about but that rarely impact beginning techs. A couple of the more interesting ones are spindle speed and third-party hard drive tools. If you have a burning desire to dive into hard drives in all their glory, you need not go any farther than StorageReview.com, an excellent site dedicated solely to hard drives.

Third-Party Partition Tools

Disk Management is a good tool and has been greatly enhanced with Windows 7, but it's still limited for some situations. Some really great third-party

tools on the market can give you incredible flexibility and power to structure and restructure your hard drive storage to meet your changing needs. They each have interesting unique features, but in general they enable you to create, change, and delete partitions on a hard drive *without* destroying any of the programs or data stored there. Slick! These programs aren't covered on the CompTIA A+ 220-802 exam, but all PC techs use at least one of them, so let's explore three of the most well-known examples: Symantec's Norton PartitionMagic, Avanquest Partition Commander Professional, and the open source Linux tool, GParted.

Probably the most well-known third-party partition tool is PartitionMagic, although it's quite dated at this point. It supports older versions of Windows but has problems with Windows Vista/7. With it, you can create, resize, split, merge, delete, undelete, and convert partitions without destroying your data. Among the additional features it advertises are the capability to browse, copy, or move files and folders between supported partitions; to expand an NTFS partition—even if it's a system partition—without rebooting; to change NTFS cluster sizes; and to add new partitions for multiple OSs by using a simple wizard.

Avanquest offers a variety of related products, one of which is the very useful Partition Commander. It supports all versions of Windows (unlike PartitionMagic) and enables you to play with your partitions without destroying your data. Among its niftier features are the capability to convert a dynamic disk to a basic disk nondestructively (which you can't do with the Microsoft-supplied Windows tools); to defrag the master file table on an NTFS partition; and to move unused space from one partition to another on the same physical drive, automatically resizing the partitions based on the amount of space you tell it to move. Figure 4.65 shows the Partition Commander dialog box for moving unused space between partitions.

• **Figure 4.65** Partition Commander

The only problem with PartitionMagic and Partition Commander is that they cost money. There's nothing wrong with spending money on a good product, but if you can find something that does the job for free, why not try it? If you think like I do, check out the GNOME Partition Editor, better known as GParted. You can find it at http://sourceforge.net/.

GParted is an incredibly powerful partition editor and does almost everything the for-pay partition editors do, but it's free. In fact, you might already have a copy lying around in the form of an Ubuntu desktop live CD. If you look closely at Figure 4.66, you'll notice that it uses strange names for the partitions, such as HDA1 or SDA2. These are Linux conventions and are well documented in GParted's Help screens. Take a little time and you'll love GParted too.

The one downside to GParted is that it is a Linux program—because no Windows version exists, you need Linux to run it. So how do you run Linux on a Windows system without actually installing Linux on your hard drive? The answer is easy—the folks at GParted will give you the tools to burn a live CD that boots Linux so you can run GParted!

A *live CD* is a complete OS on a CD. Understand this is not an installation CD like your Windows installation disc. The OS is already installed on the CD. You boot from the live CD and the OS loads into RAM, just like the OS on your hard drive loads into RAM at boot. As the live CD boots, it recognizes your hardware and loads the proper drivers into RAM so everything works. You get everything you'd expect from an OS with one big exception: a live CD does not touch your hard drive. Of course, you may run programs (such as GParted) that work on your hard drive, which makes live CDs popular with PC techs, because you can toss them into a cranky system and run utilities.

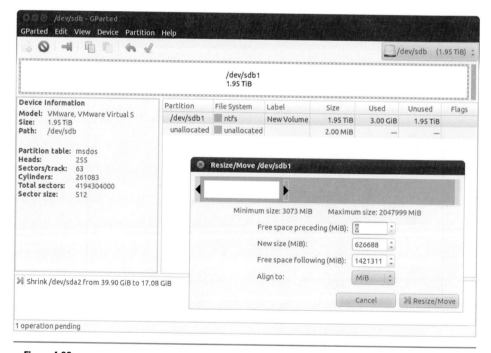

• Figure 4.66 GParted in action

The truly intrepid might want to consider using The Ultimate Boot CD (UBCD), basically a huge pile of useful freeware utilities compiled by frustrated technician Ben Burrows, who couldn't find a boot disk when he needed one. His Web site is www.ultimatebootcd.com. The UBCD has more than 100 different tools, all placed on a single live CD. It has all of the low-level diagnostic tools for all of the hard drive makers, four or five different partitioning tools, S.M.A.R.T. viewers, hard drive wiping utilities, and hard drive cloning tools (nice for when you want to replace a hard drive with a larger one). Little documentation is provided, however, and many of the tools require experience way beyond the scope of the CompTIA A+ 220-802 exam. I will tell you that I have a copy and I use it.

Chapter 4 Review

■ Chapter Summary

After reading this chapter and completing the exercises, you should understand the following about implementing hard drives.

Troubleshoot hard drive installation

- Getting a drive installed and recognized by the system takes three or four things: jumpers (PATA only), data cable, power, and CMOS setup recognizing the drive. If you miss or mess up any of these steps, you have a drive that doesn't exist according to the PC! To troubleshoot hard drives, simply work your way through each step to figure out what went wrong.

- Once you've checked the physical connections, run through these issues in CMOS. Is the controller enabled? Is the storage technology—LBA, INT13, ATA/ATAPI-6—properly set up? Similarly, can the motherboard support the type of drive you're installing? If not, you have a couple of options. You can either flash the BIOS with an upgraded BIOS from the manufacturer or get a hard drive controller that goes into an expansion slot.

Explain the partitions available in Windows

- Partitions are electronic subdivisions of physical hard drives. After partitioning, each partition must be formatted before it can be used to store files. Every hard drive must contain at least one partition, but many users choose to create multiple partitions on a single hard drive. Windows supports three partitioning schemes: master boot record (MBR), dynamic storage partitioning, and GUID partition table (GPT).

- The MBR partitioning scheme uses a master boot record and a partition table to enable the partition with a valid operating system to boot.

- MBR uses primary and extended partitions. Windows limits each MBR hard drive to a maximum of four partitions, with no more than one extended partition. Primary partitions can receive drive letters and support bootable operating systems. Extended partitions, which do not receive drive letters, house logical drives, which can receive drive letters.

- Every partition contains a partition boot sector in its first sector. During boot-up, a hard drive's MBR finds the active partition and uses the partition's boot sector to load the OS.

- Only active primary partitions can boot an operating system. Only one primary partition per hard drive can be marked as active.

- Hard drives that use the dynamic storage partitioning scheme are called dynamic disks by Microsoft. Dynamic disks use volumes rather than partitions. There are no primary or extended volumes—a volume is simply a volume.

- Dynamic disks support a total of five types of volumes: simple, spanned, striped, mirrored, and RAID 5. A simple volume is similar to a primary partition in that it can store files and can receive a drive letter or be mounted to a folder. Spanned volumes combine space from several volumes and treat them as a single volume. After one volume is full, files are written to the next volume in the span. Striped volumes are similar to spanned volumes, but files are deliberately split across volumes to increase read/write access time. Neither spanned nor striped volumes are fault tolerant. RAID 1, or mirrored volumes, use exactly two volumes that are exact duplicates of each other. You suffer a slight performance hit but make up for it with fault tolerance. RAID 5 requires at least three same-size volumes, enjoys the speed boost of striping, and is fault tolerant.

- The GUID partition table (GPT) scheme fixes several of MBR's limitations. GPT drives can have as many partitions as needed, although Windows imposes a limit of 128. GPT partitions can be larger than MBR's maximum of 2.2 TB.

- GPT includes a protective MBR to keep older utilities from damaging the partition information.

- GPT includes primary and backup copies of its GPT header and partition array.

- Other partition types are hidden and swap partitions. Hidden partitions are not visible to the operating system and are often used by PC manufacturers to store emergency restore images of the system partition. Swap partitions are used

by Linux and BSD systems for virtual memory and function much the same as Windows page files.

- Most operating systems enable you to create partitions during the installation process. To create partitions at other times, you use a dedicated partitioning tool. Older versions of Windows shipped with the command-line program FDISK for this purpose. Windows now ships with a graphical tool called Disk Management to manage partitions, convert basic disks to dynamic disks, and manage volumes. Linux uses several partitioning tools, such as FDISK (same name, but different from the Windows version) and GParted.

Discuss hard drive formatting options

- After a disk has been partitioned, it must be formatted before it can be used. Formatting creates a file system and root directory. You can use the Disk Management tool to format a partition or volume. Current versions of Windows support four file systems: FAT16, FAT32, NTFS, and exFAT (FAT64).

- The base storage area for hard drives is a sector, which can store up to 512 bytes of data. If a file is smaller than 512 bytes and does not fill a sector, the rest of the sector remains unused because only one file can reside in any one sector. If a file is more than 512 bytes, the file is split into pieces, with each piece residing in a different sector. If the sectors containing all of the pieces of a single file are not contiguous, the file is said to be fragmented.

- MS-DOS version 2.1 first supported the file allocation table (FAT). The FAT is a data structure similar to a two-column spreadsheet that tracks where data is stored on a hard drive.

- FAT comes in multiple variations, including FAT16, FAT32, and FAT64. The number indicates how many bits are available in the "left side of the FAT spreadsheet." Hard drives can use FAT16 or FAT32, while FAT64 is designed for USB flash drives.

- Every version of Windows fully supports FAT16, which uses only 16 bits to address sector locations. This translates to 2^{16}, or 64 K locations. With 64 K locations of 512-byte sectors, 64 K × 512 bytes hits the ceiling at 32 MB. For this reason, FAT16 partitions were initially limited to 32 MB. FAT16 later added a feature called clustering that treats a set of contiguous sectors as a single FAT unit. These clusters (also called file allocation units) allow a maximum partition size of 2 GB.

- Since FAT16, a cluster (rather than a sector) is the basic unit of storage. Unlike sectors, the size of a cluster is not fixed but changes with the size of the partition. Because FAT16 still supported only a maximum of 64 K storage units, the formatting program set the number of sectors in each cluster according to the size of the partition.

- After the format program creates the FAT, it tests each sector and places a special status code (FFF7) in the FAT for any bad sectors so they won't be used. Good sectors are marked with 0000. When an application saves a file, the OS starts writing the file to the first available cluster marked as good. If the entire file fits in the cluster, the OS places the end-of-file marker (FFFF) in the cluster's status area. If the file does not fit entirely in a single cluster, the OS searches for the next available cluster. Once found, its location is written to the status area of the preceding cluster holding a piece of the file, and the OS writes the next 512 bytes of the file in the available cluster. This continues until the file has been completely written and the final cluster in the chain receives the status code FFFF in the FAT. After saving the entire file, the OS lists the filename and starting cluster in the file's folder.

- As a file is split across multiple noncontiguous clusters, the file becomes fragmented. Fragmentation slows read/write access because the OS has to piece together the many fragments of the file. Every version of Windows comes with a Disk Defragmenter program that reorganizes the clusters of hard drive data so files are stored wherever possible in contiguous clusters.

- FAT32 was introduced with Windows 95 OSR2. FAT32, which uses 32 bits to describe each cluster, supports partitions up to 2 TB. FAT32 creates smaller clusters and therefore stores files more efficiently than FAT16.

- The New Technology File System (NTFS) was introduced with Windows NT and has gone through several versions. The most recent version, used since Windows 2000, is referred to as NTFS 3.1, although you'll see it referred to as NTFS 5.0/5.1. NTFS does not use a FAT such as FAT16 or FAT32, but instead uses a master file table (MFT).

- NTFS offers several major improvements over FAT, including redundancy, security, compression, encryption, disk quotas, and cluster sizing. A backup copy of the most critical parts of the MFT

151

is stored in the middle of the disk, where it is less likely to become damaged.

- With NTFS, you can protect individual files and folders by allowing only certain users or groups access to them. You can compress individual files or folders to save hard drive space and can encrypt files or folders so they are unreadable to anyone but you. You can also limit the amount of disk space per user by enforcing disk quotas. Finally, you can adjust cluster sizes to allow support of partitions up to 16 EB, though by default the limit is 16 TB.

Partition and format hard drives

- Windows XP installation discs walk you through the process of partitioning and formatting your hard drive. After accepting the license agreement, you can simply press ENTER and Windows partitions and formats your drive as one large primary partition. If you prefer to partition only a portion of the hard drive, you can do so manually by pressing the letter C to create a partition, entering the desired size in MB, and pressing ENTER. Finally, you are offered several options for formatting before the installation continues. It is recommended that you choose NTFS. Note that the disk is partitioned and formatted as a basic disk. Once Windows is installed, you can convert basic disks to dynamic disks with the Disk Management tool.

- Windows Vista/7 installation discs also walk you through the partitioning and formatting process but use a graphical user interface, thus greatly simplifying the process. When you click the Custom install button, you're taken to the partitioning screen, where you can create, delete, edit, and format partitions. You can only format partitions as NTFS off of the Vista/7 installation discs.

- All new disk drives must be initialized by Disk Management before you can use them. The initialization process places information on the drive identifying it as part of a particular system. New drives are always initialized as basic disks but can be converted to dynamic disks by right-clicking and choosing Convert to Dynamic Disk. Once initialized, you can add partitions or volumes to the drive.

- Once a disk has been initialized and partitioned, you can format it. Microsoft requires using NTFS

for any partition larger than 32 GB. Performing a Quick Format skips the checking of clusters, which results in a faster format but is risky.

- To create a mount point, right-click an unallocated section of a disk and choose New Partition or New Simple Volume. This opens the appropriately named Wizard. In the second screen, you can select a mount point rather than a drive letter. You'll need to pick an empty folder or create a new one.

- You can format any partition/volume in My Computer/Computer by right-clicking the drive and choosing Format. Alternatively, you can format partitions/volumes from the Disk Management tool. Both methods offer you options to perform a Quick Format and enable compression.

Maintain and troubleshoot hard drives

- Hard drive maintenance can be broken down into two distinct functions: checking the disk occasionally for failed clusters and keeping data organized on the drive so it can be accessed quickly.

- Microsoft offers Error-checking for scanning hard drives. It checks for bad clusters and, if found, marks them as bad so no data gets written to those areas of the hard drive. Additionally, it looks for invalid filenames and attempts to fix them, and it searches for and erases lost cluster chains.

- To run Error-checking in Windows, right-click a drive to view its Properties dialog box, choose the Tools tab, and click the Check now button. Check the box next to *Automatically fix file system errors*, but save the option to *Scan for and attempt recovery of bad sectors* for times when you actually suspect a problem.

- Run Error-checking and Disk Defragmenter once a month as preventive maintenance to keep your system running smoothly. Both are available on the Tools tab of the drive's Properties dialog box.

- The Disk Cleanup utility deletes files from the Recycle Bin, temporary Internet files, copies of downloaded Java or ActiveX applets, and other temporary files on your hard drive. You can access Disk Cleanup in all versions of Windows by choosing Start | All Programs | Accessories | System Tools | Disk Cleanup. Run Disk Cleanup once a month.

- Hard drive problems fall into four broad categories: installation errors, data corruption,

dying hard drives, and RAID issues. Installation errors can happen at any of the four steps: connectivity, CMOS, partitioning, or formatting. When troubleshooting, you should always walk back through each step and check for problems.

- Partitioning errors generally fall into two groups: failing to partition at all and making the wrong size/type of partition. You'll recognize the former type of error the first time you open My Computer/Computer after installing a drive. If you forgot to partition it, the drive won't even show up in My Computer/Computer, only in Disk Management. If you made the partition too small, that'll become painfully obvious when you start filling it up with files.

- If you try to access a drive that's not formatted, Windows displays a drive "is not accessible" error, while you'll get an "Invalid media" error from a C:\ prompt. Format the drive unless you're certain that the drive has already been formatted. Corrupted files can also create the "Invalid media" error.

- The "Trying to recover lost allocation unit" error means the drive has bad sectors. Time to replace the drive.

- If a newly installed drive fails to work, do a "mental reinstallation." If the drive does not show in CMOS autodetect, recheck the cables, master/slave jumper settings, and power. If it shows up, make sure you remembered to partition and format it. Remember the drive must be marked as Active to be bootable.

- Power surges, accidental shutdowns, corrupted installation media, and viruses are among the causes of corrupted data in individual sectors. These errors usually show while Windows is running. If core boot files become corrupted, you may see text errors such as "NTLDR is missing or corrupt," "Error loading operating system," or "Invalid BOOT.INI." Older systems may generate a "sector not found" error. The first fix for any of these problems is to run an error-checking utility.

- Almost all drives today have built-in error correction code (ECC) that constantly checks the drive for bad sectors. If it detects a bad sector, it marks the sector as bad in the drive's internal error map so it's invisible to the system. If the ECC finds a bad sector, however, you will get a corrupted data error when the computer attempts to read the bad sector.

- The powerful SpinRite utility from Gibson Research marks sectors as bad or good more accurately than ECC and does not disturb the data. When it finds a bad sector with data in it, SpinRite uses powerful algorithms that usually recover the data on all but the most badly damaged sectors. Without SpinRite, you must use a low-level formatting program supplied by the hard drive manufacturer, which will wipe out all data on the drive.

- If a hard drive is truly physically damaged, it cannot be fixed. Physical problems manifest themselves in two ways: either the drive works properly but makes a lot of noise, or the drive seems to disappear. If you hear a continuous high-pitched squeal; a series of clacks, a short pause, and then another series of clacks; or a continuous grinding or rumbling, your hard drive is about to die. Back up your critical data and replace the drive. If the drive that contains your operating system disappears, the system locks up or you get the error message "No Boot Device Present" when you try to reboot. If the problem is with a second drive, it simply stops showing up in My Computer/Computer.

- If your drive makes noise or disappears, first run the System Setup program to see if autodetect sees the drive. If it does, the drive doesn't have a physical problem. If autodetect fails, shut down the system and remove the data cable, but leave the power cable attached. Restart the system and listen to the drive. If the drive spins up, the drive is getting good power, which usually means the drive is good. Next, check for an unplugged power cord or incorrectly set jumpers. If the drive doesn't spin up, try another power connector. If it still doesn't spin up and you've triple-checked the jumpers and data cable, you have a problem with the onboard electronics and the drive is dead.

- For the most part, drive problems in a RAID array are identical to those seen on individual drives. If you're using hardware RAID and the configuration firmware doesn't recognize one of the drives, first check to make sure the drives are powered and that they are connected to the proper connections. Regardless of the reason a RAID stops working or the effects, the fix is simple. Replace the failed drive and let the RAID rebuild itself.

■ Key Terms

<div style="columns:2">

active partition *(104)*
basic disk *(103)*
chkdsk *(138)*
cluster *(111)*
data structure *(110)*
defragment *(139)*
Disk Cleanup *(141)*
disk initialization *(126)*
Disk Management *(107)*
disk quota *(116)*
dynamic disk *(103)*
encrypting file system (EFS) *(116)*
Error-checking *(138)*
error correction code (ECC) *(144)*
extended partition *(103)*
FAT32 *(115)*
FAT64 *(118)*
FDISK *(107)*
file allocation table (FAT) *(110)*
file allocation unit *(111)*
file system *(101)*
format *(101)*

fragmentation *(113)*
globally unique identifier partition table (GPT) *(106)*
high-level formatting *(110)*
logical drive *(104)*
master boot record (MBR) *(103)*
master file table (MFT) *(116)*
mirror set *(134)*
mirrored volume *(105)*
mount point *(135)*
New Technology File System (NTFS) *(116)*
partition *(101)*
partition boot sector *(103)*
partition table *(103)*
partitioning *(101)*
primary partition *(103)*
RAID 5 volume *(105)*
simple volume *(105)*
spanned volume *(105)*
stripe set *(133)*
striped volume *(105)*
volume *(105)*

</div>

■ Key Term Quiz

Use the Key Terms list to complete the sentences that follow. Not all terms will be used.

1. The MBR checks the partition table to find the _____ or bootable partition.

2. If a file is not stored in contiguous clusters, you can improve hard drive performance by using a tool to _____ the drive.

3. Instead of using a FAT, NTFS uses a(n) _____ with a backup copy placed in the middle of the disk for better security.

4. On modern versions of Windows, the best file system to choose is _____.

5. The Windows tool that attempts to fix invalid filenames, erases lost clusters, and seals off bad clusters is called _____ (or *chkdsk*).

6. The _____ partitioning scheme enables you to create more than four primary partitions without needing to use dynamic disks.

7. A logical drive must be created inside a(n) _____.

8. Only a single _____ may be set to active on one drive.

9. The _____ utility is useful for purging your system of unnecessary temporary files.

10. A(n) _____ requires exactly two volumes and is extremely fault tolerant.

Multiple-Choice Quiz

1. Which is the most complete list of file systems Windows can use?

 A. FAT16, FAT32, NTFS

 B. FAT16, FAT32, FAT64, NTFS

 C. FAT16, FAT32

 D. FAT16, NTFS

2. The Disk Cleanup utility removes which types of unneeded files?

 A. Temporary Internet files

 B. Temporary files that remain when an application is closed

 C. Programs no longer in use

 D. Both A and B

3. Which of the following correctly identifies the four possible entries in a file allocation table?

 A. Filename, date, time, size

 B. Number of the starting cluster, number of the ending cluster, number of used clusters, number of available clusters

 C. An end-of-file marker, a bad-sector marker, code indicating the cluster is available, the number of the cluster where the next part of the file is stored

 D. Filename, folder location, starting cluster number, ending cluster number

4. You receive an "Invalid media" error when trying to access a hard drive. What is the most likely cause of the error?

 A. The drive has not been partitioned.

 B. The drive has not been set to active.

 C. The drive has not been formatted.

 D. The drive has died.

5. Which of the following is an advantage of partitioning a hard drive into more than one partition?

 A. It enables a single hard drive to store more than one operating system.

 B. It protects against boot sector viruses.

 C. It uses less power.

 D. It allows for dynamic disk RAID 5.

6. What graphical program does Microsoft include with Windows to partition and format a drive?

 A. Format

 B. Disk Management console

 C. Disk Administrator console

 D. System Commander

7. Which of the following statements apply to MBR drives? (Select two.)

 A. Maximum partition size of 2.2 TB

 B. Unlimited number of partitions

 C. Cannot span partitions across multiple drives

 D. Can stripe partitions across multiple drives

8. Which of the following statements is true about extended partitions?

 A. They are optional.

 B. They are assigned drive letters when they are created.

 C. They may be set to active.

 D. Each drive must have at least one extended partition.

9. Adam has two primary partitions and wants to create a new extended partition on his MBR drive in Windows Vista, but Disk Management won't let him. Why not?

 A. Windows Vista cannot use extended partitions.

 B. MBR does not use extended partitions.

 C. He needs to set up dynamic disks.

 D. Windows Vista creates three primary partitions before automatically creating an extended partition.

10. Jaime wishes to check her hard drive for errors. What tool should she use?

 A. FDISK

 B. Format

 C. Disk Management

 D. Error-checking

11. To make your files unreadable by others, what should you use?

 A. Clustering

 B. Compression

 C. Disk quotas

 D. Encryption

12. Which of the following utilities should you run once a month to maintain the speed of your PC?

 A. Disk Defragmenter

 B. FDISK

 C. Disk Management

 D. System Commander

13. Which two terms identify a bootable partition?

 A. Master, FAT

 B. Slave, FAT

 C. Primary, Active

 D. Primary, NTFS

14. For what purpose can you use disk quotas?

 A. Limit users to a specific drive.

 B. Extend the capacity of a volume.

C. Manage dual-boot environments.

D. Limit users' space on a drive.

15. What are the requirements for booting Windows from a GPT drive? (Select all that apply.)

 A. You must use Windows Vista Business, Windows Vista Ultimate, Windows Vista Enterprise, Windows 7 Professional, Windows 7 Ultimate, or Windows 7 Enterprise.

 B. You must use a 64-bit operating system.

 C. You must use a UEFI motherboard.

 D. Your GPT disk must be a dynamic disk.

■ Essay Quiz

1. You discover that your boss's computer is using two old hard drives formatted using FAT32. Write a two- to three-paragraph memo that explains the virtues and benefits of NTFS over FAT32.

2. You've been tasked by your supervisor to teach basic hard drive partitioning to a couple of new hires. Write a short essay describing the difference between simple volumes, spanned volumes, and striped volumes. What's better? When would you use one and not the other?

3. One of your employees doesn't quite get it when it comes to computers and keeps complaining that his hard drive is stopped up, by which he most likely means "full." He installed a second hard drive by using some steps he found on the Internet, but he claims it doesn't work. On closer

examination, you determine that the drive shows up in CMOS but not in Windows—he didn't partition or format the drive! Write a short essay describing partitioning and formatting, including the tools used to accomplish this task on a second hard drive.

4. Your office has a PC shared by four people to do intensive graphics work. The hard drive has about 1 TB of free space. Write a memo on how you could use disk quotas to make certain that each user takes no more than 25 percent of the free space.

5. Your office has several computers with three 200-GB drives in them in addition to the C: drive. Write a short essay that describes how you could use spanning and mount points to make the extra drives more easily usable for your users.

Lab Projects

• Lab Project 4.1

Grab a test system with multiple drives and experiment with the partitioning tools in Windows Disk Management. Create various partition combinations, such as all primary or all extended with logical drives. Change basic disks into dynamic disks and create volumes that span multiple drives. Add to them. You get the idea—experiment and have fun!

• Lab Project 4.2

Partitioning gets all the glory and exposure in tech classes because, frankly, it's cool to be able to do some of the things possible with the Disk Management console. But the experienced tech does not forget about the other half of drive preparation: formatting. Windows offers you at least two different file systems. In this lab, you'll put them through their paces.

In at least one OS, partition a drive with two equal partitions and format one as FAT32 and the other as NTFS. Then get a couple of monster files (larger than 50 MB) and move them to those partitions. Did you notice any difference in transfer speed? Examine the drives in My Computer. Do they show the same amount of used space?

• Lab Project 4.3

Access the CMOS setup for your computer and examine the settings that apply to your hard drive(s). In particular, look at the initial screen to see if it is set to autodetect the kind of hard drive. Is the mode set to LBA or something else? Try to find a screen that includes PIO modes and examine this setting. What other screens apply to the hard drive? When you finish, be sure to choose Quit without saving.

Installing and Upgrading Windows

"Microsoft has a new version out…which according to everybody is the 'most reliable Windows ever.' To me, this is like saying that asparagus is 'the most articulate vegetable ever.'"

—DAVE BARRY

In this chapter, you will learn how to

- **Identify and implement preinstallation tasks**
- **Install and upgrade Windows XP, Windows Vista, and Windows 7**
- **Troubleshoot installation problems**
- **Identify and implement post-installation tasks**

An **operating system (OS)** provides the fundamental link between the user and the hardware that makes up the PC. Without an operating system, all of the greatest, slickest PC hardware in the world is but so much copper, silicon, and gold wrapped up as a big, beige paperweight (or, if you're a teenage boy, a big, gleaming, black paperweight with a window and glowing fluorescent lights, possibly shaped like a robot). The operating system creates the interface between human and machine, enabling you to unleash the astonishing power locked up in the sophisticated electronics of the PC to create amazing pictures, games, documents, business tools, medical miracles, and much more.

This chapter takes you through the processes for installing and upgrading Windows. It starts by analyzing the preinstallation tasks, steps not to be skipped by the wise tech. The bulk of the chapter comes in the second section, where you'll learn about installing and upgrading Windows XP, Windows Vista, and Windows 7. Not all installations go smoothly, so section three looks at troubleshooting installation issues. The final section walks you through the typical post-installation tasks.

Preparing for Installation or Upgrade

Installing or upgrading an OS is like any good story: it has a beginning, a middle, and an end. In this case, the beginning is the several tasks you need to do before you actually do the installation or upgrade. If you do your homework here, the installation process is a breeze, and the post-installation tasks are minimal.

Don't get discouraged at all of the preparation tasks. They usually go pretty fast, and skipping them can cause you gobs of grief later when you're in the middle of installing and things blow up. Well, maybe there isn't a real explosion, but the computer might lock up and refuse to boot into anything usable. With that in mind, look at the nine tasks you need to complete *before* you insert that CD or DVD. Here's the list; a discussion of each follows:

1. Identify hardware requirements.

2. Verify hardware and software compatibility.

3. Decide what type of installation to perform.

4. Determine how to back up and restore existing data, if necessary.

5. Select an installation method.

6. Determine how to partition the hard drive and what file system to use.

7. Determine your computer's network role.

8. Decide on your computer's language and locale settings.

9. Plan for post-installation tasks.

 This nine-step process was once part of the CompTIA A+ exam objectives. Starting with the 220-801 and 220-802 exams, CompTIA has dropped this process from the exams, but I've come to like it. The nine steps are practical, clear, and easy to remember. I use these as a mental checklist every time I install Windows.

Identify Hardware Requirements

Hardware requirements help you decide whether a computer system is a reasonable host for a particular operating system. Requirements include the CPU model, the amount of RAM, the amount of free hard disk space, the video adapter, the display, and the storage devices that may be required to install and run the operating system. They are stated as minimums or, more recently, as recommended minimums. Although you could install an operating system on a computer with the old minimums that Microsoft published, they were not realistic if you wanted to actually accomplish work. With the last few versions of Windows, Microsoft has published recommended minimums that are much more realistic. You will find the published minimums on the packaging and at Microsoft's Web site (www.microsoft.com). Later in this chapter, I'll also tell you what I recommend as minimums for Windows XP, Windows Vista, and Windows 7.

Verify Hardware and Software Compatibility

Assuming your system meets the requirements, you next need to find out how well Windows supports the hardware and software you intend to use under Windows. You have three sources for this information. First, the Setup Wizard that runs during the installation does a quick check of your hardware. Microsoft also provides a free utility, usually called Upgrade Advisor, which you can run on a system to see if your hardware and software will work with a newer version of Windows. Second, Microsoft provides Web sites where you can search by model number of hardware or by a software version to see if it plays well with Windows. Third, the manufacturer of the device or software will usually provide some form of information either on the product box or on their Web site to tell you about Windows compatibility. Let's look at all three information sources.

Setup Wizard/Upgrade Advisor

When you install Windows, the Setup Wizard automatically checks your hardware and software and reports any potential conflicts. It's not perfect, and if you have a critical issue (like a bad driver for your video card), Setup Wizard may simply fail. With any flavor of Windows, *first do your homework*. To help, Windows also provides a utility called Upgrade Advisor (see Figure 5.1) on the installation media (also downloadable) that you run before you attempt to install the software.

Web Sites and Lists

To ensure that your PC works well with Windows, Microsoft has put a lot of hardware and software through a series of certification programs to create a list of devices that work with Windows. The challenge is that Microsoft seems to change the name of the list with every version of Windows.

You'll occasionally hear the HCL or Windows Logo'd Products List referred to as the Windows Catalog. The Windows Catalog was a list of supported hardware Microsoft would add to the Windows XP installation media. The Windows 7 Compatibility Center Web site is the modern tech's best source, so use that rather than any printed resources.

• **Figure 5.1** Upgrade Advisor

It all began back with Windows 95 when Microsoft produced a list of known hardware that would work with their OS, called the Hardware Compatibility List (HCL). Every version of Windows up to Windows Vista contained an HCL. This list was originally simply a text file found on the install disc or downloadable from Microsoft's Web site. Over time, Microsoft created specialized Web sites where you could look up a piece of hardware or software to determine whether or not it worked with Windows. These Web sites have gone through a number of names. Microsoft's current Web site acknowledging what hardware and software works with Windows is the **Windows 7 Compatibility Center**, formerly known as the Windows Logo'd Products List (for Windows Vista) and the Windows Catalog (for Windows XP). Now the magic words are Windows 7 Compatibility Center, as shown in Figure 5.2. Here you can find information on compatible components for Windows 7.

• **Figure 5.2** Windows 7 Compatibility Center

When you install a device that hasn't been tested by Microsoft, a rather scary screen appears (see Figure 5.3). This doesn't mean the component won't work, only that it hasn't been tested. Not all component makers go through the rather painful process of getting the Microsoft approval that allows them to list their component in the Windows 7 Compatibility Center. As a general rule, unless the device is more than five years old, go ahead and install it. If it still doesn't work, you can simply uninstall it later.

Manufacturer Resources

Don't panic if you don't see your device on the official Microsoft list; many supported devices aren't on it. Check the optical disc that came with your hardware for proper drivers. Better yet, check the manufacturer's Web site

If you go looking for the Windows Catalog or Windows Logo'd Products List, you won't find them. You'll be redirected to the Windows 7 Compatibility Center (or a Web page explaining why you should upgrade to Windows 7).

The CompTIA A+ 802 exam expects you to know the different *compatibility tools* available for each OS covered. Windows XP offered the Upgrade Advisor and the Hardware Compatibility List (HCL). Windows Vista added the online Windows Logo'd Product List. Every online tool (with the exception of ftp.microsoft.com where you can find old HCLs in text format) now just points to the Windows 7 Compatibility Center.

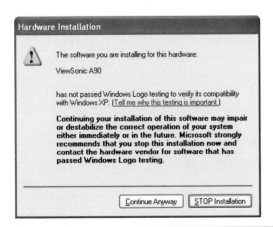

• **Figure 5.3** Untested device in Windows XP

for the most up-to-date drivers. Even when the Windows 7 Compatibility Center lists a piece of hardware, I still make a point of checking the manufacturer's Web site for newer drivers.

When preparing to upgrade, check with the Web sites of the manufacturers of the applications already installed on the previous OS. If there are software compatibility problems with the versions you have, the manufacturer should provide upgrades or patches to fix the problem.

Decide What Type of Installation to Perform

You can install Windows in several ways. A **clean installation** of an OS involves installing it onto an empty hard drive or completely replacing an existing installation. An **upgrade installation** means installing an OS on top of an earlier installed version, thus inheriting all previous hardware and software settings. You can combine versions of Windows by creating a **multiboot installation**. Installing usually involves some sort of optical disc, but other methods also exist. Let's look at all the options.

Clean Installation

A clean installation means your installation ignores a previous installation of Windows, wiping out the old version as the new version of Windows installs. A clean installation is also performed on a new system with a completely blank hard drive. The advantage of doing a clean installation is that you don't carry problems from the old OS over to the new one. The disadvantage is that you need to reinstall all your applications and reconfigure the desktop and each application to the user's preferences. You typically perform a clean installation by setting your CMOS to boot from the optical drive before your hard drive. You then boot off of a Windows installation disc, and Windows gives you the opportunity to partition and format the hard drive and then install Windows.

Upgrade Installation

In an upgrade installation, the new OS installs into the same folders as the old OS, or in tech speak, the new installs *on top of* the old. The new OS replaces the old OS, but retains your data and applications and also inherits all of the personal settings (such as font styles, desktop themes, and so on). The best part is that you don't have to reinstall your favorite programs. Many tech writers refer to this upgrade process as an **in-place upgrade**. Upgrades aren't always perfect, but the advantages make them worthwhile if your upgrade path allows it.

To begin the upgrade of Windows, you should run the appropriate program from the optical disc. This usually means inserting a Windows installation disc into your system while your old OS is running, which autostarts the installation program. The installation program will ask you whether you want to perform an upgrade or a new installation; if you select new installation, the program will remove the existing OS before installing the new one.

If you are performing an upgrade to Windows XP and for some reason the installation program doesn't start automatically, go to My Computer, open the installation disc, and locate winnt32.exe. This program starts an

Microsoft uses the term *in-place upgrade* to define an upgrade installation, so expect to see it on the 802 exam. On the other hand, Microsoft documentation also uses the term for a completely different process, called a **repair installation**, so read whatever question you get on the exam carefully for context. For repair installations, see Chapter 10.

Before starting an OS upgrade, make sure you have shut down all other open applications!

upgrade to Windows XP. For a Windows Vista or Windows 7 upgrade, open the disc in Windows Explorer and run Setup.exe in the disc's root directory, which starts the upgrade for those versions of Windows.

Multiboot Installation

A third option that you need to be aware of is the dual-boot or multiboot installation. This means your system has more than one Windows installation and you may choose which installation to use when you boot your computer. Every time your computer boots, you'll get a menu asking you which version of Windows you wish to boot. Multiboot requires that you format your active partition with a file system that every operating system you install can use. This hasn't been much of a problem since the Windows 9*x* family stopped being relevant, because there's really no reason to use anything other than NTFS.

Windows XP can be installed in a separate folder from an existing older copy of Windows, enabling you to put two operating systems on the same partition. Neither Windows Vista nor Windows 7 allows you define the install folder, so multibooting using Windows Vista or 7 requires you to put each installation on a different partition.

You'll recall from Chapter 4 that Windows Vista and Windows 7 enable you to shrink the C: partition, so if you want to dual boot but have only a single drive, you can make it happen even if Vista/7 is already installed and the C: partition takes up the full drive. Use Disk Management to shrink the volume and create another partition in the newly unallocated space. Then install another copy of Windows to the new partition.

The whole concept behind multiboot is to enable you to run multiple operating systems on a single computer. This is handy if you have an application that runs only on Windows XP, but you also want to run Windows Vista or Windows 7.

Tech Tip

Multiboot Configuration

When configuring a computer for multibooting, there are two basic rules: first, you must format the system partition in a file system that is common to all installed operating systems, and second, you must install the operating systems in order from oldest to newest.

Other Installation Methods

In medium to large organizations, more advanced installation methods are often employed, especially when many computers need to be configured identically. A common method is to place the source files in a shared directory on a network server. Then, whenever a tech needs to install a new OS, he can boot up the computer, connect to the source location on the network, and start the installation from there. This is called generically a **remote network installation**. This method alone has many variations and can be automated with special scripts that automatically select the options and components needed. The scripts can even install extra applications at the end of the OS installation, all without user intervention once the installation has been started. This type of installation is called an **unattended installation**.

Another type of installation that is very popular for re-creating standard configurations is an **image deployment**. An image is a complete copy of a hard disk volume on which an operating system and, usually, all required application software programs have been preinstalled. Images can be stored on optical discs, in which case the tech runs special software on the computer that copies the image onto the local hard drive. Images can also be stored on special network servers, in which case the tech connects to the image server using special software that copies the image from the server to the local hard drive. A leader in this technology has been Norton Ghost,

which is available from Symantec. Other similar programs are Clonezilla and Acronis's True Image.

Beginning with Windows 2000 Server, Microsoft added *Remote Installation Services* (*RIS*), which can be used to initiate either a scripted installation or an installation of an image. With Windows Server 2008 and 2008 R2, Microsoft implemented *Windows Deployment Services* (*WDS*) to replace RIS. Though they are two different systems, they work very similarly from a tech's viewpoint. These tools help with big rollouts of new systems and operating system upgrades.

Determine How to Back Up and Restore Existing Data, If Necessary

Whether you run a clean install or perform an upgrade, you may need to back up existing user data first, because things can go very wrong either way, and the data on the hard drive might be damaged. You'll need to find out where the user is currently saving data files. If they are saving onto the local hard drive, it must be backed up before the installation or replacement takes place. However, if all data has been saved to a network location, you are in luck, because the data is safe from damage during installation.

If the user saves data locally, and the computer is connected to a network, save the data, at least temporarily, to a network location until after the upgrade or installation has taken place. If the computer is not connected to a network, you have a few options for backup. For one, you can put the data on USB thumb drives. A slower option would be to copy the data to DVDs. You can also use an external hard drive, which is a handy thing for any tech to have. Wherever you save the data, you will need to copy or restore the data back to the local hard disk after the installation.

If you plan to migrate a user from one system to another, you might start the process by running the Files and Settings Transfer Wizard (Windows XP) or Windows Easy Transfer (Windows Vista and 7). You'll complete that process after the Windows installation finishes. Rather than discuss the process twice, I'll leave the full discussion on migration for the "Post-Installation Tasks" section later in this chapter.

Select an Installation Method

Once you've backed up everything important, you need to select an installation method. You have two basic choices: insert the installation disc into the drive and go, or install over a network.

Determine How to Partition the Hard Drive and What File System to Use

If you are performing a clean installation, you need to decide ahead of time how to partition the disk space on your hard disk drive, including the number and size of partitions and the file system (or systems) you will use. Actually, in the decision process, the file system comes first, and then the space issue follows, as you will see.

This was a much bigger issue back in the days when older operating systems couldn't use newer file systems, but now that every Windows OS that you could reasonably want to install supports NTFS, there's really no reason to use anything else. You still might have a reason to partition your drive, but as for choosing a file system, your work is done for you.

Determine Your Computer's Network Role

The question of your computer's network role comes up in one form or another during a Windows installation. A Windows computer can have one of several roles relative to a network (in Microsoft terms). One role, called *standalone*, is actually a non-network role, and it simply means that the computer does not participate on a network. You can install any version of Windows on a standalone computer. A standalone computer belongs to a workgroup by default, even though that workgroup contains only one member.

In a network environment, a computer must be a member of either a workgroup or a domain (if you're using Windows 7 in a workgroup on a home network, it can also belong to a homegroup).

Decide on Your Computer's Language and Locale Settings

These settings are especially important for Windows operating systems because they determine how date and time information is displayed and which math separators and currency symbols are used for various locations.

Plan for Post-Installation Tasks

After installing Windows, you may need to install the latest service pack or updates. You may also need to install updated drivers and reconfigure any settings, such as network settings, that were found not to work. You will also need to install and configure any applications (word processor, spreadsheet, database, e-mail, games, etc.) required by the user of the computer. Finally, don't forget to restore any data backed up before the installation or upgrade.

■ The Installation and Upgrade Process

At the most basic level, installing any operating system follows a fairly standard set of steps. You turn on the computer, insert an operating system disc into the optical drive, and follow the installation wizard until you have everything completed. Along the way, you'll accept the **End User License Agreement (EULA)** and enter the product key that says you're not a pirate; the product key is invariably located on the installation disc's case. At the

same time, there are nuances between installing Windows XP or upgrading to Windows 7 that every CompTIA A+ certified tech must know, so this section goes through many installation processes in some detail.

Installing or Upgrading to Windows XP Professional

Windows XP has been around for a long time with a well-established upgrade and installation process. This is the one part of the CompTIA A+ 220-802 exam where older versions of Windows may be mentioned, so be warned!

Upgrade Paths

You can upgrade to Windows XP Professional from all of the following versions of Windows:

- Windows 98 (all versions)
- Windows Me
- Windows NT 4.0 Workstation (Service Pack 5 and later)
- Windows 2000 Professional
- Windows XP Home Edition

Hardware Requirements for Windows XP

Hardware requirements for Windows XP Professional are higher than for previous versions of Windows, but are still very low by modern hardware standards.

Windows XP runs on a wide range of computers, but you need to be sure that your computer meets the minimum hardware requirements, as shown in Table 5.1. Also shown is my recommended minimum for a system running a typical selection of business productivity software.

Table 5.1	Windows XP Hardware Requirements	
Component	**Minimum for a Windows XP Computer**	**Recommended for a Windows XP Computer**
CPU	Any Intel or AMD 233 MHz or higher processor	Any Intel or AMD 300 MHz or higher processor
Memory	64 MB of RAM (though Microsoft admits XP will be somewhat crippled with only this amount)	512 MB of RAM or higher
Hard disk	1.5 GB of available hard drive space	4 GB of available hard drive space
Network	None	Modern network card
Display	Video card that supports SVGA with at least 800 × 600 resolution	Video card that supports DirectX with at least 1024 × 768 resolution
Optical drive	Any CD- or DVD-media drive	Any CD- or DVD-media drive

Hardware and Software Compatibility

You'll need to check hardware and software compatibility before installing Windows XP Professional—as either an upgrade or a new installation. Of course, if your computer already has Windows XP on it, you're spared this task, but you'll still need to verify that the applications you plan to add to the computer will be compatible. Luckily, Microsoft includes the Upgrade Advisor on the Windows XP disc.

Upgrade Advisor You would be hard-pressed these days to find a computer incapable of running Windows XP, but if you are ever uncertain about whether a computer you excavated at an archeological dig can run XP, fear not! The Upgrade Advisor is the first process that runs on the XP installation disc. It examines your hardware and installed software (in the case of an upgrade) and provides a list of devices and software that are known to have issues with XP. Be sure to follow the suggestions on this list.

You can also run the Upgrade Advisor separately from the Windows XP installation. You can run it from the Windows XP disc. Microsoft used to offer the XP Upgrade Advisor on its Web site, but searching for it now will just redirect you to the Windows 7 Upgrade Advisor, so running it from the disc is the way to go nowadays.

Booting into Windows XP Setup

The Windows XP discs are bootable, and Microsoft no longer includes a program to create a set of setup boot disks. This should not be an issue, because PCs manufactured in the past several years can boot from the optical drive. This system BIOS setting, usually described as boot order, is controlled through a PC's BIOS-based Setup program.

In the unlikely event that your lab computer can't be made to boot from its optical drive, you can create a set of six (yes, six!) Windows XP setup boot floppy disks by using a special program you can download from Microsoft's Web site. Note that Microsoft provides separate boot disk programs for XP Home and XP Professional.

Registration Versus Activation

During setup, you will be prompted to register your product and activate it. Many people confuse

 Try This!

Running the Upgrade Advisor

Upgrade Advisor has been around in one form or another for years. It's a handy, powerful tool that you should know how to run on your system, so Try This!

1. Insert the Windows XP installation disc. If Autorun is enabled, the Welcome to Microsoft Windows XP screen appears. If this does not appear, select Start | Run, enter the following (where *d* is the drive letter for the optical drive), and then click OK:

 `d:\SETUP.EXE`

2. At the Welcome to Microsoft Windows XP screen, select Check System Compatibility to start the Upgrade Advisor. On the following page, select Check My System Automatically.

3. In the Upgrade Advisor dialog box, select the first choice if you have an Internet connection. If you don't have an Internet connection, select No, Skip This Step and Continue Installing Windows. (Don't worry, you aren't really going to install yet.)

4. Click Next. The Upgrade Advisor shows the tasks that Dynamic Update is performing, and then it restarts Setup.

5. After Setup restarts, you'll be back at the same page in the Upgrade Advisor. This time, select No, Skip This Step and Continue Installing Windows, and click Next. The Upgrade Report page appears next. You can save the information in a file by clicking Save As and selecting a location.

6. Read the findings that the Upgrade Advisor presents. If a problem was found, click the Full Details button for instructions, and be sure to follow them. When you have recorded any necessary instructions, click Finish.

activation with registration, but these are separate operations. **Registration** tells Microsoft who the official owner or user of the product is, providing contact information such as name, address, company, phone number, and e-mail address. Registration is still entirely optional. Activation is a way to combat software piracy, meaning that Microsoft wishes to ensure that each license for Windows XP is used solely on a single computer. It's more formally called **Microsoft Product Activation (MPA)**.

Mandatory Activation Within 30 Days of Installation Activation is mandatory, but you can skip this step during installation. You have 30 days in which to activate the product, during which time it works normally. If you don't activate it within that time frame, it will be disabled. Don't worry about forgetting, though, because once it's installed, Windows XP frequently reminds you to activate it with a balloon message over the tray area of the taskbar. The messages even tell you how many days you have left.

Activation Mechanics Here's how product activation works. When you choose to activate, either during setup or later when XP reminds you to do it, an installation ID code is created from the product ID code that you entered during installation and a 50-digit value that identifies your key hardware components. You must send this code to Microsoft, either automatically if you have an Internet connection or verbally via a phone call to Microsoft. Microsoft then returns a 42-digit product activation code. If you are activating online, you don't have to enter the activation code; it happens automatically. If you are activating over the phone, you must read the installation ID to a representative and enter the resulting 42-digit activation code into the Activate Windows by Phone dialog box.

No personal information about you is sent as part of the activation process. Figure 5.4 shows the dialog box that opens when you start activation by clicking on the reminder message balloon.

• **Figure 5.4** Activation takes just seconds with an Internet connection.

Installing or Upgrading to Windows Vista

Preparing for a Windows Vista installation is not really different from preparing for a Windows XP installation. There are, of course, a few things to consider before installing or upgrading your system to Vista.

Upgrade Paths

Windows Vista is persnickety about doing upgrade installations with different editions; although you can upgrade to any edition of Vista from any edition of Windows XP, many upgrade paths will require you to do a clean installation of Vista. Vista's upgrade paths are so complicated that the only way to explain them is to use a grid showing the OS you're trying to upgrade from and the edition of Vista you're upgrading to. Fortunately for you, Microsoft provides such a grid, which I've re-created in Table 5.2.

 You don't really upgrade to Windows Vista Enterprise, although you can from Windows Vista Business. Because it's only available to big corporate clients, the Enterprise edition is generally installed as the first and last OS on a corporate PC.

Table 5.2	Vista's Labyrinthine Upgrade Paths			
	Vista Home Basic	**Vista Home Premium**	**Vista Business**	**Vista Ultimate**
XP Professional	Clean Install	Clean Install	Upgrade Install	Upgrade Install
XP Home	Upgrade Install	Upgrade Install	Upgrade Install	Upgrade Install
XP Media Center	Clean Install	Upgrade Install	Clean Install	Upgrade Install
XP Tablet PC	Clean Install	Clean Install	Upgrade Install	Upgrade Install
XP Professional x64	Clean Install	Clean Install	Clean Install	Clean Install

Hardware Requirements for Windows Vista

Windows Vista requires a substantially more powerful computer than XP does. Make sure your computer meets at least the minimum hardware requirements suggested by Microsoft and outlined in Table 5.3, though it would be far better to meet my recommended requirements.

Hardware and Software Compatibility

Windows Vista is markedly different from Windows XP in many very basic, fundamental ways, and this causes all sorts of difficulty with programs and device drivers designed for Windows XP. When Vista came out, you probably heard a lot of people grumbling about it, and likely they were grumbling about hardware and software incompatibility. Simply put, a lot of old

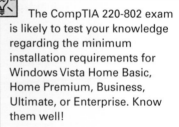 The CompTIA 220-802 exam is likely to test your knowledge regarding the minimum installation requirements for Windows Vista Home Basic, Home Premium, Business, Ultimate, or Enterprise. Know them well!

Table 5.3	Windows Vista Hardware Requirements	
Component	**Minimum for a Windows Vista Computer**	**Recommended for a Windows Vista Computer**
CPU	1 GHz 32-bit (x86) or 64-bit (x64) processor	Any dual-core Intel or AMD processor or better
Memory	512 MB of RAM for Vista Home Basic (for all other editions, 1 GB of RAM)	2 GB of RAM or higher
Hard disk	20-GB hard drive with 15 GB of available hard drive space for Vista Home Basic (for all other editions, 40 GB hard drive with 15 GB of free space)	100-GB hard drive or greater
Network	Modern network card with Internet access	Modern network card with Internet access
Display	Support for DirectX 9 graphics and 32 MB of graphics memory for Vista Home Basic (for all other editions, 128 MB of graphics memory, plus pixel shader 2.0 support, the WDDM driver, and 32 bits per pixel)	DirectX 10 capable graphics card with at least 512 MB of graphics memory
Optical drive	Any DVD-media drive	Any DVD-media drive

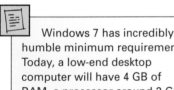

Software incompatibility in Vista was such a problem for many corporate customers and end users that Microsoft has included a *Windows XP Mode* in the higher-end editions of Windows 7, enabling most Windows XP programs to be run despite the different OS.

programs and devices don't work in Windows Vista, which is bad news for people who are still running Microsoft Word 97.

Most programs developed since Vista's release in 2007 should work, but checking the compatibility of any programs you absolutely cannot do without is always a good idea. Because the various tools for checking compatibility with Vista have disappeared in favor of tools for Windows 7, you'll need to check with the developers or manufacturers of your software and devices.

Installing or Upgrading to Windows 7

Windows 7 did not add anything new in terms of installation types. You still need to decide between a clean installation and an upgrade installation, but that's easy to do because you can only upgrade to Windows 7 from Windows Vista—and that's only if you have the same bit edition. In other words, you can upgrade 32-bit Vista to 32-bit Windows 7, but you can't upgrade 32-bit Windows Vista to 64-bit Windows 7. All other Windows editions, including Windows XP Home and Professional, require a clean installation to get Windows 7. Table 5.4 outlines the upgrade paths.

If you have Windows 7 and you want to upgrade to a higher edition with more features—from Windows 7 Home Premium to Windows 7 Ultimate, for example—you can use the built-in Windows Anytime Upgrade feature. You can find this option pinned to the Start menu. Don't forget your credit card!

Table 5.4	Installing or Upgrading to Windows 7	
Existing OS	**Can Upgrade To...**	**Can Clean Install To...**
32-bit Vista (any edition)	32-bit Windows 7 only	Any edition of Windows 7
64-bit Vista (any edition)	64-bit Windows 7 only	Any edition of Windows 7
Any pre-Vista Windows	Not allowed	Any edition of Windows 7

Hardware Requirements for Windows 7

With Windows 7, Microsoft released a single list of system requirements, broken down into 32-bit and 64-bit editions. Quoting directly from Microsoft's Windows 7 Web site, the requirements are as follows:

Windows 7 has incredibly humble minimum requirements. Today, a low-end desktop computer will have 4 GB of RAM, a processor around 2 GHz, approximately a terabyte of hard drive space, and a DirectX 11 video card with 256 or even 512 MB of graphics memory.

- 1 gigahertz (GHz) or faster 32-bit (x86) or 64-bit (x64) processor
- 1 gigabyte (GB) RAM (32-bit) or 2 GB RAM (64-bit)
- 16 GB available hard disk space (32-bit) or 20 GB (64-bit)
- DirectX 9 graphics device with WDDM 1.0 or higher driver

Make sure you memorize the list of requirements. Microsoft also added a fairly extensive list of additional requirements that vary based on the edition of Windows 7 you use. From the same Web site, they include (author's comments in brackets):

- Internet access (fees may apply). [You need Internet access to activate, register, and update the system easily.]
- Depending on resolution, video playback may require additional memory and advanced graphics hardware.

- Some games and programs might require a graphics card compatible with DirectX 10 or higher for optimal performance. [Video has improved dramatically over the years, and DirectX 9 dates back to 2004. Many games and high-definition videos need more than DirectX 9. Also, Windows Aero Desktop (aka Aero Glass) adds amazing beauty and functionality to your Desktop. You must have a video card with 128 MB of graphics memory for Aero to work.]

- For some Windows Media Center functionality a TV tuner and additional hardware may be required. [Windows Media Center works fine without a TV tuner. You can still use it to play Blu-ray Disc and DVD movies as well as video files and music. If you want to watch live TV, however, you'll need a tuner.]

- HomeGroup requires a network and PCs running Windows 7.

- DVD/CD authoring requires a compatible optical drive. [If you want to burn something to an optical disc, you need a drive that can burn discs.]

- Windows XP Mode requires an additional 1 GB of RAM and an additional 15 GB of available hard disk space.

Windows 7 is also designed to handle multiple CPU cores and multiple CPUs. Many, if not most, modern computers use multicore processors. The 32-bit editions of Windows 7 can handle up to 32 processor cores, making it an easy fact to remember for the exams. The 64-bit editions of Windows 7 support up to 256 processor cores.

In terms of multiple physical processors (found on high-end PCs), Windows 7 Professional, Ultimate, and Enterprise can handle two CPUs, whereas Windows 7 Starter and Home Premium support only one CPU.

Tech Tip

Compare and Contrast...
In this chapter, you've learned some of the different installation procedures for Windows XP, Windows Vista, and Windows 7. Keeping them straight can be hard, but if you want to avoid being tricked on the CompTIA A+ 220-802 exam, you must be able to. Review the procedures and then make sure you can identify the points of similarity and, more importantly, the differences among the three.

Upgrading Issues

A few extra steps before you pop in that installation disc are worth your time. If you plan to upgrade rather than perform a clean installation, follow these steps first:

1. Remember to check hardware and software compatibility as explained earlier in the chapter.

2. Have an up-to-date backup of your data and configuration files handy.

3. Perform a "spring cleaning" on your system by uninstalling unused or unnecessary applications and deleting old files.

4. Perform a disk scan (error-checking) and a disk defragmentation.

5. Uncompress all files, folders, and partitions.

6. Perform a virus scan, and then remove or disable all virus-checking software.

7. Disable virus checking in your system CMOS.

8. Keep in mind that if worse comes to worst, you may have to start over and do a clean installation anyway. This makes step 2 exceedingly important. Back up your data!

When dealing with RAID (in any version of Windows), make sure you have the latest drivers on hand for the installation. Put them on a thumb drive just in case the Windows installer can't detect your RAID setup.

Not all screens in the installation process are shown!

The Windows XP Clean Installation Process

A clean installation begins with your system set to boot to your optical drive and the Windows installation disc in the drive. You start your PC and the installation program loads (see Figure 5.5). Note at the bottom that it says to press F6 for a third-party SCSI or RAID driver. You only do this if you want to install Windows onto a strange drive and Windows does not already have the driver for that drive controller. Don't worry about this; Windows has a huge assortment of drivers for just about every hard drive ever made, and in the rare situation where you need a third-party driver, the folks who sell you the SCSI or RAID array will tell you ahead of time.

After the system copies a number of files, you'll see the Welcome to Setup screen (see Figure 5.6). This is an important screen! As you'll see in later chapters, techs often use the Windows installation disc as a repair tool, and this is the screen that lets you choose between installing Windows or repairing an existing installation. Because you're making a new install, just press ENTER.

You're now prompted to read and accept the EULA. Nobody ever reads this—it would give you a stomachache were you to see what you're really agreeing to—so just press F8 and move to the next screen to start partitioning the drive (see Figure 5.7).

Windows Setup

Press F6 if you need to install a third party SCSI or RAID driver...

• **Figure 5.5** Windows Setup text screen

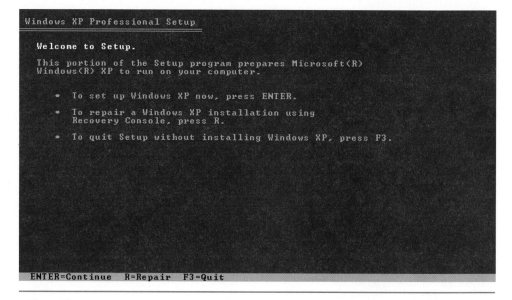

Windows XP Professional Setup

Welcome to Setup.

This portion of the Setup program prepares Microsoft(R) Windows(R) XP to run on your computer.

 • To set up Windows XP now, press ENTER.

 • To repair a Windows XP installation using Recovery Console, press R.

 • To quit Setup without installing Windows XP, press F3.

ENTER=Continue R=Repair F3=Quit

• **Figure 5.6** Welcome text screen

If your hard disk is unpartitioned, you need to create a new partition when prompted. Follow the instructions. In most cases, you can make a single partition, although you can easily make as many partitions as you wish. You can also delete partitions if you're using a hard drive that was partitioned in the past (or if you mess up your partitioning). Note that there is no option to make a primary or extended partition; this tool makes the first partition primary and the rest extended.

● **Figure 5.7** Partitioning text screen

After you've made the partition(s), you must select the partition on which to install Windows XP (sort of trivial if you only have one partition), and then you need to decide which file system format to use for the new partition.

Unless you have some weird need to support FAT or FAT32, format the partition by using NTFS (see Figure 5.8).

Setup now formats the drive and copies some basic installation files to the newly formatted partition, displaying another progress bar. Go get a book to read while you wait.

After it completes copying the base set of files to the hard drive, your computer reboots, and the graphical mode of Windows Setup begins.

Tech Tip

Save Some Space
Many techie types, at least those with big (> 500 GB) hard drives, only partition half of their hard drive for Windows. This makes it easy for them to install an alternative OS (usually Linux) at a later date.

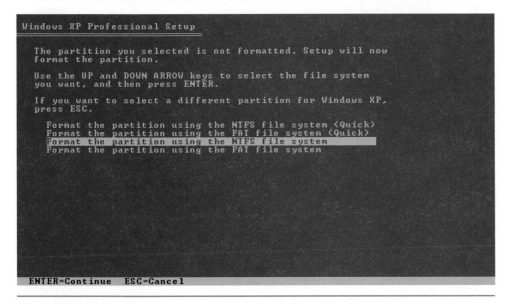

● **Figure 5.8** Choosing NTFS

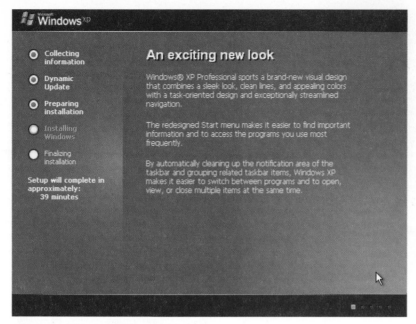

• **Figure 5.9** Beginning of graphical mode

Losing your product key is a bad idea! Document it—at least write it on the installation disc.

You will see a generic screen during the installation that looks like Figure 5.9. On the left of the screen, uncompleted tasks have a white button, completed tasks have a green button, and the current task has a red button. You'll get plenty of advertising to read as you install.

The following screens ask questions about a number of things the computer needs to know. They include the desired region and language the computer will operate in, your name and organization for personalizing your computer, and a valid **product key** for Windows XP (see Figure 5.10). The product key helps reduce piracy of the software. Be sure to enter the product key exactly, or you will be unable to continue.

Next, you need to give your computer a name that will identify it on a network. Check with your system administrator for an appropriate name. If you don't have a system administrator, just enter a simple name such as MYPC for now—you can change this at any time. You also need to create a password for the Administrator user account (see Figure 5.11). Every Windows system has an Administrator user account that can do anything on the computer. Techs will need this account to modify and fix the computer in the future.

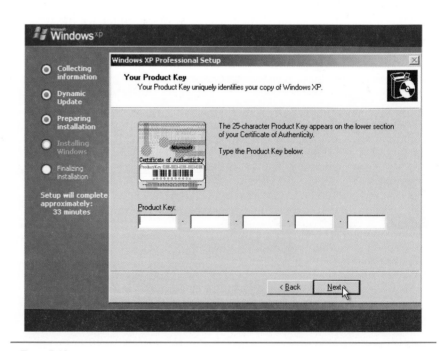

• **Figure 5.10** Product key

Figure 5.11 Computer name and Administrator password

Last, you're asked for the correct date, time, and time zone. Then Windows tries to detect a network card. If a network card is detected, the network components will be installed and you'll have an opportunity to configure the network settings. Unless you know you need special settings for your network, just select the Typical Settings option (see Figure 5.12). Relax; XP will do most of the work for you. Plus you can easily change network settings after the installation.

Even experienced techs usually select the Typical Settings option. Installation is not the time to be messing with network details unless you need to.

Figure 5.12 Selecting typical network settings

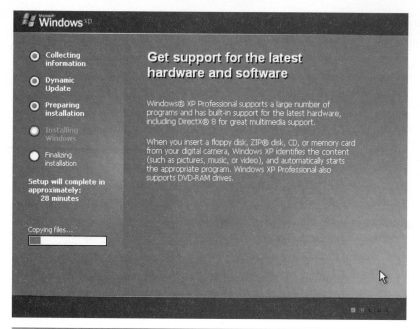

The big copy of files now begins from the CD-ROM to your hard drive. This is a good time to pick your book up again, because watching the ads is boring (see Figure 5.13).

After the files required for the final configuration are copied, XP reboots again. During this reboot, XP determines your screen size and applies the appropriate resolution. This reboot can take several minutes to complete, so be patient.

Once the reboot is complete, you can log on as the Administrator. Balloon messages may appear over the tray area of the taskbar—a common message concerns the display resolution. Click the balloon and allow Windows XP to automatically adjust the display settings.

The final message in the installation process reminds you that you have 30 days left for activation. Go ahead and activate now over the Internet or by telephone. It's painless and quick. If you choose not to activate, simply click the Close button on the message balloon. That's it! You have successfully installed Windows XP and should have a desktop with the default Bliss background, as shown in Figure 5.14.

• **Figure 5.13** The Big Copy

• **Figure 5.14** Windows XP desktop with Bliss background

Mike Meyer's CompTIA A+ Guide to 802: Managing and Troubleshooting PCs

The Windows Vista/7 Clean Installation Process

With Windows Vista, Microsoft dramatically changed the installation process. No longer will you spend your time looking at a boring blue ASCII screen and entering commands by keyboard. The Vista installer—and the installer in Windows 7 as well—has a full graphical interface, making it easy to partition drives and install your operating system. You already saw some of this process back in Chapter 4, but this chapter will go into a bit more detail.

The installation methods for Windows Vista and Windows 7 are so close to identical that it would be silly to address them as separate entries in this book (see Figure 5.15). Only the splash screens and the product-key entry dialog box have changed between Windows Vista and Windows 7! Because of this trivial difference, showing the installation process for both operating systems would waste paper. This walkthrough uses the Windows Vista screenshots just because you might never see them anywhere else.

• **Figure 5.15** Windows 7 and Vista splash screens

Just as when installing Windows XP, you need to boot your computer from some sort of Windows installation media. Usually, you'll use a DVD disc, though you can also install Vista or 7 from a USB drive, over a network, or even off of several CD-ROMs that you have to specially order from Microsoft. When you've booted into the installer, the first screen you see asks you to set your language, time/currency, and keyboard settings, as in Figure 5.16.

The next screen in the installation process is somewhat akin to the XP Welcome to Setup text screen, in that it enables techs to start the installation disc's repair tools (see Figure 5.17). Just like the completely revamped installer, the Vista and 7 repair tools are markedly different from the ones for Microsoft's previous operating systems. You'll learn more about those tools in Chapter 10, but for now all you need to know is that you

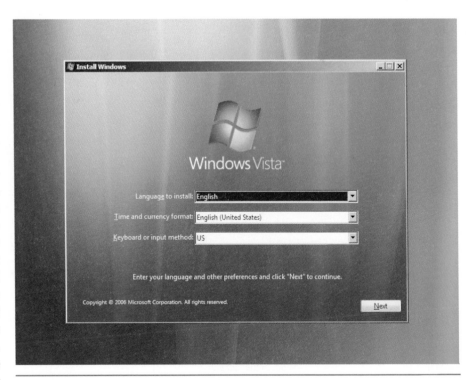

• **Figure 5.16** Windows Vista language settings screen

• Figure 5.17 The Windows Vista setup Welcome screen

• Figure 5.18 The Windows Vista product key screen

click where it says *Repair your computer* to use the repair tools. Because you're just installing Windows in this chapter, click *Install now*.

The next screen shows just how wildly different the Windows Vista and Windows 7 installation orders are. When installing Vista, you enter your product key before you do anything else, as you can see in Figure 5.18. With Windows XP (and Windows 7), this doesn't come until much, much later in the process, and there's a very interesting reason for this change.

Microsoft has dramatically altered the method they use to distribute different editions of their operating system; instead of having different discs for each edition of Windows Vista or Windows 7, every installation disc contains all of the available editions (except for Enterprise). In Windows XP, your product key did very little besides let the installation disc know that you had legitimately purchased the OS. In Windows Vista and Windows 7, your product key not only verifies the legitimacy of your purchase; it also tells the installer which edition you purchased, which, when you think about it, is a lot to ask of a randomly generated string of numbers and letters.

If you leave the product key blank and click

the Next button, you will be taken to a screen asking you which version of Windows Vista you would like to install (see Figure 5.19). (Windows 7, however, disables this option—while every version is on the disc, you can only install the edition named on the box or disc label.) And lest you start to think that you've discovered a way to install Windows without paying for it, you should know that doing this simply installs a 30-day trial of the operating system. After 30 days, you will no longer be able to boot to the desktop without entering a valid product key that matches the edition of Windows Vista/7 you installed.

After the product key screen, you'll find Microsoft's new and improved EULA, shown in Figure 5.20, which you can skip unless you're interested in seeing what's changed in the world of obtuse legalese since the release of Windows XP.

On the next page, you get to decide whether you'd like to do an upgrade installation or a clean installation (see Figure 5.21). As you learned earlier, you have to begin the Vista/7 installation process from within an older OS to use the Upgrade option, so this option will be dimmed for you if you've booted off of the installation disc. To do a clean installation of Vista/7,

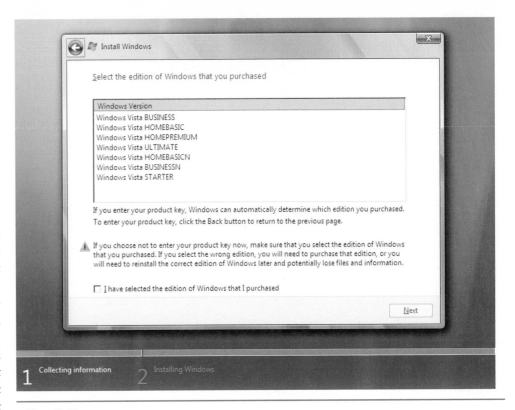

• **Figure 5.19** Choose the edition of Vista you want to install.

• **Figure 5.20** The Vista EULA

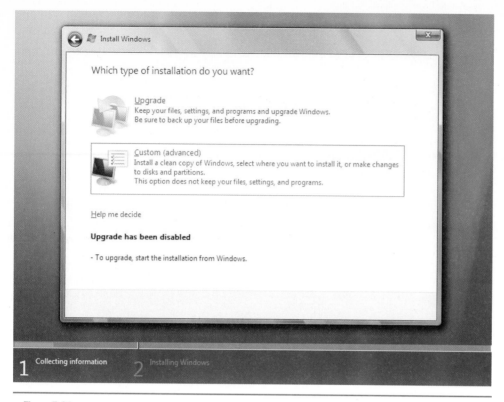

• Figure 5.21 Choose your installation type.

edit your partitions, and just generally install the OS like a pro, you choose the Custom (advanced) option.

You may remember the next screen, shown in Figure 5.22, from Chapter 4. This is the screen where you can partition your hard drives and choose to which partition you'll install Windows. From this screen, you can click the *Drive options (advanced)* link to display a variety of partitioning options, and you can click the Load Driver button to load alternative, third-party drivers. The process of loading drivers is much more intuitive than in Windows XP: you just browse to the location of the drivers you want by using Windows' very familiar browsing window (see Figure 5.23).

• Figure 5.22 The partitioning screen

Mike Meyer's CompTIA A+ Guide to 802: Managing and Troubleshooting PCs

Of course, you will most likely never have to load drivers for a drive, and if it is ever necessary, your drive will almost certainly come with a driver disc and documentation telling you that you'll have to load the drivers.

Once you've partitioned your drives and selected a partition on which to install Windows, the installation process takes over, copying files, expanding files, installing features, and just generally doing lots of computerish things. This can take a while, so if you need to get a snack or read *War and Peace*, do it during this part of the installation.

When Vista/7 has finished unpacking and installing itself, it asks you to choose a user name and picture (see Figure 5.24). This screen also asks you set up a password for your main

• **Figure 5.23** Browse for drivers.

It doesn't take *that* long to install Windows Vista. Windows 7 installation is even snappier.

• **Figure 5.24** Choose a user picture.

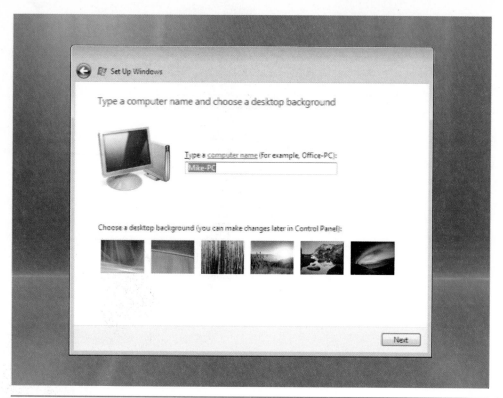

● **Figure 5.25** Choose your computer name.

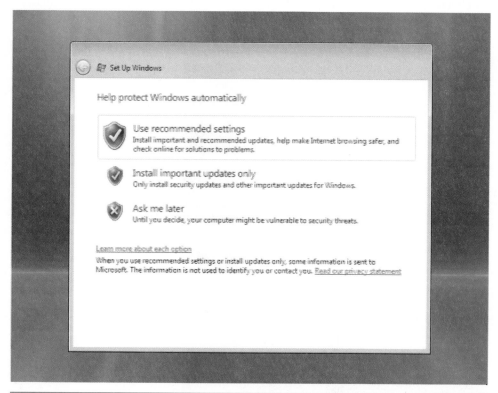

● **Figure 5.26** The automatic updates screen

user account, which is definitely a good idea if you're going to have multiple people using the computer.

After picking your user name and password, and letting Windows know how much you like pictures of kitties, you're taken to a screen where you can type in a computer name (see Figure 5.25). By default, Windows makes your computer name the same as your user name but with "-PC" appended to it, which in most cases is fine.

This is also the screen where you can change the desktop background that Windows will start up with. You can change this easily later on, so pick whatever you like and click the Next button.

At this point, Windows 7 will ask for your product activation key. On Windows Vista, you did this at the beginning of the installation.

The next page asks you how you want to set up Windows Automatic Updates (see Figure 5.26). Most users want to choose the top option, *Use recommended settings*, as it provides the most hassle-free method for updating your computer. The middle option, *Install important updates only*, installs only the most critical security fixes and updates and leaves the rest of the updates up to you.

This is useful when setting up computers for businesses, as many companies' IT departments like to test out any updates before rolling them out to the employees. You should only select the last option, *Ask me later*, if you can dedicate yourself to checking weekly for updates, as it will not install any automatically.

Next up is the time and date screen, where you can make sure your operating system knows what time it is, as in Figure 5.27. This screen should be pretty self-explanatory, so set the correct time zone, the correct date, and the correct time, and move to the next screen.

If you have your computer connected to a network while running the installer, the next screen will ask you about your current location (see Figure 5.28). If you're on a trusted network, such as your home or office network, make the appropriate selection and your computer will be discoverable on the network. If you're on, say, a Starbucks' network, choose *Public location* so the caffeine addicts around you can't see your computer and potentially do malicious things to it.

Once you're past that screen, Windows thanks you for installing it (see

• **Figure 5.27** Vista pities the fool who doesn't know what time it is.

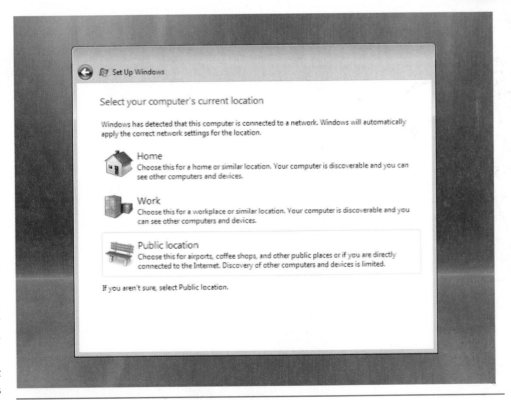

• **Figure 5.28** Tell Windows what kind of network you're on.

Figure 5.29), which is awfully polite for a piece of software, don't you think?

Lest you think you're completely out of the woods, Windows will run some tests on your computer to give it a performance rating, which, in theory, will tell you how well programs will run on your computer. You'll sometimes see minimum performance ratings on the sides of game boxes, but even then, you're more likely to need plain, old-fashioned minimum system requirements. This process can take anywhere from 5 to 20 minutes, so this is another one of those coffee-break moments in the installation process.

Once the performance test finishes, Windows Vista or Windows 7 boots up and you have 30 days to activate your new operating system.

Automating the Installation

As you can see, you may have to sit around for quite a while when installing Windows. Instead of sitting there answering questions and typing in product keys, wouldn't it be nice just to boot up the machine and have the installation process finish without any intervention on your part—especially if you have 30 PCs that need to be ready to go tomorrow morning? Fortunately, Windows offers two good options for automating the installation process: scripted installations and disk cloning.

Scripting Windows XP Installations with Setup Manager

For automating a Windows XP install, Microsoft provides *Setup Manager* to help you create a text file—called an *answer file*—containing all of your

• **Figure 5.29** Aw, shucks, Microsoft Windows Vista. Don't mention it.

• **Figure 5.30** Extracting Setup Manager from the DEPLOY cabinet file

answers to the installation questions. This enables you to do an *unattended installation*, which means you don't have to sit in front of each computer throughout the installation process.

You can find Setup Manager on the Windows installation disc in the \Support\Tools folder. Double-click the DEPLOY cabinet file, and then right-click setupmgr.cab and select Extract (see Figure 5.30). Choose a location for the file.

Setup Manager supports creating answer files for three types of setups: Unattended, Sysprep, and Remote Installation Services (see Figure 5.31). The latest version of the tool can create answer files for Windows XP Home Edition, Windows XP Professional, and Windows .NET (Standard, Enterprise, or Web Server); see Figure 5.32.

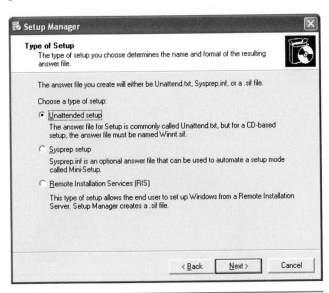

• **Figure 5.31** Setup Manager can create answer files for three types of setups.

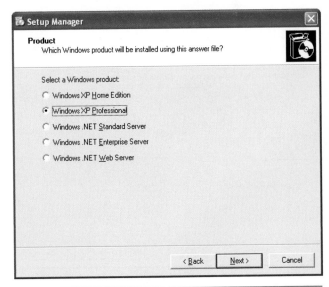

• **Figure 5.32** Setup Manager can create answer files for five versions of Windows.

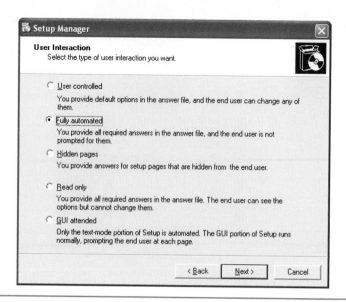

• **Figure 5.33** Setup Manager can create several kinds of answer files.

Setup Manager can create an answer file to completely automate the process, or you can use it to set default options. You'll almost always want to create an answer file that automates the entire process (see Figure 5.33).

When running a scripted installation, you have to decide how to make the installation files themselves available to the PC. Although you can boot your new machine from an installation CD, you can save yourself a lot of CD swapping if you just put the installation files on a network share and install your OS over the network (see Figure 5.34).

When you run Setup Manager, you get to answer all those pesky questions. As always, you will also have to "accept the terms of the License Agreement" (see Figure 5.35) and specify the product key (see Figure 5.36), but at least by scripting these steps you can do it once and get it over with.

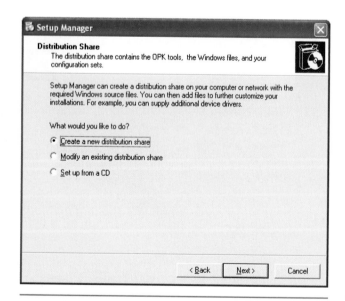

• **Figure 5.34** Choose where to store the installation files.

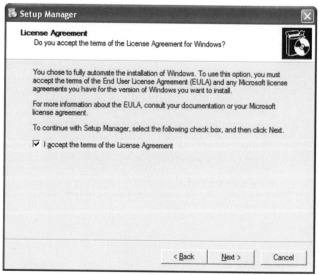

• **Figure 5.35** Don't forget to accept the license agreement.

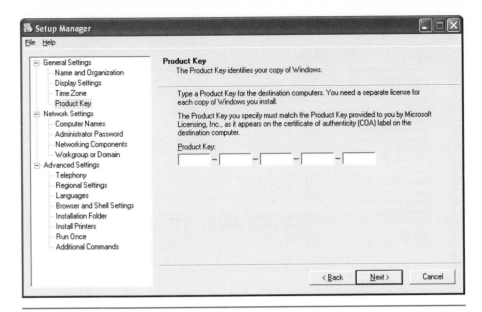

• **Figure 5.36** Enter the product key.

Now it's time to get to the good stuff, customizing your installation. Using the graphical interface, decide what configuration options you want to use: screen resolutions, network options, browser settings, regional settings, and so on. You can even add finishing touches to the installation, installing additional programs such as Microsoft Office and Adobe Reader by automatically running additional commands after the Windows installation finishes (see Figure 5.37). You can also set programs to run once (see Figure 5.38).

Remember that computer names must be unique on the network. If you're going to use the same answer files for multiple machines on the same network, you need to make sure that each machine gets its own unique name. You can either provide a list of names to use, or have the Setup program randomly generate names (see Figure 5.39).

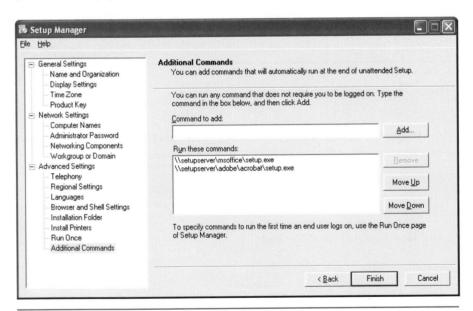

• **Figure 5.37** Running additional commands

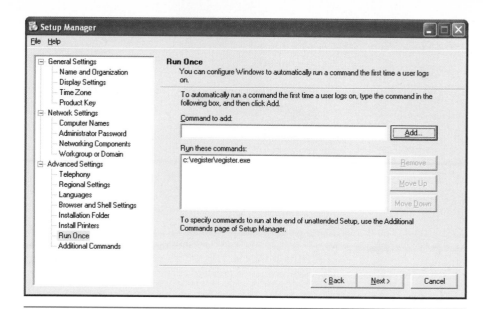

● Figure 5.38 Running a program once

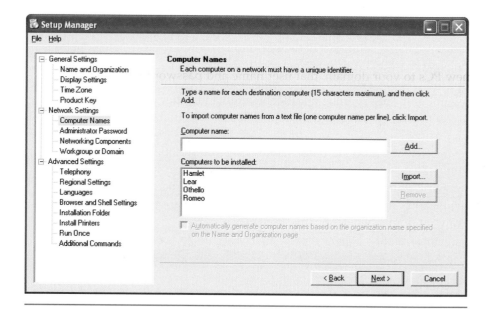

● Figure 5.39 Pick your computer names.

When you're finished, Setup Manager prompts you to save your answers as a text file. The contents of the file will look something like this:

```
;SetupMgrTag
[Data]
    AutoPartition=1
    MsDosInitiated="0"
    UnattendedInstall="Yes"

[Unattended]
    UnattendMode=FullUnattended
    OemSkipEula=Yes
```

```
    OemPreinstall=No
    TargetPath=\WINDOWS

[GuiUnattended]
    AdminPassword=414c11f760b0064 ... [out to 64 characters]
    EncryptedAdminPassword=Yes
    OEMSkipRegional=1
    TimeZone=85
    OemSkipWelcome=1
    AutoLogon=Yes
    AutoLogonCount=1

[UserData]
    ProductKey=FFFFF-FFFFF-FFFFF-FFFFF-FFFFF
    FullName="Scott"
    OrgName="Total Seminars"
    ComputerName=*

[Identification]
    JoinDomain=TOTAL
    DomainAdmin=admin09
    DomainAdminPassword=my-password
```

The list goes on for another hundred lines or so, and this is a fairly simple answer file. One thing to note is that if you provide a domain administrator's user name and password for the purpose of automatically adding new PCs to your domain, that user name and password will be in the text file in clear text:

```
[Identification]
    JoinDomain=TOTAL
    DomainAdmin=admin09
    DomainAdminPassword=my-password
```

In that case, you will want to be very careful about protecting your setup files.

Once you have your answer file created, you can start your installation with this command, and go enjoy a nice cup of coffee while the installation runs:

```
D:\i386\winnt32 /s:%SetupFiles% /unattend:%AnswerFile%
```

For `%SetupFiles%`, substitute the location of your setup files—either a local path (`D:\i386` if you are installing from a CD) or a network path. If you use a network path, don't forget to create a network boot disk so that the installation program can access the files. For `%AnswerFile%`, substitute the name of the text file you created with Setup Manager (usually `unattend.txt`).

Of course, you don't have to use Setup Manager to create your answer file. Feel free to pull out your favorite text editor and write one from scratch. Most techs, however, find it much easier to use the provided tool than to wrestle with the answer file's sometimes arcane syntax.

Automating a Windows Vista or Windows 7 Installation with the Automated Installation Kit

As of Windows Vista and Windows 7, Setup Manager is history—as is any method of automating an installation that isn't extremely complicated and intimidating. Microsoft has replaced Setup Manager with the Windows Automated Installation Kit (AIK), a set of tools that, although quite powerful, seems to have made something of a Faustian deal to obtain that power at the expense of usability (see Figure 5.40).

Writing a step-by-step guide to creating an answer file in the AIK would almost warrant its own chapter, and as the CompTIA A+ 220-802 exam doesn't cover it at all, I'm not going to go into too much gory detail. I will, however, give a brief account of the process involved.

The basic idea behind the AIK is that a tech can create an answer file by using a tool called the Windows System Image Manager, and then use that answer file to build a Master Installation file that can be burned to DVD. Vista/7's answer files are no longer simple text documents but .XML files, and the process of creating one is more complicated than it used to be. Gone are the days of simply running a wizard and modifying options as you see fit. Instead, you choose components (which represent the things you want your automated installation to do, such as create a partition, enter a certain product key, and much, much more) out of a huge, often baffling list and then modify their settings (see Figure 5.41).

Once you've selected and modified all of the components you're interested in, you have to save your answer file, copy it to a USB thumb drive, and plug that into a new computer on which you're going to install Vista/7. When you boot a computer off of the installation disc, it automatically searches all removable media for an answer file, and, finding one, uses it to automatically install itself. If you're only installing Vista/7 to this one computer, you're finished, but if you want to install it to multiple computers, you'll probably want to create a disc image based off of your Master Installation file.

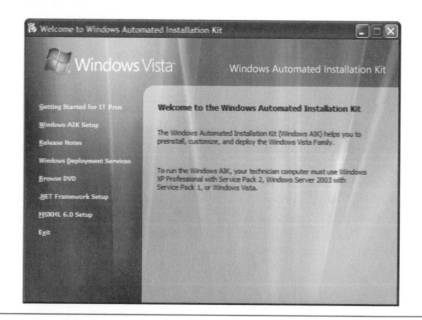

• **Figure 5.40** The Automated Installation Kit

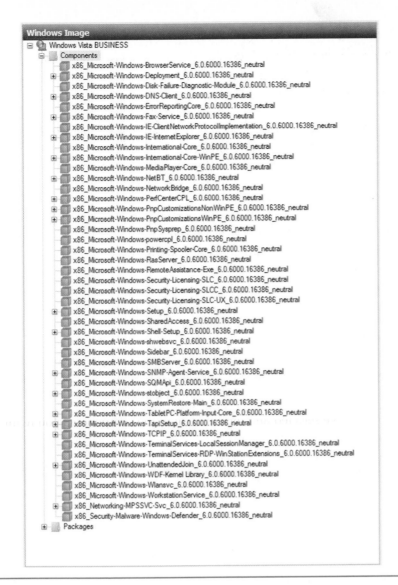

Windows Image
- Windows Vista BUSINESS
 - Components
 - x86_Microsoft-Windows-BrowserService_6.0.6000.16386_neutral
 - x86_Microsoft-Windows-Deployment_6.0.6000.16386_neutral
 - x86_Microsoft-Windows-Disk-Failure-Diagnostic-Module_6.0.6000.16386_neutral
 - x86_Microsoft-Windows-DNS-Client_6.0.6000.16386_neutral
 - x86_Microsoft-Windows-ErrorReportingCore_6.0.6000.16386_neutral
 - x86_Microsoft-Windows-Fax-Service_6.0.6000.16386_neutral
 - x86_Microsoft-Windows-IE-ClientNetworkProtocolImplementation_6.0.6000.16386_neutral
 - x86_Microsoft-Windows-IE-InternetExplorer_6.0.6000.16386_neutral
 - x86_Microsoft-Windows-International-Core_6.0.6000.16386_neutral
 - x86_Microsoft-Windows-International-Core-WinPE_6.0.6000.16386_neutral
 - x86_Microsoft-Windows-MediaPlayer-Core_6.0.6000.16386_neutral
 - x86_Microsoft-Windows-NetBT_6.0.6000.16386_neutral
 - x86_Microsoft-Windows-NetworkBridge_6.0.6000.16386_neutral
 - x86_Microsoft-Windows-PerfCenterCPL_6.0.6000.16386_neutral
 - x86_Microsoft-Windows-PnpCustomizationsNonWinPE_6.0.6000.16386_neutral
 - x86_Microsoft-Windows-PnpCustomizationsWinPE_6.0.6000.16386_neutral
 - x86_Microsoft-Windows-PnpSysprep_6.0.6000.16386_neutral
 - x86_Microsoft-Windows-powercpl_6.0.6000.16386_neutral
 - x86_Microsoft-Windows-Printing-Spooler-Core_6.0.6000.16386_neutral
 - x86_Microsoft-Windows-RasServer_6.0.6000.16386_neutral
 - x86_Microsoft-Windows-RemoteAssistance-Exe_6.0.6000.16386_neutral
 - x86_Microsoft-Windows-Security-Licensing-SLC_6.0.6000.16386_neutral
 - x86_Microsoft-Windows-Security-Licensing-SLCC_6.0.6000.16386_neutral
 - x86_Microsoft-Windows-Security-Licensing-SLC-UX_6.0.6000.16386_neutral
 - x86_Microsoft-Windows-Setup_6.0.6000.16386_neutral
 - x86_Microsoft-Windows-SharedAccess_6.0.6000.16386_neutral
 - x86_Microsoft-Windows-Shell-Setup_6.0.6000.16386_neutral
 - x86_Microsoft-Windows-shwebsvc_6.0.6000.16386_neutral
 - x86_Microsoft-Windows-Sidebar_6.0.6000.16386_neutral
 - x86_Microsoft-Windows-SMBServer_6.0.6000.16386_neutral
 - x86_Microsoft-Windows-SNMP-Agent-Service_6.0.6000.16386_neutral
 - x86_Microsoft-Windows-SQMApi_6.0.6000.16386_neutral
 - x86_Microsoft-Windows-stobject_6.0.6000.16386_neutral
 - x86_Microsoft-Windows-SystemRestore-Main_6.0.6000.16386_neutral
 - x86_Microsoft-Windows-TabletPC-Platform-Input-Core_6.0.6000.16386_neutral
 - x86_Microsoft-Windows-TapiSetup_6.0.6000.16386_neutral
 - x86_Microsoft-Windows-TCPIP_6.0.6000.16386_neutral
 - x86_Microsoft-Windows-TerminalServices-LocalSessionManager_6.0.6000.16386_neutral
 - x86_Microsoft-Windows-TerminalServices-RDP-WinStationExtensions_6.0.6000.16386_neutral
 - x86_Microsoft-Windows-UnattendedJoin_6.0.6000.16386_neutral
 - x86_Microsoft-Windows-WDF-Kernel Library_6.0.6000.16386_neutral
 - x86_Microsoft-Windows-Wlansvc_6.0.6000.16386_neutral
 - x86_Microsoft-Windows-WorkstationService_6.0.6000.16386_neutral
 - x86_Networking-MPSSVC-Svc_6.0.6000.16386_neutral
 - x86_Security-Malware-Windows-Defender_6.0.6000.16386_neutral
 - Packages

• **Figure 5.41** The list of components in the Image Monitor

To create such an image, you must use two more tools in the AIK—Windows PE and ImageX—to "capture" the installation and create a disc image from it. If the rest of the process seemed a bit complicated, this part is like solving a Rubik's cube with your teeth while balancing on top of a flagpole and juggling. Suffice it to say that the AIK comes with documentation that tells you how to do this, so with a bit of patience, you can get through it.

 Norton Ghost is not the only disk imaging software out there, but it is so widely used that techs often refer to disk cloning as "ghosting the drive."

Sysprep

Cloning a Windows PC works great for some situations, but what if you need to send the same image out to machines that have slightly different hardware? What if you need the customer to go through the final steps of the Windows installation (creating a user account, accepting the license agreement, etc.)? That's when you need to combine a scripted setup with cloning by using the System Preparation Tool, **Sysprep**, which can undo portions of the Windows installation process.

After installing Windows and adding any additional software (Microsoft Office, Adobe Acrobat, Yahoo Instant Messenger, etc.), run Sysprep (see Figure 5.42) and then create your disk image by using the cloning application of your choice. The first time a new system cloned from the image boots, an abbreviated version of setup, Mini-Setup, runs and completes the last few steps of the installation process: installing drivers for hardware, prompting the user to accept the license agreement and create user accounts, and so on. Optionally, you can use Setup Manager to create an answer file to customize Mini-Setup, just as you would with a standard scripted installation.

Installing Windows over a Network

Techs working for big corporations can end up installing Windows a lot. When you have a hundred PCs to take care of and Microsoft launches a new version of Windows, you don't want to have to walk from cubicle to cubicle with an installation disc, running one install after the other. You already know about automated installations, but network installations take this one step further.

Imagine another scenario. You're still a tech for a large company, but your boss has decided that every new PC will use an image with a predetermined set of applications and configurations. You need to put the image on every workstation, but most of them don't have optical drives. Network installation saves the day again!

The phrase "network installation" can involve many different tools depending on which version of Windows you use. Most importantly, the machines that receive the installations (the clients) need to be connected to a server. That server might be another copy of Windows XP, Vista, or 7; or it might be a fully fledged server running Windows Server 2003, 2008, or 2008 R2. The serving PC needs to host an image, which can be either the default installation of Windows or a custom image, often created by the network administrator.

All of the server-side issues should be handled by a network administrator—setting up a server to deploy Windows installations and images goes beyond what the CompTIA A+ 220-802 exam covers.

PXE

On the client side, you'll need to use the *Preboot Execution Environment* (*PXE*). PXE uses multiple protocols such as IP, DHCP, and DNS to enable your computer to boot from a network location. That means the PC needs

Tech Tip

RIS and WDS

Windows Server 2003 uses Remote Installation Services to enable network installations, while Windows Server 2008 and 2008 R2 use Windows Deployment Services, as mentioned earlier in the chapter. Both services combine several powerful tools that enable you to customize and send installation files over the network to the client PC. These tools are aimed more at enterprise networks dealing in hundreds of PCs and are managed by network professionals.

• **Figure 5.42** Sysprep, the System Preparation Tool

no installation disc or USB drive. Just plug your computer into the network and go! Okay, it's a little more complicated than that.

Booting with PXE To enable PXE, you'll need to enter your BIOS System Setup. Find the screen that configures your NIC (which changes depending on your particular BIOS). If there is a PXE setting there, enable it. You'll also need to change the boot order so that the PC boots from a network location first.

When you reboot the PC, you'll see the familiar first screens of the boot process. At some point, you should also see an instruction to "Press F12 for network boot." (It's almost always F12.) The PC will attempt to find a server on the network to which it can connect. When it does, you'll be asked to press F12 again to continue booting from the network, as you can see in Figure 5.43.

Depending on how many images are prepared on the server, you'll either be taken directly to the Windows installation screen or be asked to pick from multiple images. Pick the option you need, and everything else should proceed as if you were installing Windows from the local optical drive.

> Not every NIC supports PXE. To boot from a network location without PXE, you can create boot media that forces your PC to boot from a network location.

```
Network boot from Intel E1000
Copyright (C) 2003-2008  VMware, Inc.
Copyright (C) 1997-2000  Intel Corporation

CLIENT MAC ADDR: 00 0C 29 D7 9B 6B  GUID: 564DCC2E-04EA-ACE1-381B-5140E8D79B6B
CLIENT IP: 10.12.14.51  MASK: 255.0.0.0  DHCP IP: 10.12.14.10
GATEWAY IP: 10.12.14.1

Downloaded WDSNBP...

Press F12 for network service boot
_
```

• **Figure 5.43** Network boot

▪ Troubleshooting Installation Problems

The term "installation problem" is rather deceptive. The installation process itself almost never fails. Usually, something else fails during the process that is generally interpreted as an "install failure." Let's look at some typical installation problems and how to correct them.

Text Mode Errors

If you're going to have a problem with a Windows XP installation, this is the place to get one. It's always better to have the error right off the bat as opposed to when the installation is nearly complete. Text mode errors most often take place during clean installations and usually point to one of the following problems:

RAID Array Not Detected

If Windows fails to detect a RAID array during the text mode portion of the Windows XP installation, this could be caused by Windows not having the proper driver for the hard drive or RAID controller. If the hard drives show up properly in the RAID controller setup utility, then it's almost certainly a driver issue. Get the driver disc from the manufacturer and run setup again. Press F6 when prompted very early in the Windows XP installation process.

Nothing happens right away when you push F6, but later in the process you'll be prompted to install the drivers.

No Boot Device Present When Booting Off the Windows Installation Disc

Either the startup disc is bad or the CMOS is not set to look at that optical drive first.

Windows Setup Requires XXXX Amount of Available Drive Space

There's a bunch of stuff on the drive already.

Not Ready Error on Optical Drive

You probably just need to give the optical drive a moment to catch up. Press R for retry a few times. You may also have a damaged installation disc, or the optical drive may be too slow for the system.

A Stop Error (Blue Screen of Death) After the Reboot at the End of Text Mode

This may mean you didn't do your homework in checking hardware compatibility, especially the BIOS. I'll tell you more about stop errors in Chapter 10, but if you encounter one of these errors during installation, check out the Microsoft Knowledge Base.

Graphical Mode Errors

Graphical mode errors are found in all versions of Windows and can cause a whole new crop of problems to arise.

> Because partitioning and formatting occur during the graphical mode of Windows Vista and Windows 7 installation, failure to detect a RAID array points to drivers not loaded. The same driver issue applies, just like it did in Windows XP.

Hardware Detection Errors

Failure to detect hardware properly by any version of Windows Setup can be avoided by simply researching compatibility beforehand. Or, if you decided to skip that step, you might be lucky and only have a hardware detection error involving a noncritical hardware device. You can troubleshoot this problem at your leisure. In a sense, you are handing in your homework late, checking out compatibility and finding a proper driver after Windows is installed.

Every Windows installation depends on Windows Setup properly detecting the computer type (motherboard and BIOS stuff, in particular) and installing the correct hardware support. Microsoft designed Windows to run on several hardware platforms using a layer of software tailored specifically for the hardware, called the **hardware abstraction layer (HAL)**.

Can't Read CAB Files

This is probably the most common of all XP installation errors. **CAB files** (as in cabinet) are special compressed files, recognizable by their .cab file extension, that Microsoft uses to distribute copies of Windows. If your system can't read them, first check the installation disc for scratches. Then try copying all of the files from the source directory on the disc (\i386) into a directory on your local hard drive. Then run Windows Setup from there,

remembering to use the correct program (WINNT32.EXE). If you can't read any of the files on the installation disc, you may have a defective drive.

Lockups During Installation

Lockups are one of the most challenging problems that can take place during installation, because they don't give you a clue as to what's causing the problem. Here are a few things to check if you get a lockup during installation.

Unplug It

Most system lockups occur when Windows Setup queries the hardware. If a system locks up once during setup, turn off the computer—literally. Unplug the system! Do *not* press CTRL-ALT-DEL. Do *not* press the Reset button. Unplug it! Then turn the system back on, boot into Setup, and rerun the Setup program. Windows will see the partial installation and restart the installation process automatically. Microsoft used to call this *Smart Recovery*, but the term has faded away over the years.

Optical Drive, Hard Drive

Bad optical discs, optical drives, or hard drives may cause lockups. Check the optical disc for scratches or dirt, and clean it up or replace it. Try a known good disc in the drive. If you get the same error, you may need to replace the drive.

Log Files

Windows generates a number of special text files called **log files** that track the progress of certain processes. Windows creates different log files for different purposes. In Windows XP, the two most important log files are

- Setuplog.txt tracks the complete installation process, logging the success or failure of file copying, Registry updates, reboots, and so on.

- Setupapi.log tracks each piece of hardware as it is installed. This is not an easy log file to read, as it uses plug and play code, but it will show you the last device installed before Windows locked up.

Windows Vista and Windows 7 create about 20 log files each, organized by the phase of the installation. Each phase, however, creates a setuperr.log file to track any errors during that phase of the installation.

Windows stores these log files in the Windows directory (the location in which the OS is installed). These operating systems have powerful recovery options, so the chances of your ever actually having to read a log file, understand it, and then get something fixed as a result of that understanding are pretty small. What makes log files handy is when you call Microsoft or a hardware manufacturer. They *love* to read these files, and they actually have people who understand them. Don't worry about trying to understand log files for the CompTIA A+ 802 exam; just make sure you know the names of the log files and their location. Leave the details to the übergeeks.

■ Post-Installation Tasks

You might think that's enough work for one day, but your task list has a few more things. They include updating the OS with patches and service packs, upgrading drivers, restoring user data files, and migrating and retiring.

Patches, Service Packs, and Updates

Someone once described an airliner as consisting of millions of parts flying in close formation. I think that's also a good description for an operating system. And we can even carry that analogy further by thinking about all of the maintenance required to keep an airliner safely flying. Like an airliner, the parts (programming code) of your OS were created by different people, and some parts may even have been contracted out. Although each component is tested as much as possible, and the assembled OS is also tested, it's not possible to test for every possible combination of events. Sometimes a piece is simply found to be defective. The fix for such a problem is a corrective program called a **patch**.

In the past, Microsoft provided patches for individual problems. They also accumulated patches until they reached some sort of critical mass and then bundled them together as a **service pack**. They still do this. But they also make it easier for you to find and install the appropriate patches and service packs, which, when combined, are called *updates*. They make these updates available at their Web site or on optical disc. Many organizations make the updates available for distribution from network servers. Immediately after installing Windows, install the latest updates on the computer. Chapter 8 covers this process more fully.

Upgrading Drivers

Even if you did all your preinstallation tasks, you may decide to go with the default drivers that come with Windows and then upgrade them to the latest drivers after the fact. This is a good strategy because installation is a complicated task that you can simplify by installing old but adequate drivers. Maybe those newest drivers are just a week old—waiting until after the Windows installation to install new drivers gives you a usable driver to go back to if the new driver turns out to be a lemon.

Restoring User Data Files (If Applicable)

Remember when you backed up the user data files before installation? You don't? Well, check again, because now is the time to restore that data. Your method of restoring depends on how you backed up the files in the first place. If you used a third-party backup program, you need to install it before you can restore those files, but if you used the Windows Backup utility (Windows XP) or the Backup and Restore Center (Windows Vista and Windows 7), you are in luck, because they are installed by default (with the

exception of Windows XP Home edition). If you did something simpler, such as copying to optical discs or a network location, all you have to do is copy the files back to the local hard disk. Good luck!

Migrating and Retiring

Seasons change and so does the state of the art in computing. At a certain point in a computer's life, you'll need to retire an old system. This means you must move the data and users to a new system or at least a new hard drive—a process called **migration**—and then safely dispose of the old system. Microsoft offers a few tools to accomplish this task, and because it's important to know about them for the CompTIA A+ 220-802 exam (not to mention for your next new computer purchase), I'm going to go over them.

Files and Settings Transfer Wizard

You've already heard a bit about the **Files and Settings Transfer Wizard (FSTW)** back in Chapter 2, but the CompTIA A+ 802 exam expects you to have more than just a passing knowledge of it. When migrating to a new system, you would run the Files and Settings Transfer Wizard on the newer computer (assuming the newer computer is running Windows XP; more on the Windows Vista and Windows 7 migration options later), which would then use the wizard to pull files off of the older computer. You start the wizard by going to Accessories | System Tools in Windows XP's All Programs menu. Once you've fired it up, you're presented with the screen in Figure 5.44.

When you click the Next button on the wizard's first screen, you're asked whether the computer you're using is the new or old computer, as in Figure 5.45.

• **Figure 5.44** The Files and Settings Transfer Wizard's initial screen

• **Figure 5.45** Is this the new computer or your old one?

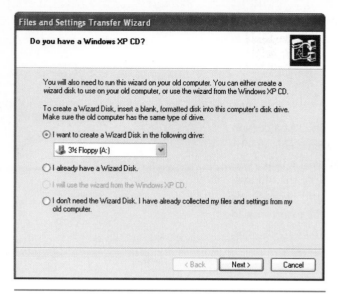

• **Figure 5.46** Creating a Wizard Disk

Note that the old computer can be running any version of Windows all the way back to Windows 95. Older Windows operating systems didn't come with the Files and Settings Transfer Wizard installed, so if you're migrating from an older version of Windows, you'll have to either install the wizard onto the older computer with the XP disc or create a Wizard Disk that will enable you to do the same thing. You're given the option to create such a disk by clicking Next with New computer selected, as in Figure 5.46.

Once you've either created a Wizard Disk (or told the wizard that you're going to install the wizard from the XP CD), you're taken to a screen that asks where to look for the files and settings that you've collected (see Figure 5.47). The first two options are slightly outdated, because the first refers to a direct serial connection, now a rarity in the personal computing world, and the second asks for a floppy disk, though you can use it with USB thumb drives as well. The third option is the most likely candidate for a migration, because it enables you to look for your older computer on your home network.

Meanwhile, to actually determine which files and settings are going to be transferred, you need to run the wizard on your old computer. If you're migrating from another Windows XP machine, you need to tell the wizard where it's being run; otherwise, you skip to the next step, which asks how you want to transfer the files (see Figure 5.48). The best option is to transfer them over a home network, but you can also save the files on a USB thumb drive or simply on a folder on your computer, though, obviously, that doesn't do a lot for transferring the files.

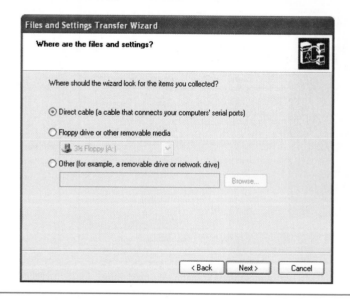

• **Figure 5.47** Where are the files and settings?

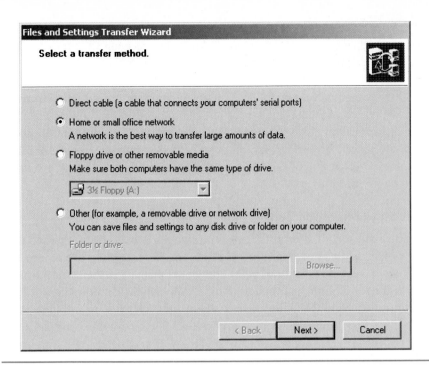

• **Figure 5.48** How will you transfer the files?

When you click Next, the wizard shows its default list of folders and settings to save, but being the savvy PC tech you are, you'll probably want to customize which folders are migrated. You can do that by checking the box that says *Let me select a custom list of files and settings when I click Next* (see Figure 5.49).

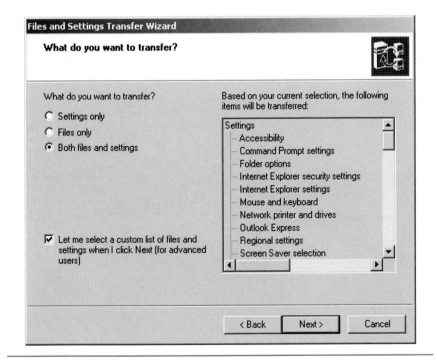

• **Figure 5.49** The files and settings you're going to transfer

Chapter 5: Installing and Upgrading Windows

If you've checked that box, the next page enables you to add additional settings and browse for additional folders, files, or even file types to back up, making it pretty easy to simply back up every .MP3 on your computer (see Figure 5.50). Neat, huh?

Once you click Next on that screen, the wizard begins the actual transfer process, which can take quite a lot of time depending on how much stuff you're transferring. This is an excellent time to, for example, read the complete works of Pliny the Elder, or, even more usefully, to memorize all of the previous chapters of this book word-for-word, because you'll probably have plenty of time.

User State Migration Tool

If you're the sort of computer user who demands maximum functionality and power from your operating system, you'll probably want to use the **User State Migration Tool (USMT)**. The USMT has all of the same features as the Files and Settings Transfer Wizard, but with much more control over advanced configurations for the new computer. Its primary use is in businesses because it has to be run in a Windows Server domain. In practice, if you're migrating a single user, use the FSTW. If you need to migrate multiple users, the USMT is the tool.

Windows Easy Transfer

With Windows Vista and Windows 7, Microsoft has upgraded the Files and Settings Transfer Wizard, calling it **Windows Easy Transfer**. Windows Easy Transfer comes native in Vista/7 and can be downloaded and installed on Windows XP as well. Windows Easy Transfer is located in the System Tools subfolder of the Accessories folder in your Programs menu. The first screen

As a reminder from Chapter 2, the CompTIA A+ exam competencies mention that the very old Windows NT (that's the version before Windows 2000, which in turn preceded Windows XP) came with the *User Data Migration Tool* (*UDMT*) that facilitated migrating users from an earlier version, just like the USMT. This tool *does not exist* on current OSs, but it might show up as a wrong answer choice.

• **Figure 5.50** Customizing the transfer

Mike Meyer's CompTIA A+ Guide to 802: Managing and Troubleshooting PCs

of Windows Easy Transfer simply gives you a bit of information about the process, so there's not really much to do there.

When you click Next, you're taken to a screen that asks if you want to start a new transfer or continue an old one (see Figure 5.51). If you've already set up your old computer to transfer the files, select the latter option; if you haven't, select the former.

If you choose to start a new transfer, the process is very similar to the Files and Settings Transfer Wizard: you select whether you're using your new or old computer and then follow the same basic steps as before. There are some differences, of course—network security is improved by using Transfer Keys to protect your files from others on the network, there's an option to use a special Easy Transfer Cable to transfer your files between USB ports, and the order of some screens is changed around a bit—but if you understand the Files and Settings Transfer Wizard transfer process, Windows Easy Transfer shouldn't be too difficult.

Migration Practices

When talking about migration or retirement in terms of security, you need to answer one question: What do you do with the old system or drive?

All but the most vanilla new installations have sensitive data on them, even if it's simply e-mail messages or notes-to-self that would cause embarrassment if discovered. Most PCs, especially in a work environment, contain a lot of sensitive data. You can't just format C: and hand over the drive.

Follow three principles when migrating or retiring a computer. First, migrate your users and data information in a secure environment. Until

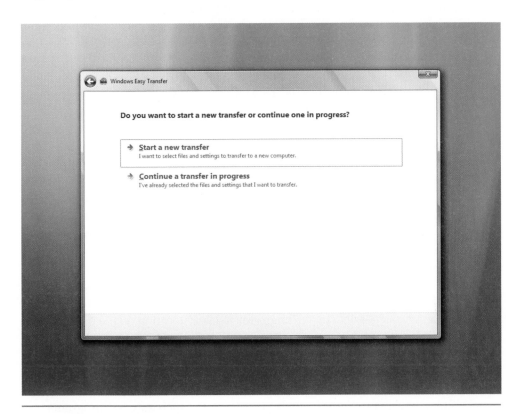

• **Figure 5.51** Start a new transfer or continue one?

you get passwords properly in place and test the security of the new system, you can't consider that system secure. Second, remove data remnants from hard drives that you store or give to charity. Third, recycle the older equipment; don't throw it in the trash. PC recyclers go through a process of deconstructing hardware, breaking system units, keyboards, printers, and even monitors into their basic plastics, metals, and glass for reuse.

The easiest way for someone to compromise or access sensitive data is to simply walk up and take it when you're not looking. This is especially true when you are in the process of copying information to a new, unprotected system. Don't set a copy to run while you go out to lunch, but rather be there to supervise and remove any remnant data that might still reside on any mass storage devices, especially hard drives.

Data Destruction

You might think that, as easy as it seems to be to lose data, you could readily get rid of data if you tried. That's not the case with flash memory or magnetic media, though, such as hard drives. When you delete something in Windows, or even empty the Recycle Bin, the "deleted" data remains on your storage device until new data overwrites it, or replaces it. (This "deleted" data is also what you see as free space in Windows.) This can be a big security hole when you dispose of a drive.

Cleaning a drive completely is very difficult. You can either physically destroy the hard drive or *sanitize* it using a software utility. Physical destruction isn't complicated—you bust up the drive into tiny little bits. Tools to accomplish this include drive shredders, drills, electromagnets, and degaussing tools (which reduce or remove the magnetic fields that store data on HDDs). Keep in mind that, as hard drives advance and pack more data into smaller spaces, you'll need to break the hard drive into smaller pieces to prevent anyone from recovering your data.

Sanitizing your drive means that the hard drive will still function once the data has been destroyed. There are several more or less effective ways to do this.

The CompTIA A+ 220-802 exam wants you to know the difference between a standard format and a *low-level format*. You already learned about standard formatting back in Chapter 4, so how is low-level formatting different? With older drives (pre-1990s), low-level formatting would create the physical marks on the disk surface so that the drive knew where to store data; in the process, it erases the data from the drive. This was initially done at the factory, but utilities existed to repeat this operation later. As drives became more complex, hard drive manufacturers disabled the ability to perform low-level formats outside the factory.

Today, the term "low-level formatting" is often used to describe a *zero-fill* or *overwrite* operation. This process returns the drive to a state as close to like-new as possible by writing zeros to every location on the disk.

You can also use a *drive wiping* utility to erase any old, deleted data that hasn't been overwritten yet. Simply put, this overwrites the free space on your drive with junk data that is more difficult to restore. Piriform's CCleaner is a data sanitizing utility that can erase your Web browsing history, erase your recent activity in Windows (such as what programs you ran), and even scrub your hard drive's free space to make deleted file unrecoverable (see Figure 5.52).

● **Figure 5.52** Piriform's CCleaner showing files to be removed

Recycle

An important and relatively easy way to be an environmentally conscious computer user is to *recycle*. Recycling products such as paper and printer cartridges not only keeps them out of overcrowded landfills, but also ensures that the more toxic products are disposed of in the right way. Safely disposing of hardware containing hazardous materials, such as computer monitors, protects both people and the environment.

Anyone who's ever tried to sell a computer more than three or four years old learns a hard lesson: they're not worth much, if anything at all. It's a real temptation to take that old computer and just toss it in the garbage, but never do that!

First of all, many parts of your computer—such as your computer monitor—contain hazardous materials that pollute the environment. Luckily, thousands of companies now specialize in computer recycling and will gladly accept your old computer. If you have enough computers, they might even pick them up. If you can't find a recycler, call your local municipality's waste authority to see where to drop off your system.

An even better alternative for your old computer is donation. Many organizations actively look for old computers to refurbish and to donate to schools and other organizations. Just keep in mind that the computer can be too old—not even a school wants a computer more than five or six years old.

No Installation Is Perfect

Even when the installation seems smooth, issues may slowly surface, especially in the case of upgrades. Be prepared to reinstall applications or deal with new functions that were absent in the previous OS. If things really fall apart, you can go back to the previous OS or, if you have an OEM computer (one built by, for example, Dell or HP instead of by you), your computer likely came with either a special recovery partition on its hard drive or a set of recovery discs that you can utilize to restore your operating system to its factory settings. You usually invoke a system recovery by hitting a certain key during boot-up—usually F10 or F11—and then following a set of prompts.

The procedures I've laid out in this chapter may seem like a lot of work—how bad could it be to grab an installation disc, fling a copy of Windows onto a system, and, as the saying goes, let the chips fall where they may? Plenty bad, is how bad. Not only is understanding these procedures important for the CompTIA A+ 220-802 exam; these procedures can also save your, ah, hide, once you're a working PC tech and you're tasked to install the latest version of Windows on the boss's new computer!

Chapter 5 Review

■ Chapter Summary

After reading this chapter and completing the exercises, you should understand the following about installing and upgrading Windows.

Identify and implement preinstallation tasks

- Identify hardware requirements, making sure your computer meets the recommended minimums for CPU, RAM, free hard disk space, video adapter, display, and other components. Check the Windows Compatibility Center at the Microsoft Web site to verify that the Windows version you're installing supports the hardware and application software you will run.

- A clean installation means your installation ignores a previous installation of Windows, wiping out the old version as the new version of Windows installs. You must reinstall all applications and reconfigure user preferences. In an upgrade installation, the new OS is installed in the directory where the old OS was located. The new OS retains the hardware and software settings of the old OS, including user preferences. Before you upgrade, back up any data that the user has saved on the local hard drive.

- Use the most advanced file system your version of Windows supports unless you are planning a multiboot configuration. Windows Vista/7 will not multiboot with another OS on the same partition.

Install and upgrade Windows XP, Windows Vista, and Windows 7

- To install Windows XP from the CD, you must boot directly to the optical drive. If this isn't possible, you can create a set of six setup boot floppy disks.

- You can install Windows Vista/7 from a DVD, a USB drive, specially ordered CD-ROMs, over a network, or by using a disc image.

- During installation, you will be prompted for registration information, including your name, address, and other details. Registration is optional.

- Designed to prevent a Windows license from being used for more than one PC, Microsoft Product Activation (MPA) is *mandatory* within 30 days of installing Windows XP, Vista, or 7, or the operating system will be disabled. You can activate the OS by using an Internet connection or by calling Microsoft. You give Microsoft an installation code—a 50-digit value that identifies your key hardware components—and Microsoft gives you a 42-digit product activation code.

- To do a clean installation of Windows XP, boot the computer to the Windows installation disc, which will copy files to your hard drive. Remove the disc. The system reboots, and Windows loads system devices and displays the Welcome to Setup screen. When prompted, accept the End User License Agreement (EULA). If necessary, create a new partition (default size or smaller). After you select the partition where Windows should be installed and the file system to use (NTFS is recommended), Setup copies files to the Windows folder and appropriate subfolders. Several reboots later and you're good to go.

- Installing Windows Vista/7 is very different from installing XP, but most of the concepts are the same. You still boot the computer from the installation disc, accept a EULA, partition your system drive, and enter a product key. You just do all those things in a different order and by using a graphical user interface instead of a primitive text mode.

- You can automate the installation process through scripted installations and disk cloning. Windows XP can use Setup Manager to help you create an answer file that contains all of the answers to the installation questions, such as computer name, locale, screen resolution, and so on. Windows Vista/7 comes with the Automated Installation Kit (AIK) that you can use to create an answer file. It's a substantially more complex tool than the older Setup Manager.

- With disc cloning, you simply take an existing PC and make a full copy of the drive, including all data, software, and configuration files. You can then transfer that copy to as many machines as you like, essentially creating clones of the original machine.

Troubleshoot installation problems

- Although the installation process itself rarely fails, you may encounter an installation failure caused by something else. Text mode errors during a clean installation may range from "No Boot Device Present" (the startup disk is bad or CMOS is not set to look at the appropriate drive first), to "Drive C: does not contain a Valid FAT Partition" (there is no partition or a partition Windows cannot use), to insufficient space on the drive. If you get a "Not Ready Error on Optical Drive," you could have a damaged installation disc or a slow optical drive that needs to catch up. A stop error (Blue Screen of Death) after the reboot at the end of the text mode points to a hardware incompatibility problem.

- Graphical mode errors indicate a different set of problems than text mode errors. Windows Setup must be able to detect the computer type (especially the motherboard and BIOS) and install the correct hardware abstraction layer (HAL). You may get a hardware detection error if Windows Setup fails to detect a device. If it is a noncritical piece of hardware, you can work on this problem later. This error may be solved by finding the proper driver.

- Probably the most common XP installation problem is failure to read the compressed Windows OS distribution files called CAB files. Try copying these files to your local hard drive and running the Setup program from there.

- If the system locks up during installation, do *not* press CTRL-ALT-DEL or the Reset button to restart the installation. Instead, unplug the system and then turn it back on so Windows will recognize a partial installation and go to the Safe Recovery mode, where it can often complete the installation. A bad disc, optical drive, or hard drive can cause an installation lockup.

- During installation, Windows creates several log files. The two files of interest are setuplog.txt, which tracks the installation process (logging success and failures), and setupapi.log, which tracks each piece of hardware as it is installed and shows you the last device installed before Windows locked up.

Identify and implement post-installation tasks

- The first essential tasks post installation include updating Windows by applying patches you download from Microsoft and updating drivers for hardware to the latest and hopefully most stable versions.

- After updating, you can go through the process of restoring a user's files through the various backup utilities available or by using the Files and Settings Transfer Wizard (FSTW) or Windows Easy Transfer.

- When migrating data to a new computer, it's important to follow three principles: migrate in a secure environment, remove data remnants when disposing of hard drives, and recycle old equipment.

- Completely removing data from a hard drive is difficult. You can either physically destroy the drive or use disk utilities that wipe or overwrite any data on the drive.

- When getting rid of old computer parts, it's important to recycle or donate them. This is helpful not only to the environment, but also to the community.

■ Key Terms

CAB files *(194)*

clean installation *(162)*

disk cloning *(190)*

End User License Agreement (EULA) *(165)*

Files and Settings Transfer Wizard (FSTW) *(197)*

hardware abstraction layer (HAL) *(194)*

image deployment *(163)*

in-place upgrade *(162)*

log files *(195)*

Microsoft Product Activation (MPA) *(168)*

migration *(197)*

multiboot installation *(162)*

operating system (OS) *(158)*

patch *(196)*

product key *(174)*

registration *(168)*

remote network installation *(163)*

repair installation *(162)*

service pack *(196)*

Sysprep *(191)*

unattended installation *(163)*
Upgrade Advisor *(167)*
upgrade installation *(162)*

User State Migration Tool (USMT) *(200)*
Windows Easy Transfer *(200)*
Windows 7 Compatibility Center *(161)*

■ Key Term Quiz

Use the Key Terms list to complete the sentences that follow. Not all terms will be used.

1. If you do not complete the _____ within 30 days, Windows stops working.

2. If you have a new hard drive with nothing on it, you will likely choose to do a(n) _____.

3. A(n) _____ is a fix for a single problem with the OS, while a(n) _____ is a combination of fixes.

4. If you wish to have only one OS and keep the applications and configuration of the current system, you should choose to do a(n) _____ of the new OS.

5. Microsoft uses compressed _____ to distribute installation files.

6. The _____ is a list of hardware devices and services that are guaranteed to work on Windows 7.

7. During the Windows installation, you will need to agree to a legal document called the _____.

8. If you're not sure your system can support Windows, run the _____.

9. Windows tracks the installation progress with a set of text files called _____.

10. Windows XP, Vista, and 7 have tools for migrating user files and settings. The tool in Windows Vista and Windows 7 is called _____.

■ Multiple-Choice Quiz

1. Which of the following is an advantage of running Windows on NTFS as opposed to FAT32?

 A. Security

 B. Support for DOS applications

 C. Long filenames

 D. Network support

2. Ricardo's Windows XP installation has failed. What file should he check to see what files failed to copy?

 A. Install.log

 B. Setup.log

 C. Setup.txt

 D. Setuplog.txt

3. If you do not complete the activation process for Windows XP, Vista, or 7, what will happen to your computer?

 A. Nothing. Activation is optional.

 B. The computer will work fine for 30 days and then Windows will be disabled.

 C. Microsoft will not know how to contact you to provide upgrade information.

 D. You will have to use a floppy disk set to boot to Windows.

4. After you have completed a Windows installation and verified that the system starts and runs okay, what should you do next?

 A. Do nothing. You're through.

 B. Install *World of Warcraft* and enjoy.

 C. Install productivity applications and restore data.

 D. Install the latest service pack or updates along with any updated drivers.

5. If Windows locks up during the installation, what should you do?

 A. Press CTRL-ALT-DEL to restart the installation process.

 B. Push the Reset button to restart the installation process.

C. Press the ESC key to cancel the installation process.

D. Unplug the computer and restart the installation process after plugging it back in.

6. You can *upgrade* directly to Windows 7 Professional 64-bit from which of these operating system editions?

 A. Windows XP Professional

 B. Windows Vista Home Premium 64-bit

 C. Windows XP 64-bit

 D. Windows Vista Ultimate 32-bit

7. If you get an error message saying that the Setup program cannot read the CAB files, what should you do?

 A. Copy the CAB files from the Windows installation disc to your local hard drive and run the Setup program from there.

 B. Skip this step because the CAB files are not necessary to install Windows successfully.

 C. Go to the Microsoft Web site and download the latest version of the CAB File Wizard.

 D. Cancel the installation process and keep your old operating system because your hardware does not meet the minimum requirements.

8. If you receive a graphical mode error in a Windows XP installation saying that Windows failed to detect a noncritical piece of hardware, what should you do?

 A. You need to remove the hardware device or replace it with one that is compatible with the OS.

 B. You can probably solve the problem after the installation is complete by finding the proper driver.

 C. You will get a stop error and be unable to complete the installation process.

 D. You should reboot the computer and restart the installation.

9. A customer has a laptop with Windows Vista Ultimate installed on the C: drive, the only hard drive on the laptop. She has a copy of Windows 7 Home Premium and wants to try it, but doesn't want to lose the extra features of Vista Ultimate. What's the best solution?

A. Install Windows 7 normally. The two operating systems can be installed on the same partition.

B. Boot to the Windows Vista disc, delete the primary partition, and repartition the drive to have two primary partitions. Install Windows Vista on the C: partition. Install Windows 7 on the D: partition.

C. Run Disk Management and shrink the C: partition. Create a new primary partition. Install Windows 7 in the new partition.

D. She cannot dual boot Windows Vista and Windows 7 on the same drive.

10. If you are experiencing problems with Windows XP and wish to install Windows 7, what type of installation is required?

 A. Clean installation

 B. Upgrade installation

 C. Network installation

 D. Image deployment

11. Which of the following tools can help you more efficiently install multiple copies of Windows 7?

 A. Automated Installation Kit

 B. Windows Easy Transfer

 C. Upgrade Advisor

 D. Activation key

12. What should you do before upgrading your copy of Windows to the latest version? (Select two.)

 A. Download the latest patches and updates.

 B. Check the Windows Compatibility Center Web site.

 C. Back up your data.

 D. Check the setup log files.

13. When the text mode of Windows XP Setup completes and the computer reboots to continue in graphical mode, what must you enter to continue the installation?

 A. Activation key

 B. CPU ID

 C. Registration information

 D. Product key

14. The Norton Ghost software is most helpful with which method of installation?

 A. Clean installation

 B. Upgrade installation

 C. Network installation

 D. Image deployment

15. Which setting affects the way currency and math separators display?

 A. Currency

 B. Language

 C. Locale

 D. Date/Time

■ Essay Quiz

1. You've been tasked to teach some new hires how to do a rollout of the latest version of Windows. Write a short essay that outlines what the newbies need to know to upgrade ten machines. You can assume that the network roles, language, and locale settings will stay the same. Make an argument for a clean, upgrade, or multiboot installation.

2. The same group of newbies will need help with post-installation tasks, so write a second memo that tells them what to do after installing.

3. Your boss has decided to go higher-tech on you and wants the next rollout of ten Windows machines to be automatic, rather than have techs sit through the whole process. Select one of the three methods outlined in the chapter for automating the installation process and make a case for one over the other two.

4. Your boss decided to upgrade her computer from Windows XP to Windows 7 Professional, but Windows keeps crashing in the middle. Write a short note discussing what could be happening so you can walk her through the installation troubleshooting over the phone.

Lab Projects

• Lab Project 5.1

Get the latest version of Windows and install it on your PC. Determine whether you will need to perform a clean installation or can use the upgrade option. Remember to check the Windows Compatibility Center Web site to make sure your existing hardware and software will be compatible. Back up your data, too! After the installation finishes, run through the post-installation tasks outlined in the chapter. Did you run into any problems along the way?

• Lab Project 5.2

On a non-essential PC, try upgrading from Windows XP to Windows Vista to Windows 7. This isn't usually recommended, but see what sort of oddities you pick up along the way. Create a user account in Windows XP. Does it survive in Windows 7? Do your documents, photos, and other data remain in the same folders in each OS, or do they move? Experiment with different features in each version and see how things have changed.

Windows Under the Hood

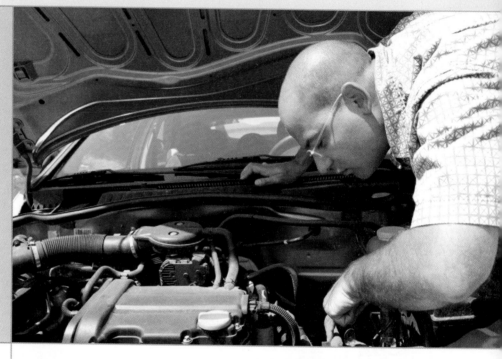

"Something's wrong with my CPU. My Register must be off because Windows is all blue and stuff and I can't log in. I need to get to my Internet. Please help."

—ANONYMOUS TECH CALL

In this chapter, you will learn how to

- **Work with the Registry**
- **Understand and observe in detail the Windows boot process**
- **Control processes and services**
- **Explore Windows tools for programmers**

W indows is powerful, easy to use, surprisingly idiot proof, backward compatible, and robust. A large part of Windows' power is hidden—*under the hood*—in programs and processes that Microsoft doesn't want normal users to see. For the record, I think hiding anything that normal users don't need to access is a smart idea; they can't break what they can't find. Technicians, on the other hand, need to not only understand these processes and programs but also know how to use them, configure them, and fix them when needed. Let's start with one of the most famous and most important items under the hood: the Registry.

■ Registry

The **Registry** is a huge database that stores everything about your PC, including information on all of the hardware in the PC, network information, user preferences, file types, and virtually anything else you might run into with Windows. Almost any form of configuration you do to a Windows system involves editing the Registry. Every version of Windows stores the numerous Registry files (called *hives*) in the \%SystemRoot%\System32\ config folder and each user account folder. Fortunately, you rarely have to access these massive files directly. Instead, you can use a set of relatively tech-friendly applications to edit the Registry.

The CompTIA A+ 220-802 certification exam does not expect you to memorize every aspect of the Windows Registry. You should, however, understand the basic components of the Registry, know how to edit the Registry manually, and know the best way to locate a particular setting.

Accessing the Registry

Before you look in the Registry, let's look at how you access the Registry directly by using a Registry editor. Once you know that, you can open the Registry on your machine and compare what you see to the examples in this chapter.

Before Windows XP, Windows came with two Registry editors: regedt32 .exe and the much older regedit.exe. You started either of these programs by going to a command prompt and typing its filename.

The reason for having two different Registry editors is long and boring, and explaining it would require a very dull 15-minute monologue about how the Registry worked in Windows 9*x* and Windows NT. Suffice it to say that starting with Windows XP, Microsoft eliminated the entire two-Registry-editor nonsense by creating a new regedt32 that includes strong search functions. No longer are there two separate programs, but interestingly, entering either regedit or regedt32 at a command prompt (or in the Start | Run dialog box or Start | Search bar) brings up the same program, so feel free to use either program name. You may also dispense with calling the Registry Editor by its filename and use its proper title.

 You might see either regedit or regedt32 on the exam as the way to access the Registry Editor.

Registry Components

The Registry is organized in a tree structure similar to the folders in the PC. Once you open the Registry Editor in Windows, you will see five main subgroups, or **root keys**:

- HKEY_CLASSES_ROOT
- HKEY_CURRENT_USER
- HKEY_USERS
- HKEY_LOCAL_MACHINE
- HKEY_CURRENT_CONFIG

• **Figure 6.1** Typical Registry root keys, subkeys, and values

Try opening one of these root keys by clicking on the plus sign to its left; note that more subkeys are listed underneath. A subkey also can have other subkeys, or *values*. Values define aspects of the subkey. Figure 6.1 shows an example of a subkey with some values. Notice that the Registry Editor shows only keys—root keys and subkeys—on the left and values on the right. Each of the root keys has a specific function, so let's take a look at them individually.

HKEY_CLASSES_ROOT

This root key defines the standard *class objects* used by Windows. A class object is a named group of functions that defines what you can do with the object it represents. Pretty much everything that has to do with files on the system is defined by a class object. For example, the Registry uses two class objects to define the popular MP3 sound file.

If you search my computer's Registry for the .PDF file extension, you will find a class object that associates the .PDF file extension with the name "FoxitReader.Document" (see Figure 6.2). Unless you use the popular Foxit Reader for your PDFs, you'll see a different program name, but the process still works.

So what are the properties of FoxitReader.Document? That's what the HKEY_CLASSES_ROOT root key is designed to handle. Search this section again for "FoxitReader.Document" (or whatever it said in the value for your PDF file) and look for a subkey called "open." This subkey tells the system everything it needs to know about a particular software item, from which program to use to open a file (its **file association**), to the type of icon used to show the file, to what to show when you right-click on that file type (see Figure 6.3).

Name	Type	Data
(Default)	REG_SZ	FoxitReader.Document
Content Type	REG_SZ	application/pdf

• **Figure 6.2** Association of .PDF with Foxit Reader

Name	Type	Data
ab (Default)	REG_SZ	"C:\Program Files\Foxit Software\Foxit Reader\Foxit Reader.exe" "%1"

Although it is possible to change most of these settings in the Registry Editor, the normal way is to choose more user-friendly methods. Select a data file, right-click on the data file, and click Properties. Click the Change

• **Figure 6.3** PDF file settings

button on the General tab to open the Open with dialog box. From there, you can select the program you want to use. If Windows knows of another program designed for that file type, it will show you these alternative programs. If not, you can simply browse for the program you want to use (see Figure 6.4).

HKEY_CURRENT_USER and HKEY_USERS

Windows is designed to support more than one user on the same PC, storing personalized information such as desktop colors, screensavers, and the contents of the desktop for every user that has an account on the system. HKEY_CURRENT_USER stores the current user settings, and

• **Figure 6.4** Changing the file association the easy way

HKEY_USERS stores all of the personalized information for all users on a PC. While you certainly can change items such as the screensaver here, the better way is to right-click on the desktop and select Properties.

HKEY_LOCAL_MACHINE

This root key contains all the data for a system's non-user-specific configurations. This encompasses every device and every program in your PC.

HKEY_CURRENT_CONFIG

If the values in HKEY_LOCAL_MACHINE have more than one option, such as two different monitors, this root key defines which one is currently being used. Because most people have only one type of monitor and similar equipment, this area is almost never touched.

Talkin' Registry

When describing a Registry setting, we use a simple nomenclature. For example, I recently moved my copy of *World of Warcraft* from my C: drive to my D: drive and was having problems when the program started. I went online to www.blizzard.com (home of Blizzard Entertainment, the folks who make *World of Warcraft*) and contacted the support staff, who gave me instructions to access the Registry and make this change:

> "Go to HKLM\SOFTWARE\Blizzard Technologies\World of Warcraft and change the GamePath object and the InstallPath object to reflect the new drive letter of your new WoW location."

To do so, I fired up regedit. Using this nomenclature, I was able to find the location of these Registry settings. Figure 6.5 shows this location. Compare this image to the path described in the instructions from Blizzard. Note that HKEY_LOCAL_MACHINE is abbreviated as HKLM. You will see this abbreviation on the exam!

To describe the location of a specific Registry value, like where the Blizzard tech told me to go, requires a little bit of repetition. To wit, in the previous example, World of Warcraft is a subkey to Blizzard Technologies, which is in turn a subkey to the root key HKLM. The World of Warcraft subkey has four values. All keys have the (Default) value, so in this case the World of Warcraft subkey offers three functional values.

Values must have a defined type of data they store:

- **String value** These are the most flexible type of value and are very common. You can put any form of data in these.

- **Binary value** These values store nothing more than long strings of ones and zeros.

- **DWORD value** These values are like Binary values but are limited to exactly 32 bits.

- **QWORD value** These values are like Binary values but are limited to exactly 64 bits.

● **Figure 6.5** Editing the Registry to move World of Warcraft to a new drive

There are other types of values, but these four are used for 98 percent of all Registry entries.

Manual Registry Edits

There's little motivation for you to go into the Registry and make manual edits unless you've done some research that tells you to do so. When you do find yourself using the Registry Editor to access the Registry, you risk breaking things in Windows: applications might not start, utilities might not work, or worst of all, your computer might not boot. To prevent these problems, always make a backup of the Registry before you change anything. Once the backup is in a safe place (I like to use a thumb drive, personally), reboot the system to see if the changes you made had the desired result. If it worked, great. If not, you'll need to restore the old Registry settings using your backup. Let's watch this in action.

One of the more common manual Registry edits is to delete autostarting programs. I want to prevent three programs installed by my Logitech GamePanel keyboard and mouse from autostarting. The most common place for making this change is here:

HKLM\SOFTWARE\Microsoft\Windows\CurrentVersion\Run

Opening the Registry Editor and going to this subkey, you'll see something like Figure 6.6.

Before I delete these keys, I'm going to save a copy of my Registry. The Registry Editor's Export feature enables you to save either the full Registry or only a single root key or subkey (with all subkeys and values under it). Select Run from the left pane and then click File | Export. Save the subkey as a Registration file with the extension .reg. Be sure to put that file somewhere you'll remember. Should you need to restore that key, use the File |

• **Figure 6.6** Mike's Run subkey

Import command, or just right-click on the icon as shown in Figure 6.7 and click Merge.

Command-line Registry Editing Tools

Windows includes a couple of command-line tools to edit the Registry (plus a lot more in the PowerShell). The two that you might need on occasion are reg and regsrv32.

The reg command is a full Registry editing tool. You can view Registry keys and values, import and export some or all of a Registry, and even compare two different versions of a Registry. The tool is so powerful that it has multiple levels of help so you can tailor a command to accomplish very tight Registry edits. For example, typing **reg /?** brings up a list of 12 specific operations that you can search for help on, such as reg query /? and reg add /?.

The regsrv32 command, in contrast with reg, can modify the Registry in only one way, adding (or *registering*) dynamic link library (DLL) files as command components. For the scoop on what regsrv32 does, please see "Component Services" later in the chapter for a description of the graphical tool that does the same thing. Only the 32-bit versions of Windows have the regsrv32 command, by the way.

• **Figure 6.7** Merging keys from a backup file

If the command-line interface is new to you, you might want to flag this section of Chapter 6 and skip it for now, then return to it after reading about the command line and how it works in Chapter 9.

■ The Boot Process

The Windows installation creates a number of specific files and folders that the OS needs to run a PC. Some of these files and folders are directly on the root of the C: drive; others can be elsewhere. The best way to remember the locations of these files and folders and to know their importance to the OS is by looking at how they interact to boot the PC.

Booting Windows XP differs dramatically from booting Windows Vista/7. Windows XP was the last Microsoft operating system to use a very old boot process known as ntldr (NT Loader). Windows Vista introduced

the far more flexible, complex, and powerful Windows Boot Manager (or **bootmgr**), which Windows 7 also uses. The great difference between these two boot managers requires us to look at both in more depth.

The Windows XP Boot Process

Windows XP distinguishes between the files that start the operating system (called the *system files*) and the rest of the operating system files (by default in the \Windows folders). The system files (memorize these!) consist of three required files: ntldr, boot.ini, and ntdetect.com. If you're using a SCSI hard drive, there's a fourth file called ntbootdd.sys. The ntldr (pronounced *NT loader*) file begins the boot process.

You know from Chapter 4 that making a drive bootable requires an active, primary partition, right? Let's look at the process in a PC with a hard drive partitioned as C: and D:.

The CPU wakes up and runs the system BIOS, and then the BIOS sends out a routine that looks on the first bootable drive's partition table for a boot sector marked as active. This is usually the C: drive. The boot sector takes over from BIOS and reads the master file table (MFT) in the bootable partition. The MFT points to the location of the Windows XP system files. Windows XP calls the primary active partition the *system partition* or the *system volume* (if it's a dynamic disk).

We're almost booted, but to complete the process, we need to take a moment to learn about some more critical Windows XP files: the Windows boot files and the Windows system files. The Windows XP *boot files* consist of ntoskrnl.exe (the Windows kernel), the \Winnt\System32\Config\System file (which controls the loading of device drivers), and the device drivers. Although these files are the core of the Windows XP operating system, they are not capable of booting, or starting, the system. For that feat, they require ntldr, ntdetect.com, and boot.ini—the system files.

The system files start the PC and then, at the end of that process, point the CPU to the location of the boot files. The CPU goes over and chats with ntoskrnl, and the GUI starts to load. The operating system is then up and running, and you're able to do work.

The odd part about all of this is that Microsoft decided to make the OS files mobile. The Windows XP operating system files can reside on any partition or volume in the PC. The \Windows folder, for example, could very well be on drive D:, not drive C:. Whichever drive holds the core OS files is called the *boot partition* or *boot volume*. This can lead to a little confusion when you say the system files are on the C: drive and Windows is on the D: drive, but that's just the way it is. Luckily, the vast majority of Windows XP systems have the system partition and the boot partition both on the same big C: partition.

You know the general process now, so let's look more specifically at the makeup and function of the individual files involved in the boot process.

 To see these files, go into My Computer and open the C: drive. Go to Tools | Folder Options. Click *Show hidden files and folders*, uncheck the *Hide protected operating system files (Recommended)* option, and click OK. Now when you return to viewing the folder in My Computer, you will see certain critical files that Windows otherwise hides from you to prevent you from accidentally moving, deleting, or changing them in some unintended way.

ntldr

When the system boots up, the master boot record (MBR) or MFT on the hard drive starts the ntldr program. The **ntldr** program then launches Windows XP. To find the available OSs, the ntldr program must read the

boot.ini configuration file. To do so, it loads its own minimal file system, which enables it to read the boot.ini file off of the system partition.

boot.ini

The **boot.ini** file is a text file that lists the OSs available to ntldr and tells ntldr where to find the boot partition (where the OS is stored) for each of them. The boot.ini file has sections defined by headings enclosed in brackets. A basic boot.ini file in Windows XP looks like this:

```
[boot loader]
timeout=30
default=multi(0)disk(0)rdisk(0)partition(1)\WINDOWS
[operating systems]
multi(0)disk(0)rdisk(0)partition(1)\WINDOWS="Microsoft
Windows XP Professional" /fastdetect
```

A more complex boot.ini file may look like this:

```
[boot loader]
timeout=30
default=multi(0)disk(0)rdisk(0)partition(1)\WINDOWS
[operating systems]
multi(0)disk(0)rdisk(0)partition(1)\WINDOWS="Microsoft
Windows XP Professional" /fastdetect
multi(0)disk(0)rdisk(0)partition(1)\WINNT="Microsoft Windows
2000 Professional" /fastdetect
```

Such a boot.ini file would result in the boot menu that appears in Figure 6.8.

This crazy `multi(0)disk(0)rdisk(0)partition(1)` is an example of the Advanced RISC Computing (ARC) naming system. It's a system that's designed to enable your PC to boot Windows from any hard drive, including removable devices. Let's take a quick peek at each ARC setting to see how it works.

• **Figure 6.8** Boot loader in Windows XP showing dual-boot configuration

`Multi(x)` is the number of the adapter and always starts with 0. The adapter is determined by the boot order you set in your CMOS setting. For example, if you have one PATA controller and one SATA controller, and you set the system to boot first from the PATA controller, any drive on that controller will get the value `multi(0)` placed in its ARC format. Any SATA drive will get `multi(1)`.

`Disk(x)` is only used for SCSI drives, but the value is required in the ARC format, so with ATA systems it's always set to `disk(0)`.

`Rdisk(x)` specifies the number of the disk on the adapter. On a PATA drive, the master is `rdisk(0)` and the slave is `rdisk(1)`. On SATA drives, the order is usually based on the number of the SATA connection printed on the motherboard, though some systems allow you to change this in CMOS.

`Partition(x)` is the number of the partition or logical drive in an extended partition. The numbering starts at 1, so the first partition is `partition(1)`, the second is `partition(2)`, and so on.

`\WINDOWS` is the name of the folder that holds the boot files. This is important to appreciate! The ARC format looks at the folder, so there's no problem running different editions of Windows XP on a single partition. You can simply install them in different folders. Of course, you have other limitations, such as file system type, but in general, multibooting with Windows is pretty easy. Better yet, this is all handled during the installation process.

> You can't boot multiple installations of Windows Vista or Windows 7 from a single partition because their setup programs don't allow you to choose the installation directory.

ARC format can get far more complicated. SCSI drives get a slightly different ARC format. For example, if you installed Windows on a SCSI drive, you might see this ARC setting in your boot.ini file:

```
scsi(0)disk(1)rdisk(0)partition(1)
```

If you want to boot to a SCSI drive, Windows adds a fourth file to your system files called ntbootdd.sys. This file only exists if you want to boot to a SCSI drive. Most people don't boot to a SCSI, so don't worry if you don't see this file with the other three system files.

On rare occasions, you might find yourself needing to edit the boot.ini file. Any text editor handily edits this file, but most of us prefer to edit boot.ini via the System Setup dialog box. In Windows XP, open the System applet from the Control Panel. Click the Advanced tab and then click the Startup and Recovery button. The boot.ini options show up at the top (see Figure 6.9).

Boot.ini has some interesting switches at the end of the ARC formats that give special instructions on how the operating system should boot. Sometimes Windows puts these in automatically, and sometimes you will add them manually for troubleshooting. Here are a few of the more common ones:

- **/bootlog** Tells Windows to create a log of the boot process and write it to a file called ntbtlog.txt.

- **/cmdcons** Tells Windows to start the Recovery Console (see Chapter 10 for a discussion of the Recovery Console).

• **Figure 6.9** The boot.ini options

- **/lastknowngood** Tells Windows to boot the Last Known Good set of files.

- **/noexecute** Newer CPUs come with Data Execute Protection (DEP) to prevent unruly programs from causing system lockups. The setting for this, /noexecute=optin, is the default on Windows systems.

ntdetect.com

If ntldr determines that you have chosen to start Windows XP, it boots the system into protected mode and then calls on **ntdetect.com** to detect the installed hardware on the system. Ntldr then refers to the boot.ini file to locate the Windows boot files.

Critical Boot Files

Naming all the critical boot files for Windows XP is akin to naming every muscle in the human body—completely possible, but time-consuming and without any real benefit. A few of the *most* important files certainly deserve a short mention.

Once ntldr finishes detections, it loads ntoskrnl.exe, hal.dll, some of the Registry, and some basic device drivers; then it passes control to the ntoskrnl.exe file. Ntoskrnl.exe completes the Registry loading, initializes all device drivers, and starts the winlogon.exe program, which displays the Windows XP logon screen (see Figure 6.10).

Take the time to memorize the primary boot files and the boot process for Windows XP. Most boot errors are easily repaired if you know which files are used for booting and in which order they load.

The Recovery Console can be used to restore damaged, corrupted, or missing ntldr and ntdetect.com files from the Windows XP installation disc.

• **Figure 6.10** Where do you want to go today?

In Windows Vista, bootmgr resides in the root directory of the boot drive. Windows 7, however, keeps bootmgr in the special 100-MB system partition you learned about in Chapter 4. If you are using a UEFI system, the helpfully named EFI system partition contains a special version of bootmgr called bootmgr.efi.

The Windows Vista/7 Boot Process

Windows Vista and Windows 7 have a very different boot process than previous versions of Windows. For one thing, Vista/7 supports both BIOS and UEFI, whereas older versions of Windows did not, so things are a bit more complex right off the bat. So not only is there a totally new boot process, this newer Windows Vista/7 boot process varies between two slightly different boot processes: one for systems using BIOS and one for systems with UEFI.

The very first thing that happens when you power on a system with Vista/7 is that either the BIOS or the UEFI starts up. The difference between BIOS and UEFI systems is in what happens next.

- In a BIOS-based system, the BIOS uses its boot order to scan a hard drive for a master boot record (MBR). The MBR holds a small bit of file system boot code that scans the partition table for the system partition and then loads its boot sector. The boot sector in turn contains code that does nothing but point the boot process toward a file called bootmgr (pronounced *Boot Manager*, or "boot mugger" if you're trying to make nerds laugh).

- In a UEFI system, on the other hand, neither the MBR/GUID partition table (GPT) nor the file system boot code is run, and UEFI simply loads bootmgr directly.

If you've ever run a dual-boot system with Vista or 7 as one of the operating systems, you're probably already somewhat familiar with bootmgr; one of its jobs is displaying that "Which operating system do you want to load?" screen and then loading the appropriate operating system. When bootmgr starts, it reads data from a **Boot Configuration Data (BCD)** file that contains information about the various operating systems installed on the system as well as instructions for how to actually load (bootstrap) them. Once an operating system is selected (or immediately if only one is present), bootmgr loads a program called winload.exe, which readies your system to load the operating system kernel itself rather like the way you clean up your house before Aunt Edna comes to visit. It does this by loading into memory the hardware abstraction layer, the system Registry, and the drivers for any boot devices before the operating system itself takes over.

Once the operating system process (called ntoskrnl.exe) takes over, it loads up all of the various processes and systems that comprise Windows, the Windows logo comes up, and you're happily computing, completely oblivious to all of the complex electronic communication that just took place inside your computer.

Tech Tip

Bootmgr Is Missing!

If you use Windows Vista/7 long enough, you may encounter an error message saying that Windows cannot boot because bootmgr is missing. This message is generated when the boot sector code is unable to locate bootmgr, which can be caused by file system corruption, a botched installation, or viruses.

 Unlike Windows XP, the boot files and the system files must all reside on the same partition in Vista/7.

 The BCD file replaces the boot.ini file used in previous operating systems and can be altered by using the command-line tool bcdedit.exe.

Processes and Services and Threads, Oh My!

In order to do work, CPUs run threads—bits of programs that are fed into the CPU. Let's see how all of this looks from Windows' point of view.

In Windows, programs are executable files waiting on a mass storage device. When you start a program, Windows loads it into RAM as a process. Once there, the CPU reads the process and the process tells the CPU which chunks of code to run. Dealing with processes in their many forms is a big part of understanding what's happening "under the hood."

Windows is a multitasking operating system, running lots of processes simultaneously. Many of these processes appear in a window (or full screen) when you open them and end when you close that window. These processes are called applications. There's also an entire class of processes that, due to the nature of their job, don't require a window of any form. These processes run invisibly in the background, providing a large number of necessary support roles. Collectively, these are called *services*. Let's look at applications, services, and processes and the tools we use to control them.

 For the purposes of the CompTIA A+ 220-802 exam, I'm simplifying things a little, but know that processes, services, and threads can get a lot more complicated.

 All versions of Windows use services.

Task Manager

The Windows **Task Manager** is the one-stop-shop for anything you need to do with applications, processes, and, if you're using Windows Vista or Windows 7, services (see Figure 6.11). The quick way to open the Task Manager

• **Figure 6.11** Task Manager in Windows 7

• **Figure 6.12** Task Manager in Windows XP

is to press CTRL-SHIFT-ESC. There are two other ways to open the Task Manager that you might see on the CompTIA A+ 220-802 exam: go to Start | Run or Start | Search, type **taskmgr**, and press ENTER; or press CTRL-ALT-DELETE and select Task Manager.

If you're running Windows XP, the Task Manager is similar (see Figure 6.12) but lacks a few handy features offered in Windows Vista and Windows 7's Task Manager. I'll cover these differences in this section.

Applications

The **Applications** tab shows all the running applications on your system. If you're having trouble getting an application to close normally, this is the place to go. To force an application to shut down, select the naughty application and click End Task, or right-click on the application and select End Task from the context menu. Be careful when using this feature! There is no "Are you sure?" prompt and it's easy to accidently close the wrong application.

There are two other handy buttons on the Applications tab:

- Switch To enables you to bring any program to the front (very handy when you have a large number of applications running).

- New Task is a lifesaver of a tool, enabling you to start any program you wish, as long as you know the filename of the program. One of the most common uses for New Task is to restart your desktop in Windows XP. If your desktop crashes, the Task Manager usually still works. Click on New Task and type in **explorer**. Sadly, this doesn't work in Windows Vista or Windows 7, but New Task is still a handy tool to start programs, especially if you don't have access to the Start menu.

Remember that everything is a process, so every application is also listed in the Processes tab. Right-click on an application and select Go To Process to open the Processes tab and see which process is running the application.

Processes

If you really want to tap the power of the Task Manager, you need to click on the **Processes** tab (see Figure 6.13). Since everything is a process, and the Processes tab shows you every running process, this is the one place that enables you to see everything running on your computer.

All processes have certain common features that you should recognize:

- A process is named after its executable file, which usually ends in .exe but can also end with other extensions.

- All processes have a user name to identify who started the process. A process started by Windows has the user name System.

- All processes have a Process Identifier (PID). To identify a process, you use the PID, not the process name. The Task Manager doesn't show the PID by default. Click on View | Select Columns and select the PID (Process Identifier) checkbox to see the PIDs (see Figure 6.14).

The Task Manager provides important information about processes. It shows the amount of CPU time (percentage) and the amount of RAM (in kilobytes) the process is using. Most processes also provide a description to help you understand what the process is doing, although you'll probably need to scroll right to see this information (see Figure 6.15).

You'll notice that almost all of the processes have the same user name. By default, the Task Manager shows only processes associated with the current user. Click on *Show processes from all users* to see every process on the system (see Figure 6.16). Note that some

Figure 6.13 Processes tab in Windows 7

Figure 6.14 Processes tab showing the PID column in Windows 7

Figure 6.15 Processes details in Windows 7

Image Name	PID	User Name	CPU	Working Set (Memo...	Description
System Idle Process	0	SYSTEM	99	24 K	Percentage of time the processor is idle
System	4	SYSTEM	00	5,384 K	NT Kernel & System
svchost.exe	152	SYSTEM	00	192,852 K	Host Process for Windows Services
smss.exe	320	SYSTEM	00	1,404 K	Windows Session Manager
svchost.exe	360	SYSTEM	00	49,792 K	Host Process for Windows Services
csrss.exe	416	SYSTEM	00	5,976 K	Client Server Runtime Process
wininit.exe	488	SYSTEM	00	4,932 K	Windows Start-Up Application
csrss.exe	512	SYSTEM	00	19,824 K	Client Server Runtime Process
aaHMSvc.exe *32	516	SYSTEM	00	5,600 K	aaHMSvc
services.exe	544	SYSTEM	00	13,208 K	Services and Controller app
lsass.exe	560	SYSTEM	00	17,092 K	Local Security Authority Process
lsm.exe	568	SYSTEM	00	4,872 K	Local Session Manager Service
svchost.exe	704	SYSTEM	00	11,168 K	Host Process for Windows Services
winlogon.exe	756	SYSTEM	00	8,608 K	Windows Logon Application
svchost.exe	812	NETWORK SERVICE	00	10,216 K	Host Process for Windows Services
MsMpEng.exe	876	SYSTEM	00	75,580 K	Antimalware Service Executable
atiesrxx.exe	952	SYSTEM	00	5,012 K	AMD External Events Service Module
svchost.exe	996	LOCAL SERVICE	00	22,784 K	Host Process for Windows Services
svchost.exe	1036	LOCAL SERVICE	00	14,072 K	Host Process for Windows Services
plugin-container.exe *32	1108	michaels	00	15,228 K	Plugin Container for Firefox
svchost.exe	1220	NETWORK SERVICE	00	19,956 K	Host Process for Windows Services
xnview.exe *32	1276	michaels	00	62,996 K	XnView for Windows
PresentationFontCache.exe	1284	LOCAL SERVICE	00	49,264 K	PresentationFontCache.exe
ngserver.exe *32	1328	SYSTEM	00	13,612 K	Symantec Ghost Configuration Server
mDNSResponder.exe	1340	SYSTEM	00	6,592 K	Bonjour Service
sqlservr.exe	1376	NETWORK SERVICE	00	13,636 K	SQL Server Windows NT - 64 Bit

☑ Show processes from all users

End Process

Processes: 82 CPU Usage: 0% Physical Memory: 48%

• **Figure 6.16** Processes from all users in Windows 7

of the processes show a user name of Local Service or Network Service. As you might imagine, those are services!

Now that you understand the basics, let's watch the Task Manager do its magic with processes. If you select a process and click the End Process button, you'll instantly end that process. If the process is an application, that application will close.

Closing processes is important, but to take it even further, you need to select a process and right-click on it to see a number of options. If you select a process that's an application (the name of the process is a strong clue—winword.exe is Microsoft Word), you see something like Figure 6.17.

Open File Location takes you to wherever the file is located. This is extremely helpful when you're looking at a mysterious process and are trying to find out what it's doing on your computer.

You already know what End Process does. End Process Tree is extremely important but also complex, so let's save that for later.

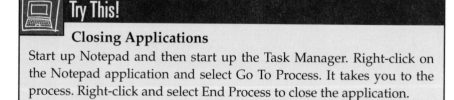

Try This!

Closing Applications

Start up Notepad and then start up the Task Manager. Right-click on the Notepad application and select Go To Process. It takes you to the process. Right-click and select End Process to close the application.

Mike Meyer's CompTIA A+ Guide to 802: Managing and Troubleshooting PCs

Debug is grayed out unless you're running a Windows debugger program—see the explanation of dump files below.

UAC Virtualization gives older programs that weren't written to avoid accessing protected folders a way to do so by making a fake protected folder. In most cases, Windows handles this automatically, but there are rare cases where you'll need to set this manually. Again, you won't do this on your own—you'll be on the phone with the tech support for some software company and they'll tell you how to use UAC Virtualization.

Dump files show the status of the program at the moment you click Create Dump File. Programmers use special debugging utilities to read dump files to analyze problems with programs. The only time you'd ever use this option is if you're having problems with a program and the support people ask you to make a dump file.

Set Priority gives you the ability to devote more or less processor time to a process (see Figure 6.18). This is very handy when you have a process that is slowing down your machine or if you have a process that is running too slowly and you want to speed it up.

Messing with priorities can get complicated quickly. The best idea here is to just increase the priority of a single

• **Figure 6.17** Processes detail of the right-click

Setting any single process to Realtime priority will often bring the entire system to a crawl as no other process gets much CPU time—avoid Realtime priority.

• **Figure 6.18** Process priority

Figure 6.19 Turning off affinity to the first two cores

process you need to run faster or reduce the priority of a single process you need to run slower, without touching any other priorities.

Set Affinity is a handy way to give a process more CPU time without messing with priorities. Windows tends to use your first two CPUs more heavily than the others. If you have more than two cores on your CPU and you have a single process that uses a lot of CPU time, try unchecking the affinity checkbox for the first two cores to force the process to only use your other cores (see Figure 6.19).

The Properties option isn't too exciting. It's the same as if you were to right-click on the executable file and select Properties in Windows Explorer. Go to Service(s) will move you to the Services tab of the Task Manager, showing you any and all services associated with the process. Depending on the process, it could use no services or multiple services. This is a great tool for those "Program won't start because associated services aren't running" situations. Figure 6.20 shows what happens when you use Go to Service(s) for a process called lsass.exe.

Let's get back to the End Process Tree option. It's very common for a single process to be dependent on other processes (or for a process to start other processes). This creates a tree of dependencies. Sadly, the Task Manager doesn't give you any clue as to what processes depend on other processes,

Figure 6.20 Services associated with the lsass.exe process

Mike Meyer's CompTIA A+ Guide to 802: Managing and Troubleshooting PCs

but it still gives you the option to End Process Tree, which ends not only the process, but any process it depends on. At first glance, this is scary since it's very common for many processes to depend on one important process. Microsoft makes this less scary, as it will not let you kill a process tree for the most important system processes.

Even so, it would be nice to actually *see* what processes you're about to kill, wouldn't it? That's when the popular (and free) Process Explorer, written by Mark Russinovitch, is your go-to tool (see Figure 6.21)

Think of Process Explorer as the Task Manager on steroids. It's very powerful, and a lot of techs use it instead of the Task Manager. It isn't on the CompTIA A+ 220-802 exam, but it should be. Instead of just listing all of the processes, Process Explorer uses a tree structure so you can see all the dependencies.

Services

If you've got Windows Vista or Windows 7, you can use the **Services** tab in the Task Manager to work with services directly (see Figure 6.22). Here, services can be stopped or started, and you can go to the associated process.

The best way to see services in action is to use the Services Control Panel applet. To open it, click on the Services button at the bottom of the Services tab in the Task Manager or go to Control Panel | Administrative Tools | Services. Figure 6.23 shows the Services applet running in Windows 7.

Look closely at Figure 6.23. Each line in this applet is an individual service. Services don't have their own window, so you use the Services applet to start, stop, and configure them. You can see if a service is running by reading the Status column. To configure a service, right-click on the service name. The context menu enables you to start, stop, pause, resume, or restart

The Windows XP Task Manager lacks all of these context menu options except for End Process, End Process Tree, Debug, and Set Priority.

Process Explorer does so much more than just show a tree structure. Download a copy and play with it. You'll see why it's so popular.

 You can open the Services applet from the Start | Run dialog box or Start | Search bar. Type **services.msc** and press ENTER.

• **Figure 6.21** Process Explorer

Figure 6.22 Services tab in Task Manager

You can start or stop any service at a command prompt by typing **net start** (or **stop**) *service name*.

any service. Click on Properties to see a dialog box similar to the one shown in Figure 6.24.

Of the four tabs you see in the Properties dialog box, General and Recovery are by far the most used. The General tab provides the name of the service, describes the service, and enables you to stop, start, pause, or resume the service. You can also define how the service starts: Manual (you go here to start it), Automatic (starts at beginning of Windows boot), Disabled (prevents the service from starting in any fashion), or Automatic (delayed start), which starts the service at boot but only after pretty much everything else has started.

Performance

For optimization purposes, the Task Manager is a great tool for investigating how hard your RAM and CPU are working at any given moment and why. Click the **Performance** tab to reveal a handy screen with the most commonly used information: CPU usage, available physical memory, size of the disk cache, commit charge (memory for programs), and kernel memory (memory used by Windows). Figure 6.25 shows a system with an eight-core processor, which is why you see eight graphs under CPU Usage History. A system with a single-core processor would have a single screen.

Figure 6.23 Services applet

● **Figure 6.24** Service Properties dialog box

● **Figure 6.25** Task Manager Performance tab

Image Name	User Name	CPU	Working Set (Memo...
blender.exe	michaels	93	262,908 K
vmware.exe *32	michaels	00	75,612 K
vmware-vmx.exe		00	711,328 K
MOM.exe	michaels	00	4,744 K
vmware-unity-helper.exe *32	michaels	00	26,520 K
taskmgr.exe	michaels	00	30,364 K

• **Figure 6.26** CPU usage

Not only does the Task Manager tell you how much CPU and RAM usage is taking place, it also tells you what program is using those resources. Let's say your system is running slowly. You open the Task Manager and see that your CPU usage is at 100 percent. You then click on the Processes tab to see all the processes running on your system. Click on the CPU column heading to sort all processes by CPU usage to see who's hogging the CPU (see Figure 6.26). If necessary, shut down the program or change its priority to fix the issue.

Networking and Users

The other two tabs in the Task Manager, Networking and Users, enable you to see network use at a glance and see which users' accounts are currently logged on to the local machine. The Networking tab is a good first spot to look if you think the computer is running slowly on the network. If there's little activity displayed, then it's not traffic from your computer that's causing the slowdown, so you need to look elsewhere. Chapter 12 covers network troubleshooting in a lot more detail, so we'll leave the Networking tab alone for now.

The Users tab enables you to log off other users if you have the proper permissions. You can also log off from here. There's not much else to say, but since the CompTIA A+ 220-802 exam objectives want this tab used in a scenario, here's one hypothetical. Another user is still logged on and left a critical file open that you need to access. Logging the user off forces his or her applications to close and makes the file available. Of course, unsaved changes will be lost, so use caution here.

The tasklist and taskkill Commands

The two command-line utilities **tasklist** and taskkill enable you to work with tasks, similarly to what you can do with the Task Manager. The tasklist command enables you to view running processes on a local or remote system. Open up a command prompt and type **tasklist**. The following is a partial example of the output:

```
C:\Users\mike>tasklist
```

The CompTIA A+ 802 exam objectives mention a command-line utility called *tlist*. Tasklist replaced tlist back in Windows XP, but for some reason CompTIA included it anyway.

Image Name	PID	Session Name	Session#	Mem Usage
System Idle Process	0	Services	0	24 K
System	4	Services	0	940 K
smss.exe	268	Services	0	340 K
csrss.exe	372	Services	0	2,388 K
wininit.exe	444	Services	0	968 K
csrss.exe	452	Console	1	9,788 K
winlogon.exe	500	Console	1	2,420 K

```
services.exe          544 Services          0      4,536 K
svchost.exe           756 Services          0      4,320 K
MsMpEng.exe           828 Services          0     42,164 K
atiesrxx.exe          904 Services          0        824 K
notepad.exe          3932 Console           0      6,612 K
```

You can kill a process using the taskkill command. See the notepad.exe listing in the preceding tasklist output? You can kill the process using either the name or the PID, as shown here:

Performance Console

The Task Manager is good for identifying current problems, but what about problems that happen when you're not around? What if your system is always running at a CPU utilization of 20 percent—is that good or bad? Windows XP provides a tool called the **Performance console** that logs resource usage so you can track items such as CPU and RAM usage over time. Performance is an MMC console file, perfmon.msc, so you call it from Start | Run or through the Performance icon in Administrative Tools. Use either method to open the Performance console (see Figure 6.27). As you can see, there are two nodes, System Monitor and Performance Logs and Alerts.

Objects and Counters

To begin working with the Performance console, you need to understand two terms: object and counter. An **object** is a system component that is given

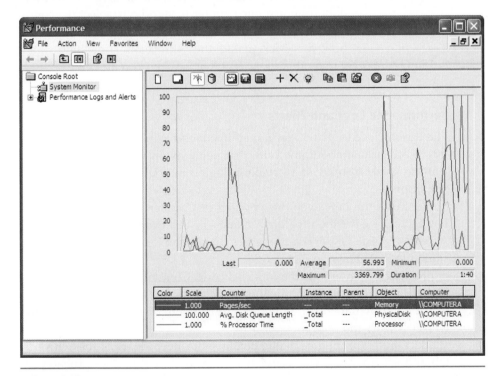

● **Figure 6.27** Performance console

• **Figure 6.28** Add Counters dialog box

a set of characteristics and can be managed by the operating system as a single entity. A **counter** tracks specific information about an object. For example, the Processor object has a counter, %Processor Time, that tracks the percentage of elapsed time the processor uses to execute a non-idle thread. Many counters can be associated with an object.

System Monitor

System Monitor gathers real-time data on objects such as memory, physical disk, processor, and network, and displays this data as a graph (line graph), histogram (bar graph), or simple report. When you first open the Performance console, System Monitor shows data in graph form. The data displayed is from the set of three counters listed below the chart. If you want to add counters, click the Add button (the one that looks like a plus sign) or press CTRL-I to open the Add Counters dialog box. Click the Performance object drop-down list and select one of the many different objects you can monitor. The Add Counters dialog box includes a helpful feature: you can select a counter and click the Explain button to learn about the counter, as shown in Figure 6.28. Try that now.

Even with just three counters selected, the graph can get a little busy. That's where one of my favorite System Monitor features shines. If you want the line of charted data from just one counter to stand out, select the counter in the list below the graph and then press CTRL-H. See how this trick makes the %Processor Time line stand out in Figure 6.29? Imagine how useful that is when you are monitoring a dozen counters.

Performance Logs and Alerts

The **Performance Logs and Alerts** snap-in enables Windows to create a written record of just about anything that happens on your system. Do you want to know if someone is trying to log on to your system when you're not around?

To create the new event log, right-click Counter Logs and select New Log Settings. Give the new log a name—in this example, "Unauthorized Accesses." Click OK, and a properties dialog box for the new log appears, similar to that shown in Figure 6.30.

To select counters for the log, click Add Counters and then select the *Use local computer counters* radio button. Select Server from the Performance object pull-down menu and then select Errors Logon from the list of counters; click Add and then click Close.

Back in the properties dialog box for your new log, click the Schedule tab and set up when you want this thing to start running—probably at the end of the workday today. Then select when it should stop logging—probably tomorrow morning when you start work. Click the Log Files tab to see where the log file will be saved—probably C:\PerfLogs—and make a

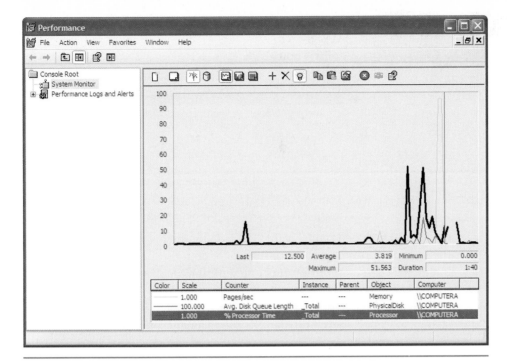

• **Figure 6.29** Pressing CTRL-H makes one set of data stand out.

• **Figure 6.30** Creating a new performance log

note of the filename. The filename will consist of the name you gave the log and a number. In this example I named the new performance log "Unauthorized Accesses," so the filename is Unauthorized Accesses_000001.blg.

When you come back in the morning, open the Performance console, select Performance Logs and Alerts, and then select Counter Logs. Your

Stopping the performance log

log should be listed on the right. The icon by the log name will be green if the log is still running or red if it has stopped. If it has not stopped, select it and click the Stop button (the one with the black square, circled in Figure 6.31).

To view the log, open the Performance console, select System Monitor, change to Report view, and load the file as a new source by using the log's properties dialog box.

Performance Tools in Windows Vista and Windows 7

Microsoft improved on the Performance console dramatically with Reliability and Performance Monitor in Windows Vista and yet again with Performance Monitor in Windows 7. **Reliability and Performance Monitor** still has a complete Performance console with all the objects and counters you see in Windows XP, but it adds an excellent Resource Overview, a Reliability Monitor tool, and a much more flexible way to use counters with Data Collector Sets and Reports. **Performance Monitor** in Windows 7 functions almost identically to Reliability and Performance Monitor in Windows Vista, but Microsoft pulled out the Reliability tool to make the remaining tool smaller and tighter.

You can open Reliability and Performance Monitor/Performance Monitor by starting the Performance Information and Tools applet in Control Panel. The initial screen is the *Rate and improve your computer's performance* screen (see Figure 6.32), which shows how your computer's hardware stacks up in the Windows Experience Index. Click the Advanced tools link in the left task area. Then click on Open Reliability and Performance Monitor or Open Performance Monitor, depending on the Windows version. You can also open the tool by going to Start | Search bar, typing **perfmon.msc**, and pressing ENTER.

Reliability and Performance Monitor in Windows Vista opens to a Resource Overview screen (see Figure 6.33). Think of the Resource Overview as an advanced Task Manager, giving details on CPU, hard drive, network, and memory usage.

When you click on one of the four bars, you get details on exactly which processes are using those resources—a powerful tool when you suspect a

The Windows Experience Index runs on a scale from 1.0 to 7.9 and gives you a pretty good gauge of the relative strengths and weaknesses of a system. The system in Figure 6.32, for example, has a CPU near the top of the chart (it's an Intel Core i7) and lots of fast RAM (8 GB), but a relatively modest hard drive. So the next obvious upgrade to this system would be to move from a platter-based drive to a solid-state drive. Disk performance would certainly jump dramatically.

Mike Meyer's CompTIA A+ Guide to 802: Managing and Troubleshooting PCs

• **Figure 6.32** Performance Information and Tools showing the computer's rating on the Windows Experience Index

• **Figure 6.33** Resource Overview in Windows Vista

The Reliability Monitor tool gives you an overview of how a PC has behaved over time, showing important events such as application or OS crashes. You can find the tool in Windows 7 as part of the Action Center Control Panel applet.

• **Figure 6.34** Network bar in Resource Overview

program might be hogging something! Figure 6.34 shows the Network bar opened to reveal the processes using the network and how much data each is sending.

Performance Monitor in Windows 7 opens to a more modest screen that displays some text about Performance Monitor and a System Summary

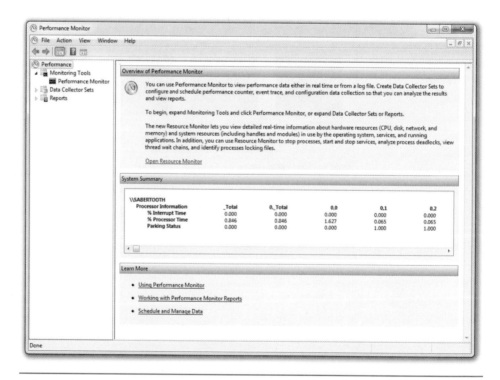

• **Figure 6.35** Initial Performance Monitor screen in Windows 7

(see Figure 6.35). You can get to the Overview screen by clicking the Open Resource Monitor link on the main screen. Aside from orienting the graphical screens on the right rather than on the top, the tool is the same as the Resource Overview in Windows Vista (see Figure 6.36).

The Performance Monitor option you can select under Monitoring Tools in either version of the OS is simply a re-creation of the Performance console and works as described earlier for Windows XP (see Figure 6.37). This is a great tool for quick checks on specific counters.

Microsoft included Data Collector Sets in Reliability and Performance Monitor, groupings of counters you can use to make reports. You can make your own Data Collector Sets (User Defined) or you

• **Figure 6.36** Resource Monitor displaying CPU usage

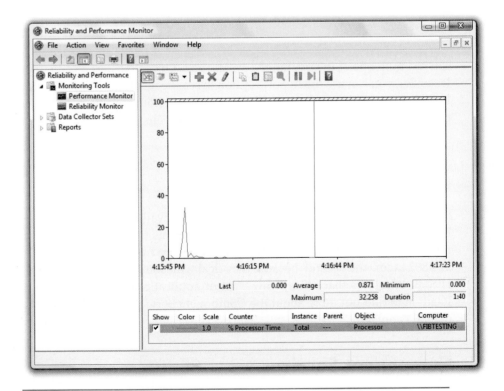

• **Figure 6.37** Reliability and Performance Monitor

● **Figure 6.38** Sample report

The CompTIA A+ 802 exam isn't going to ask too many detailed questions on either Performance Monitor or Reliability and Performance Monitor. That doesn't mean you can ignore these amazing tools! Make sure you understand that these tools give you the power to inspect anything happening on your system to help you diagnose problems.

can just grab one of the predefined system sets. Once you start a Data Collector Set, you can use the Reports option to see the results (see Figure 6.38). Data Collector Sets not only enable you to choose counter objects to track, but also enable you to schedule when you want them to run.

■ Tools for Programmers

Back in Chapter 2, I discussed many of the tools available under Administrative Tools in Control Panel. I left out two applets that I want to discuss now for two reasons: first, because they're covered on the CompTIA A+ 220-802 exam, and second, because they deal with some low-level functionality in Windows that affects how a lot of applications are programmed. Read on to find out more about the Component Services and Data Sources (ODBC) applets.

Component Services

To understand all that **Component Services** can do would require a huge amount of information—far greater than the scope of CompTIA's A+

220-802 exam. Simply put, as long as Windows has existed, Microsoft has come up with many tools (with names like COM, DCOM, and COM+) to enable programmers to share data objects (an element of programs) between applications on a single computer. Over time, this sharing was extended so that you could share objects between computers on a network.

In almost all cases, this object sharing doesn't require you to do anything more than install an application that uses these features. Component Services is there, however, for those very rare times when something's either wrong or a programmer needs you to make manual changes (see Figure 6.39). If you have a company that creates in-house or buys custom applications, there's a better than good chance that you'll be firing up Component Services and working with programmers, manually installing programs, and tweaking those programs to get them to work the way you wish. Professional, third-party applications (the kind you buy in stores) should automatically configure any of these programs during the installation process, making it extremely rare that you'll need to go into Component Services.

Every version of Windows has Component Services, but there's no ready-to-go icon in Windows XP or Windows Vista. You'll need to make a custom MMC and load Component Services from there.

Data Sources

One of the oldest and most common motivations to make networks is the idea of a number of computers accessing one or more shared databases. These computers might not all be running the same operating system, nor

• **Figure 6.39** Component Services in Windows 7

Chapter 6: Windows Under the Hood

will they always use the same application to access those databases. That's where Open Database Connectivity (ODBC) really shines. ODBC is a coding standard that enables programmers to write databases and the applications that use them in a way that they can query ODBC to see how to locate and access a database without any concern about what application or operating system is used.

Microsoft's tool to configure ODBC is called **ODBC Data Source Administrator** (see Figure 6.40). Data Source Administrator enables you to create and manage entries called Data Source Names (DSNs) that point ODBC to a database. DSNs are used by ODBC-aware applications to query ODBC to find their databases. Keep in mind that you'll rarely go into Data Source Administrator unless you're making your own shared databases.

• **Figure 6.40** Data Source Administrator in Windows 7

■ Chapter Summary

After reading this chapter and completing the exercises, you should understand the following about Windows under the hood.

Work with the Registry

■ The Registry is a huge database that stores everything about your PC, including information on all of the hardware in the PC, network information, user preferences, file types, and more. Registry files are stored in the \%SystemRoot%\System32\config folder.

■ To edit the Registry, you use regedt32 (or regedit), also known as the Registry Editor.

■ The Registry is organized in a tree structure similar to the folders on a PC. The five root keys of the Registry are HKEY_CLASSES_ROOT, HKEY_CURRENT_USER, HKEY_USERS, HKEY_LOCAL_MACHINE, and HKEY_CURRENT_CONFIG.

■ Root keys are divided into subkeys, which are divided into values. In the Registry Editor, keys are listed on the left and values are listed on the right.

■ The Registry Editor's export feature enables you to save either the full registry or only a single rootkey or subkey (with all subkeys and values under it).

Understand and observe in detail the Windows boot process

■ The Windows installation creates several files and folders that an OS needs to run a PC.

■ Each version of Windows boots differently. Windows XP was the last version of Windows to use the ntldr boot process. Windows Vista and Windows 7 boot using Windows Boot Manager (bootmgr).

■ Windows XP distinguishes between the files that start the OS (system files) and the rest of the OS files. The system files include ntldr (NT Loader), boot.ini, and ntdetect.com. If you boot from a SCSI hard drive, you also need ntbootdd.sys.

■ To boot Windows XP, the CPU wakes up and runs the system BIOS. BIOS looks for the first bootable drive's partition table and finds a boot sector

marked as active. The boot sector takes control from BIOS and reads the master file table (MFT). The MFT points to the Windows XP system files. The system files point to the boot files (which include ntoskrnl.exe, the \Winnt\System32\Config\System file, and the device drivers) and the GUI loads. The OS is then up and running and ready to work.

■ The Windows XP OS files can reside on any partition or volume in the PC.

■ Windows Vista and Windows 7 use a very different boot process than Windows XP. Windows Vista/7 supports both BIOS and UEFI; the process is slightly different between the two.

■ In a BIOS-based system, BIOS loads, and looks for the master boot record (MBR). The MBR scans for a system partition and loads the boot sector. The boot sector points to the Boot Manager (bootmgr) and Windows loads.

■ In a UEFI system, neither the MBR/GPT nor the file system boot code is run. UEFI simply loads Boot Manager directly.

■ In addition to booting Windows, Boot Manager is also responsible for controlling dual-boot systems. The Boot Configuration Data (BCD) file contains information about the various OSs installed on the system, along with instructions for how to load each of them.

Control processes and services

■ In Windows, programs are executable files waiting on a mass storage device. When you start a program, Windows loads it into RAM as a process. The CPU reads the process and the process tells the CPU which chunks of code to run.

■ The Windows Task Manager is the one-stop-shop for anything to do with applications, processes, and services (Windows Vista/7). To open the Task Manager, press CTRL-SHIFT-ESC or CTRL-ALT-DELETE and select Task Manager. Alternatively, go to Start | Run or Start | Search, type **taskmgr**, and press ENTER.

- The Applications tab shows all the running applications on your system. Here, you can force an unruly application to shut down. You can also switch to open applications, start a new task (open an application), or see the appropriate process for the application.

- The Processes tab lists all the running processes, including any running applications and services. The list of processes shows the name and the user who started the process. You can also display the Process Identifier (PID), which is how Windows refers to each process.

- From the Processes tab, you can end a process, find the executable associated with the process, debug, set UAC Virtualization, create a dump file, set priority and affinity, and see the associated services.

- The Task Manager will show you all the services on your computer, but for more options, you should use the Services applet in Administrative Tools. Here you can start, stop, and configure all of your services. You can also set if and when the service will load when you boot Windows.

- The Performance tab shows you CPU usage, memory usage, and the size of the disk cache. You can switch to the Processes tab to see which process is using your resources.

- The Users tab enables you to log off your own account or another user's account.

- The tasklist command is the command-line version of the Task Manager. Here, you can view and end processes by name or PID.

- The Performance console enables you to create logs that track CPU, memory, and other resource usages over time. To track these resources, you must set up objects (the resources you wish to track) and counters (the measurements used to track the objects).

- System Monitor gathers real-time data on objects such as memory, physical disk, processor, and network, and displays this data as a graph (line graph), histogram (bar graph), or simple report. Think of System Monitor as a more detailed, customizable Task Manager.

- The Performance Logs and Alerts snap-in enables Windows to create a written record of just about anything that happens on your system.

- Reliability and Performance Monitor in Windows Vista and Performance Monitor in Windows 7 improve on Windows XP's Performance console. They include the older console, but add the Resource Overview/Resource Monitor, Reliability Monitor (Vista only), and Data Collector Sets and Reports.

- Think of the Resource Overview/Resource Monitor as an advanced Task Manager, giving details on CPU, hard drive, network, and memory usage. When you click on one of the four bars, you get details on exactly which processes are using those resources—a powerful tool when you suspect a program might be hogging something.

- Microsoft included Data Collector Sets in Reliability and Performance Monitor/Performance Monitor, groupings of counters you can use to make reports. You can make your own Data Collector Sets (User Defined) or you can just grab one of the predefined system sets.

Explore Windows tools for programmers

- Component Services enables programmers to share data objects between applications on a single computer or over a network. Professional, third-party applications (the kind you buy in stores) should automatically configure any of these programs during the installation process, making it extremely rare that you'll need to go into Component Services.

- ODBC is a coding standard that enables programmers to write databases and the applications that use them in a way that they can query ODBC to see how to locate and access a database without any concern about what application or operating system is used. Microsoft's tool to configure ODBC is called Data Source Administrator. Data Source Administrator enables you to create and manage entries called Data Source Names (DSNs) that point ODBC to a database.

Key Terms

<div style="columns:2">

Applications *(222)*
Boot Configuration Data (BCD) *(221)*
boot.ini *(218)*
bootmgr *(217)*
Component Services *(238)*
counter *(232)*
file association *(212)*
ntdetect.com *(220)*
ntldr *(217)*
object *(231)*
ODBC Data Source Administrator *(240)*
Performance *(228)*

Performance console *(231)*
Performance Logs and Alerts *(232)*
Performance Monitor *(234)*
Processes *(222)*
Registry *(211)*
Reliability and Performance Monitor *(234)*
root keys *(211)*
Services *(227)*
System Monitor *(232)*
Task Manager *(221)*
tasklist *(230)*

</div>

Key Term Quiz

Use the Key Terms list to complete the sentences that follow. Not all terms will be used.

1. The Windows XP boot process uses _____ to track all of the installed operating systems.

2. _____ is a command-line version of the Task Manager.

3. The _____ tab in the Task Manager displays overall CPU and memory usage.

4. The Performance console requires a(n) _____ and a(n) _____ to create logs about resource usage.

5. When you open the Registry Editor, you will see the five _____ on the left side of the window.

6. You can right-click on an item in the _____ tab of the Task Manager to see the associated services.

7. Windows 7 uses _____, instead of ntldr, to boot the OS.

8. The _____ tracks everything about your computer, from file types to user preferences.

9. You can open the _____ directly by pressing CTRL-SHIFT-ESC.

10. When programmers need to use objects across multiple applications, they turn to _____.

Multiple-Choice Quiz

1. Which of the following tabs is *not* found in the Task Manager?

 A. Applications

 B. Processes

 C. Services

 D. Objects

2. Which of the following root keys contains the data for a system's non-user-specific configurations?

 A. HKEY_LOCAL_MACHINE

 B. HKEY_USERS

 C. HKEY_CURRENT_USER

 D. HKEY_CLASSES_ROOT

3. What replaced the role of boot.ini in the Windows Vista/7 boot process?

 A. Processes

 B. ntldr

C. Boot Configuration Data

D. Data Sources

4. What is the name of the command-line command for killing tasks?

 A. kill

 B. taskkill

 C. processkill

 D. appkill

5. With what is every application and service in Windows associated?

 A. An object

 B. A counter

 C. A component

 D. A process

6. Which of the following are organized inside the Registry's root keys? (Select two.)

 A. Subkeys

 B. Subfolders

 C. Values

 D. Objects

7. Which of the following programs reads the boot.ini file to launch Windows XP?

 A. Reliability and Performance Monitor

 B. bootmgr

 C. ntldr

 D. Tasklist

8. Which of the following options are available when you right-click on a process in the Task Manager's Processes tab? (Select two.)

 A. Start Service

 B. Go to Service(s)

 C. Go To Process

 D. Set Priority

9. Mark wants to monitor a PC that's been having performance issues overnight. He needs something that will record the data while he's away from the computer. Which tool should he use?

 A. Performance Logs and Alerts

 B. Task Manager

 C. System Monitor

 D. Registry

10. Which of the following statements about booting in Windows 7 is true?

 A. BIOS does not use bootmgr.

 B. UEFI looks for the MBR, which finds the boot code that launches bootmgr.

 C. BIOS looks for the MBR, which finds the boot code that launches bootmgr.

 D. UEFI does not use bootmgr.

11. From which tab in the Task Manager can you set priority and affinity from a context menu?

 A. Services

 B. Applications

 C. Performance

 D. Processes

12. What is the name of the coding standard that enables programmers to write databases and applications that interact independently of the operating system used?

 A. Open Database Connectivity

 B. Services

 C. Component Services

 D. Reliability and Performance Monitor

13. How do you open the Registry Editor from the command prompt? (Select two.)

 A. regedit

 B. regedt32

 C. regeditor

 D. rgstry

14. Which of the following is *not* a system file necessary for booting Windows XP?

 A. ntldr

 B. boot.ini

 C. ntdetect.com

 D. bootmgr.efi

15. Which of the following key combinations opens the Task Manager?

 A. CTRL-ALT-SHIFT

 B. SHIFT-F5

 C. CTRL-SHIFT-ESC

 D. WINDOWS LOGO-PAUSE/BREAK

Essay Quiz

1. You work for a company that uses both Windows XP and Windows 7 machines. The Windows XP machines need to boot using BIOS, but the Windows 7 systems have been set up with UEFI. Your non-tech boss wants to know more about how Windows works. Explain to him the boot processes for both Windows XP and Windows 7 (with UEFI).

2. Your coworker Mike just discovered the Task Manager. He's been wreaking havoc on his applications, starting and stopping services, and killing processes left and right. You notice his behavior and decide to clue him in on how processes really work. Explain the differences and connections between applications, processes, and services.

3. Your boss wants you to help him disable several startup programs that have been slowing down his PC. He thinks the best way for you to do this is in the Registry. Before you begin your work, explain to him the importance and the dangers of the contents of the Registry.

Lab Projects

• Lab Project 6.1

The Task Manager is a powerful utility. Open it and take a look around. In the Applications tab, right-click on an application and select Go To Process. On the Processes tab, right-click on a process and select Go to Service(s). Explore these connections until you understand how it all fits together. This is also a great time to try ending a task or killing a process.

• Lab Project 6.2

Try tracking your CPU and RAM usage over time. Open the Performance tool in any current version of Windows and set up some objects and counters to monitor the information. How does this tool differ from the Task Manager's Performance tab?

NTFS, Users, and Groups

"Only the insecure strive for security."

—Wayne Dyer

In this chapter, you will learn how to

■ **Create and administer Windows users and groups**

■ **Define and use NTFS permissions for authorization**

■ **Share a Windows computer securely**

■ **Secure PCs with User Account Control**

If you asked me what keeps Windows the number one operating system in the world, I'd say "Windows is the easiest operating system for securing resources, individual computers, and entire networks." Windows gets it right when it comes to protection. Using a combination of user accounts and groups that tie into the NTFS file system, Windows provides incredibly powerful file and folder protection. This user/group/NTFS combo scales from a single computer up to a network of computers spanning the world. Windows doesn't just stop at files and folders, either.

To understand security in Windows, you need to see it from Windows' point of view. In Windows, sharing files between users on a single machine and sharing files with users over a network are the same. When learning about users, groups, and NTFS permissions, however, it's helpful to think about a single PC. To that end, this chapter focuses on Windows security from the point of view of a single, or *standalone*, machine. I may dip into networks and domains from time to time, especially when the only differences are cosmetic, but Chapter 18 will revisit these topics in more detail and show you how the same tools scale up to help you protect a computer in a networked environment.

Authentication with Users and Groups

We've discussed the concept of users and groups in earlier chapters, but have you ever considered what user accounts and passwords actually do? To better understand their roles, you need to know two terms: authentication and authorization. **Authentication** is the process by which you determine a person at your computer is who he says he is and then grant him entry into the computer. In Windows, authentication is handled by a password-protected user account. Once a user is authenticated, he needs **authorization**, which controls what an authenticated user can and cannot do on a system. Authorization for Windows' files and folders is controlled by the NTFS file system, which assigns permissions to users, groups, or both.

Microsoft's answer to the authentication/authorization process is amazing. Inside every Windows computer is a database of user accounts—an encrypted list of user names with their associated password—who are allowed access to the system. Each of these individual records is called a **local user account**. If you don't have a local user account created on a particular system, you won't be able to log on to that computer (see Figure 7.1).

Tech Tip

Principle of Least Privilege

A good security practice to determine what type of user account to give to a specific person is the principle of least privilege. *In essence, you want to give users just enough—but no more—permissions to accomplish their tasks. Giving more than needed begs for problems or accidents and should be avoided.*

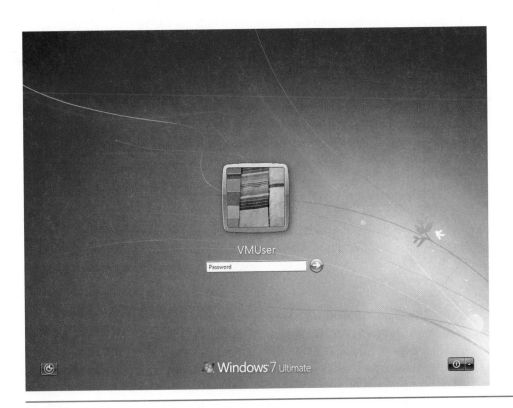

• **Figure 7.1** Windows logon screen

Every local user account needs a password (even if it's blank) and needs to belong to a group. Configuring these attributes requires tools in Windows for creating and managing users and groups. The tools used in Windows XP, however, are not the same as the tools used in Windows Vista or Windows 7. Each version of Windows includes one or two ways to deal with users and groups. Home editions of Windows (such as Windows XP Home Edition, Windows Vista Home Basic and Home Premium, and Windows 7 Home Premium) include a basic tool, while the professional editions of Windows (Windows XP Professional; Windows Vista Business, Ultimate, and Enterprise; and Windows 7 Professional, Ultimate, and Enterprise) include an extra, more advanced utility. That's a lot to learn about, and I'll explain all of these tools later in the chapter. First, I want to explain passwords and groups, which are common to users across all versions of Windows.

To create and manage users, you must have administrator privileges.

Passwords

Passwords are the ultimate key to protecting your computer. If someone learns your user name and password, they can log on to your computer. Even if the user account has only limited permissions—perhaps it can only read files, not edit them—you still have a security breach. Remember: for a hacker, just getting into the computer is half the battle.

Protect your passwords. Never give out passwords over the phone. If a user forgets a password, the network administrator should reset it to a complex combination of letters and numbers. The user should then change the password to something he or she wants, according to the parameters set by the administrator.

Make your users choose good passwords. I once attended a security seminar, and the speaker had everyone stand up. She then began to ask questions about our passwords—if we responded yes to the question, we were to sit down. She began to ask questions such as

"Do you use the name of your spouse as a password?" and

"Do you use your pet's name?"

By the time she had asked about 15 questions, only 6 people out of some 300 were still standing. The reality is that most of us choose passwords that are amazingly easy to hack. Make sure you use a **strong password**: at least eight characters in length, including letters, numbers, and punctuation symbols.

Using non-alphanumeric characters makes any password much more difficult to crack, for two reasons. First, adding non-alphanumeric characters forces the hacker to consider many more possible characters than just letters and numbers. Second, most password crackers use a combination of common words and numbers to hack passwords.

Because non-alphanumeric characters don't fit into common words or numbers, a character such as an exclamation point defeats these common-word hacks. Not all systems allow you to use characters such as @, $, %, or \, however, so you need to experiment.

CompTIA also recommends that you should have users change passwords at regular intervals. Although this concept sounds good on paper, it is a hard policy to maintain in the real world. For starters, users tend to forget passwords when they change a lot. This can lead to an even bigger security problem because users start writing passwords down.

If your organization forces you to change passwords often, one way to remember the password is to use a numbering system. I worked at a company that required me to change my password at the beginning of each month, so I did something very simple. I took a root password—let's say it was "m3y3rs5"—and simply added a number to the end representing the current month. So when June rolled around, for example, I would change my password to "m3y3rs56." It worked pretty well!

Windows enables logged-on users to create a **password reset disk** they can use if they forget a password. This is very important to have. If you lose your password and an administrator resets it, you might not have access to all of the files you had access to before, especially if they were encrypted. When you reset a password with a password reset disk, you can log on with the new password and still have access to previously encrypted files.

Best of all, password reset disks enable users to fix their own passwords. Encourage your users to create this disk; they only have this power if they create a password reset disk *before* they forget the password! Windows Vista and Windows 7 have an obvious option in the Tasks list to *Create a password reset disk*. You need a USB flash drive to create the disk. If by some chance you still have a floppy drive, you can use a floppy disk—which is where the term "disk" in password reset disk came from.

In addition to supporting password reset disks, Windows 7 enables you to create a password hint for your accounts. This clue appears after your first logon attempt fails (see Figure 7.2).

Be aware that if your computer is a member of a domain, you cannot use password reset disks or password hints to recover your password. In

 Every secure organization sets up various security policies and procedures to ensure that security is maintained. Windows has various mechanisms to implement such things as requiring a strong password, for example. Chapter 18 goes into detail about setting up Local Policies and Group Policy.

 Blank passwords or passwords that are easily visible on a sticky note provide no security. Always insist on non-blank passwords, and do not let anyone leave a password sitting out in the open.

• **Figure 7.2** Password hint on the Windows 7 logon screen

those cases, the network administrator has to reset your password on the domain controller.

Groups

A **group** is a collection of user accounts that can define the capabilities of its members. A single account can be a member of multiple groups. Groups are an efficient way of managing multiple users, especially when you are dealing with a whole network of accounts.

Groups make Windows administration much easier in two ways. First, you can assign a certain level of access for a file or folder to a group instead of to just a single user account. You can make a group called Accounting, for example, and put all the accounting user accounts in that group. If a person quits, you don't need to worry about assigning all of the proper access levels when you create a new account for his or her replacement. After you make an account for the new person, just add his account to the appropriate access group! Second, Windows provides numerous built-in groups with various access levels already predetermined. As you might imagine, there are differences among the versions of Windows, as described next.

Groups in Windows XP

Windows XP Professional provides seven built-in groups: Administrators, Power Users, Users, Backup Operators, Replicator, Everyone, and Guests. These built-in groups have a number of preset capabilities. You cannot delete these groups. Here's what you need to know about the five most important groups:

- **Administrators** Any account that is a member of the **Administrators group** has complete administrator privileges. Administrator privileges grant complete control over a machine. It is common for the primary user of a Windows system to have her account in the Administrators group.

- **Power Users** Members of the **Power Users group** are almost as powerful as Administrators, but they cannot install new devices or access other users' files or folders unless the files or folders specifically provide them access.

- **Users** Members of the **Users group** cannot edit the Registry or access critical system files. They can create groups, but can manage only those they create.

- **Everyone** This group applies to any user who can log on to the system. You cannot edit this group.

- **Guests** The **Guests group** enables someone who does not have an account on the system to log on by using a guest account. You might use this feature at a party, for example, to provide casual Internet access to guests, or at a library terminal. Most often, the guest account remains disabled.

If you're running Windows XP Professional on a Windows domain, all of the groups listed previously are included, plus other specialized groups like HelpServicesGroup and Remote Desktop Users.

Windows XP Home Edition uses groups like its big, professional brother, but never shows the user. In fact, Home Edition only enables you to use three groups: Administrators, Users, and Guests. You'll understand more when I explain how to manage users in Windows XP, but for now, know that groups are severely limited in the Home Edition of Windows XP.

Groups in Windows Vista and Windows 7

The professional editions of Windows Vista (Business, Ultimate, and Enterprise) and Windows 7 (Professional, Ultimate, and Enterprise) offer the same groups found in Windows XP Professional and throw in a lot more. Some of the default groups, such as Distributed COM Users, target specific roles in certain industries and mean little for the average user or tech. Other specific groups enable people to check on the performance and reliability of a computer without gaining access to any of the documents on the computer. These groups include Event Log Readers, Performance Log Users, and Performance Monitor Users. These groups provide excellent levels of access for technicians to help keep busy Vista/7 machines healthy.

 Windows Vista Enterprise and Windows 7 Enterprise users will almost always log on to a domain.

Like Windows XP, the home editions of Windows Vista and 7 (Home Basic and Home Premium) offer only three groups: Administrators, Users, and Guests. Administrators and Guests function as they do in all of the other versions of Windows. Members of the Users group, on the other hand, are called **standard users** and differ significantly from the limited users of Windows XP infamy. Standard users are prevented from harming the computer or uninstalling applications, but can run most applications. Technicians don't have to run over to standard user accounts to enable access to common tasks such as printing or doing e-mail.

Simple Tools for Managing Users

While I've already covered some of what makes users and groups so powerful, Microsoft understood that everyday users wanted user accounts, too. Remember that, beyond all of the permissions and administrative privileges, user accounts also create personal folders for a user's files, such as his My Documents, My Photos, and My Music folders. To that end, every version and edition of Windows includes these simple tools for managing users, all of which are found in the Control Panel. You'll learn about a more advanced tool in the next section of this chapter.

Managing Users in Windows XP

Windows XP provides the **User Accounts applet** in the Control Panel for basic user and group management. Here you can create new users, delete users, change passwords, and so forth.

User Accounts hides the complete list of users using a simplistic reference to account types that is actually a reference to the user account's group membership. An account that is a member of the local Administrators group is called a **computer administrator**; an account that belongs only to the Local Users group is called a **limited user** account. Which users the applet displays depends on which type of user is currently logged on

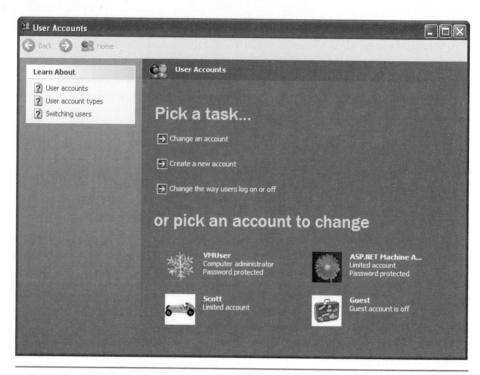

● **Figure 7.3** User Accounts dialog box showing a computer administrator, a couple of limited accounts, and the guest account (disabled)

(see Figure 7.3). When an administrator is logged on, the administrator sees both types of accounts and the guest account. Limited users see only their own account in User Accounts.

Windows XP requires you to create a second account that is a member of the Administrators group during the initial Windows installation. This is for simple redundancy—if one administrator is not available or is not able to log on to the computer, another one can.

Creating users is a straightforward process. You need to provide a user name (a password can and should be added later), and you need to know which type of account to create: computer administrator or limited. To create a new user in Windows XP, open the User Accounts applet from the Control Panel and click *Create a new account*. On the *Pick an account type* page, you can create either type of account (see Figure 7.4). Simply follow the prompts on the screen. After

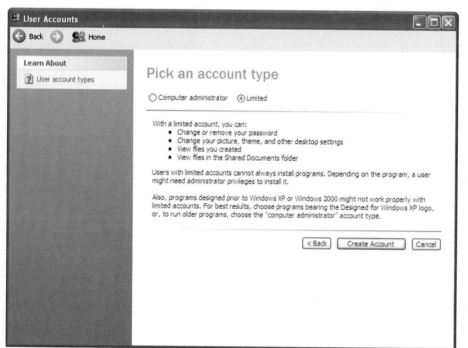

● **Figure 7.4** The Pick an account type page showing both options available

you create your local accounts, you'll see them listed when you open the User Accounts applet.

Head back to the User Accounts applet and look at the *Change the way users log on and off* option. Select it to see two checkboxes (see Figure 7.5). If you select the *Use the Welcome screen* checkbox, Windows brings up the friendly **Welcome screen** shown in Figure 7.6 each time users log on. If this box is unchecked, you'll get the classic logon screen (see Figure 7.7).

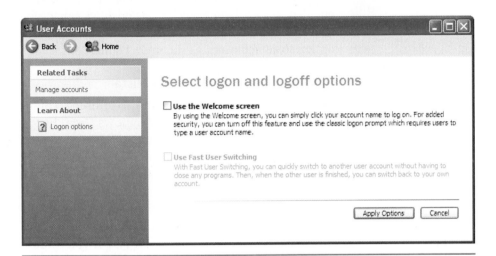

● **Figure 7.5** Select logon and logoff options

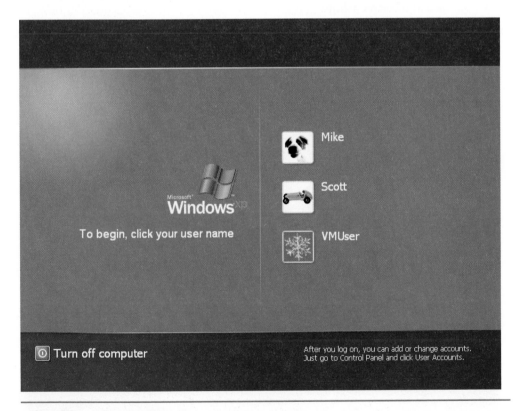

● **Figure 7.6** Welcome screen with three accounts

● **Figure 7.7** Classic logon screen, XP style

The second option, Use Fast User Switching, enables you to switch to another user without logging off of the currently running user, a feature appropriately called **Fast User Switching**. This option is handy when two people actively share a system, or when someone wants to borrow your system for a moment but you don't want to close all of your programs. This option is only active if you have the *Use the Welcome screen* checkbox enabled. If Fast User Switching is enabled, when you click the Log Off button on the Start menu, you get the option to switch users, as shown in Figure 7.8.

Managing Users in Windows Vista

Microsoft made some major changes to user accounts and the applet used to create and modify them in Windows Vista. Just as with Windows XP, you create three accounts when you set up a computer: guest, administrator, and a local account that's a member of the Administrators group. That's about where the similarities end.

To add or modify a user account, you have numerous options depending on which Control Panel view you select and which edition and update of Vista you have installed. If your machine is on a workgroup, you'll see the User Accounts and Family Safety applet (see Figure 7.9). If you connect to a domain, the default Control Panel Home view offers the User Accounts applet (see Figure 7.10). The options in each applet differ as well, as you can see in the screenshots.

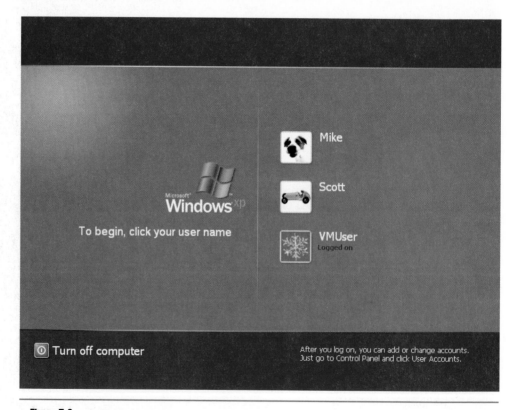

● **Figure 7.8** Switching users on the Welcome screen

• Figure 7.9 User Accounts and Family Safety applet in the Control Panel Home in Windows Vista Home Premium

• Figure 7.10 User Accounts applet in the Control Panel Home in Windows Vista Ultimate

Most techs almost immediately change the Control Panel view to Classic, but even there the different versions of Windows—and whether you're logged on to a workgroup or a domain—give you different versions of the User Accounts applet. Figure 7.11 shows the User Accounts applet in Windows Vista Business in a domain environment. Figure 7.12 shows the applet in Windows Vista Home Premium.

• **Figure 7.11** User Accounts applet in Windows Vista Business

• **Figure 7.12** User Accounts applet in Windows Vista Home Premium

The Tasks links on the left are similar between editions of Windows (with the addition of Parental Controls in the Home Premium edition), but the main options differ a lot. This chapter focuses on standalone machines, so we'll look more closely at the options included with Vista Home Premium.

Windows Vista Home Premium uses Vista's version of the Welcome screen for logging on, so each user account has a picture associated with it. You can change the picture from the User Accounts applet. You can also change the name of the user account here and alter the account type, demoting an account from administrator to standard user, for example.

To add a user in Windows Vista, open the User Accounts applet. You may need to open User Accounts and Family Safety first. Click *Manage another account* and select *Create a new account*. Give the account a user name and select a user account type. Then click Create Account.

At least one account must be an administrator account. If you try to demote the sole administrator account, you'll find the option dimmed.

User Account Control Windows XP made it too easy—and, in fact, almost necessary—to make your primary account on a computer an administrator account. Because limited users can't do common tasks, such as running certain programs, installing applications, updating applications, updating Windows, and so on, most users simply created an administrator-level account and logged on. Such accounts have full control over the computer, so any malware that slipped in with the account could do a lot more harm.

Microsoft addressed this problem with the **User Account Control (UAC)**, a feature that enables standard users to do common tasks and provides a permissions dialog box when standard users *and* administrators do certain things that could potentially harm the computer (such as attempt to install a program). We'll discuss UAC in detail at the end of this chapter.

Parental Controls With **Parental Controls**, an administrator account can monitor and limit the activities of any standard user in Windows Vista (and Windows 7), a feature that gives parents and managers an excellent level of control over the content their children and employees can access (see Figure 7.13). Activity Reporting logs applications run or attempted to run, Web sites visited or attempted to visit, any kind of files downloaded, and more. You can block various Web sites by type or specific URL, or you can allow only certain Web sites, a far more powerful option.

Parental Controls enable you to limit the time that standard users can spend logged on. You can specify acceptable and unacceptable times of day when standard users can log on. You can restrict access both to types of games and to specific applications. If you like playing rather gruesome games filled with monsters and blood that you don't want your kids to play, for example, you can simply block any games with certain ESRB (Entertainment Software Rating Board) ratings, such as E for Everyone, T for Teen, or M for Mature or Mature 17+.

• **Figure 7.13** Parental Controls

Managing Users in Windows 7

Windows 7 handles user creation in a manner very similar to Windows Vista, continuing the use of the User Accounts Control Panel applet. The Windows 7 applet is virtually identical to the one used in Windows Vista.

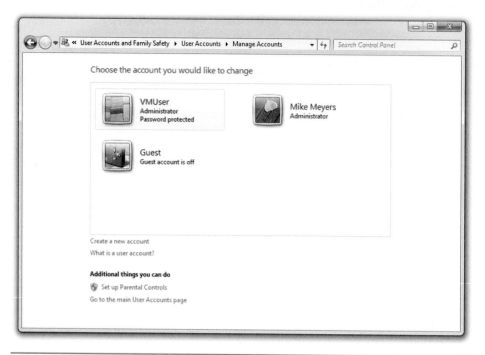

To create a user account, open the User Accounts applet and select *Manage another account* to see something like Figure 7.14.

Click on *Create a new account* to see your options for making a new account (see Figure 7.15). Note that this applet only enables you to make administrator accounts (in the Administrators group) or standard users (in the Users group).

While smaller, less sophisticated systems can get away with putting all their users into one of these two groups, you'll need to turn to Local Users and Groups to take full advantage of the power of Windows' users and groups.

• **Figure 7.14** Manage Accounts

• **Figure 7.15** Adding a new user

Advanced User Management

The professional editions of Windows include the **Local Users and Groups** tool, a more powerful tool for working with user accounts. You can get to Local Users and Groups via Control Panel | Administrative Tools | Computer Management. From here, you can create, modify, and remove users and groups. Keep in mind, however, that this advanced tool will not hold your hand like the Control Panel applets. Think of the Local Users and Groups tool as a bike without the training wheels of the User Accounts applet. Figure 7.16 shows the Local Users and Groups tool in Windows Vista with Groups selected.

To add a group, simply right-click on a blank spot in the Groups folder and select New Group. This opens the New Group dialog box, where you can type in a group name and description in their respective fields (see Figure 7.17).

To add users to this group, click the Add button. The dialog box that opens varies a little in name among the three operating systems, though they all contain the same functionality (see Figure 7.18).

• **Figure 7.16** Local Users and Groups in Windows Vista

• **Figure 7.17** New Group dialog box in Windows Vista

You can add more than just users to a group. Windows uses multiple *object* types to define what you can add. Object types include user accounts, groups, and computers. Each object type can be added to a group and assigned permissions. The short story of how to add a user account is to click the Advanced button to expand the dialog box and then click the Find Now button (see Figure 7.19).

You can either add group membership to a user's properties or add a user to a group's properties.

- To add group membership to a user account, select the Users folder, right-click a user account you want to change, and select Properties from the context menu. Then select the Member Of tab on the user account's Properties dialog box (see Figure 7.20). Click Add to add group membership.

- To add users via the group's properties, select the Groups folder. Right-click on a group and select Properties. Beneath the Members list, click the Add button to search for and add user accounts to the group.

You can also use either method to remove users. This level of flexibility makes the Local Users and Groups tool much more powerful and useful than the User Accounts Control Panel applets.

• **Figure 7.18** Select Users, Computers, or Groups dialog box in Windows Vista

• **Figure 7.19** Select Users, Computers, or Groups dialog box with Advanced options expanded to show user accounts

• **Figure 7.20** Properties dialog box of a user account, where you can change group memberships for that account

■ Authorization Through NTFS

User accounts and passwords provide the foundation for securing a Windows computer, enabling users to authenticate onto a PC. After you've created a user account, you need to determine what the user can do with the available resources (files, folders, applications, and so on). We call this process *authorization*. Windows uses the powerful NT File System (NTFS) to protect its resources. Let's delve into the amazing world of NTFS to see how this powerful file system protects your folder and files.

NTFS Permissions

In Windows, every folder and file on an NTFS partition has a list that contains two sets of data. First, the list details every user and group that has access to that file or folder. Second, the list specifies the level of access that each user or group has to that file or folder. The level of access is defined by a set of restrictions called NTFS permissions. **NTFS permissions** define exactly what any particular account can or cannot do to the file or folder and are thus quite detailed and powerful. You can make it possible, for example, for a person to edit a file but not delete it. You can configure NTFS permissions to enable someone to create a folder and not allow other people to make subfolders.

Here are a few rules about NTFS permissions:

1. You may see the NTFS permissions on a folder or file by accessing the file's or folder's Properties dialog box and opening the Security tab.

2. NTFS permissions are assigned both to user accounts and groups, although it's considered a best practice to assign permissions to groups and then add user accounts to groups instead of adding permissions directly to individual user accounts.

3. Whoever creates a folder or a file has complete control over that folder or file.

4. Administrators do not automatically have complete control over every folder and file. If an administrator wants to access a folder or file they do not have permission to access, they may go through a process called Take Control.

 Cross Check

Creating NTFS

You learned a lot about NTFS back in Chapter 4, so dust off your memory and see if you can answer these questions. What tool do you use to create partitions and format them? How do you set the format type? How does FAT32 security stack up against NTFS security?

NTFS file and folder permissions are so complicated that entire books have been written on them! Fortunately, the CompTIA A+ 220-802 exam tests your understanding of only a few basic concepts of NTFS permissions: Ownership, Take Ownership permission, Change permission, folder permissions, and file permissions.

- **Ownership** When you create a new file or folder on an NTFS partition, you become the *owner* of that file or folder. Owners can do anything they want to the files or folders they own, including changing the permissions to prevent anybody, even administrators, from accessing them.

- **Take Ownership permission** With the Take Ownership special permission, anyone with the permission can seize control of a file or folder. Administrator accounts have Take Ownership permission for everything. Note the difference here between owning a file and accessing a file. If you own a file, you can prevent anyone from accessing that file. An administrator whom you have blocked, however, can take that ownership away from you and *then* access that file!

- **Change permission** Another important permission for all NTFS files and folders is the Change permission. An account with this permission can give or take away permissions for other accounts.

- **Folder permissions** Let's look at a typical folder on my Windows 7 system to see how this one works. My E: drive is formatted as NTFS, and on it I created a folder called E:\Mike. I set the permissions for the E:\Mike folder by right-clicking on the folder, selecting Properties, and clicking the Security tab (see Figure 7.21).

- **File permissions** File permissions are similar to Folder permissions. We'll talk about File permissions right after we cover Folder permissions.

In Windows, just about everything in the computer has a Security tab in its Properties dialog box, and every Security tab contains two main areas. The top area shows the list of accounts that have permissions for that resource. The lower area shows exactly what permissions have been assigned to the selected account.

Here are the standard permissions for a folder:

- **Full Control** Enables you to do anything you want.

- **Modify** Enables you to do anything except delete files or subfolders, change permissions, or take ownership.

- **Read & Execute** Enables you to see the contents of the folder and any subfolders.

- **List Folder Contents** Enables you to see the contents of the folder and any subfolders. (This permission seems the same as the Read & Execute permission, but it is only inherited by folders.)

- **Read** Enables you to view a folder's contents and open any file in the folder.

- **Write** Enables you to write to files and create new files and folders.

The Security tab lets you set permissions.

File permissions are quite similar to folder permissions, with the main difference being the Special Permissions option, which I'll talk about a bit later in the chapter.

- **Full Control** Enables you to do anything you want.
- **Modify** Enables you to do anything except take ownership or change permissions on the file.
- **Read & Execute** Enables you to open files and applications.
- **Read** Enables you to open files.
- **Write** Enables you to open and write to the file.

Take some time to think about these permissions. Why would Microsoft create them? Think of situations where you might want to give a group Modify permission. Also, you can assign more than one permission. In many situations, we like to give users both the Read and Write permissions.

Permissions are cumulative. If you have Full Control on a folder and only Read permission on a file in the folder, you get Full Control permission on the file.

Don't panic about memorizing special permissions; just appreciate that they exist and that the permissions you see in the Security tab cover the vast majority of our needs.

Windows editions for home use have only a limited set of permissions you can assign. As far as folder permissions go, you can assign only one: Make This Folder Private. To see this in action, right-click a file or folder and select Sharing and Security from the options. Note that you can't just select Properties and see a Security tab as you can in the professional-oriented editions of Windows. Windows home editions do not have file-level permissions.

Permission Propagation

Permissions present an interesting challenge when you're moving and copying files. Techs need to understand what happens to permissions in several circumstances:

- Copying data within one NTFS-based partition
- Moving data within one NTFS-based partition
- Copying data between two NTFS-based partitions
- Moving data between two NTFS-based partitions
- Copying data from an NTFS-based partition to a FAT- or FAT32-based partition
- Moving data from an NTFS-based partition to a FAT- or FAT32-based partition

Do the permissions stay as they were on the original resource? Do they change to something else? Microsoft would describe the questions as such: Do inheritable permissions propagate? Ugh. CompTIA describes the process with the term **permission propagation**, which I take to mean "what happens to permissions on an object when you move or copy that object."

In Windows 7, if you access a folder's Properties dialog box, click on the Security tab, and then click the Advanced button, you'll see a little checkbox that says *Include inheritable permissions from this object's parent*. In other words, a user receives the parent folder's permissions for any files or subfolders created in that folder—a feature called **inheritance**. All versions of Windows have inheritance turned on by default, which most of the time is a good idea. However, there might be times where you want to turn off inheritance. Deselecting this option enables you to stop users from getting a specific permission via inheritance. Windows also provides explicit Deny functions for each option (see Figure 7.22). Deny overrules inheritance.

Let's look at our list of six things techs need to know to see what happens when you copy or move an object, such as a file or folder.

1. Copying within a partition creates two copies of the object. The object in the original location *retains* its permissions, unchanged. The copy of the object in the new location *inherits* the permissions from that new location. The new copy can have different permissions than the original.

2. Moving within a partition creates one copy of the object. That object *retains* its permissions, unchanged.

3. Copying from one NTFS partition to another creates two copies of the object. The object in the original location *retains* its permissions, unchanged. The copy of the object in the new location *inherits* the permissions from that new location. The new copy can have different permissions than the original.

4. Moving from one NTFS partition to another creates one copy of the object. The object in the new location *inherits* the permissions from that new location. The newly moved file can have different permissions than the original.

5. Copying from an NTFS-based partition to a FAT- or FAT32-based partition creates two copies of the object. The object in the original location *retains* its permissions, unchanged. The copy of the object in the new location has no permissions at all.

6. Moving from an NTFS-based partition to a FAT- or FAT32-based partition creates one copy of the object. That object has no permissions at all.

From a tech's standpoint, you need to be aware of how permissions can change when you move or copy files and, if in doubt about a sensitive file, check it before you sign off to a client. Having a top secret document totally locked down on a hard drive doesn't do you a lot of good if you put that document on a thumb drive to transport it and the thumb drive is FAT32!

Techs and Permissions

Techs, as a rule, hate NTFS permissions. You must have administrative privileges to do almost anything on a Windows machine, such as install updates, change drivers, and install applications; most administrators hate

• **Figure 7.22** Special permissions

giving out administrative permissions (for obvious reasons). If an administrator does give you administrative permission for a PC, and something goes wrong with that system while you're working on it, you immediately become the primary suspect!

If you're working on a Windows system administered by someone else, make sure he understands what you are doing and how long you think it will take. Have the administrator create a new account for you that's a member of the Administrators group. Never ask for the password for a permanent administrator account! That way, you won't be blamed if anything goes wrong on that system: "Well, I told Janet the password when she installed the new hard drive…maybe she did it!" When you have fixed the system, *make sure the administrator deletes the account you used*.

This "protect yourself from passwords" attitude applies to areas other than just doing tech support on Windows. PC support folks get lots of passwords, scan cards, keys, and ID tags. New techs tend to get an "I can go anywhere and access anything" attitude, and this is dangerous. I've seen many jobs lost and friendships ruined when a backup suddenly disappears or a critical file gets erased. Everybody points to the support tech in these situations. In physical security situations, make other people unlock doors for you. In some cases, I've literally asked the administrator or system owner to sit behind me, read a magazine, and be ready to punch in passwords as needed. What you don't have access to can't hurt you.

■ Sharing a Windows PC Securely

User accounts, groups, and NTFS work together to enable you to share a Windows PC securely with multiple user accounts. You can readily share files, folders, programs, and more. More to the point, you can share only what should be shared, locking access to files and folders that you want to make private. Each version of Windows handles multiple user accounts and sharing among those accounts differently, so let's look at Windows XP, Windows Vista, and Windows 7 separately and then finish with a look at a few other sharing and security issues.

Sharing in Windows XP

Microsoft tried to make secure sharing in Windows XP easier than it was in previous versions of Windows. To this end, Microsoft included several features. Each user account gets a series of folders in My Documents that the user can share and administrators can access. Windows XP also comes with a set of pre-made folders called **Shared Documents** that are accessible by all of the users on the computer. Also, Windows XP comes with simple file sharing enabled by default, which makes the option to share or not pretty easy. Finally, Windows XP Professional provides the option to use the full NTFS permissions and make customized shares possible.

Making Personal Documents Secure

The fact that most users of Windows XP computers will be computer administrators rather than limited users creates a bit of an issue with computers

shared by many users. By default, administrators can see all of the contents of Documents and Settings, where the My Documents folder for each user account resides. You can override this option in the My Documents Properties dialog box. Selecting the option to *Make this folder private* blocks the contents from anyone accessing them (see Figure 7.23).

Note that an administrator can take ownership of anything, so the only true way to lock down your data is to encrypt it. In the My Documents Properties dialog box, select the General tab and then click the Advanced button to open the Advanced Attributes dialog box. Click the checkbox next to *Encrypt contents to secure data* and that'll handle the encryption. Just make sure you have a password reset disk if you're going to use encryption to secure your files.

Shared Documents

You can use the Shared Documents folders to move files and folders among many users of a single machine. Every account can access the Shared Documents folder and the subfolders within, such as Shared Music and Shared Pictures (see Figure 7.24). Because new folders inherit the permissions of parent folders, by default any new subfolder you create in Shared Documents can be accessed by any account.

Simple File Sharing

With **simple file sharing**, you essentially have one local sharing option, and that's to put anything you want to share into the Shared Documents folder or one of its subfolders. To share a folder over a network, you only have a couple of options as well, such as to share or not and, if so, to give full control to everybody. Note that the sharing option is enabled in Figure 7.25. It's pretty much all or nothing.

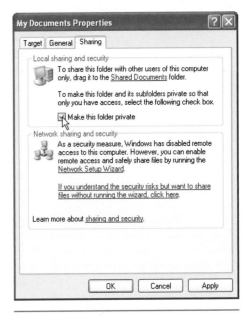

• **Figure 7.23** Making personal documents secure from prying eyes

• **Figure 7.24** Shared Music Properties dialog box

• **Figure 7.25** Folder shared, but seriously not secure

Windows XP Home and Media Center only give you the simple file sharing method, so the sharing of files and folders is straightforward. Windows XP Professional, on the other hand, enables you to turn off simple file sharing and unlock the true power of NTFS and permissions. To turn off simple file sharing, open a view of Windows Explorer (such as My Documents), choose Tools | Folder Options, and select the View tab. The very last option on the View tab is *Use simple file sharing (Recommended)*. Deselect that option, as in Figure 7.26, and then click OK.

When you access sharing and security now, you'll see a more fully formed security dialog box (see Figure 7.27).

Sharing in Windows Vista

Microsoft tweaked the settings for sharing a single PC with multiple users in Windows Vista to fix the all-or-nothing approach offered by simple file sharing; Vista enables you to target shared files and folders to specific user accounts. Microsoft beefed up the standard user account (as you read about earlier in the chapter) so users could access what they needed to get meaningful work done. Plus they expanded the concept of the Shared Documents folder into the Public folders.

Targeted Sharing

To share a folder or file with specific users—or with everyone, for that matter—you simply right-click on it and select Share. This opens the File Sharing dialog box, where you can select specific user accounts from a drop-down list (see Figure 7.28).

Once you select a user account, you can then choose what permission level to give that user. You have three choices: Reader, Contributor,

When you add a Windows XP Professional system to a domain, simple file sharing is disabled. You must use the full power of NTFS.

If the computer in question is on a Windows domain, the File Sharing dialog box differs such that you can search the network for user accounts in the domain. This makes it easy to share throughout the network.

• **Figure 7.26** Turning off simple file sharing

• **Figure 7.27** Full sharing and security options in Windows XP

or Co-owner (see Figure 7.29). *Reader* simply means the user has read-only permissions. *Contributor* gives the user read and write permissions and the permission to delete any file the user contributed to the folder. (Contributor only works at the folder level.) *Co-owner* enables the user to do anything.

Public Folders

Public folders offer another way to share files and folders. Anything you want to share with all other users on the local machine—or, if on a network, throughout the network—simply place it in the Public folder or one of the many subfolders, such as Public Documents or Public Pictures (see Figure 7.30). Note that the Public folder does not give you any control over what someone accessing the files contained within can do with those files.

● **Figure 7.28** File Sharing dialog box on a standalone machine

Like in Windows XP, NTFS sharing is alive and well in Windows Vista.

Sharing in Windows 7

Windows 7 keeps the file sharing options of Windows Vista and adds homegroups to the mix. You may not have heard of homegroups, so here's a quick overview: Instead of sharing individual files or folders, you can

● **Figure 7.29** Permissions options

• **Figure 7.30** Shared folders in the Public folder

use HomeGroup to share libraries, such as your Documents or Music libraries. Any files in your shared libraries will be automatically accessible by everyone in the homegroup, though you can also use more specific permissions. You'll need a password to join a homegroup, so any shared data will be secure.

Locating Shared Folders

Before you walk away from a computer, you should check for any unnecessary or unknown (to you) shared folders on the hard drives. This enables you to make the computer as secure as possible for the user. When you open My Computer or Computer, shared folders don't just jump out at you, especially if they're buried deep within the file system. A shared C: drive is obvious, but a shared folder all the way down in D:\temp\backup\Simon\secret share would not be obvious, especially if none of the parent folders were shared.

Windows comes with a handy tool for locating all of the shared folders on a computer, regardless of where they reside on the drives. The Computer Management console in the Administrative Tools has a Shared Folders option under System Tools. In that are three options: Shares, Sessions, and Open Files. Select Shares to reveal all of the shared folders (see Figure 7.31).

You can double-click on any share to open the Properties dialog box for that folder. At that point, you can make changes to the share—such as users and permissions—just as you would from any other sharing dialog box.

• **Figure 7.31** Shared Folders tool in Computer Management

Administrative Shares

A close glance at the screenshot in Figure 7.31 might have left some of you with raised eyebrows and quizzical looks. What kind of share is ADMIN$ or C$?

Every version of Windows since Windows NT comes with several default shares, notably all hard drives—not optical drives or removable devices, such as thumb drives—plus the %systemroot% folder—usually C:\Windows—and a couple of others, depending on the system. These **administrative shares** give local administrators administrative access to these resources, whether they log on locally or remotely. (In contrast, shares added manually are called *local shares*.)

Administrative shares are odd ducks. You cannot change the default permissions on them. You can delete them, but Windows will re-create them automatically every time you reboot. They're hidden, so they don't appear when you browse a machine over the network, though you can map them by name. Keep the administrator password safe, and these default shares won't affect the overall security of the computer.

Administrative shares have been exploited by malware programs, especially because many users who set up their computers never give the administrator account a password. Starting with Windows XP Home, Microsoft changed the remote access permissions for such machines. If you log on to a computer remotely as administrator with no password, you get guest access rather than administrator access. That neatly nips potential exploits in the bud.

Protecting Data with Encryption

The scrambling of data through **encryption** techniques provides the only true way to secure your data from access by any other user. Administrators can use the Take Ownership permission to seize any file or folder on a computer, even those you don't actively share. Thus you need to implement other security measures for that data that needs to be ultra secure. Depending on the version of Windows, you have between zero and three encryptions tools: Windows Home editions (Windows XP Home Edition, Windows Vista Home Basic and Home Premium, and Windows 7 Home Premium) have basically no security features; Windows XP Professional uses the Encrypting File System to, well, encrypt files; and Windows Vista/7 Ultimate and Enterprise add an encryption system that can encrypt entire hard drives.

Encrypting File System

The professional editions of Windows (Windows XP Professional; Windows Vista Business, Ultimate, and Enterprise; and Windows 7 Professional, Ultimate, and Enterprise) offer a feature called the **Encrypting File System (EFS)**, an encryption scheme that any user can use to encrypt individual files or folders on a computer. The home editions of Windows do not enable encryption through the built-in tools, though you have the option to use third-party encryption methods, such as TrueCrypt, to lock down data.

To encrypt a file or folder takes but a moment. You right-click the file or folder you want to encrypt and select Properties. In the Properties dialog box for that object, select the General tab and click the Advanced button (see Figure 7.32) to open the Advanced Attributes dialog box. Click the checkbox next to *Encrypt contents to secure data* (see Figure 7.33). Click OK to close the Advanced Attributes dialog box and then click OK again on the Properties dialog box, and you've locked that file or folder from any user account aside from your own.

Encryption is just one possible *attribute* of a file. You can also make files hidden, read-only, and more, all from a file or folder's Properties dialog box. You'll learn more about attributes in Chapter 9.

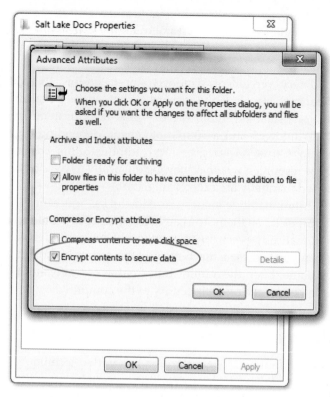

• **Figure 7.32** Click the Advanced button on the General tab

• **Figure 7.33** Selecting encryption

As long as you maintain the integrity of your password, any data you encrypt by using EFS is secure from prying. That security comes at a potential price, though, and your password is the key. The Windows security database stores the password (securely, not plain text, so no worries there), but that means access to your encrypted files is based on that specific installation of Windows. If you lose your password or an administrator resets your password, you're locked out of your encrypted files permanently. There's no recovery. Also, if the computer dies and you try to retrieve your data by installing the hard drive in another system, you're likewise out of luck. Even if you have an identical user name on the new system, the security ID that defines that user account will differ from what you had on the old system.

And one last caveat. If you copy an encrypted file to a disk formatted as anything but NTFS, you'll get a prompt saying that the copied file will not be encrypted. If you copy to a disk with NTFS, the encryption stays. The encrypted file—even if on a removable disk—will only be readable on your system with your login.

> Remember the password reset disk we discussed earlier in the chapter? If you use EFS, you simply must have a valid password reset disk in the event of some horrible catastrophe.

BitLocker Drive Encryption

Windows Vista/7's Ultimate and Enterprise editions offer full drive encryption through **BitLocker Drive Encryption**. BitLocker encrypts the whole drive, including every user's files, so it's not dependent on any one account. The

beauty of BitLocker is that if your hard drive is stolen, such as in the case of a stolen portable computer, all of the data on the hard drive is safe. The thief can't get access, even if you have a user on that laptop that failed to secure his or her data through EFS.

BitLocker requires a special Trusted Platform Module (TPM) chip on the motherboard to function. The TPM chip validates on boot that the Vista/7 computer has not changed—that you still have the same operating system installed, for example, and that the computer wasn't hacked by some malevolent program. The TPM also works in cases where you move the BitLocker drive from one system to another.

If you have a legitimate BitLocker failure (rather than a theft) because of tampering or moving the drive to another system, you need to have a properly created and accessible recovery key or recovery password. The key or password is generally created at the time you enable BitLocker and should be kept somewhere secure, such as a printed copy in a safe or a file on a network server accessible only to administrators.

To enable BitLocker, double-click the BitLocker Drive Encryption icon in the Classic Control Panel, or select Security in Control Panel Home view and then click *Protect your computer by encrypting data on your disk* (see Figure 7.34).

Tech Tip

TrueCrypt

TrueCrypt is an open-source disk encryption application with versions available for just about every operating system. You can use TrueCrypt to encrypt an entire partition or you can create an encrypted volume into which you can securely store data. The beauty of the encrypted volume is that it acts like a folder that you can move around or toss on a USB flash drive. You can take the volume to another system and, as long as you have the password and TrueCrypt installed on the other system, read the contents of the encrypted volume. If the thumb drive is big enough, you can even put a copy of TrueCrypt on it and run the program directly from the thumb drive, enabling you to read the contents of the encrypted volume—as long as you know the proper password.

TrueCrypt has some limitations, such as a lack of support for dynamic disks and some problems with multiboot systems, but considering the price—free, though donations are cheerfully accepted—and the amazing power, it's hard not to love the program. This discussion of TrueCrypt barely scratches the surface of what the application can do, so check it out at www .truecrypt.org. If you're running Windows XP Home or Windows Vista/7 Home Premium, you can't get a better tool for securing your data.

• **Figure 7.34** Enabling BitLocker Drive Encryption

User Account Control

When picking the poster child for the "327 Reasons We Hated Vista" list, I'll bet most folks put Vista's *User Account Control* (*UAC*) at the very top. Vista's UAC manifested as a pop-up dialog box that seemed to appear every time you tried to do *anything* on a Windows Vista system (see Figure 7.35).

• **Figure 7.35** UAC in action. Arrgh!

• **Figure 7.36** UAC equivalent on a Mac

It's too bad that UAC got such a bad rap. Not only is UAC an important security update for Windows Vista and Windows 7, but it is also a common feature in both Mac OS and Linux/Unix. Figure 7.36 shows the equivalent feature on a Mac.

If every other major operating system uses something like UAC, why was Microsoft slammed so hard when they unveiled UAC in Windows Vista? The reason is simple: Windows users are spoiled rotten, and, until UAC came along, the vast majority of users had no idea how risky their computing behavior was.

The problem started years ago when Microsoft created NTFS. NTFS uses robust user accounts and enables fine control over how users access files and folders—but at a cost: NTFS in its pure form is somewhat complicated. To share a folder, you need to make sure the person accessing that folder has a user account and that you've configured the NTFS permissions to give that user the permissions needed to do whatever he or she wants to do (see Figure 7.37).

User accounts have always been a bit of a challenge. The only account that can truly do *anything* on a Windows system is the administrator. Sure, you can configure a system with groups and assign NTFS permissions to those groups—and this is commonly done on large networks with a full-time IT staff—but what about small offices and home networks? These users almost never have the skill sets to deal with the complexities of users and groups, which often results in systems where the user accounts are all assigned administrator privileges by default—and that's when it gets dangerous (see Figure 7.38).

UAC in Windows Vista

User Account Control enables users to know when they are about to do something that has serious consequences. The Microsoft TechNet library

("Understanding and Configuring User Account Control in Windows Vista") provides examples of common actions that require Administrator privileges:

- Installing and uninstalling applications
- Installing a driver for a device (e.g., a digital camera driver)
- Installing Windows Updates
- Configuring Parental Controls
- Installing an ActiveX control
- Adjusting Windows Firewall settings
- Changing a user's account type
- Modifying UAC settings in the Security Policy Editor snap-in (secpol.msc)
- Configuring Remote Desktop access
- Adding or removing a user account
- Coping or moving files into the Program Files or Windows directory
- Scheduling Automated Tasks
- Restoring system backed-up files
- Configuring Automatic Updates
- Browsing to another user's directory

• **Figure 7.37** Typically confusing settings for NTFS permissions

• **Figure 7.38** The danger of administrator privileges in the wrong hands!

• **Figure 7.39** Power Users group—almost never used at the small office/
home level

Before Vista, Microsoft invented the idea of the Power Users group to give users almost all of the power of an administrator account (to handle most of the situations just described) without actually giving users the full power of the account. Assigning a user to the Power Users group still required someone who knew how to do this, however, so most folks at the small office/home level simply ignored the Power Users group (see Figure 7.39).

Clearly, Microsoft needed a better method to prevent people from running programs that they should not run. If users have the correct privileges, however—or the ability to "escalate" their privileges to that of an administrator—then they should be able to do what they need to do as simply as possible. Microsoft needed to make the following changes:

- The idea of using an administrator account for daily use needed to go away.

- Any level of account should be able to do anything as easily as possible.

- If a regular account wants to do something that requires administrator privileges, the user of the regular account will need to enter the administrator password.

- If a user with administrator privileges wants to run something that requires administrator privileges, the user will not have to reenter his or her password, but the user will have to respond to an "Are you sure?"-type dialog box so he or she appreciates the gravity of the action—thus, the infamous UAC dialog box.

How UAC Works

UAC works for both standard user accounts and administrator accounts. If a standard user attempts to do something that requires administrator privileges, he or she sees a UAC dialog box that prompts for the administrator password (see Figure 7.40).

If a user with administrator privileges attempts to do something that requires administrator privileges, a simpler UAC dialog box appears, like the one shown in Figure 7.41.

• **Figure 7.40** Prompting for an administrator password in Vista

• Figure 7.41 Classic UAC prompt

Interestingly, Vista has not one but four different UAC prompts, depending on the program/feature you wish to run, as outlined in Table 7.1.

The official name for the UAC dialog box is the "UAC consent prompt." When the UAC consent prompt appears in Vista, the rest of the desktop darkens and you cannot take any other action until you respond to the consent prompt.

Table 7.1	UAC Prompts in Windows Vista
UAC Classification	Type of Program
Blocked	A program that has been blocked by a security policy
Unverified	An unknown third-party program
Verified	A digitally signed, third-party program or non-core OS program
Published by Vista	A program that is a core part of the operating system

Blocked programs generate a scary-looking, red-bannered dialog box like the one shown in Figure 7.42. Note you can click OK in Windows Vista (or Close in Windows 7) or look at more details (if available).

• Figure 7.42 Blocked program

Chapter 7: NTFS, Users, and Groups

• Figure 7.43 Unverified program

• Figure 7.44 Verified program

Unverified programs lack any form of certificate to validate. In this case, you get a yellow-bannered dialog box warning you the application is unsigned and giving you two options: allow the program to run (Yes) or not (No). See Figure 7.43 for an example of this.

Verified programs aren't part of the core of Vista and are usually written by third parties. These programs do have valid, verified certificates. You can identify the dialog box by its gray-blue banner (see Figure 7.44).

Published by Vista programs are written as part of the core of Vista and show up with a teal-bannered dialog box (see Figure 7.45).

UAC uses small shield icons to warn you ahead of time that it will prompt you before certain tasks, as shown in Figure 7.46. Microsoft updated this somewhat redundant feature in Windows 7, as you'll soon see.

UAC gives users running a program an opportunity to consider their actions before they move forward. It's a good thing, but spoiled Windows users aren't accustomed to something that makes them consider their actions. As a result, one of the first things everyone learned how to do when Vista came out was to turn off UAC.

• Figure 7.45 Published by Vista

• **Figure 7.46** Shield icons in the Control Panel

How to Turn Off UAC

You can turn off UAC in a number of ways in Windows. Here are the two most common ways:

1. In the User Accounts Control Panel applet, you'll see an option to *Turn User Account Control on or off* (see Figure 7.47). Select this option and uncheck the checkbox to turn UAC off. Check the checkbox to turn it on again.

2. Open up the System Configuration utility (msconfig) and select *Disable UAC* on the Tools tab, as shown in Figure 7.48. You'll have to reboot for the changes to take effect. Note you can also turn on UAC from the System Configuration utility.

• **Figure 7.47** Turning User Account Control on or off

• **Figure 7.48** Disabling UAC in the System Configuration utility

Chapter 7: NTFS, Users, and Groups

UAC in Windows Vista worked well, but it startled users. Suddenly, users had to deal with UAC, and they didn't like that. Most users simply turned UAC off and added it to the reasons to not like Windows Vista.

UAC in Windows 7

Microsoft may be a huge company, but it still knows how to react when its customers speak out about features they don't like. Windows 7 unveiled a more refined, less "in-your-face" UAC that makes the feature much easier to use.

All references to Control Panel applets in Windows 7 assume you are using the Small Icon view.

• **Figure 7.49** Change User Account Control settings option

• **Figure 7.50** Four levels of UAC

Make sure you know what each of the four UAC levels does.

A More Granular UAC

Microsoft did some research on why UAC drove users nuts, concluding that the problem wasn't UAC itself but the "I'm constantly in your face or you can turn me off and you get no help at all" aspect. To make UAC less aggressive, Microsoft introduced four UAC levels. To see these levels, go to the User Accounts applet and select *Change User Account Control settings*, as shown in Figure 7.49. When you select this option, you see the dialog box in Figure 7.50.

In Figure 7.50, you can see a slider with four levels. The top level (Always notify) means you want UAC to work exactly as it does in Vista, displaying the aggressive consent form every time you do anything that typically requires administrator access. The bottom option (Never notify) turns off UAC. The two levels in the middle are new and are very similar. Both of them do the following:

- Don't notify me when I make changes.

- Notify me only when programs try to makes changes.

The only difference is in *how* they show the change. The second-from-top level will display the typical consent form, but only when programs try to make changes. The third-from-top level displays a consent form, but where the normal consent form dims your desktop and doesn't allow you to do anything but address the form, this consent form just pops up like a normal dialog box.

Program Changes Versus Changes I Make

So what's the difference between a program making a change and you making a change? Take a look at Figure 7.51. In this case, Windows 7 is set

• **Figure 7.51** Darkened UAC

to the second-from-top option. A program (the very safe and, judging by the color of the banner, verified) Adobe Download Manager is attempting to install a feature into Internet Explorer. Because this is a program trying to make changes, the UAC consent form appears and darkens the desktop.

> The default behavior for UAC in Windows 7 is the second-from-top option, which results in a screen similar to Figure 7.51.

If you lower the UAC to the third-from-top option, you still see a consent form, but now it acts like a typical dialog box, as shown in Figure 7.52.

A program such as the Adobe program described earlier is very different from a feature *you* want to change. Notice the shields, as shown earlier in Figure 7.49.

Each of these options isn't a program—each is merely a feature built into Windows. Those shields tell you that clicking the feature next to a shield will require administrator privileges. If you were to pick the Vista-strength UAC option, you'd get a UAC consent prompt when you click one of those features. If you set UAC to any of the three lower settings, however, you'd go straight to that feature without *any* form of UAC consent prompt. Of course, this isn't true if you don't have administrator privileges. If you're a standard user, you'll still be prompted for a password, just as in Vista.

• **Figure 7.52** Non-darkened UAC

Overall, the improvements to UAC in Windows 7 show that it has a place on everyone's computer. UAC might cause an occasional surprise or irritation, but that one more "Are you sure?" could mean the difference between safe and unsafe computing. So go ahead, turn UAC back on in Windows 7! It's well worth the small inconvenience.

Chapter 7 Review

■ Chapter Summary

After reading this chapter and completing the exercises, you should understand the following about securing Windows resources.

Create and administer Windows users and groups

■ The key to protecting your data is based on two related processes: authentication and authorization. Authentication is the process by which you determine a person at your computer is who he says he is. The most common way to authenticate is by using a user name and password. Once a user is authenticated, he needs authorization, the process that states what a user can and cannot do on that system. Authorization, at least for files and folders, is controlled by the NTFS file system, which assigns permissions to users and groups.

■ Passwords are the ultimate key to protecting your computer. If someone learns your user name and password, they can log on to your computer. Protect your passwords. Never give out passwords over the phone. If a user forgets or loses a password, the network administrator should reset the password to a complex combination of letters and numbers. The user should then change the password to something he or she wants, according to the parameters set by the administrator.

■ Make sure you use strong passwords: at least eight characters in length, including letters, numbers, and punctuation symbols.

■ Windows enables currently logged-on users to create a password reset disk they can use if they forget a password. This is very important to have. If you lose your password and an administrator resets it, you might not have access to all of the files you had access to before, especially if they were encrypted. When you reset a password with a password reset disk, you can log on with the new password and still have access to previously encrypted files. Windows 7 can provide a password hint if you fail to use the proper password on your first attempt to log on.

■ A group is a collection of accounts that can define the capabilities of its members. A single account can be a member of multiple groups. Groups are an efficient way of managing multiple users, especially when you are dealing with a whole network of accounts.

■ Windows XP Professional provides seven built-in groups: Administrators, Power Users, Users, Backup Operators, Replicator, Everyone, and Guests. These built-in groups have a number of preset capabilities. You cannot delete these groups. Windows XP Home Edition only enables you to use three groups: Administrators, Users, and Guests.

■ The professional editions of Windows Vista (Business, Ultimate, and Enterprise) and Windows 7 (Professional, Ultimate, and Enterprise) offer the same groups found in Windows XP Professional and throw in a lot more. Some group types enable people to check on the performance and reliability of a computer but without gaining access to any of the documents on the computer. These groups include Event Log Readers, Performance Log Users, and Performance Monitor Users and provide excellent levels of access for technicians to help keep busy Vista/7 machines healthy.

■ Windows XP uses the User Accounts applet in the Control Panel to create and manage user accounts. User Accounts hides the complete list of users, using a simplistic reference to account types that is actually a reference to a user account's group membership. An account that is a member of the local Administrators group is called a computer administrator; an account that belongs only to the Local Users group is called a limited user account.

■ Creating users is a straightforward process. You need to provide a user name (a password can and should be added later), and you need to know which type of account to create: computer administrator or limited.

■ You can opt out of the Welcome screen and thus require a user to type both a user name and a password. You can also enable or disable Fast User Switching—a feature that enables you to switch to another user account without logging out and thus having to close open programs.

■ To add or modify a user account in Windows Vista, you have numerous options depending on which Control Panel view you select and which edition

and update of Vista you have installed. Windows Vista Business and Ultimate, for example, in the default Control Panel Home view, offer the User Accounts applet. Windows Vista Home Premium, in contrast, gives you the User Accounts and Family Safety applet. The Tasks links on the left are similar between editions of Windows, with the addition of Parental Controls in the Home Premium edition, but the main options differ a lot.

- Windows Vista Home Premium uses Vista's version of the Welcome screen for logging on, so each user account has a picture associated with it. You can change the picture from the User Accounts applet. You can also change the name of the user account here and alter the account type.

- With Parental Controls, an administrator account can monitor and limit the activities of any standard user in Windows Vista/7, a feature that gives parents and managers an excellent level of control over the content their children and employees can access. Parental Controls enable you to limit the time that standard users can spend logged on, for example. You can specify acceptable and unacceptable times of day when standard users can log on.

- Creating a user account in Windows 7 is virtually identical to the process in Windows Vista. Windows 7 uses the User Accounts Control Panel applet to manage users.

- The professional editions of Windows enable you to add, remove, and modify users and groups using the advanced Local Users and Groups tool found in the Computer Management console of the Administrative Tools.

Define and use NTFS permissions for authorization

- In Windows, every folder and file on an NTFS partition has a list that contains two sets of data: every user and group that has access to that file or folder, and the level of access each user or group has to that file or folder. A set of detailed and powerful restrictions called NTFS permissions define exactly what any particular account can or cannot do to the file or folder.

- When you create a new file or folder on an NTFS partition, you become the owner of that file or folder, which means you can do anything you want to it, including changing the permissions to prevent anybody, even administrators, from accessing it. The special Take Ownership

permission enables an account to seize control of a file or folder. Administrator accounts have Take Ownership permission for everything. Change permission–equipped accounts can give or take away permissions for other accounts.

- In Windows, just about everything in the computer has a Security tab in its Properties dialog box. Every Security tab contains a list of accounts that have permissions for that resource, and the permissions assigned to those accounts. The standard permissions for a folder are Full Control, Modify, Read & Execute, List Folder Contents, Read, and Write. The standard file permissions are Full Control, Modify, Read & Execute, Read, and Write. Permissions are cumulative.

- Moving or copying objects such as files and folders can have an effect on the permissions of those objects, something that techs need to understand. If you copy or move an object from one NTFS partition to another, the new object inherits the permissions associated with the new location. If you copy an object within a partition, the newly created copy inherits the permissions associated with the new location, but the original copy retains its permissions. Any object that you put on a FAT or FAT32 partition loses any permissions because FAT and FAT32 don't support NTFS permissions.

Share a Windows computer securely

- User accounts, groups, and NTFS work together to enable you to share a Windows PC securely with multiple user accounts. You can readily share files, folders, programs, and more. You can share only what should be shared, locking access to files and folders that you want to make private.

- The fact that most users of Windows XP computers will be computer administrators rather than limited users creates a bit of an issue with a computer shared by many users. By default, administrators can see all of the contents of Documents and Settings, where the My Documents folders for each user account reside. Selecting the option to *Make this folder private* in the My Documents Properties dialog box blocks anyone from accessing the contents.

- Use the Shared Documents or Public folders to move files and folders among many users of a single machine. Every account can access the Shared Documents/Public folders and the subfolders within.

- With simple file sharing, you essentially have one local sharing option, and that's to put anything you want to share into the Shared Documents folder or one of its subfolders. To share a folder over a network, you only have a couple of options as well, such as to share or not and, if so, to give full control to everybody. Windows XP Professional enables you to disable simple file sharing and have full control over sharing and permissions.

- Windows Vista enables you to permit specific user accounts to access shared resources and to set the level of access permitted, such as Reader, Contributor, or Co-owner. Vista also uses the Public folder, similar to Shared Documents from Windows XP, which contains multiple shared folders. Any user account can access the Public folder.

- Windows 7 enables you to share libraries using homegroups. Homegroups are secured using a common password.

- You can locate shared folders on your PC using the Shared Folders tool in Administrative Tools.

- Default shares, including all hard drives and the %systemroot% folder, are called administrative shares. They give local administrators access to these resources, whether they log on locally or remotely.

- The scrambling of data through encryption techniques provides the only true way to secure your data from access by any other user. The professional editions of Windows enable a feature called the Encrypting File System (EFS), an encryption scheme that any user can use to encrypt individual files or folders on a computer. The home editions of Windows do not enable encryption.

- Windows Vista/7 Ultimate and Enterprise editions offer full drive encryption through BitLocker Drive Encryption. BitLocker encrypts the whole drive, including every user's files, so it's not dependent on any one account. BitLocker requires a special Trusted Platform Module (TPM) chip on the motherboard to function. The TPM chip validates on boot that the Vista/7 computer hasn't changed and that you still have the same operating system installed.

Secure PCs with User Account Control

- Windows XP made it almost necessary to make your primary account on a computer an administrator account, because limited users can't do common tasks such as installing applications or updating Windows. In Windows Vista, Microsoft rolled out User Account Control to better control access.

- For any action that requires administrator privileges, a dialog box will appear. Standard users need to enter an administer password to continue. Administrators only need to approve the action.

- Windows Vista uses four different UAC prompts: Blocked, Unverified, Verified, and Published by Vista.

- Windows uses small shield icons to warn you if something creates a UAC prompt.

- Windows 7 improved Vista's overactive UAC prompts by establishing four levels of security: Always notify, Notify me only when programs try to make changes to my computer, Notify me only when programs try to make changes to my computer (do not dim my desktop), and Never notify.

■ Key Terms

administrative shares *(271)*

Administrators group *(250)*

authentication *(247)*

authorization *(247)*

BitLocker Drive Encryption *(272)*

computer administrator *(251)*

Encrypting File System (EFS) *(271)*

encryption *(271)*

Fast User Switching *(254)*

group *(250)*

Guests group *(250)*

inheritance *(264)*

limited user *(251)*

local user account *(247)*

Local Users and Groups *(259)*

NTFS permissions *(261)*

Parental Controls *(257)*

password reset disk *(249)*

permission propagation *(264)*

Power Users group *(250)*

■ Key Term Quiz

Use the Key Terms list to complete the sentences that follow. Not all terms will be used.

1. The _____ enables you to manage user accounts in Windows 7.

2. To log on to a standalone Windows PC, you need a(n) _____.

3. An account that belongs only to the Local Users group in Windows XP is called a(n) _____.

4. On the _____, you can click on an icon and type a password to log on to the computer.

5. A(n) _____ is a collection of user accounts that share the same access capabilities.

6. The _____ enables standard users to perform common tasks and provides

a permissions dialog box when standard users and administrators do certain things that could potentially harm the computer.

7. By default, any file you drop into a folder on an NTFS drive gets the same permissions as those assigned to the folder, a feature called

_____.

8. The _____ feature of Windows XP Home means you can share or not share a folder. You don't have any finer control than that.

9. Windows Vista has the _____ available for sharing files and folders with other users of a particular computer.

10. The _____ enables you to scramble a file or folder and thus hide the contents from anyone, even an administrator.

■ Multiple-Choice Quiz

1. What process determines the identity of a user?

 A. Authentication

 B. Authorization

 C. Identification

 D. Indemnification

2. Which of the following user account types can create other user accounts?

 A. Administrator

 B. Limited user

 C. Restricted user

 D. Standard user

3. To which of the following groups does a standard user in Windows XP belong by default?

 A. Limited Users

 B. Power Users

 C. Restricted Users

 D. Users

4. Which utility enables you to add users and groups in Windows 7 Professional?

 A. User Account Control

 B. User Accounts applet

 C. Users and Groups applet

 D. Local Users and Groups

5. Which of the following is the strongest password?

 A. 5551212

 B. Spot01

 C. 43*xv

 D. 479love*

6. Which tool would enable a user to recover his encrypted files if he forgets his password?

 A. BitLocker

 B. Encrypting File System

 C. Password reset disk

 D. Password restore disk

7. Which of the following groups can you assign a user to in Windows Vista Home Premium? (Select two.)

 A. Administrators

 B. Power Users

 C. Replicators

 D. Users

8. Which tool in Windows Vista and Windows 7 enables an administrator to create a log that shows all of the applications a user runs or attempts to run?

 A. Create Log

 B. NTFS

 C. Parental Controls

 D. User Account Control

9. Which of the following is *not* a standard NTFS permission?

 A. Copy

 B. Full Control

 C. Modify

 D. Read & Execute

10. As a member of the accounting group, John has Write permission to the Database folder; as a member of the technicians group, John has Read permission to the Database folder. What permission or permissions does John have to the Database folder?

 A. Read only

 B. Write only

 C. Read and Write

 D. Full Control

11. When you copy a file from one folder on the C: drive to another folder on the C: drive, by default what permissions will the copy of that file have if the C: drive is formatted with NTFS?

 A. The copy will retain the permissions the original file has.

 B. The copy will inherit the permissions of the new location.

 C. The copy will lose all permissions.

 D. You can't do that.

12. On a Windows Vista Business computer, where can you place files that other users can access easily?

 A. Public Documents

 B. Public folder

 C. Shared Documents

 D. Shared folder

13. John wants to share a folder in Windows 7 with Liz but wants to make sure she can delete only files she creates in that folder, not the ones he creates. What permission level should he use?

 A. Contributor

 B. Co-owner

 C. Full Control

 D. Reader

14. Which tool in certain Windows Vista and Windows 7 editions enables you to encrypt the contents of a drive, including folders of users other than you?

 A. BitLocker

 B. Drive Encryptor

 C. Encrypting File System

 D. TrueCrypt

15. In Windows 7, how do the two middle levels of UAC security differ?

 A. One creates a prompt for verified programs; the other creates a prompt for unverified programs.

 B. One uses a consent prompt that blocks all other actions; the other uses a consent prompt that does not block other actions.

 C. One creates a prompt that requires a password; the other creates a prompt that does not require a password.

 D. One uses a prompt for standard users only; the other uses a prompt for all users.

◼ Essay Quiz

1. Your boss has tasked you with setting up five Windows 7 workstations, each to be used by three different users. Write a short essay on procedures or policies that should be implemented at each workstation to ensure that each user can share files that need to be shared but can also keep private files that need to be private.

2. Your company has a shared database in Windows Vista. Management must have full access to the database. The salespeople need to be able to access the database and make changes, but can't delete the database. All other employees should be able to read the contents of the database, but not make any changes. Write a short essay describing what groups and permissions you would need to set to make this work.

3. You have a computer with three users, plus an administrator. The three users need to be able to add documents to a folder, but only the administrator should be allowed to see the contents of those documents. Write a short essay describing how you would set up the folder, user accounts, groups, and permissions to make this work.

Lab Projects

• Lab Project 7.1

Take a single computer and create multiple user accounts and groups. Create some shared folders and change permissions on those folders to vary what different user accounts can do. Then experiment. Try to make as many different access types as you can.

• Lab Project 7.2

Experiment with permission propagation. On a computer with two hard drives, both formatted as NTFS, go through the process of copying and moving files and folders—with differing permissions—between folders on a single drive and between the two drives. Note carefully how permissions change or do not change with each step.

• Lab Project 7.3

On a computer with multiple user accounts, experiment with encryption. Encrypt files with one user account and then place those files into shared folders. What happens? Can other accounts access those files? Can they see the filenames? What about the administrator account? Go through the process of taking ownership to see if you can recover the contents of the encrypted files.

• Lab Project 7.4

On a Windows Vista or Windows 7 Ultimate computer, experiment with BitLocker on a second hard drive. Make note of what happens when you remove the drive and put it into another computer. How can you access the data that's been encrypted?

Maintaining and Optimizing Windows

chapter 8

"Chaos is inherent in all compounded things. Strive on with diligence."

—BUDDHA

In this chapter, you will learn how to

- **Perform maintenance tasks in Windows**
- **Optimize Windows**
- **Prepare Windows for problems**

Every computer running a Windows operating system requires both occasional optimization to keep the system running snappily and ongoing maintenance to make sure nothing goes wrong. Microsoft uses its decades of experience with operating systems to search for ways to make the tasks of maintaining and optimizing surprisingly easy and very automatic, but there's still plenty to do to keep things humming along.

The chapter covers maintenance and optimization, so let's make sure you know what these two terms mean. *Maintenance* means jobs you do from time to time to keep Windows running well, such as running hard drive utilities. CompTIA sees *optimization* as jobs you do to your Windows system to make it better—a good example is updating drivers to make hardware perform better. This chapter covers the standard maintenance and optimization activities performed on Windows and the tools techs use to perform them.

Even the best maintained, most perfectly optimized computer is going to run into trouble. Hard drives crash, naïve coworkers delete files, and those great new video card drivers sometimes fail. The secret isn't to try to avoid trouble, because trouble will find you, but rather to make sure you're ready to deal with problems when they arise. This is one area that very few users do well, and it's our jobs as techs to make recovery from trouble as painless as possible. Microsoft gives us plenty of tools to prep for problems—we just need to make sure we use them.

■ Maintaining Windows

Maintaining Windows can be compared to maintaining a new automobile. Of course, a new automobile comes with a warranty, so most of us just take it to the dealer to get work done. In this case, however, *you* are the mechanic, so you need to think as an auto mechanic would think. First, an auto mechanic needs to apply recalls when the automaker finds a serious problem. For a PC tech, that means installing the latest system patches released by Microsoft. You also need to check on the parts that wear down over time. On a car, that might mean changing the oil or rotating the tires. In a Windows system, that includes keeping the hard drive and Registry organized and uncluttered.

Windows Patch Management

There's no such thing as a perfect operating system, and Windows is no exception. From the moment Microsoft releases a new version of Windows, malware attacks, code errors, new hardware, new features, and many other issues compel Microsoft to provide updates, known more generically as *patches* in the computing world, to the operating system. The process of keeping software updated in a safe and timely fashion is known as *patch management*. Microsoft has been a leader in the process of patch management for decades. Microsoft's primary distribution tool for handling patch management is a Web site and a Control Panel applet called Windows Update.

Windows Update separates the available fixes into distinct types: updates and service packs. **Updates** are individual fixes that come out fairly often, on the order of once a week or so. Individual updates are usually fairly small, rarely more than a few megabytes. A **service pack** is a large bundle of updates plus anything else Microsoft might choose to add. Service packs are invariably large (hundreds of megabytes) and are often packaged with Windows, as shown in Figure 8.1.

Windows Update checks your system, grabs the updates, and patches your system automatically. Even if you don't want to allow Windows Update to run automatically, it'll nag you about updates until you patch your system. Microsoft provides the Windows Update service for all versions of Windows.

You might be asked about installing service packs and updates on the CompTIA A+ 220-802 exam. Pay attention to the steps listed here.

• **Figure 8.1** Windows 7 with Service Pack 1

Windows Update in Windows XP

You can start Windows Update when your computer is connected to the Internet. Start the utility at Start | All Programs | Windows Update. When you run Windows Update manually, the software connects to the Microsoft Web site and scans your computer to determine which updates you may need. Within a few seconds or minutes, depending on your connection speed, you'll get a straightforward screen like the one shown in Figure 8.2.

You have several choices here, although two are most obvious. If you click the Express button, Windows Update will grab any high-priority updates—these are security patches—and install them on your computer. If you click the Custom button, you can select from a list of optional updates.

Figure 8.3 shows the updater with a list of patches and security updates. You can scroll through the list and review the description of each update. You can deselect the checkbox next to a patch or update, and Windows Update will not download or install it. If you click the Clear All button, as you might suspect, all the updates will be unchecked and not installed. When you click Install Updates, all the updates remaining in the list will be installed.

● **Figure 8.2** Microsoft Windows Update page

● **Figure 8.3** Choose updates to be installed.

• **Figure 8.4** Accessing Windows Update in Windows 7

Windows Update in Windows Vista and Windows 7

Starting with Windows Vista, Microsoft changed Windows Update from a Web page to a Control Panel applet called—surprise!—Windows Update. Windows Update is virtually identical in both Windows Vista and Windows 7, so I'll just show it to you in Windows 7. Microsoft thoughtfully placed a shortcut to the applet in the Start menu, as shown in Figure 8.4.

Windows Update can run automatically (we'll cover that next), so you'll probably see new updates to install every time you open the applet. There are three common types of updates:

- **Important** These updates address critical security or stability issues and are the most critical. You can configure Windows Update to install these updates automatically.

- **Recommended** A recommended update is an added feature or enhancement that is not critical. You can configure Windows Update to install these updates automatically.

- **Optional** These include device drivers, language packs, and other nonessential updates. You must install these updates manually.

Figure 8.5 shows you what Windows Update looks like in Windows 7. Note that the Important update is Windows 7 Service Pack 1.

• **Figure 8.5** Windows Update in Windows 7

Installing an update is as easy as selecting the updates you want to install and clicking OK. If you don't want to install a specific update, and don't want to look at it every time you open Windows Update, you can hide it. To hide an update, right-click on the update you wish to hide and select Hide update (see Figure 8.6).

• **Figure 8.6** Hiding an update

Installing updates is only one part of this applet. You can find more options listed on the left side of the applet.

- **Control Panel Home** Returns you to the Control Panel
- **Check for updates** Manually checks for new updates
- **Change settings** Enables you to configure automatic updating
- **View update history** Shows you every update applied to the system and any that failed to install properly
- **Restore hidden updates** Reveals hidden updates

Automatic Updates in Windows XP

Updates are so important that Microsoft gives you the option to update Windows automatically through the **Automatic Updates** feature. Actually, it nags you about it! Soon after installing Windows XP (a day or two, in my experience), a message balloon will pop up from the taskbar suggesting that you automate updates (see Figure 8.7). If you click this balloon, the Automatic Updates Setup Wizard runs, with which you can configure the update program. You say you've never seen this message balloon but would like to automate the update process? No problem. Right-click My Computer (on the Start menu), select Properties, click the Automatic Updates tab, and select Automatic Update options. Or, open the Control Panel and double-click the Automatic Updates icon. Whenever your computer connects to the Web, it checks the Windows Update page.

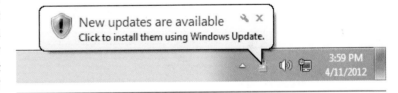

• **Figure 8.7** Windows Update balloon message in Windows XP

What happens next depends on the setting you choose. You have four choices:

- **Automatic (recommended)** Windows Update will simply keep your computer patched up and ready to go. This is the best option for most users, although it's not necessarily good for users of portable computers. Nobody wants to log into a slow hotel Wi-Fi connection and have most of your bandwidth sucked away by Automatic Updates downloading hot fixes!

- **Download updates for me, but let me choose when to install them** Windows Update downloads all patches in the background and then, when complete, tells you about them. You have the option at that point to install or not install.

- **Notify me but don't automatically download or install them** Windows Update simply flashes a dialog box that tells you updates are available but does not download anything until you say go. This is the best option for users of portable computers. You can download files when it's convenient for you, such as when you're home and not traveling on business.

- **Turn off Automatic Updates** This does precisely what is advertised. You get neither automatic patches nor notification that patches are available. Only use this option on a system that does not or cannot connect to the Internet. If you're online, your computer needs to be patched!

Automatic Updates in Windows Vista and Windows 7

Windows Vista and Windows 7 take automatic updates to a much higher level. Click on Change settings in the Windows Update dialog box to see the available options, listed next (see Figure 8.8).

• **Figure 8.8** Windows Update Change settings

Mike Meyer's CompTIA A+ Guide to 802: Managing and Troubleshooting PCs

- **Important updates** The choices in this drop-down list are almost identical to the four radio button options in Windows XP:

 - Install updates automatically (recommended)

 - Download updates but let me choose whether to install them

 - Check for updates but let me choose whether to download and install them

 - Never check for updates (not recommended)

- **Recommended updates** This option is enabled by default, but you can turn off the automatic installation of recommended updates. Most users leave it on, but paranoid admins like to turn this off.

- **Who can install updates** By default, all users can install updates. Uncheck this box to restrict installing updates to users with administrative privileges.

- **Microsoft Update** By default, the automatic update process includes updates for other Microsoft products, such as Microsoft Office. Unchecking this box disables these updates.

- **Software notifications** When enabled, you'll receive detailed information about any new Microsoft software. These show up as moderately obnoxious pop-ups in the system tray.

You need to decide whether or not you want to automatically install updates. Microsoft has a good track record for providing relatively fast, robust, and safe updates, but there have been a few rather infamous exceptions. As a result, there are always a few nerdier techs (like your humble author) who prefer to download the update and wait to see if there's any problems before installing it.

Managing Temporary Files with Disk Cleanup

You should run the Disk Cleanup utility regularly to make sure you've cleared out the junk files that accumulate from daily use. All that late-night Web surfing doesn't just use up time; it also uses up disk space, leaving behind hundreds of temporary Internet files. Those, and other bits and pieces (such as those "deleted" files still hanging around in your Recycle Bin), can add up to a lot of wasted disk space if you don't periodically clean them out.

You can reach this tool through the Start menu (Start | All Programs | Accessories | System Tools), or you can open My Computer or Computer, right-click the drive you want to clean up, and select Properties. You'll find the Disk Cleanup button in the middle of the General tab.

When you click the Disk Cleanup button, the application first calculates the space you can free up and then displays the Disk Cleanup dialog box, which tells you how much disk space it can free up—the total amount possible as well as the amount you'll get from each category of files it checks. Windows Vista and Windows 7 also ask if you want to clean up all the files on the computer or just your files. In Figure 8.9, the list of files to delete only has a few categories checked, and the actual amount of disk space to be gained by allowing Disk Cleanup to delete these files is much smaller than the estimate. As you select and deselect choices, watch this value change.

Try This!

Running Disk Cleanup

Your computer will thank you if you get rid of a bunch of unnecessary files and clean things up, so try this! Follow the instructions in the text and run Disk Cleanup. Is your computer noticeably snappier afterwards?

• **Figure 8.9** Disk Cleanup dialog box

If you scroll down through the list, you will see a choice to compress old files. What do you know—Disk Cleanup does more than just delete files! In fact, this file compression trick is where Disk Cleanup really, uh, cleans up. This is one of the few choices where you will gain the most space. The other big heavyweight category is Temporary Internet Files, which Disk Cleanup will delete. Try Disk Cleanup on a computer that gets hours of Internet use every day and you'll be pleased with the results.

Registry Maintenance

Your Registry is a huge database that Windows updates every time you add a new application or hardware or make changes to existing applications or hardware. As a result, the Registry tends to be clogged with entries that are no longer valid. These usually don't cause any problems directly, but they can slow down your system. Interestingly, Microsoft does not provide a utility to clean up the Registry. To clean your Registry, you need to turn to a third-party utility. Quite a few Registry cleaner programs are out there, but my favorite, as you might recall from Chapter 5, is the freeware CCleaner by Piriform (see Figure 8.10). You can download the latest copy at www.piriform.com/ccleaner/.

• **Figure 8.10** CCleaner

Before you start cleaning your Registry with wild abandon, keep in mind that all Registry cleaners are risky in that they may delete something you want in the Registry. Because Microsoft makes changes to the Registry for every version of Windows, make sure your utility supports the Windows version you're running. This is especially true for any 64-bit version of Windows! I've used CCleaner for a while and it has worked well for me—your experience may differ.

 CCleaner also helps clean all of the most common Web browsers and a number of popular applications.

Error-Checking and Disk Defragmentation

Keeping drives healthy and happy is a key task for every tech. Error-checking and Disk Defragmenter, discussed way back in Chapter 4, are the key Windows maintenance tools used to accomplish this task.

When you can't find a software reason (and there are many possible ones) for a problem such as a system freezing on shutdown, the problem might be the actual physical hard drive. The tool to investigate that is Error-checking. You can run Error-checking by using the chkdsk command from a command line, from the Start | Run dialog box, or from the Start | Search bar. You can also access the tool through the GUI by opening My Computer or Computer, right-clicking on the drive you want to check, selecting Properties, and then clicking the Tools tab. Click *Check now* to have Error-checking scan the drive for bad sectors, lost clusters, and similar problems, and repair them if possible.

Run Disk Defragmenter (see Figure 8.11) on a regular basis to keep your system from slowing down due to files being scattered in pieces on your hard drive. Before you click the Defragment button in Windows XP/7, click the Analyze button to have Windows analyze the disk and determine if defragmentation is actually necessary. (The Analyze button was removed from the Windows Vista disk defragmenter.) If you use Windows Vista/7, your system is defragged automatically.

Error-checking and Disk Defragmenter are such critical maintenance features that you really should have them run automatically. Read on to see how to schedule these and other critical jobs.

• **Figure 8.11** Vista Disk Defragmenter

Scheduling Maintenance

Maintenance only works properly when you do it at regular intervals. Depending on the version of Windows installed, you can schedule maintenance jobs to run automatically. The CompTIA 220-802 exam objectives define three areas for you to consider for scheduled maintenance: backups, defragmentation, and check disks (Error-checking). For the most part, we use Task Scheduler, although this depends on the task and the version of Windows.

Task Scheduler/Scheduled Tasks

Two versions of Task Scheduler are available: Windows XP runs Version 1.0, and Windows Vista and Windows 7 run Version 2.0. Microsoft calls it **Scheduled Tasks** in Windows XP, and **Task Scheduler** in Windows Vista/7. To open Scheduled Tasks in Windows XP, go to Start | Programs | Accessories | System Tools | Scheduled Tasks. To open Task Scheduler in Windows Vista and Windows 7, open the Administrative Tools applet and double-click Task Scheduler. You can also access it via Start | All Programs | Accessories | System Tools | Task Scheduler. In both versions, you can choose an executable program and define when you want that program to run. The key to running scheduled maintenance is to know the names of the executable programs and any special switches you may need to enter. Figures 8.12 and 8.13 show Scheduled Tasks running a backup at a certain time of day.

Version 2.0 is much more powerful and flexible than Windows XP's Version 1.0, dividing tasks into triggers, actions, and conditions. *Triggers* are actions or schedules that start a program. *Actions* are steps that define both the program to run and how it is to run. *Conditions* are extra criteria that must be met for the program to run. (Is the system idle? Is it connected to the Internet?) Figure 8.14 shows the Conditions tab for a sample task. To create a basic task in Windows Vista/7, all you need to do is name it, set how often it should run, and decide what it should do.

As you'll see in the following sections, many Windows utilities include built-in scheduling options. Here's the twist, though: they're still using Schedule Tasks/Task Scheduler. If you set up an automated defragmentation

> The CompTIA A+ 220-802 exam may use either name for the utility for scheduling maintenance in Windows. Remember that Windows XP labels the tool *Scheduled Tasks*; Windows Vista and Windows 7 label it *Task Scheduler*.

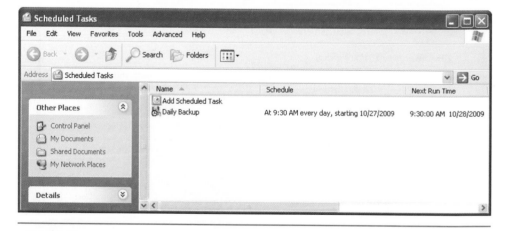

• **Figure 8.12** Windows XP Scheduled Tasks (Version 1.0)

from within Disk Defragmenter, for example, you can open up Task Scheduler and see it listed as a scheduled task. Neat!

Scheduling Backups

The backup utility varies depending on your version of Windows: in Windows XP, it's the Backup Utility (ntbackup); in Windows Vista, it's called the Backup and Restore Center, and in Windows 7, it's called Backup and Restore. You'll learn more about each of these tools later in the chapter, but right now, let's talk about scheduling regular backups of your data.

The fastest way to schedule a backup using the Backup Utility in Windows XP is to use the Backup or Restore Wizard (which I'll explain later in detail). After you configure which files to back up, where to store them, and all of that, you'll arrive at the Completing the Backup or Restore Wizard screen. Click the Advanced button to open a second set of options. The last of the advanced options you can set in the Backup or Restore Wizard is when you want the backup to run. You can set it to run now, later at a specified time, or use the Set Schedule button to configure regular backups at a time and frequency of your choosing.

Windows Vista/7's Backup and Restore Center/Backup and Restore applet includes a scheduler, too. Near the end of the Set Up Backup Wizard, after you've selected which folders to back up, you can click on *Change schedule* to set when and how often you want Windows to create the backup, just like in Windows XP (though Windows Vista/7 don't bury it under multiple buttons this time). It's that easy.

• **Figure 8.13** Daily Backup Schedule in Windows XP

• **Figure 8.14** Conditions tab in Windows 7 Task Scheduler (Version 2.0)

How often should you back up your files? If you're creating new documents, downloading music, and taking lots of digital photos, you'll want to back up your files weekly. If you're a casual, Internet-browsing, Solitaire-playing PC user, you're probably safe making a new backup once a month.

Scheduling Defragmentation

You can schedule Disk Defragmenter to run automatically using the Task Scheduler in Windows XP and from inside the utility itself in Windows Vista/7.

To defragment your hard drive on a schedule using Windows XP's Task Scheduler, double-click on Add Scheduled Task, which opens the Scheduled Task Wizard. Click Next. A list of default programs appears, but Disk Defragmenter doesn't make the cut. Click the Browse button and find the Disk Defragmenter executable, called defrag.exe, in the System32 folder. Click Open. You'll then name the task, set how often Task Scheduler should perform the task, and set the time and days it should run. You'll also be asked to enter a user name and password—the task runs as if it were run from that user's account. Once you complete the Wizard, a dialog box appears showing you all the information you configured. To set the Disk Defragmenter to defragment the C: drive, type **C:** at the end of the Run box, next to C:\Windows\System32\defrag .exe, as shown in Figure 8.15.

• **Figure 8.15** Scheduling a disk defragmentation in Windows XP

The CompTIA A+ 802 exam calls the Disk Defragmenter program "Defrag," the common tech slang term for it.

Windows Vista/7's version of Disk Defragmenter includes a scheduler, just like Backup and Restore. To access Disk Defragmenter's scheduler, open the Start menu, type **defrag**, and press ENTER. You can start defragging right away or modify/disable the task in the Disk Defragmenter: Modify Schedule dialog box (see Figure 8.16).

• **Figure 8.16** Windows 7 Disk Defragmenter scheduler

It's best to run Disk Defragmenter every evening if possible. If you're using Vista/7, take advantage of the "only run when idle" condition to keep Disk Defragmenter from interrupting possibly more important tasks.

Scheduling Error-checking (Check Disk)

The tool you know and love as Error-checking appears on the CompTIA A+ 220-802 exam objectives as *Check disk* and chkdsk (the command-line version of the tool). Regardless of what you call Error-checking, setting up Task Scheduler to run it automatically is a good thing.

Using the technique you just learned to set up a scheduled task with Disk Defragmenter, create another scheduled task to run Error-checking. Its executable is called chkdsk.exe (see Figure 8.17). There are two switches you should use: /F to repair sectors and /R to tell Error-checking to attempt to recover data on known bad sectors.

Opinions vary on how often you should run Error-checking as a scheduled task. For the CompTIA 220-802 exam, a monthly check is a good idea. For the real world, you should run Error-checking when you suspect a problem with your drives.

System Configuration

Techs use the **System Configuration utility** (also known by its executable name, **msconfig**) to edit and troubleshoot operating system and program startup processes and services. To start the System Configuration utility, go to the Start | Run dialog box or the Start | Search bar, enter **msconfig**, and click OK or press ENTER (see Figure 8.18). The program runs automatically in Windows XP; in

> No versions of Windows run Error-checking automatically, so you'll need to set up a task on the computer if you wish to do so.

• **Figure 8.17** Scheduling Error-checking in Windows XP

• **Figure 8.18** The Windows Vista System Configuration utility

Vista/7, you need to provide the necessary credentials, depending on the User Account Control (UAC) setup.

The System Configuration utility in Windows XP offers quick access to troubleshoot and edit the boot.ini file. System Configuration in Windows Vista and Windows 7 no longer has that ability, but it still offers a number of handy features, distributed across the following tabs:

- **General** Select the type of startup you would like to use for the next boot. You can perform a normal startup with all programs and services launching normally, a diagnostic startup with only basic devices and services, or a custom boot.

- **Boot** This tab contains advanced boot features. Here you can see every copy of Windows you have installed, set a default OS, or delete an OS from the boot menu. You can set up a safe boot, or adjust advanced options like the number of cores or amount of memory to use.

- **Services** This tab is identical to the Services tab in the Task Manager. You can enable or disable any or all services running on your PC.

- **Startup** This tab enables you to enable or disable any startup programs (programs that load when you launch Windows). This is perhaps the most useful tab, especially if Windows is slow to load on your PC.

- **Tools** This tab lists many of the tools and utilities available in Windows, including Event Viewer, Performance Monitor, Command Prompt, and so on. There's nothing here that you can't find elsewhere in Windows, but it's a handy list all the same.

System Information

Windows comes with a handy built-in utility known as the **System Information tool** (see Figure 8.19) that collects information about hardware resources, components, and the software environment. When it finishes doing that, it provides a nice and tidy little report, enabling you to troubleshoot and diagnose any issues and conflicts. As with many other tools you can access from the Start | Run dialog box or Start | Search bar, the CompTIA A+ 802 exam refers to System Information by its executable, **msinfo32**.

You can start System Information in one of the following ways:

- Choose Start | Programs or All Programs | Accessories | System Tools | System Information.

- In Windows XP, choose Start | Run, then type **msinfo32**, and click OK. In Windows Vista/7, go to Start | Search bar, type **msinfo32**, and press ENTER.

It is also important to note that you can use System Information to gather information about remote computers by selecting View | Remote Computer and then entering the remote computer's network machine name. Under Tools, you even get quick access to System Restore and the DirectX Diagnostic Tool, a tool for checking your video card that Chapter 11 discusses.

You simply cannot run a computer today without a large number of security programs to protect you from malicious attacks from spyware, malware, viruses, and hacking. In fact, the installation, monitoring, and updating of these programs (and possibly even hardware) is so important that they get their own chapter. Head to Chapter 18 for a complete discussion of how to keep your computer safe!

• **Figure 8.19** System Information

■ Optimizing Windows

Maintenance is about keeping Windows' performance from degrading with time and use. Of course, you don't just want to keep trouble at bay—you want to make your systems better, stronger, faster! Anything you do that makes Windows better than it was before, such as adding a piece of software or hardware to make something run better, is an optimization.

Installing and Removing Software

Probably the most common optimization performed on any PC is adding and removing applications. Installing and removing software is part of the normal life of any PC. Each time you add or remove software, you are making changes and decisions that can affect the system beyond whatever the program does, so it pays to know how to do it right.

Installing Software

Most application programs are distributed on optical discs (although this is slowly changing). Windows supports **Autorun**, a feature that enables the operating system to look for and read a special file called—wait for it—autorun.inf. Immediately after a removable media device (optical disc or thumb drive) is inserted into your computer, whatever program is listed in autorun.inf runs automatically. Most application programs distributed on removable media have an autorun file that calls up the installation program.

Sometimes, however, you need to institute the installation sequence yourself. Perhaps the installation disc lacks an Autorun installation program, or perhaps Windows is configured so that you must start programs

on optical discs manually. In some cases, a disc may contain more than one program, and you must choose which of them to install. Regardless of the reason, you can begin the installation manually by using the **Add or Remove Programs** applet in the Control Panel in Windows XP. Click the Add New Programs button (see Figure 8.20), follow the prompts, and provide the media or location of the files. In Windows Vista and 7, Microsoft has replaced the Add or Remove Programs applet with **Programs and Features**, which does not have the Add New Programs feature.

With Windows Vista/7, UAC complicates the installation process a bit. You will most likely be prompted by UAC when installing an application, giving you time to review what is happening to your system in case you did not approve of the program being installed. If you are using an administrator account, you can simply click Continue and finish the installation. Should you be logged in with a less privileged account, you will need to enter a user name and password of an account with administrative privileges. Some installers have trouble letting UAC know that they need more privileges and simply fail no matter what account you are logged in with. In those cases, it is best to right-click the installer icon and select *Run as administrator* to give the installer the access it expects from the start.

Assuming all is well, you typically must accept the terms of a software license before you can install an application. These steps are not optional; the installation simply won't proceed until you accept all terms the software manufacturer requires and, in many cases, enter a correct code. You may also be asked to make several decisions during the installation process. For example, you may be asked where you would like to install the program and if you would like certain optional components installed. Generally speaking, it is best to accept the suggested settings unless you have a very specific reason for changing the defaults.

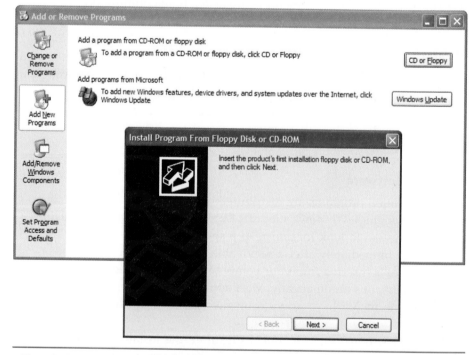

• **Figure 8.20** Result of clicking the Add New Programs button

Removing Software

Each installed application program takes up space on your computer's hard drive, and programs that you no longer need waste space that could be used for other purposes. Removing unnecessary programs can be an important piece of optimization.

You remove a program from a Windows PC in much the same manner as you install it. That is, you use the application's own uninstall program, when possible. You normally find the uninstall program listed in the application's folder in the All Programs section of the Start menu, as shown in Figure 8.21.

If an uninstall program is not available, use the appropriate Windows Control Panel applet you learned about earlier to remove the software. Figure 8.22 shows this applet in Windows 7. You select the program you want to remove and click the Uninstall/Change button or Change/Remove button. Windows displays a message warning you that the program will be permanently removed from your PC. If you're certain you want to continue, click Yes.

You may then see a message telling you that a shared file that appears to no longer be in use is about to be deleted, and asking your approval. Generally speaking, it's safe to delete such files. If you do not delete them, they will likely be orphaned and remain unused on your hard disk forever. In some cases, clicking the Uninstall/Change or Change/Remove button starts the application's install program (the one you couldn't find before) so you can modify the installed features. This is a function of

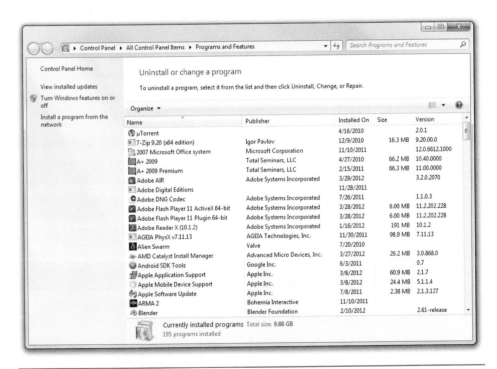

• **Figure 8.21** Uninstall me!

• **Figure 8.22** Programs and Features applet

• **Figure 8.23** Windows Components Wizard

• **Figure 8.24** Windows Features dialog box in Vista

The Uninstall/Change and Change/Remove buttons change depending on the program. Not all programs can be changed.

the program you're attempting to remove. The end result should be the removal of the application and all of its pieces and parts, including files and Registry entries.

Adding or Removing Windows Components/Features

When you installed Windows, it included certain features by default. It installed Notepad, modem support, and games on your computer. You can remove these Windows components from your system if you like, and add other components as well. If you're adding components in Windows XP, you'll need a copy of your installation disc, or another location where the Windows source files are stored. This task really hasn't changed from previous versions of Windows.

To add or remove a Windows component in Windows XP, open the Add/Remove Programs applet in the Control Panel. From here, select Add/Remove Windows Components, which opens the Windows Components Wizard (see Figure 8.23). You can select an installed program here. You can see how frequently it is used, how much disk space it uses, and (sometimes) the last time it was used.

In Windows Vista/7, open the Programs and Features applet in the Control Panel, and then click the *Turn Windows features on or off* option on the Tasks list. Click Continue if prompted by UAC and you will be presented with the Windows Features dialog box (see Figure 8.24). To toggle a feature on or off, simply click its checkbox. Unlike Windows XP, you no longer need to have the installation disc to turn on features.

Try This!

Adding and Removing Windows Components

You owe it to yourself to master the skills on adding and removing Windows components, so try this! Follow the instructions in the text and add something to a Windows PC. Check to make sure it works. Then go through the process to remove it afterward. Better?

Installing/Optimizing a Device

The processes for optimizing hardware in Windows are absolutely identical between the versions, even down to the troubleshooting utilities, and are very similar to the steps for installing a new device. The installation process is covered in every chapter of this book that deals with one type of device or another, so this section concentrates on the issues that fit best under optimization.

The CompTIA A+ 220-802 exam tests you on installing and optimizing devices.

Updating Drivers

Device manufacturers occasionally update their drivers. Most of these updates fix problems, but many updates incorporate new features. Whatever the case, when one of your devices gets an updated driver, it's your job to install it. Windows Update provides an easy method to update drivers from manufacturers that take advantage of the service. If you are using Windows XP, you usually need to select the Custom option to see these updates because the Express option only installs high-priority updates. When you click on the Custom option, look under Hardware, Optional (on the left) to see if Windows has any driver updates (see Figure 8.25).

If you are using Vista/7, you will need to click *View available updates* to see if any drivers are available for your system. No matter which version of Windows you have, you should research all driver updates before

• **Figure 8.25** Optional Hardware updates

Figure 8.26 The More information link—don't trust it.

you install them. In theory, the best way to do this research is to click on the More information button next to the driver (see Figure 8.26) to get the details on what's new with a particular driver, but this rarely seems to produce good information. Instead, go to the manufacturer's Web site and read up on what that driver provides, and then download the latest driver there.

If Windows does not put a driver update in the Windows Update tool, how do you know a device needs updating? The trick is to know your devices. Video card manufacturers update drivers quite often. Get in the habit of registering your video card with the manufacturer to stay up to date. Any very new device is also a good candidate for an update. When you buy that new cool toy for your system, make a point to head over to the manufacturer's Web site and see if any updates have come out since it was packaged for sale. That happens more often than you might think!

Once a driver is installed, test it hard. Use the new features or capabilities that motivated you to install the new driver in the first place. Make the hardware that the driver supports do everything, and look for any problems. If anything goes wrong, you can roll back a bad driver in Device Manager, as described a bit later in the chapter.

Figure 8.27 A digitally signed driver

Driver Signing

Device drivers become part of the operating system and thus have the potential to cause lots of problems if they're written poorly. To protect Windows systems from bad device drivers, Microsoft uses **driver signing**, which means that each driver has a digital signature. Any drivers included on the Windows installation media or Windows Update are digitally signed. Once you have installed a driver, you can look at its Properties dialog box to confirm that it was digitally signed. Figure 8.27 shows a digitally signed network card driver.

When an unsigned driver is detected during hardware installation in Windows XP, you'll see the message in Figure 8.28 offering you the choice to stop or continue the installation. Signed drivers are more or less a sure thing, but that doesn't mean unsigned ones are a problem—just consider the source of the driver and ensure that your device works properly after installation.

You can control how Windows XP behaves when drivers are being installed. Click the Driver Signing button on the Hardware tab of the System Properties dialog box to display the Driver Signing Options dialog box shown in Figure 8.29. If you select Ignore, Windows will install an unsigned driver without warning you. If you select Warn, you will be prompted when Windows detects an unsigned driver during driver installation, and you will be given the opportunity to either stop or continue the installation. Choosing Block will prevent the installation of unsigned drivers.

The default Driver Signing setting is Warn. This is also the default setting during installation, so you will always be warned when Windows detects an unsigned driver during Windows installation. This is no problem for a standard installation, when you are sitting at the computer, responding to all prompts—but it is a problem for automated, unattended installations. This is a good reason to check out all your device drivers before installing Windows.

Windows Vista and Windows 7 have eliminated the driver signing options. With these versions of Windows, all installed drivers are inspected for a digital signature and you are prompted with a warning if the driver is unsigned (see Figure 8.30). In 64-bit versions of Windows, all drivers must be signed. No exceptions. Microsoft wants to keep tight controls on the drivers to improve stability.

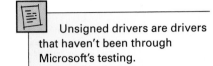
Unsigned drivers are drivers that haven't been through Microsoft's testing.

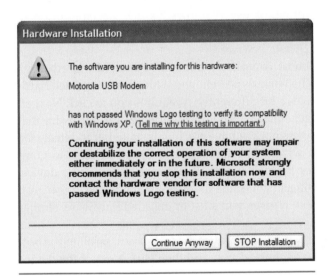

• **Figure 8.28** Stop or continue installation of an unsigned driver

• **Figure 8.29** Driver Signing Options dialog box

• Figure 8.30 Unsigned driver in Windows 7

• Figure 8.31 Rolling back to the previous driver

Device Manager

You've worked with **Device Manager** in other chapters when installing and troubleshooting devices; it's also the tool to use when optimizing device drivers. Right-click on a device in Device Manager to display the context menu. From here you can update or uninstall the driver, disable the device, scan for hardware changes, or display the Properties dialog box. When you open the Properties dialog box, you'll see several tabs that vary according to the specific device. Most have General, Driver, Details, and Resources. The tab that matters most for optimization is the Driver tab.

The Driver tab has buttons labeled Driver Details, Update Driver, Roll Back Driver, and Uninstall. Windows Vista/7 also include a Disable option, which does exactly what you think it does. Driver Details lists the driver files and their locations on disk. Update Driver opens the Hardware Update Wizard—not very useful given that the installation programs for almost all drivers do this automatically. The Roll Back Driver option is a different story. It enables you to remove an updated driver, thus rolling back to the previous driver version. Roll Back Driver (see Figure 8.31) is a life saver when you install a new driver and suddenly discover it's worse than the driver it replaced! Uninstall removes the driver.

Adding a New Device

Windows should automatically detect any new device you install in your system. If Windows does not detect a newly connected device, use Windows XP's or Windows Vista's Add Hardware Wizard, which you can find in the Add Hardware applet, or use Windows 7's *Add a device* option in the Devices and Printers applet to get the device recognized and drivers installed (see Figure 8.32).

Windows Vista/7 almost completely automated the Add Hardware/ Add a Device Wizards. The wizards present you with a list of detected hardware. Windows XP behaves a bit differently; it requires you to click Next on the Welcome screen to get started. The wizard searches for hardware that has been connected but does not yet have a driver installed. If it detects the device, select it, and the wizard installs the driver. You may have to point to the source location for the driver files. If it does not detect the device, which is very likely, it will ask you if the hardware is connected. When you answer yes and click Next, it gives you a list of installed hardware, similar to Figure 8.33.

If the device is in the list, select it and click Next. If not, scroll to the bottom and select *Add a new hardware device*, and then click Next. If the device is a printer, network card, or modem, select *Search for and install the hardware automatically* and click Next. In that case, once the wizard detects the device and installs the driver, you're finished. If you do see your device on the list, your best hope is to select *Install the hardware that I manually select from a list*. In the subsequent screens, select the appropriate device category,

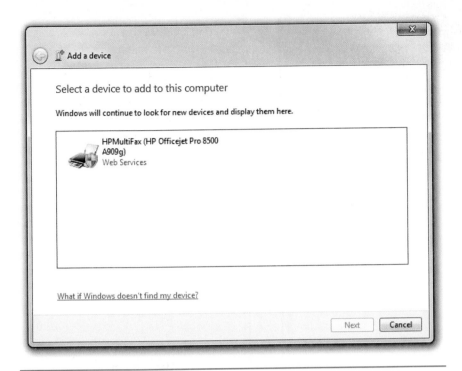

• **Figure 8.32** Adding a device in Windows 7

select the device manufacturer and the correct model, and respond to the prompts from the Add Hardware Wizard to complete the installation.

Performance Options

One optimization you can perform on all Windows versions is setting Performance Options. **Performance Options** are used to configure CPU, RAM, and virtual memory (page file) settings. To access these options in Windows XP, right-click My Computer and select Properties, click the Advanced tab, and click the Settings button in the Performance section of that tab. In Windows Vista/7, right-click Computer and select Properties, and then click the *Advanced system settings* link in the Tasks list. On the Advanced tab, click the Settings button in the Performance section.

The Performance Options dialog box has three tabs: Visual Effects, Advanced, and Data Execution Prevention (see Figure 8.34). The Visual Effects tab enables you to adjust visual effects that impact performance, such as animations, thumbnails, and transparencies. Try clicking the top three choices in turn and watch the list of settings. Notice the tiny difference between the first two choices (*Let Windows choose what's best for my computer* and *Adjust for best appearance*). The third choice, *Adjust for best performance*, turns off all visual effects, and the fourth option is an invitation to make your own adjustments. If you're on a computer that barely supports Windows, turning off visual effects can make a

• **Figure 8.33** List of installed hardware in Windows XP

311

Figure 8.34 Windows XP Performance Options dialog box

Figure 8.35 Advanced tab of Performance Options dialog box

huge difference in the responsiveness of the computer. For the most part, though, just leave these settings alone.

The Advanced tab, shown in Figure 8.35, has three sections: Processor scheduling, Memory usage (Windows XP only), and Virtual memory. Under the Processor scheduling section, you can choose to adjust for best performance of either Programs or Background services. The Memory usage settings enable you to allocate a greater share of memory to programs or to the system cache. The Virtual memory section of this tab enables you to modify the size and location of the page file. Microsoft dropped the Memory usage settings option in Windows Vista and Windows 7.

Microsoft introduced *Data Execution Prevention* (*DEP*) with Windows XP Service Pack 2. DEP works in the background to stop viruses and other malware from taking over programs loaded in system memory. It doesn't prevent viruses from being installed on your computer, but makes them less effective. By default, DEP monitors only critical operating system files in RAM, but the Data Execution Prevention tab enables you to have DEP monitor all running programs. It works, but you'll take a performance hit. Like other options in the Performance Options dialog box, leaving the default DEP settings is the best option most of the time.

Hardware Profiles

Windows XP has an interesting feature called **Hardware Profiles**. There are many unique situations, mainly with portable computers, where a user is motivated to not have all of their hardware devices running at all times. Imagine a user who has a laptop with a wireless network card. She also has

• **Figure 8.36** Default Hardware Profiles

a docking station in her office that includes a wired NIC. When the user is plugged into the docking station, she wants to use the wired connection, and when disconnected, she wants to use the wireless connection. In Windows XP, you can create two hardware profiles: one where the wired network card is disabled in Device Manager and another where the wireless network card is disabled.

You can inspect hardware profiles by going to the System applet in the Control Panel, selecting the Hardware tab, and then clicking Hardware Profiles (see Figure 8.36). All Windows XP systems have one hardware profile by default.

You can make a second profile by copying the default profile. If you have more than one profile, Windows XP will prompt you with a text menu every time you boot the computer, similar to the one shown in Figure 8.37.

There was a tremendous uproar from a small group of impassioned hardware profile fans when Microsoft decided to drop the feature from Windows Vista and Windows 7.

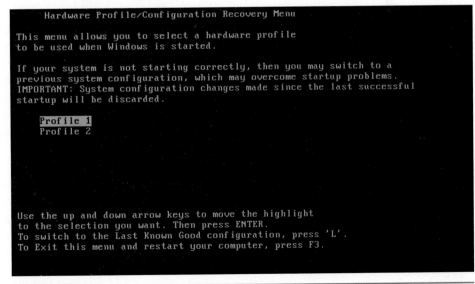

• **Figure 8.37** Hardware Profile boot menu

Preparing Windows for Problems

Techs need to prepare for problems. You must have critical system files and data backed up and tools in place for the inevitable glitches. Different versions of Windows enable you to prepare for problems differently. Windows includes multiple backup systems that do different things. Each backup system enables you to:

- Back up personal data
- Back up local copies of critical system state information
- Restore a backup if your system won't boot

Backing Up Personal Data

The most important data on your computer is the personal data: your documents, e-mail messages and contacts, Web favorites, photographs, and other files. To handle backing up personal data, every version of Windows comes with some form of backup utility. There are big differences between the backup included in Windows XP and the backup included in Windows Vista and Windows 7, so let's break up the idea of backing up personal data between Windows XP and Windows Vista/7.

Backup Utility for XP (ntbackup)

Windows XP's **Backup Utility** (popularly known by the name of the executable program, **ntbackup**) provides almost all the tools you need to back up files and folders. It has come a long way from its origins in Windows NT. The ntbackup program supports a greater variety of devices, enabling you to back up to network drives, local drives, tape, and removable disks (but not optical discs). Most folks, however, still turn to third-party utilities to create system, e-mail, browser, and personal data backups.

You can start NTBackup by navigating the Start menu to Accessories | System Tools, or by clicking the Backup Now button on the Tools tab of the local disk's Properties dialog box. I prefer to start it from Start | Run with the command **ntbackup**. Click the Backup Wizard button to run the Backup Wizard. To use the Windows XP version in Advanced Mode, click Advanced Mode on the opening screen (see Figure 8.38). To have it always open in Advanced Mode, deselect the *Always start in wizard mode* checkbox. If the program is in Advanced Mode and you want to run it as a wizard, click the Wizard Mode link to open the Backup or Restore Wizard.

To create a backup, start the Backup Utility, click Advanced Mode, and choose the Backup tab. Check the boxes next to the drives and files you want to include in the backup. To include your system state information, such as Registry and boot files (which you should do), click the System State checkbox. To specify where to put the backup file you're creating, either type the path and file name in the *Backup media or file name* box or click Browse, select a location, type the file name, and click Save. Click Start Backup. Choose whether you want to append this backup to a previous one or overwrite it. Click Advanced to open the Advanced Backup Options dialog box, select *Verify data after backup*, and click OK. Click Start Backup again. A dialog box

The Backup Utility is not included in the default installation of Windows XP Home. You must install it manually from the Windows CD-ROM.

shows you the utility's progress. When it finishes, click Close and then close the Backup Utility.

NTBackup gives you three choices after you click Advanced Mode: Backup Wizard (Advanced), Restore Wizard (Advanced), and Automated System Recovery Wizard (see Figure 8.39). First, I'm going to dive into the Backup Wizard and Automated System Recovery Wizard. Then we'll look at tape backups and more backup options.

Backup Wizard (Advanced) If you run the Backup Wizard and click the Next button on the Welcome screen, you'll open the dialog box in Figure 8.40. You have three options here. The first two are fairly self-explanatory: You can back up everything or just selected drives and files.

• **Figure 8.38** Choosing to run the Backup Wizard in Advanced Mode

The third option needs some explanation. The *Only back up the System State data* radio button enables you to save "other" system-critical files. This option really makes sense for Windows Server systems because it saves Active Directory information (which your Windows XP systems do not store) as well as other critical, server-specific functions. (I cover more on these topics in Chapter 12.)

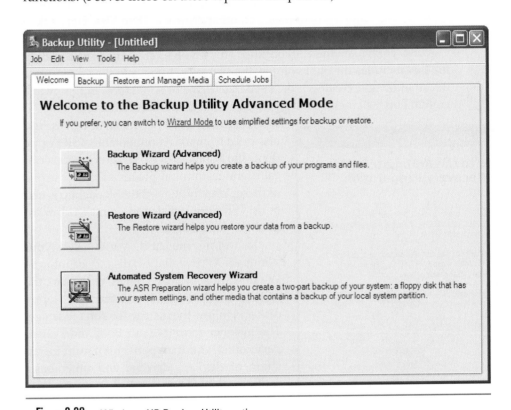

• **Figure 8.39** Windows XP Backup Utility options

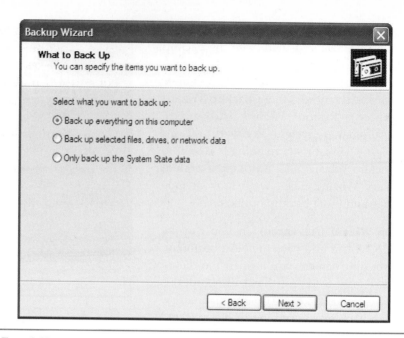

● **Figure 8.40** Backup Wizard options

Windows XP Automated System Recovery (ASR) The Windows XP **Automated System Recovery (ASR)** is your last line of defense when restoring functionality to your PC (see Figure 8.41). It backs up your boot and system volumes (meaning your C: drive, in most cases) and the system state information—the Registry, boot files, and other critical system files. Here's how it works.

First, you create the ASR backup. This involves creating a large backup file that includes the boot volume, the system volume, and the system state information and placing it on a separate drive or some form of removable media. This will include all applications and user data on that one drive—it won't back up extra partitions or drives. You also need to create a nonbootable ASR floppy disk. The floppy disk stores information critical to the restoration process. Don't lose one of these items, either—the ASR backup is tied to its ASR floppy disk and won't work without both components.

To restore the ASR, you'll need your Windows XP installation disc. Boot into the Windows installer and press F2 to start the ASR restore process. Insert the ASR floppy disk and follow the instructions on the screen. The installer formats your boot and system partition(s), and then performs a mini-installation of devices, drivers, and other basic configurations. Then the ASR Recovery Wizard launches, asking for the location of that backup file you made. Point it to the file, and the restoration process will complete.

● **Figure 8.41** Creating an ASR backup

Tape Backup The odd fact that Microsoft never updated the Backup or Restore Wizard in Windows XP to enable you to back up to optical discs of any sort has kept alive the practice of tape backups. Tape drives connect to the ATA or SCSI bus, just like optical drives, but rather than using a shiny CD-R or DVD+R disc, you have to back up to magnetic tape (see Figure 8.42).

There are a large number of different tape formats, but CompTIA lists only one technology, Digital Linear Tape (DLT), in the CompTIA A+ Acronyms list. DLT was a popular tape format from the 1980s up to the early 2000s, with capacities from 10 MB in the early versions up to (arguably) around 800 GB. DLT is rarely used anymore, and CompTIA should have removed this from the CompTIA A+ exam competencies.

Tape drive manufacturers have done pretty much everything they can do to make tape backups as fast as possible, but the technology suffers from two huge drawbacks. First, it's tape, which means all data must be stored and restored in sequential access. The drive has to go through Files 1 and 2 before reaching File 3, in other words. Second, tape is painfully slow in comparison to hard drives, optical drives, or Flash-media drives. With plenty of cheap online, hard drive, and recordable optical media options available for backup, though, tape's days are numbered.

Backup Options The goal of backing up data is to ensure that when a system dies, there will be an available, recent copy you can use to restore the system. You could simply back up the complete system at the end of each day—or whatever interval you feel is prudent to keep the backups fresh—but complete backups can be a tremendous waste of time and materials. Instead of backing up the entire system, take advantage of the fact that not all of the files will be changed in any given period; much of the time you only need to back up what's changed since your last backup. Recognizing this, most backup software solutions have a series of options available beyond the complete backup.

The key to understanding backups other than the full backup is *attributes*, 1-bit storage areas that all files have. The most common attributes are hidden (don't show the file in Computer or when `dir` is typed at the command line), system (it's a critical file for the system), read-only (can't erase it), and archive. These attributes were first used in FAT-formatted drives in

The CompTIA A+ 220-802 exam lists *repair disk* as an objective even though the Emergency Repair Disk (ERD) tool was phased out with Windows 2000. If it comes up, know that the ERD was a much simpler version of Windows XP's ASR that backed up critical system and boot files. See also Chapter 10 on creating a *system repair disc*, an optical disc used for restoring critical backups.

Windows Explorer (My Computer in Windows XP, Computer in Vista/7) by default does not show much about files in any view, even when you select Details from the View menu or from the Change your view pull-down menu. The Details view is highly customizable, however, and can reveal a phenomenal amount and variety of information about files.

To customize your view, right-click the column bar (the bar that says Name, Size, Type, Date Modified, and so forth) to look at the default choices. You'll see everything from Attributes, Owner, Author, and Title to file type–specific information such as Genre, Duration, and Bit Rate (for music files). What you see in the initial options differs according to the version of Windows. If the default extra view options don't get your motor revving, selecting the More option brings up a menu offering many more view options! For the purposes of this section, click the Attributes box to display file and folder attributes.

• **Figure 8.42** Backup tapes

the DOS era, but they are still completely supported by all file formats. The *archive bit* works basically like this: Whenever a file is saved, the archive bit is turned on. Simply opening a file affects the current state of the archive bit. Backup programs usually turn off a file's archive bit when the file is backed up. In theory, if a file's archive bit is turned off, there's a good backup of that file on some tape. If the archive bit is turned on, it means that the file has been changed since it was last backed up (see Figure 8.43).

Archive bits are used to perform backups that are not full backups. The following backup types are most often supported:

- A *normal backup* is a full backup. Every file selected is backed up, and the archive bit is turned off for every file backed up. This is the standard "back it all up" option.

- A *copy backup* is identical to a normal backup, with the important distinction being that the archive bits are *not* changed. This is used (although not often) for making extra copies of a previously completed backup.

- An *incremental backup* includes only files with the archive bit turned on. In other words, it copies only the files that have been changed since the last backup. This backup turns off the archive bits.

- A *differential backup* is identical to an incremental backup, except that it doesn't turn off the archive bits.

- A *daily backup*, also known as a *daily copy backup*, makes copies of all the files that have been changed that day. It does not change the archive bits.

The motivation for having both the incremental and differential backups may not be clear at first glance—they seem so similar as to be basically the same. Incremental seems the better option at first. If a file is backed up, you

Be sure you know the types of backups, including which ones change the archive bits and which ones do not.

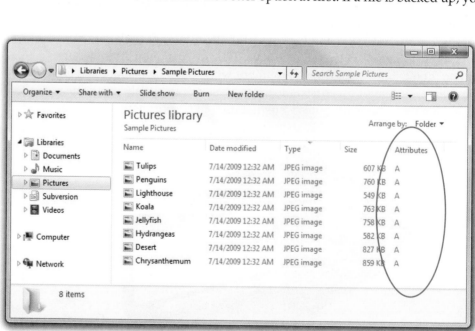

• **Figure 8.43** The archive bit on these files is on.

would want to turn off the archive bit, right? Well, maybe. But there is one scenario where that might not be too attractive. Most backups do a big weekly normal backup, followed by daily incremental or differential backups at the end of every business day. Figure 8.44 shows the difference between incremental and differential backups.

Notice that a differential backup is a cumulative backup. Because the archive bits are not set, it keeps backing up all changes since the last normal backup. This means the backup files will get progressively larger throughout the week (assuming a standard weekly normal backup). The incremental backup, by contrast, only backs up files changed since the last backup. Each incremental backup file will be relatively small and also totally different from the previous backup file.

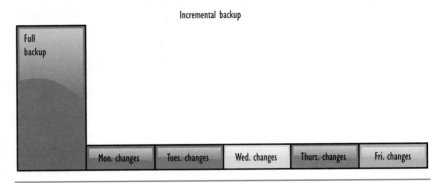

• **Figure 8.44** Incremental versus differential

Let's assume that the system is wiped out on a Thursday morning. How can you restore the system to a useful state?

If you're using an incremental backup, you will first have to restore the last weekly backup you ran on Monday, then the Tuesday backup, and then the Wednesday backup before the system is restored to its Thursday morning state. The longer the time between normal backups, the more incremental backups you must restore.

Using the same scenario but assuming you're doing differential instead of incremental backups, you only need the weekly backup and then the Wednesday backup to restore your system. A differential backup always requires only two backups to restore a system. Suddenly, the differential backup looks better than the incremental! On the other hand, one big benefit of incremental over differential is backup file size. Differential backup files are massive compared to incremental ones.

Backup and Restore Center for Windows Vista/7

Microsoft retired the ntbackup program with Windows XP, replacing it with the more automated and simpler **Backup and Restore Center** (Windows Vista) and *Backup and Restore* (Windows 7) Control Panel applets. The ntbackup program required you to choose the files you wanted to back up as well as the type of backup (incremental, differential, or normal). Windows Vista and Windows 7 no longer ask those questions, at least not directly. In Windows Vista, you can either back up files or back up your computer (Figure 8.45). Both choices will first ask you where you want to store the backup (Figure 8.46).

• **Figure 8.45** Backup options in Vista

• **Figure 8.46** Backup location in Vista

Windows Vista and Windows 7 do not back up to tape drives.

Unlike ntbackup, Windows Vista and Windows 7 don't support backing up to tape. Acceptable options for backup media include flash drives, optical discs of all sorts, or even over a network. You can even copy the backup to any hard drive, as long as it's not the drive you're backing up.

As the name implies, the *Back up computer* option backs up your entire computer to a system image. All you need to do is pick a destination for the image (optical drive, hard drive, or network location) and Windows

• **Figure 8.47** Types of files to back up

takes care of the rest. Choosing the *Back up files* option is another matter entirely. Clicking this button doesn't bring up a directory tree like you saw in ntbackup. Instead, you see the screen shown in Figure 8.47.

The *Back up files* option in Vista only enables you to back up personal information for all users. If you want to back up any installed applications, or even Windows itself, don't bother using the *Back up files* option that comes with Windows Vista.

Windows 7's Backup and Restore utility includes a number of noteworthy improvements over Windows Vista's. First of all, Microsoft changed the look of the main screen (Figure 8.48).

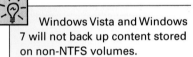

Windows Vista and Windows 7 will not back up content stored on non-NTFS volumes.

• **Figure 8.48** Windows 7 Backup and Restore

● **Figure 8.49** What do you want to back up?

Windows image files use the .wim extension.

Clicking the *Set up backup* link in Windows 7 opens a dialog box asking you to choose your backup location—very similar to Vista's backup. After selecting your backup location and clicking *Next*, you then see the screen shown in Figure 8.49.

If you select *Let Windows choose (recommended)*, you'll get a backup similar to the Vista backup, but with one very important difference. You'll back up each user's personal data, but Windows 7 doesn't stop there. Assuming you have enough space in your backup location, Windows 7 will automatically add a system image that includes the entire Windows operating system, every installed program, all device drivers, and even the registry.

Selecting *Let me choose* is equally interesting. Unlike Vista's selection, Windows 7 enables you to pick individual users' files to back up (Figure 8.50).

By selecting a user, you can choose libraries or the user's personal folders to back up, as shown in Figure 8.51. Also note the checkbox that gives you the option to make a system image, just as if you selected the *Let Windows choose (recommended)* option.

● **Figure 8.50** Backup showing a list of users

• **Figure 8.51** Single user, showing some of the user's libraries/folders

Once you complete the wizard, Windows starts backing up your files. While the backup runs, you can monitor its process with an exciting and handy progress bar (Figure 8.52). If you can't handle that much excitement, you can close the backup window while the OS backs up files. The process can take a long time, many hours with a modern system with a large hard drive.

> You can also choose to create just a system image in Windows 7. From the Backup and Restore applet, select *Create a system image*. It works like the system image function in Windows Vista.

• **Figure 8.52** Backup in progress …

Chapter 8: Maintaining and Optimizing Windows

 Try This!

Creating a System Image

If you have a copy of Windows 7 installed and a handy second hard drive with enough free space to hold the contents of your primary drive, try this! Install the second hard drive and run the Backup and Restore applet. Create a system image and then bask in how easy it is to keep your system secure in Windows 7!

System Restore

Every technician has war stories about the user who likes to add the latest gadget and cool software to his computer. Then he's amazed when things go very, very wrong: the system locks up, refuses to boot, or simply acts weird. This guy also can't remember what he added or when. All he knows is that you should be able to fix it—fast.

This is not news to the folks at Microsoft, and they have a solution to this problem. It's called **System Restore**, and they first introduced it in Windows Me, with further refinements in Windows XP. The System Restore tool enables you to create a **restore point**, a copy of your computer's configuration at a specific point in time. If you later crash or have a corrupted OS, you can restore the system to its previous state.

To create a restore point in Windows XP, go to Start | All Programs | Accessories | System Tools | System Restore. When the tool opens, select *Create a restore point* and then click Next. Type in a description on the next screen (see Figure 8.53). There's no need to include the date and time because the System Restore adds them automatically. Click Create and you're finished.

System Restore in Windows Vista/7 is much more automatic, with the operating system making a number of restore points automatically. To make your own restore point, right-click Computer and select Properties, and then click the *System protection* link in the Tasks list. On the System Protection tab, click the Create button to open the dialog box shown in Figure 8.54.

If you click the System Restore button, you might be surprised at how many system restore points are already made for you (see Figure 8.55).

The System Restore tool creates some of the restore points automatically, including every time you install new software. Thus, if installation of a program causes your computer to malfunction, simply restore the system to a time point prior to that installation, and the computer should work again.

During the restore process, only settings and programs are changed. No data is lost. Your computer includes all programs and settings as of the restore date. This feature is absolutely invaluable for overworked techs. A simple restore fixes many user-generated problems.

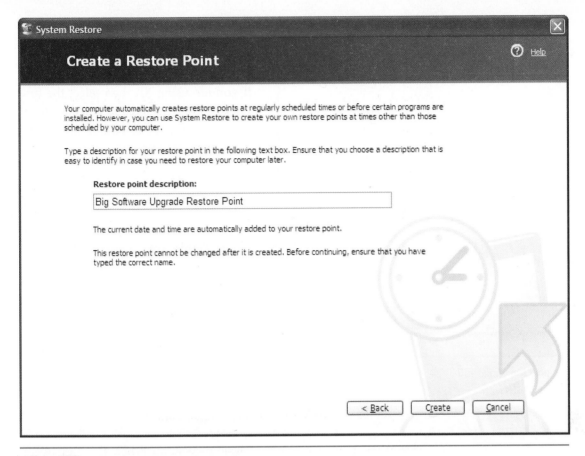

- **Figure 8.53** Creating a restore point in Windows XP

- **Figure 8.54** Creating a manual restore point in Windows 7

To restore to a previous time point, start the System Restore Wizard by choosing Start | All Programs | Accessories | System Tools | System Restore. If you are using XP, then select the first radio button, *Restore my computer to an earlier time,* and click Next. In Windows Vista and Windows 7, just click the Next button. Figure 8.56 shows a calendar with restore points. Any day with a boldface date has at least one restore point. In Windows Vista/7 this calendar was replaced with a simple list, as you saw in Figure 8.55. These points are created after you add or remove software or install Windows updates and during the normal shutdown of your computer. Select a date on the calendar, select a restore point from the list on the right, and click Next.

• **Figure 8.55** Restore points in Windows 7

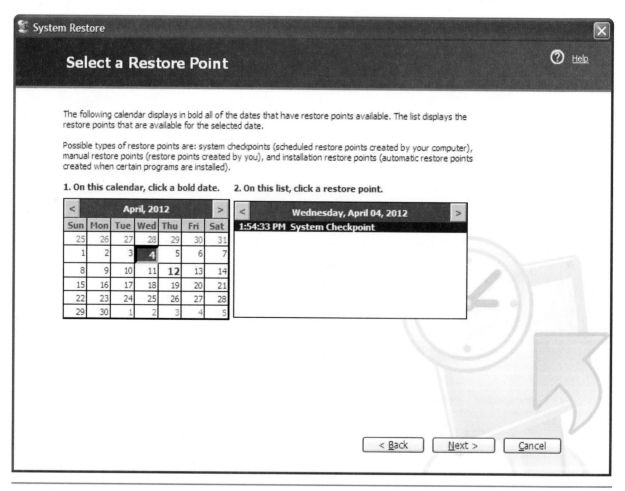

• **Figure 8.56** Calendar of restore points in Windows XP

Mike Meyer's CompTIA A+ Guide to 802: Managing and Troubleshooting PCs

The last screen before the system is restored shows a warning. It advises you to close all open programs and reminds you that Windows will shut down during the restore process. It also states that the restore operation is completely reversible. Thus, if you go too far back in time, you can restore to a more recent date.

You don't have to count on the automatic creation of restore points. You can open System Restore at any time and simply select *Create a restore point*. Consider doing this before making changes that might not trigger an automatic restore point, such as directly editing the Registry.

System Restore is turned on by default and uses some of your disk space to save information on restore points. To turn System Restore off or change the disk space usage in Windows XP, open the System Properties applet in Control Panel and select the System Restore tab (Figure 8.57). In Windows Vista/7, right-click Computer and select Properties, and then click the *System protection* link in the Tasks list. On the System Protection tab, click the Configure button.

• **Figure 8.57** System Restore tab in System Properties applet

Chapter 8 Review

■ Chapter Summary

After reading this chapter and completing the exercises, you should understand the following about maintaining and optimizing Windows.

Perform maintenance tasks in Windows

- Windows Update retrieves updates and service packs from the Internet and patches your system. Keeping your system updated prevents viruses and malicious software from exploiting vulnerabilities in your operating system.

- Every version of Windows is capable of Automatic Updates. You can configure the time, frequency, and number of updates to download and/or install.

- Disk Cleanup clears out the junk files that accumulate from daily use. You can reach this tool through the Start menu (Start | All Programs | Accessories | System Tools), or you can open My Computer or Computer, right-click the drive you want to clean up, select Properties, and click the Disk Cleanup button.

- Keeping your Registry clean ensures that your system continues to run efficiently and without errors. Unfortunately, Microsoft doesn't offer any built-in Registry cleaner tools, so you have to use third-party tools such as CCleaner to perform this task.

- When you can't find a software reason for a problem such as a system freezing on shutdown, the problem might be the actual physical hard drive. The tool to investigate that is Error-checking. You can perform Error-checking from a command line or the Start | Run dialog box (or Start | Search bar) using the chkdsk command.

- Run Disk Defragmenter on a regular basis to keep your system from slowing down because of files scattered in pieces on your hard drive.

- Maintenance only works properly when it's done at regular intervals. You can use Task Scheduler/ Schedule Tasks to schedule regular maintenance on your computer, though many utilities include built-in scheduling interfaces.

- The System Configuration utility enables techs to edit and troubleshoot operating system and program startup processes and services. Prior to Windows Vista, the System Configuration utility also offered quick access to troubleshoot and edit the boot.ini file.

- Windows comes with the System Information tool, which collects information about hardware resources, components, and the software environment. When it finishes doing that, it provides a nice and tidy little report, allowing you to troubleshoot and diagnose any issues and conflicts. You can also use System Information to gather information about remote computers by simply selecting View | Remote Computer and then entering the remote computer's network machine name.

Optimize Windows

- Windows supports Autorun, a feature that enables it to look for and read a special file called Autorun immediately after an optical disc is inserted, and then run whatever program is listed in autorun.inf. If you need to install a program manually, however, you can use the Add or Remove Programs applet in the Control Panel. In Windows Vista and 7, Microsoft has replaced the Add or Remove Programs applet with Programs and Features, which does not have the Add New Programs feature.

- With Windows Vista/7, you most likely will be prompted by UAC when installing an application. This is to give you time to review what is happening to your system in case you did not approve of the program being installed.

- Each installed application program takes up space on your computer's hard drive, and programs that you no longer need simply waste space that could be used for other purposes. Removing unnecessary programs can be an important piece of optimization. You remove programs by using the Add or Remove Programs or Programs and Features applet in the Control Panel. Select the desired program from the list of installed programs and click Uninstall.

- The third function of the Add or Remove Programs applet/Programs and Features applet is to add

or remove Windows components and features. In Windows XP, this is done by selecting Add/ Remove Windows Components, which opens the Windows Components Wizard. In Windows Vista/7, this is done by clicking the *Turn Windows features on or off* option on the Tasks list.

- Windows Update provides an easy method to update drivers from manufacturers that take advantage of the service. If you are using Windows XP, the only trick to this is that you usually need to select the Custom option to see these updates because Windows only installs high-priority updates when using the Express option. When you click on the Custom option, look under Hardware, Optional (on the left) to see if Windows has any driver updates. If you are using Vista/7, you will need to click *View available updates* to see if any drivers are available for your system.

- Device drivers become part of the operating system and thus have the potential to cause lots of problems if they're written poorly. To protect Windows systems from bad device drivers, Microsoft uses driver signing, which means that each driver has a digital signature. When an unsigned driver is detected during hardware installation, you'll see a message offering you the choice to stop or continue the installation. Signed drivers are more or less a sure thing, but that doesn't mean unsigned ones are a problem—just consider the source of the driver when installing it.

- You can control how Windows XP behaves when drivers are being installed by clicking the Driver Signing button on the Hardware tab of the System Properties dialog box. This displays the Driver Signing Options dialog box. If you select Ignore, Windows will install an unsigned driver without warning you. Windows Vista and Windows 7 have eliminated the driver signing options. In 64-bit versions of Windows, all drivers must be signed. No exceptions.

- Right-clicking on a device in Device Manager displays the context menu. From here you can update or uninstall the driver, disable the device, scan for hardware changes, or display the Properties dialog box. The Driver tab has buttons labeled Driver Details, Update Driver, Roll Back Driver, and Uninstall. Windows Vista/7 add the Disable button. The Roll Back Driver option enables you to remove an updated driver, thus rolling back to the previous driver version.

- Windows should automatically detect any new device you install in your system. If not, use the Add Hardware Wizard (or simply Add Hardware if using Vista or Add a device in Windows 7) to get the device recognized and drivers installed. You'll find it on the Hardware tab of the System Properties dialog box in Windows XP and Vista. In Windows 7, use the hdwwiz.exe program to get to the same tool.

- One optimization you can perform on all Windows versions is setting Performance Options. Performance Options are used to configure CPU, RAM, and virtual memory (page file) settings. The Performance Options dialog box has three tabs: Visual Effects, Advanced, and Data Execution Prevention. The Visual Effects tab enables you to adjust visual effects that impact performance. The Advanced tab has three sections: Processor scheduling, Memory usage, and Virtual memory.

- Microsoft introduced Data Execution Prevention (DEP) with Windows XP Service Pack 2. DEP works in the background to stop viruses and other malware from taking over programs loaded in system memory. It doesn't prevent viruses from being installed on your computer, but makes them less effective.

- Hardware Profiles in Windows XP enable you to switch several hardware configurations at once during the Windows boot process.

Prepare Windows for problems

- The most important data on your computer is the personal data: your documents, e-mail messages and contacts, Web favorites, photographs, and other files. To handle backing up personal data, every version of Windows comes with some form of backup utility.

- The Windows XP Backup Utility (ntbackup) provides almost all the tools you need to back up files and folders. The ntbackup program supports a variety of devices, enabling you to back up to network drives, local drives, tape, and removable disks (but not optical discs).

- The Windows XP Automated System Recovery (ASR) enables you to create a backup of your system. This backup includes a floppy disk and backup media containing the system and boot volume(s) and system state information.

- The archive bit works like this: Whenever a file is saved, the archive bit is turned on. Simply opening a file affects the current state of the archive bit. Backup programs usually turn off a file's archive bit when the file is backed up. If the archive bit is turned on, it means that the file has been changed since it was last backed up.

- A normal backup is a full backup. Every file selected is backed up, and the archive bit is turned off for every file backed up.

- A copy backup is identical to a normal backup, except that the archive bits are *not* changed. This is used (although not often) for making extra copies of a previously completed backup.

- An incremental backup includes only files with the archive bit turned on. In other words, it copies only the files that have been changed since the last backup. This backup turns off the archive bits.

- A differential backup is identical to an incremental backup, except that it doesn't turn off the archive bits.

- A daily backup, also known as a daily copy backup, makes copies of all the files that have been changed that day. It does not change the archive bits.

- Microsoft replaced ntbackup in Windows Vista with the Windows Backup and Restore Center, and with Backup and Restore in Windows 7. Both utilities have only two options: create a backup or restore from a previous backup. Vista/7 no longer support tape backups, nor do they let you choose between differential and incremental backups.

- You can use the System Restore tool to create a restore point, a copy of your computer's configuration at a specific point in time. If your computer later crashes or has a corrupted OS, you can restore the system to its previous state. During the restore process, only settings and programs are changed. No data is lost. Your computer will include all programs and settings as of the restore date. System Restore is turned on by default and uses some of your disk space to save information on restore points.

Key Terms

Add or Remove Programs *(304)*
Automated System Recovery (ASR) *(316)*
Automatic Updates *(293)*
Autorun *(303)*
Backup and Restore Center *(319)*
Backup Utility (ntbackup) *(314)*
Device Manager *(310)*
Disk Cleanup *(295)*
driver signing *(308)*
Hardware Profiles *(312)*
Performance Options *(311)*

Programs and Features *(304)*
restore point *(324)*
Scheduled Tasks *(298)*
service pack *(289)*
System Configuration utility (msconfig) *(301)*
System Information tool (msinfo32) *(302)*
System Restore *(324)*
Task Scheduler *(298)*
update *(289)*
Windows Update *(289)*

Key Term Quiz

Use the Key Terms list to complete the sentences that follow. Not all terms will be used.

1. In Windows Vista and 7, you use the _____ applet to add and remove programs.

2. Windows XP uses the _____ to create a backup of the system, using both a floppy disk and a backup medium such as tape, but the restore side involves completely reinstalling the operating system.

3. To change which programs and services start with Windows, you would use the _____.

4. If installing a new driver causes problems in your system, _____ enables you to roll back the driver to a previously installed version.

5. Microsoft occasionally packages several updates for Windows together into a(n) _____.

6. You can use _____ to disable certain graphical flourishes, such as animations, transparencies, and more.

7. While Windows Update is an important part of your arsenal against bugs, viruses, and other problems, you should configure _____ so that Windows regularly downloads and installs the updates for you.

8. Windows XP includes a neat feature called _____ that enables you to switch several hardware configurations at once during the Windows boot process.

9. When you insert an optical disc into your PC, Windows uses the _____ feature to start the disc automatically.

10. Microsoft uses _____ to protect PC users from installing bad drivers.

■ Multiple-Choice Quiz

1. Which tool in Windows XP Home loaded by default can you use to back up essential system files?
 A. Emergency Repair Disk
 B. Backup and Recovery Wizard
 C. System Restore
 D. Recovery Console

2. Mark loaded a new video card on his system, but now everything looks very bad. What should he do first?
 A. Go to Event Viewer and check the log
 B. Go to Device Manager
 C. Go to the printed manual
 D. Call tech support

3. Which of the following should be your first choice to remove an application that you no longer need?
 A. Delete the program files
 B. Use the uninstall program that came with the application
 C. Use the Add or Remove Programs applet or the Programs and Features applet.
 D. Use the Registry Editor to remove references to the application

4. Which of the following backup features does Windows 7 not support? (Select two.)
 A. System Restore
 B. Backup and Restore
 C. Tape Backup
 D. Setting differential vs. incremental backups

5. What program can you use to keep your systems patched and up-to-date?
 A. Windows Dispatcher
 B. Windows Patcher
 C. Windows Update
 D. Windows Upgrade

6. Pam needs to connect a hard drive controller to her new Windows 7 64-bit computer but is unable to because of the older, unsigned driver. What can she do to make Windows load her driver?
 A. Start the computer in Disable Driver Signature Enforcement mode.
 B. Install the driver in Windows XP compatibility mode.
 C. She's plain out of luck.
 D. Use the Legacy Driver option in Device Manager.

7. Diane complains that her system seems sluggish and she keeps running out of disk space. What tool can you use to get rid of unnecessary files and compress older files? Select the best answer.
 A. Disk Cleanup
 B. Disk Doctor
 C. File Manager
 D. Registry Cleaner

8. Alberto installs a video card into a Windows XP computer and it seems to work just fine until he tries to run a game. Then he gets low-end graphics and it just doesn't look right. What might he try to fix the problem? Select the best answer.

 A. Check the video card manufacturer's Web site and download updated drivers

 B. Check the video card manufacturer's Web site and download the FAQ

 C. Run the Driver Update utility

 D. Reinstall Windows

9. Which of the following operating systems enables you to back up files to a tape using the included backup utility?

 A. Windows Vista Business

 B. Windows 7 Professional

 C. Windows 7 Ultimate

 D. Windows XP Professional

10. Which of the following commands opens the System Information tool?

 A. msconfig

 B. msinfo

 C. msinfo32

 D. mscnfg32

11. Mark wants to run Error-checking on his Windows 7 machine once every week. Which tool enables him to set Windows to do this automatically?

 A. msconfig

 B. Startup Repair

 C. Hardware Profiles

 D. Task Scheduler

12. Restoring an Automated System Recovery backup in Windows XP requires which three components? (Select three.)

 A. Windows XP installation disc

 B. ASR floppy disk

 C. ASR backup media

 D. A recent system restore point

13. From which utility can you run the Windows Memory Diagnostic Tool?

 A. Automated System Recovery

 B. Device Manager

 C. System Recovery Options

 D. msconfig

14. When performing automatic updates, Windows uses which feature to download additional updates for other Microsoft products?

 A. Software notifications

 B. msinfo32

 C. Microsoft Update

 D. Registry

15. Joan recently bought a new gamepad and used the Add a Device wizard to install it, but it still won't work. What should she do next? (Select two.)

 A. Check the manufacturer's Web site for updated drivers

 B. Run the Automated System Recovery tool to return the PC to a functioning state

 C. Use a restore point in System Restore to return the PC to a functioning state

 D. Run Windows Update to search for new drivers

■ Essay Quiz

1. Your company's CEO is concerned about the backup policy in place for your file servers—namely, that there isn't one. He has asked you for advice, so write him a report about the types of backups available, how they work, and the storage requirements for each.

2. Your boss wants you to write a brief essay on how your users should back up their data for protection against accidental loss. Half the users have Windows XP PCs; the other half are running Windows 7 Professional. Keep in mind that your target audience is users, not trained technicians, so you should go for the user-level tools.

3. You've been tasked with organizing the standard maintenance routines for the Boston office's 16 Windows 7 Professional PCs. Write a couple of paragraphs describing the tools available and how often each should be run.

4. Your friend Steve got a new Windows 7 computer, but it's so loaded with trial-version software from the manufacturer that it confuses him. He wants to unload some of these useless programs, but he doesn't want to trash his new PC. Write a brief essay describing the tool(s) he needs to use to uninstall the programs and clean up afterward.

Lab Projects

• Lab Project 8.1

You learned that restore points are copies of your system's configuration at a specific point in time. You know that Windows automatically creates some restore points. But there may be situations when you would like to have a copy of the current system configuration. That's why Microsoft also allows users to create a restore point at any time. Review the process, decide on a description, and then create a restore point. Note that it automatically includes the date and time when you created it.

• Lab Project 8.2

After reading this chapter you know how critical it is to keep patches, updates, and service packs current to help the computer stay healthy and to protect it from viruses that may exploit flaws in the operating system. Now's a good time to make sure your operating system is current. Run the Windows Update utility and decide which updates to install. (Now, don't you feel better about your system?)

Working with the Command-Line Interface

"You wanted to know who I am, Zero Cool? Well, let me explain the New World Order. Governments and corporations need people like you and me. We are Samurai...the Keyboard Cowboys...and all those other people who have no idea what's going on are the cattle.... Moooo."

—THE PLAGUE, *HACKERS* (1995)

In this chapter, you will learn how to

- **Explain the operation of the command-line interface**
- **Execute fundamental commands from the command line**
- **Manipulate files from the command line**

Whenever I teach a class of new techs and we get to the section on working with the command line, I'm invariably met with a chorus of moans and a barrage of questions and statements. "Why do we need to learn this old stuff?" "We're running Windows 7, not Windows 3.1!" "Is this ritualistic hazing appropriate in an IT class?"

For techs who master the interface, the command line provides a powerful, quick, and elegant tool for working on a PC. Learning that interface and understanding how to make it work is not only useful, but also necessary for all techs who want to go beyond baby-tech status. You simply cannot work on all PCs without knowing the command line! I'm not the only one who thinks this way. The CompTIA A+ 220-802 certification exam tests you on a variety of command-line commands for doing everything from renaming a file to rebuilding a system file.

If you're interested in moving beyond Windows and into other operating systems such as Linux, you'll find that pretty much all of the serious work is done at a command prompt. Even the Apple Mac operating system (OS), for years a purely graphical operating system, now supports a command prompt. Why is the command prompt so popular? Well, for three reasons: First, if you know what you're doing, you can do most jobs more quickly by typing a text command than by clicking through a graphical user interface (GUI). Second, a command-line interface doesn't take much operating system firepower, so it's the natural choice for jobs where you don't need or don't want (or can't get to, in the case of Linux) a full-blown GUI for your OS. Third, text commands take very little bandwidth when sent across the network to another system.

So, are you sold on the idea of the command prompt? Good! This chapter gives you a tour of the Windows command-line interface, explaining how it works and what's happening behind the scenes. You'll learn the concepts and master essential commands, and then you'll work with files and folders throughout your drives. The chapter wraps up with a brief section on encryption and file compression in the "Beyond A+" section. A good tactic for absorbing the material in this chapter is to try out each command or bit of information as it is presented. If you have some experience working with a command prompt, many of these commands should be familiar to you. If the command line is completely new to you, please take the red pill and join me as we step into the matrix.

Historical/Conceptual

Operating systems existed long before PCs were invented. Ancient, massive computers called *mainframes* and *minicomputers* employed sophisticated operating systems. It wasn't until the late 1970s that IBM went looking for an OS for a new *microcomputer*—the official name for the PC—the company was developing, called the IBM Personal Computer. After being rebuffed by a company called Digital Research, IBM went to a tiny company that had written a popular new version of the programming language called BASIC. IBM asked the company president if he could create an OS for the IBM PC. Although his company had never actually written an OS, he brazenly said "Sure!" That man was Bill Gates, and the tiny company was Microsoft.

After shaking hands with IBM representatives, Bill Gates hurriedly began to search for an OS based on the Intel 8086 processor. He found a primitive OS called *Quick-and-Dirty Operating System* (*QDOS*), which was written by a one-man shop, and he purchased it for a few thousand dollars. After several minor changes, Microsoft released it as MS-DOS (Microsoft Disk Operating System) version 1.1. Although primitive by today's standards, MS-DOS 1.1 could provide all of the functions an OS needed. Over the years, MS-DOS went through version after version until the last Microsoft version, MS-DOS 6.22, was released in 1994. Microsoft licensed MS-DOS to PC makers so they could add their own changes and then rename the program. IBM called its version PC-DOS.

DOS used a **command-line interface**. You typed a command at a prompt, and DOS responded to that command. When Microsoft introduced Windows 95 and Windows NT, many computer users and techs thought that the command-line interface would go away, but techs not only continued to use the command line, they also *needed it* to troubleshoot and fix problems. With Windows 2000, it seemed once again that the command line would die, but again, that just didn't turn out to be the case.

Finally recognizing the importance of the command-line interface, Microsoft beefed it up in Windows XP and then again in Windows Vista. (The command-line interface in Windows 7 is essentially the same as in Windows Vista, but Microsoft added a whole new interface called Power-Shell. See the "Beyond A+" section of this chapter for more details.) The command line in Windows XP and in Vista/7 offers commands and options for those commands that go well beyond anything seen in previous Microsoft operating systems. This chapter starts with some essential concepts of the command line and then turns to more specific commands.

802

■ Deciphering the Command-Line Interface

So how does a command-line interface work? It's a little like having an Instant Message conversation with your computer. The computer tells you it's ready to receive commands by displaying a specific set of characters called a **prompt**.

```
Computer: Want to play a game?
Mike: _
```

You type a command and press ENTER to send it.

```
Mike: What kind of game?
Computer: _
```

The PC goes off and executes the command, and when it's finished, it displays a new prompt, often along with some information about what it did.

```
Computer: A very fun game...
Mike: _
```

Once you get a new prompt, it means the computer is ready for your next instruction. You can give the computer commands in the GUI of Windows as well, just in a different way, by clicking buttons and menu options with your mouse instead of typing on the keyboard. The results are basically the same: you tell the computer to do something and it responds.

When you type in a command from the command line, you cause the computer to respond. As an example, suppose you want to find out the contents of a particular folder. From the command line, you'd type a command (in this case **dir**, but more on that in a minute), and the computer would respond by displaying a screen like the one in Figure 9.1.

In the Windows GUI, you would open My Computer or Computer and click the C: drive icon to see the contents of that directory. The results might look like Figure 9.2, which at first glance isn't much like the command-line screen; however, simply by choosing a different view (see Figure 9.3), you can make the results look quite a bit like the command-line version, albeit much prettier (see Figure 9.4). The point here is that whichever interface you use, the information available to you is essentially the same.

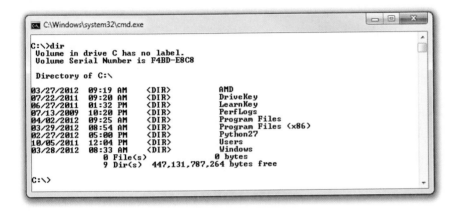

• **Figure 9.1** Contents of C: directory from the command line

• **Figure 9.2** Contents of C: in Computer—Icon view

Chapter 9: Working with the Command-Line Interface

● **Figure 9.3** Selecting Details view in Computer

● **Figure 9.4** Contents of C: in Computer—Details view

> **Try This!**
>
> ### Opening GUI Programs from the Command Prompt
>
> Keep in mind as you go through this chapter that the command line is just another tool for communicating with the operating system. Windows responds whether you're clicking or typing and sometimes does both, so try this! At a command prompt: type **notepad** and press the ENTER key. What happens?
>
> The graphical program Notepad opens up, just as if you'd double-clicked its icon!
>
> Here's another: type **explorer** and press ENTER. Voilá! Internet Explorer loads. Windows just responds.

Accessing the Command Line

Before you can use the command-line interface, you have to open it. You can use various methods to do this, depending on the flavor of Windows you are using. Some methods are simpler than others; just make sure that you know at least one, or you'll never get off the starting line!

One easy way to access the command-line interface in Windows XP is by using the **Run dialog box**. Click the Start button, and then select Run. Type **cmd** or **command** and press the ENTER key (see Figure 9.5). If you are using Windows Vista or Windows 7, you access the command-line interface through the Start menu Search bar with the same two commands. A window pops up on your screen with a black background and white text—this is the command-line interface. Alternatively, buried in the Start menu of *most* computers, under Programs/All Programs | Accessories, is a link to the command-line interface; it's called *Command Prompt*. These links, just like the Run dialog box, pull up a nice command line–interface window (see Figure 9.6, which shows the Windows XP version). If you are displaying the command-line interface in Windows Vista or Windows 7, notice that you'll see a newer version number and copyright date. Also notice that the default user profile folder in the later editions is C:\Users*User name*, as shown in Figure 9.7, rather than C:\Documents and Settings*User name* as in Windows XP. To close the command line–interface window, you can either click the Close box in the upper-right corner, as on any other window, or simply type **exit** at any command prompt and press ENTER.

• **Figure 9.5** Type **cmd** in the Run dialog box to open a command line–interface window in Windows XP.

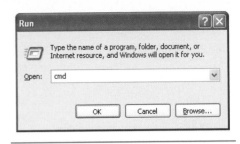

• **Figure 9.6** The command line–interface window with a C:\ prompt

• **Figure 9.7** The Windows 7 command line–interface window

If you attempt to enter at the Windows Vista/7 command prompt a command that requires elevated or administrative privileges, you receive a UAC "Windows needs your permission to continue" dialog box (you learned about UAC in Chapter 7). You can also "manually" run a command with elevated privileges by right-clicking a command-prompt shortcut and then selecting *Run as administrator*. If you are prompted for administrator password or credentials, enter them as needed.

You can also create an administrator shortcut to the Windows Vista/7 command prompt by right-clicking on the desktop and selecting New | Shortcut. Then for the location of the item, type **cmd** and click Next. Type **cmd** to name the shortcut, and click Finish. Your shortcut appears on the desktop. Next, right-click the shortcut and select the Advanced button. In the Advanced Properties dialog box, check the *Run as administrator* box and click OK. You have now created a Windows Vista/7 command-prompt shortcut that will always run with administrative privileges.

Try This!

Accessing the Command Line

This chapter will be much more fun if you follow along with your own command line, so Try This! Using one of the methods outlined in this section, access a command prompt in Windows. Just remember that everything you do at the prompt can affect the functioning of your PC. So don't delete stuff if you don't know what it's for.

• **Figure 9.8** Command prompt indicating focus on the C:\Diploma\APLUS\ folder

You can hold down the F5 or F8 key during boot-up to access the Windows Advanced Boot Options menu. This has an option to boot to Safe Mode with Command Prompt, which loads the GUI into Safe Mode and then overlays that with a command-line interface for rapid access to a prompt. This saves you the step of going to Start | Run and typing cmd.

The Command Prompt

The command prompt is always *focused* on a specific folder. This is important because any commands you issue are performed *on the files in the folder* on which the prompt is focused. For example, if you see a prompt that looks like the following line, you know that the focus is on the root directory of the C: drive:

```
C:\>
```

If you see a prompt that looks like Figure 9.8, you know that the focus is on the C:\Diploma\APLUS\ folder of the C: drive. The trick to using a command line is first to focus the prompt on the drive and folder where you want to work.

Filenames and File Formats

Windows manifests each program and piece of data as an individual file. Each file has a name, which is stored with the file on the drive. Windows inherits the idea of files from older operating systems—namely DOS—so a quick review of the old-style DOS filenames helps in understanding how Windows filenames work. Names are broken down into two parts: the filename and the extension. In true DOS, the filename could be no longer than eight characters, so you'll often see oddly named files on older systems. The extension, which is optional, could be up to three characters long in true DOS, and most computer programs and users continue to honor that old limit, even though it does not apply to modern PCs. No spaces or other illegal characters (/ \ [] | ÷ + = ; , * ?) could be used in the filename or extension. The filename and extension are separated by a period, or *dot*. This naming system was known as the **8.3 (eight-dot-three) naming system**.

Here are some examples of acceptable true DOS filenames:

fred.exe	system.ini	file1.doc
driver3.sys	janet	code33.h

Here are some unacceptable true DOS filenames:

4charext.exec	waytoolong.fil	bad÷char.bat	.no

I mention the true DOS limitations for a simple reason: *backward compatibility*. Starting with Windows 9x, Windows versions did not suffer from the 8.3 filename limitation. Instead they supported filenames of up to 255 characters (but still with the three-character extension) by using a trick called long filenames (LFN). Windows systems using LFN retained complete backward compatibility by automatically creating two names for every file, an 8.3 filename and a long filename. Modern Windows systems similarly support backward compatibility in file naming.

Whether you're running an ancient DOS system or the latest edition of Windows 7, the extension is very important, because the extension part of the filename tells the computer the type or function of the file. Program files use the extension .exe (for executable) or .com (for command). Anything that is not a program is some form of data to support a program. Different programs use different types of data files. The extension usually indicates which program uses that particular data file. For example, Microsoft Word

uses the extension .docx (.doc for Microsoft Office versions before 2007), while WordPerfect uses .wpd and PowerPoint uses .pptx (.ppt for Microsoft Office PowerPoint versions prior to 2007). Graphics file extensions, in contrast, often reflect the graphics standard used to render the image, such as .gif for CompuServe's Graphics Interchange Format or .jpg for the JPEG (Joint Photographic Experts Group) format.

Changing the extension of a data file does not affect its contents, but without the proper extension, Windows won't know which program uses it. You can see this clearly in My Computer. Figure 9.9 shows a folder with two identical image files. The one on top shows a thumbnail because Windows recognizes this as a JPEG image; the one on the bottom shows a generic icon because I deleted the extension. Windows' GUI doesn't show file extensions by default. Figure 9.10 shows the contents of that same folder from the command line.

All files are stored on the hard drive in binary format, but every program has its own way of reading and writing this binary data. Each unique method of binary organization is called a file *format*. One program cannot read another program's files unless it can convert the other program's format into its format. In the early days of DOS, no programs were capable of performing this type of conversion, yet people wanted to exchange files. They wanted some type of common format that any program could read. The answer was a special format called **American Standard Code for Information Interchange (ASCII)**.

The ASCII standard defines 256 eight-bit characters. These characters include all of the letters of the alphabet (uppercase and lowercase), numbers, punctuation, many foreign characters (such as accented letters for French and Spanish—é, ñ, ô—and other typical non-English characters), box-drawing characters, and a series of special characters for commands such as a carriage return, bell, and end of file (see Figure 9.11). ASCII files, more commonly known as *text files*, store all data in ASCII format. The ASCII standard, however, is for more than just files. For example, when you press a key, the keyboard

• **Figure 9.9** What kind of file is the one on the lower right?

• **Figure 9.10** One file has no extension.

• **Figure 9.11** ASCII characters

sends the letter of that key to the PC in ASCII code. Even the monitor outputs in ASCII when you are running DOS.

ASCII was the first universal file format. Virtually every type of program—word processors, spreadsheets, databases, presentation programs—can read and write text files. However, text files have severe limitations. A text file can't store important information such as shapes, colors, margins, or text attributes (bold, underline, font, and so on). Therefore, even though text files are fairly universal, they are also limited to the 256 ASCII characters.

Even in the most basic text, you need to perform a number of actions beyond just printing simple characters. For example, how does the program reading the text file know when to start a new line? This is where the first 32 ASCII characters come into play. These first 32 characters are special commands (actually, some of them are both commands and characters). For example, the ASCII value 7 can be either a large dot or a command to play a note (bell) on the PC speaker. ASCII value 9 is a Tab. ASCII value 27 is an Escape.

ASCII worked well for years, but as computers became used worldwide, the industry began to run into a problem: there are a lot more than 256 characters used all over the world! Nobody could use Arabic, Greek, Hebrew, or even Braille. In 1991, the Unicode Consortium, an international standards group, introduced Unicode. Basic **Unicode** is a 16-bit code that covers every character for the most common languages, plus a few thousand symbols. With Unicode you can make just about any character or symbol you might imagine—plus a few thousand more you'd never even think of. The first 256 Unicode characters are the same as ASCII characters, making for easy backward compatibility.

Try This!

Make Some Unicode!

A lot of e-mail programs can use Unicode characters, as can Internet message boards such as my Tech Forums. You can use Unicode characters to accent your writing or simply to spell a person's name correctly—Martin *Acuña*—when you address him. Working with Unicode is fun, so Try This!

1. Open a text editing program such as Notepad in the Windows GUI.

2. Hold down the ALT key on your keyboard and, referring to Figure 9.11, press numbers on your keyboard's number pad to enter special characters. For example, pressing ALT-164 should display an *ñ*, whereas ALT-168 shows a *¿*.

3. If you have access to the Internet, surf over to the Tech Forums (www.totalsem.com/techforum/index.php) and say howdy. Include some Unicode in your post, of course!

Drives and Folders

When working from the command line, you need to be able to focus the prompt at the specific drive and folder that contains the files or programs with which you want to work. This can be a little more complicated than it seems.

At boot, Windows assigns a drive letter (or name) to each hard drive partition and to each floppy or other disk drive. The first floppy drive, if installed, is called A:, and the second, if installed, is called B:. Hard drives usually start with the letter C: and can continue to Z: if necessary. Optical drives by default get the next available drive letter after the last hard drive. Windows enables you to change the default lettering for drives, so you're

likely to see all sorts of lettering schemes. On top of that, you can mount a hard drive as a volume in another drive, as you'll recall from Chapter 4.

Whatever the names of the drives, Windows uses a hierarchical directory tree to organize the contents of these drives. All files are put into groups Windows calls *folders*, although you'll often hear techs use the term *directory* rather than *folder*, a holdover from the true DOS days. Any file not in a folder *within* the tree—that is, any file in the folder at the root of the directory tree—is said to be in the **root directory**. A folder inside another folder is called a *subfolder*. Any folder can have multiple subfolders. Two or more files with the same name can exist in different folders on a PC, but two files in the same folder cannot have the same name. In the same way, no two subfolders under the same folder can have the same name, but two subfolders under different folders can have the same name.

When describing a drive, you use its letter and a colon. For example, the hard drive would be represented by C:. To describe the root directory, put a backslash (\) after the C:, as in C:\. To describe a particular directory, add the name of the directory. For example, if a PC has a directory in the root directory called Test, it is C:\Test. Subdirectories in a directory are displayed by adding backslashes and names. If the Test directory has a subdirectory called System, it is shown like this: C:\Test\System. This naming convention provides for a complete description of the location and name of any file. If the C:\Test\System directory includes a file called test2.txt, it is C:\Test\System\test2.txt.

The exact location of a file is called its **path**. The path for the test2.txt file is C:\Test\System. Here are some examples of possible paths:

```
C:\Program Files
C:\WINNT\system32\1025
F:\FRUSCH3\CLEAR
A:\Reports
D:\
```

Here are a few items to remember about folder names and filenames:

- Folders and files may have spaces in their names.
- The only disallowed characters are the following eleven: * " / \ [] : ; | = ,
- Files aren't required to have extensions, but Windows won't know the file type without an extension.
- Folder names may have extensions—but they are not commonly used.

■ Mastering Fundamental Commands

It's time to try using the command line, but before you begin, a note of warning is in order: the command-line interface is picky and unforgiving. It will do what you *say*, not what you *mean*, so it always pays to double-check that those are one and the same before you press ENTER and commit the command. One careless keystroke can result in the loss of crucial data, with

Tech Tip

Directory Trees

It helps to visualize a directory tree as upside down, because in geekspeak, the trunk, or root directory, is described as "above" the folders that divide it, and those subfolders "below" root are spoken of as being "above" the other subfolders inside them. For example, "The file is in the Adobe folder under Program Files."

no warning and no going back. In this section, you'll explore the structure of commands and then play with four commands built into all versions of Microsoft's command-line interface: dir, cd, md, and rd.

Structure: Syntax and Switches

All commands in the Windows command-line interface use a similar structure and execute in the same way. You type the name of the command, followed by the target of that command and any modifications of that command that you want to apply. You can call up a modification by using an extra letter or number, called a **switch** or *option*, which may follow either the command or the target, depending on the command. The proper way to write a command is called its **syntax**. The key with commands is that you can't spell anything incorrectly or use a \ when the syntax calls for a /. The command line is completely inflexible, so you have to learn the correct syntax for each command.

[*command*] [*target (if any)*] [*switches*]

or

[*command*] [*switches*] [*target (if any)*]

How do you know what switches are allowed? How do you know whether the switches come before or after the target? If you want to find out the syntax and switches used by a particular command, always type the command followed by /? to get help:

[command name] /?

Viewing Directory Contents: The dir Command

The **dir command** shows you the contents of the directory where the prompt is focused. If you're like most techs, you'll use dir more often than any other command at the command prompt. When you open a command-line window in Windows, it opens focused on your user folder. You will know this because the prompt in Windows XP will look like this: C:\Documents and Settings\username> and the prompt in Windows Vista/7 looks like C:\Users*User name*>. By typing **dir** and then pressing the ENTER key (remember that you must always press ENTER to execute a command from the command line), you will see something like Figure 9.12 in Windows XP.

• **Figure 9.12** Results for dir in a user's folder

If you are following along on a PC, remember that different computers contain different files and programs, so you will absolutely see something different from what's shown in Figure 9.12! If a lot of text scrolls quickly down the screen, try typing **dir /p** (pause). Don't forget to press ENTER. The dir /p command is a lifesaver when you're looking for something in a large directory. Just press SPACEBAR to display the next screen.

When you type a simple dir command, you will see that some of the entries look like this:

```
09/04/2012    05:51 PM              63,664 bambi.jpg
```

All of these entries are files. The dir command lists the creation date, creation time, file size in bytes, filename, and extension. Any entries that look like this are folders:

```
12/31/2012    10:18 AM     <DIR>          WINDOWS
```

The dir command lists the creation date, creation time, <DIR> to tell you it is a folder, and the folder name. If you ever see a listing with <JUNCTION> instead of <DIR>, you're looking at a hard drive partition that's been mounted as a folder instead of a drive letter:

```
08/06/2012    02:28 PM     <JUNCTION>     Other Drive
```

Now type the **dir /w** command. Note that the dir /w command shows only the filenames, but they are arranged in five columns across your screen. Finally, type **dir /?** to see the screen shown in Figure 9.13, which lists all possible switches for the command.

Tech Tip

Do You Need Spaces?

Some commands give you the same result whether you include spaces or not. Typing **dir/p** *or* **dir /p**, *for example, provides the same output. Some commands, however,* require *spaces between the command and switches. In general, get into the habit of putting spaces between your command and switches and you won't run into problems.*

Extra text typed after a command to modify its operation, such as /w or /p after dir, is called a *switch*. Almost all switches can be used simultaneously to modify a command. For example, try typing **dir /w /p**.

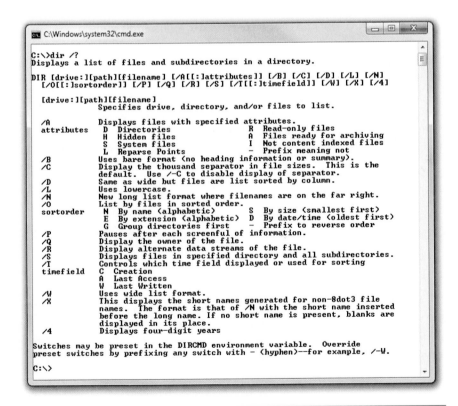

• **Figure 9.13** Typing **dir /?** lists all possible switches for the dir command.

Chapter 9: Working with the Command-Line Interface

Typing any command followed by /? brings up a help screen for that particular command. Although these help screens can sometimes seem a little cryptic, they're useful when you're not familiar with a command or you can't figure out how to get a command to do what you need. Even though I have almost every command memorized, I still refer to these help screens; you should use them as well. If you're really lost, type **help** at the command prompt for a list of commands you may type. Once you find one, type **help** and then the name of the command. For example, if you type **help dir**, you'll see the screen shown in Figure 9.13.

Changing Directory Focus: The cd Command

You can use the **cd (or chdir) command** to change the focus of the command prompt to a different directory. To use the cd command, type **cd** followed by the name of the directory on which you want the prompt to focus. For example, to go to the C:\Obiwan directory, you type **cd\obiwan** and then press ENTER. If the system has an Obiwan directory, the prompt changes focus to that directory and appears as C:\Obiwan>. If no Obiwan directory exists or if you accidentally type something like **obiwam**, you get the error "The system cannot find the path specified." If only I had a dollar for every time I've seen those errors! I usually get them because I've typed too fast. If you get this error, check what you typed and try again.

To return to the root directory, type **cd** and press ENTER. You can use the cd command to point the prompt to any directory. For example, you could type **cd\fred\backup\test** from a C:\ prompt, and the prompt would change to C:\Fred\Backup\Test\>—assuming, of course, that your system *has* a directory called C:\Fred\Backup\Test.

Once the prompt has changed, type **dir** again. You should see a different list of files and directories. Every directory holds different files and subdirectories, so when you point the prompt to different directories, the dir command shows you different contents.

The cd command allows you to use a space instead of a backslash, a convenient shortcut. For example, you could go to the C:\Windows directory from the root directory simply by typing **cd windows** at the C:\ prompt. You can use the cd [space] command to move one level at a time, like this:

```
C:\>cd fred
C:\Fred\>cd backup
C:\Fred\Backup>cd test
```

Or, you can jump multiple directory levels in one step, like this:

```
C:\>cd fred\backup\test
C:\Fred\Backup\Test>
```

A final trick: If you want to go *up* a single directory level, you can type **cd** followed immediately by two periods. So, for example, if you're in the C:\Fred\Backup directory and you want to move up to the C:\Fred directory, you can simply type **cd..** and you'll be there:

```
C:\Fred\Backup>cd..
C:\Fred>
```

Take some time to move the prompt focus around the directories of your PC, using the cd and dir commands. Use dir to find a directory, and then use cd to move the focus to that directory. Remember, cd\ always gets you back to the root directory.

Moving Between Drives

The cd command is *not* used to move between drives. To get the prompt to point to another drive ("point" is command-line geekspeak for "switch its focus"), just type the drive letter and a colon. If the prompt points at the C:\Sierra directory and you want to see what is on the USB thumb drive (E:), just type **e:** and the prompt will point to the USB drive. You'll see the following on the screen:

```
C:\Sierra>e:
E:\>
```

To return to the C: drive, just type **c:** and you'll see the following:

```
E:\>c:
C:\Sierra>
```

Note that you return to the same directory you left. Just for fun, try typing in a drive letter that you know doesn't exist. For example, I know that my system doesn't have a W: drive. If I type in a nonexistent drive on a Windows system, I get the following error:

```
The system cannot find the drive specified.
```

Try inserting a CD or DVD and use the cd command to point to its drive. Type **dir** to see the contents of the optical disc. Type **cd** to move the focus to any folders on the optical disc. Now return focus to the C: drive.

Using the dir, cd, and drive letter commands, you can access any folder on any storage device on your system. Make sure you can use these commands comfortably to navigate inside your computer.

Making Directories: The md Command

Now that you have learned how to navigate in a command-prompt world, it's time to start making stuff, beginning with a new directory.

To make a directory, use the **md (or mkdir) command**. To create a directory called Steam under the root directory C:, for example, first type **cd** to ensure that you are in the root directory. You should see the prompt

```
C:\>
```

Now that the prompt points to the root directory, type **md Steam** to create the directory:

```
C:\>md Steam
```

Once you press ENTER, Windows executes the command, but it won't volunteer any information about what it did. You must use the dir command to see that you have, in fact, created a new directory. Note that the Steam directory in this example is not listed last, as you might expect.

```
C:\>dir
 Volume in Drive C is
 Volume Serial Number is 1734-3234
 Directory of C:\

09/01/2012    8:11 AM    <DIR>           ATI
06/10/2012   08:11 AM    <DIR>           Intel
10/04/2012   10:22 PM    <DIR>           Steam
09/11/2012   11:32 AM    <DIR>           NVIDIA
08/06/2012   02:28 PM    <JUNCTION>      Other Drive
09/14/2012   11:15 AM    <DIR>           PerfLogs
09/14/2012   11:11 AM    <DIR>           Program Files
09/14/2012   11:11 AM    <DIR>           Program Files (x86)
09/12/2012   08:32 PM                21 statusclient.log
07/31/2012   10:40 PM               153 systemscandata.txt
03/13/2012   09:54 AM         1,111,040 t3h0
04/21/2012   04:19 PM    <DIR>           temp
09/24/2012   12:11 AM    <DIR>           Users
07/12/2012   10:18 AM    <DIR>           Windows
              3 File(s)      1,111,214 bytes
             10 Dir(s)   2,294,182,881,834   bytes free
```

What about uppercase and lowercase? Windows supports both in file and folder names but rarely makes any distinction with commands. Use the md command to make a folder called steam (note the lowercase) and see what happens. This also happens in the graphical Windows. Go to your desktop and try to make two folders, one called STEAM and the other called steam, and see what Windows tells you.

To create a Files subdirectory in the Steam directory, first use the cd\ command to point the prompt to the Steam directory:

cd\steam

Then run the md command to make the Files directory:

md Files

Make sure that the prompt points to the directory in which you want to make the new subdirectory before you execute the md command. When you're finished, type **dir** to see the new Files subdirectory. Just for fun, try the process again and add a Games directory under the Steam directory. Type **dir** to verify success.

Removing Directories: The rd command

Removing subdirectories works exactly like making them. First, get to the directory that contains the subdirectory you want to delete, and then execute the rd (or rmdir) command. In this example, let's delete the Files subdirectory in the C:\Steam directory. First, get to where the Files directory is located—C:\Steam—by typing **cd\steam**. Then type **rd files**. If you received no response from Windows, you probably did it right! Type **dir** to check that the Files subdirectory is gone.

The plain rd command will not delete a directory in Windows if the directory contains files or subdirectories. If you want to delete a directory that contains files or subdirectories, you must first empty that directory by

using the del (for files) or rd (for subdirectories) command. You can use the rd command followed by the /s switch to delete a directory as well as all files and subdirectories. The rd command followed by the /s switch is handy but dangerous, because it's easy to delete more than you want. When deleting, always follow the maxim "Check twice and delete once."

Let's delete the Steam and Games directories with rd followed by the /s switch. Because the Steam directory is in the root directory, point to the root directory with **cd**. Now execute the command **rd c:\steam /s**. In a rare display of mercy, Windows responds with the following:

```
C:\>rd steam /s
steam, Are you sure (Y/N)?
```

Press the Y key and both C:\Steam and C:\Steam\Games are eliminated.

 Make sure you know how to use md, rd, and cd for the CompTIA A+ 220-802 exam.

Try This!

Working with Directories

PC techs should be comfortable creating and deleting directories. To get some practice, Try This!

1. Create a new directory in the root directory by using the make directory command (md). Type **cd** to return to the root directory. At the command prompt, make a directory called Jedi:

   ```
   C:\>md Jedi
   ```

2. As usual, the prompt tells you nothing; it just presents a fresh prompt. Do a dir (that is, type the **dir** command) to see your new directory. Windows creates the new directory wherever it is pointing when you issue the command, whether or not that's where you meant to put it. To demonstrate, point the prompt to your new directory by using the cd command:

   ```
   C:\>cd jedi
   ```

3. Now use the make directory command again to create a directory called Yoda:

   ```
   C:\Jedi>md Yoda
   ```

 Do a dir again, and you should see that your Jedi directory now contains a Yoda directory.

4. Type **cd** to return to the root directory so you can delete your new directories by using the remove directory command (rd):

   ```
   C:\>rd /s jedi
   ```

 In another rare display of mercy, Windows responds with the following:

   ```
   jedi, Are you sure <Y/N>?
   ```

5. Press Y to eliminate both C:\Jedi and C:\Jedi\Yoda.

Administrator: C:\Windows\system32\cmd.exe - dir /p

```
04/10/2009  11:27 PM            950,272 mblctr.exe
01/19/2008  12:33 AM            275,968 mcbuilder.exe
11/02/2006  07:35 AM             73,376 mciavi.drv
11/02/2006  04:46 AM             82,944 mciavi32.dll
11/02/2006  04:46 AM             38,912 mcicda.dll
11/02/2006  04:46 AM             36,352 mciqtz32.dll
11/02/2006  04:46 AM             23,552 mciseq.dll
11/02/2006  07:35 AM             25,264 mciseq.drv
11/02/2006  04:46 AM             23,040 mciwave.dll
11/02/2006  07:35 AM             28,160 mciwave.drv
04/10/2009  11:32 PM            438,744 mcupdate_GenuineIntel.dll
01/19/2008  12:34 AM            129,024 McxDriv.dll
03/16/2007  11:54 PM              6,656 md5c.exe
04/09/2007  01:23 PM             28,040 mdimon.dll
01/19/2008  12:34 AM            205,312 mdminst.dll
11/02/2006  04:45 AM             88,064 MdRes.exe
01/19/2008  12:33 AM            128,512 MdSched.exe
04/10/2009  11:28 PM            356,864 MediaMetadataHandler.dll
11/02/2006  02:09 AM             39,274 mem.exe
04/10/2009  11:28 PM          2,868,224 mf.dll
11/02/2006  04:46 AM             41,984 mf3216.dll
11/02/2006  04:46 AM            924,944 mfc40.dll
11/02/2006  04:46 AM            924,944 mfc40u.dll
04/10/2009  11:28 PM          1,135,104 mfc42.dll
06/17/1998  06:08 PM             53,248 MFC42ENU.DLL
04/10/2009  11:28 PM          1,160,704 mfc42u.dll
03/18/2003  09:20 PM          1,060,864 mfc71.dll
03/18/2003  09:12 PM          1,047,552 mfc71u.dll
Press any key to continue . . .
```

• **Figure 9.14** The mem.exe program displayed in the System32 folder

Administrator: C:\Windows\system32\cmd.exe

```
C:\Windows\System32>mem

    655360 bytes total conventional memory
    655360 bytes available to MS-DOS
    580912 largest executable program size

   1048576 bytes total contiguous extended memory
         0 bytes available contiguous extended memory
    941056 bytes available XMS memory
           MS-DOS resident in High Memory Area

C:\Windows\System32>
```

• **Figure 9.15** Running mem in Windows Vista 32-bit

Windows includes a lot of command-line tools for specific jobs such as starting and stopping services, viewing computers on a network, converting hard drive file systems, and more. This book discusses these task-specific tools in the chapters that reflect their task. Chapter 10 goes into detail on the versatile and powerful net command, for example. You'll read about the convert command in Chapter 18. I couldn't resist throwing in two of the more interesting tools, compact and cipher, in the "Beyond A+" section of this chapter.

Running a Program

To run a program from the command line, simply change the prompt focus to the folder where the program is located, type the name of the program, and then press the ENTER key on your keyboard. Try this safe example. Go to the C:\Windows\System32 folder—the exact name of this folder varies by system. Type **dir /p** to see the files one page at a time. You should see a file called mem.exe if you're running a 32-bit version of Windows (see Figure 9.14).

As mentioned earlier, all files with extensions .exe and .com are programs, so mem.exe is a program. To run the mem.exe program, just type the filename, in this case **mem**, and press ENTER (see Figure 9.15). Note that you do not have to type the .exe extension, although you can. Congratulations! You have just run your first program from the command line.

■ Working with Files

This section deals with basic file manipulation. You will learn how to look at, copy, move, rename, and delete files. The examples in this section are based on a C: root directory with the following files and directories:

```
C:\>dir
 Volume in drive C has no label.
 Volume Serial Number is 4C62-1572

 Directory of C:\

05/26/2009  11:37 PM                 0 AILog.txt
05/29/2009  05:33 PM             5,776 aoedoppl.txt
05/29/2009  05:33 PM             2,238 aoeWVlog.txt
07/12/2009  10:38 AM    <DIR>          books
07/15/2009  02:45 PM             1,708 CtDrvStp.log
07/12/2008  04:46 AM    <DIR>          Documents and Settings
06/04/2009  10:22 PM    <DIR>          Impressions Games
09/11/2008  11:32 AM    <DIR>          NVIDIA
08/06/2009  02:28 PM    <JUNCTION>     Other Drive
01/03/2009  01:12 PM    <DIR>          pers-drv
09/14/2008  11:11 AM    <DIR>          Program Files
09/12/2009  08:32 PM                21 statusclient.log
07/31/2009  10:40 PM               153 systemscandata.txt
03/13/2009  09:54 AM         1,111,040 t3h0
04/21/2009  04:19 PM    <DIR>          temp
```

```
01/10/2008  07:07 PM    <DIR>          WebCam
12/31/2007  10:18 AM    <DIR>          WINDOWS
09/14/2008  12:48 PM    <DIR>          WINNT
01/03/2008  09:06 AM    <DIR>          WUTemp
              7 File(s)      1,120,936 bytes
             12 Dir(s)  94,630,002,688 bytes free
```

Because you probably don't have a PC with these files and directories, follow the examples but use what's on your drive. In other words, create your own folders and copy files to them from various folders currently on your system.

Attributes

Remember way back in Chapter 2 when you had to make changes to the folder options in My Computer/Computer to see hidden and system files? You were actually seeing files with special attributes.

All files have four special values, or **attributes**, that determine how programs (such as My Computer in Windows XP or Computer in Windows Vista/7) treat the file in special situations. The first attribute is the hidden attribute. If a file is hidden, it is not displayed when you issue the dir command. Next is the read-only attribute. A file with a **read-only attribute** cannot be modified or deleted. Third is the system attribute, which is used only for Windows XP system files such as ntldr and boot.ini. In reality, it does nothing more than provide an easy identifier for these files. Fourth is the archive attribute, which is used by backup software to identify files that have been changed since their last backup.

Up to this point in the chapter, you've used commands wrapped up in a single executable file called *cmd.exe*. The cmd.exe program all by itself, in other words, enables you to access the command-line interface and use built-in or *internal* commands such as dir, cd, md, and so forth. Several common command-line commands, in contrast, use their own executable. We call these *external* commands.

The external command-line program **attrib.exe** enables you to inspect and change file attributes. To inspect a file's attributes, type the **attrib** command followed by the name of the file. To see the attributes of the file AILog.txt, for example, type **attrib ailog.txt**. The result is

```
A       AILog.txt
```

The letter *A* stands for archive, the only attribute of AILog.txt.

Go to the C:\ directory and type **attrib** by itself. You'll see a result similar to the following:

```
C:\>attrib
A               C:\AILog.txt
A               C:\aoedoppl.txt
A               C:\aoeWVlog.txt
A     H         C:\AUTOEXEC.BAT
A     SH        C:\boot.ini
A     H         C:\CONFIG.SYS
A               C:\CtDrvStp.log
A     SH        C:\hiberfil.sys
A     SHR       C:\IO.SYS
A     SHR       C:\MSDOS.SYS
```

```
A   SHR     C:\NTDETECT.COM
A   SHR     C:\ntldr
A   SH      C:\pagefile.sys
A           C:\statusclient.log
A           C:\systemscandata.txt
A           C:\t3h0
```

The letter *R* means read-only, *H* is hidden, and *S* is system. Hey! There are some new files there. That's right, some were hidden. Don't panic if you see a number of files different from those just listed. No two C:\ directories are ever the same. In most cases, you'll see many more files than just these. Notice that important files such as ntldr and ntdetect.com in Windows XP have the system, hidden, and read-only attributes set. Microsoft does this to protect them from accidental deletion.

You also use the attrib command to change a file's attributes. To add an attribute to a file, type the attribute letter preceded by a plus sign (+) as an option, and then type the filename. To delete an attribute, use a minus sign (–). For example, to add the read-only attribute to the file AILog.txt, type this:

attrib +r ailog.txt

To remove the archive attribute, type this:

attrib -a ailog.txt

You can add or remove multiple attributes in one command. Here's an example of removing three attributes from the ntdetect.com file:

attrib -r -s -h ntdetect.com

You can also automatically apply attrib to matching files in subdirectories by using the /s switch at the end of the statement. For example, if you

Try This!

Working with Attributes

It's important for you to know that everything you do at the command line affects the same files at the GUI level, so Try This!

1. Go to My Computer or Computer and create a folder called Test in the root directory of your C: drive.

2. Copy a couple of files into that folder and then right-click one to see its properties.

3. Open a command-line window and navigate to the C:\Test folder. Type **dir** to see that the contents match what you see in My Computer/Computer.

4. From the command line, change the attributes of one or both files. Make one a hidden file, for example, and the other read-only.

5. Now go back to My Computer/Computer and access the properties of each file. Any changes?

have lots of files in your My Music folder that you want to hide, but they are neatly organized in many subdirectories, you could readily use attrib to change all of them with a simple command. Change directories from the prompt until you're at the My Music folder and then type the following:

attrib +h *.mp3 /s

When you press the ENTER key, all your music files in My Music and any My Music subdirectories will become hidden files.

 You should know how to use attrib for the CompTIA A+ 220-802 exam.

Wildcards

Visualize having 273 files in one directory. A few of these files have the extension .docx, but most do not. You are looking only for files with the .docx extension. Wouldn't it be nice to be able to type the dir command in such a way that only the .docx files come up? You can do this by using wildcards.

A **wildcard** is one of two special characters—asterisk (*) and question mark (?)—that you can use in place of all or part of a filename, often so that a command-line command will act on more than one file at a time. Wildcards work with all command-line commands that take filenames. A great example is the dir command. When you execute a plain dir command, it finds and displays all of the files and folders in the specified directory; however, you can also narrow its search by adding a filename. For example, if you type the command **dir ailog.txt** while in your root (C:\) directory, you get the following result:

```
C:\>dir ailog.txt
 Volume in drive C has no label.
 Volume Serial Number is 4C62-1572
 Directory of C:\
05/26/2009  11:37 PM                 0 AILog.txt
               1 File(s)             0 bytes
               0 Dir(s)  94,630,195,200 bytes free
```

If you just want to confirm the presence of a particular file in a particular place, this is very convenient. But suppose you want to see all files with the extension .txt. In that case, you use the * wildcard, like this: **dir *.txt**. A good way to think of the * wildcard is "*I don't care.*" Replace the part of the filename that you don't care about with an asterisk (*). The result of dir *.txt would look like this:

```
 Volume in drive C has no label.
 Volume Serial Number is 4C62-1572

 Directory of C:\

05/26/2009  11:37 PM                 0 AILog.txt
05/29/2009  05:33 PM             5,776 aoedoppl.txt
05/29/2009  05:33 PM             2,238 aoeWVlog.txt
07/31/2008  10:40 PM               153 systemscandata.txt
               4 File(s)         8,167 bytes
               0 Dir(s)  94,630,002,688 bytes free
```

Wildcards also substitute for parts of filenames. This dir command will find every file that starts with the letter *a*:

```
C:\>dir a*.*
 Volume in drive C has no label.
 Volume Serial Number is 4C62-1572

 Directory of C:\

05/26/2009  11:37 PM                 0 AILog.txt
05/29/2009  05:33 PM             5,776 aoedoppl.txt
05/29/2009  05:33 PM             2,238 aoeWVlog.txt
               3 File(s)          8,014 bytes
               0 Dir(s)  94,629,675,008 bytes free
```

We've used wildcards only with the dir command, but virtually every command that deals with files will take wildcards. Let's examine the ren and del commands and see how they use wildcards.

Renaming Files

To rename files, you use the **ren (or rename) command**, which seems pretty straightforward. To rename the file img033.jpg to park.jpg, type the following and then press the ENTER key:

ren img033.jpg park.jpg

"That's great," you might be thinking, "but what about using a more complex and descriptive filename, such as Sunny day in the park.jpg?" Type what should work, like this:

ren img033.jpg Sunny day in the park.jpg

But you'll get an error message (see Figure 9.16). Even the tried-and-true method of seeking help by typing the command followed by /? doesn't give you the answer.

You can use more complicated names by putting them in quotation marks. Figure 9.17 shows the same command that failed but now succeeds because of the quotation marks.

• **Figure 9.16** Rename failed me

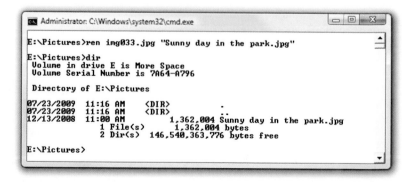

• **Figure 9.17** Success at last.

Deleting Files

To delete files, you use the **del (or erase) command**. (They're identical commands that you can use interchangeably.) Deleting files is simple—maybe too simple. Windows users enjoy the luxury of retrieving deleted files from the Recycle Bin on those "Oops, I didn't mean to delete that" occasions everyone encounters at one time or another. The command line, however, shows no such mercy to the careless user. It has no function equivalent to the Windows Recycle Bin. Once you have erased a file, you can recover it only by using a special recovery utility such as Norton's UNERASE. Again, the rule here is to *check twice and delete once*.

To delete a single file, type the **del** command followed by the name of the file to delete. To delete the file ailog.txt, for example, type this:

del ailog.txt

Although nothing appears on the screen to confirm it, the file is now gone. To confirm that the ailog.txt file is no longer listed, use the dir command.

As with the dir command, you can use wildcards with the del and erase commands to delete multiple files. For example, to delete all files with the extension .txt in a directory, you would type this:

del *.txt

To delete all files with the filename config in a directory, type **del config.***. To delete all of the files in a directory, you can use the popular *.* wildcard (often pronounced "star-dot-star"), like this:

del *.*

This is one of the few command-line commands that elicits a response. Upon receiving the del *.* command, Windows responds with "Are you sure? (Y/N)," to which you respond with a Y or N. Pressing Y erases every file in the directory, so use *.* with care!

Don't confuse deleting *files* with deleting *directories*. Use del to delete files; it will not remove directories. Use rd to delete directories.

> You'll be tested on del, erase, and rd on the CompTIA A+ 220-802 exam.

Copying and Moving Files

Being able to copy and move files in a command line is crucial to all technicians. Because of its finicky nature and many options, the copy command is also rather painful to learn, especially if you're used to dragging icons in Windows. The following tried-and-true, five-step process makes it easier, but the real secret is to get in front of a C:\ prompt and just copy and move files around until you're comfortable. Keep in mind that the only difference between copying and moving is whether the original is left behind (copy) or not (move). Once you've learned the **copy command**, you've also learned the **move command**!

Mike's Five-Step copy/move Process

I've been teaching folks how to copy and move files for years by using this handy process. Keep in mind that hundreds of variations on this process exist. As you become more confident with these commands, try doing a

copy /? or move /? at any handy prompt to see the real power of the commands. But first, follow this process step by step:

1. Point the command prompt to the directory containing the file(s) you want to copy or move.

2. Type **copy** or **move** and a space.

3. Type the *name(s)* of the file(s) to be copied/moved (with or without wildcards) and a space.

4. Type the *path* of the new location for the file(s).

5. Press ENTER.

Let's try an example. The directory C:\Steam contains the file readme.txt. Copy this file to a USB thumb drive (E:).

1. Type **cd\steam** to point the command prompt to the Steam directory.

   ```
   C:\>cd\steam
   ```

2. Type **copy** and a space.

   ```
   C:\Steam>copy
   ```

3. Type **readme.txt** and a space.

   ```
   C:\Steam>copy readme.txt
   ```

4. Type **e:**.

   ```
   C:\Steam>copy readme.txt e:\
   ```

5. Press ENTER.

The entire command and response would look like this:

```
C:\Steam>copy readme.txt e:\
1 file(s) copied
```

If you point the command prompt to the E: drive and type **dir**, the readme.txt file will be visible. Let's try another example. Suppose 100 files are in the C:\Docs directory, 30 of which have the .doc extension, and suppose you want to move those files to the C:\Steam directory. Follow these steps:

1. Type **cd\docs** to point the command prompt to the Docs directory.

   ```
   C:\>cd\docs
   ```

2. Type **move** and a space.

   ```
   C:\Docs>move
   ```

3. Type ***.doc** and a space.

   ```
   C:\Docs>move *.doc
   ```

4. Type **c:\steam**.

   ```
   C:\Docs>move *.doc c:\steam
   ```

5. Press ENTER.

   ```
   C:\Docs>move *.doc c:\steam
   30 file(s) copied
   ```

The power of the copy/move command makes it rather dangerous. The copy/move command not only lets you put a file in a new location; it also lets you change the name of the file at the same time. Suppose you want to copy a file called autoexec.bat from your C:\ folder to a thumb drive, for example, but you want the name of the copy on the thumb drive to be auto1.bat. You can do both things with one copy command, like this:

```
copy c:\autoexec.bat e:\auto1.bat
```

Not only does the autoexec.bat file get copied to the thumb drive, but the copy also gets the new name auto1.bat.

As another example, move all of the files with the extension .doc from the C:\Docs directory to the C:\Back directory and simultaneously change the .doc extension to .sav. Here is the command:

```
move c:\docs\*.doc c:\back\*.sav
```

This says, "Move all files that have the extension .doc from the directory C:\Docs into the directory C:\Back, and while you're at it, change their file extensions to .sav." This is very handy, but very dangerous!

Let's say, for example, that I made one tiny typo. Here I typed a semicolon instead of a colon after the second C:

```
move c:\docs\*.doc c;\back\*.sav
```

The command line understands the semicolon to mean "end of command" and therefore ignores both the semicolon and anything I type after it. As far as the command line is concerned, I typed this:

```
move c:\docs\*.doc c
```

This, unfortunately for me, means "take all of the files with the extension .doc in the directory C:\Docs and copy them back into that same directory, but squish them all together into a single file called c." If I run this command, Windows gives me only one clue that something went wrong:

```
move c:\docs\*.doc c
1 file(s) copied
```

See "1 file(s) copied"? Feeling the chilly hand of fate slide down my spine, I do a dir of the directory, and I now see a single file called c, where there used to be 30 files with the extension .doc. All of my .doc files are gone, completely unrecoverable.

xcopy

The standard copy and move commands can work only in one directory at a time, making them a poor choice for copying or moving files in multiple directories. To help with these multi-directory jobs, Microsoft added the **xcopy command**. (Note that there is no xmove, only xcopy.)

The xcopy command works similarly to copy, but xcopy has extra switches that give it the power to work with multiple directories. Here's how it works. Let's say I have a directory on my C: drive called \Data. The \Data directory has three subdirectories: \Jan, \Feb, and \Mar. All of these directories, including the \Data directory, contain about 50 files. If I wanted

to copy all of these files to my D: drive in one command, I would use xcopy in the following manner:

```
xcopy c:\data d:\data /s
```

Because xcopy works on directories, you don't have to use filenames as you would in copy, although xcopy certainly accepts filenames and wildcards. The /s switch, the most commonly used of all of the many switches that come with xcopy, tells xcopy to copy all subdirectories except for empty ones. The /e switch tells xcopy to copy empty subdirectories. When you have a lot of copying to do over many directories, xcopy is the tool to use.

robocopy

Microsoft introduced the **robocopy command**—short for Robust File Copy—many years ago as an add-on tool for Windows Server to enable techs to manage files and folders more quickly and efficiently than with xcopy or copy. The robocopy command, now included in Windows Vista and Windows 7, is powerful indeed, enabling you to, for example, copy the files and folders from one computer to another across a network, fully replicating the structure on the destination system *and* deleting anything on that system that wasn't part of the copy. It can do this with a simple command.

The robocopy syntax does not resemble that of copy or xcopy, so if you're going to use the tool, you need to unlearn a few things. Here's the basic syntax:

```
robocopy source destination [file [file]...] [options]
```

Here's an example of the command in action. The following command would copy all files and subfolders from a local machine's D:\testserver\newwebsite folder to a shared folder on the remote server \\webhost\companywebsite.

```
robocopy d:\testserver\newwebsite \\webhost\companywebsite
/mir
```

The /mir switch, for mirror, tells robocopy to copy everything from the source and make the destination mirror it. That means robocopy will also delete anything in the destination that doesn't match the source folders and files.

If that were it, robocopy would be powerful, but that's not even the tip of the iceberg. The robocopy command can copy encrypted files. It enables an administrator to copy files even if the administrator account is expressly denied access to those files. It will also resume copying after an interruption, and do so at the spot it stopped. For the full syntax, type the following:

robocopy /?

Their power and utility make the del, copy/move, xcopy, and robocopy commands indispensable for a PC technician, but that same power and utility can cause disaster. Only a trained Jedi, with The Force as his ally...well, wrong book, but the principle remains: Beware of the quick and easy keystroke, for it may spell your doom. Think twice and execute the command once. The data you save may be yours!

Know copy, xcopy, and robocopy for the CompTIA A+ 220-802 exam.

And Even More Tools, Utilities, and Commands

As a proficient IT technician in the field, you need to be familiar with a whole slew of command-line tools and other important utilities. The CompTIA A+ 220-802 exam focuses in on several of them, and although many have been discussed in detail in previous chapters, it is extremely important that you understand and practice with chkdsk, format, sfc, and shutdown.

chkdsk (/f /r)

The **chkdsk (checkdisk) command** scans, detects, and repairs hard drive– and volume-related issues and errors. You can run the chkdsk utility from a command prompt with the switches /f and /r. The /f switch attempts to fix volume-related errors, while the /r switch attempts to locate and repair bad sectors. To run successfully, chkdsk needs direct access to a drive. In other words, the drive needs to be "unlocked." For example, if you run chkdsk /f /r and chkdsk does not consider your drive unlocked, you will receive a "cannot lock current drive" message, meaning that another process has the drive locked and is preventing chkdsk from locking the drive itself. After this, chkdsk presents you with the option to run it the next time the system restarts (see Figure 9.18).

• **Figure 9.18** The chkdsk /f /r utility and switches on a locked drive

```
Administrator: C:\Windows\system32\cmd.exe

C:\>format /?
Formats a disk for use with Windows.

FORMAT volume [/FS:file-system] [/V:label] [/Q] [/A:size] [/C] [/X] [/P:passes]
FORMAT volume [/V:label] [/Q] [/F:size] [/P:passes]
FORMAT volume [/V:label] [/Q] [/T:tracks /N:sectors] [/P:passes]
FORMAT volume [/V:label] [/Q] [/P:passes]
FORMAT volume [/Q]

  volume          Specifies the drive letter (followed by a colon),
                  mount point, or volume name.
  /FS:filesystem  Specifies the type of the file system (FAT, FAT32, exFAT, NTFS,
                  or UDF).
  /V:label        Specifies the volume label.
  /Q              Performs a quick format. Note that this switch overrides /P.
  /C              NTFS only: Files created on the new volume will be compressed
                  by default.
  /X              Forces the volume to dismount first if necessary.  All opened
                  handles to the volume would no longer be valid.
  /R:revision     UDF only: Forces the format to a specific UDF version
                  (1.02, 1.50, 2.00, 2.01, 2.50).  The default
                  revision is 2.01.
  /D              UDF 2.50 only: Metadata will be duplicated.
  /A:size         Overrides the default allocation unit size. Default settings
                  are strongly recommended for general use.
                  NTFS supports 512, 1024, 2048, 4096, 8192, 16K, 32K, 64K.
                  FAT supports 512, 1024, 2048, 4096, 8192, 16K, 32K, 64K,
                  (128K, 256K for sector size > 512 bytes).
                  FAT32 supports 512, 1024, 2048, 4096, 8192, 16K, 32K, 64K,
                  (128K, 256K for sector size > 512 bytes).
                  exFAT supports 512, 1024, 2048, 4096, 8192, 16K, 32K, 64K,
                  128K, 256K, 512K, 1M, 2M, 4M, 8M, 16M, 32M.

                  Note that the FAT and FAT32 files systems impose the
                  following restrictions on the number of clusters on a volume:

                  FAT: Number of clusters <= 65526
                  FAT32: 65526 < Number of clusters < 4177918

                  Format will immediately stop processing if it decides that
                  the above requirements cannot be met using the specified
                  cluster size.

                  NTFS compression is not supported for allocation unit sizes
                  above 4096.

  /F:size         Specifies the size of the floppy disk to format (1.44)
  /T:tracks       Specifies the number of tracks per disk side.
  /N:sectors      Specifies the number of sectors per track.
  /P:passes       Zero every sector on the volume passes times. This switch is
                  not valid with /Q

C:\>
```

• **Figure 9.19** Using format /? at the command prompt

format

After the previous chapters, you should have an expert-level knowledge of (or, at the very least, a passing familiarity with) formatting and partitioning hard drives. Formatting, you may remember, prepares a partition or volume so it can hold an operating system or data. We have already discussed the various built-in Windows utilities available to provide the formatting of drives, and you no doubt know that many third-party formatting tools are out there. In this chapter, you just need to become familiar with the format command and its switches.

The **format command**, you may have guessed, enables you to format disks from the command line. The very best way to familiarize yourself with the format command and its available switches is simply to enter **format /?** from the command prompt. Your results should be similar to those displayed in Figure 9.19.

Although the new CompTIA A+ 220-802 exam focuses primarily on GUI operating system formatting utilities and options, you should familiarize yourself with the format command and its switches by practicing them on a test system you are literally not afraid to wipe out. Besides, you never know what skeletons CompTIA may pull out of the closet.

hostname

The **hostname command** is the most straightforward of all command-line commands. If you type **hostname** at the command prompt, it will display the name of your computer, also known as the hostname. When I type **hostname**, for example, it prints "MikePC."

sfc (System File Checker)

The Windows **sfc (System File Checker)**, or simply sfc.exe, scans, detects, and restores important Windows system files, folders, and paths. Techs often use the sfc utility from within a working version of Windows or from a Windows installation disc to restore a corrupt Windows environment. If you run sfc and it finds issues, it attempts to replace corrupted or missing files from cached DLLs located in the %WinDir%\System32\Dllcache\ directory. Without getting very deep into the mad science involved, just know that you can use sfc to correct corruption. To run sfc from a command prompt,

enter **sfc /scannow**. To familiarize yourself with sfc's switches, enter **sfc /?** (see Figure 9.20).

shutdown

The **shutdown command** enables you to do exactly that to a local or remote computer, namely, shut it down. The cool part of the tool is that you can use a number of switches to control and report the shutdown. A network administrator could use this tool to restart a computer remotely, for example with a few keystrokes, like this:

```
shutdown /r /m \\testserver
```

The /r switch tells shutdown to have the computer reboot rather than just shut down. If you want to see the full syntax for shutdown, type the following:

shutdown /?

• **Figure 9.20** Checking sfc options with sfc /? at a command prompt

Beyond A+

Using Special Keys

You might find yourself repeatedly typing the same commands, or at least very similar commands, when working at a prompt. Microsoft has provided a number of ways to access previously typed commands. Type the **dir** command at a command prompt. When you get back to a prompt, press F1, and the letter *d* appears. Press F1 again. Now the letter *i* appears after the *d*. Do you see what is happening? The F1 key brings back the previous command one letter at a time. Pressing F3 brings back the entire command at once. Now try running these three commands:

dir /w
attrib
md fred

Now press the UP ARROW key. Keep pressing it till you see your original dir command—it's a history of all your old commands. Now use the RIGHT ARROW key to add /p to the end of your dir command. Windows command history is very handy.

The compact and cipher Commands

Windows offers two cool commands at the command-line interface: compact and cipher. The compact command displays or alters the compression of files on NTFS partitions. The cipher command displays or alters the encryption of folders and files on NTFS partitions. If you type just the command with no added parameters, **compact** and **cipher** display the compression state and the encryption state, respectively, of the current directory and any files it contains. You may specify multiple directory names, and you may use wildcards, as you learned earlier in the chapter. You must add parameters to make the commands change things. For example, you add /c to compress and /u to uncompress directories and/or files with the compact command, and you add /e to encrypt and /d to decrypt directories and/or files with the cipher command. When you do these operations, you also mark the directories involved so that any files you add to them in the future will take on their encryption or compression characteristics. In other words, if you encrypt a directory and all its files, any files you add later will also be encrypted. Same thing if you compress a directory. I'll run through a quick example of each.

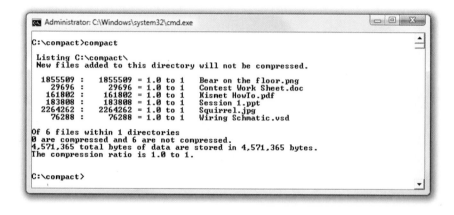

• **Figure 9.21** The compact command with no switches

compact

First let's try the compact command. Figure 9.21 shows the result of entering the compact command with no switches. It displays the compression status of the contents of a directory called compact on a system's C: drive. Notice that after the file listing, compact helpfully tells you that 0 files are compressed and 6 files (all of them) are not compressed, with a total compression ratio of 1.0 to 1.

If you enter the compact command with the /c switch, it compresses all of the files in the directory, as shown in Figure 9.22. Look closely at the list-

• **Figure 9.22** Typing **compact /c** compresses the contents of the directory.

ing. Notice that it includes the original and compressed file sizes and calculates the compression ratio for you. Notice also that the JPG and PNG files (both compressed graphics files) didn't compress at all, while the Word file and the PowerPoint file compressed down to around a third of their original sizes. Also, can you spot what's different in the text at the bottom of the screen? The compact command claims to have compressed *seven* files in *two* directories! How can this be? The secret is that when it compresses all of the files in a directory, it must also compress the directory file itself, which is "in" the C: directory above it. Thus it correctly reports that it compressed seven files: six in the compact directory, and one in the C: directory.

Typing **compact** again shows you the directory listing, and now there's a *C* next to each filename, indicating that the file is compressed (see Figure 9.23).

Okay, now suppose you want to uncompress a file—say a PowerPoint file, Session 1.ppt. To do this, you must specify the decompression operation, using the /u switch and the name of the file you want decompressed, as shown in Figure 9.24. Note that compact reports the successful decompression of one file only: Session 1.ppt. You could do the same thing in reverse, using the /c switch and a filename to compress an individual file.

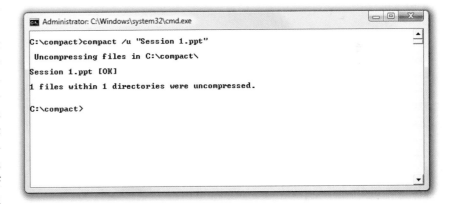

• **Figure 9.23** The contents of C:\compact have been compressed.

• **Figure 9.24** Typing **compact /u "Session 1.ppt"** decompresses only that file.

cipher

The cipher command is a bit complex, but in its most basic implementation, it's pretty straightforward. Figure 9.25 shows two steps in the process. Like the compact command, the cipher command simply displays the current state of affairs when entered with no switches. In this case, it displays the encryption state of the files in the E:\Work Files\Armor Pictures directory. Notice the letter *U* to the left of the filenames, which tells you they are unencrypted. The second command you can see on the screen in Figure 9.25 is this:

```
E:\Work Files\Armor Pictures>cipher /e /a
```

This time the cipher command carries two switches: /e specifies the encryption operation, and /a says to apply it to the *files* in the directory, not just the directory itself. As you can see, the command-line interface is actually pretty chatty in this case. It reports that it's doing the encryption and

then tells you what it's done, and it even warns you that you should clean up any stray unencrypted bits that may have been left in the directory.

To confirm the results of the cipher operation, enter the **cipher** command again, as shown in Figure 9.26. Note that the *U* to the left of each filename has been replaced with an *E*, indicating an encrypted file. The other indication that this directory has been encrypted is the statement above the file listing:

```
New files added to this directory will not be encrypted.
```

Remember that the cipher command works on directories first and foremost, and it works on individual files only when you specifically tell it to do so.

• **Figure 9.25** Typing **cipher /e /a** encrypts the contents of the directory.

• **Figure 9.26** The cipher command confirms that the files were encrypted.

That's great, but suppose you want to decrypt just *one* of the files in the Armor Pictures directory. Can you guess how you need to alter the command? Simply add the filename of the file you want to decrypt after the command and the relevant switches. Figure 9.27 shows the cipher command being used to decipher dsc_4255.dng, a single file.

PowerShell

Microsoft introduced an add-on command-line interface called PowerShell for Windows XP and finally integrated it into Windows 7 as a more powerful replacement for the traditional command-line interface. PowerShell enables you to do all the typical command-line activities, such as dir, cd, md, and so on, but brings a series of vastly more powerful tools called *cmdlets* that enable you to accomplish some amazing tasks. Figure 9.28 shows two commands that do the same thing by default—show the contents of a directory: dir and get-childitem.

With dir, you know you can search for items in a directory, such as "find all the JPEG files in a folder" with this command:

```
dir *.jpg
```

- **Figure 9.27** Typing **cipher /d /a dsc_4255.dng** decrypts only that file.

PowerShell lets you dial it all the way to 11, though, with a few more characters on a search string. The following command will find all the JPEG files on the entire computer, plus all the mentions of .jpg files in any document format, such as Word, PowerPoint, and Acrobat:

```
get-childitem . -include *.jpg -recurse -force
```

Just in case you want to know what each piece of that string in the cmdlet means, here's the scoop: get-childitem is the main command. The dot <.> indicates the current directory and all its subdirectories, while –include tells the command to fetch the file type indicated next, in this case *.jpg. –recurse makes the command repeat, and –force retrieves hidden files too. It's like dir on steroids!

To open PowerShell in Windows 7, simply type **powershell** in the Search bar and press ENTER. To use the tool in Windows XP or Windows Vista, you'll need to download it from Microsoft. Just go to Microsoft.com and search for **PowerShell download**. You'll find it readily enough. You might also need to install the .NET 2.0 framework if you're on an older machine. You can find that at the same Web site. Good luck!

- **Figure 9.28** Simple commands in PowerShell

Chapter 9 Review

■ Chapter Summary

After reading this chapter and completing the exercises, you should understand the following about the command-line interface.

Explain the operation of the command-line interface

■ The text-based DOS-like user interface, known as the command-line interface, functions as a basic installation and troubleshooting tool for techs in Windows. When you use a command-line interface, the computer tells you it's ready to receive commands by displaying a specific set of characters called a prompt. You type a command and press ENTER to send it. The OS goes off and executes the command, and when it's finished, it displays a new prompt, often along with some information about what it did. The new prompt means the computer is ready for your next instruction.

■ You can access the command-line interface in Windows XP by clicking Start | Run to open the Run dialog box, and then typing **cmd** or **command** and pressing ENTER. In Windows Vista or Windows 7, you enter one of the same commands in the Start menu Search bar. You can also click Start | Programs/All Programs | Accessories | Command Prompt. To close the command line–interface window, either click the Close box in the upper-right corner of the window or type **exit** at the prompt and press ENTER.

■ The command prompt is always focused on some directory, and any commands you issue are performed *on the files in the directory* on which the prompt is focused. Make sure you focus the prompt's attention on the drive and directory in which you want to work.

■ Windows manifests each program and piece of data as an individual *file*. Each file has a name, which is stored with the file on the drive. Names are broken down into two parts: the filename and the extension. In true DOS, the filename could be no longer than eight characters. The extension, which is optional, could be up to three characters long. No spaces or other illegal characters (/ \ [] | ÷ + = ; , * ?) could be used in the filename or extension. The filename and extension are separated by a period, or dot. This naming system

is known as the "eight-dot-three" (8.3) naming system. All versions of Windows starting with 9*x* allow filenames of up to 255 characters.

■ The filename extension tells the computer the type or function of the file. Program files use the extension .exe (for executable) or .com (for command). If the file is data, the extension indicates which program uses that particular data file. Graphics files most often reflect the graphics standard used to render the image, such as .gif or .jpg. Changing the file extension does not change the data in the file. The Windows GUI doesn't show the file extensions by default.

■ All files are stored on the hard drive in binary format, but every program has a unique method of binary organization, called a file format. One program cannot read another program's files unless it can convert the other program's file format into its file format.

■ ASCII (American Standard Code for Information Interchange) was the first universal file format. The ASCII standard defines 256 eight-bit characters, including all of the letters of the alphabet (uppercase and lowercase), numbers, punctuation, many foreign characters, box-drawing characters, and a series of special characters for commands, such as a carriage return, bell, and end of file. ASCII files, often called text files, store all data in ASCII format. The keyboard sends the characters you press on the keyboard to the PC in ASCII code. Even the monitor outputs in ASCII when you are running a command line.

■ As a rule, the OS treats the first 32 ASCII values as commands. Some of them are both commands and characters. How these first 32 values are treated depends on the program that reads them.

■ Unicode supports thousands of 16-bit characters. The first 256 Unicode characters are the same as the complete 256 ASCII character set, which maintains backward compatibility.

■ At boot, the OS assigns a drive letter to each hard drive partition and to each floppy or other disk drive. The first floppy drive, if installed, is called A:, and the second, if installed, is called B:. Hard drives start with the letter C: and can continue to

Z: if necessary. Optical drives usually get the next available drive letter after the last hard drive.

- Windows uses a hierarchical directory tree to organize the contents of these drives. All files are put into groups called directories. Windows also uses directories, but it calls them folders. Any file not in a directory *within* the tree—which is to say, any file in the directory at the root of the directory tree—is said to be in the root directory. Directories inside directories are called subdirectories. Any directory can have multiple subdirectories. Two or more files or subdirectories with the same name can exist in different directories on a PC, but two files or subdirectories in the same directory cannot have the same name.

- When describing a drive, you use its assigned letter, such as C: for the hard drive. To describe the root directory, add a backslash (\), as in C:\. To describe a particular directory, add the name of the directory after the backslash. To add a subdirectory after the directory, add another backslash and then the subdirectory's name. This naming convention provides for a complete description of the location and name of any file. The exact location of a file is called its path.

Execute fundamental commands from the command line

- The command-line interface will do what you *say*, not what you *mean*, so it always pays to double-check that those are the same before you press ENTER. One careless keystroke can result in the loss of crucial data, with no warning and no going back.

- The dir command shows you the contents of the directory on which the prompt is focused. The dir command lists the filename, extension, file size in bytes, and creation date/time. The dir /p command pauses after displaying a screen's worth of the directory contents; press the SPACEBAR to display the next screen. The dir /w command shows you filenames only, arranged in columns, with directory names in square brackets.

- Extra text typed after a command to modify its operation, such as /w or /p after dir, is called a switch. Almost all switches can be used simultaneously to modify a command. Typing any command followed by /? brings up a help screen for that particular command.

- You can use the cd command to change the focus of the command prompt to a different directory.

Type **cd** followed by the name of the directory on which you want to focus the prompt, and press ENTER. If no such directory exists or if you mistyped the name, Windows will report "The system cannot find the path specified." To return to the root directory, type **cd** and press ENTER. The cd command also allows you to use a space instead of a backslash. The cd command is not used to move between drives; to point the prompt to another drive, type the drive letter and a colon.

- To make a directory, use the md (or mkdir) command. Once you press ENTER, the OS executes the command, but it won't volunteer any information about what it did. You must use the dir command to see that you have, in fact, created a new directory. Make sure that the prompt points to the directory in which you want to make the new subdirectory before you execute the md command.

- To remove a directory, first point the prompt at the directory that contains the subdirectory you want to delete, and then execute the rd (or rmdir) command. If you get no response, you probably did it right, but use the dir command to be sure. The rd command will not delete a directory if it contains files or subdirectories; you must first empty that directory by using the del (for files) or rd (for subdirectories) command. The rd command followed by the /S switch deletes the directory as well as all files and subdirectories.

Manipulate files from the command line

- All files have four special values, or attributes, that determine how they will act in special situations: hidden, read-only, system, and archive. You can set these attributes through software. If a file is hidden, it will not be displayed when the dir command is performed. A read-only file cannot be modified or deleted. The system attribute, which is used only for system files such as ntldr and ntdetect.com found in Windows XP, provides an easy identifier for these files. The archive attribute is used by backup software to identify files that have been changed since their last backup.

- attrib.exe is an external program with which you can inspect and change file attributes. Type the **attrib** command followed by the name of the file and press ENTER. In the resulting list of files, letter codes indicate each file's attributes, if any: *A* stands for archive, *R* means read-only, *H* is hidden, and *S* is system. The attrib command can change a file's

attributes. To add an attribute to a file, type the attribute letter preceded by a plus sign (+), and then the filename. To delete an attribute, use a minus sign (–). Multiple attributes can be added or removed in one command.

- Wildcards are two special characters, asterisk (*) and question mark (?), that you can use in place of all or part of a filename to make a command act on more than one file at a time. Wildcards work with all command-line commands that take filenames. The asterisk (*) wildcard replaces any part of a filename, before and/or after the period. The ? wildcard replaces any single character. Virtually every command that deals with files will take wildcards.

- Use the ren (or rename) command to rename files and folders. If the new name contains spaces, enclose the name in quotation marks.

- To delete files, you use the del or erase command. del and erase are identical commands and can be used interchangeably. del will not erase directories. To delete a single file, type the **del** command followed by the name of the file. No confirmation will appear on the screen. To delete all of the files in a directory, you can use the *.* (star-dot-star) wildcard. Upon receiving the del *.* command, Windows responds with "Are you sure? (Y/N)," to which you respond with a *Y* or *N*. Pressing Y erases every file in the directory. It pays to check twice before you delete, because the command line has no function equivalent to the Windows Recycle Bin that allows you to retrieve an accidentally deleted file; once a file has been erased, you can recover it only by using a special recovery utility.

- The copy and move commands are used to copy and move files. The only difference between them is whether the original file is left behind (copy) or not (move). Type **copy** or **move** and a space. Point the prompt to the directory containing the file(s) to be copied or moved. Type the *name(s)* of the file(s) to be copied/moved (with or without wildcards) and a space. Type the *path* of the new location for the file(s). Press ENTER. The copy/move command not only lets you put a file in a new location; it also lets you change the name of the file at the same time.

- Check for the common typo of substituting a semicolon for a colon, because the semicolon means "end of command" and therefore ignores both the semicolon and anything you type after it.

- The xcopy command works similarly to copy but has extra switches that give xcopy the power to work with multiple directories. Because xcopy works on directories, you don't have to use filenames as you would in copy, although you can use filenames and wildcards. The /s switch tells xcopy to copy all subdirectories except empty ones. The /e switch tells it to copy empty subdirectories.

- The robocopy command acts like copy on steroids, enabling you to copy full directories, including structures, and even erase anything that doesn't match on the destination drive.

- A plethora of tools, utilities, and commands are available to prepare, maintain, detect, and/or correct operating system file structures. Many of these, including chkdsk, format, sfc, and shutdown, can be started or run from a command prompt and/or from the Windows GUI.

■ Key Terms

<div style="display: flex;">
<div>

8.3 naming system *(340)*

American Standard Code for Information Interchange (ASCII) *(341)*

attrib.exe *(351)*

attributes *(351)*

cd (chdir) command *(346)*

chkdsk (checkdisk) command *(359)*

command-line interface *(336)*

copy command *(355)*

del (erase) command *(355)*

dir command *(344)*

</div>
<div>

format command *(360)*

hostname command *(360)*

md (mkdir) command *(347)*

move command *(355)*

path *(343)*

prompt *(336)*

read-only attribute *(351)*

rd (rmdir) command *(348)*

ren (rename) command *(354)*

robocopy command *(358)*

root directory *(343)*

</div>
</div>

Run dialog box *(339)*
sfc (System File Checker) *(360)*
shutdown command *(361)*
switch *(344)*

syntax *(344)*
Unicode *(342)*
wildcard *(353)*
xcopy command *(357)*

■ Key Term Quiz

Use the Key Terms list to complete the sentences that follow. Not all terms will be used.

1. The _____ tells you it's ready to receive commands by displaying a specific set of characters called a(n) _____.

2. Extra text you type after a command to modify its operation is called a(n) _____.

3. The first universal file format was called _____.

4. The _____ shows you the contents of the directory that currently has focus.

5. Each file's _____ determine how programs (such as My Computer or Computer) treat the file in special situations.

6. The _____ enables you to restart a computer remotely from the command line.

7. An external program that enables you to inspect and change file attributes is _____.

8. The asterisk is a special character called a(n) _____ that you can use in place of part of a filename when executing a command-line command.

9. Use the _____ to rename a file.

10. To move a file from the root directory into a subfolder, use the _____.

■ Multiple-Choice Quiz

1. Which of the following is an illegal character in a Windows filename?

 A. * (asterisk)

 B. . (dot)

 C. – (dash)

 D. _ (underscore)

2. Which command pauses after displaying a screen's worth of directory contents?

 A. dir p

 B. pdir

 C. pd

 D. dir /p

3. Which of the following commands will delete all of the files in a directory?

 A. del *.*

 B. del all

 C. del ?.?

 D. del *.?

4. Which command do you use to change the focus of the command prompt to a different directory?

 A. dir /n

 B. cddir

 C. cd

 D. dir /c

5. Which attribute keeps a file from being displayed when the dir command is performed?

 A. Hidden

 B. Archive

 C. Read-only

 D. Protected

6. What command enables you to make a new directory in a Windows 7 Professional system?

 A. mf

 B. mkfol

 C. md

 D. makedir

7. What commands can you type at the Run dialog box to access the command-line interface in Windows XP? (Select two.)

 A. cmd

 B. command

 C. msdos

 D. prompt

8. Joey wants to change the name of a file from start.bat to hammer.bat. Which of the following commands would accomplish this feat?

 A. ren hammer.bat start.bat

 B. ren start.bat hammer.bat

 C. rename /s start.bat hammer.bat

 D. rename /s hammer.bat start.bat

9. What is the name for the rules for typing a command correctly?

 A. Protocol

 B. Syntax

 C. Legacy

 D. Instruction set

10. What is the command to make myfile.txt read-only?

 A. attrib myfile.txt +r

 B. attrib myfile.txt –r

 C. readonly myfile.txt

 D. myfile.txt /readonly

11. What is the maximum number of characters in a Windows filename?

 A. 8

 B. 255

 C. 65,536

 D. No limit

12. What user profile directory is displayed at a Windows Vista command prompt by default?

 A. C:\All Users*User name*

 B. C:\Users*User name*

 C. C:\Documents and Settings*User name*

 D. C:\Windows\system32\drivers\etc

13. How do you run a command at the Windows 7 command prompt with elevated or administrative privileges?

 A. Enter an elevated username and password at the command prompt.

 B. Right-click a command-prompt shortcut and then select Run as PowerUser.

 C. Right-click a command-prompt shortcut and then select Run as administrator.

 D. When prompted, enter a valid root or supervisor password.

14. What tool would you use at a Windows 7 command prompt to manage files and folders more quickly and efficiently than with xcopy or copy?

 A. recopy

 B. copynow

 C. attrib

 D. robocopy

15. What tool enables you to reboot a computer from the command line?

 A. boot

 B. reboot

 C. restart

 D. shutdown

Essay Quiz

1. You've been tasked to teach some newbie techs, whose only computer experience involves Windows, about the beauty and power of the command line. For their first lesson, write a short essay explaining how the command-line interface works, including the directory structure, filename limitations, and interaction with the command prompt.

2. You work the help desk at a college computing center. Some applications that the students must use are run from a command line. Write a memo for the help desk personnel explaining how to use the dir, cd, md, del, and rd commands, including any appropriate cautions.

3. Your coworker needs to remove the hidden attribute from a file called payroll.xls that is stored in the Employee directory on the D: drive. Write an e-mail explaining how to open a command-line window, navigate to the file, verify its presence, and remove the hidden attribute.

4. You've been tasked to teach some newbie techs, whose only computer experience involves Windows, about the beauty and power of the command line. For their second lesson, write a short essay explaining how wildcards work.

5. Write a brief essay explaining in your own words how to use Mike's Five-Step copy/move process. Give an example.

Lab Projects

• Lab Project 9.1

For each of the following files, translate the location into a path you can type at a command prompt.

1. A file named beach.jpg in the subdirectory Pictures in the directory Eziba on the primary floppy drive:

2. A file named blackdog.wav in the subdirectory Ledzep in the subdirectory Rock in the directory Music on the C: drive:

3. A file named weapon.pcx in the subdirectory Bobafett in the subdirectory Players in the subdirectory Baseq2 in the directory Quake2 on the D: drive:

4. A file named autoexec.bat in the root directory on a standard PC with a single hard drive:

5. A file named meyers.doc in the subdirectory Contracts in the subdirectory Legal in the directory Accounts on a CD-ROM on a system with one hard drive, one CD-ROM drive, and one floppy drive:

• Lab Project 9.2

To practice making/removing directories and copying/moving files, do the following:

1. Open a command-line window and point to the root directory, C:.

2. Use the md command to create a directory called Whales. Use the cd command to point to the new directory. Use the md command again to create a subdirectory of Whales called Mobydick. Use the cd command to point to the new subdirectory.

3. Populate the Mobydick subdirectory with files by opening Notepad and creating a "dummy" file called ahab.txt. Save it in the Mobydick subdirectory.

4. Use the move command to move the file ahab.txt to the Whales directory. Use the dir command to confirm that the move was successful. Use the copy command to put a copy of ahab.txt back into the Mobydick subdirectory while leaving a copy in Whales. Again use dir to confirm the operation.

5. Use the rd command to delete the Mobydick subdirectory. Did it work? Why not? Use the rd command with the /s switch to solve the problem.

Troubleshooting Windows

"Chaos is inherent in all compounded things. Strive on with diligence."

—BUDDHA

In this chapter, you will learn how to

- **Troubleshoot Windows boot problems**
- **Troubleshoot Windows GUI problems**
- **Troubleshoot Windows application problems**

This chapter looks at Windows problems from the ground up. It starts with catastrophic failure—a PC that won't boot—and then discusses ways to get past that problem. The next section covers the causes and workarounds when the Windows GUI fails to load. Once you can access the Windows GUI, the many Windows diagnostic and troubleshooting tools that you've spent so much time learning about come to your fingertips. The chapter finishes with a discussion on application problems.

■ Failure to Boot

When Windows fails to boot, you need to determine whether the problem relates to hardware or software. You'll recall from Chapter 4 that a hard drive needs proper connectivity and power, and that CMOS must be configured correctly. If not, you'll get an error like the one in Figure 10.1. We'll look more closely at these sorts of scenarios in the first part of this section as a refresher.

But after the drive powers on and the POST completes successfully, the computer tries to boot to an OS. Failure at *this* point gives you an entirely different set of errors such as *NTLDR is Missing* or *BOOTMGR is missing* (see Figure 10.2). You need a totally different set of tools from the ones used to troubleshoot hardware or CMOS issues. Windows XP and Windows Vista/7 boot differently, so to troubleshoot these failures to boot you need to know both processes and the tools available. We'll look at this type of scenario in the second part of this section.

• **Figure 10.1** If you see this screen, the problem is with hardware. Windows hasn't even started trying to boot.

• **Figure 10.2** Scary error

Failure to Boot: Hardware or Configuration

Most failed boot scenarios require you to determine where the fault occurred: with the hardware and configuration, or in Windows. This is a pretty straightforward problem. Imagine that a user calls and says "My PC won't boot" or "My computer is dead." At this point, your best tools are knowledge of the boot process and asking lots of questions. Here are some I use regularly:

"What displays on the screen—if anything—after you press the power button on the case?"

"What do you hear—if anything—after you press the power button on the case?"

"Is the PC plugged in?"

"Do you smell anything weird?"

Hardware problems can give you a blank screen on bootup, so follow the tried and true troubleshooting methodology for hardware. Make sure everything is plugged in and turned on. If the PC is new, as in less than 30 days old, you know it might have suffered a burn-in failure. If the customer smells something, one of the components might have fried. Try replacing with known good devices: RAM, power supply, CPU, hard drive, motherboard.

If the user says that the screen says "No boot device detected" and the system worked fine before, it *could* mean something as simple as the computer has attempted to boot to an incorrect device, such as to something other than the primary hard drive. This scenario happens all the time. Someone plugs a thumb drive into a USB port and CMOS is configured to boot to removable media before hard drives. The first few times it happened to me, I nearly took my machine apart before experiencing that head-slapping moment. I removed the thumb drive and then watched Windows boot normally.

> The CompTIA A+ 802 exam objectives list "Invalid boot disk" as a symptom of a Windows problem, but it's more typical of a CMOS or hardware issue.

Failure to Boot: Windows XP

Windows boot errors take place in those short moments between the time POST ends and the *Loading Windows* screen begins. For Windows XP to start loading the main operating system, the critical system files ntldr, ntdetect.com, and boot.ini must reside in the root directory of the C: drive, and boot.ini must point to the Windows boot files. In a scenario where any of these requirements isn't in place, the system won't get past this step. Here are some of the common error messages you see at this point:

No Boot Device Present

NTLDR Bad or Missing

Invalid BOOT.INI

These text errors take place very early in the startup process. That's your big clue that you have a boot issue. If you get to the Windows splash screen and then the computer locks up, that's a whole different game, so know the difference.

> The CompTIA A+ 802 exam objectives describe these error messages as "Missing NTLDR" and "Missing Boot.ini." The intent is the same, so don't be surprised by the slight difference in wording.

If you are in a failure to boot scenario where you get one of the catastrophic error messages with a Windows XP system, you have a three-level

process to get back up and running. You first should attempt to repair. If that fails, attempt to restore from a backup copy of Windows. If restore either is not available or fails, your only recourse is to rebuild. You will lose data at the restore and rebuild phases, so you definitely want to spend a lot of energy on the repair effort first! Follow this process when faced with a corrupted system files or missing operating system scenario.

Attempt to Repair by Using the Recovery Console

To begin troubleshooting one of these errors, boot from the installation CD-ROM. You have three options from the initial screen: set up Windows XP, repair using the Recovery Console, and quit Setup (see Figure 10.3). The **Recovery Console**, as you'll recall from earlier chapters, provides a command-line interface for working with Windows before the GUI starts. Press R to start the Recovery Console.

When you select the Recovery Console, you will see a message about ntdetect, another message that the Recovery Console is starting up, and then you are greeted with the following message and command prompt:

```
Microsoft Windows XP<TM> Recovery Console.
The Recovery Console provides system repair and recovery
functionality.
Type Exit to quit the Recovery Console and restart the computer.

1: C:\WINDOWS
Which Windows XP installation would you like to log onto
<To cancel, press ENTER>?
```

The cursor is a small, white rectangle sitting to the right of the question mark on the last line. If you are not accustomed to working at the command prompt, this may be disorienting. If there is only one installation of Windows XP on your computer, type the number **1** at the prompt and press the ENTER key. If you press ENTER before typing in a valid selection, the Recovery Console will cancel and the computer will reboot. The only choice you can

```
Windows XP Professional Setup

  Welcome to Setup.

  This portion of the Setup program prepares Microsoft(R)
  Windows(R) XP to run on your computer.

     •  To set up Windows XP now, press ENTER.

     •  To repair a Windows XP installation using
        Recovery Console, press R.

     •  To quit Setup without installing Windows XP, press F3.
```

```
  ENTER=Continue   R=Repair   F3=Quit
```

• **Figure 10.3** Initial Windows XP Setup screen

 Try This!

Installing the Recovery Console

If you like to be proactive, you can install the Recovery Console on your hard drive so that it is one of your startup options and does not require the Windows XP CD-ROM to run. First, you need to log on to the system with the administrator account. Next, grab a Windows XP installation CD-ROM and drop it in your system. If the Autorun function kicks in, just click the No button. To install the Recovery Console and make it a part of your startup options, click the Start button, select Run, and type the following (if your CD-ROM drive uses a different drive letter, substitute it for the D: drive):

d:\i386\winnt32 /cmdcons

Then just follow the instructions on the screen. If you are connected to the Internet, allow the Setup program to download updated files. From now on, every time the system boots, the OS selection menu will show your Windows OS and the Microsoft Windows Recovery Console. It may also show other choices if yours is a multiboot computer.

make in this example is 1. Having made that choice, the screen displays a new line, followed by the cursor:

```
Type the Administrator password:
```

Enter the Administrator password for that computer and press ENTER. The password does not display on the screen; you see asterisks in place of the password. The screen still shows everything that has happened so far, unless something has happened to cause an error message. It now looks like this:

```
Microsoft Windows XP<TM> Recovery Console.
The Recovery Console provides system repair and recovery
functionality.
Type Exit to quit the Recovery Console and restart the computer.

1: C:\WINDOWS
Which Windows XP installation would you like to log onto
<To cancel, press ENTER>? 1
Type the Administrator password: ********
C:\Windows>
```

By now, you've caught on and know that there is a rectangular prompt immediately after the last line. Now what do you do? Use the Recovery Console commands, of course. The Recovery Console uses many of the commands that work in the Windows command-line interface that you explored in Chapter 9, as well as some commands uniquely its own. Table 10.1 lists common Recovery Console commands.

The Recovery Console shines in the business of manually restoring Registries, stopping problem services, rebuilding partitions (other than the system partition), and using the expand program to extract copies of corrupted files from an optical disc or floppy disk.

Table 10.1 Common Recovery Console Commands

Command	Description
attrib	Changes attributes of selected file or folder
cd (or chdir)	Displays current directory or changes directories
chkdsk	Runs CheckDisk utility
cls	Clears screen
copy	Copies from removable media to system folders on hard disk. No wildcards
del (or delete)	Deletes service or folder
dir	Lists contents of selected directory on system partition only
disable	Disables service or driver
diskpart	Creates/deletes partitions
enable	Enables service or driver
extract	Extracts components from .cab files
fixboot	Writes new partition boot sector on system partition
fixmbr	Writes new master boot record (MBR) for partition boot sector
format	Formats selected disk
listsvc	Lists all services on system
logon	Enables you to choose which Windows installation to log on to if you have more than one
map	Displays current drive letter mappings
md (or mkdir)	Creates a directory
more (or type)	Displays contents of a text file
rd (or rmdir)	Removes a directory
ren (or rename)	Renames a single file
systemroot	Makes current directory system root of drive you're logged on to
type	Displays contents of a text file

Using the Recovery Console, you can reconfigure a service so that it starts with different settings, format partitions on the hard drive, read and write on local FAT or NTFS partitions, and copy replacement files from a floppy or optical disc. The Recovery Console enables you to access the file system and is still constrained by the file and folder security of NTFS, which makes it a more secure tool to use than some third-party solutions.

The Recovery Console also works great for fixing three items: repairing the MBR, reinstalling the boot files, and rebuilding boot.ini. Let's look at each of these.

A bad boot sector usually shows up as a No Boot Device error. If it turns out that this isn't the problem, using the Recovery Console command to fix it won't hurt anything. At the Recovery Console prompt, just type

fixmbr

This fixes the master boot record.

Missing system files are usually indicated by the error *NTLDR bad or missing*. Odds are good that if ntdlr is missing, so are the rest of the system files. To fix this, get to the root directory (cd\—remember that from

Chapter 9?) and type the following line (substituting the drive letter of the optical drive for *d:* in the example):

copy d:\i386\ntldr

Then type this line:

copy d:\i386\ntdetect.com

This takes care of two of the big three and leads us to the last issue, rebuilding boot.ini. If the boot.ini file is gone or corrupted, run this command from the Recovery Console:

bootcfg /rebuild

The Recovery Console will try to locate all installed copies of Windows and ask you if you want to add them to the new boot.ini file it's about to create. Say yes to the ones you want.

If all goes well with the Recovery Console, do a thorough backup as soon as possible (just in case something else goes wrong). If the Recovery Console does not do the trick, the next step is to restore Windows XP.

Attempt to Restore

If you've been diligent about backing up, you can attempt to restore to an earlier, working copy of Windows. Assuming you made an Automated System Recovery (ASR) backup, this will restore your system to a previously installed state, but you should use it as a last resort. You lose everything on the system that was installed or added after you created the ASR disk. If that's the best option, though, follow the steps outlined in Chapter 8.

Rebuild

If faced with a full system rebuild, you have several options, depending on the particular system. You could simply reboot to the Windows CD-ROM and install right on top of the existing system, what's called a *repair installation*. To avoid losing anything important, though, you'd be better off swapping the C: drive for a blank hard drive and installing a clean version of Windows.

Most OEM systems come with a misleadingly named *Recovery CD* or *recovery partition*. The Recovery CD is a CD-ROM that you boot to and run. The recovery partition is a hidden partition on the hard drive that you activate at boot by holding down a key combination specific to the manufacturer of that system. (See the motherboard manual or users' guide for the key combination and other details.) Both "recovery" options do the same thing—restore your computer to the factory-installed state. If you run one of these tools, *you will wipe everything off your system*—all personal files, folders, and programs will go away! Before running either tool, make sure all important files and folders are backed up on an optical disc or spare hard drive.

To use the Windows XP System Restore, you need to be able to get into Windows. "Restore" in the context used here means to give you an option to get into Windows.

When you attempt to install Windows XP onto a system with Windows XP already installed, the setup process will detect the previous OS and prompt you to repair or install a fresh copy of Windows.

Failure to Boot: Windows Vista and Windows 7

Two critical boot files risk corruption in Windows Vista and Windows 7, bootmgr and bcd, both of which you can fix with one tool, bcdedit. You can use this tool in the Windows Recovery Environment.

WinPE and the Death of the Recovery Console

With Windows Vista, Microsoft upgraded the installation environment from the 16-bit text mode environment used in every previous version of Windows to 32- and 64-bit. This upgrade enabled the Windows installation process to go graphical and support features such as a mouse pointer and clickable elements, rather than relying on command-line tools. Microsoft calls the installation environment the **Windows Preinstallation Environment** (**WinPE** or *Windows PE*).

> Although here I discuss only how WinPE helps boot repair, know that WinPE goes much further. WinPE can assist unattended installations, network installations, and even booting diskless workstations on a network.

With Windows PE, you can boot directly to the Windows DVD. This loads a limited-function graphical operating system that contains both troubleshooting and diagnostic tools, along with installation options. The Windows installation media is called a **Live DVD** because WinPE loads directly from disc into memory and doesn't access or modify the hard drive.

When you access Windows PE and opt for the troubleshooting and repair features, you open a special set of tools called the **Windows Recovery Environment** (**WinRE** or *Windows RE*). The terms can get a little confusing because of the similarity of letters, so mark this: Windows RE is the repair tools that run within Windows PE. WinPE powers WinRE. Got it? Let's tackle WinRE.

> Microsoft also refers to the Windows Recovery Environment as the *System Recovery Options menu*. It's unclear as of this writing which label CompTIA will use.

Enter Windows RE

It would be unfair to say that the Windows Recovery Environment only replaces the Recovery Console. WinRE includes an impressive, powerful set of both automated and manual utilities that collectively diagnoses and fixes all but the most serious of Windows boot problems. Although WinRE does all the hard work for you, you still need to know how to access and use it. When faced with a failure to boot scenario in Windows Vista or Windows 7, WinRE is one of your primary tools.

Getting to Windows RE

In Windows 7, you can access WinRE in three ways. (See the Exam Tip for Windows Vista options.) First, you can boot from the Windows installation media and select *Repair*. Second, you can use the *Repair Your Computer* option on the Advanced Boot Options (F8) menu (see Figure 10.4). Third, you can create a system repair disc before you have problems. Go to Control Panel | System and Security | Backup and Restore and select *Create a system repair disc*, which opens the dialog box shown in Figure 10.5.

> Windows Vista does not have the Repair Your Computer option on the Advanced Boot Options menu. You can either use a Windows installation media or, if you have SP1 or later, make a bootable system repair disc.

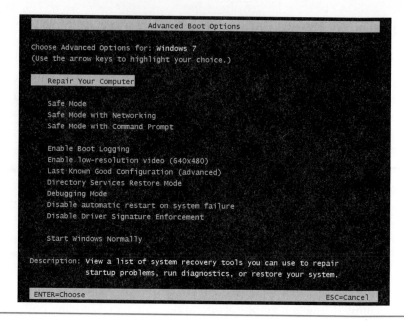

• **Figure 10.4** Selecting Repair Your Computer in the Advanced Boot Options menu

• **Figure 10.5** Making a system repair disc in Windows 7

Although any of these methods works fine, I recommend that you access WinRE from the Windows installation media for three reasons:

- The hard drive can be so messed up that you won't make it to the Advanced Boot Options menu.

- Accessing WinRE using the Repair Your Computer option in the Advanced Boot Options menu requires a local administrator password.

- Using a bootable disc enables you to avoid any malware that might be on the system.

Using Windows RE

No matter how you choose to access the Windows Recovery Environment, the main menu looks the same (see Figure 10.6). You have five options in WinRE:

- Startup Repair

- System Restore

- System Image Recovery (Windows 7) or Windows Complete PC Restore (Vista)

- Windows Memory Diagnostics (Tool) (only Vista includes "Tool" in the name)

- Command Prompt

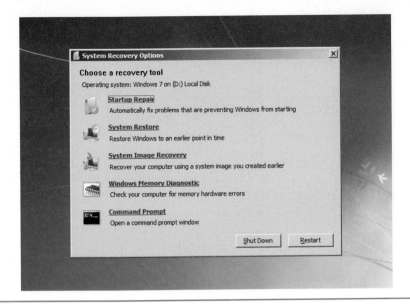

• **Figure 10.6** Recovery Environment main screen

The name of the third option differs between Windows 7 and Windows Vista, though the intent—rebuilding from a backup—is the same. I'll talk about how these options differ a little later in the chapter.

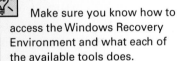

Make sure you know how to access the Windows Recovery Environment and what each of the available tools does.

Startup Repair The **Startup Repair** utility serves as a one-stop, do-it-all option (see Figure 10.7). When run, it performs a number of repairs, including:

- Repairs a corrupted Registry by accessing the backup copy on your hard drive

- Restores critical system and driver files

- Runs the equivalent of the Recovery Console's fixboot and fixmbr

- Rolls back any non-working drivers

- Uninstalls any incompatible service packs and patches

- Runs chkdsk

- Runs a memory test to check your RAM

Startup Repair fixes almost any Windows boot problem. In fact, if you have a system with one hard drive containing a single partition with Windows Vista or Windows 7 installed, you'd have trouble finding something it *couldn't* fix. Upon completion, Startup Repair shows the screen shown in Figure 10.8.

Note the link in Figure 10.8 that says *View diagnostic and repair details*. This opens a text file called srttrail.txt that lists exactly what

• **Figure 10.7** Startup Repair in action

the program found, what it fixed, and what it failed to do. It may look cryptic, but you can type anything you find into Google for more information. I've reproduced the beginning of the (very long) srttrail.txt file here:

```
Startup Repair diagnosis and repair log
---------------------------
Last successful boot time: 7/14/2012 2:37:43 AM (GMT)
Number of repair attempts: 6

Session details
---------------------------
System Disk = \Device\Harddisk0
Windows directory = C:\Windows
AutoChk Run = 0
Number of root causes = 1

Test Performed:
---------------------------
Name: Check for updates
Result: Completed successfully. Error code =  0x0
Time taken = 32 ms

Test Performed:
---------------------------
Name: System disk test
Result: Completed successfully. Error code =  0x0
Time taken = 0 ms
```

In Windows 7, Startup Repair starts automatically if your system detects a boot problem. If you power up a Windows system and see the screen shown in Figure 10.9, Windows has detected a problem in the startup process.

Personally, I think this menu pops up way too often. If you fail to shut down your computer properly, for example, this menu appears. In this case,

The *View advanced options for system recovery and support* link simply returns you to the main screen.

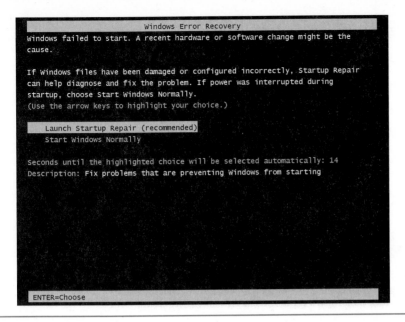

```
                        Windows Error Recovery
Windows failed to start. A recent hardware or software change might be the
cause.

If Windows files have been damaged or configured incorrectly, Startup Repair
can help diagnose and fix the problem. If power was interrupted during
startup, choose Start Windows Normally.
(Use the arrow keys to highlight your choice.)

      Launch Startup Repair (recommended)
      Start Windows Normally

Seconds until the highlighted choice will be selected automatically: 14
Description: Fix problems that are preventing Windows from starting

ENTER=Choose
```

• **Figure 10.9** Windows Error Recovery

you can save time by booting normally. When in doubt, however, go ahead and run Startup Repair. It can't hurt anything.

A powerful tool like Startup Repair still doesn't cover everything. You may have specific needs that require more finesse than a single, do-it-all approach. In many cases, you've already discovered the problem and simply want to make a single fix. You might want to perform a system restoration or check the memory. For this, we'll need to explore the other four options available in WinRE.

> If you have trouble booting your computer, you should try Startup Repair first.

System Restore System Restore does the same job here it has done since Microsoft first introduced it in Windows Me, enabling you to go back to a time when your computer worked properly. Placing this option in Windows RE gives those of us who make many **restore points**— snapshots of a system at a given point of time—a quick and handy way to return our systems to a previous state (see Figure 10.10).

System Image Recovery/Windows Complete PC Restore Windows 7's backup tools differ from Windows Vista's. Note Figure 10.11, which shows the Windows Vista Recovery Environment menu on the left next to the Windows 7 Recovery Environment on the right. The third WinRE option differs. Windows Vista uses the Windows Complete PC Restore utility, whereas Windows 7 includes the System Image Recovery tool.

With an image in hand, you can use the Windows Complete PC Restore/System Image Recovery tool to restore your system after a catastrophe.

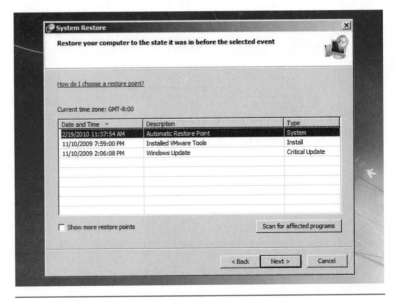

• **Figure 10.10** System Restore points

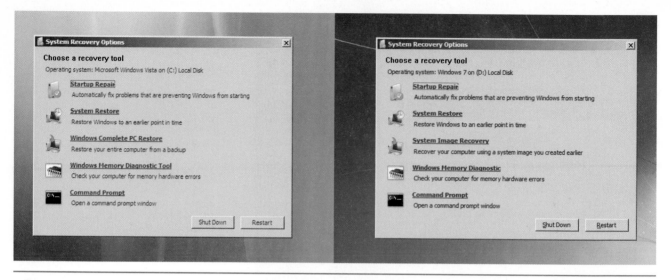

• **Figure 10.11** The WinRE options in Windows Vista (left) and Windows 7 (right)

The CompTIA A+ 802 exam objectives use the phrase *recovery image*, which conflates separate tools in Windows 7. You can use Backup and Restore to create a system image and a system repair disc. You can use the system repair disc to get to the System Image Recovery that uses the system image on the second disc to write a "fixed" or previously working version of Windows 7 to the hard drive. Got all that?

If you have the drive containing the system image plugged in when you first run the wizard, it should detect your latest backup and present you with the dialog box shown in Figure 10.12. If it doesn't list a system image or it lists the wrong one, you can select an image from another date on the same disk or even a remote network share.

After you select the image you want to restore, the utility presents you with a few more options, as shown in Figure 10.13. Most importantly, you can choose to format and repartition disks. With this option selected, the utility wipes out the existing partitions and data on all disks so the restored system will get the same partitions that the backed-up system had.

After you click Finish on the confirmation screen (see Figure 10.14), which also contains a final warning, the restore process begins (see Figure 10.15). The utility removes the old system data and then copies the backed-up system image to the hard drive(s). Once the process completes, your system reboots and should start up again with all of your data and programs just where you left them when you last backed up.

Windows Memory Diagnostics (Tool) Bad RAM causes huge problems for any operating system, creating scenarios where computers get Blue Screens of Death (BSoDs), system lockups, and continuous reboots. Starting with Windows Vista, Microsoft added a memory tester to the Windows Recovery Environment. When you click the Windows Memory Diagnostic (Tool) link from the main WinRE screen, it prompts you to *Restart now and check for problems (recommended)* or *Check for problems the next time I start my*

• **Figure 10.12** Selecting a system image

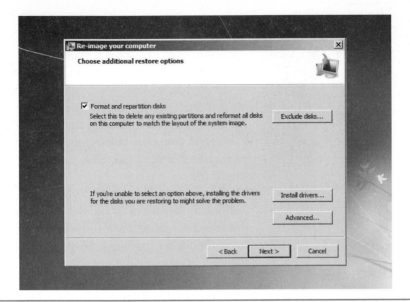

• **Figure 10.13** Additional restore options

• **Figure 10.14** Confirming your settings

• **Figure 10.15** Restoring your computer

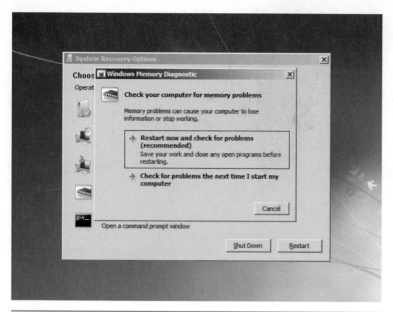

• **Figure 10.16** Windows Memory Diagnostic screen

You can also find the Windows Memory Diagnostics Tool in the Control Panel under System and Security | Administrative Tools, or start it from an administrative command prompt using the **mdsched** command.

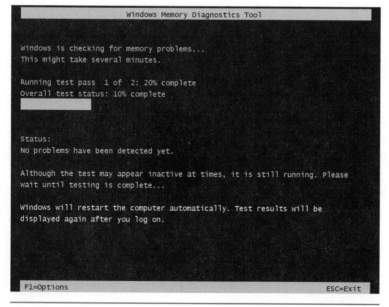

• **Figure 10.17** Windows Memory Diagnostics Tool running

computer (see Figure 10.16). It doesn't really matter which option you choose, but if you think you need to test the system's RAM, that probably means you should do it now.

Once you restart, your system immediately starts running the Windows Memory Diagnostics Tool, as shown in Figure 10.17. While the program runs, you can press F1 to see the Memory Tester options (see Figure 10.18).

The tool lists three important Test Mix options at the top of the screen: Basic, Standard, and Extended. *Basic* runs quickly (about one minute) but performs only light testing. *Standard*, the default choice, takes a few minutes and tests more aggressively. *Extended* takes hours (you should let it run overnight), but it will very aggressively test your RAM.

This tool includes two other options: Cache and Pass Count. The *Cache* option enables you to set whether the tests use the CPU's built-in cache as well as override the default cache settings for each test type. Simply leave Cache set at Default and never touch it. *Pass Count* sets the number of times each set of tests will run. This option defaults to 2.

After the tool runs, your computer reboots normally. You can open Event Viewer to see the results (see Figure 10.19).

Sadly, I've had rather poor results with the Windows Memory Diagnostics Tool. We keep lots of bad RAM around the labs here at Total Seminars, and, when put to the test, we were unable to get this tool to do anything other than give us a BSoD or lock up the system. We still turn to tried-and-tested tools such as the free Memtest86+ when we're worried about bad RAM.

Command Prompt The last, most interesting, and easily nerdiest option in the WinRE menu is Command Prompt. Unlike the Recovery Console, the WinRE command prompt is a true 32- or 64-bit prompt that functions similarly to the regular command prompt. WinRE's command prompt, however, includes an important utility (bootrec) that you can't find in the regular command prompt. The WinRE command prompt also lacks a large number of the command-prompt tools you'd have in a regular Windows command prompt (though all the important ones remain). Let's begin by looking at the bootrec command. After that, we'll look at some other utilities that the WinRE command prompt offers.

```
                  Windows Memory Diagnostics Tool - Options

Test Mix:

    Basic
    Standard
    Extended

Description: The Standard tests include all the Basic tests, plus LRAND,
             Stride6 (cache enabled), CHCKR3, WMATS+, and WINVC.

Cache:

    Default
    On
    Off

Description: Use the default cache setting of each test.

Pass Count (0 - 99):   2

Description: Set the total number of times the entire test mix will
             repeat (0 = infinite).

  TAB=Next                F10=Apply                        ESC=Cancel
```

• **Figure 10.18** Windows Memory Diagnostics Tool options

It's important for you to understand that the CompTIA A+ 220-802 exam does not expect you to know everything about all these command-prompt utilities. The exam expects that you do know these things, however:

- Which utilities are available and their names
- How to access these utilities (WinRE, regular command prompt)
- What these utilities basically do
- Some of the basic switches used for these utilities
- With higher-level support, that you can fix computers using these tools (being led by a specialist tech over the phone, for example)

You can find out more about Memtest86+ here: www.memtest.org.

The Startup Repair tool runs many of these command-prompt utilities automatically. You need to use the WinRE command prompt only for unique situations where the Startup Repair tool fails.

• **Figure 10.19** Event Viewer results

The **bootrec** command is a Windows Recovery Environment troubleshooting and repair tool that repairs the master boot record, boot sector, or BCD store. It replaces the old fixboot and fixmbr Recovery Console commands and adds two more repair features:

- **bootrec /fixboot** Rebuilds the boot sector for the active system partition
- **bootrec /fixmbr** Rebuilds the master boot record for the system partition
- **bootrec /scanos** Looks for Windows installations not currently in the BCD store and shows you the results without doing anything
- **bootrec /rebuildmbr** Looks for Windows installations not currently in the BCD store and gives you the choice to add them to the BCD store

With ntldr, you could access the boot.ini text file to see the Windows boot order. With boot.ini replaced by the BCD store, you can use a tool called **bcdedit** to see how Windows boots. Running bcdedit by itself (without switches) shows the boot options. The following boot information comes from a system with a single copy of Windows installed. Note there are two sections: the *Windows Boot Manager* section describes the location of bootmgr and the *Windows Boot Loader* section describes the location of the winload.exe file.

Instead of editing the boot .ini text file, Windows Vista/7 includes the bcdedit program for editing the BCD store.

```
Windows Boot Manager
--------------------
identifier              {bootmgr}
device                  partition=\Device\HarddiskVolume1
description             Windows Boot Manager
locale                  en-US
inherit                 {globalsettings}
default                 {current}
resumeobject            {d4539c9b-481a-11df-a981-
a17cb98be35c}
displayorder            {current}
toolsdisplayorder       {memdiag}
timeout                 30

Windows Boot Loader
-------------------
identifier              {current}
device                  partition=C:
path                    \Windows\system32\winload.exe
description             Windows 7
locale                  en-US
inherit                 {bootloadersettings}
recoverysequence        {d4539c9d-481a-11df-a981-
a17cb98be35c}
recoveryenabled         Yes
osdevice                partition=C:
systemroot              \Windows
resumeobject            {d4539c9b-481a-11df-a981-
a17cb98be35c}
nx                      OptIn
```

To make changes to the BCD store, you need to use switches:

- **bcdedit /export <filename>** exports a copy of the BCD store to a file. This is a very good idea whenever you use bcdedit!

- **bcdedit /import <filename>** imports a copy of the BCD store back into the store.

If you look carefully at the previous bcdedit output, you'll notice that each section has an identifier such as {bootmgr} or {current}. You can use these identifiers to make changes to the BCD store using the /set switch. Here's an example:

```
BCDEDIT /SET {current} path \BackupWindows\system32\winload.exe
```

This changes the path of the {current} identifier to point to an alternative winload.exe.

The bcdedit command supports multiple OSs. Notice how this BCD store has three identifiers: {bootmgr}, {current}, and {ntldr}—a fairly common dual-boot scenario.

```
Windows Boot Manager
--------------------
identifier              {bootmgr}
device                  partition=D:
description             Windows Boot Manager
locale                  en-US
inherit                 {globalsettings}
default                 {current}
resumeobject            {60b80a52-8267-11e0-ad8a-
bdb414c1bf84}
displayorder            {ntldr}
                        {current}
toolsdisplayorder       {memdiag}
timeout                 30

Windows Legacy OS Loader
------------------------
identifier              {ntldr}
device                  partition=D:
path                    \ntldr
description             Earlier Version of Windows

Windows Boot Loader
-------------------
identifier              {current}
device                  partition=C:
path                    \Windows\system32\winload.exe
description             Windows 7
locale                  en-US
inherit                 {bootloadersettings}
recoverysequence        {60b80a54-8267-11e0-ad8a-
bdb414c1bf84}
recoveryenabled         Yes
osdevice                partition=C:
systemroot              \Windows
resumeobject            {60b80a52-8267-11e0-ad8a-
bdb414c1bf84}
nx                      OptIn
```

A BCD store like this will cause the following menu to pop up at boot (see Figure 10.20).

You can use the bcdedit command to change the display order of the menu. If you wanted to add Windows XP to the beginning of the list, type this command:

bcdedit /displayorder {WindowsXP} /addfirst

You can also use bcdedit to set the default OS:

bcdedit /default {current}

You can even remove one of the identifiers, preventing others from booting to that OS:

bcdedit /delete {WindowsXP}

You can find EasyBCD at www.neosmart.net.

The bcdedit command is a tricky tool to use. To make your life easier, consider using the popular EasyBCD program from NeoSmart Technologies. You can run EasyBCD only from within a normal Windows boot, not the WinRE, but it provides more power and safety than bcdedit (see Figure 10.21).

The command prompt also includes **diskpart**, a fully featured partitioning tool. This tool lacks many of the safety features built into Disk Management, so proceed with caution. You can, for example, delete any partition of any type at any time. Starting diskpart opens a special command prompt as shown here:

```
C:\Windows\system32>diskpart
Microsoft DiskPart version 6.1.7600
Copyright (C) 1999-2008 Microsoft Corporation.
On computer: MIKESPC
DISKPART>
```

You can list volumes (or partitions on Basic disks):

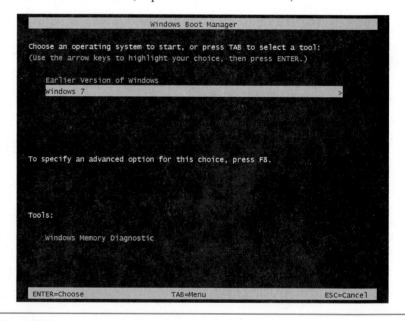

• **Figure 10.20** bootmgr showing available versions of Windows

● **Figure 10.21** EasyBCD at work

```
DISKPART> list volume
  Volume ###  Ltr  Label        Fs     Type       Size     Status    Info
  ---------   ---  ---------    -----  ---------  -------  -------  -----
  Volume 0    D                        DVD-ROM      0 B    No Media
  Volume 1    C    New Volume  NTFS    Partition  1397 GB  Healthy  System

DISKPART>
```

Select a volume to manipulate (you may also select an entire drive):

```
DISKPART> select volume 1
Volume 1 is the selected volume.
DISKPART>
```

You can run commands at the diskpart prompt to add, change, or delete volumes and partitions on drives, mount or dismount volumes, and even manipulate software-level RAID arrays.

Run the **clean** command at the diskpart prompt to wipe all partition and volume information off the currently selected disk. This tool handles nasty corruptions that simply won't let Windows boot and serves as my last-ditch step before I toss a drive.

Commands available at the diskpart prompt handle volumes and partitions, but you still need a tool for handling file systems. Both WinRE and the regular command prompt provide all of the typical utilities such as

copy, move, del, and format. One tool, however—fsutil—does a few more interesting jobs:

- Typing **fsinfo** provides a detailed query about the drives and volumes.

- Typing **fsutil dirty <drivename>** tells you if Windows considers the drive to be "dirty"—meaning you need to run autochk at the next reboot. When Windows detects an error in the file system for a drive, it flags that drive as a *dirty drive* or *dirty volume*. The disk checking utility autochk runs after a reboot and before Windows loads and will correct errors in the file system of a drive.

- Typing **fsutil repair initiate <drive letter>** runs a basic version of chkdsk without rebooting.

■ Failure to Load the GUI

Assuming that Windows gets past the boot part of the startup, it then begins to load the graphical Windows OS. You will see the Windows startup image on the screen, hiding everything until Windows loads the desktop (see Figure 10.22).

Several issues can create a scenario where the graphical interface fails to load. Windows can hang during the GUI-loading phase because of buggy device drivers or Registry problems. Even autoloading programs can cause the GUI to hang on load. The first step in troubleshooting these sorts of scenarios is to use one of the Advanced Startup options (covered later in the chapter) to try to get past the hang spot and into Windows.

If faced with a scenario where the GUI files have become corrupted, what CompTIA calls a "Missing Graphical Interface" problem, your only choices are to restore from backup or rebuild from the installation media.

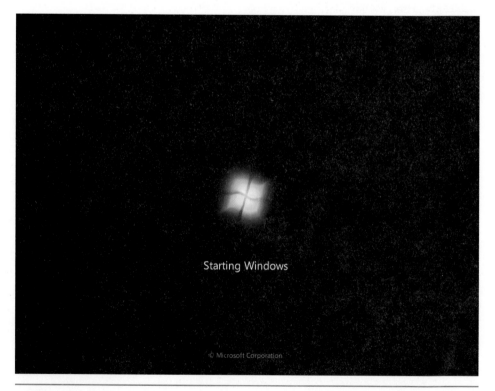

• **Figure 10.22** GUI time!

Device Drivers

Device driver problems that stop Windows GUI from loading look pretty scary. Figure 10.23 shows the infamous Windows *Stop error*, better known as the **Blue Screen of Death (BSoD)**. The BSoD only appears when something causes an error from which Windows cannot recover. The BSoD is not limited to device driver problems, but device drivers are one of the reasons you'll see the BSoD.

Whenever faced with a scenario where you get a BSoD, read what it says. Windows BSoDs tell you the name of the file that caused the problem and usually suggests a recommended action. Once in a while these are helpful.

BSoD problems due to device drivers almost always take place immediately after you've installed a new device and rebooted. Take out the device and reboot. If Windows loads properly, head over to the manufacturer's Web site. A new device producing this type of problem is a serious issue that should have been caught before the device was released. In many cases, the manufacturer will have updated drivers available for download or will recommend a replacement device.

The second indication of a device problem that shows up during the GUI part of startup is a freeze-up: the Windows startup screen just stays there and you never get a chance to log on. If this happens, try one of the Advanced Startup Options, covered following the Registry.

```
A problem has been detected and windows has been shut down to prevent damage
to your computer.

NO_MORE_IRP_STACK_LOCATIONS

If this is the first time you've seen this Stop error screen,
restart your computer. If this screen appears again, follow
these steps:

Check to make sure that any new hardware or software is properly installed.
If this is a new installation, ask your hardware or software manufacturer
for any windows updates you might need.

If problems continue, disable or remove any newly installed hardware
or software. Disable BIOS memory options such as caching or shadowing.
If you need to use Safe Mode to remove or disable components, restart
your computer, press F8 to select Advanced Startup Options, and then
select Safe Mode.

Technical information:

*** STOP: 0x00000035 (0x00000000,0xF7E562B2,0x00000008,0xC00000000)

***     wdmaud.sys - Address F7E562B2 base at F7E56000, DateStamp 36B047A5
```

• **Figure 10.23** BSoD

> Viruses can cause the GUI to fail or make it appear to be missing. One nasty one running around recently, for example, caused what appeared to be a BSoD warning of imminent hard drive controller failure. Even after getting rid of the virus, Windows appeared devoid of any graphical elements at all: no Start button, icons, or files even in Computer. That's because the virus had changed the attributes of every file and folder on the hard drive to hidden! See Chapter 9 for the attrib command; see Chapter 18 for recovery techniques for virus-attacked computers.

Registry

The Registry files load every time the computer boots. Windows does a pretty good job of protecting your Registry files from corruption, but from time to time something may slip by Windows and it will attempt to load a bad Registry. These errors may show up as BSoDs that say "Registry File Failure" or text errors that say "Windows could not start." Whatever the case, when you run into these sorts of scenarios, you need to restore a good Registry copy. The best way to do this is the Last Known Good Configuration boot option (see the upcoming section). If that fails, you can restore an earlier version of the Registry through the Recovery Console in Windows XP or through Windows RE in Windows Vista/7.

Replacing the Registry in Windows XP

Boot to the Windows installation CD-ROM, get to the Recovery Console, and type these commands to restore a Registry. Notice I didn't say "your"

Registry in the previous sentence. Your Registry is corrupted and gone, so you need to rebuild.

```
delete c:\windows\system32\config\system
delete c:\windows\system32\config\software
delete c:\windows\system32\config\sam
delete c:\windows\system32\config\security
delete c:\windows\system32\config\default

copy c:\windows\repair\system c:\windows\system32\config\system
copy c:\windows\repair\software c:\windows\system32\config\software
copy c:\windows\repair\sam c:\windows\system32\config\sam
copy c:\windows\repair\security c:\windows\system32\config\security
copy c:\windows\repair\default c:\windows\system32\config\default
```

Replacing the Registry in Windows Vista/7

Windows Vista and Windows 7 keep a regular backup of the Registry handy in case you need to overwrite a corrupted Registry. By default, the RegIdleBackup task runs every 10 days, so that's as far back as you would lose if you replaced the current Registry with the automatically backed-up files. Of course, it would be better if you kept regular backups too, but at least the damage would be limited. You can find the backed-up Registry files in \Windows\System32\config\RegBack (see Figure 10.24).

To replace the Registry, boot to the Windows DVD to access Windows RE and get to the Command Prompt shell. Run the **reg** command to get to a reg prompt. From there, you have numerous commands to deal with the Registry. The simplest is probably the *copy* command. You know the location of the backed-up Registry files. Just copy the files to the location of the main Registry files—up one level in the tree under the \config folder.

• **Figure 10.24** The backed-up Registry files located in the RegBack folder

Advanced Startup Options

If Windows fails to start up, use the Windows **Advanced Startup Options** menu to discover the cause. To get to this menu, restart the computer and press F8 after the POST messages but before the Windows logo screen appears. Windows XP's Startup options are a tad different from Windows Vista's and Windows 7's. Central to these advanced options are Safe Mode and Last Known Good Configuration. Here's a rundown of the menu options.

Windows 9*x* had an option for step-by-step confirmation, but that is not a choice in Windows XP/Vista/7. Look for it as a wrong answer on the exam!

Safe Mode (All Versions)

Safe Mode starts up Windows but loads only very basic, non–vendor-specific drivers for mouse, 640 × 480 resolution monitor (in XP) and 800 ×

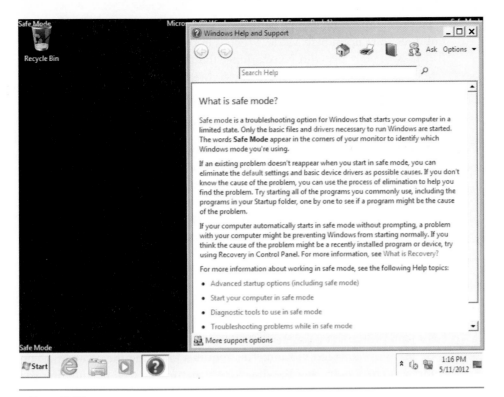

• **Figure 10.25** Safe Mode

600 resolution monitor (Vista and 7), keyboard, mass storage, and system services (see Figure 10.25).

Once in Safe Mode, you can use tools such as Device Manager to locate and correct the source of the problem. When you use Device Manager in Safe Mode, you can access the properties for all the devices, even those that are not working in Safe Mode. The status displayed for the device is the status for a normal startup. Even the network card will show as enabled. You can disable any suspect device or perform other tasks, such as removing or updating drivers. If a problem with a device driver is preventing the operating system from starting normally, check Device Manager for warning icons that indicate an unknown device.

There is no safety or repair feature in any version of Windows that makes the OS boot to Safe Mode automatically. In most cases, Windows automatically booting to Safe Mode indicates that someone has set the System Configuration utility to force Windows to do so. Type **msconfig** at the Start | Search or Start | Run option and press ENTER to open the System Configuration utility, and then deselect the Safe boot or Boot to Safe Mode check box (see Figure 10.26).

The CompTIA A+ 802 exam objectives mention a scenario where Windows boots directly to Safe Mode. This can only happen if a tech specifically makes a change to the System Configuration utility.

Safe Mode with Networking (All Versions)

This mode is identical to plain Safe Mode except that you get network support. I use this mode to test

• **Figure 10.26** Uncheck Safe boot

for a problem with network drivers. If Windows won't start up normally but does start up in Safe Mode, I reboot into Safe Mode with Networking. If it fails to start up with Networking, the problem is a network driver. I reboot back to Safe Mode, open Device Manager, and start disabling network components, beginning with the network adapter.

Safe Mode with Command Prompt (All Versions)

When you start Windows in this mode, rather than loading the GUI desktop, it loads the command prompt (cmd.exe) as the shell to the operating system after you log on, as shown in Figure 10.27. From here you can run any of the commands you learned about in Chapter 9, plus a lot of utilities as well. Error-checking runs fine as chkdsk, for example. Disk Defragmenter probably runs even faster when you type **defrag** followed by a drive letter at the command prompt than it does from the graphical version of the tool.

Safe Mode with Command Prompt is a handy option to remember if the desktop does not display at all, which, after you have eliminated video drivers, can be caused by corruption of the explorer.exe program. From the command prompt, you can delete the corrupted version of explorer.exe and copy in an undamaged version. This requires knowing the command-line commands for navigating the directory structure, as well as knowing the location of the file you are replacing. Although Explorer is not loaded, you can load other GUI tools that don't depend on Explorer. All you have to do is enter the correct command. For instance, to load Event Viewer, type **eventvwr.msc** at the command line and press ENTER.

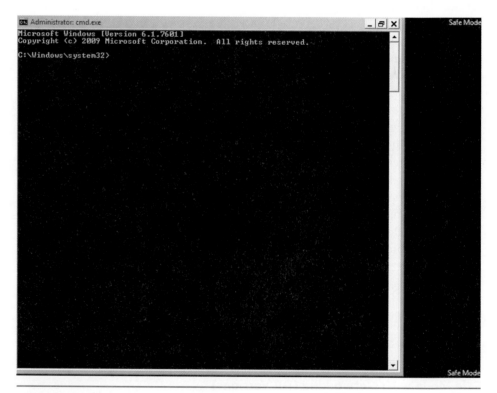

• **Figure 10.27** Safe Mode with Command Prompt

Enable Boot Logging (All Versions)

This option starts Windows normally and creates a log file of the drivers as they load into memory. The file is named Ntbtlog.txt and is saved in the %SystemRoot% folder. If the startup failed because of a bad driver, the last entry in this file may be the driver the OS was initializing when it failed.

Reboot and go into the Recovery Console or WinRE. Use the tools there to read the boot log (**type ntbtlog.txt**) and disable or enable problematic devices or services.

Enable VGA Mode (XP)/Enable Low-Resolution Mode (Vista and 7)

Enable VGA Mode/Enable Low-Resolution Mode starts Windows normally, but only loads a default VGA driver. If this mode works, it may mean you have a bad driver, or it may mean you are using the correct video driver but it is configured incorrectly (perhaps with the wrong refresh rate and/or resolution). Whereas Safe Mode loads a generic VGA driver, this mode loads the driver Windows is configured to use but starts it up in standard VGA mode rather than using the settings for which it is configured. After successfully starting in this mode, open the Display applet and change the settings.

Last Known Good Configuration (All Versions)

When Windows' startup fails immediately after installing a new driver but before you have logged on again, try the Last Known Good Configuration option. This option applies specifically to new device drivers that cause failures on reboot.

Directory Services Restore Mode (All Versions)

The title says it all here; this option only applies to Active Directory domain controllers, and only Windows Server versions can be domain controllers. I have no idea why Microsoft includes this option. If you choose it, you simply boot into Safe Mode.

Debugging Mode (All Versions)

If you select this choice, Windows starts in kernel debug mode. It's a super-techie thing to do, and I doubt that even über techs do debug mode anymore. To do this, you have to connect the computer you are debugging to another computer via a serial connection, and as Windows starts up, a debug of the kernel is sent to the second computer, which must also be running a debugger program.

Disable Automatic Restart on System Failure (All Versions)

Sometimes a BSoD will appear at startup, causing your computer to spontaneously reboot. That's all well and good, but if it happens too quickly, you might not be able to read the BSoD to see what caused the problem. Selecting *Disable automatic restart on system failure* from the Advanced Startup Options menu stops the computer from rebooting on Stop errors. This gives you the opportunity to write down the error and hopefully find a fix.

Disable Driver Signature Enforcement (Vista and 7)

Windows Vista and 7 require that all very low-level drivers (kernel drivers) must have a Microsoft driver signature. If you are using an older driver to connect to your hard drive controller or some other low-level feature, you must use this option to get Windows to load the driver. Hopefully you will always check your motherboard and hard drives for Windows compatibility and never have to use this option.

Start Windows Normally (All Versions)

This choice will simply start Windows normally, without rebooting. You already rebooted to get to this menu. Select this if you changed your mind about using any of the other exotic choices.

Reboot (All Versions)

This choice will actually do a soft reboot of the computer.

Return to OS Choices Menu (All Versions)

On computers with multiple operating systems, you get an OS Choices menu to select which OS to load. If you load Windows and press F8 to get the Advanced Startup Options menu, you'll see this option. Choosing it returns you to the OS Choices menu, from which you can select the operating system to load.

Troubleshooting Tools in the GUI

Once you're able to load into Windows, whether through Safe Mode or one of the other options, the whole gamut of Windows tools is available for you. In the previous scenario where a bad device driver caused the startup problems, for example, you can open Device Manager and begin troubleshooting just as you've learned in previous chapters. If you suspect some service or Registry issue caused the problem, head on over to Event Viewer and see what sort of logon events have happened recently. Let's go there first.

Event Viewer

When you get into the GUI, one of the first tools you should use is Event Viewer to see what's causing the problems on your computer. **Event Viewer** is Windows' default tattletale program, spilling the beans about a number of interesting happenings on the system. With a little tweaking, Event Viewer turns into a virtual recording of anything you might ever want to know about on your system.

Keep in mind that Event Viewer is a powerful tool for more than just troubleshooting Windows—it's a powerful tool for security as well, as you'll see in Chapter 18. But for now let's examine Event Viewer, both in Windows XP and in Windows 7 (the Vista version of Event Viewer is almost identical to the version in Windows 7), to see what we can do with this amazing utility.

Windows XP Event Viewer You can find Event Viewer in the Administrative Tools applet in the Control Panel. By default, Event Viewer has

three sections: Application, Security, and System. If you've downloaded Internet Explorer 7 or later, you'll see a fourth option for the browser, Internet Explorer (see Figure 10.28). Each of these sections stores certain types of events, as described next.

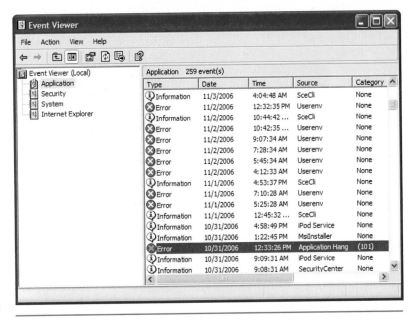

• **Figure 10.28** Event Viewer

■ **Application** As the name implies, the Application section stores events specific to applications. There are three types of events recorded: Errors, Warnings, and Information. Errors, marked with a red *X*, are the most serious, reflecting events that prevent the application from working properly. Warnings, marked with an exclamation point over a triangle, are for events that aren't preventing the application from running but may do so in the future. Information events are merely record keeping, letting you know that a program, driver, or service ran successfully.

■ **Security** Security records events that Microsoft calls *audits*. Audits record anything to do with security, such as the number of logon events. All audits are listed as either successful or failed. There a thousands of audits available on a Windows system, the vast majority of which are turned off by default but can be turned on in Administrative Tools | Local Security Policy. Since these are security issues, we'll cover the Security section as well as auditing in Chapter 18.

■ **System** The System section is similar to the Application section in that you have Errors, Warnings, and Information, but the events listed here are specific only to the operating system.

When something goes wrong with Windows, it's common for techs to turn to Event Viewer first. Let's say an application fails to load. A common use for Event Viewer is to view the application to see what happened (see Figure 10.29). One very cool feature of Event Viewer is that you can click the link to take you

• **Figure 10.29** Typical application error message

to the online Help and Support Center at Microsoft.com, and the software reports your error (see Figure 10.30), checks the online database, and comes back with a more or less useful explanation (see Figure 10.31).

Event Viewer might reveal problems with applications failing to load, a big cause of Windows loading problems (see Figure 10.32). It might also reveal problems with services failing to start. Finally, Windows might run into problems loading DLLs. You can troubleshoot these issues individually or you can use System Restore to load a restore point that predates the bugginess.

Windows Vista/7 Event Viewer Windows Vista/7 adds an easy-to-use interface to Event Viewer (while retaining the old Windows XP style if you prefer it). Opening Event Viewer (System and Security | Administrative Tools | Event Viewer)

● **Figure 10.30** Details about to be sent

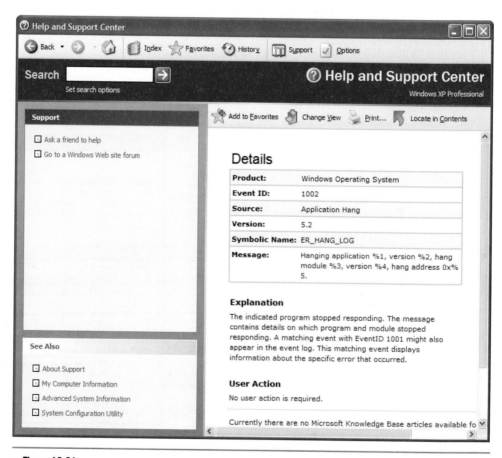

● **Figure 10.31** Help and Support Center being helpful

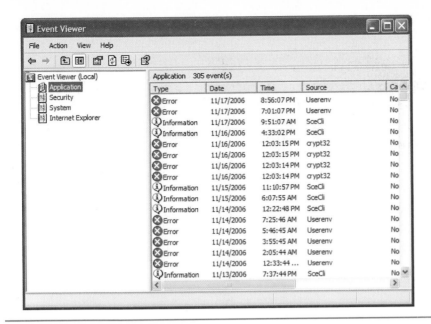

• **Figure 10.32** Event Viewer in Windows XP showing some serious application errors!

shows you a very different interface from the one you've seen in Windows XP (see Figure 10.33).

Note the four main bars in the center pane: Overview, Summary of Administrative Events, Recently Viewed Nodes, and Log Summary. Pay special attention to the Summary of Administrative Events. It breaks down the events into different levels: Critical, Error, Warning, Information, Audit Success, and Audit Failure. Figure 10.34 shows a typical Summary with the Warning Events opened. You can then click any event to see a dialog box describing the event in detail. Microsoft refers to these as *Views*.

• **Figure 10.33** Windows 7 Event Viewer default screen

• **Figure 10.34** Warning Events open

Windows 7's Event Viewer still includes the classic logs you saw in Windows XP (Application, Security, and System) but leans heavily on Views to show you the contents of the logs. Views filter existing log files, making them great for custom reports using beginning/end times, levels of errors, and more. You can use the built-in Views or easily create custom Views, as shown in Figure 10.35.

Remember, you still record all data to logs. Logs in Windows 7 still have the same limitations that logs in earlier versions of Windows had. They have a maximum size, a location, and a behavior for when they get too big (such as overwrite the log or make an error). Figure 10.36 shows a typical Log Properties dialog box in Windows 7.

Windows 7's Event Viewer remains largely untouched in terms of the data collected, but Microsoft did a great job of making that data much easier to understand and use.

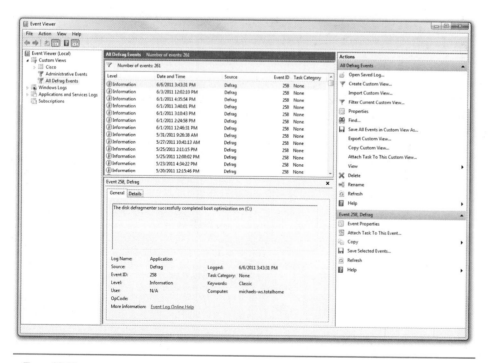

• **Figure 10.35** Created custom Views

Only users with Administrator privileges can make changes to log files in Event Viewer.

If you run into a scenario where a device has failed and this created problems with Windows' startup, you would turn to the primary Windows tool for hardware issues: Device Manager. We've covered Device Manager in chapters specific to hardware, so there's no need to go into it yet again here.

• **Figure 10.36** Log Properties dialog box in Windows 7

Autoloading Programs

Windows loves to autoload programs so they start at boot. Most of the time this is an incredibly handy option, used by every Windows PC in existence. The problem with autoloading programs is that when one of them starts behaving badly, you need to shut off that program! Use the System Configuration utility to temporarily stop programs from autoloading. If you want to make the program stop forever, go into the program and find a load on startup option (see Figure 10.37).

If you can't find a load on startup option in your application, run the Registry Editor and go to where most applications autoload:
 HKEY_LOCAL_MACHINE\
SOFTWARE\Microsoft\Windows\
CurrentVersion\Run

Services

Windows loads a number of services as it starts. In a scenario where any critical service fails to load, Windows tells you at this point with an error message. The important word here is *critical*. Windows will not report *all* service failures at this point. If a service that is less than critical to Windows doesn't start, the OS usually waits until you try to use a program that needs that

• **Figure 10.37** Typical load on startup option

service before it prompts you with an error message (see Figure 10.38).

To work with your system's services, go to the Control Panel | Administrative Tools | Services and verify that the service you need is running. If not, turn it on. Also notice that each service has a Startup Type—Automatic, Manual, or Disabled—that defines when it starts. It's very common to find that a service has been set to Manual when it needs to be set to Automatic so that it starts when Windows boots (see Figure 10.39).

Task Manager and Command-Line Options

Task Manager is a great place to go to shut down errant processes that won't otherwise close properly. Task Manager enables you to see all applications or programs currently running or to close an application that has stopped working. You remember how to get to it, right? Press CTRL-SHIFT-ESC to open it directly or CTRL-ALT-DELETE to get to a list of action items, one of which opens Task Manager.

If you're unable to get to Task Manager or are comfortable with the command line, you can get to a command prompt (like in the Recovery Console or Windows Recovery Environment) and type the command **tasklist** to find the names and process IDs of all the running processes. You can then run **taskkill** to end any process either by filename or by process ID. If you're in the Windows PowerShell, the commands are *tasklist* and *kill*.

System Files

Windows lives on dynamic link library (DLL) files. Almost every program used by Windows—and certainly all of the important ones—call on DLL files to do most of the heavy lifting that makes Windows work.

Windows protects all of the critical DLL files very carefully, but once in a while you may get an error saying Windows can't load a particular DLL. Although rare, the core system files that make up Windows itself may become corrupted, preventing Windows from starting properly. You usually see something like "Error loading XXXX.DLL," or sometimes a program you need simply won't start when you double-click its icon. In these cases, the tool you need is the **System File Checker** that you learned about in Chapter 9. Use it to check and replace a number of critical files, including the ever-important DLL cache.

System Restore

System Restore is the final step in recovering from a major Windows meltdown. Earlier in the chapter, you learned that you can use System Restore from the Windows Recovery Environment, but don't forget that you can

• **Figure 10.38** Service error

• **Figure 10.39** Autostarting a service

> Newly installed DLLs must be entered into the Registry via a process cleverly called *registration*. In most cases DLLs will register themselves, but on rare occasions you might need to manually register a DLL using the command-line tool regsvr32 that you learned about in Chapter 6.

also use restore points from within Windows. Follow the process explained in Chapter 8.

Troubleshooting Tools in Windows Vista and Windows 7

Windows Vista and Windows 7 include amazing utilities designed to help you support your system. Many of these tools first appeared in Windows Vista, but Windows 7 either refined them or made them easily accessible. These Control Panel tools perform a number of different jobs, from telling you what's happening on the system to showing you how well a system's performance stacks up to other computers.

Problem Reports and Solutions (Windows Vista) and Action Center (Windows 7) centralize a lot of useful information about the status of your computer. The Performance and Information Tools applet tells you just how powerful your computer really is. Let's take a look at this crazy mixture of utilities in alphabetical order and explore the scenarios appropriate for their use.

Problem Reports and Solutions

If a computer is having a problem, wouldn't it be great to tell the people who are in charge of the program you're having that problem so they can fix it? That's the idea behind *Windows Error Reporting*. There's a good chance that, like many users, you've run into errors that look something like Figure 10.40.

The problem with these errors is that, while they might help Microsoft, they traditionally do little to help us fix the computer. Windows Error Reporting was a one-way tool, until Microsoft upgraded it with Vista to a much more powerful, two-way tool that gives developers a way to give you ways to fix computers.

The **Problem Reports and Solutions** Control Panel applet in Windows Vista lists all Windows Error Reporting issues (plus a few easy-to-check items like firewall and antimalware status), as shown in Figure 10.41. You click on the solution and, in many cases, the problem is fixed.

• **Figure 10.40** Crash.exe has stopped working.

● Figure 10.41 Problem Reports and Solutions

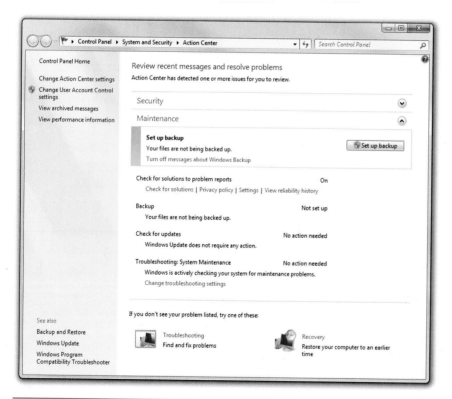

● Figure 10.42 Action Center

Action Center

Problem Reports and Solutions is a good tool but lacks some refinements. For example, once you fix a problem, you have to delete the problem from the list manually. Also, there are a number of issues that don't have anything to do with Windows Error Reporting that just make sense to combine, such as Microsoft Troubleshooter and System Restore. Microsoft realized that they could organize the solutions to make it easier for you to choose what you wanted to do. **Action Center** in Windows 7 provides a one-page aggregation of event messages, warnings, and maintenance messages that, for many techs, might quickly replace Event Viewer as the first place to look for problems. Unlike Event Viewer, Action Center separates issues into two sections, Security and Maintenance, making it easier to scan a system quickly (see Figure 10.42).

Action Center only compiles the information, taking data from well-known utilities such as Event Viewer, Windows Update, Windows Firewall, and UAC and placing it into an easy-to-read format. If you wish, you can tell Action Center where to look for information by selecting *Change Action Center settings* (see Figure 10.43).

If you see a problem, Action Center includes plenty of links to get you to the utility you need. From the Action Center applet, you get direct links to the following tools:

- UAC settings
- Performance Information and Tools
- Backup and Restore
- Windows Update
- Troubleshooting Wizard
- System Restore

Although Action Center does little more than reproduce information from other utilities, it makes finding problems quick and easy. Combined with quick links to most of the utilities you'll need, Action Center should become your base of operations when something goes wrong on your Windows 7 PC.

Performance Information and Tools

Techs must often answer difficult questions like "Why is my machine running so slowly?" Before Windows Vista, we could only use Performance Monitor baselines or third-party tools. Neither of these options worked very well. Baselines required you to choose the right counters—choosing

• **Figure 10.43** Change Action Center settings

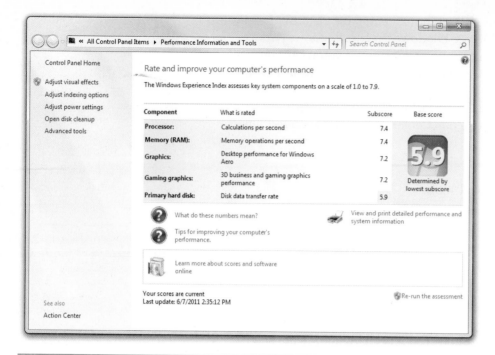

Rate and improve your computer's performance

The Windows Experience Index assesses key system components on a scale of 1.0 to 7.9.

Component	What is rated	Subscore	Base score
Processor:	Calculations per second	7.4	
Memory (RAM):	Memory operations per second	7.4	5.9
Graphics:	Desktop performance for Windows Aero	7.2	Determined by lowest subscore
Gaming graphics:	3D business and gaming graphics performance	7.2	
Primary hard disk:	Disk data transfer rate	5.9	

Your scores are current
Last update: 6/7/2011 2:35:12 PM

• **Figure 10.44** Performance Information and Tools

the wrong counters made useless and sometimes even distracting logs. Third-party tools often measured one aspect of a system (like video quality) very well but didn't help much when you wanted an overview of your system.

This changed with Microsoft's introduction of the Performance Information and Tools Control Panel applet (see Figure 10.44).

The **Performance Information and Tools** applet doesn't fix anything. It just provides a relative feel for how your computer stacks up against other systems using the Windows Experience Index. Windows bases this on five components:

- **Processor** Calculations per second
- **Memory (RAM)** Memory operations per second
- **Graphics** Desktop performance for Windows Aero
- **Gaming graphics** 3-D business and gaming graphics performance
- **Primary hard disk** Disk data transfer rate

Each component generates a subscore. These values range from 1 to 5.9 for Windows Vista and 1 to 7.9 for Windows 7. Microsoft determines the calculations that generate these numbers, so I don't know exactly what it takes to give, for example, a CPU a score of 6.1. Your system's Base score is based on the lowest subscore.

The Performance Information and Tools applet won't fix anything, but tells you which component is the weakest link in overall performance.

■ Application Problems

Programmers want to write applications that work well, enable you to accomplish a specific task, and be good enough to earn your money. But PCs are complicated and programmers can't get it right every time with every combination of hardware and software.

Application problems show up in several ways. The typical scenario has the application failing to install or uninstall. Operating system version issues can cause compatibility problems. Another typical scenario is where an application tries to access a file and that file is either missing or won't open. The least common problems come from sloppy or poorly written

> You can't change a subscore in the Windows Experience Index without making some kind of hardware change.

> Every once in a while you'll get an application that reports an error if the clock settings in Windows don't match. This can cause the application not to run. Likewise, if a computer has a failing battery and is offline for a while, the BIOS time and settings will be off. You'll get a brief "error" noting the change when you connect that computer to a network timeserver. This is both a hardware issue (failing battery) and an application issue. When the Windows clock resets, so does the BIOS time and settings.

code that causes the application or the operating system to crash. Finally, corrupted applications can corrupt data too, but Windows has tools for recovering previous versions of files and folders.

Application Installation Problems

Almost all Windows programs come with some form of handy installer. When you insert the disc, Windows knows to look for a text file called autorun.inf that tells it which file to run off the disc, usually setup.exe. If you download the application, you'll need to double-click it to start the installation. Either way, you run the installer and the program runs. It almost couldn't be simpler.

A well-behaved program should always make itself easy to uninstall as well. In most cases, you should see an uninstallation option in the program's Start menu area; and in all cases (unless you have an application with a badly configured installer), the application should appear in either the Add/Remove Programs applet or the Programs and Features applet (see Figure 10.45) in the Control Panel.

Programs that fail to install usually aren't to blame in and of themselves. In most cases, a problem with Windows prevents them from installing, most notably the lack of some other program that the application needs so it can operate. One of the best examples of this is the popular Microsoft .NET Framework. .NET is an extension to the Windows operating system that includes support for a number of features, particularly powerful interface tools and flexible database access. Programs written to incorporate .NET require the proper version of the framework installed to function. Many such programs attempt to install the .NET framework when you install the program, but this doesn't always work. If .NET is missing or if the version of .NET you are using is too old (there have been a number of .NET versions since it came

The fact that Windows looks for the autorun.inf file by default when you insert a disc creates a security issue. Someone could put a malicious program on a disc and write an autorun.inf file to point to the virus. Insert the disc and boom! There goes your clean PC. Of course, if someone has access to your computer and is fully logged on with administrator privileges, then you've already lost everything, with or without a disc-born program, so this "big" security issue is pretty much not an issue at all. Nevertheless, you should know that to turn off this behavior in Windows requires opening the Registry Editor and changing up to six different settings.

Remember that you need local administrator privileges to install applications in all versions of Windows.

• **Figure 10.45** Programs and Features Control Panel applet

• Figure 10.46 .NET error

out in 2002), you can get some of the most indecipherable errors in the history of Windows applications.

Figure 10.46 shows one such example in Windows 7 where the VMware vSphere client fails due to the wrong .NET version. Too bad the error doesn't give you any clues!

These types of errors invariably require you to go online and do Web searches, using the application name and the error. No matter how bad the error, someone else has already suffered from the same problem. The trick is to find out what they did to get around it.

Problems with Uninstalling

The single biggest problem with uninstalling is that people try to uninstall without administrator privileges. If you try to uninstall and get an error, log back on as an administrator and you should be fine. Don't forget you can right-click on most uninstallation menu options on the Programs menu and select *Run as administrator* to switch to administrator privileges (see Figure 10.47).

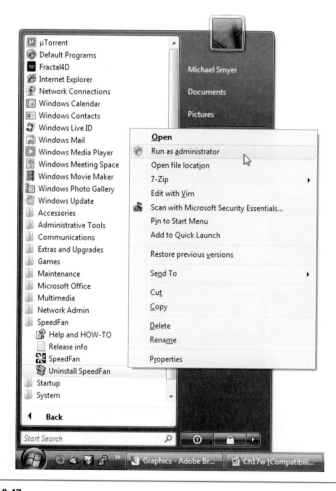

• Figure 10.47 Selecting Run as administrator from the context menu

Compatibility

Most applications are written with the most recent version of Windows in mind, but as Windows versions change over time, older programs have difficulty running in more recent Windows versions. In some cases, such as the jump from Windows Vista to Windows 7, the changes are generally minor enough to cause few if any compatibility problems. In other cases, say a program written back when Windows 98 was around, the underpinnings of the OS differ so much that you have to perform certain steps to ensure that the older programs run. Windows XP, Windows Vista, and Windows 7 provide different forms of **compatibility modes** to support older applications.

Windows XP handles compatibility using the aptly named Compatibility tab (see Figure 10.48) in every executable program's Properties dialog box (right-click on the executable file and click Properties). Select the version of Windows you want Windows XP to emulate, and in many cases that is all you need to do to make that older program work (see Figure 10.49).

You can also set other settings on the Compatibility tab, such as the following located under Display settings:

- **Run in 256 colors** Many old Windows programs were designed to run in 256 colors. Later versions of Windows that support more colors can confuse these older programs.

- **Run in 640 × 480 screen resolution** A few (badly written) older programs assume the screen to be at 640 × 480 resolution. This setting enables them to work.

- **Disable visual themes** Windows themes change a program window's title bar, fonts, and menus, which might make problems for some programs.

• **Figure 10.48** XP Compatibility tab

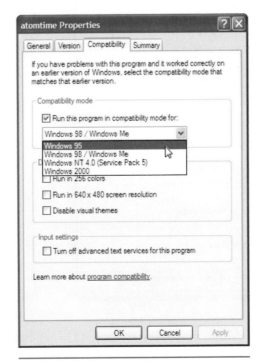

• **Figure 10.49** Compatibility mode options in Windows XP

Windows Vista and Windows 7 add some important improvements to the Compatibility tab. Both add more recent OS options to the Compatibility mode drop-down menu. Figure 10.50 shows the many options available in Windows 7.

The newer Compatibility tab also adds some new options (see Figure 10.51) to help older programs run:

- **Disable desktop composition** Disables all display features such as Aero. More advanced Windows display features often bog down older programs.

- **Disable display scaling on high DPI settings** Turns off automatic resizing of a program's windows if you're using any high DPI (dots per inch) font. This was added because many programs with large fonts would look bizarre if resized.

- **Run this program as an administrator** As stated, enables you to run the program as an administrator. If this option isn't available, log on as an administrator to see it.

- **Change settings for all users** Clicking this button applies compatibility changes made to a program to every user account on the machine. Otherwise, the settings are only for the current user.

If you need to make things 100 percent compatible with Windows XP and you have Windows 7 (Professional, Ultimate, and Enterprise only)

• **Figure 10.50** Compatibility mode options in Windows 7

• **Figure 10.51** Windows 7 Compatibility tab

installed on your system, you can download Windows XP Mode. **Windows XP Mode** is nothing more than a premade Windows XP SP3 virtual machine that runs under Microsoft's popular (and free) virtualization program, Windows Virtual PC (see Figure 10.52).

We'll wait until Chapter 19 for a complete discussion of virtualization and how it works, but for now it's important to appreciate that Windows XP Mode is nothing more than a copy of Windows XP. You can install programs in this virtual machine, access the Internet, print to your printers—everything that you can do with a real computer.

The secret to using compatibility mode isn't much of a secret at all: if the program doesn't run, try a compatibly mode. If you want to be really careful, do a Web search on your application before you try to run it. Compatibility mode is a handy tool to get older applications running.

Missing File or Incorrect File Version

An application may rely on other files, in particular DLL files. Sometimes the application installer will bring specially formatted versions of common DLL or other files to Windows, overwriting the previous versions. Later applications might look for the earlier version of the DLL and fail when it's not found.

You'll experience this sort of scenario with error messages such as "missing DLL" or "cannot open file *xyz.*" The usual fix for either issue is to perform an Internet search for the missing DLL or file that fails to open, along with the name of the program you're trying to use.

• **Figure 10.52** Windows XP Mode

Crashing Programs

Occasionally, a program gets released that isn't ready for prime time and the error-prone code causes the application to crash or even causes the operating system to crash. I've seen this most often with games rushed to market near the winter holidays. The results of this rushed code can be pretty spectacular. You're right in the middle of a thrilling fight with the bad guy and then what happens? A crash to desktop (CTD).

Poorly written or buggy programs can have awful effects on you and your clients. Some of the scenarios caused by such programs are the computer locking up or unexpectedly shutting down. The system might spontaneously shut down and restart. That kind of improper shutdown can cause problems, especially to open files and folders.

The problem here is that all this crashing can be caused by hardware and driver problems, not just application problems. You've got to keep in mind all of these things as you approach troubleshooting a crash.

Here's a typical scenario where you need to troubleshoot broadly first. If you're playing a graphically intensive game that happens to be huge and takes up a lot of RAM, what could the problem be if the screen locks up and Windows locks up too? It could be that the program ran a routine that clashed with some other application or used a Windows feature improperly. It could be that the video card was marginal and failed when taxed too much. It could be that the system accessed a section of RAM that had gone bad.

In that same scenario, though, where the game runs but degrades the overall performance of Windows, what could cause that problem? That points more squarely at the application side of things rather than the hardware or drivers, especially if the computer successfully runs other programs. The bottom line with crash issues is to keep an open mind and not rule out anything without testing it first.

> One error common on older systems, still mentioned on the CompTIA A+ 802 exam, but largely absent or invisible on modern systems, is a *general protection fault* (*GPF*). A GPF occurs when a program tries to do something not permitted, like writing to protected memory or something else Windows doesn't like. This can cause an error message to appear or can even crash the computer. You are very unlikely to encounter a GPF today.

Volume Shadow Copy Service and System Protection

One of the big headaches to a failure with an application isn't so much the application itself but any data it may have corrupted. Sure, a good backup or a restore point might save you, but these can be a hassle. Unless the data was specifically saved (in the backup), there's a chance you don't have a backup in the first place. Microsoft came to your rescue in Windows Vista (Business, Ultimate, and Enterprise only) and Windows 7 (all editions) with a feature called System Protection.

This amazing feature is powered by Volume Shadow Copy Service (VSS), a feature introduced in Windows XP and used by ntbackup. VSS enables the operating system to make backups of any file, even one that is in use. In Windows Vista and 7, VSS is also used by **System Protection**, enabling you to access previous versions of any data file or folder. Try right-clicking on any data file and selecting *Restore previous versions*, which opens the file's Properties dialog box with the Previous Versions tab displayed, as shown in Figure 10.53.

If any of the following criteria are met, you will have at least one previous version in the list:

- The file or folder was backed up using the backup program.
- You created a restore point.
- The file or folder was changed.

You must make sure System Protection is enabled as well. Go to the System Protection tab in the System Properties dialog box (see Figure 10.54) to see if the feature is enabled (it should be running by default).

System Protection falls in the category generically called *file recovery software*, and does an outstanding job. You can also get many third-party utilities that accomplish general file recovery. I've used Recuva from Piriform many times, for example, to get "deleted" data off a hard drive or RAID array.

Keep in mind that System Protection doesn't have to be only for recovery of corrupted data files caused by bad applications. It's also a great tool to recover previous versions of files that users accidently overwrite.

The System Protection tab also enables you to load a restore point and to create restore points manually, very handy features.

• **Figure 10.53** Previous Versions tab

• **Figure 10.54** System Protection tab

Chapter 10 Review

■ Chapter Summary

After reading this chapter and completing the exercises, you should understand the following about troubleshooting Windows.

Troubleshoot Windows boot problems

■ If you see an "NTLDR is Missing" or "BOOTMGR is missing" error, you first want to check your hardware configuration. Check the screen—what do you see? Is the PC plugged in? These are all common problems. If that doesn't work, you should use either Windows XP's Recovery Console or Windows Vista/7's Recovery Environment (also known as the System Recovery Options menu).

■ The Recovery Console works as a command-line utility. Many of its commands are those familiar to DOS users, but some new commands have also been added. Because the file for the Recovery Console is on the system partition in a folder called cmdcons, this program is useless for system partition crashes, but it is excellent for restoring Registries, stopping problem services, or using the expand program to extract copies of files from an optical disc or floppy disk. You can also use it to partition and format hard drives and read and write on local FAT or NTFS volumes. It's also good for repairing the MBR, reinstalling the boot files, and rebuilding boot.ini.

■ A bad boot sector usually shows up as a No Boot Device error. If it turns out that this isn't the problem, the Recovery Console command to fix it won't hurt anything. At the Recovery Console prompt, just type **fixmbr**, which fixes the master boot record.

■ The second problem the Recovery Console is best at fixing is missing system files, usually indicated by the error "NTLDR bad or missing." To fix this, get to the root directory (**cd**) and type the following line: **copy d:\i386\ntldr**. Then type **copy d:\i386\ntdetect.com**. To rebuild the boot.ini file, type **bootcfg /rebuild**.

■ Automated System Recovery can restore your system to a previously installed state, but you should use it as a last resort. You lose everything on the system that was installed or added after you created the ASR disk.

■ When rebuilding your Windows installation, you're best off swapping the C: drive for a blank hard drive and installing a clean version of Windows. You may also have a Recovery CD or recovery partition that came with your computer. These tools can restore your PC to its factory settings.

■ Windows Vista/7 do not use the Recovery Console. Instead, you boot to the Windows Preinstallation Environment (Windows PE). Here, you can boot directly to the Windows installation disc or access a set of repair tools known as the Windows Recovery Environment (Windows RE). Windows RE is also called the System Recovery Options menu.

■ From Windows RE, you can access Startup Repair, System Restore, System Image Recovery/ Windows Complete PC Restore, Windows Memory Diagnostics (Tool), and the Command Prompt.

■ The Startup Repair utility enables you to repair a corrupted Registry, restore critical system files, roll back nonfunctioning drivers, uninstall incompatible service packs and patches, and more. In Windows 7, Startup Repair runs automatically if the system detects a boot problem.

■ System Restore enables you to return your system to a previous state.

■ The System Image Recovery/Windows Complete PC Restore tools use a system image to restore the files, applications, and settings for your PC. You will need to use the Backup and Restore Center/ Backup and Restore applet in Control Panel to make a system image first.

■ The Windows Memory Diagnostics (Tool) checks for bad RAM that may be causing BSoDs, system lockups, or continuous reboots. This tool isn't perfect, and can sometimes cause more problems than it fixes. Check out Memtest86+ for another solution.

■ Unlike the Recovery Console in Windows XP, the Command Prompt in Windows RE is fully featured. It also adds an important utility called bootrec, which enables you to troubleshoot the master boot record, boot sector, and BCD store. You can also work with the boot configuration data using the bcdedit command.

Troubleshoot Windows GUI problems

- Several issues can cause Windows to hang during the GUI-loading phase, such as buggy device drivers, Registry problems, and even autoloading programs.

- If you get errors like "Registry File Failure" or "Windows could not start," you should try restoring a good copy of the Registry. You can do this manually or by using the Last Known Good Configuration boot option from the Advanced Startup Options menu. To get to the Advanced Startup Options menu, restart the computer and press F8 after the POST messages but before the Windows logo screen appears. From here, you can start your computer into Safe Mode or into the Last Known Good Configuration.

- From the Advanced Startup Options menu, you can boot your computer into Safe Mode. Safe Mode uses basic, non–vendor-specific drivers for mouse, display, keyboard, storage, and system services. You can also use Safe Mode with Networking and Safe Mode with Command Prompt, which enable networking and the command prompt, respectively.

- Enable Boot Logging creates a log of the boot process as the drivers are loaded into memory. The file is named Ntbtlog.txt and is saved in the %SystemRoot% folder.

- Enable VGA Mode in Windows XP and Enable Low-Resolution Mode in Windows Vista/7 boot into Windows normally but disable your normal display driver and use a standard one instead.

- Last Known Good Configuration loads the configuration of Windows that existed immediately before you installed the most recent device driver.

- Directory Services Restore Mode is designed for use with Active Directory domain controllers. Debugging Mode sends a debug of the kernel to a second computer. Both of these tools are only used in very specific circumstances.

- With the Disable Automatic Restart on System Failure mode, you can prevent Windows from automatically rebooting after a BSoD. You can also use the Disable Driver Signature Enforcement mode to use devices without signed drivers that Windows Vista/7 would otherwise prevent you

from using. You can also start Windows normally, reboot, or return to the OS Choices menu.

- Event Viewer in Window shows you all sorts of interesting happenings on the system. You can record application events, security events, and system events. One of these recorded events may be able to tell you why the system crashed, locked up, or otherwise failed.

- The System Configuration utility enables you to keep individual programs and services from autoloading, but it does not actually remove the programs/services.

- Windows loads a number of services as it starts. If any critical service fails to load, Windows will tell you at this point with an error message.

- Task Manager is a great place to go to shut down errant processes that won't otherwise close properly. If you're unable to get to Task Manager or are comfortable with the command line, you can use the tasklist and taskkill commands to do the same thing.

- Windows protects all of its critical DLL files very carefully, but once in a while you may get an error saying Windows can't load a particular DLL. In these cases, the tool you need is the System File Checker. Use it to check a number of critical files, including the ever-important DLL cache, and replace any corrupted ones.

- The Problem Reports and Solutions Control Panel applet in Windows Vista lists all Windows Error Reporting issues and shows the status of your firewall and antimalware software. In Windows 7, Microsoft enhanced this tool and created the Action Center. The Action Center performs all of the same functions as the Problem Reports and Solutions applet, but adds the Microsoft Troubleshooter, System Restore, and several other messages and warnings.

- While the Performance Information and Tools applet doesn't fix anything, it does provide you a relative feel for how your machine stacks up against other systems. Using the Windows Experience Index, the applet ranks your processor, RAM, graphics, and hard disk on a scale of 1 to 5.9 for Windows Vista and on a scale of 1 to 7.9 for Windows 7.

Troubleshoot Windows application problems

- Programs that fail to install usually aren't to blame in and of themselves. In most cases, a problem with Windows prevents them from installing, most notably the lack of some other program that the application needs so it can operate. If you get an error while trying to uninstall a program, log back on as an administrator and try again.

- Most applications are written with the most recent version of Windows in mind, but as Windows versions change over time, older programs have difficulty running in more recent Windows versions. You can use compatibility modes to emulate older versions of Windows. Other compatibility settings include lowering the resolution, lowering the number of colors, disabling themes, and so on.

- If you see an error message about a missing DLL file, use the Internet to search for the missing file and find the popular solution.

- If your applications crash repeatedly, it could be bad programming. It could also be a hardware or driver problem that causes the application to crash. You'll need to check both software and hardware to find out why applications crash to desktop.

- Windows Vista Business, Ultimate, and Enterprise and all editions of Windows 7 use Volume Shadow Copy Service, which enables the OS to make backups of any files, even one that is in use. Windows Vista/7 also use System Protection, which enables you to access previous versions of any data file or folder.

Key Terms

Action Center *(406)*
Advanced Startup Options *(394)*
bcdedit *(388)*
Blue Screen of Death (BSoD) *(393)*
bootrec *(388)*
compatibility mode *(411)*
diskpart *(390)*
Event Viewer *(398)*
Last Known Good Configuration *(397)*
Live DVD *(379)*
Performance Information and Tools *(408)*
Problem Reports and Solutions *(405)*

Recovery Console *(375)*
restore point *(383)*
Safe Mode *(394)*
Startup Repair *(381)*
System File Checker *(404)*
System Protection *(414)*
System Restore *(383)*
Task Manager *(404)*
Windows Preinstallation Environment (WinPE) *(379)*
Windows Recovery Environment (WinRE) *(379)*
Windows XP Mode *(413)*

Key Term Quiz

Use the Key Terms list to complete the sentences that follow. Not all terms will be used.

1. The _____ tool enables you to view and modify the BCD store.

2. Use the _____ to check and replace any corrupted critical Windows files, such as DLLs.

3. If Windows fails but you have *not* logged on, you can select _____ to restore the computer to the way it was the last time a user logged on.

4. To start Windows using only the most basic and essential drivers and services, use

 _____.

5. The _____, accessed by pressing CTRL-SHIFT-ESC once, enables you to see all applications or programs currently running or to close an application that has stopped working.

6. Use the _____ in Windows 7 to see an aggregation of event messages, warnings, and maintenance messages.

7. In Windows Vista and Windows 7, you can use the _____ feature to recover previous versions of corrupted or deleted files.

8. To run a program written for Windows XP in a Windows 7 computer, use _____ if you encounter problems.

9. The _____ applet provides a relative feel for how your computer stacks up against other systems using the Windows Experience Index.

10. While Windows XP provides the Recovery Console troubleshooting environment, Windows Vista and Windows 7 include the

_____ .

■ Multiple-Choice Quiz

1. Mark loaded a new video card on his system, but now everything looks very bad. What should he do first?

 A. Go to Event Viewer and check the log

 B. Go to Device Manager

 C. Go to the printed manual

 D. Call tech support

2. Which utility is useful in identifying a program that is hogging the processor?

 A. Task Manager

 B. Device Manager

 C. System Monitor

 D. System Information

3. You've just installed a software update, rebooted, and now your system experiences random crashes. Which utility should you use first to try to fix the problem?

 A. Automated System Restore

 B. Device Manager

 C. System Restore

 D. Recovery Console

4. You suspect your system is failing to boot because of a corrupt master boot record. Which utility is the best to fix this?

 A. Automated System Restore

 B. Device Manager

 C. System Restore

 D. Recovery Console

5. What command should you run to check and fix corrupt system files, DLLs, and other critical files?

 A. cmdcons /fixboot

 B. sfc /scannow

 C. chkdsk /r

 D. defrag –a

6. You get a tech call from a distraught Windows XP user who can't get into Windows. He says he has a Recovery CD from the manufacturer and plans to run it. What would you suggest?

 A. Run the Recovery CD to restore the system

 B. Run the Recovery CD to return the system to the factory-installed state

 C. Try to get the computer to boot into Safe Mode

 D. Reinstall Windows by using a Windows XP disc

7. Which of the following points to a hardware or CMOS problem rather than an OS problem with a PC that won't boot.

 A. A black screen with the error message "invalid boot disk"

 B. A black screen with the error message "NTLDR Bad or Missing"

 C. A black screen with the error message "Invalid BOOT.INI"

 D. A black screen with the error message "Invalid BCD"

8. John's computer has an error that says bootmgr is corrupted. What tool can he use to fix this problem?

 A. bcdedit

 B. chkdsk

 C. config.sys

 D. regedit

9. What does Microsoft call the 32- or 64-bit installation environment in Windows 7?

 A. WinEE

 B. WinPE

 C. WinRE

 D. Recovery Console

10. Ralph suspects a bad RAM stick is causing Windows to fail to boot. What default Windows tool can he use to check the RAM?

 A. MEMMAKER

 B. Memtest86+

 C. Windows RAM Diagnostic Tool

 D. Windows Memory Diagnostics Tool

11. If you create a system image from Windows 7's Backup and Restore applet, what gets backed up?

 A. Everything

 B. Essential system files and personal information for all users

 C. Personal information for all users

 D. Personal information for all users and a full system image

12. Which of the following commands will repair a damaged master boot record in a Windows 7 PC?

 A. bootrec /fixboot

 B. bootrec /fixmbr

 C. fixboot

 D. fixmbr

13. Ellen tries to boot into Windows but the computer crashes at the logon screen. What tool should she use first to try to fix the problem?

 A. Boot to the Windows DVD, get to WinRE, and type **clean** at the diskpart prompt

 B. Boot to the Windows DVD, get to WinRE, and run Startup Repair

 C. Reboot the PC, press F8 to open the Advanced Startup Options menu, and select Safe Mode

 D. Reboot the PC, press F8 to open WinRE, and select Safe Mode

14. Which feature in Windows 7 enables you to right-click a file or folder and restore previous versions of that file or folder?

 A. Reversion

 B. System Protection

 C. System Revert

 D. Undelete

15. Which of the following can cause a computer to lock up or unexpectedly shut down? (Select two.)

 A. Bad RAM

 B. Poorly written application

 C. Windows Installer

 D. Windows remote shutdown

■ Essay Quiz

1. Your team needs to present a case for updating the primary company computers from Windows XP to Windows 7. Your role is to discuss and contrast the recovery tools in case of system crashes. Write an essay on how the recovery tools work in Windows 7 compared to how the recovery tools work in Windows XP.

2. The Registry Editor is the universal tool for editing the Registry in all versions of Windows (covered on the CompTIA A+ 220-802 exam). Your boss needs an explanation of the Registry

and how the Registry Editor can be used to back up and restore the Registry files. Explain these things to your boss. Don't forget to tell the boss how to load the Registry Editor!

3. Write an essay that contrasts the three Safe Mode options available in the Advanced Startup Options menu. Why would you use anything but straight-up Safe Mode? Provide a scenario in your answer for why Safe Mode with Command Prompt might offer better troubleshooting options than Safe Mode with Networking.

Lab Projects

• Lab Project 10.1

On your test system, put the Windows recovery tools to the test. You can do this project in any of the relevant versions of Windows. Back up the system. Create a system image if you're using Windows 7.

Create a system repair disc. Make some catastrophic change to Windows, then boot to the system repair disc and run through the recovery process.

• Lab Project 10.2

Similar to Lab Project 10.1, put the System Protection tool in Windows 7 to the test. Delete some files. Right-click on the folder they were deleted from and select *Restore previous version*. What happens? Go further. Delete a whole folder, then select *Restore* *previous version* from the folder in which that deleted folder resided. What happens? Try both exercises again, but this time empty the Recycle Bin before trying to restore. What happens now?

11 Video

chapter

*"Video killed the radio star
Video killed the radio star
In my mind and in my car
We can't rewind, we've gone
too far."*

—THE BUGGLES, "VIDEO KILLED THE
RADIO STAR," *THE AGE OF PLASTIC*

In this chapter, you will learn how to

- **Install and configure video**
- **Troubleshoot basic video problems**

The term *video* encompasses a complex interaction among numerous parts of the PC, all designed to put a picture on the screen. The monitor or video display shows you what's going on with your programs and operating system. It's the primary output device for the PC. The video card or display adapter handles all of the communication between the CPU and the monitor (see Figure 11.1). The operating system needs to know how to handle communication between the CPU and the display adapter, which requires drivers specific for each card and proper setup within Windows. Finally, each application needs to be able to interact with the rest of the video system.

Knowing how to get this process working is an important part of becoming a PC tech. As such, you'll begin this chapter by looking at the process of installing and configuring video. After that, you'll take a look at what to do when things go wrong with your video hardware.

• Figure 11.1 Typical monitor and video card

■ Installing and Configuring Video

Once you've purchased your new video card and monitor, you need to install them into your system. As long as you have the right connection to your video card, installing a monitor is straightforward. The challenge comes when installing the video card.

During the physical installation of a video card, watch out for two possible issues: long cards and proximity of the nearest expansion card. Some high-end video cards simply won't fit in certain cases or block access to needed motherboard connectors such as the SATA sockets. There's no clean fix for such a problem—you simply have to change at least one of the components (video card, motherboard, or case). Because high-end video cards run very hot, you don't want them sitting right next to another card; make sure the fan on the video card has plenty of ventilation space. A good practice is to leave the slot next to the video card empty to allow better airflow (see Figure 11.2). (Many high-end video cards come as double-wide cards with built-in air vents, so you don't have any choice but to take up double the space.)

Try This!

Install a Video Card

Installing a video card is basically just like installing any other expansion card. That said, get a video card and Try This!

1. Find the PCIe x16 slot on your motherboard.

2. Press the video card firmly down into the PCIe x16 slot and secure it by screwing in the case retention screw. Plug the monitor into the video card and power up the system. If your PC seems dead after installing the card, or you get beep codes, try reseating the video card.

Once you've properly installed the video card and connected it to the monitor, you've conquered half the territory for making the video process work properly. You're ready to tackle the drivers and tweak the operating system, so let's go!

Software

Configuring your video software is usually a two-step process. First you need to load drivers for the video card. Then you need to open the Control Panel and go to the Display applet (Windows XP/7) or Personalization applet (Windows Vista) to make your adjustments. Let's explore how to make the video card and monitor work in Windows.

• Figure 11.2 Installing a video card

Drivers

Just like any other piece of hardware, your video card needs a driver to function. Video card drivers install pretty much the same way as all of the other drivers we've discussed thus far: either the driver is already built into Windows or you must use the installation media that comes with the video card.

Video card makers are constantly updating their drivers. Odds are good that any video card more than a few months old has at least one driver update. If possible, check the manufacturer's Web site and use the driver located there if there is one. If the Web site doesn't offer a driver, it's usually best to use the installation media. Always avoid using the built-in Windows driver as it tends to be the most dated.

We'll explore driver issues in more detail after we discuss the Display and Personalization applets. Like so many things about video, you can't fully understand one topic without understanding at least one other!

Using the Display and Personalization Applets

With the driver installed, you're ready to configure your display settings. The Display applet or Personalization applet on the Control Panel is your next stop. The **Display applet** and **Personalization applet** provide convenient, central locations for all of your display settings, including resolution, refresh rate, driver information, and color depth.

The default Display applet window in Windows XP, called the Display Properties dialog box (see Figure 11.3), has five tabs: Themes, Desktop, Screen Saver, Appearance, and Settings. The first four tabs have options you can choose to change the look and

• Figure 11.3 Display Properties dialog box in Windows XP

feel of Windows and set up a screensaver; the fifth tab is where you make adjustments that relate directly to your monitor and video card.

The Personalization applet in Windows Vista offers functions similar to the Display applet, but each function manifests as a clickable option rather than as a separate tab (see Figure 11.4). Four of the seven options mirror the look and feel options of earlier versions of Windows, such as Window Color and Appearance, Desktop Background, Screen Saver, and Theme. The last option, Display Settings, is where you make adjustments to your monitor and video card. Two options, Sounds and Mouse Pointers, don't concern us at all at this time.

With Windows 7, Microsoft created a more visually oriented Personalization applet (see Figure 11.5). Most users typically want to change only their background or theme rather than anything else, so those options are front and center. Other options are in the Tasks panel on the left or in the Display applet, which is different than Windows XP's display applet.

Whether discussing tabs or options, the functions on all three applets are pretty much the same, so let's do this in one discussion. I'll point out any serious differences among the versions.

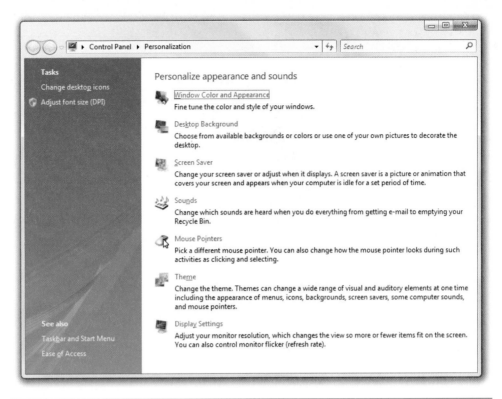

• **Figure 11.4** Personalization applet in Windows Vista

• **Figure 11.5** Personalization applet in Windows 7

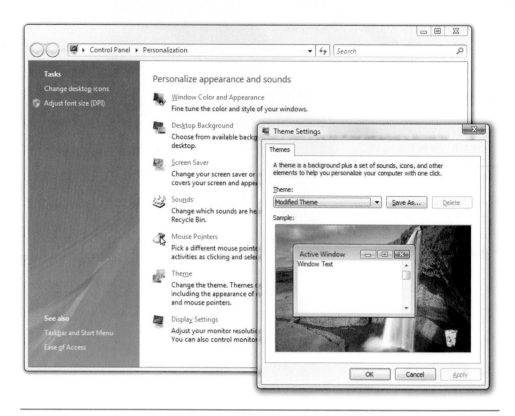

● **Figure 11.6** Theme option in the Windows Vista Personalization applet

Making the Screen Pretty

Three tabs/options in the Display/Personalization applet have the job of adjusting the appearance of the screen: Themes/Theme, Desktop/Desktop

● **Figure 11.7** Desktop tab on Display Properties dialog box

Background, and Appearance/Window Color and Appearance. Windows 7 simplifies this process by making those adjustments available on the Personalization screen, as you saw in Figure 11.5. Windows themes are preset configurations of the look and feel of the entire Windows environment (see Figure 11.6).

The Desktop tab in Windows XP (see Figure 11.7) or Desktop Background link in Windows Vista/7 defines the background color or image. In Windows XP, it also includes the handy Customize Desktop button that enables you to define the icons as well as any Web pages you want to appear on the desktop. Windows Vista/7 give you the option to position the image on the screen (see Figure 11.8), and the *Change desktop icons* option in the Tasks list in the Personalization applet enables you to choose which system icons (such as Computer, Recycle Bin, and Network) show up on your desktop, as well as which graphical icons they use.

The last of the tabs for the look and feel of the desktop in Windows XP is the Appearance tab. Think of the Appearance tab as the way to fine-tune the theme to your liking. The main screen gives only a few options—the real power is when you click the Advanced button to open the Advanced Appearance dialog box (see Figure 11.9). Using this dialog box, you may adjust almost

• **Figure 11.8** Desktop Background options in Windows 7

• **Figure 11.9** Advanced Appearance dialog box in Windows XP

● **Figure 11.10** Window Color and Appearance options in Windows 7

● **Figure 11.11** Screen Saver Settings in Windows 7

everything about the desktop, including the types of fonts and colors of every part of a window.

The Window Color and Appearance option in Windows Vista is a little simpler on the surface, enabling you to change the color scheme, intensity, and transparency. Windows 7 shows similar controls following the Windows Color link (see Figure 11.10). You can unlock the full gamut of options, though, by clicking the *Open classic appearance properties for more color options* link in Windows Vista or *Advanced appearance settings* in Windows 7.

Screen Saver

At first glance, the Screen Saver tab/option seems to do nothing but set the Windows screensaver—no big deal, just about everyone has set a screensaver (see Figure 11.11). But another option on the Screen Saver tab gets you to one of the most important settings of your system: power management. Click on the Power button or *Change power settings* option to get to the Power Options Properties dialog box or Power Options applet (see Figure 11.12).

• **Figure 11.12** Power Options applet in Windows 7

The tabs and options define all of the power management of the system. Power management is a fairly involved process, so we'll save the big discussion for where we need to save power the most: Chapter 15.

Settings Tab/Display Settings Applet/Display Applet

The Settings tab in Windows XP and the Display Settings applet in Windows Vista (see Figure 11.13) are the centralized location for configuring all of your video settings in Windows XP/Vista. From the main screen you can adjust both the resolution and the color depth. Windows only displays resolutions and color depths that your video card/monitor combination can accept and that are suitable for most situations. Everyone has a favorite resolution, and higher isn't always better. Especially for those with trouble seeing small screen elements, higher resolutions can present a difficulty— already small icons are *much* smaller at 1280 × 1024 than at 800 × 600. Try

• **Figure 11.13** Display Settings applet and Settings tab

Change the appearance of your display

Detect
Identify

Display: 1. GR276HL ▾
Resolution: 1366 × 927 ▾

Advanced settings

Make text and other items larger or smaller
What display settings should I choose?

OK Cancel Apply

• **Figure 11.14** Display applet in Windows 7

all of the resolutions to see which you like—just remember that LCD monitors look sharpest at their native resolution (usually the highest listed).

Clicking the Display link in the Tasks list of the Personalization applet in Windows 7 takes you to a simpler interface, again designed to give you quick access to only features you might commonly want to change. Changing the font size is centrally featured, but links in the top left of the task pane enable you to drill down to more advanced options, such as setting the color depth (see Figure 11.14).

Another option you may see in the Settings tab/Display Settings applet is multiple monitors. To see the same feature options in Windows 7, click the *Change display settings* link in the Display applet. Windows supports the use of two (or more) monitors. These monitors may work together like two halves of one large monitor, or the second monitor might simply show a duplicate of what's happening on the first monitor. Multiple monitors are handy if you need lots of screen space but don't want to buy a really large, expensive monitor (see Figure 11.15).

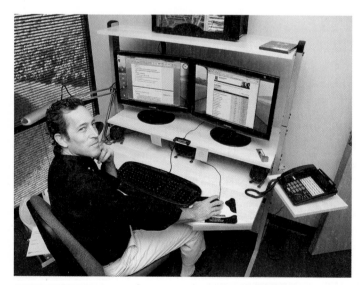

• **Figure 11.15** My editor hard at work with dual monitors

There are two ways to set up multiple monitors: plug in two or more video cards or use a single video card that supports multiple monitors. Both methods are quite common and work well. Multiple monitors are easy to configure: just plug in the monitors and Windows should detect them. Windows will show the monitors in the applet, as shown in Figure 11.16 for Windows 7. By default, the second monitor is not enabled. To use the second monitor, just select *Extend my Windows desktop onto this monitor* in Windows XP, *Extend the desktop onto this monitor* in Windows Vista, or use the Multiple displays dropdown box and select *Extend these displays* in Windows 7.

If you need to see more advanced settings, click on...that's right, the Advanced or Advanced Settings button in Windows XP/Vista, or on the Advanced settings link in the Screen Resolution dialog box in Windows 7. The title of the dialog

• **Figure 11.16** Enabling multiple monitors

box that opens reflects the monitor and video card. As you can see in Figure 11.17, this particular computer uses a pair of Samsung SyncMaster T220 monitors running off of an ATI Radeon 5750 video card.

 All LCD monitors have a fixed refresh rate.

The two tabs you're most likely to use are the Adapter and Monitor tabs. The Adapter tab gives detailed information about the video card, including the amount of video memory, the graphics processor, and the BIOS information (yup, your video card has a BIOS, too!). You can also click on the List All Modes button to change the current mode of the video card, although any mode you may set here, you can also set in the sliders on the main screen.

If you're still using a CRT, you'll find the Monitor tab a handy place. This is where you can set the refresh rate (see Figure 11.18). Windows only shows refresh rates that the monitor says it can handle, but many monitors can take a faster—and therefore easier on the eyes—refresh rate. To see all of the modes the video card can support, uncheck the *Hide modes that this monitor cannot display* option.

If you try this, always increase the refresh rate in small increments. If the screen looks better, use it. If the screen seems distorted or disappears, wait a moment and Windows will reset to the original refresh rate. Be careful when using modes that Windows says the monitor cannot display. Pushing a CRT past its fastest refresh rate for more than a minute or two can damage it.

• **Figure 11.17** Advanced video settings, Adapter tab

• **Figure 11.18** Advanced video settings, Monitor tab

• **Figure 11.19** Third-party video tab

Most video cards add their own tab to the Advanced dialog box. In the case of the tab shown in Figure 11.19, you'd need to click on the Catalyst Control Center button to see more settings for the video card. What you see here varies by model of card and version of driver, but here's a list of some of the more interesting settings you might see.

Color Correction Sometimes the colors on your monitor are not close enough for your tastes to the actual color you're trying to create. In this case you use color correction to fine-tune the colors on the screen to get the look you want.

Rotation All monitors are by default wider than they are tall. This is called *landscape mode*. Some LCD monitors can be physically rotated to facilitate users who like to see their desktops taller than they are wide (*portrait mode*). Figure 11.20 shows the author's LCD monitor rotated in portrait mode. If you want to rotate your screen, you must tell the system you're rotating it.

Modes Most video cards add very advanced settings to enable you to finely tweak your monitor. These very dangerous settings have names such as "sync polarity" or "front porch" and are outside the scope of both CompTIA A+ certification and the needs of all but the most geeky techs. These settings are mostly used to display a non-standard resolution. Stay out of those settings!

Working with Drivers

Now that you know the locations of the primary video tools within the operating system, it's time to learn about fine-tuning your video. You need to know how to work with video drivers from within the Display (Windows XP/7) and Personalization (Windows Vista) applets, including how to update them, roll back updates, and uninstall them.

Windows is very persnickety when it comes to video card drivers. You can crash Windows and force a reinstallation simply by installing a new video card and not uninstalling the old card's drivers. This doesn't happen every time, but certainly can happen. As a basic rule, always uninstall the old card's drivers before you install drivers for a new card.

When you update the drivers for a card, you have a choice of uninstalling the outdated drivers and then installing new drivers—which makes the process the

same as for installing a new card—or you can let Windows flex some digital muscle and install the new ones right over the older drivers.

To update your drivers, go to the Control Panel and double-click the Display applet (Windows XP and Windows 7) or click the Personalization applet and click Display Settings (Windows Vista). In the Display Properties dialog box in Windows XP, select the Settings tab and click the Advanced button. In Windows Vista's Display Settings dialog box, select the Monitor tab and click the Advanced Settings button. In the Display applet for Windows 7, click *Change display settings* in the Tasks list and then click the *Advanced settings* link. In the dialog box that appears (all versions), click the Adapter tab and then click the Properties button. In the Properties dialog box for your adapter (see Figure 11.21), select the Driver tab and then click the Update Driver button to run the Hardware Update wizard.

3-D Graphics

No other area of the PC world reflects the amazing acceleration of technological improvements more than **3-D graphics**—in particular, 3-D gaming—which attempts to create images with the same depth and texture as objects seen in the real world. We are spectators to an amazing new world where software and hardware race to produce new levels of realism and complexity displayed on the computer screen. Powered by the wallets of tens of millions of PC gamers always demanding more and better, the video industry constantly introduces new video cards and new software titles that make today's games so incredibly realistic and fun. Although the gaming world certainly leads the PC industry in 3-D technologies, many other PC applications—such as *Computer Aided Design* (*CAD*) programs—quickly snatch up these technologies, making 3-D more useful in many ways other than just games. In this section, we'll add to the many bits and pieces of 3-D video encountered over previous chapters in the book and put together an understanding of the function and configuration of 3-D graphics.

Before the early 1990s, PCs did not mix well with 3-D graphics. Certainly, many 3-D applications existed, primarily 3-D design programs such as AutoCAD and Intergraph, but these applications would often run only on expensive, specialized hardware—not so great for casual users.

The big change took place in 1992 when a small company called id Software created a new game

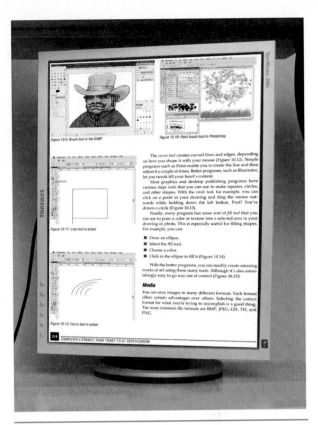

• **Figure 11.20** Portrait mode

• **Figure 11.21** Adapter Properties dialog box

• **Figure 11.22** *Wolfenstein 3D*

• **Figure 11.23** Each figure had a limited number of sprites.

called *Wolfenstein 3D* (see Figure 11.22). They launched an entirely new genre of games, now called *first-person shooters* (*FPSs*), in which the player looks out into a 3-D world, interacting with walls, doors, and other items, and shoots whatever bad guys the game provides.

Wolfenstein 3D shook the PC gaming world to its foundations. That this innovative format came from an upstart little company made *Wolfenstein 3D* and id Software into overnight sensations. Even though their game was demanding on hardware, they gambled that enough people could run it to make it a success. The gamble paid off for John Carmack and John Romero, the creators of id Software, making them the fathers of 3-D gaming.

Early 3-D games used fixed 3-D images called **sprites** to create the 3-D world. A sprite is nothing more than a bitmapped graphic such as a BMP file. These early first-person shooters would calculate the position of an object from the player's perspective and place a sprite to represent the object. Any single object had only a fixed number of sprites—if you walked around an object, you noticed an obvious jerk as the game replaced the current sprite with a new one to represent the new position. Figure 11.23 shows different sprites for the same bad guy in *Wolfenstein 3D*. Sprites weren't pretty, but they worked without seriously taxing the 486s and early Pentiums of the time.

The second generation of 3-D games began to replace sprites with true 3-D objects, which are drastically more complex than sprites. A true 3-D object is composed of a group of points called **vertices**. Each vertex has a defined X, Y, and Z position in a 3-D world. Figure 11.24 shows the vertices for a video game character in a 3-D world.

The computer must track all of the vertices of all of the objects in the 3-D world, including the ones you cannot currently see. Keep in mind that objects may be motionless in the 3-D world (a wall, for example), may have animation (such as a door opening and closing), or may be moving (like bad monsters trying to spray you with evil alien goo). This calculation process is called *transformation* and, as you might imagine, is extremely taxing to most CPUs. Intel's SIMD and AMD's 3DNow! processor extensions were expressly designed to perform transformations.

Once the CPU has determined the positions of all vertices, the system begins to fill in the 3-D object. The process begins by drawing lines (the 3-D term is *edges*) between vertices to build the 3-D object into many triangles. Why triangles? Well, mainly by consensus of game developers. Any shape works, but triangles make the most sense from a mathematical standpoint. I could go into more depth here, but that would require talking about trigonometry, and I'm gambling you'd rather not read that detailed a description! All 3-D games use triangles to connect vertices. The 3-D process then

groups triangles into various shapes called **polygons**. Figure 11.25 shows the same model as Figure 11.24, now displaying all of the connected vertices to create a large number of polygons.

Originally, the CPU handled these calculations to create triangles, but now special 3-D video cards do the job, greatly speeding up the process.

The last step in second-generation games was texturing. Every 3-D game stores a number of image files called **textures**. The program wraps textures around an object to give it a surface. Textures work well to provide dramatic detail without using a lot of triangles. A single object may take one texture or many textures, applied to single triangles or groups of triangles (polygons). Figure 11.26 shows the finished warrior.

True 3-D objects, more often referred to as *rendered*, immediately created the need for massively powerful video cards and much wider data buses. Intel's primary motivation for creating AGP was to provide a big enough pipe for massive data pumping between the video card and the CPU. Intel gave AGP the ability to read system RAM to support textures. If it weren't for 3-D games, AGP (and probably even PCIe) would almost certainly not exist.

3-D Video Cards

No CPU of the mid-1990s could ever hope to handle the massive processes required to render 3-D worlds. Keep in mind that to create realistic movement, the 3-D world must refresh at least 24 times per second. That means that this entire process, from transformation to texturing, must repeat once every 1/24th of a second! Furthermore, although the game re-creates each screen, it must also keep score, track the positions of all of the

• **Figure 11.24** Vertices for a video game warrior

• **Figure 11.25** Connected vertices forming polygons on a 3-D character

• **Figure 11.26** Video game warrior with textures added

objects in the game, provide some type of intelligence to the bad guys, and so on. Something had to happen to take the workload off the CPU. The answer came from video cards.

Video cards were developed with smart onboard GPUs. The GPU helped the CPU by taking over some, and eventually all, of the 3-D rendering duties. These video cards not only have GPUs but also have massive amounts of RAM to store textures.

But a problem exists with this setup: How do we talk to these cards? This is done by means of a device driver, of course, but wouldn't it be great if we could create standard commands to speed up the process? The best thing to do would be to create a standardized set of instructions that any 3-D program could send to a video card to do all of the basic work, such as "make a cone" or "lay texture 237 on the cone you just made."

The video card instructions standards manifested themselves into a series of **application programming interfaces (APIs)**. In essence, an API is a library of commands that people who make 3-D games must use in their programs. The program currently using the video card sends API commands directly to the device driver. Device drivers must know how to understand the API commands. If you were to picture the graphics system of your computer as a layer cake, the top layer would be the program making a call to the video card driver that then directs the graphics hardware.

Several APIs have been developed over the years, with two clear winners among all of them: OpenGL and DirectX. The **OpenGL** standard was developed for UNIX systems but has since been *ported*, or made compatible with, a wide variety of computer systems, including Windows and Apple computers. As the demand for 3-D video became increasingly strong, Microsoft decided to throw its hat into the 3-D graphics ring with its own API, called DirectX. We look at DirectX in depth in the next section.

Although they might accomplish the same task (for instance, translating instructions and passing them on to the video driver), every API handles things just a little bit differently. In some 3-D games, the OpenGL standard might produce more precise images with less CPU overhead than the DirectX standard. In general, however, you won't notice a large difference between the images produced by OpenGL and DirectX.

DirectX and Video Cards

In the old days, many applications communicated directly with much of the PC hardware and, as a result, could crash your computer if not written well enough. Microsoft tried to fix this problem by placing all hardware under the control of Windows, but programmers balked because Windows added too much work for the video process and slowed down everything. For the most demanding programs, such as games, only direct access of hardware would work.

This need to "get around Windows" motivated Microsoft to unveil a new set of protocols called **DirectX**. Programmers use DirectX to take control of certain pieces of hardware and to talk directly to that hardware; it provides the speed necessary to play the advanced games so popular today. The primary impetus for DirectX was to build a series of products to enable Windows to run 3-D games. That's not to say that you couldn't run 3-D games in Windows *before* DirectX; rather, it's just that Microsoft wasn't involved in the API rat race at the time and wanted to be. Microsoft's goal

in developing DirectX was to create a 100-percent stable environment, with direct hardware access, for running 3-D applications and games within Windows.

DirectX is not only for video; it also supports sound, network connections, input devices, and other parts of your PC. Each of these subsets of DirectX has a name, such as DirectDraw, Direct3D, or DirectSound.

- **DirectDraw** Supports direct access to the hardware for 2-D graphics
- **Direct3D** Supports direct access to the hardware for 3-D graphics—the most important part of DirectX
- **DirectInput** Supports direct access to the hardware for joysticks and other game controllers
- **DirectSound** Supports direct access to the hardware for waveforms
- **DirectMusic** Supports direct access to the hardware for MIDI devices
- **DirectPlay** Supports direct access to network devices for multiplayer games
- **DirectShow** Supports direct access to video and presentation devices

Microsoft constantly adds to and tweaks this list. As almost all games need DirectX and all video cards have drivers to support DirectX, you need to verify that DirectX is installed and working properly on your system. To do this, use the **DirectX Diagnostic Tool (dxdiag)**, as shown in Figure 11.27.

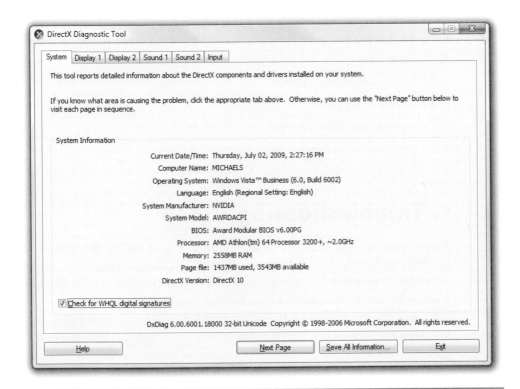

• **Figure 11.27** The DirectX Diagnostic Tool

In Windows XP, you can find it in the System Information program. After you open System Information (it usually lives in the Accessories | System Tools area of the Start menu), click the Tools menu and select DirectX Diagnostic Tool.

For Windows Vista/7, go to Start and type **dxdiag** in the Search bar. Press ENTER to run the program.

The System tab gives the version of DirectX. The system pictured in Figure 11.27 runs DirectX 10.

Cross Check

Keeping DirectX Updated

I always have the latest version of DirectX installed on my system. In my experience, each new version adds functionality and increases stability—both items are extremely important to me. Most versions of Windows have a tool for updating important system files, so flip back to Chapter 8 and run through the steps for updating. What tool should you use to update?

So, what does DirectX do for video cards? Back in the bad old days before DirectX became popular with the game makers, many GPU makers created their own chip-specific APIs. 3dfx had Glide, for example, and S3 had ViRGE. This made buying 3-D games a mess. There would often be multiple versions of the same game for each card. Even worse, many games never used 3-D acceleration because it was just too much work to support all of the different cards.

That all changed when Microsoft beefed up DirectX and got more GPU makers to support it. That in turn enabled the game companies to write games by using DirectX and have them run on any card out there. The bottom line: When Microsoft comes out with a new version of DirectX, all of the GPU companies hurry to support it or they will be left behind.

Trying to decide what video card to buy gives me the shakes—too many options! One good way to narrow down your buying decision is to see what GPU is hot at the moment. I make a point to check out these Web sites whenever I'm getting ready to buy, so I can see what everyone says is the best.

- http://arstechnica.com
- www.hardocp.com
- www.tomshardware.com
- www.sharkyextreme.com

■ Troubleshooting Video

People tend to notice when their monitors stop showing the Windows desktop, making video problems a big issue for technicians. Users might temporarily ignore a bad sound card or other device, but will holler like crazy when the screen doesn't look the way they expect. To fix video problems quickly, the best place to start is to divide your video problems into two groups: video cards/drivers and monitors.

Troubleshooting Video Cards/Drivers

Video cards rarely go bad, so the vast majority of video card/driver problems are bad or incompatible drivers or incorrect settings. Always make sure you have the correct driver installed. If you're using an incompatible driver, Windows defaults to good old 640 × 480, 16-color VGA mode or you might get a Blue Screen of Death (BSoD) as soon as Windows starts to load. A driver that is suddenly corrupted usually doesn't show the problem until the next reboot. If you reboot a system with a corrupted driver, Windows will do one of the following: go into VGA mode, blank the monitor, lock up, or display a garbled screen with weird color patterns or a very distorted image. Whatever the output, reboot into Safe mode and roll back or delete the driver. Keep in mind that more advanced video cards tend to show their drivers as installed programs under Add or Remove Programs in Windows XP or Programs and Features in Windows Vista/7, so always check there first before you try deleting a driver by using Device Manager. Download the latest driver and reinstall.

Video cards are pretty durable, but they have two components that do go bad: the fan and the RAM. Lucky for you, if either of these goes out, it tends to show the same error—bizarre screen outputs followed shortly by a screen lockup. Usually Windows keeps running; you may see your mouse pointer moving around and windows refreshing, but the screen turns into a huge mess (see Figure 11.28).

• **Figure 11.28** Serious video problem

Bad drivers sometimes also make this error, so always first try going into Safe mode to see if the problem suddenly clears up. If it does, you do not have a problem with the video card!

Excessive heat inside the case, even with the video card fan running at full blast, can create some interesting effects. The computer could simply shut down due to overheating. You'll recognize this possible cause because the computer will come back up in a minute or two, but then shut down again as you use it hard and it heats up again. Sometimes the screen will get bizarre artifacts or start distorting. Check your case fans and make sure nothing is too close to the video card. You might need to blow out (outdoors!) the dust from filters, vents, and fans.

The last and probably most common problem is nothing more than improperly configured video settings. Identifying the problem is just common sense—if your monitor is showing everything sideways, someone messed with your rotation settings; if your gorgeous wallpaper of a mountain pass looks like an ugly four-color cartoon, someone lowered the color depth. You'll need to reset the color depth to a more appropriate setting. In Windows XP, open the Display Properties. In Windows Vista, go to Personalization | Display Settings. In Windows 7, go to Display | Change display settings | Advanced settings, then open the Monitor tab.

The one serious configuration issue is pushing the resolution too high. If you adjust your resolution and then your monitor displays an error message such as "Input Signal Out of Range," just wait. Windows will automatically put your settings back after a few seconds if you don't click on anything.

Troubleshooting Monitors

Because of the inherent dangers of the high-frequency and high-voltage power required by monitors, and because proper adjustment requires specialized training, this section concentrates on giving a support person the information necessary to decide whether a trouble call is warranted. Virtually no monitor manufacturers make schematics of their monitors available to the public, because of liability issues regarding possible electrocution. To simplify troubleshooting, look at the process as three separate parts: common monitor problems, external adjustments, and internal adjustments.

Common Monitor Problems

Although I'm not super comfortable diving into the guts of a monitor, you can fix a substantial percentage of monitor problems yourself. The following list describes the most common monitor problems and tells you what to do—even when that means sending it to someone else.

- Almost all CRT and LCD monitors have replaceable controls. If the Brightness knob or Menu button stops working or seems loose, check with the manufacturer for replacement controls. They usually come as a complete package.

- For problems with ghosting, streaking, and/or fuzzy vertical edges, check the cable connections and the cable itself. These problems rarely apply to monitors; more commonly, they point to the video card.

- If one color is missing, check cables for breaks or bent pins. Check the front controls for that color. If the color adjustment is already maxed out, the monitor will require internal service.

- As monitors age, they lose brightness. If the brightness control is turned all of the way up and the picture seems dim, the monitor will require internal adjustment. This is a good argument for power-management functions. Use the power switch or the power-management options in Windows to turn off the monitor after a certain amount of time.

Common Problems Specific to CRTs

The complexity of CRTs compared to LCDs requires us to look at a number of monitor problems unique to CRTs. Most of these problems require opening the monitor, so be careful! When in doubt, take it to a repair shop.

- Most out-of-focus monitors can be fixed. Focus adjustments are usually on the inside, somewhere close to the flyback transformer. This is the transformer that provides power to the high-voltage anode.

- Hissing or sparking sounds are often indicative of an insulation rupture on the flyback transformer. This sound is usually accompanied by the smell of ozone. If your monitor has these symptoms, it definitely needs a qualified technician. Having replaced a flyback transformer once myself, I can say it is not worth the hassle and potential loss of life and limb.

- Big color blotches or discoloration on the display are an easy and cheap repair. Find the Degauss button and use it. If your monitor doesn't have a Degauss button, you can purchase a special tool called a degaussing coil at any electronics store.

- Bird-like chirping sounds occurring at regular intervals usually indicate a problem with the monitor power supply.

- Suppose you got a good deal on a used 19-inch monitor, but the display is kind of dark, even though you have the brightness turned up all the way. This dim image points to a dying CRT. So, how about replacing the CRT? Forget it. Even if the monitor was free, it just isn't worth it; a replacement tube runs into the hundreds of dollars. Nobody ever sold a monitor because it was too bright and too sharp. Save your money and buy a new monitor.

- If the monitor displays only a single horizontal or vertical line, the problem is probably between the main circuit board and the yoke, or a blown yoke coil. This definitely requires a service call.

- A single white dot on an otherwise black screen means the high-voltage flyback transformer is most likely shot. Take it into the repair shop.

External Adjustments

Monitor adjustments range from the simplest—brightness and contrast—to the more sophisticated—pincushioning and trapezoidal adjustments. The

external controls provide users with the opportunity to fine-tune the monitor's image. Many monitors have controls for changing the tint and saturation of color, although plenty of monitors put those controls inside the monitor. Better monitors enable you to square up the visible portion of the screen with the monitor housing.

Finally, most monitors have the ability to **degauss** themselves with the push of a button. Over time, the shadow mask picks up a weak magnetic charge that interferes with the focus of the electron beams. This magnetic field makes the image look slightly fuzzy and streaked. Most monitors have a special built-in circuit called a *degaussing coil* to eliminate this magnetic buildup. When the degaussing circuit is used, an alternating current is sent through a coil of wire surrounding the CRT, and this current generates an alternating magnetic field that demagnetizes the shadow mask. You activate the degaussing coil by using the Degauss button or menu selection on the monitor. Degaussing usually makes a rather nasty thunk sound and the screen goes crazy for a moment—don't worry, that's normal.

> ⚠️ Internal CRT adjustments should be left to the professional monitor techs.

Troubleshooting LCDs

With the proliferation of LCD panels in the computing world, PC techs need to have some understanding of what to do when they break. Some of the components you can fix, including replacing some of the internal components. I tend to use monitor repair shops for most LCD issues, but let's take a look.

An LCD monitor may have bad pixels. A bad pixel is any single pixel that does not react the way it should. A pixel that never lights up is a *dead pixel*, a pixel that is stuck on pure white is a lit pixel, and a pixel on a certain color is a stuck pixel. You cannot repair bad pixels; the panel must be replaced. All LCD panel makers allow a certain number of bad pixels, even on a brand-new LCD monitor! You need to check the warranty for your monitor and see how many they allow before you may return the monitor.

- If your LCD monitor cracks, it is not repairable and must be replaced.

- A flickering image with an LCD usually points to either a very inexpensive panel with too much light bleed from the backlight or a dying CCFL backlight. LEDs don't flicker, so you won't see this issue with those types of LCDs. Replace the backlight if necessary.

- A dim image, especially on only the top or bottom half of the screen, points to a dead or dying backlight in a multibacklight system. Replace as necessary.

- If the LCD goes dark but you can still barely see the image under bright lights, you lost either the backlight or the inverter. In many cases, especially with super-thin panels, you'll replace the entire panel and backlight as a unit. On the other hand, an inverter can be on a separate circuit board that you can replace, such as the one pictured in Figure 11.29.

- If your LCD makes a distinct hissing noise, an inverter is about to fail. Again, you can replace the inverter if need be.

CCFL backlight Power supply/inverters

Timing control Main board/logic

• **Figure 11.29** LCD components labeled

Be careful if you open an LCD to work on the inside. The inverter can bite you in several ways. First, it's powered by a high-voltage electrical circuit that can give you a nasty shock. Worse, the inverter will retain a charge for a few minutes after you unplug it, so unplug and wait for a bit. Second, inverters get very hot and present a very real danger of burning you at a touch. Again, wait for a while after you unplug it to try to replace it. Finally, if you shock an inverter, you might irreparably damage it. So use proper ESD-avoidance techniques.

Bottom line on fixing LCD monitors? You can find companies that sell replacement parts for LCDs, but repairing an LCD is difficult, and there are folks who will do it for you faster and cheaper than you can. Search for a specialty LCD repair company. Hundreds of these companies exist all over the world.

Cleaning Monitors

Cleaning monitors is easy. Always use antistatic monitor wipes or at least a general antistatic cloth. Some LCD monitors may require special cleaning equipment. Never use window cleaners that contain ammonia or any liquid because getting liquid into the monitor may create a shocking experience! Many commercial cleaning solutions will also melt older LCD screens, which is never a good thing.

Safety Concerns

Aside from avoiding the inside of a CRT, the biggest safety issues involve moving and recycling monitors. Always practice good cable management, especially if you have the back of the monitor area exposed to traffic. One accidental hook of a monitor cable could cause it to come crashing to the floor. They don't do too well with impact.

CRTs are heavy, even the small ones, and the ones likely still in use are probably the graphics workstation 20+-inch units. Use proper lifting techniques (use your legs, not your back) and be careful when you place the monitor on lighter-weight shelves or stands. Monitor stands all have weight limitations.

CompTIA is not much interested in mounting LCD monitors to wall mounts, but all of the wall mounts have fairly strict weight limitations as well. Don't hang that lovely new 24-inch panel on a mount designed to handle the weight of a 17-inch unit!

Finally, you should always take a monitor—CRT or LED—to a proper recycling center. They have toxic chemicals such as lead and mercury and should never be placed in a landfill.

Troubleshooting Playback

One of the odd "video" issues techs run into today is when a Blu-ray Disc or downloaded HD movie won't play and the user gets the error message that his or her display won't play that media. Figure 11.30 shows the dreaded message from iTunes that says you can't play the movie you just rented.

Note the fine print under the generic comment: ". . . display that supports HDCP." The HDCP part is the key here.

• **Figure 11.30** HDCP erro

Intel created the High-bandwidth Digital Content Protection (HDCP) standard to help movie makers ensure copyright protection and stop pirates from stealing copyright-protected content. It's not just the monitor that must support HDCP; every part of the connection between the video card and the monitor must support it. The monitor that captured the screenshot in Figure 11.30 most assuredly is HDCP compliant, as is the video card. The error appeared because the monitor connects to the video card through a VGA cable.

Only HDMI, DVI, and DisplayPort cables support HDCP. VGA does not, which is one of the major differences among the standards. Note also that HDCP can bite you when using converters too, like Mini HDMI to Standard HDMI, so always check that as well.

Beyond A+

• **Figure 11.31** DLP chip (photo courtesy of Texas Instruments)

DLP

Digital Light Processing (*DLP*) displays use a chip covered in microscopically small mirrors (see Figure 11.31).

These individual mirrors move thousands of times per second toward and away from a light source. The more times per second they move toward a light source, the whiter the image; the fewer times they move, the grayer the image. See Figure 11.32 for a diagram of how the mirrors would appear in a microscopic close-up of the chip. The lamp projects through a color wheel onto the DLP chip. The DLP chip creates the image by moving the tiny mirrors, which in turn reflect onto the screen.

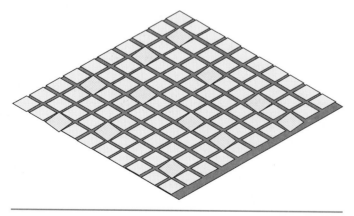

• **Figure 11.32** Microscopic close-up of DLP showing tiny mirrors— note that some are tilted.

DLP was very popular for a time in home theater systems, as it makes an amazingly rich image. DLP has had very little impact on PC monitors, but has had great success in projectors. DLP projectors are much more expensive than LCD projectors, but many customers feel the extra expense is worth the image quality.

Chapter Summary

After reading this chapter and completing the exercises, you should understand the following about video.

Install and configure video

- During the physical install of a video card, be conscious of long cards and proximity to other PCI cards. Long cards simply don't fit in some cases, and close proximity to other expansion cards can cause overheating.

- Video card drivers install pretty much the same as all other drivers: either the driver is already built into Windows or you must use the installation media that comes with the video card.

- As a basic rule, always uninstall an old video card's drivers before you install drivers for a new card.

- The Display applet (Windows XP) or Personalization applet (Windows Vista) provides a convenient, central location for adjusting all of your display settings, including resolution, refresh rate, driver information, and color depth. Windows 7 splits its display controls across both the Display applet and the Personalization applet.

- In Windows XP's Display applet, the Screen Saver tab provides access to the power-management settings. In Windows Vista and Windows 7, this is an option in the Personalization applet.

- The Settings tab in Windows XP's Display applet provides access for configuring all of your video settings, such as resolution, color depth, and dual monitor configuration. The Settings tab also provides an Advanced button for access to the Monitor tab. The Monitor tab enables you to set the refresh rate for your CRT monitor. Most video cards add their own tabs to the Advanced section. In Windows Vista, all of these controls are contained within the Personalization | Display Settings option. In Windows 7, these controls are found within the Display | Change display settings option.

- You can configure dual monitors by using a video card with two monitor connectors or by using two video cards. Either way, once both monitors are connected, you can enable the second monitor in Windows XP from the Display applet's Settings tab, in Windows Vista from the Personalization | Display Settings option, and in Windows 7 from the Display | Change display settings option.

- Early 3-D games used sprites to create a 3-D world. Later games replaced sprites with true 3-D objects composed of vertices. Bitmap textures are used to tile a section of the screen to provide a surface in the 3-D world.

- Video cards use a series of APIs to translate instructions for the video device driver. If you were to picture the graphics system of your computer as a layer cake, the top layer would be the program making a call to the graphics hardware. The next layer is the API. The device driver comes next, and way down at the base of the cake is the actual graphics hardware: RAM, graphics processor, and RAMDAC. OpenGL and DirectX are the most popular APIs.

- DirectX includes several subsets, including DirectDraw, Direct3D, DirectInput, DirectSound, DirectMusic, DirectPlay, and DirectShow. You can verify your DirectX installation via the DirectX Diagnostics Tool, which is found in Windows XP under the Tools menu of the System Information utility and in Windows Vista/7 by typing **dxdiag** in the Start | Search bar.

Troubleshoot basic video problems

- Video problems may be divided into two categories: video cards/drivers and monitors.

- If your screen is black or garbled, or Windows freezes after you install a video card driver, reboot into Safe mode and roll back or delete the driver. Check Add or Remove Programs in Windows XP and Programs and Features in Windows Vista/7 first, as many video card drivers show up there. If Safe mode doesn't fix the problem, you may have a bad video card that needs to be replaced.

- All monitors have replaceable hardware controls (knobs and buttons). Check with the manufacturer for replacement parts. Ghosting, streaking, or fuzzy images may mean a bad or improperly connected video cable, or the video card may be the cause.

- Because monitors have high-voltage power that can harm or kill you, always leave it to the trained professional to work inside the monitor. Many CRT monitors have a button to degauss themselves. When the shadow mask picks up a weak magnetic charge, it interferes with the focus of the electron beams, making the monitor appear fuzzy or streaked. A built-in circuit called a degaussing coil generates an alternating magnetic field that eliminates the magnetic buildup on the shadow mask.

- Clean CRT monitors with an antistatic monitor wipe. Never use window cleaners or other liquids. LCD monitors need special cleaning equipment or a soft, damp cloth.

- Common monitor problems are often related to cable breaks or bent pins. Monitors also lose brightness over time, especially if you are not using the power-management functions.

- For best performance, keep the screen clean, use power management, don't block the ventilation slots, and don't leave the monitor on all of the time, even with a screensaver. If the monitor is dead, use proper disposal methods.

- A cracked LCD monitor must be replaced. If the LCD screen goes dark, starts to hiss, or develops bad pixels, it is best to either replace the monitor or find a company specializing in LCD repair.

Key Terms

3-D graphics *(433)*

application programming interfaces (APIs) *(436)*

degauss *(442)*

DirectX *(436)*

DirectX Diagnostic Tool (dxdiag) *(437)*

Display applet *(424)*

OpenGL *(436)*

Personalization applet *(424)*

polygons *(435)*

sprites *(434)*

textures *(435)*

vertices *(434)*

Key Term Quiz

Use the Key Terms list to complete the sentences that follow. Not all terms will be used.

1. A(n) _____ is an image applied on top of a 3-D model.

2. In Windows Vista and 7, you can change your desktop image using the _____.

3. DirectX is one of a number of _____, programs that translate instructions for the video device driver.

4. Before computer games used 3-D graphics, they would use _____.

5. A 3-D model is made up of _____ at its most basic level.

6. If your monitor displays big color blotches, it indicates that you should _____ the monitor to eliminate the magnetic buildup on the shadow mask.

7. Vertices joined together create shapes called _____.

8. To check which version of DirectX you have, you would use the _____.

9. _____ is a 3-D graphics API originally developed for UNIX.

■ Multiple-Choice Quiz

1. If one of the colors is missing on the monitor and you cannot fix the problem by adjusting the front controls, you should then check for _____.

 A. A refresh rate that is set higher than that recommended by the manufacturer

 B. A corrupted video driver

 C. A broken cable or bent pins

 D. Misconvergence

2. What are some signs of a corrupted video card driver? (Select all that apply.)

 A. Garbled video

 B. Windows boots into VGA mode

 C. You lose Internet connectivity

 D. Monitor goes blank

3. Which of the following problems would make it impossible to repair an LCD monitor?

 A. A blown yoke coil

 B. A broken LCD panel

 C. A bad flyback transformer

 D. Misconvergence

4. A computer that keeps shutting down after a few minutes of heavy 3-D gaming is probably suffering from:

 A. Overheating

 B. Bad RAM

 C. Improperly installed video card

 D. VGA mode

5. What should you use to clean CRT monitors?

 A. Window cleaner

 B. Water

 C. Bleach

 D. Microfiber cloth

6. If the monitor displays only a single horizontal or vertical line, the problem is likely to be caused by a _____.

 A. Bad flyback transformer

 B. Blown yoke coil

 C. Bad monitor power supply

 D. Bad electron gun

7. When should you open a CRT monitor to work inside it?

 A. If the screen goes dark

 B. If the degausser stops working

 C. You should never open a CRT monitor

 D. If the power cord needs replacing

8. In Windows XP, how do you get to the power management settings?

 A. Control Panel | Power Management

 B. Through the Screen Saver tab of the Display applet

 C. The Power Management icon in the notification area

 D. Control Panel | Power Options

9. How would you check what version of DirectX you have installed?

 A. dxdiag

 B. dxver

 C. directxdiag

 D. dxconfig

10. Which video connectors support HDCP?

 A. DisplayPort

 B. VGA

 C. HDMI

 D. DVI

11. What is the most popular API used by 3-D game developers?

 A. DirectX

 B. OpenGL

 C. DigitalDirector

 D. RAMDAC

12. What tool enables you to test 3-D video in a modern PC?

 A. DirectX

 B. dxdiag

 C. OpenGL

 D. NVIDIA

13. Which Control Panel applet in Windows 7 enables you to change settings involving how the monitor shows text and the Windows theme that determines the colors of boxes and other visual items?

 A. Display

 B. Personalization

 C. System

 D. Visualization

Essay Quiz

1. The editor of your company's newsletter has asked you to prepare a short article for next month's edition that explains how to care for monitors to extend their lifespan. Explain at least four things that the average user can do.

2. Dave and Shannon disagree about whether the monitor should stay on all of the time or not. Dave says it's okay to leave the monitor on as long as you have a screensaver. Shannon disagrees, saying the monitor will become dim and burn out sooner if you leave it on. Dave thinks that leaving it on actually extends its life because turning the monitor on and off is bad for it. They've called you to save their monitor and their marriage. What will you tell them?

3. You've been tasked to write a guide for new users of Windows 7, specifically how to tailor their screens to suit their eyes and sensibilities. Write a short essay discussing the appropriate Control Panel applets and the various things they can do.

4. Your company just hired two new technicians. You've been tapped to teach them what they can and cannot do to troubleshoot and repair an LCD monitor. What will you tell them?

Lab Projects

• Lab Project 11.1

If you just received a $500 bonus and decided to buy a new video system for your computer, what would you select? Go to the local computer store or to Web sites such as www.newegg.com and pick out the best combination of monitor and video card that you can buy with your bonus. Now imagine that you also received a $200 birthday gift and have decided to purchase an even better graphics card and monitor. Which ones will you select now that you have $700 to spend?

• Lab Project 11.2

Monitors are not the only output device for the computer. Research one of the following devices and prepare a short essay for the class about how the device works and its features, cost, and connections.

- Rearview projectors
- Plasma monitors
- Touch screens

Ethernet and TCP/IP

In this chapter, you will learn how to

- **Install and troubleshoot structured cabling**
- **Explain the basics of TCP/IP**

Networks dominate the modern computing environment. A vast percentage of businesses have PCs connected in a small local area network (LAN), and big businesses simply can't survive without connecting their many offices into a single wide area network (WAN). Even the operating systems of today demand networks. Windows XP, Vista, and 7, for example, come out of the box *assuming* you'll attach them to the Internet just to make them work past 30 days (product activation), and they get all indignant if you don't.

Because networks are so common today, every good tech needs to know the basics of networking technology, operating systems, implementation, and troubleshooting. Accordingly, this chapter teaches you how to build and troubleshoot a basic network. First, let's move beyond basic switches and UTP cables with RJ-45 connectors and discover how real-world networks connect using alternatives to RJ-45, such as fiber. You'll see how professionals use a concept called "structured cabling" with wired networks to ensure their reliability and ease of use. I'll even show you the tools needed to make your own structured cable system.

The second part of this chapter gets down and dirty into TCP/IP and how Windows uses it in a typical network. I'll break down the TCP/IP protocol so you can appreciate how it works.

Next, we'll go through the process of setting up a small network from start to finish. This includes details on planning a network, installing and configuring NICs, setting up switches, configuring TCP/IP—everything you need so that Windows will enable you to share folders, printers, libraries, and so on.

The chapter closes with a popular topic: troubleshooting a network. Windows comes with plenty of powerful tools to help you when the network stops functioning. I'll show you the tools and combine that with a troubleshooting process that helps you get a network up and running again.

This chapter only covers local area networks, such as a group of computers in a single office. We'll save connecting to the Internet for Chapter 14. But be ready! You need to understand everything in this chapter before you can take the next step and connect to the Internet.

Beyond Basic Ethernet Cabling

Ethernet is the dominant networking technology, and unshielded twisted-pair (UTP) wired Ethernet networks using RJ-45 connectors are the most dominant form of Ethernet. We're going to look at several network technologies, starting with alternatives to UTP, touring some of the more unique devices you might see in a network, and learning about proper cabling.

Know your cable types for the CompTIA A+ 220-802 exam: STP, UTP, CAT 3, CAT 5, CAT 5e, and CAT 6. Recall the differences between plenum-grade cable and PVC-sheathed cables.

Alternative Connections

UTP is very popular, but Ethernet, as well as other types of networks, can use alternative cabling that you need to be able to identify. Every CompTIA A+ certified tech needs to know about fiber optic cabling and coaxial cable, so let's start there.

Fiber Optic

Fiber optic cable is a very attractive way to transmit Ethernet network frames. First, because it uses light instead of electricity, fiber optic cable is immune to electrical problems such as lightning, short circuits, and static. Second, fiber optic signals travel much farther, 2000 meters or more (compared with 100 meters on UTP). Most fiber Ethernet networks use *62.5/125 multimode* fiber optic cable. All fiber Ethernet networks that use this type of cabling require two cables. Figure 12.1 shows three of the more common connectors used in fiber optic networks. Square *SC* connectors are shown in the middle and on the right, and the round *ST* connector is on the left.

Like many other fiber optic connectors, the SC and ST connectors are half-duplex, meaning data flows only one way—hence the need for two cables in a fiber installation. Newer and higher-end fiber installations use connectors with names like LC or MT-RJ.

Tech Tip

Crossover Cables
You can hook two network cards directly together using a special UTP cable called a **crossover cable**. *A crossover cable is a standard UTP cable with one RJ-45 connector using the 568A standard and the other using the 568B standard. This reverses the signal between sending and receiving wires and thus does the job of a hub or switch. Crossover cables work great as a quick way to network two PCs. You can purchase a crossover cable at any computer store.*

Cables can also be full-duplex, meaning that they transfer data both ways. Most modern NICs are autosensing, so that they work with both types of cables.

• **Figure 12.1** Typical fiber optic cables with connectors

> 💡 Know fiber connector types and the difference between multimode and single-mode fiber.

> 💡 There are a number of Ethernet standards that use fiber optic cable instead of UTP.

• **Figure 12.2** Typical coax

Multimode and Single-Mode Light can be sent down a fiber optic cable as regular light or as laser light. Each type of light requires totally different fiber optic cables. Most network technologies that use fiber optics use light-emitting diodes (LEDs) to send light signals. These use *multimode* fiber optic cabling. Multimode fiber transmits multiple light signals at the same time, each using a different reflection angle within the core of the cable. The multiple reflection angles tend to disperse over long distances, so multimode fiber optic cables are used for relatively short distances.

Network technologies that use laser light use *single-mode* fiber optic cabling. Using laser light and single-mode fiber optic cables allows for phenomenally high transfer rates over long distances. Except for long-distance links, single-mode is currently quite rare; if you see fiber optic cabling, you can be relatively sure it is multimode.

There are close to 100 different Ethernet fiber optic cabling standards, with names like 1000BaseSX and 10GBaseSR. The major difference is the speed of the network (there are also some important differences in the way systems interconnect, and so on). If you want to use fiber optic cabling, you need a fiber optic switch and fiber optic network cards, and they're not cheap. The fiber optic cabling itself is delicate, expensive, and difficult to use, so it is usually reserved for use in data centers and is rarely used to connect desktop PCs.

Fiber networks follow the speed and distance limitations of their networking standard, so it's hard to pin down precise numbers on true limitations. Multimode overall is slower and has a shorter range than single-mode. A typical multimode network runs at 10, 100, or 1000 Mbps, though some can go to 10,000 Mbps. Distances for multimode runs generally top out at ~600 meters. With single-mode, speed and distance—depending on the standard—can blow multimode away. The record transmission speed in 2011, for example, was 100 *terabits* per second and that was over 100 *miles*!

Coax/BNC

Early versions of Ethernet ran on **coaxial cable** instead of UTP. While the Ethernet standards using coax are long gone, coax lives on in the networking world, primarily for cable modems and satellite connections. Coax cable consists of a center cable (core) surrounded by insulation. This in turn is covered with a *shield* of braided cable (see Figure 12.2). The center core actually carries the signal. The shield effectively eliminates outside interference. The entire cable is then surrounded by a protective insulating cover.

Coax cables are rated using an RG name. There are hundreds of RG ratings for coax, but the only two you need to know for the CompTIA A+ 802 exam are RG-59 and RG-6. Both standards are rated by impedance, which is measured in ohms. Both RG-6 and RG-59 have a 75-ohm impedance. Both of these coax cables are used by your cable television, but RG-59 is thinner and doesn't carry data quite as far as RG-6. The RG rating is clearly marked on the cable.

• **Figure 12.3** BNC connector

• **Figure 12.4** F-type connector

Coax most often uses two different types of connectors. A BNC connector (see Figure 12.3) uses a quarter twist connector, and an F-type connector uses a screw connector. BNC is uncommon, but F-type is on the back of all cable modems and most televisions (see Figure 12.4).

> There is no hard limit to how fast coaxial cable can transmit data. Most cable broadband Internet implementations, however, top out at around 50 Mbps.

Network Devices

Now that we've covered the various wires and connectors used in networking, let's look at the devices that connect all those wires together.

Hubs

Hubs were the main interconnection for older Ethernet networks (see Figure 12.5). Any incoming signal on any port on a hub is re-created (repeated) and sent out on every connected port on the hub. The downside to hubs is that all connected devices have to share the total bandwidth. Hubs are extremely rare today, having been replaced by switches.

• **Figure 12.5** Typical hubs

Switches

Switches are the current most common interconnection for Ethernet networks (see Figure 12.6). A **switch** looks like a hub, but a switch automatically creates point-to-point connections between any two computers. By separating every connection, each computer can use the full bandwidth of the switch.

Bridges

If someone knows Morse code, it doesn't matter what medium you use to communicate the patterns of a coded method. You can blink a flashlight in his or her face, beat on a bongo drum, or tap into a telegraph machine: the person will understand the code. Ethernet functions

• **Figure 12.6** Typical switch

similarly. The code for Ethernet is the same no matter what medium transfers that message. That means you can easily connect two Ethernet networks that use completely different media internally, such as UTP to fiber or maybe UTP to wireless. In these cases you need a device called a bridge. A **bridge** will always have two interfaces, one interface for each of the different media (see Figure 12.7).

Networked Attached Storage (NAS)

You already know that networks enable you to share files and services with multiple PCs. In most cases, network administrators store files on a server system. This server might be a dedicated file server—a machine running Windows Server 2008 R2, for example—or it might just be someone's regular Windows machine with a shared folder. You can also use a *networked attached storage* (*NAS*) system. A NAS is basically a headless system (no monitor, no keyboard, and no mouse) that you plug into a network (Figure 12.8). A NAS is almost totally self-configuring, requiring only a name and network type (domain/workgroup).

Understand that a NAS only does one thing: share its hard drives. Almost all NAS devices use some form of Web interface for configuration, enabling you to control the NAS from a Web browser on any PC in the network.

There are hundreds of different NAS solutions to choose from. For most people, the big criteria are storage capacity, RAID options, and ease of configuration.

> We tend to use the term *network appliance* for any headless computer (that is, one with no direct interface) designed to do very specific duties. A NAS box is a perfect example of a network appliance.

• **Figure 12.7** Typical bridge

• **Figure 12.8** Typical NAS

Routers

A **router** connects LANs together using the TCP/IP protocol. By definition, a router must have at least two connections—one into a network, and one out to another network. Some more powerful routers have many more connections. Figure 12.9 shows a typical home router.

• **Figure 12.9** Typical home router

The CompTIA A+ 220-802 exam assumes you have a basic understanding of how routers work. To detail the process, I'll need to dive a bit deeper into TCP/IP. Check out the "TCP/IP" section later in this chapter.

The CompTIA A+ 802 exam expects you to know the differences between hubs, routers, switches, bridges, and access points.

Structured Cabling

If you want a functioning, dependable, real-world network, you need a solid understanding of a set of standards collectively called **structured cabling**. These standards, defined by the Telecommunications Industry Association/Electronic Industries Alliance (TIA/EIA)—yes, the same folks who tell you how to crimp an RJ-45 onto the end of a UTP cable—give professional cable installers detailed standards on every aspect of a cabled network, from the type of cabling to use to standards on running cable in walls, even the position of wall outlets.

The CompTIA A+ 802 exam requires you to understand the basic concepts involved in installing network cabling and to recognize the components used in a network. The CompTIA A+ 802 exam does not, however, expect you to be as knowledgeable as a professional network designer or cable installer. Your goal should be to understand enough about real-world cabling systems to communicate knowledgeably with cable installers and to perform basic troubleshooting. Granted, by the end of this section, you'll know enough to try running your own cable (I certainly run my own cable), but consider that knowledge extra credit.

A structured cabling system is useful for more than just computer networks. You'll find structured cabling defining telephone networks and video conferencing setups, for example.

The idea of structured cabling is to create a safe, reliable cabling infrastructure for all of the devices that may need interconnection. Certainly this applies to computer networks, but also to telephone, video—anything that might need low-power, distributed cabling.

You should understand three issues with structured cabling. Cable basics start the picture, with switches, cabling, and PCs. You'll then look at the components of a network, such as how the cable runs through the walls and where it ends up. This section wraps up with an assessment of connections leading outside your network.

Cable Basics—A Star Is Born

Before going through this chapter, consider a LAN in its most basic configuration: a switch, some UTP cable, and a few PCs—in other words, a typical physical star network (see Figure 12.10).

• **Figure 12.10** A switch connected by UTP cable to two PCs

No law of physics prevents you from placing a switch in the middle of your office and running cables on the floor to all the computers in your network. This setup works, but it falls apart spectacularly when applied to a real-world environment. Three problems present themselves to the network tech. First, the exposed cables running along the floor are just waiting for someone to trip over them, giving that person a wonderful lawsuit opportunity. Simply moving and stepping on the cabling will, over time, cause a cable to fail due to wires breaking or RJ-45 connectors ripping off cable ends. Second, the presence of other electrical devices close to the cable can create interference that confuses the signals going through the wire. Third, this type of setup limits your ability to make any changes to the network. Before you can change anything, you have to figure out which cables in the huge rat's nest of cables connected to the switch go to which machines. Imagine *that* troubleshooting nightmare!

"Gosh," you're thinking (okay, I'm thinking it, but you should be, too), "there must be a better way to install a physical network." A better installation would provide safety, protecting the star from vacuum cleaners, clumsy coworkers, and electrical interference. It would have extra hardware to organize and protect the cabling. Finally, the new and improved star network installation would feature a cabling standard with the flexibility to enable the network to grow according to its needs and then to upgrade when the next great network technology comes along. That is the definition of structured cabling.

Structured Cable Network Components

Successful implementation of a basic structured cabling network requires three essential ingredients: a telecommunications room, horizontal cabling, and a work area. Let's zero in on one floor of a typical office. All the cabling runs from individual PCs to a central location, the **telecommunications room** (see Figure 12.11). What equipment goes in there—a switch or a telephone system—is not the important thing. What matters is that all the cables concentrate in this one area.

All cables run horizontally (for the most part) from the telecommunications room to the PCs. This cabling is called, appropriately, **horizontal cabling**. A single piece of installed horizontal cabling is called a **run**. At the opposite end of the horizontal cabling from the telecommunications room is the work area. The **work area** is often simply an office or cubicle that potentially contains a PC and a telephone. Figure 12.12 shows both the horizontal cabling and work areas.

Telecommunications room

• **Figure 12.11** Telecommunications room

Each of the three parts of a basic star network—the telecommunications room, the horizontal cabling, and the work area(s)—must follow a series of strict standards designed to ensure that the cabling system is reliable and easy to manage. The cabling standards set by TIA/EIA enable techs to make sensible decisions on equipment installed in the telecommunications room, so let's tackle horizontal cabling first, and then return to the telecommunications room. We'll finish up with the work area.

Horizontal Cabling A horizontal cabling run is the cabling that goes more or less horizontally from a work area to the telecommunications room. In most networks, this cable is a CAT 5e or better UTP, but when you move into structured cabling, the TIA/EIA standards define a number of other aspects of the cable, such as the type of wires, number of pairs of wires, and fire ratings.

• **Figure 12.12** Horizontal cabling and work area

Solid Core Versus Stranded Core All UTP cables come in one of two types: solid core or stranded core. Each wire in **solid core** UTP uses a single solid wire. With **stranded core**, each wire is actually a bundle of tiny wire strands. Each of these cable types has its benefits and downsides. Solid core is a better conductor, but it is stiff and will break if handled too often or too roughly. Stranded core is not quite as good a conductor, but it will stand up to substantial handling without breaking. Figure 12.13 shows a close-up of solid and stranded core UTP.

TIA/EIA specifies that horizontal cabling should always be solid core. Remember, this cabling is going into your walls and ceilings, safe from the harmful effects of shoes and vacuum cleaners. The ceilings and walls enable you to take advantage of the better conductivity of solid core without the

A single piece of cable that runs from a work area to a telecommunications room is called a *run*. In most networks, this cable is CAT 5e or better UTP.

The Telecommunications Industry Association/Electronic Industries Alliance (TIA/EIA) establishes various industry-wide standards in the technology sector.

• **Figure 12.13** Solid and stranded core UTP

• **Figure 12.14** A short equipment rack

Equipment racks evolved out of the railroad signaling racks from the 19th century. The components in a rack today obviously differ a lot from railroad signaling, but the 19-inch width has remained the standard for well over 100 years.

• **Figure 12.15** A floor-to-ceiling rack

risk of cable damage. Stranded cable also has an important function in a structured cabling network, but I need to discuss a few more parts of the network before I talk about where to use stranded UTP cable.

The Telecommunications Room

The telecommunications room is the heart of the basic star. This room is where all the horizontal runs from all the work areas come together. The concentration of all this gear in one place makes the telecommunications room potentially one of the messiest parts of the basic star. Even if you do a nice, neat job of organizing the cables when they are first installed, networks change over time. People move computers, new work areas are added, network topologies are added or improved, and so on. Unless you impose some type of organization, this conglomeration of equipment and cables decays into a nightmarish mess.

Fortunately, the TIA/EIA structured cabling standards define the use of specialized components in the telecommunications room that make organizing a snap. In fact, it might be fair to say that there are too many options! To keep it simple, we're going to stay with the most common telecommunications room setup and then take a short peek at some other fairly common options.

Equipment Racks The central component of every telecommunications room is one or more equipment racks. An **equipment rack** provides a safe, stable platform for all the different hardware components. All equipment racks are 19 inches wide, but they vary in height from two- to three-foot-high models that bolt onto a wall (see Figure 12.14) to the more popular floor-to-ceiling models (see Figure 12.15).

You can mount almost any network hardware component into a rack. All manufacturers make rack-mounted switches that mount into a rack with a few screws. These switches are available with a wide assortment of ports and capabilities. There are even rack-mounted servers, complete with slide-out keyboards, and rack-mounted uninterruptible power supplies (UPSs) to power the equipment (see Figure 12.16).

All rack-mounted equipment uses a height measurement known simply as a **U**. A U is 1.75 inches. A device that fits in a 1.75-inch space is called a 1U; a device designed for a 3.5-inch space is a 2U; and a device that goes into a 7-inch space is called a 4U. Most rack-mounted devices are 1U, 2U, or 4U. The rack in Figure 12.15 is called a 42U rack to reflect the total number of Us it can hold.

Patch Panels and Cables Ideally, once you install horizontal cabling, you should never move it. As you know, UTP horizontal cabling has a solid core, making it pretty stiff. Solid core cables can handle some rearranging,

• **Figure 12.16** A rack-mounted UPS

but if you insert a wad of solid core cables directly into your switches, every time you move a cable to a different port on the switch, or move the switch itself, you will jostle the cable. You don't have to move a solid core cable many times before one of the solid copper wires breaks, and there goes a network connection!

Luckily for you, you can easily avoid this problem by using a patch panel. A **patch panel** is simply a box with a row of female connectors (ports) in the front and permanent connections in the back, to which you connect the horizontal cables (see Figure 12.17).

• **Figure 12.17** Typical patch panels

The most common type of patch panel today uses a special type of connecter called a **110 block**, or sometimes a *110-punchdown block*. UTP cables connect to a 110 block using a **punchdown tool**. Figure 12.18 shows a typical punchdown tool, and Figure 12.19 shows the punchdown tool punching down individual strands.

The punchdown block has small metal-lined grooves for the individual wires. The punchdown tool has a blunt end that forces the wire into the groove. The metal in the groove slices the cladding enough to make contact.

Not only do patch panels prevent the horizontal cabling from being moved, but they are also your first line of defense in organizing the cables. All patch panels have space in the front for labels, and these labels are the network tech's best friend! Simply place a tiny label on the patch panel to identify each cable, and you will never have to experience that sinking feeling of standing in the telecommunications room of your nonfunctioning network, wondering which cable is which. If you want to be a purist, there is an official, and rather confusing, TIA/EIA labeling methodology called TIA/EIA 606, but a number of real-world network techs simply use their own internal codes (see Figure 12.20).

The CompTIA A+ 220-802 exam expects you to know that a punchdown tool is used for securing UTP connections to a punchdown block. It's not until you go for CompTIA Network+ certification that you'll be expected to know how to use these tools.

• **Figure 12.18** Punchdown tool

• **Figure 12.19** Punching down a 110 block

• **Figure 12.20** Typical patch panels with labels

Patch panels are available in a wide variety of configurations that include different types of ports and numbers of ports. You can get UTP, STP, or fiber ports, and some manufacturers combine several different types on the same patch panel. Panels are available with 8, 12, 24, 48, or even more ports.

UTP patch panels, like UTP cables, come with CAT ratings, which you should be sure to check. Don't blow a good CAT 6 cable installation by buying a cheap patch panel—get a CAT 6 patch panel! A higher-rated panel supports earlier standards, so you can use a CAT 6 or even CAT 6a rack with CAT 5e cabling. Most manufacturers proudly display the CAT level right on the patch panel (see Figure 12.21).

Once you have installed the patch panel, you need to connect the ports to the switch through **patch cables**. Patch cables are short (typically two- to five-foot) UTP cables. Patch cables use stranded rather than solid cable, so they can tolerate much more handling. Even though you can make your own patch cables, most people buy premade ones. Buying patch cables enables you to use different-colored cables to facilitate organization (yellow for accounting, blue for sales, or whatever scheme works for you). Most prefabricated patch cables also come with a reinforced (booted) connector specially designed to handle multiple insertions and removals (see Figure 12.22).

Making Your Own Patch Cables Although most people prefer simply to purchase premade patch cables, making your own is fairly easy. To make your own, use stranded UTP cable that matches the CAT level of your horizontal cabling. Stranded cable also requires specific crimps, so don't use crimps designed for solid cable. Crimping is simple enough, although getting it right takes some practice.

Figure 12.23 shows the two main tools of the crimping trade: an RJ-45 crimper with built-in wire stripper and a pair of wire snips. Professional cable installers naturally have a wide variety of other tools as well.

Here are the steps for properly crimping an RJ-45 onto a UTP cable. If you have some crimps, cable, and a crimping tool handy, follow along!

> The CompTIA A+ 802 exam expects you to know that a cable tech uses a crimper or crimping tool to attach an RJ-45 to the end of a UTP cable.

• **Figure 12.21** CAT level on patch panel

• **Figure 12.22** Typical patch cable

• **Figure 12.23** Crimper and snips

• **Figure 12.24** Properly stripped cable

1. Cut the cable square using RJ-45 crimpers or scissors.

2. Strip off one-half inch of plastic jacket from the end of the cable (see Figure 12.24).

3. Slowly and carefully insert each individual wire into the correct location according to either TIA/EIA 568A or B (see Figure 12.25). Unravel as little as possible.

4. Insert the crimp into the crimper and press (see Figure 12.26). Don't worry about pressing too hard; the crimper has a stop to prevent you from using too much pressure.

Figure 12.27 shows a nicely crimped cable. Note how the plastic jacket goes into the crimp.

• **Figure 12.25** Inserting the individual strands

• **Figure 12.26** Crimping the cable

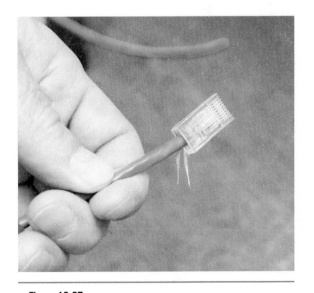

• **Figure 12.27** Properly crimped cable

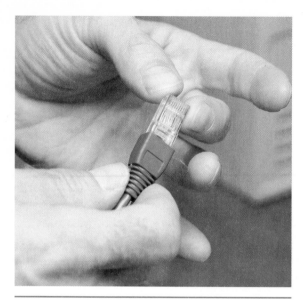

• **Figure 12.28** Adding a boot

A good patch cable should include a boot. Figure 12.28 shows a boot being slid onto a newly crimped cable. Don't forget to slide each boot onto the patch cable *before* you crimp both ends!

After making a cable, you need to test it to make sure it's properly crimped. We use a handy cable tester (a kind of multimeter), available in any good electronics store, to verify all the individual wires are properly connected and in the correct location (see Figure 12.29).

The Work Area

From a cabling standpoint, a work area is nothing more than a wall outlet that serves as the termination point for horizontal network cables: a convenient insertion point for a PC and a telephone. (In practice, of course, the term "work area" includes the office or cubicle.) A wall outlet itself consists of one or two female jacks to accept the cable, a mounting bracket, and a faceplate. You connect the PC to the wall outlet with a patch cable (see Figure 12.30).

The female RJ-45 jacks in these wall outlets also have CAT ratings. You must buy CAT-rated jacks for wall outlets to go along with the CAT rating of the cabling in your network. In fact, many network connector manufacturers use the same connectors, often 110 punchdowns, in the wall outlets that they use on the patch panels (see Figure 12.31). These modular outlets significantly increase the ease of installation.

The last step is connecting the PC to the wall outlet. Here again, most folks use a patch cable. Its stranded cabling stands up to the abuse caused by moving PCs, not to mention the occasional kick.

The work area may be the simplest part of the structured cabling system, but it is also the source of most network failures. When a user can't access the network and you suspect a broken cable, the first place to look is the work area.

• **Figure 12.29** Typical tester

• **Figure 12.30** Typical work area outlet

• Figure 12.31 Punching down a modular jack

■ TCP/IP

The **Transmission Control Protocol/Internet Protocol (TCP/IP)** is the primary protocol of most modern networks, including the Internet. For a PC to access the Internet, it must have TCP/IP loaded and configured properly. TCP/IP has become so predominant that most network folks use it even on networks that do not connect to the Internet. Although TCP/IP is powerful, it is also a bit of a challenge to set up. So whether you are installing a modem for a dial-up connection to the Internet or setting up 500 computers on their own private *intranet*, you must understand some TCP/IP basics. You'll go through the following basic sections of the protocol and then you'll look at specific steps to install and configure TCP/IP.

Network Addressing

Any network address must provide two pieces of information: it must uniquely identify the machine and it must locate that machine within the larger network. In a TCP/IP network, the IP address identifies the PC and the network on which it resides. If you look at an IP address, it's not apparent which part of the address identifies the network and which part is the unique identifier of the computer. Let's review IP addresses and then see how they identify PCs and networks.

IP Addresses

TCP/IP networks don't identify PCs by name, but by IP address. The **IP address** is the unique identification number for your system on the network. IP addresses consist of four sets of eight binary numbers (octets), each set separated by a period. This is called *dotted-decimal notation*. So, instead of a computer being called SERVER1, it gets an address like so:

202.34.16.11

Written in binary form, the address would look like this:

```
11001010.00100010.00010000.00001011
```

To make the addresses more comprehensible to users, the TCP/IP folks decided to write the decimal equivalents:

```
00000000 = 0
00000001 = 1
00000010 = 2
...
11111111 = 255
```

Subnet Mask

Part of every IP address identifies the network (the network ID), and another part identifies the local computer (the host ID, or host) on the network. A NIC uses a value called the **subnet mask** to distinguish which part of the IP address identifies the network ID and which part of the address identifies the host. The subnet mask blocks out (or masks) the network portion of an IP address.

Let's look at a typical subnet mask: 255.255.255.0. When you compare the subnet mask to the IP address, any part that's all 255s is the network ID. Any part that's all zeros is the host ID. Look at the following example:

IP address: 192.168.4.33

Subnet mask: 255.255.255.0

Because the first thee octets are 255, the network ID is 192.168.4 and the host ID is 33.

Every computer on a single LAN must have the same network ID and a unique host ID. That means every computer on the preceding network must have an IP address that starts with 192.168.4. Every computer on the network must have a unique IP address. If two computers have the same IP address, they won't be able to talk to each other, and other computers won't know where to send data. This is called an *IP conflict*.

You can never have an IP address that ends with a 0 or a 255, so for the preceding example, we can have addresses starting at 192.168.4.1 and ending at 192.168.4.254: a total of 254 addresses. But what if you have more than 254 computers? Well, you just take a 255 out of the subnet mask like this:

255.255.0.0

If the IP address is 192.168.4.33, then we now have a network ID of 192.168 and a host of 4.33. We can have addresses ranging from 192.168.0.1

to 192.168.255.254. (Notice the 0 and the 255? You can have 0s and 255s in an IP address, just not at the end of the IP address.)

So how many addresses can you have now? Well, let's count them out:

192.168.0.1

192.168.0.2

...

192.168.0.254

192.168.1.1

192.168.1.2

...

192.168.255.253

192.168.255.254

You would have a total of 65,534 addresses on your network. So with a subnet mask of 255.255.255.0, you get 254 addresses and a network ID of 192.168.4; and with a subnet mask of 255.255.0.0, you get 65,534 addresses and a network ID of 192.168. That just leaves one big question: who picks the network ID?

Class Licenses

The folks who organized IP addressing way back in the 1970s came up with a way to pass out network IDs using something called *class licenses*. IP addresses are divided into class licenses that correspond with the potential size of the network: Class A, Class B, and Class C. Class A licenses were intended for huge companies and organizations, such as major multinational corporations, universities, and governmental agencies. Class B licenses were assigned to medium-size companies, and Class C licenses were designated for smaller LANs.

Class A networks use the first octet to identify the network address and the remaining three octets to identify the host. Class B networks use the first two octets to identify the network address and the remaining two octets to identify the host. Class C networks use the first three octets to identify the network address and the last octet to identify the host. Table 12.1 lists range (class) assignments.

You'll note that the IP address ranges listed in Table 12.1 skip from 126.x.x.x to 128.x.x.x. That's because the 127 address range (i.e., 127.0.0.0–127.255.255.255) is reserved for network testing (loopback) operations. (We usually just use the address 127.0.0.1 for loopback purposes and call it the *localhost* address, but any address that starts with *127* will work just as well.) That's not the only reserved range, either! Each network class has a specific IP address range reserved for *private* networks—traffic from these networks doesn't get routed to the Internet at large. Class A's private range goes from 10.0.0.0 to 10.255.255.255. Class B has two private address ranges: 172.16.0.0 up to 172.31.255.254 for private

Table 12.1	Class A, B, and C Addresses		
Network Class	Address Range	No. of Network Addresses Available	No. of Host Nodes (Computers) Supported
A	1–126	129	16,777,214
B	128–191	16,384	65,534
C	192–223	2,097,152	254

 Pinging the loopback is the best way to test whether a NIC is working properly. To test a NIC's loopback, the other end of the cable must be in a working switch or you must use a loopback device such as a loopback adapter/plug.

Private IP addresses are very commonly used on LANs. But if private IP addresses are blocked by routers, how can we use them if we want to get on the Internet? It's a neat little trick called NAT, which shares one public IP address among all the computers on a private network.

addresses and 169.254.0.0 to 169.254.255.254 to accommodate the **Automatic Private IP Addressing (APIPA)** function (discussed later in the chapter). Class C's private addresses range from 192.168.0.0 to 192.168.255.254.

The default subnet mask for Class A addresses is 255.0.0.0; for Class B, it's 255.255.0.0; and for Class C, 255.255.255.0. For example, in the Class B IP address 131.190.4.121 with a subnet mask of 255.255.0.0, the first two octets (131.190) make up the network ID, and the last two (4.121) make up the host ID.

Interconnecting Networks with Routers

Now that you have a basic understanding of IP addressing, let's go back and watch a router in action. Let's take a look at a typical network: four computers and a networked printer all connected to a single switch (see Figure 12.32).

When network nerds draw out a network, they tend not to draw every device. Instead, they make a circle with the network ID and the subnet mask, as shown in Figure 12.33.

If you have two networks, just make two circles. Routers read IP addresses of incoming traffic and forward the traffic to the proper port. Since routers interconnect network IDs, we draw routers as boxes between networks, as shown in Figure 12.34

To make a router connect two networks requires a configuration process. There are a lot of different routers out there, from cheap home routers to multimillion-dollar routers that connect the big pipes of the Internet. The CompTIA A+ 220-802 exam only tests on a few basic settings on simple home routers. While we'll save the real configuration of routers for Chapter 14, there's one thing that's very important to understand now: every port

• **Figure 12.32** Typical network

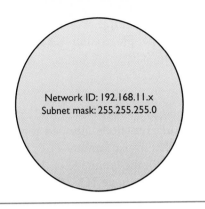

• **Figure 12.33** Same network shown as a circle

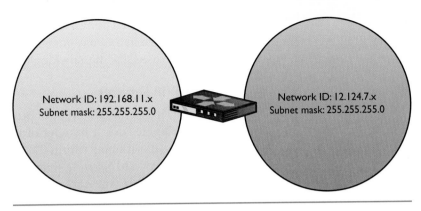

• **Figure 12.34** Router between two networks

on a router is a member of a different network ID. Let's zoom in on the router in Figure 12.34 and see how the ports are set up, as shown in Figure 12.35. Note that each router gets the first address in the network ID. This isn't a law of physics, just good manners. Keep in mind that the IP address for the router is usually the default gateway for all the computers for that network.

• **Figure 12.35** Router graphic in detail

TCP/UDP

When moving data from one system to another, the TCP/IP protocol suite needs to know if the communication is connection-oriented or connectionless. When you want to be positive that the data moving between two systems gets there in good order, use a connection-oriented application. If it's not a big deal for data to miss a bit or two, then connectionless is the way to go. The connection-oriented protocol used with TCP/IP is called the *Transmission Control Protocol* (*TCP*). The connectionless one is called the *User Datagram Protocol* (*UDP*).

Let me be clear: you don't *choose* TCP or UDP. The people who developed the applications decide which protocol to use. When you fire up your Web browser, for example, you're using TCP because Web browsers use a protocol called HTTP. HTTP is built on TCP.

Over 95 percent of all TCP/IP applications use TCP—that's why we call the protocol suite "TCP/IP" and not "UDP/IP." TCP gets an application's data from one machine to another reliably and completely. As a result, TCP comes with communication rules that require both the sending and receiving machines to acknowledge the other's presence and readiness to send and receive data.

UDP is the "fire and forget" missile of the TCP/IP protocol suite. UDP doesn't possess any of the extras you see in TCP to make sure the data is received intact. UDP works best when you have a lot of data to send that doesn't need to be perfect or when the systems are so close to each other that the chances of a problem occurring are too small to bother worrying about.

Besides the physical ports on your computer and router, a networking *port* is also a 16-bit number (between 0 and 65,535) assigned to a TCP/IP session (or connection). The port number determines the software protocol used and how to handle the data packet. You'll learn more about ports in Chapter 14.

A few dropped frames on a Voice over IP call, for example, won't make much difference in the communication between two people. So there's a good reason to use UDP: it's smoking fast compared to TCP.

TCP/IP Services

TCP/IP is a different type of protocol. Although it supports File and Printer Sharing, it adds a number of unique sharing functions, lumped together under the umbrella term **TCP/IP services**. The most famous TCP/IP service is called *Hypertext Transfer Protocol* (*HTTP*), the language of the World Wide Web. If you want to surf the Web, you must have TCP/IP. But TCP/IP supplies many other services beyond just HTTP. By using a service called Telnet, for example, you can access a remote system as though you were actually in front of that machine.

Another example is a handy utility called ping. The **ping** command enables one machine to check whether it can communicate with another machine. Figure 12.36 shows an example of ping running on a Windows 7 system. Isn't it interesting that many TCP/IP services run from a command prompt? Good thing you know how to access one! I'll show you other services in a moment.

• **Figure 12.36** The ping command in action

The goal of TCP/IP is to link any two hosts (remember, a *host* is just a computer in TCP/IP lingo), whether the two computers are on the same LAN or on some other network within the WAN. The LANs within the WAN are linked together with a variety of connections, ranging from basic dial-ups to dedicated high-speed (and expensive) data lines (see Figure 12.37). To move traffic between networks, you use routers (see Figure 12.38). Each host sends traffic to the router only when that data is destined for a remote network, cutting down on traffic across the more expensive WAN links. The host makes these decisions based on the destination IP address of each packet.

TCP/IP Settings

TCP/IP has a number of unique settings that you must configure correctly to ensure proper network functionality. Unfortunately, these

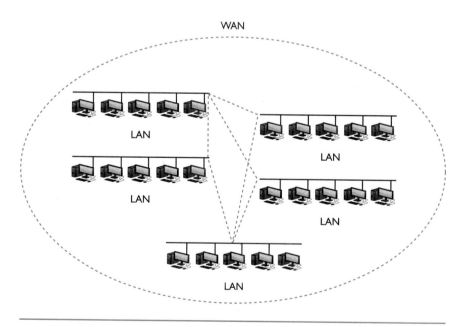

• **Figure 12.37** WAN concept

settings can be quite confusing, and there are several of them. Not all settings are used for every type of TCP/IP network, and it's not always obvious where you go to set them.

In Windows, you can configure network settings from the appropriate networking applet. To open Network Connections in Windows XP, either right-click on My Network Places and select Properties or open the Control Panel and select Network Connections (see Figure 12.39). In Windows Vista and Windows 7, either right-click on Network and select Properties or open the Control Panel and select Network and Sharing Center. In Windows Vista, you'll also need to click the *Manage network connections* link, and in Windows 7, you'll need to click *Change adapter settings*.

The CompTIA A+ 802 exam assumes that someone else, such as a tech support person or some network guru, will tell you the correct TCP/IP settings for the network. Your only job is to understand roughly what those settings do and to know where to enter them so the system works.

• **Figure 12.38** Typical router

The CompTIA A+ 220-802 exam has a rather strange view of what you should know about networking. Take a lot of time practicing how to get to certain network configuration screens. Be ready for questions that ask, "Which of the following steps will enable you to change a particular value?"

DHCP To understand the **Dynamic Host Configuration Protocol (DHCP)**, you must first remember that every machine must be assigned an IP address, a subnet mask, a default gateway, and at least one DNS server. These settings can be added manually by using the TCP/IP Properties dialog box. When you set the IP address manually, the IP address will not change and is called a **static IP address** (see Figure 12.40).

DHCP enables you to create a pool of IP addresses that are given temporarily to machines. DHCP is especially handy for networks of a lot of laptops that join and leave the network on a regular basis. Why give a machine that is on the network for only a few hours a day a static IP address? For that reason, DHCP is quite popular. If you add a NIC to a Windows system, the default TCP/IP settings are set to use DHCP. When you accept those

• **Figure 12.39** Network Connections showing dial-up and LAN connections

• **Figure 12.40** Setting a static IP address

• Figure 12.41 Automatically obtaining an IP address

automatic settings, you're really telling the machine to use DHCP (see Figure 12.41).

To use DHCP you need a DHCP server. A DHCP server can be a program running on any computer in your network, but most commonly it's a feature added to routers.

TCP/IP Tools

All versions of Windows come with handy tools to test and configure TCP/IP. Those you're most likely to use in the field are ping, ipconfig, nslookup, and tracert. All of these programs are command-line utilities. Open a command prompt to run them; if you just place these commands in the Run or Search dialog box, you'll see the Command Prompt window open for a moment and then quickly close!

ping You've already encountered ping, a really great way to see if you can talk to another system. Here's how it works. Get to a command prompt and type **ping** followed by an IP address or by a DNS name, such as **ping www.chivalry.com**. Press the ENTER key on your keyboard and away it goes! Figure 12.42 shows the common syntax for ping.

The ping command has a few useful options beyond the basics. The first option is the –t switch. If you use the –t switch, ping continuously sends ping packets until you stop it with the break command (CTRL-C). The second option is the –l switch, which enables you to specify how big a ping packet to send. This helps in diagnosing specific problems with the routers between your computer and the computer you ping.

ipconfig Windows offers the command-line tool **ipconfig** for a quick glance at your network settings. From a command prompt, type **ipconfig/ all** to see all of your TCP/IP settings (see Figure 12.43).

When you have a static IP address, ipconfig does little beyond reporting your current IP settings, including your IP address, subnet mask, default gateway, DNS servers, and WINS servers. When using DHCP, however, ipconfig is also the primary tool for releasing and renewing your IP address. Just type **ipconfig /renew** to get a new IP address or **ipconfig /release** to give up the IP address you currently have.

nslookup The **nslookup** command is a powerful command-line program that enables you to determine exactly what information the DNS server is

• Figure 12.42 The ping command's syntax

You can do some cool stuff with nslookup, and consequently some techs absolutely love the tool. It's way outside the scope of CompTIA A+ certification, but if you want to play with it, type **help** at the nslookup prompt and press ENTER to see a list of common commands and syntax.

```
C:\Windows\system32\cmd.exe

C:\>ipconfig /all

Windows IP Configuration

    Host Name . . . . . . . . . . . . : Windows7
    Primary Dns Suffix  . . . . . . . :
    Node Type . . . . . . . . . . . . : Hybrid
    IP Routing Enabled. . . . . . . . : No
    WINS Proxy Enabled. . . . . . . . : No
    DNS Suffix Search List. . . . . . : totalhome

Ethernet adapter Local Area Connection:

    Connection-specific DNS Suffix  . : totalhome
    Description . . . . . . . . . . . : Intel(R) PRO/1000 MT Network Connection
    Physical Address. . . . . . . . . : 00-0C-29-04-A5-F7
    DHCP Enabled. . . . . . . . . . . : Yes
    Autoconfiguration Enabled . . . . : Yes
    Link-local IPv6 Address . . . . . : fe80::5d74:16a0:f201:2f37%10(Preferred)
    IPv4 Address. . . . . . . . . . . : 192.168.4.23(Preferred)
    Subnet Mask . . . . . . . . . . . : 255.255.255.0
    Lease Obtained. . . . . . . . . . : Thursday, April 26, 2012 11:19:24 AM
    Lease Expires . . . . . . . . . . : Wednesday, May 02, 2012 11:19:24 AM
    Default Gateway . . . . . . . . . : 192.168.4.1
    DHCP Server . . . . . . . . . . . : 192.168.4.12
    DHCPv6 IAID . . . . . . . . . . . : 234884137
    DHCPv6 Client DUID. . . . . . . . : 00-01-00-01-12-0E-1C-C7-00-0C-29-04-A5-F7
    DNS Servers . . . . . . . . . . . : 192.168.4.12
    NetBIOS over Tcpip. . . . . . . . : Enabled

Tunnel adapter isatap.totalhome:

    Media State . . . . . . . . . . . : Media disconnected
    Connection-specific DNS Suffix  . : totalhome
    Description . . . . . . . . . . . : Microsoft ISATAP Adapter
    Physical Address. . . . . . . . . : 00-00-00-00-00-00-00-E0
    DHCP Enabled. . . . . . . . . . . : No
    Autoconfiguration Enabled . . . . : Yes

Tunnel adapter Local Area Connection* 11:

    Connection-specific DNS Suffix  . :
    Description . . . . . . . . . . . : Teredo Tunneling Pseudo-Interface
    Physical Address. . . . . . . . . : 00-00-00-00-00-00-00-E0
    DHCP Enabled. . . . . . . . . . . : No
    Autoconfiguration Enabled . . . . : Yes
    IPv6 Address. . . . . . . . . . . : 2001:0:5ef5:79fd:8cd:348:3f57:fbe8(Preferred)
    Link-local IPv6 Address . . . . . : fe80::8cd:348:3f57:fbe8%12(Preferred)
    Default Gateway . . . . . . . . . : ::
    NetBIOS over Tcpip. . . . . . . . : Disabled

C:\>
```

• **Figure 12.43** An ipconfig /all command on Windows 7

giving you about a specific host name. Every version of Windows makes nslookup available when you install TCP/IP. To run the program, type **nslookup** from the command prompt and press the ENTER key (see Figure 12.44). Note that this gives you a little information and that the prompt has changed. That's because you're running the application. Type **exit** and press the ENTER key to return to the command prompt.

tracert The **tracert** utility shows the route that a packet takes to get to its destination. From a command line, type **tracert** followed by a space and an IP address or URL. The output describes the route from your machine to the destination machine, including all devices the packet passes through and how long each hop between devices takes (see Figure 12.45). The tracert command can come in handy when you have to troubleshoot bottlenecks. When users complain of difficulty reaching a particular

```
C:\Windows\system32\cmd.exe - nslookup

C:\>nslookup
Default Server:  totalhomedc2.totalhome
Address:  192.168.4.12

> totalsem.com
Server:  totalhomedc2.totalhome
Address:  192.168.4.12

Non-authoritative answer:
Name:    totalsem.com
Address:  216.40.231.195

>
```

• **Figure 12.44** The nslookup command in action

```
C:\Windows\system32\cmd.exe                                                    _ □ X

C:\>tracert chivalry.com

Tracing route to chivalry.com [69.94.71.175]
over a maximum of 30 hops:

  1    <1 ms    <1 ms    <1 ms  Router.totalhome [192.168.4.1]
  2   122 ms   116 ms   116 ms  adsl-208-190-121-38.dsl.hstntx.swbell.net [208.190.121.38]

  3   120 ms   125 ms    43 ms  12.83.37.149
  4    48 ms    48 ms    49 ms  gar25.dlstx.ip.att.net [12.122.85.233]
  5    48 ms    48 ms    48 ms  192.205.34.142
  6    89 ms    89 ms    89 ms  OLM-LLC.Vlan495.asr1.JFK1.gblx.net [64.212.32.166]
  7    91 ms    90 ms    90 ms  gi1-1.corea.trum.fastdns.net [69.94.1.69]
  8    88 ms    88 ms    88 ms  chivalry.com [69.94.71.175]

Trace complete.

C:\>
```

• **Figure 12.45** The tracert command in action

Try This!

Running tracert

Ever wonder why your e-mail takes *years* to get to some people but arrives instantly for others? Or why some Web sites are slower to load than others? Part of the blame could lie with how many hops away your connection is from the target server. You can use tracert to run a quick check of how many hops it takes to get to somewhere on a network, so Try This!

1. Run tracert on some known source, such as www.microsoft.com or www.totalsem.com. How many hops did it take? Did your tracert time out or make it all of the way to the server?

2. Try a tracert to a local address. If you're in a university town, run a tracert on the campus Web site, such as www.rice.edu for folks in Houston, or www.ucla.edu for those of you in Los Angeles. Did you get fewer hops with a local site?

destination by using TCP/IP, you can run this utility to determine whether the problem exists on a machine or connection over which you have control, or if it is a problem on another machine or router. Similarly, if a destination is completely unreachable, tracert can again determine whether the problem is on a machine or router over which you have control.

Configuring TCP/IP

By default, TCP/IP is configured to receive an IP address automatically from a DHCP server on the network (and automatically assign a corresponding subnet mask). As far as the CompTIA A+ 220-802 exam is concerned, Network+ techs and administrators give you the IP address, subnet mask, and default gateway information and you plug them into the PC. That's about it, so here's how to do it manually:

1. In Windows XP, open the Control Panel and double-click the Network Connections applet. Double-click the Local Area Connection icon. In Windows Vista/7, open the Control Panel and go to the Network and Sharing Center applet. In Windows Vista, click the *Manage network connections* link, and in Windows 7, click *Change adapter settings*. After that, double-click the Local Area Network icon.

2. Click the Properties button, highlight Internet Protocol (TCP/IP), and click the Properties button. In Windows Vista/7, you should highlight Internet Protocol Version 4 (TCP/IPv4), as opposed to

IPv6, which you'll learn about later in this chapter.

3. In the Properties dialog box (see Figure 12.46), click the radio button next to *Use the following IP address*.

4. Enter the IP address in the appropriate fields.

5. Press the TAB key to skip down to the Subnet mask field. Note that the subnet mask is entered automatically, although you can type over this if you want to enter a different subnet mask.

6. Optionally, enter the IP address for a default gateway.

7. Optionally, enter the IP addresses of a primary DNS server and a secondary DNS server. (Figure 12.46 uses the Google DNS servers.)

8. Click the OK button to close the Properties dialog box.

9. Click the Close button to exit the Local Area Connection Status dialog box.

• **Figure 12.46** Setting up IP

Automatic Private IP Addressing

Windows supports a feature called Automatic Private IP Addressing (APIPA) that automatically assigns an IP address to the system when the client cannot obtain an IP address automatically. The Internet Assigned Numbers Authority, the nonprofit corporation responsible for assigning IP addresses and managing root servers, has set aside the range of addresses from 169.254.0.1 to 169.254.255.254 for this purpose.

If the computer system cannot contact a DHCP server, the computer randomly chooses an address in the form of 169.254.*x.y* (where *x.y* is the computer's identifier) and a 16-bit subnet mask (255.255.0.0) and broadcasts it on the network segment (subnet). If no other computer responds to the address, the system assigns this address to itself. When using APIPA, the system can communicate only with other computers on the same subnet that also use the 169.254.*x.y* range with a 16-bit mask. APIPA is enabled by default if your system is configured to obtain an IP address automatically.

A computer system on a network with an active DHCP server that has an IP address in this range usually indicates a problem connecting to the DHCP server.

IPv6

When the early developers of the Internet set out to create an addressing or naming scheme for devices on the Internet, they faced several issues. Of course they needed to determine how the numbers or names worked, and for that they developed the Internet Protocol and IP addresses. But beyond that, they had to determine how many computers might exist in the future, and then make the IP address space even bigger to give Internet naming longevity. But how many computers would exist in the future?

Keep in mind that TCP/IP development took place back in the early 1970s. There were fewer than 1000 computers in the entire *world* at the time,

but that didn't keep the IP developers from thinking big! They decided to go absolutely crazy (as many people considered it at the time) and, in 1979, created the **Internet Protocol version 4 (IPv4)** 32-bit IP address space, creating approximately 4 billion IP addresses. That should have been fine for the foreseeable future!

It wasn't. First, the TCP/IP folks wasted huge chunks of IP addresses due to classful addressing and an easygoing method of parceling out IP addresses. Second, the Internet reached a level of popularity far beyond the original developers' imaginations. By the mid-1980s, the rate of consumption for IP addresses started to worry the Internet people and the writing was on the wall for IPv4's 32-bit addressing.

As a result, the Internet Engineering Task Force (IETF) developed a new IP addressing scheme called **Internet Protocol version 6 (IPv6)** that is slowly replacing IPv4. IPv6 extends the 32-bit IP address space to 128 bits, allowing up to 2^{128} addresses! That should hold us for the foreseeable future! This number—close to 3.4×10^{38} addresses—is something like all the grains of sand on Earth or 1/8 of all the molecules in the atmosphere.

Although they achieve the same function—enabling computers on IP networks to send packets to each other—IPv6 and IPv4 differ a lot when it comes to implementation. This section provides you with a quick overview to get you up to speed with IPv6 and show you how it differs from IPv4.

IPv6 Address Notation

The familiar 32-bit IPv4 addresses are written as 197.169.94.82, using four octets. The 128-bit IPv6 addresses are written like this:

2001:0000:0000:3210:0800:200C:00CF:1234

IPv6 uses a colon as a separator, instead of the period used in IPv4's dotted-decimal format. Each "group" is a hexadecimal number between 0000 and FFFF called, unofficially, a *field* or *hextet*.

A complete IPv6 address always has eight groups of four hexadecimal characters. If this sounds like you're going to type in really long IP addresses, don't worry, IPv6 offers a number of ways to shorten the address in written form.

First, leading zeros can be dropped from any group, so 00CF becomes CF and 0000 becomes 0. Let's rewrite the previous IPv6 address using this shortening method:

2001:0:0:3210:800:200C:CF:1234

Second, you can remove one or more consecutive groups of all zeros, leaving the two colons together. For example, using the :: rule, you can write the IPv6 address

2001:0:0:3210:800:200C:CF:1234

as

2001::3210:800:200C:CF:1234

You can remove any number of consecutive groups of zeros to leave a double colon, but you can only use this trick *once* in an IPv6 address.

Take a look at this IPv6 address:

FEDC:0000:0000:0000:00CF:0000:BA98:1234

If you really want to know how many IP addresses IPv6 provides, here's your number: 340,282,366,920,938,463,463,374,607,431,768,211,456.

For those who don't play with hex regularly, one hexadecimal character (for example, *F*) represents 4 bits, so four hexadecimal characters make a 16-bit group. For some reason, the IPv6 developers didn't provide a name for the "group of four hexadecimal characters," so many techs and writers have taken to calling them fields or "hextets" to distinguish them from IPv4 "octets."

IPv4 addresses use 32 bits, and IPv6 addresses use 128 bits. Be sure you can identify their address length differences and address conventions.

Using the double-colon rule, you can reduce four groups of zeros; three of them follow the FEDC and the fourth comes after 00CF. Because of the "only use once" stipulation, the best and shortest option is to convert the address to

FEDC::CF:0:BA98:1234

You may not use a second :: to represent the fourth groups of zeros—only one :: is allowed per address! This rule exists for a good reason. If more than one :: was used, how could you tell how many groups of zeros were in each group? Answer: you couldn't.

Here's an example of a very special IPv6 address that takes full advantage of the double-colon rule, the IPv6 loopback address:

::1

Without using the double-colon nomenclature, this IPv6 address would look like this:

0000:0000:0000:0000:0000:0000:0000:0001

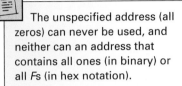

The unspecified address (all zeros) can never be used, and neither can an address that contains all ones (in binary) or all *F*s (in hex notation).

IPv6 still uses subnets, but you won't find a place to type in 255s anywhere. IPv6 uses the "/x" *Classless Inter-Domain Routing* (*CIDR*) nomenclature, where the /x refers to the number of bits in the subnet mask, just like in IPv4. Here's how to write an IP address and subnet for a typical IPv6 host:

FEDC::CF:0:BA98:1234/64

Where Do IPv6 Addresses Come From?

With IPv4, IP addresses come from one of two places: either you type in the IP address yourself (*static IP addressing*) or you use DHCP (also called *dynamic IP addressing*). With IPv6, addressing works very differently. Instead of one IP address, you can have up to three IP addresses on a single network card.

Every computer running IPv6 will always have at least a link-local address.

When a computer running IPv6 first boots up, it gives itself a *link-local address*, IPv6's equivalent to IPv4's APIPA address. Although an APIPA address can indicate a loss of network connectivity or a problem with the DHCP server, computers running IPv6 always have a link-local address. The first 64 bits of a link-local address are always FE80::. That means every address always begins with FE80:0000:0000:0000. If your operating system supports IPv6 and IPv6 is enabled, you can see this address. Figure 12.47 shows the link-local address for a typical system running the ipconfig utility.

If you want to force Windows to use the MAC address, just go to a command prompt and type this:

```
netsh interface ipv6
set global randomize
identifiers= disabled
```

The folks who designed IPv6 gave operating system makers a choice on how to make the last 64 bits of an IPv6 address. The first method uses a random value—and this is the way Windows does it. When you activate a NIC, Windows simply makes a random value for the last 64 bits of the IPv6 address. Once created, this unique 64-bit value will never change.

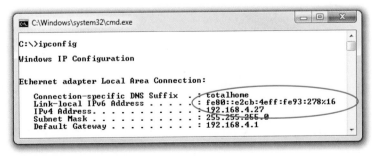

• **Figure 12.47** Link-local address in ipconfig

475

A router solicitation message uses the address FF02::2. This address is read only by other computers running IPv6 in the network. This type of address is different from a broadcast address and is called a *multicast address*. In IPv6, there is no broadcast, only multicast!

Most Windows Vista and Windows 7 machines have three IPv6 addresses: one link local address and two global addresses. One global address stays the same, while the second is a temporary address used to make it harder for your system to be tracked by IP address.

At the moment, IANA only passes out global addresses that begin with the number 2 (for example, 2001::, 2002::, and so on). As demand increases, this will certainly change, but for now, knowing a global address when you see one is easy.

• **Figure 12.48** Getting a global address

The alternative method to create the IPv6 address uses the MAC address of the network card (called the *Extended Unique Identifier, 64-bit*, or *EUI-64*). Be warned! The CompTIA A+ 220-802 exam is Windows-centric, and Windows does not use this second method by default. Even though Windows does not currently use this method by default, understanding this is critical to understanding IPv6.

IPv6 Subnet Masks

IPv6 subnets function the same as IPv4 subnets, but you need to know two new rules:

- The last 64 bits of an IPv6 address are generated randomly or using the MAC address, leaving a maximum of 64 bits for the network ID. Therefore, no subnet is ever longer than /64.

- The IANA passes out /32 subnets to big ISPs and end users who need large allotments. ISPs and others may pass out /48 and /64 subnets to end users.

Therefore, the vast majority of IPv6 subnets are between /48 and /64.

Subnet masks are just as important in IPv6 networks as they are in IPv4 networks. Unlike with IPv4 networks, however, all IPv6 networks with computers have a /64 subnet mask, so you'll rarely if ever need to make any changes manually.

Global Addresses

To get on the Internet, a system needs a second IPv6 address called a *global address*. The most common way to get a global address is to request it from the default gateway router, which must be configured to pass out global IPv6 addresses. When you plug a computer into a network, it sends out a very special packet called a *router solicitation* (*RS*) message, looking for a router (see Figure 12.48). The router hears this message and responds with a *router advertisement* (*RA*). This RA tells the computer its network ID and subnet (together called the *prefix*) and DNS server (if configured).

Once the computer gets a prefix, it generates the rest of the address just like with the link-local address. The computer ends up with a legitimate, 128-bit public IPv6 address as well as a link-local address. Figure 12.49 shows the IPv6 information in Windows 7.

Let's look at this process in detail with an example:

1. An IPv6-capable computer boots up. As it boots, it sends out a router solicitation message (FF02::2).

2. An IPv6-configured router hears the request and then sends to the computer a router advertisement containing the prefix and DNS. In this example, let's say it is 2001:470:ABCD:1/64.

3. The computer takes the prefix and adds the EUI-64 or a random value to the end of the prefix. If the MAC address is 00-0C-29-53-45-CA, then the address is 20C:29FF:FE53:45CA.

4. Putting the prefix with the last half of the address, you get the global address: 2001:470:ABCD:1:20C:29FF:FE53:45CA.

```
■■ Administrator: C:\Windows\system32\cmd.exe                              □ □ ▨

C:\>ipconfig

Windows IP Configuration

Ethernet adapter Gigabit NIC:

   Connection-specific DNS Suffix  . :
   IPv6 Address. . . . . . . . . . . : 2001:74:b8f8:1:c547:4dd3:86a3:739d
   Temporary IPv6 Address. . . . . . : 2001:74:b8f8:1:e918:a9af:c6e4:120b
   Link-local IPv6 Address . . . . . : fe80::c547:4dd3:86a3:739d%8
   IPv4 Address. . . . . . . . . . . : 192.168.4.81
   Subnet Mask . . . . . . . . . . . : 255.255.255.0
   Default Gateway . . . . . . . . . : fe80::223:4ff:fe8c:b720%8
                                       192.168.4.1
```

• **Figure 12.49** Windows system with a global IPv6 address

A global address is a true Internet address. If another computer is running IPv6 and also has a global address, it can access your system unless you have some form of firewall.

The addition of IPv6 makes programs such as ipconfig fairly complex. Take a look at Figure 12.50. With multiple NICs and both IPv4 and IPv6, the output is vast—too big to even put on a single screen.

> 💡 Computers using IPv6 need a *global* address to access the Internet.

```
■■ C:\Windows\system32\cmd.exe                                            □ □ ▨

C:\>ipconfig /all

Windows IP Configuration

   Host Name . . . . . . . . . . . . : michaels-ws
   Primary Dns Suffix  . . . . . . . : totalhome
   Node Type . . . . . . . . . . . . : Hybrid
   IP Routing Enabled. . . . . . . . : No
   WINS Proxy Enabled. . . . . . . . : No
   DNS Suffix Search List. . . . . . : totalhome

Ethernet adapter Local Area Connection:

   Connection-specific DNS Suffix  . : totalhome
   Description . . . . . . . . . . . : Realtek PCIe GBE Family Controller
   Physical Address. . . . . . . . . : E0-CB-4E-93-02-78
   DHCP Enabled. . . . . . . . . . . : Yes
   Autoconfiguration Enabled . . . . : Yes
   IPv6 Address. . . . . . . . . . . : 2001:470:baf9:1::200(Preferred)
   Link-local IPv6 Address . . . . . : fe80::e2cb:4eff:fe93:278%16(Preferred)
   IPv4 Address. . . . . . . . . . . : 192.168.4.27(Preferred)
   Subnet Mask . . . . . . . . . . . : 255.255.255.0
   Lease Obtained. . . . . . . . . . : Thursday, April 26, 2012 8:37:26 AM
   Lease Expires . . . . . . . . . . : Wednesday, May 02, 2012 8:37:25 AM
   Default Gateway . . . . . . . . . : 2001:470:baf9:1::1
                                       192.168.4.1
   DHCP Server . . . . . . . . . . . : 192.168.4.12
   DHCPv6 IAID . . . . . . . . . . . : 400608078
   DHCPv6 Client DUID. . . . . . . . : 00-01-00-01-13-57-F6-2D-E0-CB-4E-93-02-78

   DNS Servers . . . . . . . . . . . : 192.168.4.12
   NetBIOS over Tcpip. . . . . . . . : Enabled

Ethernet adapter VMware Network Adapter VMnet1:

   Connection-specific DNS Suffix  . :
   Description . . . . . . . . . . . : VMware Virtual Ethernet Adapter for VMnet
1
   Physical Address. . . . . . . . . : 00-50-56-C0-00-01
   DHCP Enabled. . . . . . . . . . . : No
   Autoconfiguration Enabled . . . . : Yes
   Link-local IPv6 Address . . . . . : fe80::250:56ff:fec0:1%19(Preferred)
   IPv4 Address. . . . . . . . . . . : 192.168.22.1(Preferred)
   Subnet Mask . . . . . . . . . . . : 255.255.255.0
   Default Gateway . . . . . . . . . :
   DHCPv6 IAID . . . . . . . . . . . : 436228182
   DHCPv6 Client DUID. . . . . . . . : 00-01-00-01-13-57-F6-2D-E0-CB-4E-93-02-78

   DNS Servers . . . . . . . . . . . : fec0:0:0:ffff::1%1
```

• **Figure 12.50** The ipconfig command with IPv6 and IPv4

Chapter 12 Review

■ Chapter Summary

After reading this chapter and completing the exercises, you should understand the following about networking.

Install and troubleshoot structured cabling

- Fiber optic Ethernet transmits light instead of electricity, achieving much greater maximum distances than other forms of Ethernet. Most fiber networks use LEDs to send light signals and use multimode fiber optic cabling. Networks that use laser light use single-mode fiber optic cabling. Laser light and single-mode cabling are used most often for very long-distance connections.

- Most fiber optic cables use one of two connectors: the square SC type or the round ST type.

- Early versions of Ethernet ran on coaxial cable instead of UTP. Coax cable consists of a center cable, or core, surrounded by insulation, covered by a shield of braided cable. Coaxial cables are rated using an RG name, with the two most popular standards being RG-6 and RG-59.

- The two common coaxial cable connectors are the BNC twist connector and the F-type screw connector.

- Hubs connected older Ethernet networks. They repeat data to every connected port.

- Switches have replaced hubs as the modern interconnection point for Ethernet networks. They create point-to-point connections between two computers.

- A bridge enables two devices with different connector types, such as UTP and fiber optic, to connect and communicate with one another.

- A network attached storage (NAS) device is a simple box that supports one or more hard drives for sharing data across a network. These are often self-configuring. A NAS is a type of network appliance.

- A router connects multiple LANs together. By definition, a router must have at least two connections: one into the network, and one out to another network.

- Structured cabling refers to a set of standards for installing wired networks, including the type of cables to be used, where to place them, how to connect them, and so on. The idea is to create a safe and reliable cabling infrastructure. Structured cabling requires three ingredients: a telecommunications room, horizontal cabling, and a work area.

- All UTP cables use either solid core or stranded core. Each wire in solid core UTP uses a single solid wire. With stranded core, each wire is actually a bundle of tiny wire strands. Each of these cable types has its benefits and downsides.

- A patch panel is a box with a row of female connectors (or ports) in the front and permanent connections in the back, where you connect your horizontal cables. Most patch panels use a 110 block.

Explain the basics of TCP/IP

- TCP/IP is the primary protocol of most modern networks, including the Internet. For a PC to access the Internet, it must have TCP/IP loaded and configured properly.

- Any network address must provide two pieces of information: it must uniquely identify the machine and it must locate that machine within the larger network. In a TCP/IP network, the IP address identifies the PC and the network on which it resides.

- Part of every IP address identifies the network (the network ID), and another part identifies the local computer (the host ID, or host) on the network. The subnet mask is a value that a NIC uses to distinguish which part of the IP address identifies the network ID and which part of the address identifies the host.

- IP addresses are divided into class licenses that correspond with the potential size of the network: Class A, Class B, and Class C. Class A licenses were intended for huge companies and organizations, such as major multinational corporations, universities, and governmental agencies. Class B licenses were assigned to medium-size companies, and Class C licenses were designated for smaller LANs.

- When you want to be positive that the data moving between two systems gets there in good order, use a connection-oriented application. If it's not a big deal for data to miss a bit or two, then connectionless is the way to go. The connection-oriented protocol used with TCP/IP is called the Transmission Control Protocol (TCP). The connectionless one is called the User Datagram Protocol (UDP).

- TCP/IP provides sharing functions called services. Well-known TCP/IP services include HTTP, the language of the World Wide Web, Telnet, and ping.

- TCP/IP requires that several settings are properly configured before you can connect to a network. A network administrator should configure these for you. These settings include your IP address, default gateway, DNS settings, and DHCP settings.

- Windows includes several tools for testing and managing TCP/IP, including ping, ipconfig, nslookup, and tracert.

- By default, TCP/IP is configured to receive an IP address automatically from a DHCP server on the network (and automatically assign a corresponding subnet mask).

- Windows supports a feature called Automatic Private IP Addressing (APIPA) that automatically assigns an IP address to the system when the client cannot obtain an IP address automatically.

- IPv6 extends the 32-bit IP address space to 128 bits, allowing up to 2^{128} (that's close to 3.4×10^{38}) addresses. The familiar 32-bit IPv4 addresses are written as 197.169.94.82, using four octets. The 128-bit IPv6 addresses are written like this: 2001:0000:0000:3210:0800:200C:00CF:1234. A complete IPv6 address always has eight groups of four hexadecimal characters.

- You may have up to three IPv6 addresses on your PC at one time: a link-local address and two global addresses.

■ Key Terms

110 block (*459*)	**punchdown tool** (*459*)
Automatic Private IP Addressing (APIPA) (*466*)	**router** (*455*)
bridge (*454*)	**run** (*456*)
coaxial cable (*452*)	**solid core** (*457*)
crossover cable (*451*)	**static IP address** (*469*)
Dynamic Host Configuration Protocol (DHCP) (*469*)	**stranded core** (*457*)
equipment rack (*458*)	**structured cabling** (*455*)
fiber optic cable (*451*)	**subnet mask** (*464*)
horizontal cabling (*456*)	**switch** (*453*)
Internet Protocol version 4 (IPv4) (*474*)	**TCP/IP services** (*468*)
Internet Protocol version 6 (IPv6) (*474*)	**telecommunications room** (*456*)
IP address (*464*)	**tracert** (*471*)
ipconfig (*470*)	**Transmission Control Protocol/Internet Protocol (TCP/IP)** (*463*)
nslookup (*470*)	**U** (*458*)
patch cable (*460*)	**work area** (*456*)
patch panel (*459*)	
ping (*468*)	

■ Key Term Quiz

Use the Key Terms list to complete the sentences that follow. Not all terms will be used.

1. HTTP and Telnet are both examples of special sharing functions called _____.

2. The command-line utility called _____ enables one machine to check whether it can communicate with another machine.

3. A center cable surrounded by insulation and covered with a shield of braided cable is called _____.

4. A computer on a(n) _____ network gets a 32-bit address.

5. A computer on a(n) _____ network gets a 128-bit address.

6. The set of standards established by the TIA/EIA regarding network cabling is called _____.

7. _____ uses light, instead of electricity, to transmit data.

8. You can use a(n) _____ to connect two different types of network media, such as coaxial and UTP.

9. A single piece of installed horizontal cabling, whether coax or fiber-optic, is called a(n) _____.

■ Multiple-Choice Quiz

1. Everything worked fine on your 1000BaseT network yesterday, but today no one can connect to the server. The server seems to be in good running order. Which of the following is the most likely problem?

 A. Someone changed all of the passwords for server access.

 B. A switch is malfunctioning.

 C. Someone's T connector has come loose on the bus.

 D. The server's cable is wired as TIA/EIA 568A and all of the others are wired as TIA/EIA 568B.

2. Simon's system can't contact a DHCP server to obtain an IP address automatically, but he can still communicate with other systems on his subnet. What feature of Windows makes this possible?

 A. Subnet masking

 B. Default gateway

 C. APIPA

 D. Client for Microsoft Networks

3. Which of the following protocols is connection-oriented?

 A. UDP

 B. HTTP

 C. TCP

 D. IP

4. What protocol runs the majority of modern networks, including the Internet?

 A. FTP

 B. WWW

 C. HTTP

 D. TCP/IP

5. What is the term used to describe where the network hardware and patch panels are kept?

 A. Drop room

 B. Telecommunications room

 C. Routing room

 D. Telecloset room

6. What determines which part of your IP address is the network ID and which part is the host ID?

 A. Dotted octet

 B. IP mask

 C. Subnet mask

 D. Default gateway

7. What class is the IP address 115.22.0.16?

 A. A

 B. B

 C. C

 D. D

8. What protocol automatically assigns IP addresses to computers on a network?

 A. DHCP

 B. DNS

 C. NAS

 D. UDP

9. When connecting a cable run onto a patch panel, which tool should you use?

 A. 110-punchdown tool

 B. Crimper

 C. TDR

 D. Tone generator

10. What is the structured cabling name for the end user's office space where network computers are set up?

 A. Backbone

 B. Building entrance

 C. Cable drop

 D. Work area

10. A(n) _____ automatically creates point-to-point connections between any two computers.

11. Which of the following describes an IPv4 address? (Select three.)

 A. Uses decimal, not hexadecimal numbers

 B. Uses periods, not colons, as separators

 C. Uses four octets

 D. Uses eight sets of characters

12. Which of the following are fiber connector types? (Select three.)

 A. LC

 B. LS

 C. MT-RJ

 D. ST

■ Essay Quiz

1. You are a tech for a small company and you get a call from Jessica, who cannot access the network anymore from her workstation. What techniques would you use to help troubleshoot her system and get her back working?

2. There are different classifications of IP addresses and different ways to assign them. Write a short essay on the difference between Class A, B, and C addresses, and how to choose either static or dynamic addressing.

3. Which types of computer network cable connections are you familiar with already? Write a short paragraph describing your experience.

4. Prepare a list of questions you would ask a large organization's network administrator regarding cabling, connections, hubs, switches, and even routers.

Lab Projects

• Lab Project 12.1

This chapter described how Windows automatically generates an IP address if there is no DHCP server. Experiment with this idea. If you have a network of Windows PCs that you can play with, make sure there is no DHCP server on the network. Use ipconfig and see what your IP address is, and try sharing it and pinging other systems. Try to share resources and access shared resources on other machines in the lab.

• Lab Project 12.2

The PC is not the only device that can connect to an Ethernet network. Do an Internet search or make a run to your local computer store and create a list of network devices. What did you find? How would they be used?

• Lab Project 12.3

Nearly every hardware manufacturer wants you to upgrade to their latest networking gear and they keep adding new features to entice you. Do a search through the bigger companies' product lists and compare the Linksys, Netgear, Microsoft, and D-Link devices:

www.linksys.com

www.netgear.com

www.microsoft.com

www.dlink.com

• Lab Project 12.4

The Internet is a big, sprawling place with big routers that move packets from place to place around the world. Using the tracert command, see how many hops it takes to get to various Web sites around the world.

Implementing and Troubleshooting Wireless Networks

"The wireless telegraph is not difficult to understand. The ordinary telegraph is like a very long cat. You pull the tail in New York, and it meows in Los Angeles. The wireless is the same, only without the cat."

—ALBERT EINSTEIN

In this chapter, you will learn how to

■ **Install and configure wireless networks**

■ **Troubleshoot wireless networks**

Wireless networks have been popular for many years now, but unlike wired networks, so much of how wireless works continues to elude people. Part of the problem might be that a simple wireless network is so inexpensive and easy to configure that most users and techs never really get into the *hows* of wireless. The chance to get away from all the cables and mess and just *connect* has a phenomenal appeal. Well, let's change all that and dive deeply into wireless networking.

Installing and Configuring Wireless Networking

The mechanics of setting up a wireless network don't differ much from a wired network. Physically installing a wireless network adapter is the same as installing a wired NIC, whether it's an internal PCI card, a PC Card, or an external USB device. Simply install the device and let plug and play handle the rest. Install the device's supplied driver when prompted, and you're practically finished.

As mentioned earlier, wireless devices want to talk to each other, so communicating with an available wireless network is usually a no-brainer. The trick is in configuring the wireless network so that only specific wireless nodes are able to use it and securing the data that's being sent through the air.

Wi-Fi Configuration

Wi-Fi networks support ad hoc and infrastructure operation modes. Which mode you choose depends on the number of wireless nodes you need to support, the type of data sharing they'll perform, and your management requirements.

Ad hoc Mode

Ad hoc mode wireless networks don't need a WAP. The only requirements in an ad hoc mode wireless network are that each wireless node be configured with the same network name (SSID) and that no two nodes use the same IP address. Figure 13.1 shows a wireless network configuration utility with ad hoc mode selected.

• **Figure 13.1** Selecting ad hoc mode in a wireless configuration utility

The only other configuration steps to take are to make sure that no two nodes are using the same IP address (this step is usually unnecessary if all PCs are using DHCP) and ensuring that the File and Printer Sharing service is running on all nodes.

Infrastructure Mode

Typically, **infrastructure mode** wireless networks employ one or more WAPs connected to a wired network segment, a corporate intranet or the Internet, or both. As with ad hoc mode wireless networks, infrastructure mode networks require that the same SSID be configured on all nodes and WAPs. Figure 13.2 shows a NETGEAR Wi-Fi configuration screen set to infrastructure mode and using WPA security.

WAPs have an integrated Web server and are configured through a browser-based setup utility. Typically, you fire up your Web browser on one of your network client workstations and enter the WAP's default IP address, such as 192.168.1.1, to bring up the configuration page. You will need to supply an administrative password, included with your WAP's documentation, to log in (see Figure 13.3). Setup screens vary from vendor to vendor and from model to model. Figure 13.4 shows the initial setup screen for a popular Linksys WAP/router.

Configure the SSID option where indicated. Channel selection is usually automatic, but you can reconfigure this option if you have particular needs in your organization (for example, if you have multiple wireless networks operating in the same area). Remember that it's always more secure to configure a unique SSID than it is to accept the well-known default one. You should also make sure that the option to allow broadcasting of the SSID is disabled. This ensures that only wireless nodes specifically configured with the correct SSID can join the wireless network.

• **Figure 13.2** Selecting infrastructure mode in a wireless configuration utility

• **Figure 13.3** Security login for Linksys WAP

To increase security even more, use **MAC filtering**. Figure 13.5 shows the MAC filtering configuration screen for a Linksys WAP. Simply enter the MAC address of a wireless node that you wish to allow (or deny) access to your wireless network. Set up encryption by turning encryption on at the WAP and then generating a unique security key. Then configure all connected wireless nodes on the network with the same key information. Figure 13.6 shows the WEP key configuration screen for a Linksys WAP.

When setting up WEP, you have the option of automatically generating a set of encryption keys or doing it manually; save yourself a headache and use the automatic method. Select an encryption level—the usual choices are either 64-bit or 128-bit—and then enter a unique passphrase and click the Generate button (or whatever the equivalent button is called on your WAP). Then select a default key and save the settings. The encryption level, key, and passphrase must match on the wireless client node or communication will fail. Many WAPs have the capability

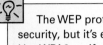 The WEP protocol provides security, but it's easily cracked. Use WPA2 or, if you have older equipment, settle for WPA until you can upgrade.

• **Figure 13.4** Linksys WAP setup screen

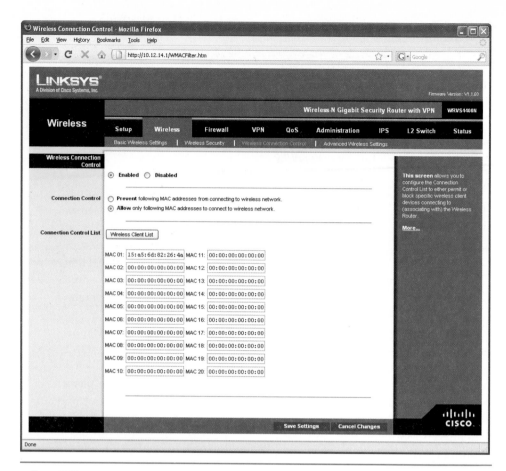

• **Figure 13.5** MAC filtering configuration screen for a Linksys WAP

• **Figure 13.6** WEP encryption key configuration screen for a Linksys WAP

to export the WEP encryption key data onto a media storage device for easy importing onto a client workstation, or you can manually configure encryption by using the vendor-supplied configuration utility, as shown in Figure 13.7.

WPA and WPA2 encryption is configured in much the same way as WEP. There are two ways to set up WPA/WPA2: Pre-shared Key (PSK) or Enterprise. WPA/WPA2-PSK is the most common for small and home networks. Enterprise is much more complex, requires extra equipment (a RADIUS server), and is only used in the most serious and secure wireless networks.

If you have the option, choose WPA2 encryption for the WAP as well as the NICs in your network. You configure WPA2 the same way you would WPA. Note that the settings such as WPA2 for the Enterprise assume you'll enable authentication by using a device called a RADIUS server (see Figure 13.8). This way, businesses can allow only people with the proper credentials to connect to their Wi-Fi networks. For home use, select the PSK version of WPA/WPA2. Use the best encryption you can. If you have WPA2, use it. If not, use WPA. WEP is always a last choice.

With most home networks, you can simply leave the channel and frequency of the WAP at the factory defaults, but in an environment with overlapping Wi-Fi signals, you'll want to adjust one or both features. To adjust the channel, find the option in the WAP configuration screens and simply change it. Figure 13.9 shows the channel option in a Linksys WAP.

With dual-band 802.11n WAPs, you can choose which band to put 802.11n traffic on, either 2.4 GHz or 5 GHz. In an area with overlapping

• **Figure 13.7** WEP encryption screen on client wireless network adapter configuration utility

Always try WPA2-PSK first. If you then have wireless computers that can't connect to your WAP, fall back to WPA-PSK.

• **Figure 13.8** Encryption screen with RADIUS option

signals, most of the traffic will be on the 2.4-GHz frequency, because most devices are either 802.11b or 802.11g. In addition to other wireless devices (such as cordless phones), microwaves also use the 2.4-GHz frequency and can cause a great deal of interference. You can avoid any kind of conflict with your 802.11n devices by using the 5-GHz frequency instead. Figure 13.10 shows the configuration screen for a dual-band 802.11n WAP.

• **Figure 13.9** Changing the channel

• **Figure 13.10** Selecting frequency

Placing the Access Point(s)

The optimal location for an access point depends on the area you want to cover, whether you care if the signal bleeds out beyond the borders, and what interference exists from other wireless sources. You start by doing a site survey. A site survey can be as trivial as firing up a wireless-capable laptop and looking for existing SSIDs. Or it can be a complex job where you hire people with specialized equipment to come in and make lots of careful plans, defining the best place to put WAPs and which wireless channels to use. To make sure the wireless signal goes where you want it to go and not where you don't, you need to use the right antenna. Let's see what types of antennas are available.

Omni-directional and Centered For a typical network, you want blanket coverage and would place a WAP with an omni-directional antenna in the center of the area (see Figure 13.11). With an omni-directional antenna, the radio wave flows outward from the WAP. This has the advantage of ease of use—anything within the signal radius can potentially access the network. Most wireless networks use this combination, especially in the consumer space. The standard straight-wire antennas that provide most omni-directional function are called **dipole antennas**.

Gaining Gain An antenna strengthens and focuses the radio frequency (RF) output from a WAP. The ratio of increase—what's called **gain**—is measured in decibels (dB). The gain from a typical WAP is 2 dB, enough to cover a reasonable area, but not a very large room. To increase that signal requires a bigger antenna. Many WAPs have removable antennas that you can replace. To increase the signal in an omni-directional and centered setup, simply replace the factory antennas with one or more bigger antennas (see Figure 13.12). Get a big enough antenna and you can crank it all the way up to 11 dB!

> If you want to know whether your local café, bookstore, airport, or other public place has a Wi-Fi access point (otherwise known as a *hotspot*), you can use a *Wi-Fi* or *wireless locator*. The locator is usually the size of your car remote and lights up or otherwise signals you whenever you are in range of a Wi-Fi access point.

• **Figure 13.11** Room layout with WAP in the center

• **Figure 13.12** Replacement antenna on WAP

• **Figure 13.13** iPAQ Bluetooth Manager software connected to a Bluetooth access point

Bluetooth network access points are a rare sight out in the real world. Today small portables, PDAs, and smartphones almost certainly connect by using a Wi-Fi or cellular network.

Bluetooth Configuration

As with other wireless networking solutions, **Bluetooth** devices are completely plug and play. Just connect the adapter and follow the prompts to install the appropriate drivers and configuration utilities (these are supplied by your hardware vendor). Once they're installed, you have little to do: Bluetooth devices seek each other out and establish the master/slave relationship without any intervention on your part.

Connecting to a Bluetooth PAN is handled by specialized utility software provided by your portable device or Bluetooth device vendor. Figure 13.13 shows a screen of an older PDA running the Bluetooth Manager software to connect to a Bluetooth access point. Like their Wi-Fi counterparts, Bluetooth access points use a browser-based configuration utility. Figure 13.14 shows the main setup screen for a Belkin Bluetooth access point. Use this setup screen to check on the status of connected Bluetooth devices; configure encryption, MAC filtering, and other security settings; and use other utilities provided by the access point's vendor.

Cellular Configuration

There is no single standard for configuring a cellular network card because the cards and software change based on your service provider. Fortunately, those same cell phone companies have made the process of installing their cards very simple. All that is required in most cases is to plug in the card and install the software.

With most cellular cards, you simply plug the card into your computer, usually via USB, and the setup program automatically launches. These cards almost always have all the required software and drivers built into the cards themselves, so there are no optical discs to worry about. Once you've installed the necessary software, launch the connection application. Follow the instructions that came with the software; in Figure 13.15, for example, double-click on the VZAccess network listed in the window. This initiates the connection to Verizon's network. You can also go to the Options menu and select Statistics to see the specifics of your connection, as shown in Figure 13.16.

The key thing to remember about cellular Internet access is that it is almost completely configured and controlled by the provider. A tech has very little to do except to make sure the cellular card is plugged in, recognized by the computer, and properly installed.

• **Figure 13.14** Belkin Bluetooth access point

• **Figure 13.15** VZAccess Manager

• **Figure 13.16** Session statistics for VZAccess Manager

■ Troubleshooting Wi-Fi

Wireless networks are a real boon when they work right, but they can also be one of the most vexing things to troubleshoot when they don't. Let's turn to some practical advice on how to detect and correct wireless hardware, software, and configuration problems.

As with any troubleshooting scenario, your first step in troubleshooting a wireless network is to break down your tasks into logical steps. Your first step should be to figure out the scope of your wireless networking problem. Ask yourself *who*, *what*, and *when*:

- Who is affected by the problem?
- What is the nature of their network problem?
- When did the problem start?

The answers to these questions dictate at least the initial direction of your troubleshooting.

So, who's affected? If all machines on your network—wired and wireless—have lost connectivity, you have bigger problems than that the wireless machines cannot access the network. Troubleshoot this situation the way you'd troubleshoot any network failure. Once you determine which wireless nodes are affected, it's easier to pinpoint whether the problem lies in one or more wireless clients or in one or more access points.

After you narrow down the number of affected machines, your next task is to figure out specifically what type of error the users are experiencing. If they can access some, but not all, network services, it's unlikely that the problem is limited to their wireless equipment. For example, if they can browse the Internet but can't access any shared resources on a server,

they're probably experiencing a permissions-related issue rather than a wireless one.

Finally, determine when the problem started. What has changed that might explain your loss of connectivity? Did you or somebody else change the wireless network configuration? For example, if the network worked fine two minutes ago, and then you changed the WEP key on the access point, and now nobody can see the network, you have your solution—or at least your culprit! Did your office experience a power outage, power sag, or power surge? Any of these might cause a WAP to fail.

Once you figure out the who, what, and when, you can start troubleshooting in earnest. Typically, your problem is going to center on your hardware, software, connectivity, or configuration.

Hardware Troubleshooting

Wireless networking hardware components are subject to the same kind of abuse and faulty installation as any other hardware component. Troubleshooting a suspected hardware problem should bring out the technician in you.

Open Windows Device Manager and look for an error or conflict with the wireless adapter. If you see a big exclamation point or a red *X* next to the device, you have a driver error. Reinstall the device driver as needed.

If you don't see the device listed at all, perhaps it is not seated properly in its expansion slot or not plugged all the way into its PC Card or USB slot. These problems are easy to fix. Just remove them and reinstall the device.

 As with all things computing, don't forget to do the standard PC troubleshooting thing and reboot the computer before you do any configuration or hardware changes!

Software Troubleshooting

Because you've already checked to confirm that your hardware is using the correct drivers, what kind of software-related problems are left to check? Two things come immediately to mind: the wireless adapter configuration utility and the WAP's firmware version.

As I mentioned earlier, some wireless devices won't work correctly unless you install the vendor-provided drivers and configuration utility before plugging in the device. This is particularly true of wireless USB devices. If you didn't do this, go into Device Manager and uninstall the device; then start again from scratch.

Some WAP manufacturers (I won't name names here, but they're popular) are notorious for shipping devices without the latest firmware installed. This problem often manifests as a device that enables clients to connect, but only at such slow speeds that the devices experience frequent timeout errors. The fix for this is to update the access point's firmware. Go to the manufacturer's Web site and follow the support links until you find the latest version. You'll need your device's exact model and serial number—this is important, because installing the wrong firmware version on your device is a guaranteed way of rendering it unusable!

Again, follow the manufacturer's instructions for updating the firmware to the letter. Typically, you need to download a small executable updating program along with a data file containing the firmware software. The process takes only minutes, and you'll be amazed at the results.

Connectivity Troubleshooting

Properly configured wireless clients should automatically and quickly connect to the desired SSID. If this isn't taking place, it's time for some troubleshooting. Most wireless connectivity problems come down to either an incorrect configuration (such as an incorrect password) or low signal strength. Without a strong signal, even a properly configured wireless client isn't going to work. Wireless clients use a multi-bar graph (usually five bars) to give an idea of signal strength: zero bars indicates no signal and five bars indicates maximum signal.

Whether configuration or signal strength, the process to diagnose and repair uses the same methods you use for a wired network. First, check the wireless NIC's link light to see whether it's passing data packets to and from the network. Second, check the wireless NIC's configuration utility. Typically the utility has an icon in your system tray/notification area that shows the strength of your wireless signal. Figure 13.17 shows Windows XP Professional's built-in wireless configuration utility—called Wireless Zero Configuration (or just Zeroconf)—displaying the link state and signal strength. Wireless Zero Configuration was first introduced with Windows XP. In Windows Vista and Windows 7, the service is called WLAN Auto-Config.

The link state defines the wireless NIC's connection status to a wireless network: connected or disconnected. If your link state indicates that your computer is currently disconnected, you may have a problem with your WAP. If your signal is too weak to receive a signal (referred to on the CompTIA A+ 220-802 exam as a "low RF signal"), you may be out of range of your access point, or there may be a device causing interference.

You can fix these problems in a number of ways. Because Wi-Fi signals bounce off of objects, you can try small adjustments to your antennas to see if the signal improves. You can swap out the standard antenna for one or more higher-gain antennas. You can relocate the PC or access point, or locate and move the device causing interference.

Other wireless devices that operate in the same frequency range as your wireless nodes can cause interference as well. Look for wireless telephones, intercoms, and so on as possible culprits. One fix for interference caused by other wireless devices is to change the channel your network uses. Another is to change the channel the offending device uses, if possible. If you can't change channels, try moving the interfering device to another area or replacing it with a different device.

Wireless Network Connection (HomeWiFi)
Speed: 54.0 Mbps
Signal Strength: Very Good
Status: Connected

11:25 AM

● **Figure 13.17** Windows XP Professional's wireless configuration utility

If you're lucky enough to have a laptop with an internally installed NIC (instead of a PC Card), your device may not have a link light.

Configuration Troubleshooting

With all due respect to the fine network techs in the field, the most common type of wireless networking problem is misconfigured hardware or software. That's right—the dreaded *user error*! Given the complexities of wireless networking, this isn't so surprising. All it takes is one slip of the typing finger to throw off your configuration completely. The things you're most likely to get wrong are the SSID and security configuration.

Verify SSID configuration on your access point first, and then check on the affected wireless nodes. With most wireless devices, you can use any characters in the SSID, including blank spaces. Be careful not to add blank

characters where they don't belong, such as trailing blank spaces behind any other characters typed into the name field.

If you're using MAC address filtering, make sure the MAC address of the client that's attempting to access the wireless network is on the list of accepted users. This is particularly important if you swap out NICs on a PC, or if you introduce a new PC to your wireless network.

Check the security configuration to make sure that all wireless nodes and access points match. Mistyping an encryption key prevents the affected node from talking to the wireless network, even if your signal strength is 100 percent! Remember that many access points have the capability to export encryption keys onto a thumb drive or other removable media. It's then a simple matter to import the encryption key onto the PC by using the wireless NIC's configuration utility. Remember that the encryption level must match on access points and wireless nodes. If your WAP is configured for 128-bit encryption, all nodes must also use 128-bit encryption.

Chapter 13 Review

■ Chapter Summary

After reading this chapter and completing the exercises, you should understand the following about wireless networking.

Install and configure wireless networks

■ The mechanics of setting up a wireless network don't differ much from a wired network. Physically installing a wireless network adapter is the same as installing a wired NIC, whether it's an internal expansion card, a PC Card, or an external USB device. Simply install the device and let plug and play handle the rest.

■ Wi-Fi networks support ad hoc and infrastructure operation modes. Which mode you choose depends on the number of wireless nodes you need to support, the type of data sharing they'll perform, and your management requirements.

■ Ad hoc mode wireless networks don't need a WAP. The only requirements in an ad hoc mode wireless network are that each wireless node be configured with the same network name (SSID) and that no two nodes use the same IP address. You may also have to select a common channel for all ad hoc nodes.

■ Typically, infrastructure mode wireless networks employ one or more WAPs connected to a wired network segment, a corporate intranet or the Internet, or both. As with ad hoc mode wireless networks, infrastructure mode networks require that the same SSID be configured on all nodes and WAPs.

■ WAPs have an integrated Web server and are configured through a browser-based setup utility. Typically, you enter the WAP's default IP address to bring up the configuration page and supply an administrative password, included with your WAP's documentation, to log in.

■ Set up WEP encryption—if that's your only option—by turning encryption on at the WAP and then generating a unique security key. Then configure all connected wireless nodes on the network with the same key information. WPA and WPA2 encryption are configured in much the same way. You may be required to input a valid user name and password to configure encryption by using WPA/WPA2.

■ As with other wireless networking solutions, Bluetooth devices are completely plug and play. Just connect the adapter and follow the prompts to install the appropriate drivers and configuration utilities. Connecting to a Bluetooth PAN is handled by specialized utility software provided by your portable device or Bluetooth device vendor.

Troubleshoot wireless networks

■ As with any troubleshooting scenario, your first step should be to figure out the scope of your wireless networking problem. Ask yourself *who*, *what*, and *when*. This helps you focus your initial troubleshooting on the most likely aspects of the network.

■ Hardware troubleshooting for Wi-Fi devices should touch on the usual hardware process. Go to Device Manager and check for obvious conflicts. Check the drivers to make sure you have them installed and up-to-date. Make certain you have proper connectivity between the device and the PC.

■ Software troubleshooting involves checking configuration settings, such as the SSID, WEP, MAC address filtering, and encryption levels. Be sure to check configuration settings on both the WAP and the wireless NIC.

■ Key Terms

ad hoc mode *(483)*

Bluetooth *(490)*

dipole antennas *(489)*

gain *(489)*

infrastructure mode *(484)*

MAC address filtering *(485)*

Key Term Quiz

Use the Key Terms list to complete the sentences that follow. Not all terms will be used.

1. A technology for setting up wireless PANs and connecting to some peripherals is called _____.

2. _____ provide omni-directional signals.

3. Computers are in _____ when they connect directly together without using a WAP.

4. The amount that an antenna increases a WAP's radio signal is called _____.

5. You can use _____ to keep unwanted computers out of your network.

6. If you need share an Internet connection or connect to a wired network through your wireless network, you would use _____.

Multiple-Choice Quiz

1. Two wireless nodes that are communicating directly with each other, without any intermediary systems or hardware, are using what wireless mode?

 A. Ad hoc

 B. Bluetooth

 C. Infrastructure

 D. 802.11

2. What security feature limits which PCs can access a wireless network based on their NICs' hard-coded addresses?

 A. WPA

 B. SSID

 C. MAC filtering

 D. WEP filtering

3. How do you install and configure most cellular WAN cards?

 A. Plug the card into a USB port and then follow the onscreen instructions.

 B. Set up CMOS to enable cellular WAN and then install the card into a PCIe slot.

 C. Plug the card into a USB port and enter your IP and cellular account information.

 D. Plug the card into an eSATA port and follow the onscreen instructions.

4. What are the two ways you can set up WPA/WPA2? (Select two.)

 A. PSK

 B. WEP

 C. Enterprise

 D. Administrator

5. What can limit wireless connectivity to a list of accepted users based on the hard-wired address of their wireless NIC?

 A. Encryption

 B. MAC filtering

 C. NWLink

 D. WEP

6. What tool can you use to find available wireless networks?

 A. WAP

 B. Wireless Detection System

 C. MAC locator

 D. Wireless locator

7. Which of these Wi-Fi security protocols is the least secure and is easily hacked?

 A. WEP

 B. WAP

 C. WINS

 D. WPA2

8. What is a cheap and easy way to extend the range of a WAP?

 A. Upgrade the antenna.

 B. Buy a WAP that advertises a longer range.

 C. You can't easily boost range.

 D. Upgrade the wireless NICs.

9. What is the technical name of a wireless network?

 A. SSID

 B. BSSID

 C. SSD

 D. WPA

10. Which of the following devices is a major source of interference for Wi-Fi networks?

 A. Cell phones

 B. Small FM radio transmitters

 C. Microwaves

 D. Fluorescent lights

■ Essay Quiz

1. You purchased a new WAP, but its range just isn't cutting the mustard. Do some research on the available types of upgrade antennas for WAPs and write a short paragraph about the different options.

2. Write a short memo about the various security options when setting up a wireless network. Remember: there's more to security than just setting up encryption!

3. Prepare a short memo to your instructor (or friend) that outlines the basic differences between WEP and WPA encryption methods. Use any standard memo format you are familiar with. Include a company or school logo on the top of the page to make the memo appear to be printed on company stationery (or "letterhead").

Lab Projects

• Lab Project 13.1

You just received a nice tax return and want to expand your home network. Your current wired home network setup consists of two Intel Core 2 Duo desktop PCs with 10/100-Mbps NICs and a relative's older laptop with both an RJ-45 port and 802.11b wireless built in. The main Internet connection coming into your home enters your more powerful desktop system first and then spreads out to a 100-Mbps switch from there. With your own money to be spent buying

equipment, you seek a solution that will satisfy your needs for a long time.

You want to buy your new equipment locally so you can set it up right away. Use the Internet to explore prices and equipment in local stores. Also check out reviews of the items you are interested in obtaining. After you have done sufficient research, prepare an itemized price list with your choices arranged like the following table:

ITEM	STORE/MODEL	PRICE	QUANTITY	TOTAL
Wireless NICs, PCI\PCIe				
Wireless NICs, PC Card				
Wireless Access Point				
Other				
TOTALS				

• Lab Project 13.2

Write a short manual for troubleshooting common wireless networking problems. Make sure there are sections for dealing with interference, increasing wireless range, fixing connection issues, and dealing with security. Include other sections as you see fit.

Implementing and Troubleshooting Networks

"The Internet? Is that thing still around?"

—Homer Simpson, *The Simpsons*

In this chapter, you will learn how to

- **Understand network organization**
- **Install and configure wired networks**
- **Troubleshoot wired networks**
- **Troubleshoot an Internet connection**

Networks are everywhere. It's been a long time since being a PC tech meant primarily fixing individual computers. These days, any tech worth a flip has to understand not only how each individual computer works, but also how groups of computers work *together*. With that in mind, this chapter looks at the various aspects of installing and troubleshooting networks.

You'll first read about the various methods used to organize computers into networks for resource sharing, and then you'll look at installing and configuring wired networks. Knowing how to install a network isn't much good if you don't know how to fix things when the network goes bad, so the next section deals with troubleshooting wired networks. The chapter ends with a look at troubleshooting connections to the biggest network of them all, the Internet.

Network Organization

Once a network is created using appropriate network technology like Ethernet, users need to be able to share resources in some organized fashion. Resources such as folders and printers need a way to determine who can and cannot use them and how they can be used. Microsoft designed Windows networks to work in one of three categories: workgroups, domains, or homegroups. (These are the Microsoft terms, but the concepts have been adopted by the entire computer industry and apply to Mac OS X and other operating systems.) These three organizations differ in control, number of machines needed, compatibility, and security.

Let's start with the oldest network organization: workgroups.

Workgroups

Workgroups are the most basic and simplistic of the three network organizations. They are also the default for almost every fresh installation of Windows. Workgroups have been around since the ancient Windows for Workgroups came out back in the early 1990s.

By default, all computers on the network are assigned to a workgroup called WORKGROUP. You can see your workgroup name by opening the System applet (press WINDOWS KEY-PAUSE or go to Start | Control Panel | System applet), as shown in Figure 14.1.

There's nothing special about the name WORKGROUP, except that every computer on the network needs the same workgroup name to be able to share resources. If you want to change your workgroup name, you need

• **Figure 14.1** Default workgroup

• **Figure 14.2** Changing the workgroup in advanced settings

Most workgroup-based Windows networks keep the default name of WORKGROUP.

to use the System applet. Click the *Change settings* button to open the System Properties dialog box. Then click the Change button to change your workgroup name (see Figure 14.2).

Workgroups lack centralized control over the network; all systems connected to the network are equals. This works well for smaller networks because there are fewer users, connections, and security concerns to think about. But what do you do when your network encompasses dozens or hundreds of users and systems? How can you control all of that?

User Names and Passwords

As you'll recall from Chapter 2, when you log on to a Windows computer, you need to enter a user name and password. Windows 7 makes this easy by giving you a pretty logon interface, as shown in Figure 14.3.

The user names and their passwords are stored in an encrypted format on your computer. User names have a number of jobs on your computer, but at this point, the job most interesting to us is to give a user access to the computer. User names work well when you access your own computer, but these same user names and passwords are used to access shared resources on other computers in the network—and that's where we run into trouble. To appreciate this problem, let's watch a typical folder share take place on a network of Windows 7 systems.

Sharing a Folder

All Windows computers can share folders and printers out of the box. Sharing a folder in Windows 7 is easy—just right-click on the folder and

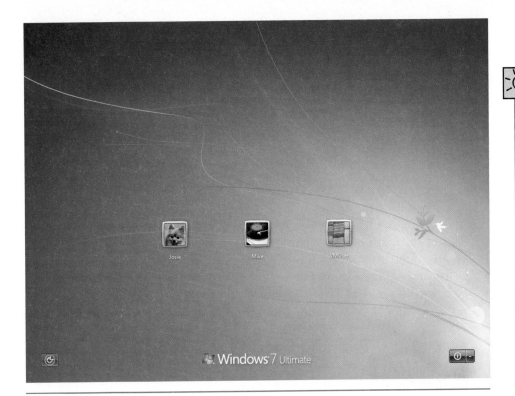

Windows XP provides a tool called the Network Setup Wizard that enables you to configure computers on a LAN to share folders and printers. This tool is especially useful on networks that use Internet Connection Sharing with a Windows XP machine as the default gateway. To run the Wizard, go to Start | Control Panel | Network and Internet Connections | Network Connections. Under Common Tasks, click Network Setup Wizard. Follow the steps in the Wizard to create a floppy disk with a small setup program used to configure other computers to share resources (folders, printers, and so on).

• **Figure 14.3** Windows 7 logon screen

select Share with | Specific people (see Figure 14.4) to get to the File Sharing dialog box. On most Windows 7 systems, you'll see options called Homegroup in the context menu—ignore these for now as they will be explained in the upcoming "Homegroups" section.

• **Figure 14.4** Accessing the Folder Sharing dialog box

By default, you'll see every user account that's currently on this system. You may give an account Read or Read/Write permission, while the person who created the folder is assigned as Owner. The following list describes these permissions:

- **Read** You can see what's in the folder. You may open files in the folder, but you can't save anything back into the folder.

- **Read/Write** Same as Read but you can save files into the folder.

- **Owner** Same as Read/Write plus you can set the permissions for other users on the folder.

All versions of Windows come with a far more powerful and much more complex form of permissions based on the NTFS file system. You may remember the big discussion of this more advanced form of permissions from Chapter 7.

So all this sharing seems to work quite nicely, except for one big issue: When you log on to your computer, you are accessing a user name and database on that computer. The accounts you are giving access to are stored on your computer, so how do you give someone from another computer access to that shared folder? You have to give that other person a valid user name and password. We use the nomenclature <computer name>\<user name> to track our logons. If you log on to Computer A as Mike, we say you are logged on to ComputerA\Mike. This nomenclature comes in very handy when networked computers become part of the process.

Figure 14.5 shows an account called Mike on Computer A. Assume there is a shared folder called Timmy on Computer A and Mike has read/write permission.

A person fires up Computer B, logging in as Fred. He opens his Network menu option and sees Computer A, but when he clicks on it he sees a network password prompt (see Figure 14.6).

Computer A\Mike

Computer B\Fred

• **Figure 14.5** Computers A and B

• **Figure 14.6** Prompt for entering user name and password

The reason is that the person is logged on as ComputerB\Fred and he needs to be logged on as ComputerA\Mike to access this folder successfully. So the user needs to know the password for ComputerA\Mike. This isn't a very pretty way to protect user names and passwords. So what can you do? You have three choices:

- You can make people log on to shares as just shown.

- You can create the same accounts (same user name and same password) on all the computers and give sharing permissions to all the users for all the shares.

- You can use one account on all computers. Everyone logs on with the same account, and then all shares are by default assigned to the same account.

Domains

Larger networks that need more control use **domains**. Opposite the decentralized nature of workgroups, domains require a specific server to control access to the network's resources. This means tracking each user, each resource, and what each user can do to each resource.

To use a domain on a network of Windows machines, you must have a computer running a version of Windows Server (see Figure 14.7). Windows Server is a completely different, much more powerful, and much more expensive version of Windows. Current editions of this specialized OS include Windows Server 2008 and Windows Server 2008 R2.

An administrator creates a domain on the Windows Server system, which makes that system the *domain controller* (*DC*). The administrator also creates new user accounts on the domain controller. These accounts are called *domain accounts*. Once a network is set up as a domain, each PC on

In addition to running domains, Windows Server enables servers to run applications that can be accessed remotely by client PCs running Windows 7 (or Vista with the appropriate update). You can access this feature using the RemoteApp and Desktop Connections Control Panel applets.

• **Figure 14.7** Windows Server

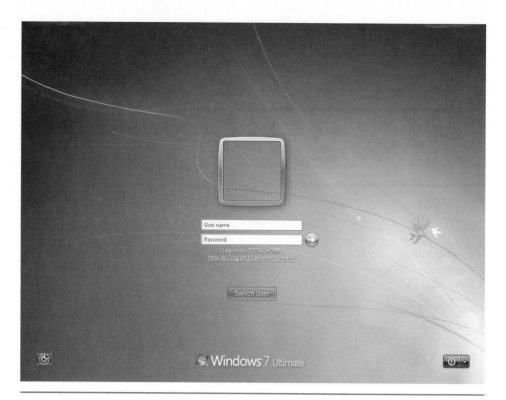

• **Figure 14.8** Domain logon screen

the network needs to join the domain (which kicks you off the workgroup). When you log on to a computer that's a member of a domain, Windows will prompt you for a user name instead of showing you icons for all the users on the network (see Figure 14.8).

When using a domain, you don't log on to your computer. Instead, you log on directly to the domain. All user accounts are stored on the domain controller, as shown in Figure 14.9. A lot of domains have names that look like Web addresses, like totalhome.com, totalhome.local, or even just total-home. Using the previous nomenclature, you can log on to a domain using <domain>\<domain user name>. If the domain totalhome.local has a user account called Mike, for example, you would use totalhome.local\Mike to log on.

One of the best features of domains is that you can log on to any computer on the domain using the same domain account. You don't have to set up local accounts on each computer. We call this feature *single sign-on*, and for most users, this is the biggest benefit to using a Windows domain.

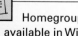
There is much more to a Windows domain than single sign-on. For the CompTIA A+ certification, however, that's the big selling point. If you want to delve deeper into Windows domains, consider pursuing the CompTIA Network+ certification or one of the Microsoft certifications.

Homegroups

The problem with workgroups is that they provide almost no security and require lots of signing on to access resources. Domains provide single sign-on and lots of security, but require special servers and lots of administration. To address this, Microsoft introduced a feature in Windows 7 called **HomeGroup**.

Homegroups are not available in Windows XP or Windows Vista.

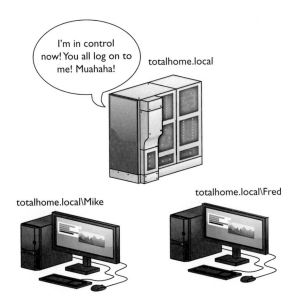

Figure 14.9 Domain network

HomeGroup uses the idea that people want to connect data, not folders. Most people want to share their music, not their My Music folder. So homegroups skip folders completely and share Windows 7 libraries.

A homegroup connects a group of computers using a common password—no special user names required. Each computer can be a member of only one homegroup at a time. Let's make a homegroup and see how this works.

To make a homegroup, open the HomeGroup Control Panel applet. Assuming you currently connect to a workgroup and haven't already created a homegroup, you'll see a dialog box like the one shown in Figure 14.10.

Click the *Create a homegroup* button to create a homegroup. You'll then see the Create a Homegroup dialog box shown in Figure 14.11.

Notice the five options: Pictures, Music, Videos, Documents, and Printers. Remember that those first four are the libraries you learned about in

You may want to review what you learned about libraries in Chapter 2.

Microsoft refers to the technology as HomeGroup, but drops the capitalization to homegroup when talking about the groups themselves. Look for it to appear either way on the CompTIA A+ 220-802 exam.

Figure 14.10 Default HomeGroup dialog box

• Figure 14.11 Create a Homegroup dialog box

Interestingly, all homegroup data is encrypted between systems.

Chapter 2? The Documents checkbox is probably not checked, but go ahead and check it to share all five things. Click Next to see the homegroup's password (see Figure 14.12)

Perhaps you've heard that you shouldn't write down passwords? Well, this password is so long that you might *need* to write it down. The dialog box even gives you a way to print it out! Click Next one more time to see the dialog box shown in Figure 14.13. This is the dialog box you will now see every time you click the HomeGroup applet in the Control Panel.

Let's look at this carefully. Notice where it says *Share libraries and printers* and, a bit lower, *How do I share additional libraries?* By default, homegroups share libraries, not individual folders. The Music, Pictures, Videos,

• Figure 14.12 The homegroup's password

● **Figure 14.13** Homegroup configured

and Documents libraries are shared by default. Although printers get their own checkbox, this setting remains the same as a normal printer share. It's just a handy place to add printer sharing, as even the most basic users like to share printers.

Once you've created a homegroup, go to another computer on the network and open the HomeGroup Control Panel applet. Assuming all the factors stated earlier, you will see a dialog box like Figure 14.14.

Click the *Join now* button, enter the password, choose which libraries you want to share with everyone else, and the new computer is in the homegroup!

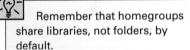
Remember that homegroups share libraries, not folders, by default.

● **Figure 14.14** HomeGroup showing an existing homegroup

• **Figure 14.15** Using homegroups

Once you create a homegroup, you can access it from Windows Explorer.

Access the files shared through a homegroup by opening Windows Explorer, as shown in Figure 14.15. To see what others are sharing, select the corresponding computer name. You can then open those libraries to see the shared folders.

Sharing more libraries is easy, and, if you'd like, you can even share individual folders. Just right-click on the library or folder and select Share with, as shown in Figure 14.16.

• **Figure 14.16** The Share with menu

Notice you have four options: Nobody, Homegroup (Read), Homegroup (Read/Write), and Specific people. The Nobody option means the item is not shared.

By sharing libraries with homegroups, Microsoft hides folders for most users, helping users share their stuff (documents, pictures, music, and videos) instead of folders. Homegroups fit a very specific world—smaller, non–domain home networks—but within that realm, they work wonderfully.

Installing and Configuring a Wired Network

Network organization and resource sharing is fun, but let's move on to the good stuff: installing and configuring a network! To have network connectivity, you need to have three things in place:

- **NIC** The physical hardware that connects the computer system to the network media

- **Protocol** The language that the computer systems use to communicate

- **Network client** The interface that allows the computer system to speak to the protocol

If you want to share resources on your PC with other network users, you also need to enable Microsoft's File and Printer Sharing. Plus, of course, you need to connect the PC to the network switch via some sort of cable (preferably CAT 6 with Gigabit Ethernet cranking through the wires, but that's just me!). When you install a NIC, by default Windows installs upon setup the TCP/IP protocol, the Client for Microsoft Networks, and File and Printer Sharing for Microsoft Networks.

Installing a NIC

The NIC is your computer system's link to the network, and installing one is the first step required to connect to a network. NICs are manufactured to operate on specific media and network types, such as 1000BaseT Ethernet. Follow the manufacturer's instructions for installation. If your NIC is of recent vintage, it will be detected, installed, and configured automatically by Windows. You might need a driver disc or a driver download from the manufacturer's Web site.

The Add Hardware Wizard in Windows XP automates installation of non–plug-and-play devices or plug-and-play devices that were not detected correctly. Start the wizard by clicking Start | Control Panel and then double-clicking the icon for the Add Hardware applet. Click the Next button to select the hardware task you wish to perform, and follow the prompts to complete the wizard. If, for some reason, Windows Vista or Windows 7 doesn't automatically detect a new NIC after you turn the PC back on, go to Start | Control Panel | Add Hardware in Windows Vista or Start | Devices and Printers and click on *Add a device* in Windows 7 to install it.

Windows Explorer also adds a *Share with* toolbar button that works exactly like the menu shown in Figure 14.16.

When you've configured your wired network, you also might need to configure your Web browser. You can do this using the Internet Options Control Panel applet. Internet Options contains several different tabs that give you access to various settings. The General tab is where you control the most basic features of Internet Explorer. The Security tab controls IE's security features. The Privacy tab controls cookies and pop-ups. The Content tab controls what your browser will and will not display. The Connections tab enables you to set up your Internet connection (broadband or dial-up), connect to a VPN (Virtual Private Network) or proxy server, or adjust LAN settings. The Programs tab contains settings for add-ons and how other programs handle HTML files and e-mail. Finally, the Advanced tab contains a bunch of advanced options for accessibility, browsing, and more security settings.

Full-Duplex and Half-Duplex

All modern NICs can run in **full-duplex** mode, meaning they can send and receive data at the same time. The vast majority of NICs and switches use a feature called *auto-sensing* to accommodate very old devices that might attach to the network and need to run in half-duplex mode. *Half-duplex* means that the device can send and receive, but not at the same time. An obvious example of a half-duplex device is the walkie-talkies you played with as a kid that required you to press and hold the orange button to transmit—at which time you couldn't hear anything. Half-duplex devices are exceedingly rare in modern computers, but you need to understand this option. Some NICs just can't handle full-duplex communication when you connect them directly to another NIC by using a crossover cable—that is, no switch. Dropping both NICs down from full-duplex or auto-sensing can sometimes enable these odd NICs to communicate.

• **Figure 14.17** Mmmm, pretty lights!

Link Lights

NICs made today have some type of light-emitting diode (LED) *status indicator* that gives information about the state of the NIC's link to whatever is on the other end of the connection. Even though you know the lights are actually LEDs, get used to calling them **link lights**, because that's the term all network techs use. NICs can have between one and four different link lights, and the LEDs can be any color. These lights give you clues about what's happening with the link and are one of the first items to check whenever you think a system is disconnected from the network (see Figure 14.17).

Switches also have link lights, enabling you to check the connectivity at both ends of the cable. If a PC can't access a network, always check the link lights first. Multispeed devices usually have a link light that tells you the speed of the connection. In Figure 14.18, the light for port 2 on the top photo is orange, for example, signifying that the other end of the cable is plugged into either a 10BaseT or 100BaseT NIC. The same port connected to a Gigabit NIC—that's the lower picture—displays a green LED.

A properly functioning link light is steady on when the NIC is connected to another device. No flickering, no on and off, just on. A link light that is off or flickering shows a connection problem.

• **Figure 14.18** Multispeed lights

Another light is the **activity light**. This little guy turns on when the card detects network traffic, so it makes an intermittent flickering when operating properly. The activity light is a lifesaver for detecting problems, because in the real world, the connection light sometimes lies to you. If the connection light says the connection is good, the next step is to try to copy a file or do something else to create network traffic. If the activity light does not flicker, you have a problem.

No standard governs how NIC manufacturers use their lights; as a result, LEDs in NICs come in an amazing array of colors and layouts. When you encounter a NIC with a number of LEDs, take a moment to try to figure out what each one means. Although different NICs have different ways of arranging and using their LEDs, the functions are always the same: link, activity, and speed.

Wake-on-LAN

A popular feature of most NICs is the ability to turn on or wake up a powered-down or sleeping PC. You'll learn more about power management in Chapter 15, but for now, know that *Wake-on-LAN* is handy when you want to wake up one or multiple computers that you aren't physically near. To wake up a PC with Wake-on-LAN, you'll need to use a second PC to send either a special pattern or a *magic packet* (a broadcast packet that essentially repeats the destination MAC address many times).

A powered-down or sleeping PC knows to look for this special pattern or packet, at least after configured to do so. In Windows XP, go to the Control Panel and open Network Connections. In Windows Vista/7, go to the Control Panel and open Network and Sharing Center. Click *Manage network connections* (Vista) or *Change adapter settings* (7) on the left. For all versions of Windows, right-click on the adapter and select Properties. Click the Configure button in the Properties dialog box and then select the Power Management tab (see Figure 14.19). To enable Wake-on-LAN, make sure the checkbox next to *Allow this device to wake the computer* is checked. Optionally, you can select *Only allow a magic packet to wake the computer*, which will instruct the NIC to ignore everything but magic packets.

Wake-on-LAN is very convenient, but it has one nasty downside. As noted in the Properties dialog box, Wake-on-LAN can wake up or turn on laptops using wireless connections, even when they aren't plugged in or are inside a carrying case. Don't let your laptop's battery die or overheat—unless you know that you'll need it, turn off Wake-on-LAN on your laptop.

Configuring a Network Client

To establish network connectivity, you need a network client installed and configured properly. Let's look at Microsoft's client.

Though no real standard exists for NIC LEDs, the CompTIA A+ 802 exam will test you on some more-or-less *de facto* LED meanings. You should know that a solid green light means connectivity, a flashing green light means intermittent connectivity, no green light means no connectivity, and a flashing amber light means there are collisions on the network (which is sometimes okay). Also, know that the first things you should check when having connectivity issues are the NIC's LEDs.

Your BIOS might also have settings for controlling Wake-on-LAN functions. Check your CMOS System Configuration tool to find out.

• **Figure 14.19** Wake-on-LAN settings on the Power Management tab

If you need to access your office network remotely, you can use what's called a Virtual Private Network (VPN). You can configure VPN access in the Internet Options applet in the Control Panel.

Installed as part of the OS installation, the Client for Microsoft Networks rarely needs configuration, and, in fact, few configuration options are available. To start it in Windows Vista/7, click Start, right-click Network, and select Properties. Then click *Manage network connections* (Vista) or *Change adapter settings* (7) on the left. In Windows XP, click Start, right-click My Network Places, and select Properties.

In all versions of Windows, the next step is to double-click the Local Area Connection icon, click the Properties button, and highlight Client for Microsoft Networks. In Windows XP/Vista, click the Properties button. Windows 7 disables this option. Note, however, that there's not much to do here. Unless told to do something by a network administrator, just leave this alone.

Sharing and Security

Windows systems can share all kinds of resources: files, folders, entire drives, printers, faxes, Internet connections, and much more. Conveniently for you, the scope of the CompTIA A+ 220-802 exam is limited to folders and printers.

Sharing Drives and Folders

All versions of Windows share drives and folders in basically the same manner. Right-click any drive or folder and choose Properties. Select the Sharing tab (see Figure 14.20). In Windows Vista/7, click the Advanced Sharing button. Select *Share this folder*, add something in the Comment or User limit fields if you wish (they're not required), and click Permissions (see Figure 14.21).

• **Figure 14.20** Windows XP Sharing tab on NTFS volume

• **Figure 14.21** Network permissions

Hey! Doesn't NTFS have all those wild permissions such as Read, Execute, Take Ownership, and all that? Yes, it does, but NTFS permissions and network permissions are totally separate beasties. Microsoft wanted Windows to support many different file systems (NTFS, FAT16, FAT32), old and new. Network permissions are Microsoft's way of enabling you to administer file sharing on any type of partition supported by Windows, no matter how ancient. Sure, your options will be pretty limited if you are working with an older file system, but you *can* do it.

If you share a folder on an NTFS drive, as you normally do these days, you must set *both* the network permissions and the NTFS permissions to let others access your shared resources. Some good news: This is actually no big deal! Just set the network permissions to give everyone full control, and then use the NTFS permissions to exercise more precise control over *who* accesses the shared resources and *how* they access them. Open the Security tab to set the NTFS permissions.

> Windows offers two types of sharing: share-level and NTFS permissions.

Accessing Shared Drives/Directories

Once you have set up a drive or directory to be shared, the final step is to access that shared drive or directory from another machine. Windows XP uses My Network Places and Windows Vista and Windows 7 use Network, although you'll need to do a little clicking to get to the shared resources (see Figure 14.22).

• **Figure 14.22** Shared resources in Network

You can also map network resources to a local resource name. For example, the FREDC share can be mapped to be a local hard drive such as E: or F:. From within any Explorer window (such as My Documents or Documents), choose Tools | Map Network Drive to open the Map Network Drive dialog box (see Figure 14.23). In Windows Vista/7, you might need to press the ALT key once to see the menu bar. Click the Browse button to check out the neighborhood and find a shared drive (see Figure 14.24).

Windows 2000 had the handy Add Network Place icon in My Network Places to add network locations you frequently access without using up drive letters. Windows XP removed the icon but added the menu option in its context bar

• **Figure 14.23** Map Network Drive dialog box in Windows 7

• **Figure 14.24** Browsing for shared folders

on the left. Windows Vista and Windows 7 have removed it altogether but have added the ability to add links to network locations to your Favorites in Windows Explorer. Simply drag the network share, or any folder for that matter, to the Favorites list in the Navigation pane on the left. Figure 14.25 shows how it looks on a Windows 7 system.

Mapping shared network drives is a common practice, as it makes a remote network share look like just another drive on the local system. The only downside to drive mapping stems from the fact that users tend to forget they are on a network. A classic example is the user who always accesses a particular folder or file on the network and then suddenly gets a "file not found" error when the workstation is disconnected from the network. Instead of recognizing this as a network error, the user often imagines the problem is a missing or corrupted file.

All shared resources should show up in My Network Places/Network. If a shared resource fails to show up, make sure you check the basics first: Is File and Printer Sharing activated? Is the device shared? Don't let silly errors fool you!

UNC

All computers that share must have a network name, and all of the resources they share must also have network names. Any resource on a network can be described by combining the name of the resource being shared and the name of the system sharing it. If a machine called SERVER1 is sharing its C: drive as FREDC, for example, the complete name would look like this:

```
\\SERVER1\FREDC
```

• **Figure 14.25** Adding a network location to the Windows 7 Navigation pane

Another command-line network utility you'll see on the CompTIA A+ 220-802 exam is **mstsc**, which runs the Remote Desktop application. This enables you to control another computer remotely over the Internet. You can also set up Remote Desktop using the Remote Settings Control Panel applet.

This is called the **universal naming convention (UNC)**. The UNC is distinguished by its use of double backslashes in front of the sharing system's name and a single backslash in front of the shared resource's name. A UNC name can also point directly to a specific file or folder:

```
\\SERVER1\FREDC\INSTALL-FILES\SETUP.EXE
```

In this example, INSTALL-FILES is a subdirectory in the shared folder FREDC (which may or may not be called FREDC on the server), and SETUP.EXE is a specific file.

net

Windows enables you to view a network quickly from the command line through the *net command*. This works great when you plug into a network for the first time and, naturally, don't know the names of the other computers on that network. To see the many options that net offers, type **net** at a command prompt and press ENTER. The view and use options offer excellent network tools.

You can think of net view as the command-line version of My Network Places/Network. When run, net view returns a list of Windows computers on the network:

```
C:\Users\Mike>net view
Server Name          Remark
-------------------------------------------------
\\SABERTOOTH
\\UBERBOX
\\SERVER1
The command completed successfully.
C:\Users\Mike>
```

Once you know the names of the computers, you type **net view** followed by the computer name. The net view command will show any shares on that machine and whether they are mapped drives:

```
C:\>net view server1
Shared resources at SERVER1
Share name  Type  Used as  Comment
-----------------------------------------------------------------
FREDC       Disk
Research    Disk  W:
The command completed successfully.
```

The net use command is a command-line method for mapping network shares. For example, if you wanted to map the Research share shown in the previous example to the X: drive, you simply type

```
C:\>net use x: \\server1\research
```

This will map drive X: to the Research share on the SERVER1 computer.

nbtstat

The nbtstat command is an old command-line utility that goes back to before Windows. It stands for NetBIOS over TCP/IP Statistics. Even though NetBIOS is long gone, it's still a great tool for learning anything "Windowsy" you want to know about your network, such as "What other workgroups or domains

are on this network?" It's also is a great tool to answer the question, "Who am I connected to right now?" Try running **nbtstat –s** to see all your connections:

```
C:\>nbtstat -s
Local Area Connection:
Node IpAddress: [192.168.15.102] Scope Id: []
                  NetBIOS Connection Table

    Local Name        State    In/Out  Remote Host        Input Output
    -----------------------------------------------------------------
    UBERBOX    <00>  Connected   Out   SABERTOOTH <20>     1KB   769B
    UBERBOX    <00>  Connected   Out   AARONV     <20>     760B  606B
    UBERBOX    <00>  Connected   Out   AARONV     <20>     950B  695B
    UBERBOX    <00>  Connected   Out   THEATER    <20>     620B  659B
    UBERBOX          Connected   In    SABERTOOTH <00>     649KB 791KB
C:\>
```

Note that nbtstat –s shows every connection, even if two computers have multiple connections. You can also use nbtstat with the –c command for a more abbreviated list:

```
C:\>nbtstat -c
Local Area Connection:
Node IpAddress: [192.168.15.102] Scope Id: []

                 NetBIOS Remote Cache Name Table

        Name           Type      Host Address    Life [sec]
    ----------------------------------------------------------
    AARONV      <20>  UNIQUE      192.168.15.100     327
    SABERTOOTH  <20>  UNIQUE      192.168.15.101     485
    THEATER     <20>  UNIQUE      192.168.15.201     380
C:\>
```

Sharing Printers

Sharing printers in Windows follows the same process as sharing drives and folders. Assuming that the system has printer sharing services loaded, in Windows XP and Vista go to the Printers folder in the Control Panel or Start menu and right-click the printer you wish to share. Select Sharing, and then click *Share this printer* and give it a name (see Figure 14.26). In Windows 7, choose Start | Devices and Printers, right-click on the printer you wish to share, select Printer properties, and then select the Sharing tab. From here it's just like XP and Vista—click *Share this printer* and you're done.

One of the most pleasant aspects of configuring a system for networking under all versions of Microsoft Windows is the amazing amount of the process that is automated. For example, if Windows detects a NIC in a system, it automatically installs the NIC driver, a network protocol (TCP/IP), and Client for Microsoft Networks. So if you want to share a resource, everything you need is automatically installed. Note that although File and Printer Sharing is also automatically installed, you still must activate it by clicking the appropriate checkbox in the Local Area Connection Properties dialog box.

• **Figure 14.26** Giving a name to a shared printer on Windows XP

Troubleshooting Wired Networks

Once you go beyond a single PC and enter the realm of networked computers, your troubleshooting skills need to take a giant leap up in quality. The secret to finding the right answer to networking problems on the CompTIA A+ 220-802 exam is to remember that the exam only asks about the skills to get a single computer back on the network. Granted, this might mean you'll need to check a switch or verify another system's connectivity, but in general, always focus your network troubleshooting answers on getting a single system up and running.

CompTIA likes to ask questions that deal with "no connectivity" or "intermittent connectivity." There are two ways to look at connectivity issues, and CompTIA A+ 220-802 exam objectives don't specify which type is covered on the exam. The first type of connectivity issue (and probably the one CompTIA means) is when your computer loses physical connectivity. The second type is when you're on the network and can't access a particular resource (you can access other resources, just not the one you want right now). Let's consider both.

Repairing Physical Cabling

"The network's down!" is one of the most terrifying phrases a network tech will ever hear. Networks fail for many reasons, and the first thing to know is that good-quality, professionally installed cabling rarely goes bad, but when it does, you need to know what to do. Let's take a moment now to discuss what to do when you think you've got a problem with your physical network.

Symptoms

Losing physical connectivity is pretty obvious in Windows. Windows XP gives you a nice pop-up message warning you that you have lost a connection, along with a red X over the network icon (see Figure 14.27). Windows Vista and Windows 7 aren't quite as obvious, displaying only the red X over the network icon in the system tray to show you're not connected (see Figure 14.28).

If you encounter this problem, first check the obvious: Is the cable unplugged at your system? At the wall outlet? Then go for the less obvious: Is the NIC disabled in Device Manager? If these checks don't solve the problem, take a peek on the other side of the cable. If you're not connected to a running switch, you're going to get the disconnect errors.

Intermittent connectivity is often the same issue, but typically is harder to figure out. Either way, read the next section to see how to get serious about testing for these pesky connectivity problems.

• **Figure 14.27** Windows XP pop-up message and red X error icon

• **Figure 14.28** Windows 7 red X error icon

Diagnosing Physical Problems

Look for errors that point to physical disconnection. A key clue that the computer may have a physical problem is that a user gets a "No server is found" error, or tries to use the operating system's network explorer utility (like Network in Windows 7) and doesn't see any systems besides his or her own.

Multiple systems failing to access the network often points to hardware problems. This is where knowledge of your network cabling helps. If all the systems connected to one switch suddenly no longer see the network, but all the other systems in your network still function, you not only have a probable hardware problem, but also have a suspect—the switch.

Check the Lights

If you suspect a hardware problem, first check the link lights on the NIC and switch. If they're not lit, you know the cable isn't connected somewhere. If you're not physically at the system in question (if you're on a tech call, for example), you can have the user check his or her connection status through the link lights or through software.

If the problem system clearly cannot connect, eliminate the possibility of a failed switch or other larger problem by checking to make sure other people can access the network, and that other systems can access the shared resource (server) that the problem system can't see. Inspect the cable running from the back of the PC to the outlet. Finally, if you can, plug the system into a known good outlet and see if it works. A veteran network tech keeps a long patch cable for just this purpose. If you get connectivity with the second outlet, you should begin to suspect the structured cable running from the first outlet to the switch. Assuming the cable is installed properly and has been working correctly before this event, a simple continuity test will confirm your suspicion in most cases.

Onboard NICs on laptops are especially notorious for breaking due to frequent plugging and unplugging. On some laptops, the NICs are easy to replace; others require a motherboard replacement.

Check the NIC

Be warned that a bad NIC can also generate a "can't see the network" problem. Use the utility provided by the OS to verify that the NIC works. If you've got a NIC with diagnostic software, run it—this software will check the NIC's circuitry. The NIC's female connector is a common failure point, so NICs that come with diagnostic software often include a special test called a **loopback test**. A loopback test sends data out of the NIC and checks to see if it comes back. Some NICs perform only an internal loopback, which tests the circuitry that sends and receives, but not the actual connecting pins. A true external loopback requires a **loopback plug** inserted into the NIC's port (see Figure 14.29). If a NIC is bad, replace it.

Cable Testing

The vast majority of network disconnection problems occur at the work area. If you've tested those connections, though, and the work area seems fine, it's time to consider deeper issues.

• **Figure 14.29** Loopback plug

With the right equipment, diagnosing a bad horizontal cabling run is easy. Anyone with a network should own a midrange time-domain reflectometer (TDR) tester such as the Fluke MicroScanner. A TDR measures impedance in network cabling. If the tester measures any impedance, something is wrong with the cable. With a little practice, you can easily determine not only whether a cable is disconnected but also where the disconnection takes place. Sometimes patience is required, especially if you've failed to label your cable runs, but you will find the problem.

When you're testing a cable run, always include the patch cables as you test. This means unplugging the patch cable from the PC, attaching a tester, and then going to the telecommunications room. Here you'll want to unplug the patch cable from the switch and plug the tester into that patch cable, making a complete test, as shown in Figure 14.30.

Testing in this manner gives you a complete test from the switch to the system. In general, a broken cable must be replaced. A bad patch cable is an easy fix, but what happens if the horizontal cable is to blame? In these cases, I get on the phone and call my local installer. If a cable is bad in one spot, the risk of it being bad in another is simply too great to try anything other than total replacement.

Toners

It would be nice to say that all cable installations are perfect and that over the years they won't tend to grow into horrific piles of spaghetti-like, unlabeled cables. In the real world, though, you might eventually find yourself having to locate or *trace* cables. Even in the best-planned networks, labels fall off ports and outlets, mystery cables appear behind walls, new cable runs are added, and mistakes are made counting rows and columns on patch panels. Sooner or later, most network techs will have to be able to pick out one particular cable or port from a stack.

When the time comes to trace cables, network techs turn to a device called a toner for help. **Toner** is the generic term for two separate devices that are used together: a tone generator and a tone probe. The **tone generator** connects to the cable using alligator clips, tiny hooks, or a network jack, and it sends an electrical signal along the wire at a certain frequency. The **tone probe** emits a sound when it is placed near a cable connected to the tone

• **Figure 14.30** Cable tester in action

generator. These two devices are often referred to by the brand-name Fox and Hound, a popular model of toner made by the Triplett Corporation (see Figure 14.31).

To trace a cable, connect the tone generator to the known end of the cable in question, and then position the tone probe next to the other end of each of the cables that might be the right one. The tone probe makes a sound when it's placed next to the right cable. Some toners have one tone probe that works with multiple tone generators. Each generator emits a separate frequency, and the probe sounds a different tone for each one. Even good toners are relatively inexpensive ($75); although inexpensive toners can cost less than $25, they tend to not work well, so spending a little more is worthwhile. Just keep in mind that if you have to support a network, you'd do best to own a decent toner.

Fixing Common Problems

Let's go back and look at the second possible meaning for a loss in connectivity. It's very common to try to connect to a shared resource and either fail or find that a shared resource you've used time and again has suddenly disappeared.

Failing to Connect to a New Resource

When you can't connect to a resource on the first try, it often points to a configuration issue. In most cases, a quick double-check of the sharing system will reveal one of the following problems (and call for the associated solution):

- You don't have the right share name? Go check at the serving system.

- You don't have the required user name/password? Ask someone who might have this knowledge, or double-check that your account has access.

- You don't have permission to use/access/connect to the shared resource? Make sure you have the correct permissions.

- You're not on the right homegroup/domain/workgroup? Check your system and the sharing system to verify which workgroup/ domain name to use. On a homegroup, make sure you've used the proper password.

- The folder or printer isn't shared? Share it!

- The folder or printer doesn't exist? Make sure the serving system still hosts the folder you want. Install the network printer if you haven't yet.

Failing to Connect to a Previously Used Resource

If you suddenly can't connect to a resource that you've used many times before, go with the easy answers first:

- Verify that you are not already connected by using **nbtstat –s**.

- Check that you can see the resource using My Network Places/ Network or **net view**.

- Check that the serving system is on.

- Check that the computer is physically connected to the serving system.

You'll see a tone probe referred to on the CompTIA A+ exam as a *toner probe*.

• **Figure 14.31** Fox and Hound

▪ Internet Troubleshooting

There isn't a person who's spent more than a few hours on a computer connected to the Internet who hasn't run into some form of connectivity problem. I love it when I get a call from someone saying "The Internet is down!" as I always respond the same way: "No, the Internet is fine. It's the way you're trying to get to it that's down." Okay, so I don't make a lot of friends with that remark, but it's actually a really good reminder of why we run into problems on the Internet. Let's review the common symptoms CompTIA lists on their objectives for the CompTIA A+ 220-802 exam and see what we can do to fix these all-too-common problems.

The dominant Internet setup for a SOHO environment consists of some box from your ISP—a cable modem, a DSL modem, etc.—that connects via Ethernet cable to a home router. This router is usually 802.11 capable and includes four Ethernet ports. Some computers in the network connect through a wire and some connect wirelessly (see Figure 14.32). It's a pretty safe assumption that CompTIA has a setup like this in mind when talking about Internet troubleshooting, and we'll refer to this setup here as well.

One quick note before we dive in— most Internet connection problems are network connection problems. In other words, everything you learned earlier in the chapter still applies here. We're not going to rehash those repair problems here. The following issues are Internet-only problems, so don't let a bad cable fool you into thinking a bigger problem is taking place.

• **Figure 14.32** Typical SOHO setup

No Connectivity

As you'll remember from earlier in the chapter, "no connectivity" has two meanings: a disconnected NIC or an inability to connect to a resource. Since you've already covered wired connectivity issues and wireless issues (in Chapter 13), let's look at lack of connectivity from a "you're on the Internet but you can't get to a Web site" point of view:

- Can you get to other Web sites? If not, go back and triple-check your local connectivity.

- Can you ping the site? Go to a command prompt and try pinging the URL as shown here:

```
C:\>ping www.cheetos1.com
Ping request could not find host www.cheetos1.com. Please check the
name and try again.
C:\>
```

The ping is a failure, but we learn a lot from it. The ping shows that your computer can't get an IP address for that Web site. This points to a DNS failure, a very common problem. To fix a failing DNS:

Go to a command prompt and type **ipconfig /flushdns**:

```
C:\>ipconfig /flushdns
Windows IP Configuration
Successfully flushed the DNS Resolver Cache.
C:\>
```

If you have Windows XP, go to the Network Connections applet in the Control Panel. Right-click on your network connection and select Repair. If you have Windows Vista/7, go to the Network and Sharing Center and click *Change adapter settings.* Right-click on your network connection and select Diagnose to run the troubleshooter (see Figure 14.33).

Try using another DNS server. There are lots of DNS servers out there that are open to the public. Try Google's famous 8.8.8.8 and 8.8.4.4.

If DNS is OK, make sure you're using the right URL. This is especially true when you're entering DNS names into applications like e-mail clients.

• **Figure 14.33** Diagnosing a network problem in Windows 7

Limited Connectivity

Limited connectivity points to a DHCP problem, assuming you're connected to a DHCP server. Run **ipconfig** and see if you have an APIPA address:

```
C:\>ipconfig
Windows IP Configuration
Ethernet adapter Local Area Connection:
        Connection-specific DNS Suffix  . :
        IP Address. . . . . . . . . . . . : 169.254.0.16
        Subnet Mask . . . . . . . . . . . : 255.255.0.0
        Default Gateway . . . . . . . . . :
C:\>
```

Uh-oh! No DHCP server! If your router is your DHCP server, try restarting the router. If you know the Network ID for your network and the IP address for your default gateway (something you should know—it's your network!), try setting up your NIC statically.

Local Connectivity

Local connectivity means you can access network resources but not the Internet. First, this is a classic symptom of a downed DHCP server since all the systems in the local network will have APIPA addresses. However, you might also have a problem with your router. In Windows XP, you need to ping the default gateway; if that's successful, ping the other port (the WAN port) on your router. The only way to determine the IP address of the other port on your router is to access the router's configuration Web page and find it (see Figure 14.34). Every router is different—good luck!

• **Figure 14.34** Router's WAN IP address

• **Figure 14.35** No WAN connection

You can learn a lot by looking at your WAN IP address. Take a look at Figure 14.35. At first glance, it looks the same as Figure 14.34, but notice that there is no IP address. Most ISPs don't provide static IP addresses—they simply give you the physical connection, and your router's WAN network card uses DHCP, just like most internal networks. If you're lucky, you can renew your DHCP address using some button on the router's configuration. If not, try resetting the cable/DSL modem. If that doesn't work, it's time to call your ISP.

Slow Transfer Speeds

No matter how fast the connection is, we all want our Internet to go faster. People expect a certain amount of wait for a large program to download or an HD video to buffer, but your connection can sometimes slow down to unacceptable speeds.

Remember that your Internet connection has a maximum speed at which it can transfer. If you divide that connection between multiple programs trying to use the Internet, all of your programs will connect very slowly.

To see what's happening on your network, open a command prompt and type **netstat**, which shows all the connections between your computer and any other computer. Here's a very simplified example of netstat output:

```
C:\>netstat
Active Connections

  Proto  Local Address          Foreign Address           State
  TCP    10.12.14.47:57788      totalfs3:microsoft-ds     ESTABLISHED
  TCP    192.168.15.102:139     Sabertooth:20508          ESTABLISHED
  TCP    192.168.15.102:50283   Theater:netbios-ssn       ESTABLISHED
  TCP    192.168.15.102:60222   dts1.google.com:https     ESTABLISHED
  TCP    192.168.15.102:60456   www.serve2.le.com:http     ESTABLISHED
  TCP    192.168.15.102:60482   64.145.92.65:http         ESTABLISHED
  TCP    192.168.15.102:60483   12.162.15.1:57080         TIME_WAIT
C:\>
```

If you look at the Foreign Address column, you'll see that most of the connections are Web pages (HTTP and HTTPS) or shared folders (microsoft-ds, netbios-ssn), but what is the connection to 12.162.15.1:57080? Not knowing every connection by heart, I looked it up on Google and found out that there was a background torrent program running on my machine. I found the program and shut it down.

When everyone on the network is getting slow Internet connectivity, it's time to check out the router. In all probability, you have too many people that need too much bandwidth—go buy more bandwidth!

You can control what's going through your router using *Quality of Service* (*QoS*). QoS is a feature that enables you to limit the bandwidth for certain types of data based on application protocol, the IP address of a computer, and all sorts of other features. Figure 14.36 is a typical router's QoS page.

• **Figure 14.36** QoS

Beyond A+

The areas covered by the CompTIA A+ 220-802 exam do a great job on the more common issues of dealing with the Internet, but a few hot topics (although beyond the scope of the CompTIA A+ 220-802 exam) are so common and important that you need to know them: online gaming, chatting, and file sharing.

Online Gaming

One of the more exciting and certainly more fun aspects of the Internet is online gaming. Competing online against a real person or people makes for some pleasant gaming. Enjoying classics such as Hearts and Backgammon with another human can be challenging and fun. Another popular genre of online gaming is the "first-person shooter." These games place you in a small world with up to 64 other players. A great example is Valve Software's *Counter-Strike: Source* (see Figure 14.37).

No discussion of online gaming is complete without talking about the most amazing game type of all: the massively multiplayer online role-playing game (MMORPG). Imagine being an elfin wizard, joined by a band of friends, all going on adventures together in a world so large that it would take a real 24-hour day to journey across it! Imagine that in this same world, 2000 to 3000 other players, as well as thousands of game-controlled

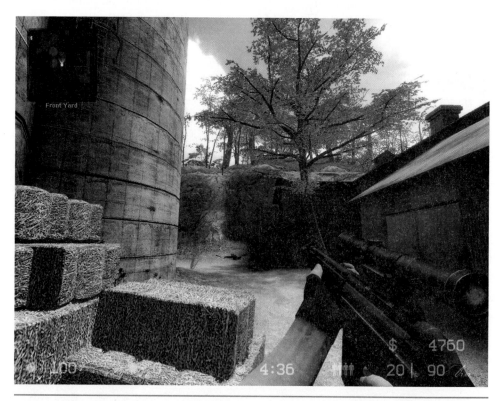

• **Figure 14.37** Counter-Strike: Source

characters, are participating! Plenty of MMOR-PGs are out there, but the most popular today is *World of Warcraft* (see Figure 14.38).

Each of these games employs good old TCP/IP to send information, using ports reserved by the game. For instance, the Quake series of games uses port 26000, while DirectX uses ports 47624 and 2300–2400.

Chat

If there's one thing we human beings love to do, it's chat. The Internet provides a multitude of ways to do so, whether by typing or actual talking. Keep in mind that chatting occurs in real time. As fast as you can type or talk, whoever is at the other end hears or sees what you have to say. To chat, however, you need some form of chat software. The oldest family of chat programs is based on the Internet Relay Chat (IRC) protocol; a very common IRC chat program is mIRC. IRC protocols allow for a number of other little extras as well, such as being able to share files.

Today, companies such as Google, AOL, Yahoo!, and Microsoft have made their own chat programs (otherwise known as instant messengers, or IMs) that not only provide text chat but also add features such as voice and video, turning your PC into a VoIP phone! Figure 14.39 shows the popular Microsoft Windows Live Messenger software.

• **Figure 14.38** My editor playing World of Warcraft

• **Figure 14.39** Windows Live Messenger in action

File Sharing

The last extra Internet function to discuss is also probably the most controversial: file sharing. File sharing started over a decade ago and consisted of a whole bunch of computers with one program loaded, such as Napster or Kazaa. The file-sharing program enables each of the computers running that program to offer files to share, such as music and movies. Once all of the file-sharing programs connect to the Internet, any of them can download any file offered by any other in the group.

File sharing through such *distributed* sharing software becomes almost anonymous and free—and that's the problem. You can share *anything*, even copyright-protected music, movies, and more. The music industry in particular has come out swinging to try to stop file-sharing practices. As a result, the music industry is working on a way to shut down those persons who share lots of files. Software developers and file sharers haven't backed down, creating Internet protocols such as BitTorrent that can share files faster and more efficiently. Figure 14.40 shows one of the more popular BitTorrent protocol programs called µTorrent (the µ is the symbol for "micro," so you pronounce it "micro torrent"). BitTorrent has many legitimate uses as well—its protocol is extremely efficient for the distribution of large files and has become the method of choice for distributing Linux distributions and is even used to distribute and patch *World of Warcraft* and *Starcraft II*!

These example programs just scratch the surface of the many applications that use the Internet. One of the more amazing aspects of TCP/IP is that its basic design is around 40 years old. We use TCP/IP in ways completely outside the original concept of its designers, yet TCP/IP continues to show its power and flexibility. Pretty amazing!

• **Figure 14.40** µTorrent

Chapter 14 Review

■ Chapter Summary

After reading this chapter and completing the exercises, you should understand the following facts about implementing and troubleshooting networks.

Understand network organization

- Microsoft designed Windows networks to work in one of three categories: workgroups, domains, or homegroups. These three organizations differ in control, number of machines needed, compatibility, and security.

- Every computer on a network needs the same workgroup name to be able to share resources. By default, all computers on the network are assigned to a workgroup called WORKGROUP. Workgroups require a valid user name and password to log on to each node in the workgroup.

- When using a domain, you don't log on to your computer. Instead, you log on directly to the domain controller, a node running Windows Server that stores all user accounts. This enables single sign-on for all resources available to your user account on the domain computers.

- Microsoft added HomeGroup to Windows 7 to simplify sharing within a small LAN. Once you add connected computers into a homegroup, sharing is simple, with no further logon required for accessing shared resources such as libraries.

Install and configure wired networks

- When you install a NIC, by default, Windows installs upon setup the TCP/IP protocol (configured for DHCP), the Client for Microsoft Networks, and File and Printer Sharing for Microsoft Networks.

- To establish network connectivity, you need a network client installed and configured properly. The Client for Microsoft Networks is installed as part of the OS installation.

- All versions of Windows share drives and folders in basically the same manner. Right-click any drive or folder, choose Properties, and then select the Sharing tab. In Windows Vista/7 click the Advanced Sharing button. Click the *Share this folder* radio button and type a share name.

- When sharing a folder on an NTFS drive, you must set the network permissions to give everyone full control, and then use the NTFS permissions (on the Security tab) to exercise more precise control over who accesses the shared resources and how they access them.

- Network resources can be mapped to a local resource name. This can be done from Windows Explorer or by right-clicking a share in My Network Places/Network and choosing Map Network Drive.

- All computers that share must have a share name, and all the resources they share must also have names. Any resource on a network can be described by combining the name of the resource being shared and the name of the system sharing it. The complete UNC name of the FREDC share on SERVER1, for example, would be \\SERVER1\FREDC.

- The nbtstat command shows you information about your network, including the workgroups or domains on the network.

- Windows provides the net utility to help you explore and diagnose a Windows network. One of the more popular options is net view, which lists other Windows systems on the network. Another popular option is the net use command to map a remote share as a network drive.

- To share a printer in Windows, open the Printers folder in the Control Panel or Start menu and right-click the printer you wish to share. Select Sharing, and then click *Share this printer* and give it a name.

Troubleshoot wired networks

- Look for errors that point to physical disconnection. A key clue that you may have a physical problem is that a user gets a "No server is found" error, or tries to use the operating system's network explorer utility (like Network in Windows 7) and doesn't see any systems besides his or her own.

- If you suspect a hardware problem, first check the link lights on the NIC and switch. If they're not lit, you know the cable isn't connected somewhere. If you're not physically at the system in question

(if you're on a tech call, for example), you can have the user check his or her connection status through the link lights or through software.

- Be warned that a bad NIC can also generate a "can't see the network" problem. Use the utility provided by your OS to verify that the NIC works. If you've got a NIC with diagnostic software, run it—this software will check the NIC's circuitry.

- A loopback test sends data out of the NIC and checks to see if it comes back. Some NICs perform only an internal loopback, which tests the circuitry that sends and receives, but not the actual connecting pins. A true external loopback requires a loopback plug inserted into the NIC's port.

- A TDR measures impedance in network cabling. If the tester measures any impedance, something is wrong with the cable.

- When you're testing a cable run, always include the patch cables as you test. This means unplugging the patch cable from the PC, attaching a tester, and then going to the telecommunications room.

- When the time comes to trace cables, network techs turn to a device called a toner for help. The tone generator connects to the cable using alligator clips, tiny hooks, or a network jack, and it sends an electrical signal along the wire at a certain frequency. The tone probe emits a sound when it is placed near a cable connected to the tone generator. These two devices are often referred to by the brand-name Fox and Hound, a popular model of toner.

Troubleshoot an Internet connection

- If you can't connect to a specific Web site, check to make sure you can connect to other Web sites. Use the ping utility to check your connection. Try changing your DNS settings if ping is unable to find an IP address for a particular Web site.

- If you have limited connectivity, check your DHCP settings. If your PC has been assigned an APIPA address, try restarting your router to receive a new IP address from the DHCP server. Otherwise, you can try to set up a static IP address.

- If you can access your local network but not the Internet, you might have a DHCP server issue. You might also have a problem with your router. Try pinging your default gateway and the WAN port of your router.

- If your connection to the Internet feels slower than usual, use the netstat tool to see which programs use the most bandwidth. Also check the number of users connecting to the Internet through the same router. You may need to implement Quality of Service (QoS) to keep more of the bandwidth available.

■ Key Terms

activity light *(513)*
domain *(505)*
full-duplex *(512)*
HomeGroup *(506)*
link lights *(512)*
loopback plug *(521)*

loopback test *(521)*
toner *(522)*
tone generator *(522)*
tone probe *(522)*
universal naming convention (UNC) *(518)*
workgroup *(501)*

■ Key Term Quiz

Use the Key Terms list to complete the sentences that follow. Not all terms will be used.

1. Windows 7 enables sharing of libraries using _____.

2. A Windows _____ enables single sign-on.

3. When troubleshooting a NIC, you'll need to crawl behind your computer and look for the _____, which should be on or blinking.

4. To test a possibly broken Ethernet port, plug in a(n) _____.

5. A NIC that can send and receive data at the same time is running in _____ mode.

6. The most common form of Windows resource sharing is the _____.

7. The _____ on a NIC tells you when it's sending or receiving data.

8. A(n) _____ and a(n) _____ are used to trace network cabling.

Multiple-Choice Quiz

1. Which OS enables you to implement HomeGroup?
 A. Mac OS X
 B. Windows XP
 C. Windows 7
 D. Windows Server

2. Which of the following is an advantage of a domain-based network over a workgroup-based network?
 A. Ease of administration
 B. Cheaper
 C. Single sign-on
 D. Faster to implement

3. Which of the following is the default network organization for a new Windows installation?
 A. LAN
 B. Workgroup
 C. Domain
 D. HomeGroup

4. Which of the following is the correct net syntax for discovering which network shares on a particular server are mapped on your computer?
 A. net view \\fileserver
 B. net \\fileserver
 C. net map \\fileserver
 D. net share \\fileserver

5. A small device that enables you to test a NIC's circuitry is called?
 A. Loopback plug
 B. Port tester
 C. Multimeter
 D. Integrated network and logic probe

6. You are down under your desk organizing some wires when you notice that the activity light on your NIC is blinking erratically. Is there a problem?
 A. Yes, the activity light should be on steadily when the computer is running.
 B. Yes, the activity light should be blinking steadily, not randomly.
 C. No, the light blinks when there is network traffic.
 D. No, the light blinks to show bus activity.

7. What is a common symptom of a bad network cable?
 A. Rapidly blinking link lights
 B. No link lights
 C. Solid on link lights
 D. Steady blinking link lights

8. What command-line utility would you run to show a list of network computers?
 A. net send
 B. show net_servers
 C. net use
 D. net view

9. You are trying to locate which patch cable in the main switch traces back to a particular computer. Which tool should you use?
 A. Tone probe
 B. Cable tester
 C. Punchdown tool
 D. Butt set

10. What benefit does full-duplex offer?
 A. It enables NICs to send and receive signals at the same time.
 B. It enables NICs to send data twice as fast.

C. It enables NICs to receive data twice as fast.

D. It enables a switch to connect to both coaxial and fiber optic cables.

11. To check to see if the Web server you are trying to reach is available or is down, which command-line utility should you use?

A. ping

B. ICS

C. Telnet

D. NAT

12. If your modem cannot connect to the Internet, which of the following can you eliminate as a cause of the problem?

A. The phone line is dead.

B. All lines on the Internet are busy.

C. You dialed the wrong number.

D. The modem is bad.

13. John tried going to www.totalsem.com with his Web browser, but the Web site wouldn't load. He opened a command-line window and typed **ping www.totalsem.com**. He received a message that the ping request couldn't find www.totalsem.com. What is the most likely reason John received this message?

A. Bad default gateway

B. DNS failure

C. Corrupted NIC driver

D. Too many applications using the Internet connection simultaneously

■ Essay Quiz

1. Leah's home network has a large number of shared folders across four different systems and she's getting tired of continually logging on to these shares. She doesn't want to install a domain. What can she do to reduce the logon hassle?

2. Your company is running a Windows 7 network as a workgroup. There are 15 computers and 15 users on the network. Your boss wants to upgrade to a Windows domain. Do some research to determine the costs involved with upgrading your network. In your report to your boss, include the cost of a new server as well as a copy of Windows Server that will support 15 computers.

3. You are a tech for a small company and you get a call from Jessica, who cannot access the network anymore from her workstation. What techniques would you use to help troubleshoot her system and get her back working?

Lab Projects

• Lab Project 14.1

A good tech should know their network. Take a tour of your network to answer the following questions:

- What is the network ID for your network?

- What is the workgroup or domain name?

- What is the default DNS server?

- What is the default gateway?

• Lab Project 14.2

It's very common for smaller Windows networks to all be members of a workgroup called WORKGROUP.

- Put every computer into a different workgroup. How does this change the ability to see computers in the network folder? How does this change the way you share folders?

- Put half the computers into one workgroup and the other half into another workgroup to see the changes as discussed in the previous question.

- Assuming you have Windows 7 systems, put some of the computers into a homegroup and leave some out of the homegroup. Can you still share folders? What happens to non–Windows 7 computers in this situation?

Portable Computing

chapter
15

"The great thing about a computer notebook is that no matter how much you stuff into it, it doesn't get bigger or heavier."

—Bill Gates, *Business @ The Speed of Thought*

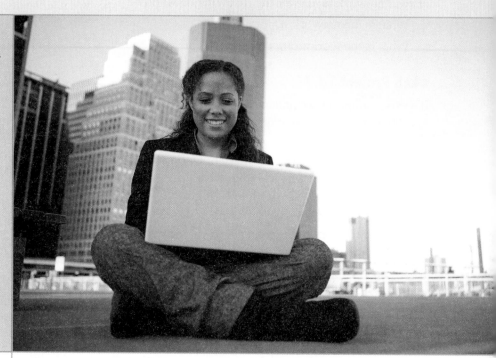

In this chapter, you will learn how to

- **Describe the many types of portable computing devices available**
- **Explain ways to expand portable computers**
- **Manage and maintain portable computers**
- **Upgrade and repair portable computers**
- **Troubleshoot portable computers**

There are times when the walls close in, when you need a change of scenery to get that elusive spark that inspires greatness...or sometimes you just need to get away from your coworkers for a few hours because they're driving you nuts! For many occupations, that's difficult to do. You need access to your documents and spreadsheets; you can't function without e-mail or the Internet. In short, you need a computer to get your job done.

Portable computing devices combine mobility with accessibility to bring you the best of both worlds; portables enable you to take some or even all of your computing capabilities with you when you go. Featuring all the bells and whistles of a desktop system, many portables offer a seamless transition from desk to café table.

This chapter looks at the classic portable computer, essentially a desktop PC transformed into a mobile format. Classic portables run Windows, Mac OS X, or some flavor of Linux.

Other portable devices, such as smartphones and tablets, run mobile operating systems designed to take advantage of small form factors and touch screens. In practice (and on the CompTIA A+ 220-802 exam), such mobile devices differ a lot from classic portable computers. These devices get their own "Mobile Devices" chapter later in the book.

Portable Computing Devices

All portable devices share certain features. For output, they use LCD screens, although these vary from 20-inch behemoths to diminutive 10-inch displays. Portable computing devices employ sound of varying quality, from bland mono playback to fairly nice faux-surround reproductions. All of them run on DC electricity stored in batteries when not plugged into an AC outlet.

When asked about portable computing devices, most folks describe the traditional clamshell **notebook** computer, such as the one in Figure 15.1, with built-in LCD monitor, keyboard, and input device (a *touchpad*, in this case). The notebook is also called a portable or a **laptop**. All the terms are synonymous. A typical laptop computer functions as a fully stand-alone PC, potentially even replacing the desktop. The one in Figure 15.1, for example, has all of the features you expect the modern PC to have, such as a fast CPU, lots of RAM, a high-capacity hard drive, an optical drive, and an adequate sound system. Attach it to a network and you can browse the Internet and send e-mail.

• **Figure 15.1** A notebook PC

Input Devices

Portable computers come with a variety of input devices. Most have a fully functional keyboard and a device to control the mouse pointer.

Keyboard Quirks

Laptop keyboards differ somewhat from those of desktop PCs, primarily because manufacturers have to cram all the keys onto a smaller form factor. They use the QWERTY format, but manufacturers make choices with key size and placement of the non-alphabet characters. Almost every portable keyboard uses a **Function (FN) key** to enable some keys to perform a third duty. Figure 15.2 compares a standard desktop keyboard with a large portable keyboard. You'll note that the latter has no separate number pad on the right. To use the number pad, you press the FN key (lower left in this case) to transform the (7, 8, 9), (U, I, O), (J, K, L), and (M) keys into the (7, 8, 9), (4, 5, 6), (1, 2, 3), and (0) keys.

 The FN key also enables you to toggle other features specific to a portable, such as network connectivity and external displays. We'll examine these options in the next section of the chapter.

• **Figure 15.2** Keyboard comparison

Pointing Devices

Portables need a way to control your mouse pointer, but their smaller size requires manufacturers to come up with clever solutions. First, portables today have USB ports and can use every type of pointing device you'd see on a desktop. Second, early portables used *trackballs*, often plugged in like a mouse and clipped to the side of the case. Other models with trackballs placed them in front of the keyboard at the edge of the case nearest the user, or behind the keyboard at the edge nearest the screen.

The next wave to hit the laptop market was IBM's **TrackPoint** device, a joystick the size of a pencil eraser, situated in the center of the keyboard (see Figure 15.3). With the TrackPoint, you can move the pointer around without taking your fingers away from the "home" typing position. You use a forefinger to push the joystick around, and then click or right-click, using two buttons below the spacebar. This type of pointing device has since been licensed for use by other manufacturers, and it continues to appear on laptops today.

• **Figure 15.3** IBM TrackPoint

By far the most common laptop pointing device found today is the **touchpad** (see Figure 15.4)—a flat, touch-sensitive pad just in front of the keyboard. To operate a touchpad, you simply glide your finger across its surface to move the pointer, and tap the surface once or twice to single- or double-click. You can also click by using buttons just below the pad. Most people get the hang of this technique after just a few minutes of practice. The main advantage of the touchpad over previous laptop pointing devices is that it uses no moving parts—a fact that can really extend the life of a hard-working laptop.

Some manufacturers today include a **multitouch** touchpad that enables you to perform actions with multiple fingers, such as scrolling up and down or swiping to another screen or desktop.

• **Figure 15.4** Touchpad on a laptop

Display Types

Laptops come in a variety of sizes and at varying costs. One major contributor to the overall cost of a laptop is the size of the LCD screen. Most laptops offer a range between 10.1-inch to 17.3-inch screens (measured diagonally), while a few offer just over 20-inch screens.

Many manufacturers are phasing out the standard 4:3 aspect ratio screen in favor of the widescreen format. **Aspect ratio** is the comparison of the screen width to the screen height. Depending on screen resolution, widescreens can have varying aspect ratios of 10:6, 16:9, 16:9.5, or 16:10.

Laptop LCD screens come in a variety of supported resolutions, described with acronyms such as XGA, WXGA, WSXGA, and more. The *W* in front of the letters indicates widescreen. Table 15.1 lists commonly supported laptop display resolutions.

Laptop LCDs are the same in almost every way as desktop LCDs with a TFT screen, an inverter (if using a CCFL backlight), and a backlight (CCFL or LED). Expect questions about laptop displays, but know that they're pretty much the same as desktop displays. The only major difference is that they contain an antenna, but we'll discuss this later in the chapter.

The two most common resolutions are WXGA for the 14- to 15-inch models and HD 1080 for the 17.3-inch models.

Table 15.1	Common Screen Resolutions	
Acronym	**Name**	**Native Resolution**
XGA	eXtended Graphics Array	1024 × 768
HD 720	HD 720	1280 × 720
WXGA (16:10)	Wide eXtended Graphics Array	1280 × 800
WXGA (16:9)	Wide eXtended Graphics Array	1366 × 768
SXGA	Super eXtended Graphics Array	1280 × 1024
SXGA+	Super eXtended Graphics Array Plus	1400 × 1050
HD 900	HD 900	1600 × 900
WSXGA+	Widescreen SXGA Plus	1680 × 1050
UXGA	Ultra eXtended Graphics Array	1600 × 1200
HD 1080	HD 1080	1920 × 1080
WUXGA	Widescreen UXGA	1920 × 1200

Laptop screens typically come with one of two types of finish: **matte** or **high-gloss**. The matte finish was the industry standard for many years and offered a good trade-off between richness of colors and the reduction of glare. The better screens have a wide viewing angle and decent response time. The major drawback for matte-finished laptop screens is that they wash out a lot in bright light. Using such a laptop at an outdoor café, for example, is almost hopeless during daylight.

Manufacturers released high-gloss laptop screens in 2006, and they rapidly took over many store shelves. The high-gloss finish offers sharper contrast, richer colors, and wider viewing angles when compared to the matte screens. Each manufacturer has a different name for high-gloss coatings. Dell calls theirs TrueLife, Acer calls theirs CrystalBrite, and HP calls theirs BrightView. The drawback to the high-gloss screens is that, contrary to what the manufacturers' claim, they pick up lots of reflection from nearby objects, including the user! So although they're usable outside during the day, you'll need to contend with increased reflection as well.

With the advent of LED backlighting for LCD panels, many manufacturers have switched back to an anti-glare screen, though they're not quite the matte screens of old. When the LED brightness is up high, these are lovely screens. (See the "Troubleshooting Portable Computers" section later in this chapter for issues specific to LED-backlit portables.)

As with other LCD technologies, most LCD/LED screens use twisted nematic (TN) technology. Some laptop screens use In-Plane Switching (IPS) panels for the greater viewing angle and better color quality. You'll find IPS panels on expensive, professional-grade desktop-replacement portables.

What you will *not* find on portable PCs are two other display technologies, plasma and organic light-emitting diode (OLED). Plasma displays demand a lot more electricity than LCDs demand and are completely inappropriate for portable PCs. OLED screens sip energy when compared to LCDs, but they're still so expensive that you'll only find them on a few smartphones today. Chapter 16 discusses OLED screen technology.

Desktop Replacements

A *desktop replacement* features a massive screen, a full-size keyboard, an optical drive (or maybe two), and plenty of hard drive space (see the portable on the left in Figure 15.5). Considering that it weighs almost as much as a mini-tower PC (or at least it feels like it does when I'm lugging it through the airport!), such a portable can be considered a **desktop replacement** because it does everything most people want to do with a desktop PC and doesn't compromise on performance just to make the laptop a few pounds lighter or the battery last an extra hour. Think power first, portability second.

The current sweet spot for desktop replacements is a 17.3-inch monitor with 16+ GB of DDR3 and either dual 1- to 2-TB HDDs or a single 512-GB to 1-TB SSD. Dedicated graphics are a must. Desktop replacements run the latest Intel high-end mobile processors and, of course, run Windows 7 64-bit edition. Such perfection in computing in a sub-8-pound format doesn't come cheap, so the question that immediately arises is, why buy a desktop replacement?

• **Figure 15.5** Desktop replacement (left) next to a standard portable computer (right)

Desktop replacements appeal to a diverse group of users. Most obviously, dedicated road warriors need to do everything on the plane, on the train, and in the hotel room. Second, having a computer that can work well on the road and in the office is convenient. Finally, some folks just prefer the compactness of a laptop. You can, after all, put it out of sight when you're finished with it and not have to dedicate space to an equally powerful desktop computer.

Netbooks

Netbooks offer a robust computing platform with low cost and long battery life. These machines usually have displays in the 10-inch range, small hard drives, and CPUs geared more for minimal power usage than raw speed.

A prime example of the netbook is the ASUS Eee PC, shown in Figure 15.6 sitting on a full-sized laptop. This netbook has a 9-inch screen, a 1.6-GHz Intel Atom CPU, and a small solid-state drive, and runs a customized Linux distribution. One distinguishing feature of these netbooks is the use of Intel's Atom processor. The Atom CPU is very useful for keeping power usage down but has much less computing power than its more power-hungry siblings. Therefore, most netbooks run either Windows 7 Starter edition or some form of Linux that is better suited for their limited resources.

• **Figure 15.6** ASUS Eee PC sitting on a normal laptop

Ultrabooks

Thin, light, and powerful, **Ultrabooks** are as much about power and portability as they are about looks. Ultrabooks are for people who can't give up the power of high-end computers but can afford to pay more for a smaller package. Intel set up the Ultrabook specifications in 2011, defining the form factor to use power-sipping Intel processors with integrated graphics. These Ultrabooks have maximum dimensions (18 to 23 mm thick, depending on the size of the screen) and a minimum battery life (5 hours). Several manufacturers are stepping into the Ultrabook market, mostly copying the thin-slice aesthetic of the MacBook Air. You won't find optical drives on these, and most use solid-state drives for storage. Some people find this limiting; those *in the know* (read: young people) won't care, as long as they can edit their HD movies while drinking at a coffee shop and looking good (see Figure 15.7).

Tablet PC is a Microsoft term and is *not* the equivalent of a tablet such as the Apple iPad or Samsung Galaxy Tab. The latter devices derive from the mobile phone market, as mentioned at the beginning of this chapter, so they're *not* PCs, but rather a unique class of mobile devices. According to Microsoft, a Tablet PC runs Windows. Chapter 16 covers mobile devices in detail.

Tablet PCs

Microsoft started the **Tablet PC** initiative way back in 2001, defining the devices as fully featured portables running a tablet-aware version of Windows and using a stylus to interact directly with the screen. Many Tablet PCs have come to market since then, fulfilling the needs of specific professions, notably medicine.

Instead of (or in addition to) a keyboard and mouse, Tablet PCs provide a screen that doubles as an input device. With a special pen, called a **stylus**, you can actually write on the screen (see Figure 15.8). Just make sure you don't grab your fancy Cross ballpoint pen accidentally and start writing on

• **Figure 15.7** Ultrabook (photo courtesy of Intel Free Press)

the screen! Unlike some touch screens, most Tablet PC screens are not pressure sensitive—you have to use the stylus to write on the screen. Tablet PCs come in two main form factors: *convertibles*, which include a keyboard that you can fold out of the way, and *slates*, which do away with the keyboard entirely. The convertible Tablet PC in Figure 15.8, for example, looks and functions just like the typical clamshell laptop shown back in Figure 15.1. But here it's shown with the screen rotated 180 degrees and snapped flat so it functions as a slate. Pretty slick!

• **Figure 15.8** A Tablet PC

Early Tablet PCs ran Windows XP Tablet edition. Windows Vista and Windows 7 support tablet features in all editions. Windows Vista and 7 have a specific Tablet PC Settings applet (see Figure 15.9) that enables you to configure the tablet to recognize handwriting, place menus conveniently for right- or left-handed users, and more.

In applications that aren't "tablet-aware," the stylus acts just like a mouse, enabling you to select items, double-click, right-click, and so on. To input text with the stylus, you can either tap keys on a virtual keyboard (shown in Figure 15.10), write in the writing utility (shown in Figure 15.11), or use speech recognition software. With a little practice, most users find the computer's accuracy in recognizing their handwriting to be sufficient for most text input, although speedy touch-typists will probably still want to use a keyboard when typing longer documents.

Tablet PCs work well when you have limited space or have to walk around and use a laptop. Anyone who has ever tried to type with one hand while walking around the factory floor and holding the laptop with the other hand will immediately appreciate the beauty of a Tablet PC. In this scenario, Tablet PCs are most effective when combined with applications designed to be used with a stylus instead of a keyboard. An inventory control program, for example, might present drop-down lists and radio buttons to the user, making a stylus the perfect input tool. With the right custom application, Tablet PCs become indispensable tools.

Microsoft encourages software developers to take advantage of a feature they call *digital ink*, which allows applications to accept pen strokes as input without first converting the pen strokes into text or mouse-clicks. In Microsoft Journal, which comes with Tablet PCs, you can write on the screen just as though you were writing on

• **Figure 15.9** Tablet PC Settings applet

• **Figure 15.10** The virtual keyboard

a paper legal pad (see Figure 15.12). Many other applications, including Microsoft Office, allow you to add ink annotations. Imagine sitting on an airplane reviewing a Microsoft Word document and simply scribbling your comments on the screen (see Figure 15.13). No more printing out hard copy and breaking out the red pen for me! Imagine running a PowerPoint presentation and being able to annotate your presentation as you go.

Many useful third-party applications are designed specifically to take advantage of the Tablet PC form factor. In fields such as law and medicine,

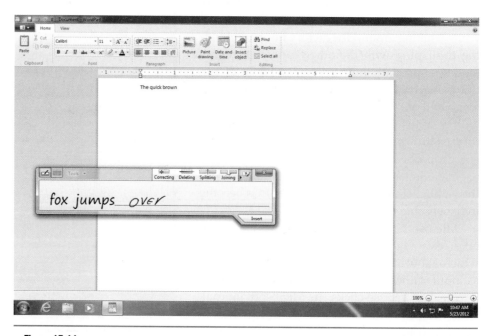

• **Figure 15.11** The writing pad

● **Figure 15.12** Microsoft Journal preserves pen strokes as digital ink.

where Tablet PCs have been especially popular, the choices are endless. One handy free utility that anyone who spends time in front of an audience (teachers, salespeople, cult leaders, and so on) will appreciate is InkyBoard (www.cfcassidy.com/Inkyboard). InkyBoard provides a virtual dry-erase board, eliminating the need to find a real board when holding meetings. Ever wished you could have a record of everything that was written on the chalkboard in a class (or business meeting)? If the professor had used Inky-Board, creating and distributing a copy would be a snap.

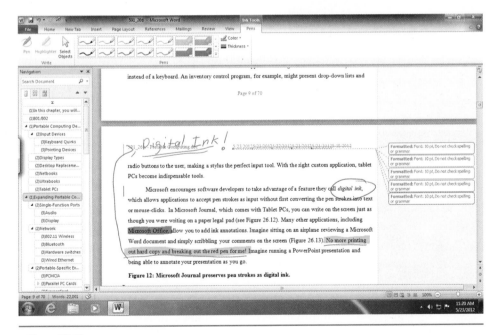

● **Figure 15.13** Microsoft Office supports digital ink.

■ Expanding Portable Computers

In the dark ages of mobile computing, you had to shell out top dollar for any device that would unplug, and what you purchased was what you got. Upgrade a laptop? Connect to external devices? You had few if any options, so you simply paid for a device that would be way behind the technology curve within a year and functionally obsolete within two.

Portable PCs today offer many ways to enhance their capabilities. Most feature external ports that enable you to add completely new functions to portables, such as attaching a scanner or mobile printer or both. You can take advantage of the latest wireless technology breakthrough simply by slipping a card into the appropriate slot on the laptop.

I'll first describe single-function ports, and then turn to networking options. Next, I'll cover card slots, and then finish with a discussion of general-purpose ports.

Single-Function Ports

All portable PCs come with one or more single-function ports. You'd have a hard time finding a portable computing device that doesn't have a speaker port, for example. Laptops invariably provide a video port such as a VGA or DVI connection for hooking up an external monitor.

Ports work the same way on portable PCs as they do on desktop models. You plug in a device to a particular port and, as long as Windows has the proper drivers, you will have a functioning device when you boot.

Audio

Portable PCs have a standard 3.5-mm audio out port and some have a similarly sized microphone in port (see Figure 15.14). You can plug in regular PC speakers or even a nice surround sound set to enable the laptop to play music just as well as a desktop computer can.

• **Figure 15.14** Standard audio ports

You control the sound (both out and in) through either the appropriate Control Panel applet in Windows or through some kind of switches on the laptop. The portable in Figure 15.15, for example, enables you to mute the speakers by pressing a special mute spot above the keyboard. Other portables use a combination of the FN key and another key to toggle mute on and off. You can also find many variations on how to control the volume coming out of the machine. Few portable PCs have a manual volume dial these days, instead relying on key combinations or special keys for control.

• **Figure 15.15** The mute spot on a laptop

Display

Most laptops support a second monitor via an analog VGA port or a digital port of some flavor, such as DVI, HDMI, Mini HDMI, Micro HDMI, or DisplayPort. With a second monitor attached, you can display Windows on only the laptop screen, on only the external monitor, or on both simultaneously. Not all portables can do all variations, but they're more common than not.

● **Figure 15.16** Laptop keyboard showing Function (FN) key that enables you to access additional key options, as on the F2 key

Most portables use the FN key plus another key on the keyboard to cycle through display options. Figure 15.16 shows a close-up of a typical keyboard with the Function key; note the other options you can access with the Function key, such as indicated on the F2 key. To engage the second monitor or to cycle through the modes, hold the Function key and press F2.

You can control how the external monitor displays through the Display applet in the Control Panel. Open Display and click on *Change display settings* (see Figure 15.17). Under the Screen Resolution panel, click the drop-down arrow next to Multiple displays (see Figure 15.18). You'll see several options. *Extend these displays* makes your desktop encompass both the laptop and the external monitor. *Duplicate these displays* places the

Although many laptops use the Function key method to cycle the monitor selections, that's not always the case. You might have to pop into the Display applet in the Control Panel to click a checkbox. Just be assured that if the laptop has a video output port, you can cycle through monitor choices!

In Windows 7, the Windows key + P keyboard shortcut switches between multiple display modes.

● **Figure 15.17** Display applet

● **Figure 15.18** Multiple display options menu

same thing on both displays. You'd use that for a presentation, for example, rather than for a work space. (The other two options shown in Figure 15.18 temporarily blank one or the other display.)

Network

It's a rare item to find a portable computer without at least one network connection option. Today's laptops come with 802.11, Bluetooth, and wired Ethernet connections. Some still have modems for connecting to older-style telephone jacks. Generally they work exactly as you've seen in previous chapters, but you may stumble into a few issues that are unique to laptops.

802.11 Wireless

Most portables today have Wi-Fi built directly into the chipset for connecting the device to a wireless access point (WAP) and from there to a bigger network, such as the Internet. The 802.11b standard is common on older laptops; newer ones use 802.11g or 802.11n.

Bluetooth

While not nearly as common as 802.11, plenty of laptops use Bluetooth as well. Bluetooth is really handy on a laptop because it gives you the ability to add wireless mice, keyboards, and headsets.

Hardware Switches

Laptops that come with 802.11 or Bluetooth have some form of on/off switch to toggle the antenna off or on so that you may use the laptop in areas where emissions aren't allowed (like a commercial aircraft). The switch may be hard wired, like the one shown in Figure 15.19, or it may be a toggle of the FN key plus another key on the keyboard. Also, if you're not using Wi-Fi or Bluetooth, turn them off to save electricity and lengthen the portable's battery life.

Wired Ethernet

Most laptops have an RJ-45 wired Ethernet connection like the one shown in Figure 15.20. These work exactly like any other Ethernet jack—they have link lights and connect via UTP cable.

There are two issues with RJ-45s on laptops. First, they do not have an on/off switch like the 802.11 and Bluetooth connections. You can turn them off just like you would turn off the NIC on a desktop: disable the NIC in Device Manager or turn the NIC off in BIOS. The other issue is the relative weakness of the physical connection. If you ever plug a laptop into a wired network and Windows doesn't see a connection, check the RJ-45 port.

• **Figure 15.19** Wireless switch

• **Figure 15.20** Ethernet port on laptop

Portable-Specific Expansion Slots

The makers of portable computers have developed methods for you to add features to a portable via specialized connections known generically as *expansion slots*. Once a common feature on laptops, these specialized expansion slots are quickly fading away due to the dominance of USB. Yet you'll still find laptops with these slots (and they're covered on the CompTIA A+ 220-802 exam), so let's take a look at expansion slots over the years.

PCMCIA

For many years, the *Personal Computer Memory Card International Association* (*PCMCIA*) established standards involving portable computers, especially when it came to expansion cards, which are generically called PC Cards. **PC Cards** are roughly credit card–sized devices that enhance and extend the functions of a portable PC. PC Cards are easy to use, inexpensive, and convenient. Figure 15.21 shows a typical PC Card.

Older portable PCs come with one or two PC Card slots, into which you insert a PC Card. Each card has at least one

• **Figure 15.21** PC Card

CompTIA uses the older term **PCMCIA cards** to describe PC Cards. Don't be shocked if you get that as an option on your exams! You'll hear many techs use the phrase as well.

Many manufacturers use the term *hot-pluggable* rather than hot-swappable to describe the ability to plug in and replace PC Cards on the fly. Look for either term on the exams.

• **Figure 15.22** PC Card slots

Tech Tip

Keeping Your PC Cards Healthy

PC Cards typically come with a hard plastic storage case. Always be sure to use this case to store the cards when you're not using them. If dust, dirt, or grime gets into the array of contacts at the end of the card, the card won't work when you try to use it next. Also, be careful when using PC Cards that extend out of the PC Card slot past the edge of your laptop. One dark night, I set my laptop on the floor with a PC Card NIC sticking out of it while I went to get a drink of water. On my way back, I accidentally stepped on the card sticking out of my laptop and nearly snapped it in half. Luckily, my laptop wasn't damaged, but the card was toast!

function, but many have two, three, or more! You can buy a PC Card that offers connections for removable media, for example, such as combination SD and CF card readers. You can also find PC Cards that enable you to plug into multiple types of networks. All PC Cards are hot-swappable, meaning you can plug them in without powering down the PC.

The PCMCIA established two versions of PC Cards, one using a parallel bus and the other using a serial bus. Each version, in turn, offers two technology variations as well as several physical varieties. This might sound complicated at first, but here's the map to sort it all out.

Parallel PC Cards

Parallel PC Cards come in two flavors, **16-bit** and **CardBus**, and each flavor comes in three physical sizes, called Type I, Type II, and Type III. The 16-bit PC Cards, as the name suggests, are 16-bit, 5-V cards that can have up to two distinct functions or devices, such as a modem/network card combination. CardBus PC Cards are 32-bit, 3.3-V cards that can have up to eight (!) functions on a single card. Regular PC Cards fit into and work in CardBus slots, but the reverse is not true. CardBus totally dominates the current PC Card landscape, but you might still run into older 16-bit PC Cards.

Type I, II, and III cards differ only in the thickness of the card (Type I being the thinnest, and Type III the thickest). All PC Cards share the same 68-pin interface, so any PC Card will work in any slot that accepts that card type. Type II cards are by far the most common of PC Cards. Therefore, most older laptops have two Type II slots, one above the other, so the computer can accept two Type I or II cards or one Type III card (see Figure 15.22).

Although PCMCIA doesn't require that certain sizes perform certain functions, most PC Cards follow their recommendations. Table 15.2 lists the sizes and typical uses of each type of PC Card.

Table 15.2	PC Card Types and Their Typical Uses			
Type	**Length**	**Width**	**Thickness**	**Typical Use**
Type I	85.6 mm	54.0 mm	3.3 mm	Flash memory
Type II	85.6 mm	54.0 mm	5.0 mm	I/O (modem, NIC, and so on)
Type III	85.6 mm	54.0 mm	10.5 mm	Hard drives

ExpressCard

Slots for **ExpressCard**, the high-performance serial version of the PC Card, have replaced PC Card slots on laptop PCs over the last decade. ExpressCard comes in two widths: 34 mm and 54 mm, called *ExpressCard/34* and *ExpressCard/54*. Figure 15.23 shows both ExpressCard varieties. Both cards are 75 mm long and 5 mm thick, which makes them shorter than all previous PC Cards and the same thickness as a Type II PC Card.

ExpressCards connect to either the USB 2.0 bus or the PCI Express bus. These differ phenomenally in speed. The amazingly slow-in-comparison USB version has a maximum throughput of 480 Mbps. The PCIe version, in contrast, roars in at 2.5 Gbps in unidirectional communication.

Table 15.3 shows the throughput and variations for the parallel and serial PC Cards currently on the market.

PCMCIA announced ExpressCard 2.0 in 2009 with speeds up to 5 Gbps and support for SuperSpeed USB 3.0, and we expected to see devices roll out in 2010, but that's not what happened. PCMCIA has dissolved and shut its offices. The USB Implementer's Forum now manages all PC Card and ExpressCard standards, and there's not likely to be any further development.

• **Figure 15.23** 34-mm and 54-mm ExpressCards

Storage Card Slots

Many portable computers offer one or more flash-memory card slots to enable you to add storage to the portable. These slots also enable the fast transfer of data from the card to the portable, and vice versa. They come in several standard varieties, such as SD, CompactFlash, and xD.

General-Purpose Ports

Laptops rarely come with all of the hardware you want. Today's laptops usually include at least USB ports to give you the option to add more hardware. Some laptops still provide legacy general-purpose expansion ports (PS/2, RS-232 serial ports, and so on) for installing peripheral hardware, while other portables focus on more modern ports like eSATA and FireWire. If you're lucky, you will have a docking station or port replicator so you don't have to plug in all of your peripheral devices one at a time.

USB, FireWire, and eSATA

Universal serial bus (USB), FireWire (or more properly, IEEE 1394), and eSATA enable users to connect a device while the PC is running—you won't have to reboot the system to install a new peripheral. With USB, FireWire, and eSATA, just plug the device in and go! Because portable PCs don't have a desktop's multiple internal expansion capabilities, USB, FireWire, and

> You can find ExpressCards that supposedly support USB 3.0. While technically these cards have USB 3.0 ports, they connect to the PCIe bus and therefore aren't capable of true USB 3.0 speeds of up to 5 Gbps.

> The small device resting in a stand in Figure 15.24 is called a *personal digital assistant* (*PDA*), a precursor to modern smartphones and tablets such as the Apple iPhone and iPad. You could view pictures, take notes, check a calendar, listen to music, and more on these devices. Expect PDA as an answer choice in exam questions, but most likely as one of the wrong answers. PDAs are rarely used today.

Table 15.3	PC Card Speeds
Standard	**Maximum Theoretical Throughput**
PC Card using 16-bit bus	160 Mbps
CardBus PC Card using PCI bus	1056 Mbps
ExpressCard using USB 2.0 bus	480 Mbps
ExpressCard using PCIe bus	2.5 Gbps

Tech Tip

USB and Handheld Computing Devices

Almost all handheld computing devices—such as iPod music players—connect to PCs through USB ports. Most come with a USB cable that has a standard connector on one end and a proprietary connector on the other. Don't lose the cable!

• **Figure 15.24** Devices attached to USB on a portable PC

Although portable PCs most often connect to port replicators via USB ports, some manufacturers have proprietary connections for proprietary port replicators. As long as such a portable PC has a USB port, you can use either the proprietary hardware or the more flexible USB devices.

eSATA are three of the more popular methods for attaching peripherals to laptops (see Figure 15.24).

Port Replicators

A **port replicator** plugs into a single port on the portable computer—often a USB port but sometimes a proprietary port—and offers uncommon and common PC ports, such as serial, parallel, USB, network, and PS/2. By plugging the port replicator into your notebook computer, you can instantly connect the computer to nonportable components such as a printer, scanner, monitor, or a full-sized keyboard. Port replicators are typically used at home or in the office with the nonportable equipment already connected. Figure 15.25 shows a Dell Inspiron laptop connected to a port replicator.

The computer can access any devices attached to the port replicator; you don't need to connect each individual device to the PC. As a side bonus, port replicators enable you to attach legacy devices, such as parallel printers,

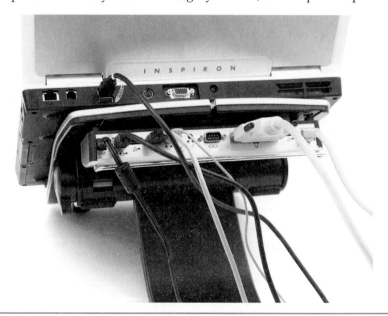

• **Figure 15.25** Port replicator for a Dell portable computer

to a new laptop that only has modern multifunction ports such as USB and FireWire and not parallel or serial ports.

Docking Stations

Docking stations resemble port replicators in many ways, offering legacy and modern single- and multi-function ports (see Figure 15.26). The typical docking station uses a proprietary connection but has extra features built in, such as a DVD drive or PC Card slot for extra enhancements. You can find docking stations for many older small laptops. A docking station makes an excellent companion to such portables.

• **Figure 15.26** Docking station

Managing and Maintaining Portable Computers

Most portable PCs come from the factory solidly built and configured. Manufacturers know that few techs outside their factories know enough to work on them, so they don't cut corners. From a tech's standpoint, your most common work on managing and maintaining portables involves taking care of the batteries and extending the battery life through proper power management, keeping the machine clean, and avoiding excessive heat.

Everything you normally do to maintain a PC applies to portable PCs. You need to keep current on Windows patches and service packs and use stable, recent drivers. Run Check Disk with some frequency, and definitely defragment the hard drive. Disk Cleanup is a must if the laptop runs Windows. That said, let's look at issues specifically involving portables.

Batteries

Manufacturers have used three types of batteries for portable PCs: **Nickel-Cadmium (Ni-Cd)**, **Nickel-Metal Hydride (Ni-MH)**, and **Lithium-Ion (Li-Ion)**. Today, only Li-Ion is used because that battery chemistry provides the highest energy density for the weight and has few problems with external factors. Let's look at each battery type briefly.

Nickel-Cadmium

Ni-Cds were the first batteries commonly used in mobile PCs, which means the technology was full of little problems. Probably most irritating was a little thing called *battery memory*, or the tendency of a Ni-Cd battery to lose a significant amount of its rechargeability if it was charged repeatedly without being totally discharged. A battery that originally kept a laptop running for two hours would eventually only keep that same laptop going for 30 minutes or less. Figure 15.27 shows a typical Ni-Cd battery.

• **Figure 15.27** Ni-Cd battery

• **Figure 15.28** Ni-MH battery

Tech Tip

Lithium Polymer

Lithium polymer (LiPO) batteries are a variation of Li-Ion that places the heart of the battery—the electrolyte—into a solid polymer shape rather than an organic solvent. This enables the batteries to take on unusual forms beyond the simple cylinder or rectangle shapes. LiPO batteries haven't replaced Li-Ion in most portable PCs (with the Apple MacBook the obvious exception), but they are used heavily in smaller electronics such as tablets, smartphones, and portable media players.

Nickel-Metal Hydride

Ni-MH batteries were the next generation of mobile PC batteries and are basically Ni-Cd batteries without most of the headaches. Ni-MH batteries are much less susceptible to memory problems, can tolerate overcharging better, can take more recharging, and can last longer between rechargings. Like Ni-Cds, Ni-MH batteries are susceptible to heat, but at least they are considered less toxic to the environment. Figure 15.28 shows a typical Ni-MH battery.

Lithium-Ion

The most common battery used today is Li-Ion. Li-Ion batteries are powerful, completely immune to memory problems, and last at least twice as long as comparable Ni-MH batteries on one charge. Sadly, they can't handle as many charges as Ni-MH types, but today's users are usually more than glad to give up total battery lifespan in return for longer periods between charges. Li-Ion batteries will explode if they are overcharged, so all Li-Ion batteries sold with PCs have built-in circuitry to prevent accidental overcharging. Lithium batteries can only be used on systems designed to use them. They can't be used as replacement batteries. Figure 15.29 shows a typical Li-Ion battery.

The Care and Feeding of Batteries

In general, keep in mind the following basics. First, always store batteries in a cool place. Although a freezer is in concept an excellent storage place, the moisture, metal racks, and food make it a bad idea. Second, keep the battery charged, at least to 70–80 percent. Third, never drain a battery all the way down unless required to do so as part of a *battery calibration* (where you, in essence, reset the battery according to steps provided by the manufacturer). Rechargeable batteries have only a limited number of charge-discharge cycles before overall battery performance is reduced. Fourth, *never* handle a battery that has ruptured or broken; battery chemicals are very dangerous. Finally, always recycle old batteries.

• **Figure 15.29** Li-Ion battery

Power Management

Many different parts are included in the typical laptop, and each part uses power. The problem with early laptops was that every one of these parts used power continuously, whether or not the system needed that device at that time. For example, the hard drive continued to spin even when it was not being accessed, and the LCD panel continued to display even when the user walked away from the machine.

The optimal situation would be a system where the user could instruct the PC to shut down unused devices selectively, preferably by defining a maximum period of inactivity that, when reached, would trigger the PC to shut down the inactive device. Longer periods of inactivity would eventually enable the entire system to shut itself down, leaving critical information loaded in RAM, ready to restart if a wake-up event (such as moving the mouse or pressing a key) told the system to restart. The system would have to be sensitive to potential hazards, such as shutting down in the middle of writing to a drive, and so on. Also, this feature could not add significantly to the cost of the PC. Clearly, a machine that could perform these functions would need specialized hardware and a specialized BIOS and operating system to operate properly. This process of cooperation among the hardware, the BIOS, and the OS to reduce power use is known generically as *power management*.

 Try This!

Recycling Old Portable PC Batteries

Got an old portable PC battery lying around? Well, you need to get rid of it, and there are some pretty nasty chemicals in that battery, so you can't just throw it in the trash. Sooner or later, you'll probably need to deal with such a battery, so Try This!

1. Do an online search to find the battery recycling center nearest to you.

2. Sometimes, you can take old laptop batteries to an auto parts store that disposes of old car batteries—I know it sounds odd, but it's true! See if you can find one in your area that will do this.

3. Many cities offer a hazardous materials disposal or recycling service. Check to see if and how your local government will help you dispose of your old batteries.

System Management Mode

Intel began the process of power management with a series of new features built into the 386SX CPU. These new features enabled the CPU to slow down or stop its clock without erasing the register information, as well as enabling power saving in peripherals. These features were collectively called **System Management Mode (SMM)**. All modern CPUs have SMM. Although a power-saving CPU was okay, power management was relegated to special "sleep" or "doze" buttons that would stop the CPU and all of the peripherals on the laptop. To take real advantage of SMM, the system needed a specialized BIOS and OS to go with the SMM CPU. To this end, Intel put forward the **Advanced Power Management (APM)** specification in 1992 and the **Advanced Configuration and Power Interface (ACPI)** standard in 1996.

Requirements for APM/ACPI

To function fully, APM and ACPI require a number of items. First, they require an SMM-capable CPU. As virtually all CPUs are SMM-capable, this is easy. Second, they need an APM-compliant BIOS that enables the CPU to shut off the peripherals when desired. The third requirement is devices

Don't limit your perception of APM, ACPI, and Energy Star just to laptops. Virtually all desktop systems and many appliances also use the power management functions.

that will accept being shut off. These devices are usually called Energy Star devices, which signals their compliance with the EPA's Energy Star standard. To be an Energy Star device, a peripheral must be able to shut down without actually turning off and show that it uses much less power than the non–Energy Star equivalent. Last, the system's OS must know how to request that a particular device be shut down, and the CPU's clock must be slowed down or stopped.

ACPI goes beyond the APM standard by supplying support for hot-swappable devices—always a huge problem with APM. This feature aside, it is a challenge to tell the difference between an APM system and an ACPI system at first glance.

APM/ACPI Levels

APM defined four power-usage operating levels for a system. These levels are intentionally fuzzy to give manufacturers considerable leeway in their use; the only real difference among them is the amount of time each takes to return to normal usage. These levels are as follows:

- **Full On** Everything in the system is running at full power. There is no power management.

- **APM Enabled** CPU and RAM are running at full power. Power management is enabled. An unused device may or may not be shut down.

- **APM Standby** CPU is stopped. RAM still stores all programs. All peripherals are shut down, although configuration options are still stored. (In other words, to get back to APM Enabled, you won't have to reinitialize the devices.)

- **APM Suspend** Everything in the PC is shut down or at its lowest power-consumption setting. Many systems use a special type of Suspend called **hibernation**, where critical configuration information is written to the hard drive. Upon a wake-up event, the system is reinitialized, and the data is read from the drive to return the system to the APM Enabled mode. Clearly, the recovery time between Suspend and Enabled will be much longer than the time between Standby and Enabled.

ACPI, the successor to APM, handles all these levels plus a few more, such as "soft power on/off," that enables you to define the function of the power button. You should familiarize yourself with the following ACPI global (G) and sleeping (S) system power state specifications for both the CompTIA A+ 802 exam and your own practical application:

- **G0 (S0)** Working state
- **G1** Sleeping state mode. Further subdivided into four *S* states:
 - **S1** CPU stops processing. Power to CPU and memory (RAM) is maintained.
 - **S2** CPU is powered down.
 - **S3** Sleep or Standby mode. Power to RAM still on.
 - **S4** Hibernation mode. Information in RAM is stored to nonvolatile memory or drive and powered off.

- **G2 (S5)** Soft power off mode. Certain devices used to wake a system—such as keyboard, LAN, USB, and other devices—remain on, while most other components are powered to a mechanical off state (G3).

- **G3** Mechanical off mode. The system and all components, with the exception of the real-time clock (RTC), are completely powered down.

Configuration of APM/ACPI

You configure APM/ACPI via CMOS settings or through Windows. Windows settings override CMOS settings. Although the APM/ACPI standards permit a great deal of flexibility, which can create some confusion among different implementations, certain settings apply generally to CMOS configuration. First is the ability to initialize power management; this enables the system to enter the APM Enabled mode. Often CMOS then presents time frames for entering Standby and Suspend modes, as well as settings to determine which events take place in each of these modes.

Many CMOS versions present settings to determine wake-up events, such as directing the system to monitor a modem or a NIC (see Figure 15.30). You'll see this feature as *Wake on LAN*, or something similar. A true ACPI-compliant CMOS provides an ACPI setup option. Figure 15.31 shows a typical modern BIOS that provides this setting.

```
                 Phoenix - AwardBIOS CMOS Utility
                              Power
┌──────────────────────────────────────────┬───────────────────┐
│            APM Configuration               │    Select Menu     │
├──────────────────────────────────────────┼───────────────────┤
│  Restore on AC Power Loss    [Power-Off]   │ Item Specific Help▶▶│
│  PWR Button < 4 secs         [Instant-Off] │                    │
│  Power Up On PCI/PCIE Devices [Disabled]   │ Set the Data, Time │
│  USB Resume from S5          [Disabled]    │ resume by Alarm.   │
│  Power On By RTC Alarm       [Enabled]     │                    │
│  Date(of Month) Alarm        [ 5]          │                    │
│  Alarm Time(hh:mm)             2 : 9 : 5   │                    │
│  Power Up By PS/2 Mouse      [Disabled]    │                    │
│  Power Up By PS/2 Keyboard   [Disabled]    │                    │
│                                            │                    │
├──────────────────────────────────────────┴───────────────────┤
│ F1:Help      ↑↓:Select Item   -/+: Change Value   F5:Setup Defaults │
│ ESC:Exit     ▶◀:Select Menu   Enter: Select SubMenu  F10:Save and Exit │
└──────────────────────────────────────────────────────────────┘
```

• **Figure 15.30** Setting a wake-up event in CMOS

In Windows XP, you can also access your power options by right-clicking on the desktop, selecting Properties, and then clicking the Power button in the Monitor power section of the Screen Saver tab. In Windows Vista and 7, right-click the desktop, select Personalize, select Screen Saver, and then click on the *Change power settings* link.

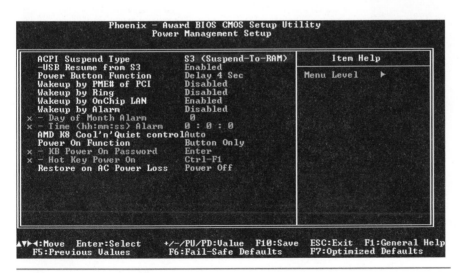

• **Figure 15.31** CMOS with ACPI setup option

• **Figure 15.32** The Windows XP Power Options
applet's Power Schemes tab

APM/ACPI settings can be found in the Control Panel applet Power Options. In Windows XP, the Power Options applet has several built-in *power schemes* such as Home/Office and Max Battery that put the system into Standby or Suspend after a certain interval (see Figure 15.32). You can also require the system to go into Standby after a set period of time or to turn off the monitor or hard drive after a time, thus creating your own custom power scheme. This is technically called adjusting the **sleep timers**.

Windows Vista and Windows 7 offer **power plans** that enable better control over power use by customizing a balanced, power saver, or high performance power plan (see Figure 15.33). You can customize a power saver plan for your laptop, for example, and configure it to turn off the display at a certain time interval while on battery or plugged in and configure it to put the computer to sleep as desired (see Figure 15.34).

Another feature, Hibernate mode, takes everything in active memory and stores it on the hard drive just before the system powers down. When the PC comes out of hibernation, Windows reloads all the files and applications into RAM. Figure 15.35 shows the Power Options Properties applet in Windows XP.

Manual Control over Power Use

Most portable PCs give you several manual options for reducing battery use in certain circumstances. We've already discussed using the on/off switch or keyboard combination for disabling the Wi-Fi antenna, for example, and shutting off Bluetooth. Laptops with backlit keyboards

• **Figure 15.33** Windows Vista Balanced, Power saver, and High performance power plan options

• **Figure 15.34** Customizing a laptop power plan in Windows Vista

will have some way you can disable this feature when it's not needed, usually with a keyboard combination. You can also reduce the output of the LCD backlight using a combination of FN and another key to eke out a few more precious minutes of computing time before you have to shut down.

• **Figure 15.35** Windows XP hibernation settings in the Power Options applet

Try This!

Adjusting Your System's Power Management

Go into the Power Options applet and take a look at the various settings. What is the current power scheme for your computer? If you're using a laptop with Windows XP, is your system still using the Home/Office Desktop power scheme? If this is the case, change the power scheme to Portable/Laptop. If you're using a laptop with Windows Vista/7, check to see if you are running a balanced or high performance power plan. If you are, change the power plan to power saver and familiarize yourself with some of the advanced power settings (click on the *Change advanced power settings* link).

Try changing the individual settings for each power scheme. For instance, set a new value for the *System standby* setting—try making your computer go into standby after five minutes. Don't worry; you aren't going to hurt anything if you fiddle with these settings.

• **Figure 15.36** Keys for adjusting screen brightness

Figure 15.36 shows a close-up of the FN-activated keys for adjusting screen brightness.

One of the best ways to conserve battery use is to plan ahead for times when you'll be unplugged. When I travel, for example, and know that I'm going to need a certain set of files stored on my file server at the office, I put those files on my laptop before I leave, while it's still plugged into the AC. It's tempting to throw the files on a thumb drive so I don't have to break out my laptop at the office, right? Or to let Dropbox do my syncing for me when I get to a Wi-Fi hotspot, but both USB and Wi-Fi use electricity.

Better than that even, Windows Vista and Windows 7 enable me to designate the files and folders I need as **offline files**, storing a local, duplicate copy of the files and folders on my hard drive. When I connect my laptop into my office network, those offline files are automatically synced with the files and folders on the file server. Anything I changed on the laptop gets written to the server. Anything anyone changed in those folders on the server gets written to my laptop. (If changes were made on both sides, a sync conflict pops up automatically, enabling you to resolve problems without fear of overwriting anything important.)

To designate a folder and its contents as offline files, right-click on the folder you want and select *Always available offline* from the menu (see Figure 15.37). The sync will occur and you're done. When you want to open the files offline, go to the Control Panel and open the Sync Center applet (see Figure 15.38). Click the *Manage offline files* link in the Tasks list to open the Offline Files dialog box (see Figure 15.39). Click the *View your offline files* button and you're in.

• **Figure 15.37** Setting up offline files

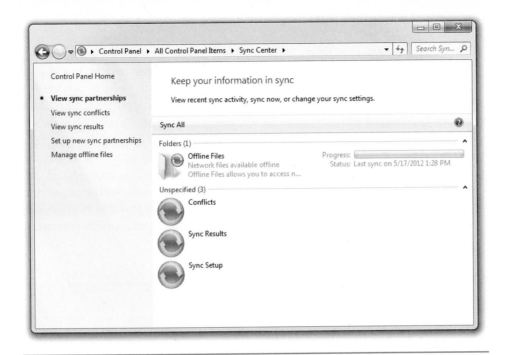

• Figure 15.38 Sync Center applet

• Figure 15.39 Offline Files dialog box

Chapter 15: Portable Computing

Cleaning

Most portable PCs take substantially more abuse than a corresponding desktop model. Constant handling, travel, airport food on the run, and so on can radically shorten the life of a portable if you don't take action. One of the most important things you should do is clean the laptop regularly. Use an appropriate screen cleaner (not a glass cleaner!) to remove fingerprints and dust from the fragile LCD panel. (Refer to Chapter 11 for specifics.)

If you've had the laptop in a smoky or dusty environment where the air quality alone causes problems, try cleaning it with compressed air. Compressed air works great for blowing out the dust and crumbs from the keyboard and for keeping PC Card sockets clear. Don't use water on your keyboard! Even a minor amount of moisture inside the portable can toast a component.

Heat

To manage and maintain a healthy portable PC, you need to deal with issues of heat. Every portable has a stack of electronic components crammed into a very small space. Unlike their desktop brethren, portables don't have lots of freely moving air space that enables fans to cool everything down. Even with lots of low-power-consumption devices inside, portable PCs crank out a good deal of heat. Excessive heat can cause system lockups and hardware failures, so you should handle the issue wisely. Try this as a starter guide:

- Use power management, even if you're plugged into the AC outlet. This is especially important if you're working in a warm (more than 80 degrees Fahrenheit) room.

- Keep air space between the bottom of the laptop and the surface on which it rests. Putting a laptop on a soft surface, such as a pillow on your lap, creates a great heat-retention system—not a good thing! Always use a hard, flat surface.

- Don't use a keyboard protector for extended amounts of time.

- Listen to your fan, assuming the laptop has one. If it's often running very fast—you can tell by the high-pitched whirring sound—examine your power management settings and your environment, and change whatever is causing heat retention.

- Speaking of fans, be alert to a fan that suddenly goes silent. Fans do fail on laptops, causing overheating and failure. All laptop fans can be replaced easily.

Protecting the Machine

Although prices continue to drop for basic laptops, a fully loaded system is still pricey. To protect your investment, you'll want to adhere to certain best practices. You've already read tips in this chapter to deal with cleaning and heat, so let's look at the "portable" part of portable computers.

Tripping

Pay attention to where you run the power cord when you plug in a laptop. One of the primary causes of laptop destruction is people tripping over the power cord and knocking the laptop off of a desk. This is especially true if you plug in at a public place such as a café or airport. Remember, the life you save could be your portable PC's!

Storage

If you aren't going to use your laptop for a while, storing it safely will go a long way toward keeping it operable when you do power it up again. Investing in a quality case is worth the extra few dollars—preferably one with ample padding. Not only will this protect your system on a daily basis when transporting it from home to office, but it will keep dust and pet hair away as well. Lastly, protect from battery leakage by removing the battery if you'll be storing your device for an extended time.

Travel

If you're traveling with a laptop, take care to guard against theft. If possible, use a case that doesn't look like a computer case. A well-padded backpack makes a great travel bag for a laptop and appears less tempting to would-be thieves. Don't forget to pack any accessories you might need, like modular devices, spare batteries, and AC adapters. Make sure to remove any disks, such as optical or floppies, from their drives. Most importantly—back up any important data before you leave!

Make sure to have at least a little battery power available. Heightened security at airports means you might have to power on your system to prove it's really a computer and not a transport case for questionable materials. And never let your laptop out of your sight. If going through an x-ray machine, request a manual search. The x-ray won't harm your computer like a metal detector would, but if the laptop gets through the line at security before you do, someone else might walk away with it. If flying, stow your laptop under the seat in front of you where you can keep an eye on it.

If you travel to a foreign country, be very careful about the electricity. North America uses ~115-V power outlets, but most of the world uses ~230-V outlets. Many portable computers have **auto-switching power supplies**, meaning they detect the voltage at the outlet and adjust accordingly. For these portables, a simple plug converter will do the trick. Other portable computers, however, have *fixed-input power supplies*, which means they run only on ~115-V or on ~230-V power. For these portables, you need a full-blown electricity converting device, either a step-down or step-up *transformer*. You can find converters and transformers at electrical parts stores, such as Radio Shack in the United States.

Shipping

Much of the storage and travel advice can be applied to shipping. Remove batteries and optical discs from their drives. Pack the laptop well and disguise the container as best you can. Back up any data and verify the warranty coverage. Ship with a reputable carrier and always request a tracking

• **Figure 15.40** Cable lock

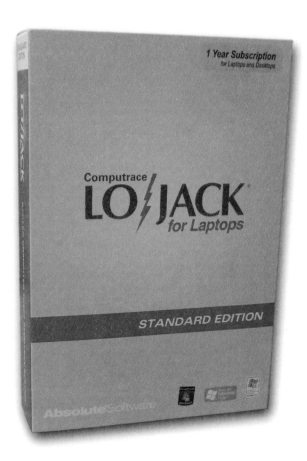

• **Figure 15.41** LoJack (photo courtesy of Absolute Software Corporation)

number and, if possible, delivery signature. It's also worth the extra couple of bucks to pay for the shipping insurance. And when the clerk asks what's in the box, it's safer to say "electronics" rather than "a new 20-inch laptop computer."

Security

The fact is, if someone really wants to steal your laptop, they'll find a way. There are, however, some things you can do to make yourself, and your equipment, less desirable targets. As you've already learned, disguise is a good idea. Although you don't need to camouflage your laptop or carry it in a brown grocery bag on a daily basis, an inconspicuous carrying case will draw less attention.

Another physical deterrent is a laptop lock. Similar to a steel bicycle cable, there is a loop on one end and a lock on the other. The idea is to loop the cable around a solid object, such as a bed frame, and secure the lock to the small security hole on the side of the laptop (see Figure 15.40). Again, if someone really wants to steal your computer, they'll find a way. They'll dismantle the bed frame if they're desperate. The best protection is to be vigilant and not let the computer out of your sight.

An alternative to physically securing a laptop with a lock is to use a software tracking system. Software makers, such as Computer Security Products, Inc., at www .computersecurity.com, offer tracking software that transmits a signal to a central office if the computer is stolen and connected to a phone line or the Internet. Even LoJack, the company famous for recovering stolen automobiles via its tracking devices, lends its name to a tracking product sold by Absolute Software (see Figure 15.41). The location of the stolen PC can be tracked, and sensitive files can even be deleted automatically with the aid of the stealth signal.

Upgrading and Repairing Laptop Computers

A competent tech can upgrade and repair portable computers to a degree, though true laptop techs are specialists. Upgrading the basics usually means breaking out the trusty screwdriver and avoiding electrostatic discharge (ESD). *Repairing* portables successfully, on the other hand, requires research, patience, organization, special tools, and documentation. Plus you need a ridiculously steady hand. This section provides an overview of the upgrade and repair process.

Disassembly Process

Disassembling a portable PC is pretty easy. Putting it back together in working condition is the hard part! You need to follow a four-step process to succeed in disassembly/reassembly.

First, *document and label every cable and screw location*. Laptops don't use standard connectors or screws. Often you'll run into many tiny screws of varying threads. If you try to put a screw into the wrong hole, you could end up stripping the screw, stripping the hole, or getting the screw wedged into the wrong place.

Second, *organize any parts you extract from the laptop*. Seriously, put a big white piece of construction paper on your work surface, lay each extracted piece out in logical fashion, and clearly mark where each component connects and what it connects to as well.

Third, *refer to the manufacturer's documentation*. I can't stress this point enough. Unlike desktop PCs, portable PCs have no standardization of internal structure. Everything in the portable is designed according to the manufacturer's best engineering efforts. Two portables from the same manufacturer might have a similar layout inside, but it's far more likely that every model differs a lot.

Finally, you need to *use the appropriate hand tools*. A portable PC, especially on the inside, will have a remarkable variety of tiny screws that you can't remove/reinsert without tiny-headed Phillips or Torx drivers. You'll need tiny pry bars—metal and plastic—to open components. Figure 15.42 shows an entry-level toolkit for a laptop tech that you can order from iFixit.com

● **Figure 15.42** Bare-minimum laptop repair tools

(more on this site in a moment). Their professional version of the toolkit has 70 tools, plus there's an expansion kit! Like I said at the beginning of the chapter, portable techs are specialists.

Now that you have the official line on the disassembly process, let's get one thing clear: A lot of manufacturers don't provide documentation to just any tech, but only to authorized repair centers. So what do you do when faced with an unfamiliar laptop that a client brought in for repair?

You have essentially three options. First, you can find a dedicated laptop tech and refer your client to that person. If the problem is exceptionally complicated and the portable in question is mission critical, that's often the best option. If you want to tackle the problem or it looks like something you should be able to do, then you go to the sources: YouTube and iFixit.com.

Every portable computer has a specific make and model. Open up a Web browser and go to YouTube. Type in precisely what you want to do, such as "replace the keyboard on a Lenovo y530," and see what pops up (see Figure 15.43). You'll most likely be in shock and awe when you get the results back, especially if the laptop in question is a couple of years old. People all over the world have to deal with broken devices, so you're not alone.

Once you've found the appropriate video or something that's close enough to enable the repair attempt, watch it. If it's too difficult for your skill level or requires a set of expensive tools, then fall back to step one and go find that dedicated tech. Otherwise, figure out what tools and parts you need. Parts specific to a laptop (as in that Lenovo keyboard in the preceding example) will need to be purchased from

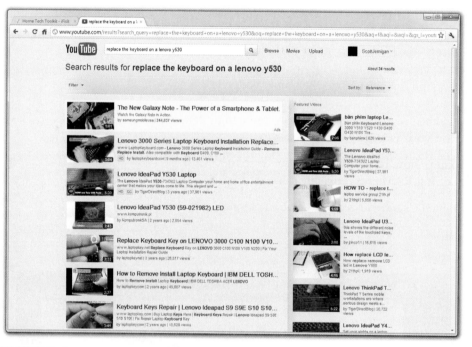

• **Figure 15.43** YouTube search result

the manufacturer. More generic parts, like hard drives, CPUs, and so on, can be purchased from Newegg (my favorite tech store) or some other online retailer.

For general tools, parts, and a lot of very detailed step-by-step instructions, I highly recommend iFixit.com. Billed as a "free repair manual you can edit," iFixit is built by techs like you who conquer a problem, document the steps, and post the details (see Figure 15.44). This means the next tech along who runs into the same problem doesn't have to reinvent the wheel. Just go to iFixit.com. The proceeds from parts and tools they sell, by the way, go toward supporting the site. It's not a for-profit enterprise.

• **Figure 15.44** Some of the Dell laptop repair walkthroughs at iFixit.com

Standard Upgrades

Every CompTIA A+ tech should know how to perform the two standard upgrades to portable computers: adding RAM and replacing a hard drive. Let's go through the steps.

RAM

Stock factory portable PCs almost always come with a minimal amount of RAM, so one of the first laptop upgrades you'll be called on to do is to add more RAM. Economy laptops running Windows 7 Home Premium routinely sit on store shelves and go home to consumers with as little as 1 GB of RAM, an amount guaranteed to limit the use and performance of the laptop. The OS alone will consume more than half of the RAM! Luckily, every decent laptop has upgradeable RAM slots. Ancient laptops use either 72-pin or 144-pin SO-DIMMs with SDRAM technology. DDR, DDR2, and DDR3 systems primarily use 200-pin SO-DIMMs (see Figure 15.45), although some laptops use micro-DIMMs.

How to Add or Replace RAM Upgrading the RAM in a portable PC requires a couple of steps. First, you need to get the correct RAM. Many older portable PCs use proprietary RAM solutions, which means you need to order directly from Dell, HP, or Sony and pay exorbitant prices for the precious extra megabytes. Most manufacturers have taken pity on consumers in recent years and use standard SO-DIMMs or

One of the most striking contrasts between portable PCs and the tablets and smartphones you'll read about in Chapter 16 is in upgradability. You can and should upgrade portable PCs. Mobile devices, on the other hand, offer almost no upgradability at all.

• **Figure 15.45** 200-pin SO-DIMM stick (front and back)

How Much RAM Is Enough?

The amount of RAM needed to run a PC—portable or otherwise—smoothly and stably depends on both the type of applications that it will run and the needs of the OS. When making a recommendation to a client about upgrading a laptop's memory, you should ask the basic questions, such as what the client plans to do on the laptop. If the laptop will be used for e-mail, word processing, and Web surfing, a medium level of RAM, such as 1–2 GB, might be adequate. If the user travels, uses a high-end digital camera, and wants to use Photoshop to edit huge images, you'll need to augment the RAM accordingly. Then add the needs of the OS to give a good recommendation. Turn to Chapter 5 and cross check your knowledge about specific OS RAM needs. What's a good minimum for Windows XP? What about Vista? How much for Windows 7?

micro-DIMMs. Refer to the manufacturer's Web site or to the manual (if any) that came with the portable for the specific RAM needed.

Second, every portable PC offers a unique challenge to the tech who wants to upgrade the RAM, because there's no standard location for RAM placement in portables. More often than not, you need to unscrew or pop open a panel on the underside of the portable (see Figure 15.46). Then you press out on the restraining clips and the RAM stick pops up (see Figure 15.47). Gently remove the old stick of RAM and insert the new one by reversing the steps.

Always remove all electrical power from the laptop before removing or inserting memory. Disconnect the AC cord from the wall outlet. Take out the battery! Failure to disconnect from power can result in a fried laptop.

Shared Memory Some laptops (and desktops) support **shared memory**. Shared memory reduces the cost of video cards by reducing the amount

• **Figure 15.46** Removing a RAM panel

• **Figure 15.47** Releasing the RAM

of memory on the video card itself. Instead of having 256 MB of RAM, the video card might have only 64 MB of RAM but be able to borrow 192 MB of RAM from the system. This equates to a 256 MB video card. The video card uses regular system RAM to make up for the loss.

The obvious benefit of shared memory is a less expensive video card (and a less expensive laptop!) with performance comparable to its mega-memory alternative. The downside is that your overall system performance will suffer because a portion of the system RAM is no longer available to programs. (The term *shared* is a bit misleading because the video card takes control of a portion of RAM. The video portion of system RAM is *not* shared back and forth between the video card processor and the CPU.) Shared memory technologies include TurboCache (developed by NVIDIA) and HyperMemory (developed by ATI).

You cannot tell if a laptop is using shared memory in Windows. You have to go to CMOS to be sure.

Some systems give you control over the amount of shared memory, while others simply allow you to turn shared memory on or off. The settings are found in CMOS setup and only on systems that support shared memory. Shared memory is not reported to Windows, so don't panic if you have 1 GB of RAM in your laptop but Windows only sees 924 MB—the missing memory is used for video.

Adding more system RAM to a laptop with shared memory will improve laptop performance. Although it might appear to improve video performance, that doesn't tell the true story. It'll improve overall performance because the OS and CPU get more usable RAM. On some laptops, you can improve video performance as well, but that depends on the CMOS setup. If the shared memory is not set to maximum by default, increasing the overall memory and upping the portion reserved for video will improve video performance specifically.

HDD/SSD

You can replace a hard disk drive (HDD) or solid-state drive (SSD) in a portable PC fairly easily, especially if the laptop is only a few years old. SATA drives in the 2.5-inch drive format now rule in all laptops. Although much smaller than regular 3.5-inch hard drives, they use all the same features and configurations. These smaller hard drives have suffered, however, from diminished storage capacity as compared to their 3.5-inch brothers. Currently, large 2.5-inch hard drives hold up to 1 TB, while the 3.5-inch hard drives can hold more than 3 TB of data!

If you have a much older laptop, it might have a PATA drive, which means you need to pay more attention to cabling and jumpers. Some PATA drive manufacturers may require you to set the drive to use a cable-select setting as opposed to master or slave, so check with the laptop maker for any special issues. Otherwise, no difference exists between 2.5-inch drives and their larger 3.5-inch brethren (see Figure 15.48).

One of the best upgrades you can make on a laptop is to go from an HDD to an SSD. Obviously, you'll get a lot less storage capacity for the money, but the trade-offs can be worth it. First, the SSD will use a lot less electricity than an HDD, thus extending battery life. Second, any SSD is rip-roaringly faster than an HDD and performance across the board will be boosted.

• **Figure 15.48** The 2.5-inch and 3.5-inch drives are mostly the same.

Comparing HDD with SSD Today

As I write this chapter, you can get roughly ten times the storage capacity on an HDD for the same cost as an SSD. In other words, $100 spent on an SSD would give me ~100 GB of storage, whereas I could purchase a 1-TB HDD for the same $100. So do some comparison shopping. What's the price point now? Are the trade-offs worth it for you or for your clients to make the switch from HDD to SSD?

The process of replacing a hard drive mirrors that of replacing RAM. You find the hard drive hatch—either along one edge or in a compartment on the underside of the computer—and release the screws (see Figure 15.49). Remove the old drive and then slide the new drive into its place (see Figure 15.50). Reattach the hatch or cover and boot the computer. Grab a Windows disc and prepare to reinstall.

• **Figure 15.49** Removing the drive compartment cover

Hardware Replacement

Once you get beyond upgrading RAM and replacing a hard drive on a portable PC, you take the plunge into the laptop repair specialty. You can replace some components by lifting them out, detaching a ribbon cable, and then reversing the steps with the replacement part. Other parts require a full teardown of the laptop to the bare bones, which presents a much greater magnitude of difficulty. Because every portable PC differs from every other one, this section provides guidance, but not concrete steps, for replacement.

Components

Replaceable components require more work than the RAM or drive upgrades, but replacing them generally falls into the category of "doable." What I call *components* are the battery, keyboard, optical drive, internal speaker, and plastic parts.

Battery If a battery's performance falls below an acceptable level, you can replace it with a battery from the manufacturer or from an aftermarket vendor. Although this should be a simple swap replacement (and usually is), you might encounter a situation where

• **Figure 15.50** Inserting a replacement drive

the real problem wasn't the battery per se, but an inadequate or malfunctioning charging system. The new battery might not give you any better performance than the old one. Try it.

Keyboard Getting a keyboard off a laptop computer often requires little pry bars, but also look for screws, clips, and so on. Keyboards connect via a tiny, short, and very delicate cable, often held down by tape. Replacing one is tricky, but doable.

Optical Drive Replacing an optical drive can present a challenge. If the drive is part of a modular system, just pop out the old drive and pop in a new one. If the drive is part of the internal chassis of the portable, on the other hand, you're looking at a full dissection. (See the "Integral Parts" section for tips on dismantling the portable.)

Speaker Like the optical drive, replacing the internal speaker or speakers on a laptop can be simple or a total pain, depending on where the speakers connect. Some laptops have speakers mounted on the outside of the chassis. You pry off the covers, pull out the little speakers, disconnect the cable, and then reverse the process for replacement speakers. If the speakers are inside the chassis, on the other hand, you need to dismantle the portable to get to them. (See the "Integral Parts" section.)

Plastic Parts Laptops have a few plastic parts that can get lost or broken. These are slot covers or card blanks designed to keep dust out of the memory card and expansion slots (see Figure 15.51). If you need to replace one of these, simply get a spare from the manufacturer or an aftermarket vendor and replace it.

Expansion Cards Not to be confused with PC Cards, many portable PCs have one or more true expansion slots for add-on cards. The more modular varieties will have a hatch on the bottom of the case that opens like the RAM hatch that gives you access to the slot(s). This enables you to change out an 802.11g wireless card, for example, for an 802.11n card, thus greatly

• **Figure 15.51** ExpressCard blank

enhancing the Wi-Fi experience on this device. Figure 15.52 shows a wide-open laptop with the expansion slot exposed.

Just like when installing RAM in a portable, you must avoid ESD and remove all electricity before you take out or put in an expansion card. Failure to remove the battery and the AC adapter can and probably will result in a shorted-out laptop motherboard, and that just makes for a bad day.

The only other consideration with expansion cards applies specifically to wireless. Not only will you need to connect the card to the slot properly, but you must reattach the antenna connection and often a separate power cable. Pay attention when you remove the card as to the placement of these vital connections.

You'll find one of two types of expansion slot in a portable. The older ones (think 2005 and earlier) use **Mini-PCI**, because PCI dominated that time period. Just about every portable since then uses PCI Express, so the laptops come with **Mini-PCIe** slots.

CPU Replacing a CPU on a modern portable takes a lot more work than replacing RAM or a Mini-PCIe expansion card, but follows the same general steps. Many CPUs mount facing the bottom of the portable, so that the venting goes away from your hands. When sitting properly on a flat surface, the heated air also goes to the back of the laptop and not toward the user. You access the CPU in this sort of system from the bottom of the portable.

As you can see in Figure 15.53, the CPU has an elaborate heat-sink and fan assembly that includes both the CPU and the chipset. Each of the pieces screws down in multiple places, plus the fan has a power connection. Aside from the tiny screws, there's no difference here in process between replacing a mobile CPU and a desktop CPU.

First, remove all power from the laptop, including the battery. Remove the hatch to expose the CPU. Remove the heat-sink and fan assembly and lift out the CPU. Replace it with another CPU, apply thermal paste, and reattach the heat-sink and fan assembly. Reconnect the fan power connector and you're good to go.

• **Figure 15.52** Mini-PCIe expansion slot on laptop

● **Figure 15.53** CPU heat-sink and fan assembly exposed

Some older laptops use passive cooling and thus have the CPU pointed up rather than down. They have a heat sink beneath the keyboard that cools everything down. With that style laptop, you remove the keyboard and heat sink to expose the CPU.

Integral Parts

Some hardware replacements require you to get serious with the laptop, opening it fully to the outside, removing many delicate parts, and even stripping it down to the bare metal chassis. I leave these repairs to the professional laptop repair folks, simply because they have the specific tools and expertise to do the job efficiently. CompTIA expects you to understand the process, though, so I've outlined it here. This pertains to four components: screen, DC jack, touchpad, and system board.

Portables open in two different ways, depending on the manufacturer. You either peel away layers from the top down, through the keyboard, or from the bottom up, through the base. Either direction requires careful attention to detail, part connectivity, and locations. You'll need a system to keep track of the dozens of tiny screws.

Every one of the replacements here requires you to detach the screen from the main chassis of the portable. Aside from finding the connection points and removing the proper screws, you need to pay attention to the connection points for the data stream to the monitor and the antenna that's in the frame of the display.

Once you have the portable stripped down, you replace whichever component you're in there to replace and then begin the process of building it back up into a coherent unit. Pay incredibly careful attention to getting data cables connected properly as you rebuild. I can't imagine a worse tech experience than replacing a touchpad and rebuilding a laptop only to have missed a connection and having to do it all over again.

The DC jack requires extra-special love when you need to replace one. The part is soldered to the main board, so to replace it means you'll need to not only strip the laptop to the bare metal, but also unsolder the old part and solder the new part. Then you'll rebuild the laptop and hope you got everything right. CompTIA cannot expect a CompTIA A+ technician to know how to do this stuff. Expect a question that explores whether it *can* be done. Rest assured, specialized techs can replace *any* component on a laptop, even the DC jack.

Troubleshooting Portable Computers

Many of the troubleshooting techniques you learned about for desktop systems can be applied to laptops. For example, take the proper precautions before and during disassembly. Use the proper hand tools, and document, label, and organize each plastic part and screw location for reassembly. Additionally, here are some laptop-specific procedures to try.

Laptop Won't Power On

- Verify AC power by plugging another electronic device into the wall outlet. If the other device receives power, the outlet is good.

- If the outlet is good, connect the laptop to the wall outlet and try to power on. If no LEDs light up, you may have a bad AC adapter. Swap it out with a known-good power adapter.

- A faulty peripheral device might keep the laptop from powering up. Remove any peripherals such as USB or FireWire devices.

Screen Doesn't Come On Properly

- If the laptop is booting (you hear the beeps and the drives), first make sure the display is turned on. Press the FN key and the key to activate the screen a number of times until the laptop display comes on. If that doesn't work, check the LCD cutoff switch—on many laptops, this is the small nub somewhere near the screen hinge that shuts the monitor off when you close the laptop—and make sure it isn't stuck in the down position.

- If the laptop display is very dim, you may have lost an inverter. The clue here is that inverters never go quietly. They can make a nasty hum as they are about to die and an equally nasty popping noise when they actually fail. Failure often occurs when you plug in the laptop's AC adapter, as the inverters take power directly from the AC adapter. It's also possible that the backlights in the LCD panel have died, though this is much less common than a bad inverter.

- If the screen won't come on or is cracked, most laptops have a port for plugging in an external monitor, which you can use to log into your laptop.

- If you plug a laptop into an external monitor and that monitor does not display, remember that you have both a hardware and an OS component to making dual displays successful. There's usually a combination of FN and another key to toggle among only portable, only external, and both displays. Plus you have the Display applet in the Control Panel to mirror or extend the desktop to a second monitor.

Tech Tip

Battery Won't Charge

If you have a laptop with a battery that won't charge up, it could be one of two things: the battery might be cooked or the AC adapter isn't doing its job. To troubleshoot, replace the battery with a known-good battery. If the new battery works, you've found the problem. Just replace the battery. Alternatively, remove the battery and run the laptop on AC only. If that works, you know the AC adapter is good. If it doesn't, replace the AC adapter.

- Many manufacturers have switched to LED displays on laptops, which has led to a phenomenon many techs thought long behind us: *flickering displays*. The LED backlights don't work quite the same as CCFL backlights, especially when you lower the brightness. This doesn't affect desktop LED displays, because they're usually so bright it doesn't matter. But portables need to be able to dim to save battery life. One technique for dimming LEDs is to have them turn on and off rapidly enough to keep the pixels lit, but slowly enough that there's a reduction in visible light and electricity use. With some of these panels, that flickering is not only noticeable, but headache and eyestrain inducing.

- There are two things you can do with a flickering LED display: crank up the brightness so that it goes away (and thus live with reduced battery life) or replace the laptop.

Wireless Doesn't Work or Works Intermittently

- If the wireless doesn't work at all, check along the front, rear, or side edges of the laptop for a physical switch that toggles the internal wireless adapter or Bluetooth adapter on and off.

- If a tech has recently replaced a component that required removal of the laptop display, dead wireless could mean simply a disconnected antenna. Most portables have the antenna built into the display panel, so check that connection.

- Try the special key combination for your laptop to toggle the wireless or Bluetooth adapter. You usually press the FN key in combination with another key.

- You might simply be out of range or, if the wireless works intermittently, then right at the edge of the range. Physically walk the laptop over to the wireless router or access point to ensure there are no out-of-range issues.

- With Bluetooth specifically, remember that the pairing process takes action or configuration on both devices to succeed. Turn on the Bluetooth device, actively seek it, and try again.

Input Problems

- If none of the keys work on your laptop, there's a good chance you've unseated the keypad connector. These connectors are quite fragile and are prone to unseating from any physical stress on the laptop. Check the manufacturer's disassembly procedures to locate and reseat the keypad.

- If you're getting numbers when you're expecting to get letters, the number lock (NUMLOCK) function key is turned on. The numlock LED should indicate the status. Turn it off.

 The troubleshooting issue known as a *ghost cursor* can mean one of two things. First, the display shows a trail of ghost cursors behind your real cursor as you move it. This might point to an aging display or an improperly configured refresh rate. Second, the cursor moves erratically, whether you are touching the touchpad or not. This probably means the touchpad has been damaged in some way and needs to be replaced.

- Laptop keyboards take far more abuse than the typical desktop keyboard, because of all those lunch meetings and café brainstorm sessions. Eating and drinking while over or around a keyboard just begs for problems. If you have a portable with sticking keys, look for the obvious debris in the keys. Use compressed air to clean them out. If you have serious goo and need to use a cleaning solution, disconnect the keyboard from the portable first. Make sure it's fully dried out before you reconnect it or you'll short it out.

- If the touchpad is having problems, a shot of compressed air does wonders for cleaning pet hair out of the touchpad sensors. You might get a cleaner shot if you remove the keyboard before using the compressed air. Remember to be gentle when lifting off the keyboard and make sure to follow the manufacturer's instructions.

- The touchpad driver might need to be reconfigured. Try the various options in the Control Panel | Mouse applet.

Chapter 15 Review

■ Chapter Summary

After reading this chapter and completing the exercises, you should understand the following about portable computers.

Describe the many types of portable computing devices available

- All portable devices share certain features: video output using LCD screens, some kind of PC sound, and DC battery power. There's no industry standard for naming the vast majority of styles of portable computing devices.

- A portable PC refers in general to the clamshell, keyboard-on-the-bottom and LCD-screen-at-the-top design that is considered the shape of mobile PCs. The terms "laptop," "notebook," and "portable" all define the same form factor.

- Portable computers come with a variety of input devices. Most have a fully functional keyboard and a device to control the mouse pointer. The basic QUERTY format is followed, but manufacturers make choices with key size and placement of the non-alphabet characters. Almost every portable keyboard uses a Function (FN) key to enable some keys to perform a third duty.

- By far the most common laptop pointing device found today is the touchpad—a flat, touch-sensitive pad just in front of the keyboard. To operate a touchpad, you simply glide your finger across its surface to move the pointer, and tap the surface once or twice to single- or double-click.

- Laptop LCD screens come in a variety of supported resolutions, described with acronyms such as XGA, WXGA, WSXGA, and more. The W in front of the letters indicates widescreen. The two most common resolutions are WXGA for the 14- to 15-inch models and HD 1080 for the 17.3-inch models. The common finish is either matte or high-gloss.

- A portable PC can be considered a desktop replacement if it does everything most people want to do with a desktop PC. Desktop replacements appeal to road warriors and people who prefer to tuck computing devices out of sight when not in use.

- Netbook portables normally weigh less than three pounds and are less than an inch in thickness. These machines usually have smaller displays, lower-capacity hard drives, and CPUs that operate at lower speeds than their more full-sized brethren.

- Ultrabooks are for people who can't give up the power of high-end computers but can afford to pay more for a smaller package. Intel set up the Ultrabook specifications in 2011, defining the form factor to use power-sipping Intel processors with integrated graphics.

- Microsoft started the Tablet PC initiative way back in 2001, defining the devices as fully featured portables running a tablet-aware version of Windows and using a stylus to interact directly with the screen. Many Tablet PCs have come to market since then, fulfilling the needs of specific professions, notably medicine.

Explain ways to expand portable computers

- Every portable PC comes with one or more single-function ports. The most common of all is the ubiquitous USB port. Additionally, the single PS/2 port on some laptops supports both keyboards and pointing devices. Most portable computing devices have a speaker port, and some have line in and microphone jacks as well. Laptops invariably provide a video port such as a VGA, HDMI, DisplayPort, or DVI connection for hooking up an external monitor.

- Most laptops support a second monitor, giving the user the option to display Windows on the laptop only, the external monitor only, or both simultaneously. Usually a special Function (FN) key on the keyboard will cycle through the monitor configurations.

- All portables offer some kind of network connectivity, such as 802.11 Wi-Fi to connect to the Internet. Wired Ethernet ports are standard issue. Bluetooth is common for connecting peripherals. Portables have some way to toggle Wi-Fi and Bluetooth off and on to conserve battery life.

- PC Cards are roughly credit card–sized devices that enhance and extend the functions of a portable PC. Still commonly known by their older name, *PCMCIA cards*, PC Cards were standard on mobile computers for years but are slowly disappearing. All PC Cards are hot-swappable.

- Parallel PC Cards come in two flavors, 16-bit and CardBus, and each flavor comes in three different physical sizes, called Type I, Type II, and Type III. Type I, II, and III cards differ only in the thickness of the card (Type I being the thinnest and Type III the thickest). Type II cards are by far the most common. All parallel PC Cards share the same 68-pin interface. The 16-bit PC Cards are 16-bit, 5-V cards that can have up to two distinct functions or devices, such as a modem/network card combination. CardBus PC Cards are 32-bit, 3.3-V cards that can have up to eight different functions on a single card. The 16-bit PC Cards will fit into and work in CardBus slots, but the reverse is not true.

- The serial ExpressCard comes in two widths: 54 mm (ExpressCard/54) and 34 mm (ExpressCard/34). Both cards are 75 mm long and 5 mm thick, which makes them shorter than all previous PC Cards and the same thickness as a Type II PC Card. ExpressCards connect to either the Hi-Speed USB 2.0 bus (480 Mbps) or a PCI Express bus (2.5 Gbps).

- Most portable PCs have one or more general-purpose expansion ports that enable you to plug in many types of devices. Older portables sport RS-232 serial and IEEE 1284 parallel ports for mice, modems, printers, scanners, external CD-media drives, and more. USB, FireWire, and eSATA are popular and widespread methods for attaching peripherals to laptops. All have easy-to-use connectors and can be hot-swapped.

- Port replicators are devices that plug into a single port (usually USB but sometimes proprietary) and offer common PC ports, such as serial, parallel, USB, network, and PS/2. Docking stations resemble port replicators in many ways, offering legacy and modern single- and multi-function ports, but have extra features built in, such as optical drives or PC Card slots.

Manage and maintain portable computers

- Portable computers use three types of batteries: Nickel-Cadmium (Ni-Cd), Nickel-Metal Hydride (Ni-MH), and Lithium-Ion (Li-Ion). Today, only Li-Ion is used because that battery chemistry provides the highest energy density for the weight and has few problems with external factors.

- Batteries should be stored in a cool place and kept charged, at least to 70–80 percent. Never drain a battery all the way down unless required to do so as part of a battery calibration. Rechargeable batteries have only a limited number of charge-discharge cycles before overall battery performance is reduced. Because batteries contain dangerous chemicals, never handle one that has ruptured. Always recycle old batteries rather than disposing of them in the trash.

- The process of cooperation among the hardware, the BIOS, and the OS to reduce power use is known generically as power management. Early laptops used power continuously, regardless of whether the system was using the device at the time. With power management features, today's laptops can automatically turn off unused devices or can shut down the entire system, leaving the information in RAM ready for a restart. To perform these power management functions requires specialized hardware, BIOS, and an operating system that supports power management.

- Starting with the 386SX, Intel introduced System Management Mode (SMM), a power management system that would make the CPU and all peripherals go to "sleep." In 1992, Intel introduced the improved Advanced Power Management (APM) specification, followed by the Advanced Configuration and Power Interface (ACPI) standard in 1996.

- To use APM or ACPI, the computer must have an SMM-capable CPU, an APM-compliant BIOS, and devices that can be shut off. Referred to as Energy Star devices, these peripherals can shut down without actually turning off. The OS must also know how to request that a particular device be shut down. ACPI extends power-saving to include hot-swappable devices.

- Virtually all laptops and desktops use power management functions. APM defines four power-usage levels, including Full On, APM Enabled, APM Standby, and APM Suspend. ACPI, the successor to APM, handles all these levels plus a few more, totaling four Global (G) and six total (S) states. Support for APM was discontinued in Windows Vista, which uses ACPI.

- Configure APM/ACPI through CMOS or through the Power Options Control Panel applet in Windows, with Windows settings overriding CMOS settings. Many CMOS versions allow configuration of wake-up events.

- Hibernation writes information from RAM to the hard drive. Upon waking up, the data is returned to RAM, and programs and files are in the same state they were in when the computer entered hibernation.

- Laptops with backlit keyboards will have some way you can disable this feature when it's not needed, usually with a keyboard combination. You can also reduce the output of the LCD backlight using a combination of FN and another key to get a few more minutes of computing time before you have to shut down.

- Use an appropriate screen cleaner (not glass cleaner) to clean the LCD screen. Use compressed air around the keyboard and PC card sockets. Never use water around the keyboard.

- To combat the inevitable heat produced by a portable computer, always use power management, keep an air space between the bottom of the laptop and the surface on which it rests, don't use a keyboard protector for an extended period of time, and be aware of your fan.

- Store portable computers in quality cases when traveling. Well-padded backpacks not only keep a laptop protected but also make a system less appealing to would-be thieves. When traveling, don't forget accessories such as AC power cords, additional batteries, or modular devices. Remove all discs from drives and make sure you have enough battery power to boot up for security personnel. If shipping your computer, go with a reputable carrier, keep your tracking number, and request a delivery signature. Use a laptop lock or a software tracking system to protect your laptop when traveling.

Upgrade and repair portable computers

- You need to follow a four-step process to succeed in disassembly/reassembly. First, document and label every cable and screw location. Second, organize any parts you extract from the laptop. Third, refer to the manufacturer's documentation. Finally, you need to use the appropriate hand tools. If you can't get information directly from the manufacturer, try various online sites, such as YouTube or iFixit, for walkthroughs on fixing laptop problems.

- Every CompTIA A+ tech should know how to perform the two standard upgrades to portable computers: adding RAM and replacing a hard drive.

- Laptops use one of four types of RAM. Most older laptops use either 72-pin or 144-pin SO-DIMMs with SDRAM technology. DDR SDRAM systems primarily use 200-pin SO-DIMMs, although you'll also find 172-pin micro-DIMMs. Every decent laptop has upgradeable RAM slots. Get the correct RAM; many portable PC makers use proprietary RAM solutions. No standard exists for RAM placement in portables. More often than not, you need to unscrew or pop open a panel on the underside of the portable and press out on the restraining clips to make the RAM stick pop up so you can remove and replace it. Always disconnect from all electrical sources before removing or inserting RAM.

- Laptops that support shared memory benefit from more affordable video cards. The video card has less built-in RAM and uses a portion of the computer's system RAM to make up the difference. Although this results in a lower cost, system performance suffers because RAM that is shared with the video card is not available to programs. NVIDIA calls their shared memory technology TurboCache and ATI calls theirs HyperMemory.

- SATA drives in the 2.5-inch drive format now rule in all laptops. Currently, the larger 2.5-inch hard drives hold up to 500+ GB, while the larger 3.5-inch hard drives hold more than 3 TB. Upgrading from an HDD to an SSD can bring remarkable gains in battery life and performance.

- Once you get beyond upgrading RAM and replacing a hard drive on a portable PC, you take the plunge into the laptop repair specialty. You

can replace some components by lifting them out, detaching a ribbon cable, and then reversing the steps with the replacement part. Other parts require a full teardown of the laptop to the bare bones, which presents a much greater level of difficulty.

- Standard tech-level repairs you should be able to do are replacing the battery, keyboard, and optical drive (usually—some are tough to get out). Others are replacing the small speakers and missing plastic parts.

- You can also open the hatch on the bottom of the case that opens like the RAM hatch to expose other parts for replacement. The same hatch might hold one or two Mini-PCIe slots, for example, and give you access to the CPU.

- Some hardware replacements require you to open a laptop, remove many delicate parts, and strip it down to the bare metal chassis. Dedicated laptop techs do these jobs, but you should know the process.

- Portables open in two different ways, depending on the manufacturer. You either peel away layers from the top down, through the keyboard, or from the bottom up, through the base. Either direction requires careful attention to detail, part connectivity, and locations. You'll need a system to keep track of the dozens of tiny screws.

Troubleshoot portable computers

- If your laptop won't power on, try a different wall outlet. If it still fails to power up, remove all peripheral devices and try again.

- If the screen doesn't come on properly, verify that the laptop is configured to use the built-in LCD screen by pressing the appropriate key to cycle through the internal and external monitors. If you hear a popping sound, you may have blown an inverter. If the screen is definitely broken, you may use an external monitor to access the laptop. One technique for dimming LEDs is to have them turn on and off rapidly enough to keep the pixels lit, but slowly enough that there's a reduction in visible light and electricity use. With some of these panels, that flickering is not only noticeable, but headache and eyestrain inducing.

- If wireless is not working, check for the physical switch on the side of the laptop that toggles power to the internal network card or Bluetooth adapter. If your laptop doesn't have a switch, check for a key combination or function key that toggles power. You also may be out of range. Physically walk the laptop closer to the wireless router or access point.

- If the keypad or touchpad doesn't work, try a shot of compressed air, reseat the physical internal connection, or reconfigure the driver settings through the Control Panel.

■ Key Terms

16-bit *(550)*

Advanced Configuration and Power Interface (ACPI) *(555)*

Advanced Power Management (APM) *(555)*

aspect ratio *(539)*

auto-switching power supply *(563)*

CardBus *(550)*

desktop replacement *(540)*

docking station *(553)*

ExpressCard *(550)*

Function (FN) key *(537)*

hibernation *(556)*

high-gloss *(540)*

laptop *(537)*

Lithium-Ion (Li-Ion) *(553)*

matte *(540)*

Mini-PCI *(572)*

Mini-PCIe *(572)*

multitouch *(539)*

netbook *(541)*

Nickel-Cadmium (Ni-Cd) *(553)*

Nickel-Metal Hydride (Ni-MH) *(553)*

notebook *(537)*

offline files *(560)*

PC Card *(549)*

PCMCIA card *(550)*

port replicator *(552)*

power plan *(558)*

shared memory *(568)*

sleep timer *(558)*

stylus *(542)*

System Management Mode (SMM) *(555)*

Tablet PC *(542)*

touchpad *(539)*

TrackPoint *(538)*

Ultrabook *(542)*

■ Key Term Quiz

Use the Key Terms list to complete the sentences that follow. Not all terms will be used.

1. A typical clamshell-style computer with built-in LCD monitor, keyboard, and input device is most commonly called a laptop or _____.

2. The _____ enables laptop keyboards to do more than two functions on a single key.

3. Many newer laptops feature _____ screens offering richer color, higher contrast, and wider viewing angles.

4. Intel set up the _____ specifications for super thin, super light, and super efficient laptops with integrated graphics and no optical drive.

5. The _____ replaced the PC Card as the external expansion slot of choice on laptops.

6. A(n) _____ plugs into a single port on the portable computer and offers uncommon and common PC ports, such as serial, parallel, USB, network, and PS/2.

7. Today's laptops use _____ for batteries because that battery chemistry provides the highest energy density for the weight.

8. Windows Vista and Windows 7 enable _____ for storing and automatically syncing files and folders between a portable and a file server.

9. Laptops using _____ are less expensive because the video card has less built-in memory, but the RAM it borrows from the system results in less memory available to programs.

10. Most laptops today have one or more _____ slots for internal expansion cards such as Wi-Fi NICs.

■ Multiple-Choice Quiz

1. Which of the following statements best describes hard drives typically found in laptops?

 A. They are 2.5-inch SATA drives, but they do not hold as much data as the 3.5-inch hard drives found in desktop PCs.

 B. They are 3.5-inch ATA drives just like those found in desktop PCs, but they usually require "cable select" settings rather than master or slave.

 C. They are 3.5-inch SATA drives that hold more data than the 2.5-inch hard drives found in desktop PCs.

 D. They are 2.5-inch PCMCIA drives, while desktops usually have 3.5-inch SCSI drives.

2. Which of the following APM power levels writes information from RAM to the hard drive and then copies the data back to RAM when the computer is activated again?

 A. Full On

 B. APM Enabled

 C. APM Standby

 D. Hibernation

3. Portable PCs typically use which of the following kinds of upgradeable RAM?

 A. 68-pin and 72-pin RIMMs

 B. 30-pin and 72-pin SIMMs

 C. 72-pin and 144-pin SO-DIMMs

 D. 30-pin and 72-pin SO-RIMMs

4. Where do you configure APM/ACPI in Windows?

 A. The Power Options applet in the Control Panel

 B. The Display applet in the Control Panel

 C. The Power Management applet in the Control Panel

 D. The Power and Devices applet in the Control Panel

5. Which of the following input devices will you most likely find on a portable PC?

 A. TrackPoint

 B. Touchpad

 C. Trackball

 D. Mouse

6. Which buses do ExpressCards use?

 A. Hi-Speed USB and FireWire

 B. Hi-Speed USB and PCI Express

 C. PCI and PCI Express

 D. Mini-PCI and Parallel

7. *Convertibles* and *slates* describe what type of device?

 A. Multicore processor

 B. Clamshell laptop computer

 C. PDA

 D. Tablet PC

8. If wireless networking is not working, what should you check?

 A. Check the switch on the side of the laptop that toggles power to the network card.

 B. Make sure the Ethernet cable is plugged into the laptop.

 C. Make sure the digitizer has been trained.

 D. Make sure Power Management is enabled.

9. Erin has an older laptop with a switch on the back that says 115/230. What does this indicate?

 A. The laptop has an auto-switching power supply.

 B. The laptop has a fixed-input power supply.

 C. The laptop has a step-down transforming power supply.

 D. The laptop has a step-up transforming power supply.

10. Which of the following display types will you most commonly find on a portable PC today? (Select two.)

 A. LCD

 B. LED

 C. OLED

 D. Plasma

11. Jake has received two replacement memory sticks for his Dell laptop. What should he do first in the upgrade process?

 A. Disconnect the AC cord and remove the battery.

 B. Flip the laptop over and remove the RAM compartment cover.

 C. Remove the memory sticks from their antistatic bags and set them on the antistatic map next to the laptop.

 D. Remove the memory sticks from the laptop.

12. Steve complains that his Windows 7 laptop still isn't snappy enough after doubling the amount of RAM. What might improve system performance?

 A. Add more RAM.

 B. Replace the power supply.

 C. Replace the battery.

 D. Replace the HDD with an SSD.

13. Jim likes his laptop but complains that his wireless seems slow compared to all the new laptops. On further inspection, you determine his laptop runs 802.11g. What can be done to improve his network connection speed?

 A. Replace the regular RAM with 802.11n RAM.

 B. Replace the display with one with a better antenna.

 C. Replace the Mini-PCIe 802.11g card with an 802.11n card.

 D. Get a new laptop, because this one can't be upgraded.

14. Edgar successfully replaced the display on a laptop (a toddler had taken a ballpoint pen to it), but the customer called back almost immediately complaining that his wireless didn't work. What could the problem be?

 A. The problems are unrelated, so it could be anything.

 B. Edgar inadvertently disconnected the antenna from the Mini-PCIe 802.11 card.

 C. Edgar replaced the display with one without an internal antenna.

 D. Edgar failed to reconnect the antenna in the new display.

15. Rafael gets a tech call from a user with a brand new laptop complaining that working on it was causing headaches. What could the problem be?

 A. The laptop uses a plasma display.

 B. The laptop uses a CRT display.

 C. The laptop uses an LED display in power saving mode.

 D. The laptop uses an LED display in full power mode.

■ Essay Quiz

1. At the upcoming training seminar for new techs, your boss wants to make sure they understand and use power management settings. You've been asked to prepare a short presentation showing the range of power management settings available in Windows XP, Vista, and 7 and demonstrating how to set them. What will you include in your presentation?

2. You've been tasked to advise your group on current portable computer technology so they can purchase ten new laptops by the end of the quarter. In a short essay, weigh the pros and cons of getting desktop replacements versus smaller laptops that would come with docking stations.

3. Your boss has a new portable computer and is planning to take it with him on a business trip to Paris. He's not all that tech-savvy or much of a traveler, so write a memo that tells him what to do or avoid while traveling, especially overseas.

4. Norm wants to upgrade his laptop's hard drive, CPU, and RAM. Because he's upgraded all of these components on his desktop, he doesn't think he'll run into much trouble. What advice will you give him about selecting the components and upgrading the laptop?

Lab Projects

• Lab Project 15.1

This chapter mentioned that, although they are more expensive, portable PCs typically provide less processing power and smaller hard drives, and in general are not as full-featured as desktop computers. Use the Internet to check sites such as www.lenovo.com, www.toshiba.com, www .dell.com, and www.hp.com to compare the best

equipped, most powerful laptop you can find with the best equipped, most powerful desktop computer you can find. How do their features and prices compare? Now find a less expensive laptop and try to find a desktop computer that is as similar as possible in terms of capabilities, and compare their prices.

• Lab Project 15.2

Continuing from the previous lab, go to the www .dell.com website and compare one of the better desktop-replacement laptops with one of the more basic laptops. List the features that are of interest to

you personally, starting with the most important and continuing down. Then use the site to begin building the perfect laptop for you. Compare your results with others and discuss what's important to you.

Mobile Devices

chapter
16

"Buyer should be aware that 'CELL' is a violent piece of work, which comes complete with zombies set in motion by bad cell phone signals that destroy the human brain."

—Stephen King

In this chapter, you will learn how to

- **Explain the features and capabilities of smartphones and tablets**
- **Explain how to configure mobile devices**
- **Describe how to secure mobile devices**

Mobile devices have revolutionized the way we work and play in recent years. Devices such as smartphones and tablets enable people to access the Internet from just about anywhere and accomplish essential tasks on the go.

This chapter explores mobile devices in detail. We'll first look at the features and capabilities of devices that are common in the mobile market. The chapter then jumps into the details of configuring the devices for personal use, doing such things as setting up e-mail and adding productivity devices. The chapter wraps with a discussion on securing mobile devices. I'm eager to jump into a topic new to this version of the CompTIA A+ certification, so let's get started.

Features and Capabilities

Modern mobile devices fall into two categories, smartphones and tablets, and both types of device have similar features and capabilities. The primary distinction between the types is that a **smartphone** is a cell phone enhanced to do things formerly reserved for fully grown PCs; a **tablet** embodies those enhanced computing features and capabilities on an expanded format and screen. Tablets generally do *not* have cellular phone capability. This section explores the common features among the devices and highlights major differences as well. We'll first look at the mobile experience, and then look at ways to add programs to and enhance the capabilities of the devices. The section finishes with ways to enhance the hardware of mobile devices, or at least the hardware's capabilities.

Mobile Experience

Mobile devices might seem, at first description, like PCs scaled down to fit in a backpack, purse, or pocket, but they bring a unique experience to users that differs substantially from the standard PC experience. Mobile devices have a default screen—like the desktop in Windows—called the **home screen** and have icons for applications (*apps*) for accomplishing specific tasks. But the first thing that will strike you when you handle one of these devices is that it's *not* the same thing as a small PC (see Figure 16.1). The most obvious difference is the interface, so we'll start there.

• **Figure 16.1** Small PC and tablet—cousins at best

● **Figure 16.2** Mobile devices have a touch interface.

Touch Interface

Mobile devices use a **touch interface**, meaning that to interact with them you touch the screen (see Figure 16.2). They don't come with a physical keyboard for typing or a mouse for clicking. (In fact, you can't add a mouse at all to most mobile devices.)

Different gestures with your fingers accomplish different tasks. To start a program, or app as they're called, you **tap** its icon, which means to poke it with your finger. If you've opened an app with multiple screens, you hold your finger on the screen and slide it across the screen, either right to left or top to bottom, depending on the type of application (see Figure 16.3). This is called a **swipe**.

Holding a finger on the home screen or on an open app screen in many devices brings up a context menu for accomplishing things like changing the background picture (the *wallpaper*), bookmarking a page, or editing. Touching different parts of the screen when in an app can offer other options, such as closing the app or pushing the app to the background (see Figure 16.4).

Many mobile devices enable you to use multiple fingers to do tasks such as expand or shrink an image on the screen (see Figure 16.5). An open long document, such as a word processing document, for example, might give you two different responses when you scroll with one or two fingers. Using one finger might select text to edit, but two-fingered scrolling might move the document up or down. Different vendors call this feature different things, but the common term is **multitouch**.

● **Figure 16.3** Swiping to move to the next screen

● **Figure 16.4** Getting a context menu by touching and holding

This multitouch interface enables you to expand or contract some content on the screen. You can **pinch** an image, for example, between two fingers and make that picture bigger or smaller according to the way your fingers move.

Screen Technology Current **capacitive** touchscreens use electrical current in your body to determine movement of your fingers across the screen. They measure the difference between the electrical charge in your body and the static charge on the screen, which is quite cool when you think about it. Capacitive touchscreens require physical contact, so gloved fingers won't work. Older technologies used **resistive** touchscreens that responded to the pressure applied to the screen. Fingers worked, but best results came from using a special pointing stick called a *stylus* (see Figure 16.6).

Mobile devices use a variety of screen types. Most tablets use some type of LCD panel, just like portable PCs and desktop monitors. The less expensive ones use twisted nematic (TN); the better ones, like the Apple iPad, use an In-Plane Switching (IPS) panel for richer colors and better viewing angles.

Some smaller devices, like the better smartphones, use a related but different technology called **organic light-emitting diode (OLED)** screens where an organic compound provides the light for the screen. Applying an electric current causes the organic layer to glow in the precise spots desired. Displaying a checkerboard pattern of black and white, in other words, only lights up the white squares. OLEDs don't use backlights at all, which means they can display true black, they're lighter, and they use less electricity than LCDs of any sort. Screens larger than half a dozen inches, as of this writing, are too expensive to make for mainstream consumer devices.

 The resistive touchscreen devices required periodic *screen calibration*, which resets the touch screen for improved accuracy. Capacitive touchscreens don't require calibration.

OLED screens use an organic compound exposed to electrical current for lighting; they don't have a traditional backlight.

• **Figure 16.5** Resizing and rotating an image using two fingers

• **Figure 16.6** Older mobile device with stylus

Orientation Mobile devices feature rectangular screens, just like desktop displays, but all of them rotate easily. Plus, the orientation of the screen rotates right along with the display, so by default, up is always up. The underlying technology, called an **accelerometer**, enables you to switch easily from portrait view to landscape view. If you want to switch from reading a book to watching a movie, just turn the device on its side (see Figure 16.7). Figure 16.8 shows a wonderful use of the accelerometer in an iPhone, turning the device into an electronic level.

Some devices feature a **gyroscope** that can detect the position of the tablet or phone in 3-D space. This enables more intuitive control over onscreen devices, such as a plane's joystick. Tilting the device forward, for example, would have the effect of pushing the plane's nose down; tilting backward "pulls back" on the stick, easing the plane's nose up. Few applications (and those primarily games) use the gyroscope as of this writing.

Mobile Operating Systems

Two operating systems power the vast majority of mobile devices. Apple **iOS** runs on all Apple devices, such as the iPhone smartphone and the iPad tablet. Google **Android** runs almost every non-Apple product. Microsoft has a very small presence in the mobile devices market, but you'll only find Windows Phone 7 on a few smartphones.

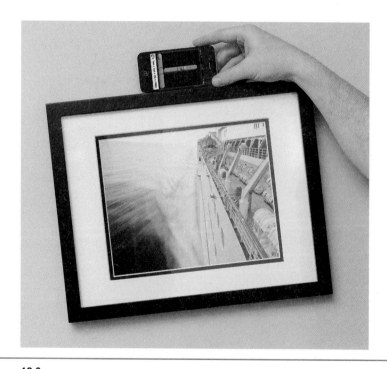

• **Figure 16.8** Hanging a picture properly

Apps

An **app** enables you to accomplish a specific task on a mobile device, such as check e-mail, surf the Web, play games, and so on. (Apps are the same thing as applications. For some reason, it's more hip to use the short term when discussing mobile devices.) Programmers write apps for specific mobile platforms and sometimes for specific devices. So an app written for a Windows Phone 7 phone, for example, won't work on an Apple iPhone, even though both are smartphones. This applies somewhat to apps written for a specific operating system as well. Apps written for an Apple iPhone can run on an Apple iPad, because both devices use Apple iOS for an operating system, but the same app optimized for the iPad will look and run better than a scaled-up iPhone app.

Different apps bring out different features of the mobile device. An electronic book reader, for example, shows an interface that appears like a book (see Figure 16.9). You swipe to change pages. A note-taking application, in contrast, will open a virtual keyboard that enables you to type as if you had a regular keyboard attached (see Figure 16.10). Finally, a racing game will turn the entire mobile device into a steering wheel, relying on the accelerometer to provide accurate turning (see Figure 16.11).

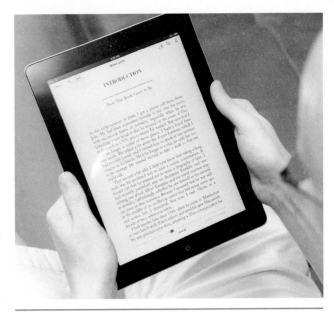

• **Figure 16.9** Reading an eBook

Multimedia

Most mobile devices today come with one or two cameras for taking digital photos and movies and for video conferencing. Manufacturers initially offered low-resolution cameras and camcorders that produced poor-quality photos and grainy videos, but some current devices offer crystal-clear high-definition videos with flash photos and optical zoom.

• **Figure 16.10** Typing on a virtual keyboard

• **Figure 16.11** Racing

• Figure 16.12 Switching from the rear camera to the front camera

Devices with two cameras, one pointed away and one pointed at the user, have some kind of button to switch when picture taking. The tablet in Figure 16.12, for example, enables the user to swap the focus of the picture-taking software by tapping the double-arrow button in the lower-right corner.

Adding Apps

Mobile devices come from the manufacturer with a certain number of vital apps installed for accessing e-mail, surfing the Web, taking notes, making entries in a calendar, and so on. Almost all of them offer multimedia apps to enable you to listen to music, take pictures, watch You-Tube videos, and view photos. You'll find instant messaging tools and, in the case of smartphones, telephone capabilities.

With no exceptions I've encountered, though, you'll want to add capabilities to the mobile device, and that means adding apps. Games are incredibly popular to add, with *Angry Birds* accounting for billions of dollars of lost worker productivity in the United States alone (see Figure 16.13). (And if you haven't played *Angry Birds*, I highly suggest downloading it right now!)

Even when the prebundled tools offer great functionality, often other software developers will take an idea and run with it to create something

> ### Tech Tip
>
> **iOS and Flash**
>
> *The one big gotcha about Apple is that none of their mobile devices support Adobe Flash, making a surprising number of Web sites not available. You simply cannot add an app that makes Flash work on an Apple iPhone or iPad.*

The GPS aspect of mobile devices goes both ways. Because mobile devices tap into the Internet or cellular phone networks, the devices have identifying numbers such as a MAC address. The cell phone companies and government agencies can use the ID or MAC address to pinpoint where you are at any given time. This feature, called geotracking, clearly has a lot of room for abuse of power, though nothing major has happened as of this writing.

• Figure 16.13 Angry Birds on an ASUS tablet

wholly unexpectedly cool. All the smartphones and nearly every tablet, for example, include some sort map tool that also includes *positioning software*. This software taps into the **Global Positioning System (GPS)** network of satellites maintained by the U.S. government to pinpoint your current location on a map (see Figure 16.14). This helps you find how to get from where you are to where you want to be.

The Internet has turned the concept of map viewing into something much more powerful courtesy of tools like Google Earth. With Google Earth, you can zoom all over the world, seeing satellite images of cities, towns, and countryside. You can access embedded images of places (see Figure 16.15) and get information via Wikipedia. Adding Google Earth (or any other app) to a mobile device follows different patterns according to the operating system and manufacturer of a specific mobile device.

Apple and Closed Source

Apple makes the most popular mobile devices in the iPhone and the iPad (smartphone and tablet, respectively). Both devices use the iOS operating system. Unlike every other manufacturer, Apple tightly controls the user experience, insisting that all developers of apps for iOS follow the same guidelines.

Apple has created a **closed source** or **single source** system, meaning that if you want to get an app for your iPhone or iPad, you can only get it from the Apple App Store (see Figure 16.16). Apple must approve any app before it goes into the App Store, and Apple reserves the right to revoke permission on any app that fails to measure up.

To add an app, select the App Store icon from the home screen. You can select from featured apps or view by category. You can check out the top 25 paid or free apps or simply search for what you want (see Figure 16.17).

Figure 16.14 GPS app showing current location (an excellent café in the Montrose neighborhood of Houston, Texas, in this example)

Don't like the idea of Big Brother knowing where you are all the time? Turn off Location Services in iOS or GPS Services on your Android. Keep in mind that turning this off will keep all applications that need this information from working.

Figure 16.15 Image in Google Earth

• **Figure 16.16** App Store

• **Figure 16.17** Searching for Google Earth

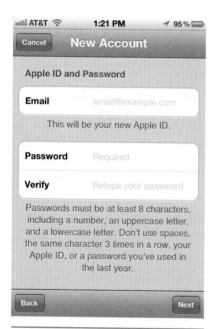

• **Figure 16.18** Creating an iCloud account

The first time you try to purchase an app through the App Store, you'll be prompted to set up an account. You can use an account that you created previously through the Apple iTunes music and video store or create a new account using the Apple iCloud service. Creating a new iCloud account takes a few steps and a lot of typing in of passwords and such (see Figure 16.18), but eventually you'll get the account figured out. You'll need a valid credit card to set up the account.

Android Experience

Google Android powers a majority of smartphones and a solid percentage of tablets, but Android differs greatly from Apple iOS in that Google gives the OS away and developers create versions suited to their devices. That means in practice that when you have a smartphone or tablet that uses Google Android for an OS, you have to amend that description to include the manufacturer as well. A Samsung tablet, in other words, uses an OS that

Try This!

Checking Out Apps

You can see the kind of apps available through Google Apps Marketplace or Google Play, even if you don't have an Android tablet, so try this! Here are the two Web sites:

https://www.google.com/enterprise/marketplace/

https://play.google.com/store

What kinds of apps do they offer? What would you want that you don't see?

differs somewhat from the OS an ASUS tablet uses. HTC, for example, uses a custom interface for its Android devices called HTC Sense that changes the look and feel of Android.

When you want to get an app for an Android device, you have alternative sources for that app. Many vendors offer a store with apps developed or customized to work with their devices. These **vendor-specific** stores enable you to get apps that should work well with your Android smartphone or tablet.

You can also go to an **open source** market for apps developed "for Android" that probably will work with your device, but there's not a guarantee that they'll work on all Android devices. Google Play, for example, offers hundreds of thousands of apps. This Wild West approach to apps makes the Android experience vastly different from the iOS experience when it comes to smartphones and tablets.

Enhancing Hardware

A mobile device is a computer, just like your desktop PC or laptop, with the same basic components doing the same basic things. The construction centers around a primary circuit board, a *motherboard*, onto which every other component is attached. Each mobile device has a CPU and GPU, though not necessarily based on the same architecture as a portable PC. The Apple iPad uses an ARM processor, for example, rather than an Intel ×86 or ×64 processor. In contrast, the ASUS Transformer featured as the Android model in this chapter uses a processor called a Tegra from NVIDIA, billed as the first mobile super processor. It features two to four CPU cores with integrated GPU, Northbridge, Southbridge, and memory controller for awesome power and serious 3-D capabilities.

Mobile devices use storage, though usually not a traditional hard disk drive (HDD) with spinning platters. More commonly, mobile devices use a *solid state drive* (*SSD*) because SSDs use much less electricity than platter-based drives. Plus they're cooler in general, just like you.

Mobile devices vary from their larger brethren in two very significant areas of importance to techs. First, none of them offer any field-serviceable parts. If something breaks, you send the device back to the manufacturer. Second, you can't upgrade them at all. Even a laptop enables you to upgrade RAM or a hard drive, for example, but the mobile device you buy is exactly what you get. You want something better? Buy a new one.

That said, every mobile device enables you to attach some kind of peripheral or external storage device. But every device offers different expansion capabilities, so it's hard to generalize about them.

The one exception to the rule that you can't generalize about mobile devices relates to sound. Every mobile device has a single 3.5-mm audio jack for plugging in earbuds or speakers (see Figure 16.19). This applies to smartphones and tablets from all vendors.

 The CompTIA A+ 220-802 objectives mention "touch flow" as if it were a standard feature of mobile operating systems. In fact, HTC's TouchFLO preceded HTC's Sense interface. TouchFLO is no longer used on HTC's Android phones.

 Microsoft has a small but growing presence in the mobile devices market with Windows Phone 7 and Windows 8. Expect the market share to increase over the coming years. Microsoft embraces an app marketplace somewhere in between that of Apple and Google, with both Microsoft-created apps and those created by other developers available through the Windows Phone Marketplace and other venues.

 Mobile devices have no field replaceable units (FRUs) and no upgradeability.

• **Figure 16.19** Earbuds plugged into a smartphone

• Figure 16.20 Recharger dongle

Apple Expansion Options

Apple devices offer the least expansion capability of all the mobile devices, so even though they dominate the marketplace, there's not much to say about them. The iPhone and iPad use a single proprietary port that's used to recharge the device and to connect the few external devices available. Figure 16.20 shows the typical use for the port, a dongle that connects to a USB AC adapter for recharging.

Early iPhones and iPads had limited multimedia capabilities, but current devices enable you to mirror the screen to a multimedia device such as a projector. This enables seamless presentations, for example, through the excellent Apple Keynote program (see Figure 16.21). The multimedia connection requires another dongle adapter (see Figure 16.22).

Android Expansion Options

Devices that use Google Android come with a variety of connections and expansion capabilities. Many offer microSD slots for adding storage in the form of the tiny flash memory cards (see Figure 16.23). Some offer bigger slots, and a few feature Micro USB or even full-sized USB ports.

Many Android devices offer a proprietary socket that mimics the functions of Apple's dongle port, providing a way to recharge the tablet or smartphone and get data from a PC to the tablet and vice versa. Figure 16.24 shows a proprietary connector for power.

Finally, many tablets sport a connector for attaching the device to an external monitor, such as a big screen or projector. (Smartphones don't generally have this connector.) Figure 16.25 shows a Micro-HDMI port and connector.

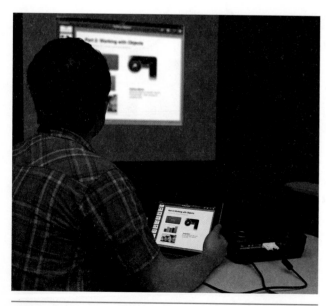

• Figure 16.21 Apple Keynote on an iPad and a projector

• Figure 16.22 Apple Digital AV Adapter

• **Figure 16.23** MicroSD card and slot

• **Figure 16.24** ASUS proprietary power connector

Bluetooth

The last way that mobile devices expand their physical capabilities is wirelessly, most often using the Bluetooth standard for adding a keyboard (all) or mouse (not with Apple products). In theory, you could attach all sorts of Bluetooth devices to the mobile device, but the reality seems limited to keyboards, headphones, and headsets. Figure 16.26 shows a diminutive Apple keyboard for the iPad and the iPad resting in a stand to make typing this chapter a little easier than using the virtual keyboard.

• **Figure 16.25** Micro-HDMI port and connector

See the "Bluetooth" subsection of the "Configuration" section later in this chapter for the steps to set up a tablet with a Bluetooth keyboard.

• **Figure 16.26** Keyboard associated with iPad

■ Configuration

Mobile devices require some setup and configuration to function seamlessly in your online life. That means you need to set up network connectivity, add Bluetooth devices, configure e-mail account(s), and enable the devices to synchronize with a PC. Let's look at all four options.

Network Connectivity

Mobile devices connect to the outside world through the cellular networks or through various 802.11 Wi-Fi standards. This section looks at standard configuration issues from the perspective of a mobile device.

When you want to connect to a Wi-Fi network, you need to turn Wi-Fi on and then actively connect to a network. If the network is properly configured with WPA or WPA2 encryption, then you also need to have the logon information to access the network. The most common way to connect is through the Settings app (see Figure 16.27). (This applies to all iOS and Android devices.)

Settings enables you to do the vast majority of configuration necessary to a mobile device. To join a network, for example, tap the Wi-Fi (or Networks) option to see available networks (see Figure 16.28). Simply select the one you want to join and type in the passphrase or passcode. Give the mobile device a moment to get IP and DNS information from the DHCP server, and you're on the network.

After you connect to a network successfully, all mobile devices store that network access information automatically, creating a *profile* of that network based on the SSID (the name of the network). This works just like with any other device that connects to a Wi-Fi network. If the SSID of a network

• **Figure 16.27** Selecting the Settings icon

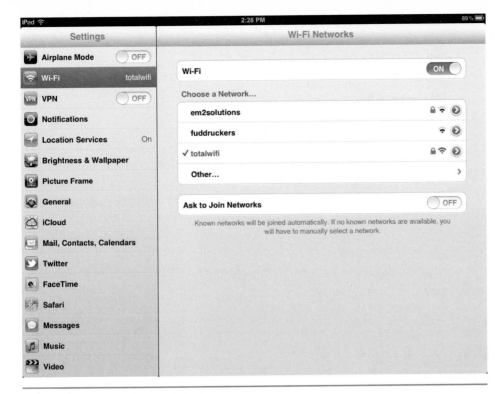

• **Figure 16.28** Browsing available networks

changes after you've connected to that network, your mobile device will fail to connect to the rechristened network. You need to delete the profile and reconnect. You do this through the Settings app by selecting the Wi-Fi network and selecting *Forget this network*.

> You can use the Settings app to turn Wi-Fi off or to go into Airplane Mode to stop the device from sending any signals out.

Data

Many mobile devices can use cellular data services to access the Internet. This way you can use your smartphone or tablet to get e-mail or browse the Web pretty much anywhere, even without a Wi-Fi hotspot.

By default, mobile devices that use cellular networks for Internet connectivity use **data roaming**, meaning they'll jump from cell tower to cell tower and from your provider to another provider without obvious notice. This is no big deal when you travel within your own country where competing providers have inexpensive roaming agreements.

Watch out for data roaming outside your country! If you travel outside of your country, your mobile device will also happily and seamlessly connect via some other available cell provider. This can lead to some shockingly huge bills from your cell phone company when you get back from that cruise or out-of-country trip. If you're going outside your cell provider's coverage area, get a plan that specifies that you're traveling. It'll still be more expensive than your regular plan, but not nearly as crazy as an accidental roaming charge.

If you don't need to connect when out of the country, turn data roaming off. You'll find the feature in the Settings app, as you might expect. You can also turn off cellular data entirely or only turn off cellular services

selectively if your device can do more than one type. (You would want to turn off cellular data, for example, if you don't have an unlimited data plan and are getting near your limits.)

Bluetooth

Pairing a Bluetooth device with a mobile device follows a similar, simple pattern through the Settings icon. You turn on Bluetooth on the smartphone or tablet, then power on the Bluetooth device. Return to the mobile device and select to pair with the Bluetooth device, and then enter the appropriate personal identification number (PIN) code. For a keyboard, for example, the smartphone or tablet will display a set of characters for you to type on the keyboard (see Figure 16.29). Once you type in the PIN code, the devices connect.

Always test the connectivity between a mobile device and a newly added Bluetooth accessory. If you've added a keyboard, for example, open up a note-taking app and start typing to make sure it works.

Most mobile devices have Bluetooth discovery disabled by default to conserve battery life. Actively seeking pairing uses electricity, as does completed pairing, so use Bluetooth when you need to use it and be prepared for the battery hit.

• **Figure 16.29** Prompting for PIN

E-Mail

Setting up e-mail offers many levels of complexity with mobile devices, primarily because of the many different types of e-mail servers out there. The process is similar to that of setting up e-mail accounts. Apple devices go through the Settings app, then the Mail, Contacts, Calendars option (see Figure 16.30). Tap the Add Account option to bring up the default e-mail options (see Figure 16.31). If you want to connect to a Microsoft Exchange Server–based e-mail account, tap the appropriate option here and type in your e-mail address, domain, username, password, and description.

If you want a more common POP3 or IMAP account set up, that's not one of Apple's default options, so you'd have to go through the Other option on the initial Add Account screen. Eventually you'll get prompted

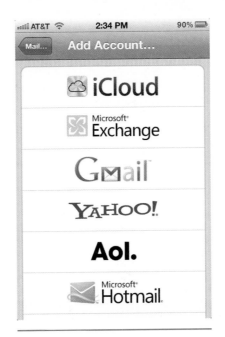

● Figure 16.30 Mail, Contacts, Calendars screen on iPhone

● Figure 16.31 Default e-mail types on iPhone

as you would expect to choose POP3 or IMAP and type in addresses for the sending and receiving servers.

Android-based tablets assume you'll have a Gmail account as your primary account, so that option is offered as a distinctive icon on the home screen (see Figure 16.32). You'll also have an Email icon for setting up Exchange, POP3, or IMAP accounts. You configure them the same way as you would a desktop e-mail application, including putting in the port setting and security type, such as SSL or TLS (see Figure 16.33).

● Figure 16.32 Gmail account option

• Figure 16.33 Setting up a secure IMAP account

Synchronization

Smartphones and tablets can **synchronize**, or **sync**, with local machines or over the Internet with cloud-based servers to keep files and data up-to-date. Older devices, such as BlackBerrys and Palm Pilots, had a specialized sync program that installed onto your PC that you could use to sync contacts, calendars, and so on. Today's devices either use a dedicated program or sync through the cloud.

Most tablets and many smartphones use a proprietary dongle for syncing through a USB port on the computer. This is the same dongle used to recharge the battery. Some devices can sync through Wi-Fi connections. Many smartphones use a micro USB to regular USB cable to connect to the PC.

iTunes and iCloud

Apple iPhones and iPads sync through Apple iTunes installed on a Mac or PC, a free program that you download from Apple. Everything, such as music, videos, contacts, pictures, and so on, can be stored locally. You can choose to back up all the apps on your iPhone or iPad to iTunes as well. This single source for backup makes it easy to recover from something catastrophic happening to your Apple device. If you replace an Apple device, for example, you can simply sync that new device and all your files, contact information, and apps copy to the new device.

In late 2011, Apple introduced a cloud-based storage solution called iCloud. With iCloud, you can have all your iPhone or iPad data backed up and thus accessible from anywhere. This includes any media purchased through iTunes and calendars, contacts, reminders, and so forth.

Apple iTunes will run on just about any Mac OS X machine. On Windows at the time of this writing, you need to be running Windows XP with Service Pack 2 or better or any later Windows OS.

The CompTIA A+ 802 competencies don't discuss hardware requirements. The only thing that's relevant to a tech is that hardware needs to scale up to play more complex media. You can play music with a 1-GHz CPU, for example, but need a 2.4-GHz CPU with two or more cores to play an HD video.

Android and Gmail

Android-based mobile devices don't have a central desktop application like Apple devices. Rather, they sync over the Internet—but only some data. Contacts, calendars, and e-mail (through Gmail) are all that sync by default. For every other type of data or media, you treat the Android device like a fat thumb drive—you drag and drop files into the appropriate folder on the smartphone or tablet.

Sync In, Sync Out

One of the radical differences between an Apple device and an Android device is in the direction of syncing (or even copying, for that matter). With Apple, you can sync files—especially media files—to the iPhone or iPad. You cannot take that Apple device, connect it to another computer, and copy files *from* it to the PC. It's a one-way street.

Android devices, in contrast, happily share like a thumb drive. You can drag and drop from an Android smartphone or tablet to any PC.

■ Security

Mobile devices almost long to roam freely, so you need to take active steps to secure them against damage, loss, or theft. Let's look at all three issues.

Preventing Damage

Mobile devices cost a fair amount of money and thus aren't disposable media for most people. That means you need to take steps to prevent damage, both physical and software-based.

For physical damage, the first step you must take is to get a protective cover or sleeve for the mobile device. It doesn't help the HD camcorder in your new iPad if you get a scratch across the lens! You'll get a scratched, blurry movie even though the camcorder is capable of much, much more. Apple makes very nice covers for iPhones and iPads, plus you can get many third-party covers and sleeves (see Figure 16.34).

Depending on the amount of money you're willing to spend, you can get covers that help protect your screen from scratches, impacts, and small amounts of water. Like to scuba with your Android device? There are waterproof cases (as opposed to a cover) that enable you to check your Facebook account from 40 feet underwater. (These are specialty devices and not very typical.)

Do the obvious to protect your devices. Don't get them anywhere near liquids. Don't run your smartphone through the wash in your trousers.

• **Figure 16.34** Putting an Apple Smart cover on an iPad

General **Passcode Lock**

Turn Passcode Off

Change Passcode

Require Passcode Immediately >

Simple Passcode ON

A simple passcode is a 4 digit number.

Siri ON

Allow access to Siri when locked with a passcode.

Erase Data OFF

• **Figure 16.35** Screen lock option in Settings

Don't even think about placing heavy objects on that ~$600 tablet! Use common sense.

Your options for software-based issues depend on your mobile platform. Android devices support a large number of antivirus applications, while iOS devices have no antivirus software. (Apple contends that such software is unnecessary on iOS.) You can also protect your mobile device with periodic *patching*, automatic updates and operating system patches from the device manufacturers.

Dealing with Loss

Losing a mobile device creates a series of issues that you need to address. First, protect your data from access by putting a good **passcode lock** on the device, which requires you to type in a series of letters, numbers, or motion patterns to unlock the mobile device each time you press the power button. Don't assume that you'll never set the phone down in the lavatory at an airport and forget about it or lose it to a thief. Most mobile devices enable you to set a passcode lock or screen lock from the Settings icon (see Figure 16.35). Do it right now! Some devices enable you to encrypt the contents of the SSD, so even if a "finder" dismantles the device to access the drive, he or she will not get your documents.

Mobile devices also have a preset number of failed login attempt restrictions that, when exceeded, lock up the mobile device. This slows down someone trying to hack into a found mobile device while you use locator services or applications to try to recover it.

• **Figure 16.36** Locating a device in iCloud

Both Apple and Google offer locator services for discovering the whereabouts of a misplaced mobile device. Google's service is okay, while Apple does a much better job with iCloud. Log in to your iCloud account and click the Find My iPhone button. (This works for both iPhones and iPads.) As soon as the device in question accesses the Internet (and thus receives an IP address and posts its MAC address), iCloud will pinpoint the location within a few yards (see Figure 16.36). Very slick!

Recovering from Theft

If your mobile device gets stolen and contains sensitive information, then you have a couple of options for dealing with it. Certainly the locator services help, but if you have credit card information or other very damaging information on your mobile device, you need to act quickly.

First, make sure you have your data backed up. You should have everything synced to a local machine and, if possible, backed up to one of the remote backup applications—like iCloud—to put your data beyond the reach of even a disaster that takes out your house. With iCloud, go into Settings and select iCloud. Tap the Storage & Backup option and turn iCloud Backup from OFF (the default) to ON (see Figure 16.37). Note that this will stop automatic backups to your local machine when you sync with iTunes.

Second, you can remotely wipe your mobile device. Apple makes it supremely easy through iCloud. Log in, locate, and nuke your device (see Figure 16.38). You may never get the device back, but at least the bad guys won't have your data.

• **Figure 16.37** Turning on remote backup

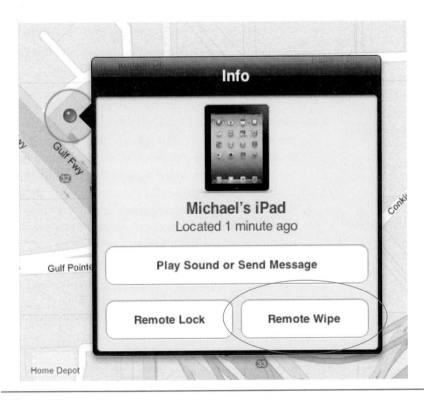

• **Figure 16.38** Remote wipe

Chapter 16 Review

■ Chapter Summary

After reading this chapter and completing the exercises, you should understand the following about mobile devices.

Explain the features and capabilities of smartphones and tablets

- The primary distinction between the two mobile device types is that a smartphone is a cell phone enhanced to do things formerly reserved for fully grown PCs, whereas a tablet embodies those enhanced computing features and capabilities on an expanded format and screen.

- Mobile devices have a default home screen and have icons for apps for accomplishing specific tasks, just like portable computers, but they use a touch interface for interaction rather than a mouse and keyboard. You interact with mobile devices by using your fingers to tap, swipe, and pinch the LCD or OLED screen. The screens reorient automatically when rotated by using their accelerometer.

- Adding an app to increase the functionality of a mobile device differs somewhat between Apple and non-Apple devices. Apple uses a closed source or single source system, meaning that if you want to get an app for your iPhone or iPad, you can only get it from the Apple App Store. With Android devices, you get apps from vendor-specific stores or an open source market for apps developed "for Android" that probably will work with your device.

- Upgrading mobile devices means only adding a few external devices rather than updating internal components. You can attach a Bluetooth keyboard, for example, but not swap out the internal memory or SSD. Mobile devices offer no field-serviceable parts.

Explain how to configure mobile devices

- Mobile devices connect to the outside world through the cellular networks or through various 802.11 Wi-Fi standards. When you want to connect to a Wi-Fi network, you need to turn Wi-Fi on and then actively connect to a network using proper authentication.

- To pair a Bluetooth device with a mobile device, turn on Bluetooth on the smartphone or tablet, then power on the Bluetooth device. Return to the mobile device to select to pair with the Bluetooth device, and then enter the appropriate PIN code.

- The Settings icon enables you to set up all sorts of types of e-mail on both iOS and Android devices. You set up an Exchange, POP3, IMAP, Gmail, or other type of e-mail account the same way you would on a desktop, with addresses for sending and receiving servers, login information, port settings, and security type, such as SSL or TLS.

- You can sync smartphones and tablets with local machines or over the Internet with cloud-based servers to keep files and data up-to-date. Apple devices use iTunes or iCloud. Android devices sync primarily with Gmail for mail and contacts.

Describe how to secure mobile devices

- Start with securing hardware and software. For preventing physical damage, the first step you must take is to get a protective cover or sleeve for the mobile device. At the time of this writing, there is no antivirus software for smartphones or tablets. About the only software protection you get is periodic, automatic updates and operating system patches from the device manufacturers.

- Use passcode locks and device finding services to protect and recover from losing your mobile device. Make sure you back up the device regularly. If the device is stolen and doesn't appear recoverable, you can wipe it from afar.

■ Key Terms

accelerometer *(588)*

Android *(588)*

app *(589)*

capacitive *(587)*

closed source *(591)*

data roaming *(597)*

geotracking *(590)*
Global Positioning System (GPS) *(591)*
gyroscope *(588)*
home screen *(585)*
iOS *(588)*
multitouch *(586)*
open source *(593)*
organic light-emitting diode (OLED) *(587)*
passcode lock *(602)*
pinch *(587)*

resistive *(587)*
single source *(591)*
smartphone *(585)*
swipe *(586)*
sync *(600)*
synchronize *(600)*
tablet *(585)*
tap *(586)*
touch interface *(586)*
vendor-specific *(593)*

■ Key Term Quiz

Use the Key Terms list to complete the sentences that follow. Not all terms will be used.

1. The default "desktop" of a mobile device is called the _____.

2. The feature that most differentiates smartphones and tablets from portable PCs is the _____.

3. The feature that enables a user to rotate a tablet and have the screen rotate with the device is called a(n) _____.

4. A program that enables you to accomplish a specific task, like play *Angry Birds*, on a tablet is called a(n) _____.

5. The _____ enables a mobile device to determine where you are on a map.

6. When you want to buy software for an Android device, you buy from the vendor or from the _____ market for Android devices.

7. Tablets respond differently when you use one or multiple fingers on the screen, a feature called _____.

8. Protect your data from access by putting a good _____ on the device, which requires you to type in a series of letters, numbers, or motion patterns to unlock the mobile device each time you press the power button.

9. A(n) _____ screen responds to pressure applied to the screen and needs to be calibrated periodically.

10. Moving your finger across the screen on a mobile device to switch the screen to the next item, such as the next page in an eBook, is called a(n) _____.

■ Multiple-Choice Quiz

1. Which operating system powers an Apple mobile device?
 A. Android
 B. iOS
 C. OS X
 D. Windows Mobile

2. Which type of display responds to the difference in electrical potential between you and the screen?
 A. Capacitive
 B. LCD
 C. IPS
 D. Resistive

3. John has a high-resolution image on his iPad of his 2-year-old son and the family dog. The image initially displays smaller than the screen, so he wants to zoom in to get the details of his son's expression. How can he accomplish this task? (Select two.)

 A. Click the mouse in the middle of the picture to select it, then use the scroll wheel on the mouse to zoom in.

 B. Tap the picture with his index finger on his son's face.

 C. Right-click the picture with his index finger on his son's face.

 D. Touch his son's face on the screen with his thumb and finger, then pinch outward to scroll in.

4. Which mobile device screen technology uses no backlight?

 A. CCFL

 B. LCD

 C. LED

 D. OLED

5. What can a government use to determine your location at a specific time as long as you're using your mobile device?

 A. *Angry Birds*

 B. Geotracking

 C. Google Earth

 D. Gyroscope

6. What are the steps involved in pairing a Bluetooth keyboard with a tablet?

 A. Enable Bluetooth on the tablet; turn on the Bluetooth device; find the device with the tablet; enter a PIN code or other pairing sequence.

 B. Turn on the Bluetooth device; find the device with the tablet; enter a PIN code or other pairing sequence.

 C. Search for a Bluetooth device from the tablet; select **pair** from the options to enable the device.

 D. Enable Bluetooth on the tablet; turn on the Bluetooth device; find the device with the tablet; select **pair** from the options to enable the device.

7. A client calls, wanting to copy his music from his iPhone to his new PC. How can he accomplish this task?

 A. Connect the iPhone to the new PC. When it shows up as a new device, right-click it and select Properties. In the Properties dialog box, select Export media files.

 B. Connect the iPhone to the new PC. Double-click it and go to the Media folder. Drag and drop the desired music to the Music library on his new PC.

 C. Access the iPhone wirelessly from the PC. Drag and drop the desired music to the Music library on his new PC.

 D. He can't.

8. A client calls and is upset that he's misplaced his iPad. The mobile device has literally thousands of client records, including business addresses, e-mail addresses, phone numbers, and, in some cases, credit card information. What is the first thing he should do?

 A. There's nothing he can do.

 B. He should call his ISP and have them track his iPad.

 C. He should access his iCloud account and wipe his iPad to erase all personal data.

 D. He should purchase another iPad and sync with his iTunes account. This automatically erases the information on the old tablet.

9. Name the primary feature that separates a smartphone from a tablet.

 A. iTunes

 B. OLED screen

 C. Capacitive touchscreen

 D. Capability to make telephone calls

10. What information do you need to connect an Android-based tablet to an IMAP account?

 A. POP3 server DNS name

 B. Username and password

 C. Username, password, sending and receiving server addresses

 D. Exchange server name, username, and password

11. Tim wants to listen to music on his iPad. Which of the following are connectivity options for his headset? (Select two.)

 A. Infrared

 B. 802.11

 C. Bluetooth

 D. 3.5-mm audio jack

12. John returned from a cruise to the Bahamas and got a bill from his cell phone company (Sprint) that was over $1000. What could have happened?

 A. John connected to the Internet with his smartphone using the cruise ship company's Wi-Fi.

 B. John's smartphone connected to the Internet in the Bahamas via a cell provider that wasn't Sprint.

 C. John used his smartphone to do Internet gambling and Sprint frowns on that activity.

 D. Bills after international trips are always reported in the currency of the country visited. When translated from Bahamian dollars to U.S. dollars, the amount is the same he normally pays.

13. Galina has an application that tracks her location for people she invites via the application to know her whereabouts. She's in another town and wants to prevent temporarily one user from knowing her location. Which of the following is the best answer?

 A. Turn off the GPS.

 B. Uninstall the application.

 C. Uninvite the person using the application.

 D. Leave her phone at home.

14. Placing your phone in a typical protective cover will *not* protect the phone from:

 A. Scratches

 B. Impact

 C. Small amounts of water

 D. Immersion in water

15. Benjamin is using his iPhone to access a Web page. When the page opens he notices that it says he needs to install Flash. Which of the following should he do?

 A. Install Flash.

 B. There's nothing he can do to access this site.

 C. Use a Flash converter.

 D. Install MacFlash.

■ Essay Quiz

1. The boss has decided that all employees should get a new tablet to increase company satisfaction. Write a short essay on why every employee should get an Apple iPad.

2. The boss has decided that all employees should get a new tablet to increase company satisfaction. Write a short essay on why every employee should get a Google Android-based tablet.

Lab Project

• Lab Project 16.1

Explore the Apple or Android apps available (seeking reviews and such on the Internet) and come up with a list of ten apps that would enable you to turn a tablet into a work device. That work can be whatever you or your instructor defines it as, such as something that enables you to create content (text, images, and so on). How much would such apps cost? Would they make you more likely to benefit from a tablet?

Troubleshooting Printers

17

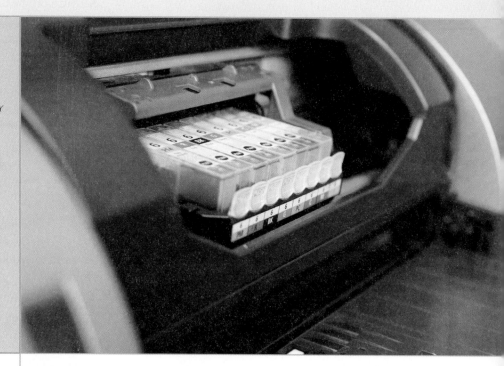

"Faster! Faster! Faster would be better!"

—Capt. Malcolm Reynolds, *Serenity*

In this chapter, you will learn how to

■ **Recognize and fix basic printer problems**

Despite all of the talk about the "paperless office," printers continue to be a vital part of the typical office. In many cases, PCs are used exclusively for the purpose of producing paper documents. Many people simply prefer dealing with a hard copy. Programmers cater to this preference by using metaphors such as *page*, *workbook*, and *binder* in their applications. The CompTIA A+ 220-802 exam strongly stresses the area of printing and expects a high degree of technical knowledge of troubleshooting all types of printers.

■ Troubleshooting Printers

As easy as printers are to set up, they are equally robust at running, assuming that you install the proper drivers and keep the printer well maintained. But printer errors do occasionally develop. Take a look at the most common print problems with Windows, as well as problems that crop up with specific printer types.

Every printer is different. Read the documentation included with your printer to learn how you can perform the tasks listed in this section.

General Troubleshooting Issues

Printers of all stripes share some common problems, such as print jobs that don't go, strangely sized prints, and misalignment. Other issues include disposing of consumables, sharing multiple printers, and crashing on power-up. Let's take a look at these general troubleshooting issues, but start with a recap of the tools of the trade.

Don't forget to check the obvious. Many printers include tiny displays that can clue you in to what's wrong. Most brands use a series of error codes that indicate the problem. Use the manual or the manufacturer's Web site to translate the error code into meaningful information.

Tools of the Trade

Before you jump in and start to work on a printer that's giving you fits, you'll need some tools. You can use the standard computer tech tools in your toolkit, plus a couple of printer-specific devices. Here are some that will come in handy:

- A **multimeter** for troubleshooting electrical problems such as faulty wall outlets

- Various cleaning solutions, such as **denatured alcohol**

- An extension magnet for grabbing loose screws in tight spaces and cleaning up iron-based toner

- An optical disc or USB thumb drive with test patterns for checking print quality

- Your trusty screwdriver—both a Phillips-head and flat-head, because if you bring just one kind, it's a sure bet that you'll need the other

If you're printing an especially complicated print job, you might get an error reading "MEM OVERFLOW" or similiar. This means that your printer needs more memory! On many printers, you can upgrade the RAM in the printer, so check your printer's documentation.

Print Job Never Prints

If you click Print but nothing comes out of the printer, first check all the obvious things. Is the printer on? Is it connected? Is it online? Does it have paper?

If you can't connect to the printer, check all cables, ports, and power involved. If everything is plugged in and ready to go, check the appropriate printer applet for your version of Windows. If you don't see the printer you are looking for, you'll need to reinstall it using the Add Printer Wizard.

If you attempt to use a printer shared by another PC, but Windows pops up with an "Access Denied" error, you might not have permission to use the printer. Go to the host PC and check the Security tab of the Printer Properties dialog box. Make sure your user account is allowed to use the printer.

Assuming the printer is in good order, it's time to look at the spooler. You can see the spooler status either by double-clicking the printer's icon in the appropriate printer Control Panel applet or by double-clicking the

Document Name	Status	Owner	Pages	Size	Submitted	Port
F28-10.tif		michaels	1	2.73 MB	2:23:06 PM 4/20/2012	
Microsoft Word - 591_28w	Printing	michaels	1/67	88.2 KB/3.45 MB	2:22:20 PM 4/20/2012	laserjet4.totalhome

2 document(s) in queue

• **Figure 17.1** Print spooler

Windows 7 includes the Print Management console, which enables you to view and modify all the printers and drivers on your PC or network. Many of Print Management's features go beyond the scope of the A+ exam, but know that it centralizes the standard printer controls in Windows 7.

tiny printer icon in the notification area if it's present. If you're having a problem, the printer icon will almost always be there. Figure 17.1 shows the print spooler open.

Print spoolers can easily overflow or become corrupt due to a lack of disk space, too many print jobs, or one of a thousand other factors. The status window shows all of the pending print jobs and enables you to delete, start, or pause jobs. I usually just delete the affected print job(s) and try again.

Print spoolers are handy. If the printer goes down, you can just leave the print jobs in the spooler until the printer comes back online. Some versions of Windows require you to select Resume Printing manually, but others automatically continue the print job(s). If you have a printer that isn't coming on anytime soon, you can simply delete the print job in the spooler window and try another printer.

If you have problems with the print spooler, you can get around them by changing your print spool settings. Go into the Printers and Faxes/Printers/Devices and Printers applet, right-click the icon of the printer in question, and choose Properties. In the resulting Properties dialog box (see Figure 17.2), choose the *Print directly to the printer* radio button and click OK; then try sending your print job again. Note that this window also offers you the choice of printing immediately—that is, starting to print pages as soon as the spooler has enough information to feed to the printer—or holding off on printing until the entire job is spooled.

If that isn't enough, try restarting the print spooler service. Open the Start menu and right-click on My Computer/Computer. Select Manage—you'll need administrator privileges to continue. In the column on the left, double-click on Services and Applications, and then click on Services. The Services console should appear in the center of the Computer Management window. Scroll down and find the service named Print Spooler. Right-click on the service and select Stop. After it has stopped, right-click on the service again and select Start. You should be able to print using the print spooler again.

Another possible cause for a stalled print job is that the printer is simply waiting for the correct paper! Laser printers in particular have settings that tell them what size paper is in their standard paper tray or trays. If the application sending a print job specifies a different paper size—for example,

• **Figure 17.2** Print spool settings

it wants to print a standard No. 10 envelope, or perhaps a legal sheet, but the standard paper tray holds only 8.5 × 11 letter paper—the printer usually pauses and holds up the queue until someone switches out the tray or manually feeds the type of paper that this print job requires. You can usually override this pause, even without having the specified paper, by pressing the OK or GO button on the printer.

The printer's default paper tray and paper size options will differ greatly depending on the printer type and model. To find these settings, go into the printer's Properties dialog box from the Printers and Faxes/Printers/Devices and Printers applet, and then select the Device Settings tab. This list of settings includes Form To Tray Assignment, where you can specify which tray (in the case of a printer with multiple paper trays) holds which size paper.

Strange Sizes

A print job that comes out a strange size usually points to a user mistake in setting up the print job. All applications have a Print command and a Page Setup interface. The Page Setup interface enables you to define a number of print options, which vary from application to application. Figure 17.3 shows the Page Setup options for Microsoft Word. Make sure the page is set up properly before you blame the printer for a problem.

If you know the page is set up correctly, recheck the printer drivers. If necessary, uninstall and reinstall the printer drivers. If the problem persists, you may have a serious problem with the printer's print engine, but that comes up as a likely answer only when you continually get the same strangely sized printouts using a variety of applications.

• **Figure 17.3** Page Setup options for Microsoft Word

MSDSs contain important information regarding hazardous materials such as safe use procedures and emergency response instructions. An MSDS is typically posted anywhere a hazardous chemical is used.

Misaligned, Garbled, or Garbage Printouts

Misaligned or garbage printouts invariably point to a corrupted or incorrect driver. Make sure you're using the right driver (it's hard to mess this up, but not impossible) and then uninstall and reinstall the printer driver. If the problem persists, you may be asking the printer to do something it cannot do. For example, you may be printing to a PostScript printer with a PCL driver. Check the printer type to verify that you haven't installed the wrong type of driver for that printer!

Dealing with Consumables

All printers tend to generate a lot of trash in the form of **consumables**. Impact printers use paper and ribbons, inkjet printers use paper and ink cartridges, and laser printers use paper and toner cartridges. In today's environmentally sensitive world, many laws regulate the proper disposal of most printer components. Be sure to check with the local sanitation department or disposal services company before throwing away any component. Of course, you should never throw away toner cartridges—certain companies will *pay* for used cartridges!

Problems Sharing Multiple Printers

If you want to use multiple printers attached to the same parallel port, you have to use a switch box. Laser printers should never be used with mechanical switch boxes. Mechanical switch boxes create power surges that can damage your printer. If you must use a switch box, use a box that switches between printers electronically and has built-in surge protection.

Crashes on Power-up

Both laser printers and PCs require more power during their initial power-up (the POST on a PC and the warm-up on a laser printer) than once they are running. Hewlett-Packard recommends a *reverse power-up*. Turn on the laser printer first and allow it to finish its warm-up before turning on the PC. This avoids having two devices drawing their peak loads simultaneously.

Troubleshooting Impact Printers

Impact printers require regular maintenance but will run forever as long as you're diligent. Keep the platen (the roller or plate on which the pins impact) clean and the printhead clean with denatured alcohol. Be sure to lubricate gears and pulleys according to the manufacturer's specifications. Never lubricate the printhead, however, because the lubricant will smear and stain the paper. Don't forget to replace the ink ribbon every so often.

Bad-looking Text

White bars going through the text point to a dirty or damaged printhead. Try cleaning the printhead with a little denatured alcohol. If the problem persists, replace the printhead. Printheads for most printers are readily available from the manufacturer or from companies that rebuild them. If the characters look chopped off at the top or bottom, the printhead probably

needs to be adjusted. Refer to the manufacturer's instructions for proper adjustment.

Bad-looking Page

If the page is covered with dots and small smudges—the "pepper look"—the platen is dirty. Clean the platen with denatured alcohol. If the image is faded, and you know the ribbon is good, try adjusting the printhead closer to the platen. If the image is okay on one side of the paper but fades as you move to the other, the platen is out of adjustment. Platens are generally difficult to adjust, so your best plan is to take it to the manufacturer's local warranty/repair center.

Troubleshooting Thermal Printers

Compared to other printer styles, thermal printers are simple to trouble-shoot and maintain. With direct thermal printers, you only need to worry about three things: the heating element, the rollers, and the paper. With thermal wax printers, you also need to care for the wax ribbon.

To clean the heating element, turn off the thermal printer and open it according to the manufacturer's instructions. Use denatured alcohol and a lint-free cloth to wipe off the heating element. You might need to use a little pressure to get it completely clean. Clean the rollers with a cloth or compressed air. You want to keep them free of debris so they can properly grip the paper. Replacing the paper is as easy as sliding off the old roll and replacing it with a new one. Remember to feed the paper through the heating element, because otherwise you won't print anything. Replacing the ribbon is similar to replacing the roll of paper; make sure to feed it past the heating element, or the printer won't work properly. Your printer's manufacturer should include any special instructions for installing a new ribbon.

Troubleshooting Inkjet Printers

Inkjet printers are reliable devices that require little maintenance as long as they are used within their design parameters (high-use machines will require more intensive maintenance). Because of the low price of these printers, manufacturers know that people don't want to spend a lot of money keeping them running. If you perform even the most basic maintenance tasks, they will soldier on for years without a whimper. Inkjets generally have built-in maintenance programs that you should run from time to time to keep your inkjet in good operating order.

Inkjet Printer Maintenance

Inkjet printers don't get nearly as dirty as laser printers, and most manufacturers do not recommend periodic cleaning. Unless your manufacturer explicitly tells you to do so, don't vacuum an inkjet. Inkjets generally do not have maintenance kits, but most inkjet printers come with extensive maintenance software (see Figure 17.4). Usually, the hardest

• **Figure 17.4** Inkjet printer maintenance screen

part of using this software is finding it in the first place. Look for an option in Printing Preferences, a selection on the Start menu, or an icon on your desktop. Don't worry—it's there!

When you first set up an inkjet printer, it normally instructs you to perform a routine (sometimes confusingly referred to as **calibration**) to align the printheads properly, wherein you print out a page and select from sets of numbered lines. If this isn't done, the print quality will show it, but the good news is that you can perform this procedure at any time. If a printer is moved or dropped or it's just been working away untended for a while, it's often worth running the alignment routine.

Inkjet Problems

Did I say that you never should clean an inkjet? Well, that may be true for the printer itself, but there is one part of your printer that will benefit from an occasional cleaning: the inkjet's printer head nozzles. The nozzles are the tiny pipes that squirt the ink onto the paper. A common problem with inkjet printers is the tendency for the ink inside the nozzles to dry out when not used even for a relatively short time, blocking any ink from exiting. If your printer is telling Windows that it's printing and feeding paper through, but either nothing is coming out (usually the case if you're just printing black text) or only certain colors are printing, the culprit is almost certainly dried ink clogging the nozzles.

Every inkjet printer has a different procedure for cleaning the printhead nozzles. On older inkjets, you usually have to press buttons on the printer to start a maintenance program. On more modern inkjets, you can access the head-cleaning maintenance program from Windows.

Another problem that sometimes arises is the dreaded multi-sheet paper grab. This is often not actually your printer's fault—humidity can cause sheets of paper to cling to each other—but sometimes the culprit is an overheated printer, so if you've been cranking out a lot of documents without stopping, try giving the printer a bit of a coffee break. Also, fan the sheets of the paper stack before inserting it into the paper tray.

Finally, check to see if excess ink overflow is a problem. In the area where the printheads park, look for a small tank or tray that catches excess ink from the cleaning process. If the printer has one, check to see how full it is. If this tray overflows onto the main board or even the power supply, it will kill your printer. If you discover that the tray is about to overflow, you can remove excess ink by inserting a twisted paper towel into the tank to soak up some of the ink. It is advisable to wear latex or vinyl gloves while doing this. Clean up any spilled ink with a paper towel dampened with distilled water.

Troubleshooting Laser Printers

Quite a few problems can arise with laser printers, but before getting into those details, you need to review some recommended procedures for *avoiding* those problems.

All inkjet inks are water-based, and water works better than alcohol to clean them up.

Cleaning the heads on an inkjet printer is sometimes necessary, but I don't recommend that you do it on a regular basis as preventive maintenance. The head-cleaning process uses up a lot of that very expensive inkjet ink—so do this only when a printing problem seems to indicate clogged or dirty printheads!

Before you service a laser printer, always, *always* turn it off and unplug it! Don't expose yourself to the very dangerous high voltages found inside these machines.

Laser Printer Maintenance

Unlike PC maintenance, laser printer maintenance follows a fairly well established procedure. Of course, you'll need to replace the toner cartridge every so often, but keeping your laser printer healthy requires following these maintenance steps.

Keep It Clean Laser printers are quite robust as a rule. A good cleaning every time you replace the toner cartridge will help that printer last for many years. I know of many examples of original HP LaserJet I printers continuing to run perfectly after a dozen or more years of operation. The secret is that they were kept immaculately clean.

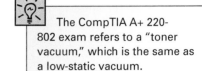

The CompTIA A+ 220-802 exam refers to a "toner vacuum," which is the same as a low-static vacuum.

Your laser printer gets dirty in two ways: Excess toner, over time, will slowly coat the entire printer. Paper dust, sometimes called **paper dander**, tends to build up where the paper is bent around rollers or where pickup rollers grab paper. Unlike (black) toner, paper dust is easy to see and is usually a good indicator that a printer needs to be cleaned. Usually, a thorough cleaning using a can of compressed air to blow out the printer is the best cleaning you can do. It's best to do this outdoors, or you may end up looking like one of those chimney sweeps from *Mary Poppins*! If you must clean a printer indoors, use a special low-static vacuum designed especially for electronic components (see Figure 17.5).

• **Figure 17.5** Low-static vacuum

Every laser printer has its own unique cleaning method, but the cleaning instructions tend to skip one little area. Every laser printer has a number of rubber guide rollers through which the paper is run during the print process. These little rollers tend to pick up dirt and paper dust over time, making them slip and jam paper. They are easily cleaned with a small amount of 90 percent or better alcohol on a fibrous cleaning towel. The alcohol will remove the debris and any dead rubber. If the paper won't feed, you can give the rollers and separator pads a textured surface that will restore their feeding properties by rubbing them with a little alcohol on a nonmetallic scouring pad.

The photosensitive drum, usually contained in the toner cartridge, can be wiped clean if it becomes dirty, but be very careful if you do so! If the drum becomes scratched, the scratch will appear on every page printed from that point on. The only repair in the event of a scratch is to replace the toner cartridge.

If you're ready to get specific, get the printer's service manual. They are a key source for information on how to keep a printer clean and running. Sadly, not all printer manufacturers provide these, but most do. While you're at it, see if the manufacturer has a Quick Reference Guide; these can be very handy for most printer problems!

Periodic Maintenance Although keeping the printer clean is critical to its health and well being, every laser printer has certain components that you need to replace periodically. Your ultimate source for determining the parts that need to be replaced (and when to replace them) is the printer manufacturer. Following the manufacturer's maintenance guidelines will help to ensure years of trouble-free, dependable printing from your laser printer.

Many manufacturers provide kits that contain components that you should replace on a regular schedule. These **maintenance kits** include sets of replacement parts, such as a fuser, as well as one or more rollers or pads.

Failure of the thermal fuse (used to keep the fuser from overheating) can necessitate replacing the fuser assembly. Some machines contain more than one thermal fuse. As always, follow the manufacturer's recommendations. Many manufacturers have kits that alert you with an alarm code to replace the fuser unit and key rollers and guides at predetermined page counts.

The fuser assembly operates at 200 to 300 degrees Fahrenheit, so always allow time for this component to cool down before you attempt to clean it.

Typically, you need to reset the page counter after installing a maintenance kit so the printer can remind you to perform maintenance again after a certain number of pages have been printed.

Some ozone filters can be cleaned with a vacuum and some can only be replaced—follow the manufacturer's recommendation. You can clean the fuser assembly with 90 percent or better denatured alcohol. Check the heat roller (the Teflon-coated one with the light bulb inside) for pits and scratches. If you see surface damage on the rollers, replace the fuser unit.

Most printers will give you an error code when the fuser is damaged or overheating and needs to be replaced; others will produce the error code at a preset copy count as a preventive maintenance measure. Again, follow the manufacturer's recommendations.

The transfer corona can be cleaned with a 90 percent denatured alcohol solution on a cotton swab. If the wire is broken, you can replace it; many just snap in or are held in by a couple of screws. Paper guides can also be cleaned with alcohol on a fibrous towel.

Laser Printer Problems

Laser printers usually manifest problems by creating poor output. One of the most important tests you can do on any printer, not just a laser printer, is called a *diagnostic print page* or an *engine test page*. You do this by either holding down the On Line button as the printer is started or using the printer's maintenance software.

Blank Paper Blank sheets of paper usually mean the printer is out of toner. If the printer does have toner and nothing prints, print a diagnostic print page. If that is also blank, remove the toner cartridge and look at the imaging drum inside. If the image is still there, you know the transfer corona or the high-voltage power supply has failed. Check the printer's maintenance guide to see how to focus on the bad part and replace it.

Dirty or Smudged Printouts If the fusing mechanism in a laser printer gets dirty, it will leave a light dusting of toner all over the paper, particularly on the back of the page. When you see toner speckles on your printouts, you should get the printer cleaned.

If the printout looks smudged, the fuser isn't properly fusing the toner to the paper. Depending on the paper used, the fuser needs to reach a certain temperature to fuse the toner. If the toner won't fuse to the paper, try using a lighter-weight paper. You might also need to replace the fuser.

Ghosting Ghost images sometimes appear at regular intervals on the printed page. This happens when the imaging drum has not fully discharged and is picking up toner from a previous image or when a previous image has used up so much toner that either the supply of charged toner is insufficient or the toner has not been adequately charged. Sometimes it can also be caused by a worn-out cleaning blade that isn't removing the toner from the drum.

Light Ghosting versus Dark Ghosting A variety of problems can cause both light and dark ghosting, but the most common source of light ghosting is "developer starvation." If you ask a laser printer to print an extremely

dark or complex image, it can use up so much toner that the toner cartridge will not be able to charge enough toner to print the next image. The proper solution is to use less toner. You can fix ghosting problems in the following ways:

- Lower the resolution of the page (print at 300 dpi instead of 600 dpi).
- Use a different pattern.
- Avoid 50 percent grayscale and "dot-on/dot-off patterns."
- Change the layout so that grayscale patterns do not follow black areas.
- Make dark patterns lighter and light patterns darker.
- Print in landscape orientation.
- Adjust print density and RET settings.
- Print a completely blank page immediately prior to the page with the ghosting image, as part of the same print job.

In addition to these possibilities, low temperature and low humidity can aggravate ghosting problems. Check your user's manual for environmental recommendations. Dark ghosting can sometimes be caused by a damaged drum. It may be fixed by replacing the toner cartridge. Light ghosting would *not* be solved in this way. Switching other components will not usually affect ghosting problems because they are a side effect of the entire printing process.

Vertical White Lines Vertical white lines usually happen when the toner is clogged, preventing the proper dispersion of toner on the drum. Try shaking the toner cartridge to dislodge the clog. If that doesn't work, replace the toner cartridge.

Blotchy Print Blotches are commonly a result of uneven dispersion of toner, especially if the toner is low. Shake the toner from side to side and then try to print. Also be sure that the printer is sitting level. Finally, make sure the paper is not wet in spots. If the blotches are in a regular order, check the fusing rollers and the photosensitive drum for any foreign objects.

Spotty Print If the spots appear at regular intervals, the drum may be damaged or some toner may be stuck to the fuser rollers. Try wiping off the fuser rollers. Check the drum for damage. If the drum is damaged, get a new toner cartridge.

Embossed Effect If your prints are getting an embossed effect (like putting a penny under a piece of paper and rubbing it with a lead pencil), there is almost certainly a foreign object on a roller. Use 90 percent denatured alcohol or regular water with a soft cloth to try to remove it. If the foreign object is on the photosensitive drum, you're going to have to use a new toner cartridge. An embossed effect can also be caused by the contrast control being set too high. The contrast control is actually a knob on the inside of the unit (sometimes accessible from the outside, on older models). Check your manual for the specific location.

Incomplete Characters You can sometimes correct incompletely printed characters on laser-printed transparencies by adjusting the print density. Be extremely careful to use only materials approved for use in laser printers.

Creased Pages Laser printers have up to four rollers. In addition to the heat and pressure rollers of the fuser assembly, other rollers move the paper from the source tray to the output tray. These rollers crease the paper to avoid curling that would cause paper jams in the printer. If the creases are noticeable, try using a different paper type. Cotton bond paper is usually more susceptible to noticeable creasing than other bonds. You might also try sending the output to the face-up tray, which avoids one roller. There is no hardware solution to this problem; it is simply a side effect of the process.

Paper Jams Every printer jams now and then. If you get a jam, always refer first to the manufacturer's jam removal procedure. It is simply too easy to damage a printer by pulling on the jammed paper! If the printer reports a jam but there's no paper inside, you've almost certainly got a problem with one of the many jam sensors or paper feed sensors inside the printer, and you'll need to take it to a repair center.

Pulling Multiple Sheets If the printer grabs multiple sheets at a time, first try opening a new ream of paper and loading that in the printer. If that works, you have a humidity problem. If the new paper angle doesn't work, check the separation pad on the printer. The separation pad is a small piece of cork or rubber that separates the sheets as they are pulled from the paper feed tray. A worn separation pad looks shiny and, well, *worn*! Most separation pads are easy to replace. Check out www.printerworks.com to see if you can replace yours.

Warped, Overprinted, or Poorly Formed Characters Poorly formed characters can indicate either a problem with the paper (or other media) or a problem with the hardware.

Incorrect media cause a number of these types of problems. Avoid paper that is too rough or too smooth. Paper that is too rough interferes with the fusing of characters and their initial definition. If the paper is too smooth (like some coated papers, for example), it may feed improperly, causing distorted or overwritten characters. Even though you can purchase laser printer–specific paper, all laser printers print acceptably on standard photocopy paper. Try to keep the paper from becoming too wet. Don't open a ream of paper until it is time to load it into the printer. Always fan the paper before loading it into the printer, especially if the paper has been left out of the package for more than just a few days.

The durability of a well-maintained laser printer makes hardware a much rarer source of character printing problems, but you should be aware of the possibility. Fortunately, it is fairly easy to check the hardware. Most laser printers have a self-test function—often combined with a diagnostic printout but sometimes as a separate process. This self-test shows whether the laser printer can properly develop an image without actually having to send print commands from the PC. The self-test is quite handy to verify the question "Is it the printer or is it the computer?" Run the self-test to check for connectivity and configuration problems.

Possible solutions include replacing the toner cartridge, especially if you hear popping noises; checking the cabling; and replacing the data cable, especially if it has bends or crimps or if objects are resting on the cable. If you have a front menu panel, turn off advanced functions and high-speed settings to determine whether the advanced functions are either not working properly or not supported by your current software configuration (check your manuals for configuration information). If these solutions do not work, the problem may not be user serviceable. Contact an authorized service center.

Beyond A+

Multifunction Peripherals

It's a common theme in computing: why have two devices that do one thing each when you can have one device that does two things? In that spirit, manufacturers started gluing various peripherals together to create *multifunction peripherals*, or *MFPs* (see Figure 17.6). These devices can include printers, scanners, fax machines, photocopiers, and more. All of your standard connection options are available, including USB, parallel, Ethernet, Wi-Fi, and more.

One of the best parts of a multifunction device is that all of these functions are available using a single connection. On the other hand, because a multifunction device is much more complicated than a single-function device, you'll probably need to follow very specific instructions and use the

• **Figure 17.6** All-in-one printer/scanner/fax machine/copier/coffee maker/iPod dock

manufacturer-supplied installation disc to get it all working. Many multifunction devices also include functions that don't require a PC at all, such as photocopying and faxing. You can even print files from a digital camera's memory card without plugging the MFP into a PC.

Chapter 17 Review

■ Chapter Summary

After reading this chapter and completing the exercises, you should understand the following aspects of printers.

Recognize and fix basic printer problems

■ When troubleshooting a printer, first check all the obvious things. Is the printer on? Is it connected? Is it online? Does it have paper? Does the printer display an error code on an LCD display? Then check the spooler status either by double-clicking the printer's icon in the Printers applet or by double-clicking the tiny printer icon in the notification area, if it's present. You may be able to bypass spooler problems by changing the printer's Properties dialog box setting to *Print directly to the printer*.

■ If you see an "Access Denied" error when trying to print using a shared printer, make sure you have permission to use that printer.

■ A print job that comes out a strange size usually points to a user mistake in setting up the print job. Use the program's Page Setup feature to fix these problems. If you know the page is set up correctly, recheck the printer drivers. Misaligned or garbage printouts invariably point to a corrupted or incorrect driver.

■ Printer manufacturers will supply an MSDS for each of their products; they provide detailed information about the potential environmental hazards associated with different components and proper disposal methods. This isn't just a printer issue—you can find an MSDS for most PC components.

■ Turn on the laser printer first and allow it to finish its warm-up before turning on the PC (a reverse power-up). This avoids having two devices drawing their peak loads simultaneously.

■ With regular maintenance, impact printers run forever. White bars going through the text point to a dirty or damaged printhead. Try cleaning the printhead with a little 90 percent or better denatured alcohol. If the characters look chopped off at the top or bottom, you probably need to adjust the printhead.

■ Thermal printers are easy to maintain. Keep the rollers and heating element clean and replace the ribbon and paper as needed.

■ Inkjet printers generally have built-in maintenance programs that you should run from time to time to keep your inkjet in good operating order. A common problem with inkjet printers is the tendency for the ink inside the nozzles to dry out when not used even for a relatively short time, blocking any ink from exiting. To clean the nozzles on older inkjets, you usually have to press buttons on the printer to start a maintenance program. On more modern inkjets, you can access the head-cleaning maintenance program from Windows.

■ Remember to clean your laser printer every time you replace the toner. Many manufacturers provide kits that contain components that you should replace on a regular schedule. These maintenance kits include sets of replacement parts, such as a fuser, as well as one or more rollers or pads.

■ One of the most important tests you can do on any printer, not just a laser printer, is called a diagnostic print page or an engine test page. There are two types of printer test: the Windows test in which you print a test page, and the printer self-test that runs from the printer itself.

■ Over time, excess toner will slowly coat a laser printer. Paper dander will build up where the paper is bent around rollers or where pickup rollers grab paper. Use a small amount of 90 percent or better alcohol on a fibrous cleaning towel to remove the debris and any dead rubber.

■ Blank sheets of paper usually mean a laser printer is out of toner. If the printer has toner and nothing prints, print a diagnostic print page. If that is also blank, remove the toner cartridge and look at the imaging drum inside. If the image is still there, you know the transfer corona or the high-voltage power supply has failed. Blotchy print is most commonly due to uneven dispersion of toner, especially if the toner is low; also check that the printer is level and the paper is completely dry.

■ Ghost images can be caused either because a laser printer's imaging drum has not fully discharged

(and is picking up toner from a previous image) or because a previous image has used up so much toner that either the supply of charged toner is insufficient or the toner has not been adequately charged. Dark ghosting can sometimes be caused by a damaged drum. It may be fixed by replacing the toner cartridge. Light ghosting would *not* be solved in this way.

- The rollers that move the paper from the source tray to the output tray crease the paper to avoid curling that would cause paper jams in the printer. If the creases are noticeable, try using a different paper type. If the printer reports a jam but there's no paper inside, you almost certainly have a problem with one of the many jam sensors or paper feed sensors. If the printer grabs multiple sheets at a time, it may be humidity, or a worn separation pad. Hardware problems are a much rarer source of character printing problems. Most laser printers have a self-test function that shows whether the laser printer can properly develop an image without having to send print commands from the PC. Run the self-test to check for connectivity and configuration problems.

Key Terms

calibration *(614)*
denatured alcohol *(609)*
error codes *(609)*
maintenance kits *(615)*

material safety data sheet (MSDS) *(612)*
multimeter *(609)*
paper dander *(615)*

Key Term Quiz

Use the Key Terms list to complete the sentences that follow. Not all terms will be used.

1. _____ is a useful cleaning solution for maintaining printers.

2. An easy-to-see sign that your printer needs to be cleaned is _____.

3. Many inkjet printers run a(n) _____ process to align their printheads.

4. Printers use various _____ to let you know what has gone wrong.

5. Many manufacturers provide _____ that contain components that you should replace on a regular schedule.

6. You can use a(n) _____ to test for electrical problems in a printer.

7. A(n) _____ tells you about potential environmental hazards and proper disposal techniques for various printer components.

Multiple-Choice Quiz

1. How can you possibly bypass printer spooler problems?

 A. Check the *Bypass print spooler* box in the printer's Properties dialog box.

 B. Disable the print spooler in the Devices and Printers applet.

 C. Change the printer's Properties dialog box setting to *Print directly to the printer*.

 D. Printer spooler problems cannot be bypassed.

2. David's impact printer is printing white bars through the text. What is most likely the problem?

 A. The ink ribbon is depleted.

 B. The printhead is dirty or damaged.

 C. The printhead isn't impacting the paper hard enough.

 D. The print spooler is sending incorrect information to the printer.

3. What should you do to your laser printer every time you replace the toner?

 A. Change the power cord.

 B. Shake the toner cartridge.

 C. Cycle the printer's power.

 D. Clean the printer.

4. Mrs. Robinson is getting an "Access Denied" error when trying to print to her networked printer. What should she check to fix the problem?

 A. Her network permissions

 B. The printer's power cable

 C. The printer's IP settings

 D. Her default printer settings

5. Frank's color inkjet printer no longer prints the color yellow, though it prints all the other colors just fine. The printer worked fine last month, the last time he printed in color. Which of the following is the most likely problem?

 A. He turned off the yellow nozzle.

 B. He has run out of yellow ink.

 C. He has a corrupt printer driver.

 D. His printer is set to monochrome mode.

6. Beth's laser printer is printing tiny specks on the paper. What should she do first?

 A. Wipe the paper with bleach.

 B. Run the printer maintenance program.

 C. Clean the nozzles.

 D. Vacuum the printer.

7. Ursula's laser printer has stopped working and is displaying this error message: "Error 81 – Service." What should she do first?

 A. Update the printer's firmware.

 B. Reinstall the printer driver.

 C. Try to find the error in the user's guide or maintenance program or online.

 D. Turn off the printer and call the manufacturer's help line.

8. Kevin's inkjet printer isn't printing blue (cyan). He checks the ink levels and sees that there's plenty of ink. What should he consider next?

 A. A printhead is jammed.

 B. A laser is blocked.

 C. A nozzle is clogged.

 D. An ink cartridge is missing.

9. The output from Diane's laser printer is fading evenly. What should she suspect first?

 A. A laser is blocked.

 B. The printer is out of toner.

 C. A nozzle is clogged.

 D. Her printer is dirty.

10. What should you check if your laser printer keeps grabbing multiple sheets even after you've loaded a new ream of paper?

 A. The RIP

 B. The erase lamp

 C. The seperator pad

 D. The transfer corona

■ Essay Quiz

1. Write a short essay detailing different problems that frequently occur with laser printers and how to resolve them.

2. Mike has an inkjet printer that seems to be refusing to print anything. Write a few paragraphs describing how he should troubleshoot this problem.

Lab Project

• Lab Project 17.1

Go online and do a search for printer maintenance kits. Create a spreadsheet detailing three different kits. Make sure to include things like the cost of the kit and what parts it contains.

Securing Computers

chapter 18

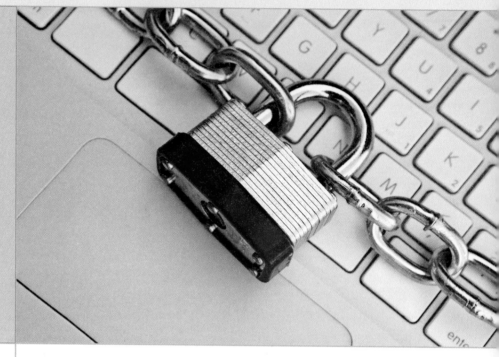

"Strategy without tactics is the slowest route to victory. Tactics without strategy is the noise before defeat."

—SUN TZU, THE ART OF WAR

In this chapter, you will learn how to

- **Explain the threats to your computers and data**
- **Describe key security concepts and technologies**
- **Explain how to protect computers from network threats**

Your PC is under siege. Through your PC, a malicious person can gain valuable information about you and your habits. He can steal your files. He can run programs that log your keystrokes and thus gain account names and passwords, credit card information, and more. He can run software that takes over much of your computer processing time and use it to send spam or steal from others. The threat is real and right now. Worse, he's doing one or more of these things to your clients as I write these words. You need to secure your computer and your users' computers from these attacks.

But what does *computer security* mean? Is it an antivirus program? Is it big, complex passwords? Sure, it's both of these things, but what about the fact that your laptop can be stolen easily or that improper ventilation can cause hard drives and other components to die?

To secure computers, you need both a sound strategy and proper tactics. From a strategic sense, you need to understand the threat from unauthorized access to local machines as well as the big threats posed when computers go onto networks. Part of the big picture means to know what policies, software, and hardware to put in place to stop those threats. From a tactical in-the-trenches sense, you need to master the details, to know how to implement and maintain the proper tools. Not only do you need to install antivirus programs in your users' computers, for example, but you also need to update those programs regularly to keep up with the constant barrage of new viruses.

■ Analyzing Threats

Threats to your data and PC come from two directions: accidents and malicious people. All sorts of things can go wrong with your computer, from users getting access to folders they shouldn't see to a virus striking and deleting folders. Files can be deleted, renamed, or simply lost. Hard drives can die, and optical discs get scratched and rendered unreadable. Accidents happen and even well-meaning people can make mistakes.

Unfortunately, a lot of people out there intend to do you harm. Add that intent together with a talent for computers, and you have a deadly combination. Let's look at the following issues:

- Unauthorized access

- Data destruction, accidental or deliberate

- Administrative access

- Catastrophic hardware failures

- Malware

- Environmental threats

Unauthorized Access

Unauthorized access occurs when a person accesses resources without permission. Resources in this case mean data, applications, and hardware. A user can alter or delete data; access sensitive information, such as financial data, personnel files, or e-mail messages; or use a computer for purposes the owner did not intend.

Not all unauthorized access is malicious—often this problem arises when users who are randomly poking around in a computer discover that they can access resources in a fashion the primary user did not intend. Unauthorized access becomes malicious when outsiders knowingly and intentionally take advantage of weaknesses in your security to gain information, use resources, or destroy data!

One of the ways to gain unauthorized access is through intrusion. You might imagine someone kicking in a door and hacking into a computer, but more often than not it's someone sitting at a home computer, trying various passwords over the Internet. Not quite as glamorous, but still....

Dumpster diving is the generic term for anytime a hacker goes through your refuse, looking for information. This is also a form of intrusion. The amount of sensitive information that makes it into any organization's trash bin boggles the mind! Years ago, I worked with an IT security guru who gave me and a few other IT people a tour of our office's trash. In one 20-minute tour of the personal wastebaskets of one office area, we had enough information to access the network easily, as well as to embarrass seriously more than a few people. When it comes to getting information, the trash is the place to look!

Shoulder surfing is another technique for gaining unauthorized access. Shoulder surfing is simply observing someone's screen or keyboard to get information, often passwords. As the name implies, it usually requires the bad guy looking over your shoulder to see what you are doing.

Social Engineering

Although you're more likely to lose data through accident, the acts of malicious users get the vast majority of headlines. Most of these attacks come under the heading of **social engineering**—the process of using or manipulating people inside the networking environment to gain access to that network from the outside—which covers the many ways humans can use other humans to gain unauthorized information. This unauthorized information may be a network login, a credit card number, company customer data—almost anything you might imagine that one person or organization may not want a person outside of that organization to access.

Social engineering attacks aren't hacking—at least in the classic sense of the word—although the goals are the same. Social engineering means people attacking an organization through the people in the organization or physically accessing the organization to get the information they need. Following are a few of the more classic types of social engineering attacks.

It's common for social engineering attacks to be used together, so if you discover one of them being used against your organization, it's a good idea to look for others.

Infiltration

Hackers can physically enter your building under the guise of someone who might have a legitimate reason for being there, such as cleaning personnel, repair technicians, or messengers. They then snoop around desks, looking for whatever they can find. They might talk with people inside the organization, gathering names, office numbers, department names—little things in and of themselves, but powerful tools when combined later with other social engineering attacks.

Dressing the part of a legitimate user—with fake badge and everything—enables malicious people to gain access to locations and thus potentially your data. Following someone through the door, for example, as if you belong, is called **tailgating**. Tailgating is a common form of infiltration.

Telephone Scams

Telephone scams are probably the most common social engineering attack. In this case, the attacker makes a phone call to someone in the organization to gain information. The attacker attempts to come across as someone inside the organization and uses this to get the desired information. Probably the most famous of these scams is the "I forgot my user name and password" scam. In this gambit, the attacker first learns the account name of a legitimate person in the organization, usually using the infiltration method. The attacker then calls someone in the organization, usually the help desk, in an attempt to gather information, in this case a password.

> **Hacker:** "Hi, this is John Anderson in accounting. I forgot my password. Can you reset it, please?"
>
> **Help Desk:** "Sure, what's your user name?"
>
> **Hacker:** "j_w_Anderson"
>
> **Help Desk:** "OK, I reset it to e34rd3."

Certainly telephone scams aren't limited to attempts to get network access. There are documented telephone scams against organizations aimed at getting cash, blackmail material, or other valuables.

Phishing

Phishing is the act of trying to get people to give their user names, passwords, or other security information by pretending to be someone else electronically. A classic example is when a bad guy sends you an e-mail that's supposed to be from your local credit card company asking you to send them your user name and password. Phishing is by far the most common form of social engineering done today.

Data Destruction

Often an extension of unauthorized access, data destruction means more than just intentionally or accidentally erasing or corrupting data. It's easy to imagine some evil hacker accessing your network and deleting all your important files, but authorized users may also access certain data and then use that data beyond what they are authorized to do. A good example is the person who legitimately accesses a Microsoft Access product database to modify the product descriptions, only to discover that she can change the prices of the products, too.

This type of threat is particularly dangerous when users are not clearly informed about the extent to which they are authorized to make changes. A fellow tech once told me about a user who managed to mangle an important database when someone gave him incorrect access. When confronted, the user said: "If I wasn't allowed to change it, the system wouldn't let me do it!" Many users believe that systems are configured in a paternalistic way that wouldn't allow them to do anything inappropriate. As a result, users often assume they're authorized to make any changes they believe are necessary when working on a piece of data they know they're authorized to access.

Administrative Access

Every operating system enables you to create user accounts and grant those accounts a certain level of access to files and folders in that computer. As an administrator, supervisor, or root user, you have full control over just about every aspect of the computer. Windows XP, in particular, makes it entirely too easy to give users administrative access to the computer, especially Windows XP Home, which has only two kinds of users: administrators and limited users. Because you can't do much as a limited user, most home and small office systems simply use multiple administrator accounts. If you need to control access, you need to use non-Home versions of Windows.

System Crash/Hardware Failure

As with any technology, computers can and will fail—usually when you can least afford for it to happen. Hard drives crash, the power fails—it's all part of the joy of working in the computing business. You need to create redundancy in areas prone to failure (such as installing backup power in case of electrical failure) and perform those all-important data backups. Chapter 8 goes into detail about using backups and other issues involved in creating a stable and reliable system.

Physical Theft

A fellow network geek once challenged me to try to bring down his newly installed network. He had just installed a powerful and expensive firewall router and was convinced that I couldn't get to a test server he added to his network just for me to try to access. After a few attempts to hack in over the Internet, I saw that I wasn't going to get anywhere that way.

So I jumped in my car and drove to his office, having first outfitted myself in a techy-looking jumpsuit and an ancient ID badge I just happened to have in my sock drawer. I smiled sweetly at the receptionist and walked right by my friend's office (I noticed he was smugly monitoring incoming IP traffic by using some neato packet-sniffing program) to his new server.

I quickly pulled the wires out of the back of his precious server, picked it up, and walked out the door. The receptionist was too busy trying to figure out why her e-mail wasn't working to notice me as I whisked by her carrying the 65-pound server box. I stopped in the hall and called him from my cell phone.

> **Me (cheerily):** "Dude, I got all your data!"
>
> **Him (not cheerily):** "You rebooted my server! How did you do it?"
>
> **Me (smiling):** "I didn't reboot it—go over and look at it!"
>
> **Him (really mad now):** "YOU <EXPLETIVE> THIEF! YOU STOLE MY SERVER!"
>
> **Me (cordially):** "Why, yes. Yes, I did. Give me two days to hack your password in the comfort of my home, and I'll see everything! Bye!"

I immediately walked back in and handed him the test server. It was fun. The moral here is simple: Never forget that the best network software

security measures can be rendered useless if you fail to protect your systems physically!

Malware

Networks are without a doubt the fastest and most efficient vehicles for transferring computer viruses among systems. News reports focus attention on the many malicious software attacks from the Internet, but a huge number of such attacks still come from users who bring in programs on optical discs and USB drives. The "Network Security" section of this chapter describes the various methods of virus infection and other malware and what you need to do to prevent such attacks from damaging your networked systems.

Environmental Threats

Your computer is surrounded by a host of dangers all just waiting to wreak havoc: bad electricity from the power company, a host of chemicals that just by the nature of your business may or may not be near your computer, dust, heat, cold, wet…it's a jungle out there!

Power

We've covered power issues extensively back in Chapter 3. Don't ever fail to appreciate the importance of surge suppressors and uninterruptible power supplies (UPSs) to protect your electronics from surges, brownouts, and blackouts. Also remember that network devices need power protection as well. Figure 18.1 shows a typical UPS protecting a network rack.

• **Figure 18.1** UPS on rack

How's the Air in There?

Proper environmental controls help secure servers and workstations from the environmental impact of excessive heat, dust, and humidity. Such *environmental controls* include air conditioning, proper ventilation, air filtration, and monitors for temperature and humidity. A CompTIA A+ technician maintains an awareness of temperature, humidity level, and ventilation, so that he or she can tell very quickly when proper levels or settings are out of whack.

A PC works best in an environment where the air is clean, dry, and room temperature. CompTIA doesn't expect you to become an environmental engineer, but it does expect you to explain and deal with how dirty, humid, or hot air can affect a computer. We've covered all of these topics to some extent throughout the book, so let's just do a quick overview with security in mind.

Dirty Air Dust and debris aren't good for any electronic components. Your typical office air conditioning does a pretty good job of eliminating the worst offenders, but not all computers are in nice offices. No matter where the computers reside, you need to monitor your systems for dirt. The best

• **Figure 18.2** Dirty fan

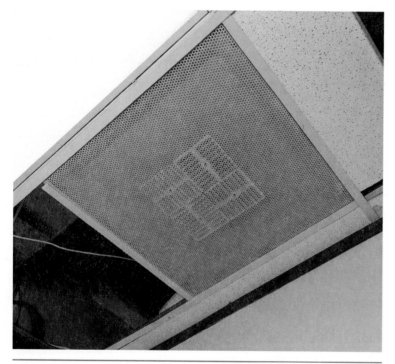

• **Figure 18.3** Air-conditioning vent in a small server closet

way to do this is observation as part of your regular work. Dust and debris will show up all over the systems, but the best place to look are the fans. Fans will collect dust and dirt quickly (see Figure 18.2).

All electronic components get dirty over time. To clean them, you need to use either compressed air or a nonstatic vacuum. So which one do you use? The rule is simple: If you don't mind dust blowing all over the place, use compressed air. If you don't want dust blowing all over the place, use a vacuum.

Equipment closets filled with racks of servers need proper airflow to keep things cool and to control dusty air. Make sure that the room is ventilated and air-conditioned (see Figure 18.3) and that the air filters are changed regularly.

If things are really bad, you can enclose a system in a dust shield. Dust shields come complete with their own filters to keep a computer clean and happy even in the worst of environments.

Temperature and Humidity Most computers are designed to operate at room temperature, which is somewhere in the area of 22°C (72°F) with the relative humidity in the 30–40 percent range. Colder and dryer is better for computers (but not for people), so the real challenge is when the temperature and the humidity go higher.

A modern office will usually have good air conditioning and heating, so your job as a tech is to make sure that things don't happen to prevent your air conditioning from doing its job. That means you're pretty much always on ventilation patrol. Watch for the following to make sure air is flowing:

- Make sure ducts are always clear of obstructions.

- Make sure ducts are adjusted (not too hot or too cold).

- Don't let equipment get too closed off from proper ventilation.

Toxic Materials

Every office is filled with chemicals, compositions that invariably get stored, spilled, or dumped. If something spills and it's not something you're

familiar with, refer to the Material Safety Data Sheet (MSDS) for proper documentation for handling and disposal. Always comply with local government regulations when dealing with chemicals, including batteries and the metals on circuit boards.

Security Concepts and Technologies

Once you've assessed the threats to your computers and networks, you need to take steps to protect those valuable resources. Depending on the complexity of your organization, this can be a small job encompassing some basic security concepts and procedures, or it can be exceedingly complex. The security needs for a three-person desktop publishing firm, for example, would differ wildly from those of a defense contractor supplying top-secret toys to the Pentagon.

From a CompTIA A+ certified technician's perspective, you need to understand the big picture (that's the strategic side), knowing the concepts and available technologies for security. At the implementation level (that's the tactical side), you're expected to know where to find such things as security policies in Windows. A CompTIA Network+ or CompTIA Security+ tech will give you the specific options to implement. (The exception to this level of knowledge comes in dealing with malicious software such as viruses, but we'll tackle that subject as the last part of the chapter.) So let's look at three concept and technology areas: access control, data classification and compliance, and reporting.

Cross Check

Securing Windows Resources
Part of establishing local control over resources involves setting up the computer properly in the first place, a topic covered in depth in Chapter 7. Check your memory of proper setup techniques from that chapter and see if you can answer these questions: How do you establish control over a computer's resources? What file system must you use?

Access Control

Access is the key. If you can control access to the data, programs, and other computing resources, you've secured your systems. **Access control** is composed of four interlinked areas that a good security-minded tech should think about: physical security, authentication, users and groups, and security policies. Much of this you know from previous chapters, but this section should help tie it all together as a security topic.

Secure Physical Area and Lock Down Systems

The first order of security is to block access to the physical hardware from people who shouldn't have access. This isn't rocket science. Lock the door to your workspace. Don't leave a PC unattended when logged in. In fact, don't ever leave a system logged in, even as a limited user. God help you if you walk away from a server still logged in as an administrator. You're tempting fate.

Employee ID badges are now so common that even relatively small organizations use them. Badges are a great way not only to control building access but also to store authentication tools such as radio frequency identification (RFID) or smart cards (see "Authentication" later in this chapter). Figure 18.4 shows a typical badge.

Be aware of the risk of shoulder surfing. One handy tool to prevent this is a privacy filter. A privacy filter is little more than a framed sheet or film that you apply to the front of your monitor. Privacy filters reduce the viewing angle, making it impossible to see the contents on the screen for anyone except those directly in front of the screen (see Figure 18.5).

Security is more of an issue when users walk away from their computers, even for a moment. When you see a user's computer logged in and unattended, do the user and your company a huge favor and lock the computer. Just walk up and press WINDOWS LOGO KEY-L on the keyboard to lock the system. It works in all versions of Windows. Better yet, make a point to make users aware of this issue so they understand the risk and can take the precaution themselves. You should also instruct them how to password-protect their screensaver. When the password feature is enabled, a user won't be able to return to the desktop until they've entered the proper password. It's a little like locking the computer, and good for those who like using screensavers.

While you're looking at a user's monitor, examine around his or her desk. Is the user writing down passwords and putting them in plain sight?

• **Figure 18.4** Typical employee badge/smart card

• **Figure 18.5** Privacy filter

If so, tell the user to get rid of them! Teach users to create easy-to-remember passwords. Are critical, personal, or sensitive documents also lying about in plain sight? The user should put them in a closed, secure place. Documents no longer needed should be shredded immediately.

Authentication

Security requires properly implemented **authentication**, which means in essence how the computer determines who can or should access it and, once accessed, what that user can do. A computer can authenticate users through software or hardware, or a combination of both.

You can categorize ways to authenticate into three broad areas: knowledge factors, ownership factors, and inherent factors. A *knowledge factor* is something the user knows, like a password or personal identification number (PIN). An *ownership factor* is something the user has, like an ID card or security token. An *inherent factor* (also called a biometric) is something that is part of the user, like a fingerprint or retinal pattern.

Multifactor authentication provides the best authentication, where a user must use two or more factors to prove his or her identity. Note that multifactor means more than one factor, not just more than one *thing*. Logging in with a user name and password is two things, for example, but because both fall into the category of what a user knows, it's not multifactor authentication.

Many organizations use *two-factor authentication*. An example is a key fob that generates a numeric key. A user authenticates by entering his or her user name and password (something you know) and is then prompted to enter the key (something you have).

Software Authentication: Proper Passwords It's still rather shocking to me to power up a friend's computer and go straight to his or her desktop, or with my married-with-kids friends, to click one of the parents' user account icons and not be prompted for a password. This is just wrong! I'm always tempted to assign passwords right then and there—and not tell them the passwords, of course—so they'll see the error of their ways when they try to log on next. I don't do it, but always try to explain gently the importance of good passwords.

You know about passwords from Chapter 7, so I won't belabor the point here. Suffice it to say that you must require that your users have proper passwords. Don't let them write passwords down or tape them to the underside of their mouse pads either!

 A popular way to remember authentication factors is to think of them as something you know (passwords), something about you (biometric), and something you have (badge, key fob, or security token).

 You can log on to any computer in a domain using one set of credentials. In addition to being a time-saver, this is also a great security feature that helps network administrators better control who can gain access to the network.

Cross Check

Proper Passwords

So, what goes into making a good password? Turning once again to Chapter 7, see if you can answer these questions: What sorts of characters should make up a password? Should you ask for a user's password when working on that user's PC? Why or why not? If you're in a secure environment and know you'll have to reboot several times, is it okay to ask for a password then? What should you do?

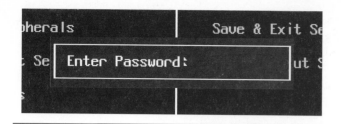

Figure 18.6 CMOS access password request

Figure 18.7 Keyboard-mounted smart card reader being used for a commercial application (photo courtesy of Cherry Corp.)

It's not just access to Windows that you need to think about. There's always the temptation for people to do other mean things, such as changing CMOS settings, opening up the case, and even stealing hard drives. Any of these actions renders the computer inoperable to the casual user until a tech can undo the damage or replace components. All modern CMOS setup utilities come with a number of tools to protect your computer, such as drive lock, intrusion detection, and of course system access passwords such as the one shown in Figure 18.6.

Hardware Authentication Smart cards and biometric devices enable modern systems to authenticate users with more authority than mere passwords. **Smart cards** are credit card–sized cards with circuitry that can identify the bearer of the card. Smart cards are relatively common for such tasks as authenticating users for mass transit systems, for example, but are fairly uncommon in computers. Figure 18.7 shows a smart card and keyboard combination.

Security tokens are devices that store some unique information that the user carries on their person. They may be digital certificates, passwords, or biometric data. They may also store an RSA token. *RSA tokens* are random-number generators that are used with user names and passwords to ensure extra security. Most security tokens come in the form of key fobs, as shown in Figure 18.8.

You can also get many types of security tokens as software. Anyone who plays *World of Warcraft* knows that there's an entire illegal industry known as "gold farmers" who like to hack accounts and steal all the hard-earned loot your character collects. It's a terrible feeling to log in to the game only to find your character cleaned out (see Figure 18.9).

Figure 18.8 RSA key fob (photo courtesy of EMC Corp.)

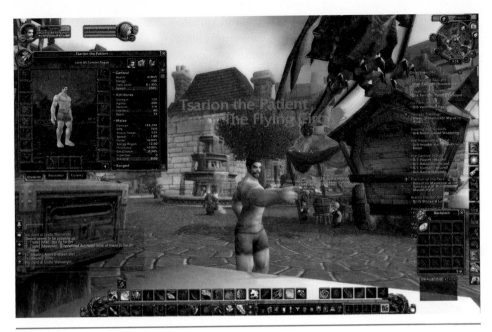

• **Figure 18.9** I've been robbed! My fine armor is gone, my bags are empty, and my bank account only has a few copper pieces!

To counter this problem, Blizzard Entertainment, the folks who own *World of Warcraft*, provide free security tokens. Most folks think "hardware" in the form of key fobs when they hear the words "security tokens," but you can also download a security token as software—Blizzard offers an app for your smartphone, as shown in Figure 18.10.

People can guess or discover passwords, but it's a lot harder to forge someone's fingerprints. The keyboard in Figure 18.11 authenticates users on a local machine by using fingerprints. Other devices that will do the trick are key fobs and retinal scanners. Devices

> How's this for full disclosure? Microsoft does not claim that the keyboard in Figure 18.11 offers any security at all. In fact, the documentation specifically claims that the fingerprint reader is an accessibility tool, not a security device. Because it enables a person to log on to a local machine, though, I think it falls into the category of authentication devices.

• **Figure 18.10** Blizzard Entertainment security token for iPhone

• **Figure 18.11** Microsoft keyboard with fingerprint accessibility

plusID™

PRIVARIS®

• **Figure 18.12** plusID (photo courtesy of Privaris, Inc.)

that require some sort of physical, flesh-and-blood authentication are called **biometric devices**.

Clever manufacturers have developed key fobs and smart cards that use RFID to transmit authentication information so users don't have to insert something into a computer or card reader. The Privaris plusID combines, for example, a biometric fingerprint fob with an RFID tag that makes security as easy as opening a garage door remotely! Figure 18.12 shows a plusID device.

For some reason, CompTIA lists *retinal scanners* as a form of biometric security. While retinal scanners do exist, I have been in hundreds of high-security facilities and have only seen one retinal scanner in operation in almost 30 years as a tech. CompTIA should remove this silly objective, but until they do, Figure 18.13 shows about the only image of a retinal scanner in operation you'll ever encounter.

NTFS, not FAT32!

The file system on a hard drive matters a lot when it comes to security. On a Windows machine with multiple users, you simply must use NTFS or you have no security at all. Not just primary drives, but also any secondary drives in computers in your care should be formatted as NTFS, with the exception of removable drives such as the one you use to back up your system.

When you run into a multiple-drive system that has a second or third drive formatted as FAT32, you can use the **convert** command-line utility to go from FAT to NTFS. The syntax is pretty straightforward. To convert a D: drive from FAT or FAT32 to NTFS, for example, you'd type the following:

```
convert d: /fs:ntfs
```

• **Figure 18.13** Retinal scanner in Half-Life 2

You can substitute a mount name in place of the drive letter in case you have a mounted volume. The command has a few extra switches as well, so at the command prompt, type **/?** after the convert command to see all of your options.

Users and Groups

Windows uses user accounts and groups as the bedrock of access control. A user account is assigned to a group, such as Users, Power Users, or Administrators, and by association gets certain permissions on the computer. Using NTFS enables the highest level of control over data resources.

Assigning users to groups is a great first step in controlling a local machine, but this feature really shines once you go to a networked environment. Let's go there now.

User Account Management Through Groups

Access to user accounts should be restricted to the assigned individuals, and those who configure the permissions to those accounts must remember the *principle of least privilege* discussed in Chapter 7: Accounts should have permission to access only the resources they need and no more. Tight control of user accounts is critical to preventing unauthorized access. Disabling unused accounts is an important part of this strategy, but good user account management goes far deeper than that.

Groups are a great way to achieve increased complexity without increasing the administrative burden on network administrators, because all operating systems combine permissions. When a user is a member of more than one group, which permissions does that user have with respect to any particular resource? In all operating systems, the permissions of the groups are *combined*, and the result is what you call the **effective permissions** the user has to access the resource. As an example, if Rita is a member of the Sales group, which has List Folder Contents permission to a folder, and she is also a member of the Managers group, which has Read and Execute permissions to the same folder, Rita will have both List Folder Contents *and* Read and Execute permissions to that folder.

Watch out for *default* user accounts and groups—they can become secret backdoors to your network! All network operating systems have a default Everyone group that can be used to sneak into shared resources easily. This Everyone group, as its name implies, literally includes anyone who connects to that resource. Windows gives full control to the Everyone group by default, for example, so make sure you know to lock this down! The other scary one is the Guest account. The Guest account is the only way to access a system without a user name and password. Unless you have a compelling reason to provide guest access, you should always make sure the Guest account is disabled.

All of the default groups—Everyone, Guest, Users—define broad groups of users. Never use them unless you intend to permit all of those folks access to a resource. If you use one of the default groups, remember to configure them with the proper permissions to prevent users from doing things you don't want them to do with a shared resource!

Security Policies

Although permissions control how users access shared resources, there are other functions you should control that are outside the scope of resources. For example, do you want users to be able to access a command prompt on their Windows system? Do you want users to be able to install software? Would you like to control what systems a user can log on to or at what time of day a user can log on? All network operating systems provide you with some capability to control these and literally hundreds of other security parameters, under what Windows calls *policies*. I like to think of policies as permissions for activities, as opposed to true permissions, which control access to resources.

A policy is usually applied to a user account, a computer, or a group. Let's use the example of a network composed of Windows XP Professional systems with a Windows Server 2008 system. Every Windows XP system has its own local policies program, which enables policies to be placed on that system only. Figure 18.14 shows the tool you use to set local policies on an individual system, called **Local Security Policy**, being used to deny the user account Danar the capability to log on locally.

Local policies work great for individual systems, but they can be a pain to configure if you want to apply the same settings to more than one PC on your network. If you want to apply policy settings *en masse*, you need to step up to Windows Active Directory domain-based **Group Policy**. By using Group Policy, you can exercise deity-like—Microsoft prefers to use the term *granular*—control over your network clients.

Want to set default wallpaper for every PC in your domain? Group Policy can do that. Want to make certain tools inaccessible to everyone except authorized users? Group Policy can do that, too. Want to control access to the Internet, redirect home folders, run scripts, deploy software, or just remind folks that unauthorized access to the network will get them nowhere fast? Group Policy is the answer. Figure 18.15 shows Group Policy; I'm about to change the default title on every instance of Internet Explorer on every computer in my domain!

That's just one simple example of the settings you can configure by using Group Policy. You can apply literally hundreds of tweaks through Group Policy, from the great to the small, but don't worry too much about familiarizing yourself with each and every one. Group Policy settings are a big topic on most of the Microsoft certification tracks, but for the purposes of the CompTIA A+ 220-802 exam, you simply have to be comfortable with the concept behind Group Policy.

When you open the Local Security Policy tool in Windows XP, note that the program is labeled "Local Security Settings," even though the icon is labeled "Local Security Policy." In Windows Vista and Windows 7, it is always called Local Security Policy.

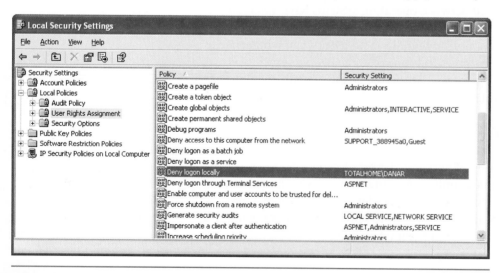

• **Figure 18.14** Local Security Policy

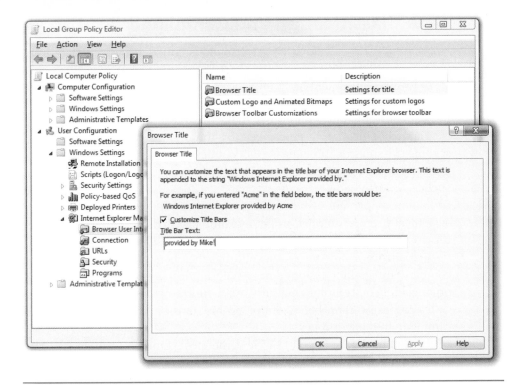

● **Figure 18.15** Using Group Policy to make IE title say "provided by Mike!"

Although I could never list every possible policy you can enable on a Windows system, here's a list of some commonly used ones:

- **Prevent Registry Edits** If you try to edit the Registry, you get a failure message.

- **Prevent Access to the Command Prompt** Keeps users from getting to the command prompt by turning off the Run command and the Command Prompt shortcut.

- **Log on Locally** Defines who may log on to the system locally.

- **Shut Down System** Defines who may shut down the system.

- **Minimum Password Length** Forces a minimum password length.

- **Account Lockout Threshold** Sets the maximum number of logon attempts a person can make before being locked out of the account.

- **Disable Windows Installer** Prevents users from installing software.

- **Printer Browsing** Enables users to browse for printers on the network, as opposed to using only assigned printers.

Although the CompTIA A+ 220-802 exam doesn't expect you to know how to implement policies on any type of network, you are expected to understand that policies exist, especially on Windows networks, and that they can do amazing things to control what users can do on their systems. If you ever try to get to a command prompt on a Windows system only to discover the Run command is dimmed, blame it on a policy, not the computer!

Data Classification and Compliance

Larger organizations, such as government entities, benefit greatly from organizing their data according to its sensitivity—what's called **data classification**—and making certain that computer hardware and software stay as uniform as possible. In addition, many government and internal regulations apply fairly rigorously to the organizations.

Data classification systems vary by the organization, but a common scheme classifies documents as public, internal use only, highly confidential, top secret, and so on. Using a classification scheme enables employees such as techs to know very quickly what to do with documents, the drives containing documents, and more. Your strategy for recycling a computer system left from a migrated user, for example, will differ a lot if the data on the drive was classified as internal use only or top secret.

Compliance means, in a nutshell, that members of an organization or company must abide by or comply with all of the rules that apply to the organization or company. Statutes with funny names such as Sarbanes-Oxley impose certain behaviors or prohibitions on what people can and cannot do in the workplace.

From a technician's point of view, the most common compliance issue revolves around software, such as what sort of software users can be allowed to install on their computers or, conversely, why you have to tell a user that he can't install the latest application that may help him do the job more effectively because that software isn't on the approved list. This can lead to some uncomfortable confrontations, but it's part of a tech's job.

The concepts behind compliance in IT are not, as some might imagine at first blush, to stop you from being able to work effectively. Rather they're designed to stop users with not quite enough technical skill or knowledge from installing malicious programs or applications that will destabilize their systems. This keeps technical support calls down and enables techs to focus on more serious problems.

Reporting

As a final weapon in your security arsenal, you need to report any security issues so a network administrator or technician can take steps to make them go away. You can set up auditing within Windows so that the OS reports problems to you. **Event Viewer** enables you to read the logs created by auditing. You can then do your work and report those problems. Let's take a look.

Auditing

The Security section of Event Viewer doesn't show you anything by default. To unlock the full potential of Event Viewer, you need to set up auditing. *Auditing* in the security sense means to tell Windows to create an entry in the Security Log when certain events happen, such as when a user logs on—called **event auditing**—or tries to access a certain file or folder—called **object access auditing**. Figure 18.16 shows Event Viewer tracking logon and logoff events.

The CompTIA A+ 220-802 exam doesn't test you on creating a brilliant auditing policy for your office—that's what network administrators do.

Event Viewer stores log files in %SystemRoot%\System32\ Config.

• **Figure 18.16** Event Viewer displaying security alerts

You simply need to know what auditing does and how to turn it on or off so you can provide support for the network administrators in the field. To turn on auditing at a local level, go to Local Security Policy in Administrative Tools. Select Local Policies and then click Audit Policy. Double-click one of the policy options and select one or both of the checkboxes in the Properties dialog box that opens. Figure 18.17 shows the Audit object access Properties dialog box.

Incidence Reporting

Once you've gathered data about a particular system or you've dealt with a computer or network problem, you need to complete the mission by telling your supervisor. This is called

• **Figure 18.17** Audit object access Properties dialog box, with Local Security Policy open in the background

incidence reporting. Many companies have pre-made forms that you simply fill out and submit. Other places are less formal. Regardless, you need to do this!

Incidence reporting does a couple of things for you. First, it provides a record of work you've accomplished. Second, it provides a piece of information that, when combined with other information you might or might not know, reveals a pattern or bigger problem to someone higher up the chain. A seemingly innocuous security audit report, for example, might match other such events in numerous places in the building at the same time and thus show that conscious, coordinated action rather than a glitch was at work.

Evidence Handling

As a tech, you'll need to deal with people who use company computers in prohibited ways. In most cases, you're not paid to be the police and should not get involved. There are times, however, where something bad—really bad—takes place on one of the systems you support, and if you're the first tech person there, everyone is going to turn to you for action.

A technician should ignore personal information in and around a person's computer. You should treat anything said to you and anything you see as a personal confidence, not to be repeated to customers, coworkers, or bosses. Here's Mike's Rule of Confidentiality: "Unless it's a felony or an imminent physical danger, you didn't see nothin'." This includes any confidential customer materials. Try not to look at anything that isn't directly related to your job. (Sometimes that's impossible, but limit your exposure.) If you're waiting on a printout at a printer and suddenly there's a bunch of printed pages coming out of the printer with employee payroll information, set it to the side and pretend you never saw it.

But what about the scary stuff? Obvious espionage? Pornography? People passing out personal information? Hacking? In these cases, you've just become the first line of defense and you need to act accordingly.

Identify the Action or Content as Prohibited Use common sense, but keep in mind that most organizations have an Acceptable Use Policy that employees must sign. The Acceptable Use Policy defines what actions employees may or may not perform on company equipment. Remember that these polices aren't just for obvious issues such as using a computer for personal use. These policies cover computers, phones, printers, and even the network itself. This policy will define the handling of passwords, e-mail, and many other issues.

Report Through Proper Channels In most cases, you'll report any prohibited actions or content directly to your supervisor. There's also a chance your company will have a security officer or incident response leader who you'll contact instead. Do *not* speak to the person committing the infraction unless your supervisor approves that contact.

Data/Device Preservation You might end up in a situation serious enough that a computer or other device becomes evidence. In these cases, the

The SANS Institute provides an excellent boilerplate Acceptable Use Policy on their Web site: www.sans.org/security-resources/policies/Acceptable_Use_Policy.pdf.

location of the system and who has touched it may come into question, so you need to establish a **chain of custody**: a documented history of who has been in possession of the system. You'll hopefully have a legal expert to guide you, but the following are fairly common rules:

1. Isolate the system. Shut down the system and store it in a place where no one else can access it.

2. Document when you took control of the system and the actions you took: shutting it down, unplugging it, moving it, and so on. Don't worry about too much detail, but you must track its location.

3. If another person takes control of the system, document the transfer of custody.

■ Network Security

Networks are under threat from the outside as well, so this section looks at issues involving Internet-borne attacks, firewalls, and wireless networking. This content is the security bread and butter for a CompTIA A+ technician, so you need to understand the concepts and procedures and be able to implement them properly.

Malicious Software

The beauty of the Internet is the ease of accessing resources just about anywhere on the globe, all from the comfort of your favorite chair. This connection, however, runs both ways, and people from all over the world can potentially access your computer from the comfort of their evil lairs. The Internet is awash with malicious software that is, even at this moment, trying to infect your systems.

The term **malware** defines any program or code (macro, script, and so on) that's designed to do something on a system or network that you don't want done. Malware comes in quite a variety of guises, such as grayware, spam, viruses, worms, macros, Trojan horses, and rootkits. Let's examine all these malware flavors and then explore how to deal with them.

Grayware

Programs that intrude unwanted into your computing experience but don't actually do any damage to your systems or data—what's called **grayware**—can make that computing experience less than perfect. On most systems, the Internet Web browser client is the most often used piece of software. Over the years, Web sites have come up with more and more ways to try to get you to see what they want you to see: their advertising. When the Web first got underway, we were forced to look at an occasional banner ad. In the past few years, Web site designers have become much more sophisticated, creating a number of intrusive and irritating ways to get you to part with your money in one form or another.

The term *adware* generally refers to programs that support themselves using revenue from ads, like all those "free" Internet game sites. Every once in a while those ads can lead to spyware installing on a system, making many authors lump adware into the grayware category.

There are basically two irritating grayware types: pop-ups and spyware. **Pop-ups** are those surprise browser windows that appear automatically when you visit a Web site, proving themselves irritating and unwanted and nothing else. **Spyware**, meanwhile, defines a family of programs that run in the background on your PC, sending information about your browsing habits to the company that installed it on your system. Of the two, spyware is much less noticeable, but far more nefarious.

Pop-Ups Getting rid of pop-ups is actually rather tricky. You've probably noticed that most of these pop-up browser windows don't look like browser windows at all. They have no menu bar, button bar, or address window, yet they are separate browser windows. HTML coding permits Web site and advertising designers to remove the usual navigation aids from a browser window so all you're left with is the content. In fact, as I'll describe in a minute, some pop-up browser windows are deliberately designed to mimic similar pop-up alerts from the Windows OS. They might even have buttons similar to Windows' own exit buttons, but you might find that when you click them, you wind up with more pop-up windows instead! What to do?

The first thing you need to know when dealing with pop-ups is how to close them without actually having to risk clicking them. As I said, most pop-ups have removed all navigation aids, and many are also configured to appear on your monitor screen in a position that places the browser window's exit button—the little X button in the upper-right corner—outside of your visible screen area. Some even pop up behind the active browser window and wait there in the background. Most annoying! To remedy this, use alternate means to close the pop-up browser window. For instance, you can right-click the browser window's taskbar icon to generate a pop-up menu of your own. Select Close, and the window should go away. You can also press ALT-TAB to bring the browser window in question to the forefront and then press ALT-F4 to close it.

Most Web browsers have features to prevent pop-up ads in the first place, but I've found that these types of applications are sometimes *too* thorough. That is, they tend to prevent *all* new browser windows from opening, even those you want to view. Applications such as AdSubtract control a variety of Internet annoyances, including pop-up windows, cookies, and Java applets, and are more configurable—you can specify what you want to allow on any particular domain address—but the fully functional versions usually cost at least something, and that much control is too confusing for most novice-level users.

Spyware Some types of spyware go considerably beyond grayware's level of intrusion. They can use your computer's resources to run *distributed computing* applications, capture your keystrokes to steal passwords, reconfigure your dial-up settings to use a different phone number at a much higher connection charge, or even use your Internet connection and e-mail address list to propagate itself to other computers in a virus-like fashion! Are you concerned yet?

Setting aside the legal and ethical issues—and there are many—you should at least appreciate that spyware can seriously impact your PC's performance and cause problems with your Internet connection. The threat is real, so what practical steps can you take to protect yourself? Let's look

at how to prevent spyware installation and how to detect and remove any installed spyware.

How does this spyware get into your system in the first place? Obviously, sensible people don't download and install something that they know is going to compromise their computers. Makers of spyware know this, so they bundle their software with some other program or utility that purports to give you some benefit.

What kind of benefit? In 2005, Movieland (otherwise known as Movieland.com and Popcorn.net) released a "handy" movie download service. They didn't tell users, of course, that everyone who installed the software was "automatically enrolled" in a three-day trial. If you didn't cancel the "trial," a pop-up window filled your screen demanding you pay them for the service that you never signed up for. The best part, however, was that you couldn't uninstall the application completely. The uninstaller redirected users to a Web page demanding money again. (Movieland was shut down in 2007.) As you can see, spyware doesn't need to force its way into a PC. Instead, it saunters calmly through the front door.

Another popular spyware method is to use pop-up browser windows crudely disguised as Windows' own system warnings (see Figure 18.18). When clicked, these may trigger a flood of other browser windows, or may even start a file download.

If Movieland was a problem back in 2005, what are the big spyware applications today? Unfortunately, I can't tell you—not because it's a secret, but because we don't know about them yet. Look at Figure 18.19: the dialog box asks the user if she trusts the Gator Corporation (a well-known spyware producer from several years ago). Because everyone eventually knew not to trust Gator, they would click No, and the company faded away several years ago. Gator, however, was incredibly well-known at the time. What about those small, unknown applications waiting in the dark corners

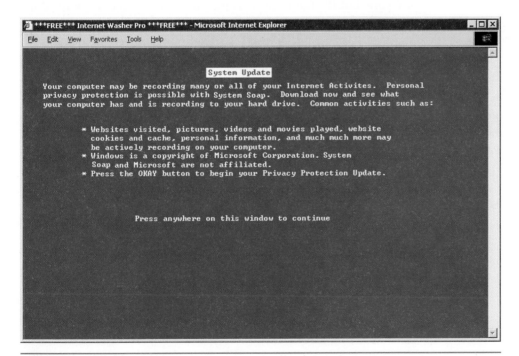

• **Figure 18.18** A spyware pop-up browser window, disguised as a Windows alert

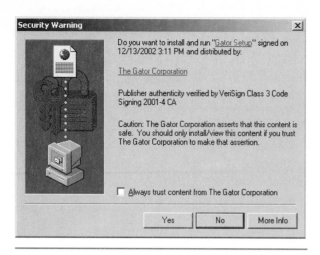

of the Internet—the ones that just might have spyware hiding inside? How do you protect yourself from them?

The lesson here is simple: *Don't install these programs*, at least not without researching the program first. Careful reading of the software's license agreement before you install a program is a good idea, but realistically, it does little to protect your PC. With that in mind, here are a couple of preventive measures you can take to keep parasitic software off of your system.

If you visit a Web site that prompts you to install a third-party application or plug-in that you've never heard of, *don't install it*. Well-known and reputable plug-ins, such as Adobe's Shockwave or Flash, are safe, but be suspicious of any others. Don't click *anywhere* inside of a pop-up browser window, even if it looks just like a Windows alert window

• **Figure 18.19** Gator Corporation's acknowledgment warning

or DOS command-line prompt—as I just mentioned, it's probably fake and the Close button is likely a hyperlink. Instead, use other means to close the window, such as pressing ALT-F4 or right-clicking the browser window's icon on the taskbar and selecting Close.

You can also install spyware detection and removal software on your system and run it regularly. Let's look at how to do that.

Some spyware makers are reputable enough to include a routine for uninstalling their software. Gator, for instance, made it fairly easy to get rid of their programs; you just used the Windows Add/Remove Programs or Programs and Features applet in the Control Panel. Others, however, aren't quite so cooperative. In fact, because spyware is so—well, *sneaky*—it's entirely possible that your system already has some installed that you don't even know about. How do you discover it?

Windows comes with Windows Defender, a fine tool for catching most spyware, but it's not perfect. The better solution is to back up Windows Defender with a second spyware removal program. There are several on the market, but two that I highly recommend are Lavasoft's Ad-Aware (see Figure 18.20) and Safer Networking's Spybot Search & Destroy.

Both of these applications work exactly as advertised. They detect and delete spyware of all sorts—hidden files and folders, cookies, Registry keys and values, you name it. Ad-Aware is free for personal use, while Spybot Search & Destroy is shareware (see Figure 18.21).

• **Figure 18.20** Lavasoft's Ad-Aware

Many times I've used both programs at the same time because one tends to catch what the other misses.

Spam

E-mail that comes into your Inbox from a source that's not a friend, family member, or colleague, and that you didn't ask for, can create huge problems for your computer and you. This unsolicited e-mail, called spam, accounts for a huge percentage of traffic on the Internet. Spam comes in many flavors, from legitimate businesses trying to sell you products to scammers who just want to take your money. Hoaxes, pornography, and get-rich-quick schemes pour into the Inboxes of most e-mail users. They waste your time and can easily offend.

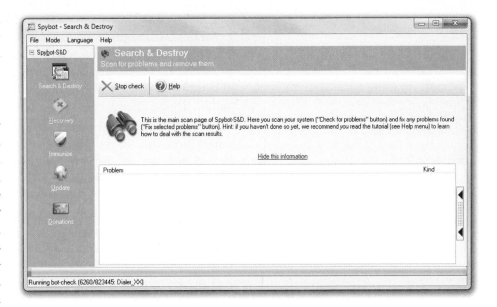

• **Figure 18.21** Spybot Search & Destroy

You can use several options to cope with the flood of spam. The first option is defense. Never post your e-mail address on the Internet. One study tested this theory and found that *over 97 percent* of the spam received during the study went to e-mail addresses they had posted on the public Internet.

Filters and filtering software can block spam at your mail server and at your computer. Google Mail has powerful blocking schemes, for example, that drop the average spam received by its subscribers by a large percentage, usually more than 90 percent. You can set most e-mail programs to block e-mail from specific people—good to use if someone is harassing you—or to specific people. You can block by subject line or keywords. Most people use a third-party antispam program instead of using the filters in their e-mail program.

 Try This!

Spybot

If you haven't done this already, do it now. Go to www.safer-networking.org and download the latest copy of Spybot Search & Destroy. Install it on your computer and run it. Did it find any spyware that slipped in past your defenses?

A lot of spam contains malware or points to dangerous Web sites. Never click on any link or open an e-mail from someone you don't know! You might just save your computer.

Spam is also notorious for phishing scams. Phishing works by sending you an e-mail message that looks legitimate, like a bill or account information, hoping you will enter important personal information. If you receive an e-mail from Amazon.com, ebay.com, or some other site (like your bank), don't click on it! Like Admiral Ackbar said in *Star Wars*, "It's a trap!"

Virus

A **virus** is a program that has two jobs: to replicate and to activate. *Replication* means it makes copies of itself, often as code stored in boot sectors or as extra code added to the end of executable programs. *Activation* is when a virus does something like erase the boot sector of a drive. A virus only replicates to other drives, such as thumb drives or optical media. It does not replicate across networks. Plus, a virus needs human action to spread.

Worm

A **worm** functions similarly to a virus, though it replicates exclusively through networks. A worm, unlike a virus, doesn't have to wait for someone to use a removable drive to replicate. If the infected computer is on a network, a worm will immediately start sending copies of itself to any other computers on the network it can locate. Worms can exploit inherent flaws in program code like *buffer overflows*, where a buffer cannot hold all the data sent to it.

Macro

A **macro** is any type of virus that exploits application macros to replicate and activate. A *macro* is also programming within an application that enables you to control aspects of the application. Macros exist in any application that has a built-in macro language, such as Microsoft Excel, that users can program to handle repetitive tasks (among other things).

Trojan Horse

A **Trojan horse** is a piece of malware that looks or pretends to do one thing while, at the same time, doing something evil. A Trojan horse may be a game, like poker, or a free screensaver. The sky is the limit. The more "popular" Trojan horses turn an infected computer into a server and then open TCP or UDP ports so a remote user can control the infected computer. Trojan horses can be used to capture keystrokes, passwords, files, credit card information, and more. Trojan horses do not replicate.

Rootkit

For a virus or Trojan horse to succeed, it needs to come up with some method to hide itself. As awareness of malware has grown, anti-malware programs make it harder to find new locations on a computer to hide malware. A **rootkit** is a Trojan horse that takes advantage of very low-level operating system functions to hide itself from all but the most aggressive of anti-malware tools. Worse, a rootkit, by definition, gains privileged access to the computer. Rootkits can strike operating systems, hypervisors, and even firmware.

The most infamous rootkit appeared a few years ago as an antipiracy attempt by Sony on its music CDs. Unfortunately for the media giant, the rootkit software installed when you played a music CD and opened a backdoor that could be used for malicious intent.

Malware Signs and Symptoms

If your PC has been infected by malware, you'll bump into some strange things before you can even run an anti-malware scan. Like a medical condition, malware causes unusual symptoms that should stand out from your everyday computer use. You need to become a PC physician and understand what each of these symptoms means.

Malware's biggest strength is its flexibility: it can look like anything. In fact, a lot of malware attacks can feel like normal PC "wonkiness"— momentary slowdowns, random one-time crashes, and so on. Knowing when a weird application crash is actually a malware attack is half the battle.

A slow PC can mean you're running too many applications at once or you've been hit with malware. How do you tell the difference? In this case, it's the frequency. If it's happening a lot, even when all of your applications are closed, you've got a problem. This goes for frequent lockups, too. If Windows starts misbehaving (more than usual), run your anti-malware application right away.

Malware, however, doesn't always jump out at you with big system crashes. Some malware tries to rename system files, change file permissions, or hide files completely. Most of these issues are easily caught by a regular anti-malware scan, so as long as you remain vigilant, you'll be okay.

Some malware even fights back, defending itself from your many attempts to remove it. If your Windows Update feature stops working, preventing you from patching your PC, you've got malware. If other tools and utilities throw up an "Access Denied" road block, you've got malware. If you lose all Internet connectivity, either the malware is stopping you or removing the malware broke your connection. In this case, you might need to reconfigure your Internet connection: reinstall your NIC and its drivers, reboot your router, and so on.

Even your browser and anti-malware applications can turn against you. If you type in one Web address and end up at a different site than you anticipated, a malware infection might have overwritten your HOSTS file. The HOSTS file overrules any DNS settings and can redirect your browser to whatever site the malware adds to the file. Most browser redirections

 While it's not necessarily a malware attack, watch out for hijacked e-mail accounts, too, belonging either to you or to someone you know. Hackers can hit both e-mail clients and Webmail users. If you start receiving some fishy (or phishy) e-mail messages, change your Webmail user name and password or scan your PC for malware.

point you to phishing scams or Web sites full of free downloads (that are, of course, covered in malware). In fact, some free anti-malware applications are actually malware—what techs call a *rogue anti-malware* program. You can avoid these rogue applications by sticking to the recommended lists of anti-malware software found online.

Watch for security alerts in Windows, either from Windows' built-in security tools or from your third-party anti-malware program. Windows XP (SP2 and later) and Windows Vista include the Security Center, a Control Panel applet that monitors your software firewall, automatic updates, malware protection, and more. Windows 7 includes a similar tool, but calls it the Action Center, which you learned about back in Chapter 10 (see Figure 18.22). You don't actually configure much using these applets; they just tell you whether or not you are protected. Both of these tools place an icon and pop up a notification in the notification area whenever Windows detects a problem. Windows XP and Vista use a red shield with a white × to notify you, while Windows 7 uses a white flag.

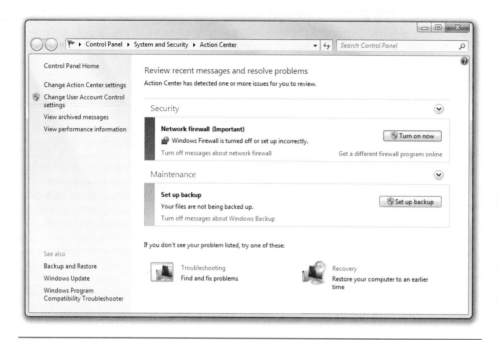

• **Figure 18.22** Windows 7 Action Center

Malware Prevention and Recovery

The only way to protect your PC permanently from getting malware is to disconnect it from the Internet and never permit any potentially infected software to touch your precious computer. Because neither scenario is likely these days, you need to use specialized anti-malware programs to help stave off the inevitable assaults. Even with the best anti-malware tools, there are times when malware still manages to strike your computer. When you discover infected systems, you need to know how to stop the spread of the malware to other computers, how to fix infected computers, and how to remediate (restore) the system as close to its original state as possible.

Dealing with Malware

You can deal with malware in several ways: anti-malware programs, training and awareness, patch management, and remediation.

At the very least, every computer should run an anti-malware program. If possible, add an appliance that runs anti-malware programs against incoming data from your network. Also remember that an anti-malware program is only as good as its updates—keep everyone's definition file (explained a bit later) up to date with, literally, nightly updates! Users must be trained to look for suspicious ads, programs, and pop-ups, and

understand that they must not click these things. The more you teach users about malware, the more aware they'll be of potential threats. Your organization should have policies and procedures in place so everyone knows what to do if they encounter malware. Finally, a good tech maintains proper incident response records to see if any pattern to attacks emerges. He or she can then adjust policies and procedures to mitigate these attacks.

Anti-Malware Programs

An **anti-malware program** such as a classic **antivirus program** protects your PC in two ways. It can be both sword and shield, working in an active seek-and-destroy mode and in a passive sentry mode. When ordered to seek and destroy, the program scans the computer's boot sector and files for viruses and, if it finds any, presents you with the available options for removing or disabling them. Antivirus programs can also operate as **virus shields** that passively monitor a computer's activity, checking for viruses only when certain events occur, such as a program executing or a file being downloaded.

Antivirus programs use different techniques to combat different types of viruses. They detect boot sector viruses simply by comparing the drive's boot sector to a standard boot sector. This works because most boot sectors are basically the same. Some antivirus programs make a backup copy of the boot sector. If they detect a virus, the programs use that backup copy to replace the infected boot sector. Executable viruses are a little more difficult to find because they can be on any file in the drive. To detect executable viruses, the antivirus program uses a library of signatures. A **signature** is the code pattern of a known virus. The antivirus program compares an executable file to its library of signatures. There have been instances where a perfectly clean program coincidentally held a virus signature. Usually the antivirus program's creator provides a patch to prevent further alarms. Now that you understand the types of viruses and how antivirus programs try to protect against them, let's review a few terms that are often used when describing certain traits of viruses.

Polymorphic/Polymorphs A **polymorph virus** attempts to change its signature to prevent detection by antivirus programs, usually by continually scrambling a bit of useless code. Fortunately, the scrambling code itself can be identified and used as the signature—once the antivirus makers become aware of the virus. One technique used to combat unknown polymorphs is to have the antivirus program create a checksum on every file in the drive. A *checksum* in this context is a number generated by the software based on the contents of the file rather than the name, date, or size of that file. The algorithms for creating these checksums vary among different antivirus programs (they are also usually kept secret to help prevent virus makers from coming up with ways to beat them). Every time a program is run, the antivirus program calculates a new checksum and compares it with the earlier calculation. If the checksums are different, it is a sure sign of a virus.

Stealth The term "stealth" is more of a concept than an actual virus function. Most **stealth virus** programs are boot sector viruses that use various methods to hide from antivirus software. The AntiEXE stealth virus hooks on to a little-known but often-used software interrupt, for example, running only when that interrupt runs. Others make copies of innocent-looking files.

One of the most important malware mitigation procedures is to keep systems under your control patched and up to date through proper *patch management*. Microsoft does a very good job of putting out bug fixes and patches as soon as problems occur. If your systems aren't set up to update automatically, then perform manual updates regularly.

The term *antivirus* (and antispyware, or anti-anything) is becoming obsolete. Viruses are only a small component of the many types of malware. Many people continue to use the term as a synonym for anti-malware.

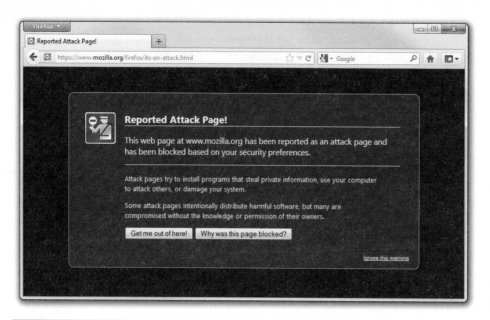

User Education

A powerful tool to prevent malware attacks and to reduce the impact of malware attacks when they happen is to educate your users. Teach users to be cautious of incoming e-mail they don't clearly recognize and to never click on an attachment or URL in an e-mail unless they are 100 percent certain of the source.

Explain to users the dangers of going to questionable Web sites and teach them how to react when they see questionable actions take place. Let's look at a few of the more evil ones. All Web browsers have built-in attack site warnings like the one shown in Figure 18.23.

• **Figure 18.23** Attack site warning

Mozilla provides a sample Web site that displays the attack site sign—a great way to show users what it looks like: www.mozilla.org/firefox/its-an-attack.html.

Nobody wants their systems infected with malware. Users are motivated and happy when you give them the skills necessary to protect themselves. The bottom line is that educated and aware users will make your life a lot easier.

Malware Prevention Tips

The secret to preventing damage from a malicious software attack is to keep from getting malware on your system in the first place. As discussed earlier, for example, all good antivirus programs include a virus shield that scans e-mail, downloads, running programs, and so on automatically (see Figure 18.24).

Use your antivirus shield. It is also a good idea to scan PCs daily for possible virus attacks. All antivirus programs include terminate-and-stay resident programs (TSRs) that run every time the PC is booted. Last but not least, know the source of any software before you load it. Although the chance of commercial, shrink-wrapped software having a virus is virtually nil (there have been a couple of well-publicized exceptions), that copy of *Call of Duty: Modern Warfare 3* you borrowed from a local hacker should definitely be inspected with care.

Keep your antivirus and anti-malware programs updated. New viruses and other malware appear daily, and your programs

• **Figure 18.24** A virus shield in action

need to know about them. The list of virus signatures your antivirus program can recognize, for example, is called the **definition file**, and you must keep that definition file up to date so your antivirus software has the latest signatures. Fortunately, most antivirus programs update themselves automatically. Further, you should periodically update the core anti-malware software programming—called the *engine*—to employ the latest refinements the developers have included.

Try This!

Scoring Excellent Anti-Malware Programs

You can download many excellent anti-malware programs for free, either for extended trial periods or for indefinite use. Since you need these programs to keep your systems happy, Try This! Download one or more anti-malware programs, such as the following:

- **Windows Defender** Windows Defender is a good antispyware program, but it won't protect you against any other form of malware. It's free with Windows, however, and better than nothing.

- **Microsoft Security Essentials** Recognizing the shortcomings of Windows Defender and no longer willing to count on users to download and install third-party programs, Microsoft offers a complete anti-malware solution called Microsoft Security Essentials. You can download this program for free from Microsoft (search for Microsoft Security Essentials). This program automatically shuts off Windows Defender when installed.

- **Malwarebytes Anti-Malware (www.malwarebytes.org)** Malwarebytes' Anti-Malware program rocks the house in terms of dealing with malicious software. They offer both a free version that scans your computer for malware and quarantines it and a PRO version that actively protects against any incoming malware. Anti-Malware is my first choice in dealing with malware on a client's computer.

- **Lavasoft Ad-Aware (www.lavasoft.com)** Ad-Aware is an excellent antispyware program. Ad-Aware will root out all sorts of files and programs that can cause your computer to run slowly (or worse).

- **Spybot Search & Destroy (www.safer-networking.org)** Spybot Search & Destroy from Safer Networking Ltd. is another superb antispyware program. Many folks use both Ad-Aware and Spybot—though sometimes the two programs detect each other as spyware!

- **AVG Anti-Virus (http://free.avg.com)** AVG offers a free version of their antivirus software for noncommercial use. Updated regularly to add the latest virus signatures, the software will keep your system clean and bug free.

Boot CD Anti-Malware Tools

If you run anti-malware software and your computer still gets infected, especially after a reboot, you need a more serious anti-malware tool. Many anti-malware companies provide bootable CDs or flash drives (or show you how to make one) that enable you to boot from a known-clean OS and run the same anti-malware software, but this time not corrupted by the malware on your system.

Malware Recovery Tips

When the inevitable happens and either your computer or one of your user's computers gets infected by malware such as a computer virus, you need to follow certain steps to stop the problem from spreading and get the computer back up safely into service. Try this five-step process.

1. Recognize
2. Quarantine
3. Search and destroy
4. Remediate
5. Educate

Recognize and Quarantine The first step is to identify and recognize that a potential malware outbreak has occurred. If you're monitoring network traffic and one computer starts spewing e-mail, that's a good sign. Or users might complain that a computer that was running snappily the day before seems very sluggish.

Many networks employ software such as the open source PacketFence that automatically monitors network traffic and can cut a machine off the network if that machine starts sending suspicious packets. You can also quarantine a computer manually, by disconnecting the network cable. Once you're sure the machine isn't capable of infecting others, you're ready to find the virus or other malware and get rid of it.

At this point, you should disable System Restore. If you make any changes going forward, you don't want the virus to be included in any saved restore points. To turn off System Restore in Windows XP, open the Start menu, right-click on My Computer, and select Properties. Switch to the System Restore tab and select Turn off System Restore. On the dialog box that pops up, confirm your selection by clicking Yes. To turn off System Restore in Windows Vista/7, open the Start menu, right-click on Computer, and select Properties. Click on the *System protection* link. In the Protection Settings section, select a drive and click on Configure. In the System Protection dialog box that opens, select *Turn off system protection*. Repeat the procedure for each hard drive on your Windows Vista/7 system.

Search and Destroy Once you've isolated the infected computer (or computers), you need to get to a safe boot environment and run anti-malware software. You can try Windows Safe Mode first, because it doesn't require anything but a reboot. If that doesn't work, or you suspect a boot sector virus, you need to turn to an external bootable source, such as a bootable CD or flash memory drive.

Get into the habit of keeping around a bootable anti-malware flash drive or optical media. If you suspect a virus or other malware, use the disc, even if your anti-malware program claims to have eliminated the problem. Turn off the PC and reboot it from the anti-malware disc. (You might have to change CMOS settings to boot to optical media.) This will put you in a clean boot environment that you know is free from any boot sector viruses. If you only support fairly recent computers, most have an option to boot to a USB flash drive, so you can put a boot environment on a thumb drive for even faster start-up speeds.

You have several options for creating the bootable optical disc or flash drive. First, some antivirus software comes in a bootable version, such as the avast! Virus Cleaner Tool (see Figure 18.25).

Second, you can download a copy of Linux that offers a live CD option such as Ubuntu. With a live CD, you boot to the CD and install a complete working copy of the operating system into RAM, never touching or accessing the hard drive, to give you full Internet-ready access to many online anti-malware sites. (You'll obviously need Internet access for those tools.) Kaspersky Labs provides a nice option at www.kaspersky.com.

Finally, you can download and burn a copy of the Ultimate Boot CD. It comes stocked with several antivirus and anti-malware programs, so you wouldn't need any other tool. Find it at www.ultimatebootcd.com. The only downside is that the anti-malware engines will quickly be out of date, as will their malware libraries.

Once you get to a boot environment, run your anti-malware program's most comprehensive scan. (Make sure you have all the latest updates for the software.) Then check all removable media that were exposed to the system, and any other machine that might have received data from the

• **Figure 18.25** avast! Virus Cleaner Tool

system or that is networked to the cleaned machine. A virus or other malicious program can often lie dormant for months before anyone knows of its presence.

E-mail is still a common source of viruses, and opening infected e-mails is a common way to get infected. Viewing an e-mail in a preview window opens the e-mail message and exposes your computer to some viruses. Download files only from sites you know to be safe and avoid the less reputable corners of the Internet, the most likely places to pick up computer infections.

Remediate Malware infections can do a lot of damage to a system, especially to sensitive files needed to load Windows, so you might need to remediate formerly infected systems after cleaning off the drive or drives. Remediation simply means that you fix things the virus or other malware harmed. This can mean replacing corrupted Windows Registry files or even startup files.

If you can't start Windows after the malware scan is finished, you need to follow the steps outlined in Chapter 10 to boot to the Recovery Console in Windows XP, or boot from the Windows Preinstallation Environment into the Windows Recovery Environment in Windows Vista or Windows 7.

In the Windows XP Recovery Console, you'll have access to tools to repair the boot sector (or *boot blocks*, as CompTIA calls them) through the fixmbr and fixboot commands. You can run bootcfg to rebuild a corrupted boot.ini file.

With the Windows Vista/7 Recovery Environment, you have access to more repair tools, such as Startup Repair, System Restore, Windows Complete PC Restore (System Image Recovery in Windows 7), and the command prompt (see Figure 18.26). Run the appropriate option for the situation and you should have the machine properly remediated in a jiffy.

Educate The best way to keep from having to deal with malware and grayware is education. It's your job as the IT person to talk to users, especially the ones whose systems you've just spent the last hour cleaning of nasties, about how to avoid these programs. Show them samples of dangerous e-mails they should not open, Web sites to avoid, and the types of programs they should not install and use on the network. Any user who understands the risks of questionable actions on their computers will usually do the right thing and stay away from malware.

Finally, have your users run antivirus and antispyware programs regularly. Schedule them while interfacing with the user so you know it will happen.

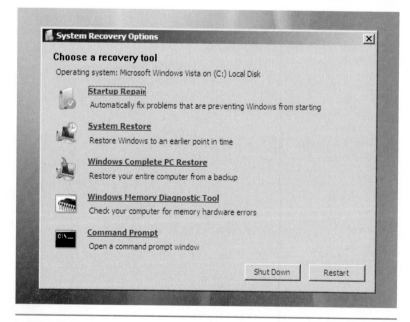

• **Figure 18.26** System Recovery options in Windows Vista

Recovery Environment

You saw the Windows Vista and Windows 7 Recovery Environments (also known as the System Recovery Options menu) back in Chapter 10, so check your memory now. What's the major difference between System Restore and Windows Complete PC Restore (System Image Recovery in Windows 7)? In what circumstances would you choose one tool over the other? What are the dangers, if any, in either tool?

Firewalls

Firewalls are an essential tool in the fight against malicious programs on the Internet. **Firewalls** are devices or software that protect an internal network from unauthorized access to and from the Internet at large. Firewalls use a number of methods to protect networks, such as hiding IP addresses and blocking TCP/IP ports.

A typical network uses one of two types of firewalls: *hardware firewalls*, often built into routers, and *software firewalls* that run on your computers. Both types of firewall protect your computer and your network. You also run them at the same time. Let's look at both a typical SOHO router's firewall features and your computer's software firewall to see how they protect your network and your computers.

Hardware Firewall Settings

Most SOHO networks use a hardware firewall, often as a feature built into a router like the Linksys model shown in Figure 18.27. A hardware firewall hides and separates your internal LAN from outside connections like the Internet by using Network Address Translation (NAT), which shares one public IP address among several computers. Routers, however, have a few other tricks up their sleeves. From the router's browser-based settings screen, you can configure a hardware firewall (see Figure 18.28). Let's walk through a few of the available settings.

A hardware firewall watches for and stops many common threats—all you have to do is turn it on (see Figure 18.29). Hardware firewalls use *Stateful Packet Inspection (SPI)* to inspect each incoming packet individually. SPI also blocks any incoming traffic that isn't in response to your outgoing traffic. You can even disable ports entirely, blocking all traffic in or out. But what if you want to allow outside users access to a Web server on the LAN? Because NAT hides the true IP address of that system, you'll need a way to allow incoming traffic past the router/firewall and a way to redirect that traffic to the right PC.

● **Figure 18.27** Linksys router as a firewall

• Figure 18.28 Default Web interface

• Figure 18.29 SPI firewall settings

Port forwarding enables you to open a port in the firewall and direct incoming traffic on that port to a specific IP address on your LAN. In the case of the Web server referenced in the previous paragraph, you would open port 80 (for HTTP packets) and instruct the router to send all incoming traffic to the server machine. Figure 18.30 shows port forwarding configured to send all HTTP packets to an internal Web server.

Port forwarding isn't the only way to open ports on a firewall. **Port triggering** enables you to open an incoming connection to one computer automatically based on a specific outgoing connection. The *trigger port* defines the outgoing connection, and the *destination port* defines the incoming connection. If you set the trigger port to 3434 and the destination port to 1234, for example, any outgoing traffic on port 3434 will trigger the router to open port 1234 and send any received data back to the PC with the original outgoing traffic. Figure 18.31 shows a router set up for port triggering of an Internet Relay Chat (IRC) server.

If you want to go beyond port forwarding and port triggering and open every port on a machine, you need a demilitarized zone (DMZ). A DMZ puts systems with the specified IP addresses outside the protection of the

• **Figure 18.30** Port forwarding

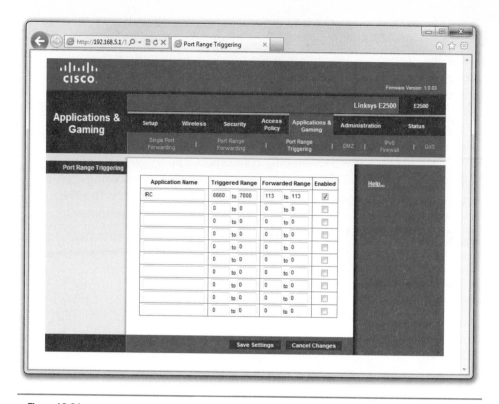

• **Figure 18.31** Port triggering

• **Figure 18.32** DMZ set up on a SOHO router

firewall, opening all ports and enabling all incoming traffic (see Figure 18.32). If you think this sounds incredibly dangerous, you are right! Any PC inside the DMZ will be completely exposed to outside attacks. Don't use it!

Software Firewalls

While a hardware firewall does a lot to protect you from outside intruders, you should also use a software firewall, such as the firewalls built into each version of Windows, called (appropriately) Windows Firewall. Windows Firewall handles the heavy lifting of port blocking, security logging, and more.

You can access Windows Firewall in Windows XP by opening the Windows Firewall applet in the Control Panel. The Windows XP's Windows Firewall applet (see Figure 18.33) looks a lot different from the one available in Windows 7 (see Figure 18.34), though their primary function remains

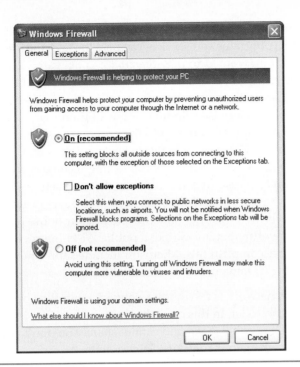

• **Figure 18.33** Windows XP's Firewall applet

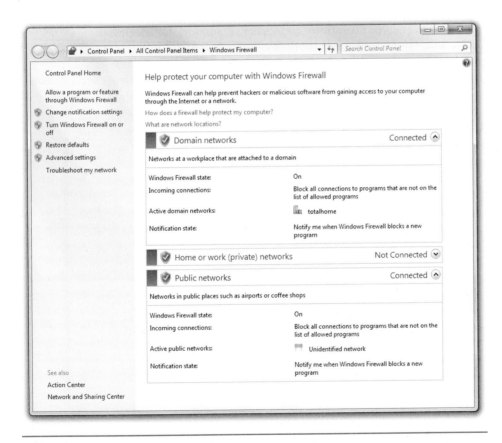

• **Figure 18.34** Windows 7 Firewall applet

the same. Configuring Windows Firewall involves turning it on or off, and choosing which programs and services can pass through the firewall, known as *exceptions*. If you wanted to play *Starcraft 2* (a PC game that requires an Internet connection), for example, it would need to be on the list of exceptions for your firewall—most programs you install add themselves to this list automatically, otherwise Windows Firewall prompts you the first time you run it and asks if you want to add the program as an exception.

The Windows XP firewall's biggest shortcoming is that it fails to consider that a single PC, especially a portable, might connect to multiple networks. You don't necessarily want the same firewall settings used for both public and private networks. Microsoft needed to develop a way for you to separate trustworthy networks (like the one in your house or at the office) from non-trustworthy networks (like a public Wi-Fi Internet connection at the airport). To accomplish this, Microsoft included three network types in Windows Vista/7: Domain, Private, and Public.

- A *Domain* network is a Windows network controlled by a Windows domain controller. In this case, the domain controller itself tells your machine what it can and cannot share. You don't need to do anything when your computer joins a domain.

- A *Private* network enables you to share resources, discover other devices, and allow other devices to discover your computer safely.

- A *Public* network prevents your computer from sharing and disables all discovery protocols.

When your computer connects to a network for the first time, Windows Vista and 7 will prompt you to choose the network type: Home, Work, or Public location (see Figure 18.35).

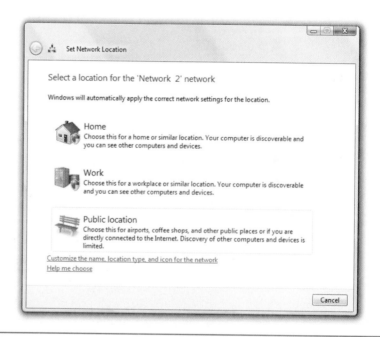

• **Figure 18.35** Set Network Location in Vista

First, notice that Domain is not an option. There's a good reason for this: If your computer is on a domain, you won't see the dialog box in Figure 18.35. When your computer joins a domain, Windows automatically sets your network location to Domain (unless your domain controller chooses something different, which is unlikely).

So what exactly does Windows do when you select Home, Work, or Public location? Windows configures Windows Firewall to block or unblock discovery and sharing services. When running on a Private (Home or Work) network, Windows enables Network Discovery and File and Printer Sharing as exceptions. When running on a Public network, Windows disables these exceptions.

In Windows Vista, Microsoft cleverly used Windows Firewall and the network type to turn services on and off, but Microsoft made one mistake: the firewall configuration and network type remain the same for every connection. If your Windows machine never changes networks, you won't have a problem. But what about machines (mainly laptops) that hop from one network to another (see Figure 18.36)? In that case, you need different firewall settings for each network the system might encounter.

In this regard, Windows 7 makes a big departure from Windows Vista. In Windows 7, the Set Network Location dialog box appears every time you connect to a new network. Windows 7 even includes three different firewall settings: one for Domains, one for Private networks (Home or Work), and one for Public networks.

Once you've picked a network type, you might want to customize the firewall settings further. If you click the Advanced Settings option in Windows Vista/7's Firewall applet, you'll discover a much deeper level of firewall configuration, one very different from the settings found in Windows XP (see Figure 18.37). In fact, it's an entirely different tool called Windows Firewall with Advanced Security.

Microsoft enhanced how Windows Vista/7 treat exceptions. In Windows XP, you can only choose a program and make it an exception, giving it permission to pass through the firewall. But programs both send and receive network data; Windows XP ignores the "inbound" and "outbound" aspect of firewalls. Windows Vista/7 takes the exceptions concept and expands it to include custom rules for both inbound and outbound data. Figure 18.38 shows the outbound rules for a typical Windows Vista/7 system.

The Network Discovery setting dictates whether a computer can find other computers or devices on a network and vice versa. Even with Network Discovery activated, several firewall settings can overrule certain connections.

• **Figure 18.36** Many machines need more than one network setting.

• **Figure 18.37** Windows Firewall with Advanced Security

• **Figure 18.38** Outbound Rules list

A rule always includes at least the following:

- The name of the program
- Group: an organizational group that helps sort all the rules
- The associated profile (All, Domain, Public, Private)
- Enabled/disabled status
- Remote and local address
- Remote and local port number

You can add, remove, and customize any rule to your liking. It quickly gets complicated, so unless you need to set a lot of custom rules, stick to the standard Windows Firewall applet.

Authentication and Encryption

You know from previous chapters that the first step in securing data is authentication through a user name and password. But when you throw in networking, you're suddenly not just a single user sitting in front of a computer and typing. You're accessing a remote resource and sending login information over the Internet. What's to stop someone from intercepting your user name and password?

Firewalls do a great job of controlling traffic coming into a network from the Internet and going out of a network to the Internet, but they do nothing to stop interceptor hackers who monitor traffic on the public Internet looking for vulnerabilities. Worse, once a packet is on the Internet itself, anyone with the right equipment can intercept and inspect it. Inspected packets are a cornucopia of passwords, account names, and other tidbits that hackers can use to intrude into your network. Because we can't stop hackers from inspecting these packets, we must turn to **encryption** to make them unreadable.

Network encryption occurs at many levels and is in no way limited to Internet-based activities. Not only are there many levels of network encryption, but each encryption level also provides multiple standards and options, making encryption one of the most complicated of all networking issues. You need to understand where encryption comes into play, what options are available, and what you can use to protect your network.

Network Authentication

Have you ever considered the process that takes place each time a person types in a user name and password to access a network, rather than just a local machine? What happens when this *network* authentication is requested? If you're thinking that when a user types in a user name and password, that information is sent to a server of some sort to be authenticated, you're right—but do you know how the user name and password get to the serving system? That's where encryption becomes important in authentication.

In a local network, authentication and encryption are usually handled by the OS. In today's increasingly interconnected and diverse networking environment, there is a motivation to enable different operating systems

to authenticate any client system from any other OS. Modern operating systems such as Windows and Mac OS X use standard authentication encryptions such as MIT's **Kerberos**, enabling multiple brands of servers to authenticate multiple brands of clients. These LAN authentication methods are usually transparent and work quite nicely, even in mixed networks.

Data Encryption

Encryption methods don't stop at the authentication level. There are a number of ways to encrypt network *data* as well. The choice of encryption method is dictated to a large degree by the method used by the communicating systems to connect. Many networks consist of multiple networks linked together by some sort of private connection, usually some kind of WAN connection such as DSL or T1. Microsoft's encryption method of choice for this type of network is called **IPSec** (derived from *IP security*). IPSec provides transparent encryption between the server and the client. IPSec also works in VPNs, but other encryption methods are more commonly used in those situations.

Application Encryption

When it comes to encryption, even TCP/IP applications can get into the swing of things. The most famous of all application encryptions is Netscape's **Secure Sockets Layer (SSL)** security protocol, which is used to create secure Web sites. Microsoft incorporates SSL into its more far-reaching **HTTPS** (HTTP over SSL) protocol. These protocols make it possible to create the secure Web sites people use to make purchases over the Internet. You can identify HTTPS Web sites by the *https://* (rather than http://) included in the URL (see Figure 18.39).

To make a secure connection, your Web browser and the Web server must encrypt their data. That means there must be a way for both the Web server and your browser to encrypt and decrypt each other's data. To do this, the server sends a public key to your Web browser so the browser knows how to decrypt the incoming data. These public keys are sent in the form of a **digital certificate**. This certificate is signed by a trusted authority that guarantees that the public key you are about to get is actually from the Web server and not from some evil person trying to pretend to be the Web server. A number of companies issue digital certificates to Web sites, probably the most famous being VeriSign, Inc.

Your Web browser has a built-in list of trusted authorities. If a certificate comes in from a Web site that uses one of these highly respected companies, you won't see anything happen in your browser; you'll just go to the secure Web page, where a small lock will appear in the corner of your browser. Figure 18.40 shows the list of trusted authorities built into the Firefox Web browser.

If you receive a certificate from someone *not* listed in your browser, however, the browser will warn you and ask you if you wish to accept the certificate, as shown in Figure 18.41.

What you do here is up to you. Do you wish to trust this certificate? In most cases, you simply say yes, and this certificate is added to your SSL cache of certificates. An accepted certificate may become invalid, however, usually because of something boring; for instance, it may go out of date or

• Figure 18.39 A secure Web site

• Figure 18.40 Trusted authorities

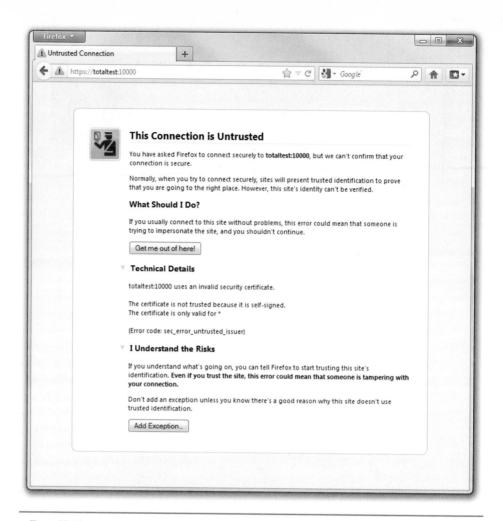

• **Figure 18.41** Incoming certificate

the public key may change. This never happens with the "big name" certificates built into your browser—you'll see this more often when a certificate is used, for example, in-house on a company intranet and the administrator forgets to update the certificates. If a certificate goes bad, your browser issues a warning the next time you visit that site. To clear invalid certificates, you need to clear the SSL cache. The process varies in every browser, but in Internet Explorer, go to the Content tab under Internet Options and click the *Clear SSL state* button (see Figure 18.42).

Wireless Issues

Wireless networks add a whole level of additional security headaches for techs to face, as you know from Chapter 13. Some of the points to remember or to go back and look up are as follows:

- Set up wireless encryption, at least WEP but preferably WPA or the more secure WPA2, and configure clients to use it.

- Disable DHCP and require your wireless clients to use a static IP address.

- If you need to use DHCP, only allot enough DHCP addresses to meet the needs of your network, to avoid unused wireless connections.

- Change the WAP's SSID from default.

- Filter by MAC address to allow only known clients on the network.

- Change the default user name and password. Every hacker has memorized the default user names and passwords.

- Update the firmware as needed.

- If available, make sure the WAP's firewall settings are turned on.

- **Figure 18.42** Internet Options Content tab in Internet Explorer

Cross Check

Securing Wireless Networks

Wireless networks are all the rage right now, from your local Starbucks to the neighbors around you. Securing wireless networks has, therefore, become an area that CompTIA A+ certified technicians must master. You read a lot about wireless networks in Chapter 13, so turn there now and see if you can answer these questions.

What is the minimum level of encryption to secure a wireless network? What types of wireless will you find for connecting at your local coffee shop?

Chapter 18 Review

■ Chapter Summary

After reading this chapter and completing the exercises, you should understand the following about computer security.

Explain the threats to your computers and data

- Threats to your data come from two sources: accidents and malicious people.

- Unauthorized access occurs when a user accesses resources in an unauthorized way. Not all unauthorized access is malicious and some is even accidental. Authorized access can lead to data destruction by users who do not intend to be malicious. When users have access to a file or database, they typically believe the system won't let them make any changes they are not authorized to make.

- Most computer attacks are accomplished through social engineering rather than hacking. Telephone scams are one of the most common social engineering tactics. Dumpster diving involves physically going through an organization's trash looking for documents that might reveal user names, passwords, or other sensitive information. Be sure to secure your computer equipment in a locked room to prevent physical theft.

- Computers, hard drives, and power all fail. As a tech, you need to plan for redundancy in these areas. You also need to protect your computers against viruses distributed through the network and removable media. You should implement good access policies and implement methods for tracking computer usage.

- Protect your PC from environmental dangers such as power surges, dirty or humid air, heat, or toxic hazards.

Describe key security concepts and technologies

- Controlling access to programs, data, and other computing resources is the key to securing your system. Access control includes four interlinked areas requiring your attention: physical security, authentication, users and groups, and security policies.

- Store computers with sensitive data in a locked room and never walk away from your computer while logged on. Log out or lock the computer by pressing WINDOWS LOGO KEY-L. Some companies lock down computer rooms with ID badges that act as key cards, using RFID or smart cards for authentication. Be aware of those around you in the space, and watch out for shoulder surfers looking at your monitor while you work.

- The three forms of authentication include knowledge factors (something the user knows, like a password or PIN), ownership factors (something the user has, like a key or card), and inherent factors (something about the user, such as a fingerprint).

- Accounts should be given permissions to access only what they need and no more. Unused accounts should be disabled.

- When a user account is a member of several groups, and permissions have been granted to groups, the user account will have a set of combined permissions that may conflict. The resulting permissions that ultimately control access are referred to as the effective permissions.

- Make sure to lock down the default Everyone group of which all users are automatically members. Never use the default Everyone or Users groups or the default Guest account unless you intend to permit all those accounts access to resources.

- Policies control permissions for activities, such as installing software, accessing a command prompt, or logging on at a particular time of day. A policy is usually applied to a user account, computer account, or a group. Use the Local Security Policy tool to manage policies for an individual computer.

- Group Policy enables you to control such things as deploying software or setting each computer in a domain to use the same wallpaper. Commonly used policies include Prevent Registry Edits, Prevent Access to the Command Prompt, Log On Locally, and Minimum Password Length.

- Data classification systems vary by the organization, but a common scheme classifies

documents as public, internal use only, highly confidential, top secret, and so on. Using a classification scheme enables employees such as techs to know very quickly what to do with documents, drives containing documents, and more.

- Compliance means that members of an organization or company must abide by or comply with all of the rules that apply to the organization or company. From a technician's point of view, the most common compliance issue revolves around software, such as what sort of software users can be allowed to install on their computers. Compliance keeps technical support calls down and enables techs to focus on more serious problems.

- Use Event Viewer to track activity on your system. By default, the Security section doesn't show you everything, so it is good practice to enable event auditing and object access auditing. Event auditing creates an entry in the Security Log when certain events happen, such as a user logging on, while object access auditing creates entries in response to object access, such as someone trying to access a certain file or folder.

- Incidence reporting means telling your supervisor about the data you've gathered regarding a computer or network problem. This provides a record of what you've done and accomplished. It also provides information that, when combined with other information you may or may not know, may reveal a pattern or bigger problem to someone higher up the chain.

- Try to avoid any personal information on a PC. If you find something private (that isn't illegal), ignore it and forget about it. If you find something illegal, you must follow the proper procedures. If a device you work on becomes evidence in legal proceedings, isolate the system and document everything that happens going forward. Pay special attention to the chain of custody, or whoever is currently in control of the machine.

Explain how to protect computers from network threats

- Malware includes grayware, spam, viruses, worms, macros, Trojan horses, and rootkits, all of which can wreak havoc on your system.

- Irritating Web browser problems include pop-ups and spyware. Many pop-ups remove the navigation aids from the browser window or mimic Windows dialog boxes. To safely close a pop-up, right-click the pop-up's taskbar icon and choose Close, or press ALT-TAB until the pop-up window is active and then press ALT-F4 to close it.

- Spyware can use your computer's resources to run distributed computing applications, capture keystrokes to steal passwords, or worse. Spyware typically disguises itself as useful utilities, so be vigilant about what you install. Some spyware can be removed via Add Remove Programs, but for stubborn spyware, use a third-party tool such as Lavasoft's Ad-Aware or Safer Networking's Spybot Search & Destroy.

- Unsolicited e-mail is called spam. Never post your e-mail address on the Internet; over 97 percent of spam goes to e-mail addresses posted online. Spam filters can block spam at the mail server or at your computer. You can set most e-mail programs to block e-mail sent from specific people or to a specific person.

- A virus is a piece of malicious software that is passed from computer to computer and is designed to attach itself to another program on your computer. A worm is a freestanding program that takes advantage of security flaws and copies itself over and over again, thereby bogging down a network.

- A macro is any type of virus that exploits application macros to replicate and activate. Trojan horses are freestanding programs that do something other than the user expects it to do when run, such as expecting a game to run but erasing CMOS settings instead.

- A rootkit is a Trojan horse that takes advantage of very low-level operating system functions to hide itself from all but the most aggressive of anti-malware tools. Rootkits can strike operating systems, hypervisors, and even firmware.

- To help protect a computer from malware, make sure to run up-to-date antivirus software, use a firewall, and apply all security patches for your software and operating system. Run Windows Update automatically, or at least weekly if you choose to configure it for manual updates.

- Antivirus software works in active mode to scan your file system for viruses and in passive mode by monitoring your computer's activity and checking for viruses in response to an action, such as running a program or downloading a file. The

software detects boot sector viruses by comparing the drive's boot sector to a standard boot sector. To detect executable viruses, a library of virus signatures is used.

- Polymorph viruses attempt to change their signature to prevent detection by antivirus software. Fortunately, the scrambled code itself can be used as a signature. A checksum, based on file contents, can be created for every file on the drive. If the checksum changes, it is a sign of a virus infection. Most stealth viruses are boot sector viruses that hide from antivirus software.

- The best way to prevent damage from a virus is to keep from getting a virus in the first place. Use your passive antivirus shield, scan the PC daily, know where software has come from before you load it, and keep your antivirus definitions updated. Don't view e-mail messages in a preview window, and only download files from sites you know to be safe.

- Some of the common symptoms of a malware infection include: browser redirections, crashes, unresponsiveness, changed file permissions, hidden files, missing system files, and so on.

- When the inevitable happens and either your computer or one of your user's computers is infected by a computer virus or other malware, you need to follow a process to stop the problem from spreading and get the computer back up safely into service. First, recognize the symptoms of a computer malware attack, such as a suddenly very sluggish computer. Follow up by quarantining the infected computer to make certain the virus or other malware doesn't spread. Third, boot the computer in Safe Mode or an alternative safe boot

environment and run anti-malware software. To finish up, remediate the formerly infected machine by fixing boot sector problems and so on, and educate your users so infection doesn't happen again.

- Hardware firewalls protect networks by hiding IP addresses and blocking TCP/IP ports. Port forwarding and port triggering enable traffic to pass through the firewall on specific ports to specific machines.

- Windows XP and later come with a built-in software firewall that is accessible from the Windows Firewall Control Panel applet.

- Encryption makes network packets unreadable by hackers who intercept network traffic. You are especially vulnerable when using the Internet over a public network. Modern operating systems use Kerberos to encrypt authentication credentials over a local network.

- Network data can be encrypted similar to authentication credentials. Microsoft's encryption method of choice is called IPSec. Netscape's Secure Sockets Layer (SSL) creates secure Web sites. Microsoft's HTTPS protocol incorporates SSL into HTTP. Web sites whose URL begins with https:// (rather than http://) are used to encrypt credit card purchases.

- To secure a wireless network, use wireless encryption and disable DHCP. Require wireless clients to use a static IP address, or allot only enough DHCP addresses to meet the needs of your network. Definitely change the default administrator user name and password on the WAP!

■ Key Terms

access control *(631)*

anti-malware program *(651)*

antivirus program *(651)*

authentication *(633)*

biometric device *(636)*

chain of custody *(643)*

compliance *(640)*

convert *(636)*

data classification *(640)*

definition files *(653)*

digital certificate *(666)*

dumpster diving *(626)*

effective permissions *(637)*

encryption *(665)*

event auditing *(640)*

Event Viewer *(640)*

firewall *(657)*

grayware *(643)*

Group Policy *(638)*

HTTPS *(666)*

incidence reporting *(642)*
IPSec *(666)*
Kerberos *(666)*
Local Security Policy *(638)*
macro *(648)*
malware *(643)*
object access auditing *(640)*
phishing *(627)*
polymorph virus *(651)*
pop-up *(644)*
port forwarding *(659)*
port triggering *(659)*
remediation *(656)*
rootkit *(649)*
Secure Sockets Layer (SSL) *(666)*

shoulder surfing *(626)*
signature *(651)*
smart card *(634)*
social engineering *(626)*
spam *(647)*
spyware *(644)*
stealth virus *(651)*
tailgating *(626)*
telephone scam *(627)*
Trojan horse *(648)*
unauthorized access *(625)*
virus *(648)*
virus shield *(651)*
worm *(648)*

■ Key Term Quiz

Use the Key Terms list to complete the sentences that follow. Not all terms will be used.

1. Mary's company routinely labels data according to its sensitivity or potential danger to the company if someone outside accesses the data. This is an example of _____.

2. A(n) _____ masquerades as a legitimate program, yet does something different than what is expected when executed.

3. Antivirus software uses updatable _____ to identify a virus by its _____.

4. Enable _____ to create Event Viewer entries when a specific file is accessed.

5. Although not all _____ is malicious, it can lead to data destruction.

6. Most attacks on computer data are accomplished through _____.

7. A(n) _____ protects against unauthorized access from the Internet.

8. Many companies authenticate access to secure rooms using an ownership factor such as a(n) _____.

9. Before making a credit card purchase on the Internet, be sure the Web site uses the _____ security protocol, which you can verify by checking for the _____ protocol in the address bar.

10. A virus that changes its signature to prevent detection is called a(n)_____.

■ Multiple-Choice Quiz

1. What is the process of using or manipulating people to gain access to network resources?

 A. Cracking

 B. Hacking

 C. Network engineering

 D. Social engineering

2. Which of the following might offer good hardware authentication?

 A. Strong password

 B. Encrypted password

 C. NTFS

 D. Smart card

3. Which of the following tools would enable you to stop a user from logging on to a local machine but still enable him to log on to the domain?

 A. AD Policy filter

 B. Group Policy Auditing

 C. Local Security Policy

 D. User Settings

4. Which hardware firewall feature enables incoming traffic on a specific port to reach an IP address on the LAN?

 A. Port forwarding

 B. NAT

 C. DMZ

 D. Multifactor authentication

5. Zander downloaded a game off the Internet and installed it, but as soon as he started to play he got a Blue Screen of Death. Upon rebooting, he discovered that his My Documents folder had been erased. What happened?

 A. He installed spyware.

 B. He installed a Trojan horse.

 C. He broke the Group Policy.

 D. He broke the Local Security Policy.

6. Which of the following should Mary set up on her Wi-Fi router to make it the most secure?

 A. NTFS

 B. WEP

 C. WPA

 D. WPA2

7. A user account is a member of several groups, and the groups have conflicting rights and permissions to several network resources. The culminating permissions that ultimately affect the user's access are referred to as what?

 A. Effective permissions

 B. Culminating rights

 C. Last rights

 D. Persistent permissions

8. What is true about virus shields?

 A. They automatically scan e-mails, downloads, and running programs.

 B. They protect against spyware and adware.

 C. They are effective in stopping pop-ups.

 D. They can reduce the amount of spam by 97 percent.

9. What does Windows use to encrypt the user authentication process over a LAN?

 A. PAP

 B. TPM

 C. HTTPS

 D. Kerberos

10. Which threats are categorized as social engineering? (Select all that apply.)

 A. Telephone scams

 B. Dumpster diving

 C. Trojan horses

 D. Spyware

11. A user calls to complain that his computer seems awfully sluggish. All he's done so far is open his e-mail. What should the tech do first?

 A. Educate the user about the dangers of opening e-mail.

 B. Quarantine the computer so the suspected virus does not spread.

 C. Run antivirus software on the computer.

 D. Remediate the infected system.

12. Which of the following are good examples of remediation? (Select two.)

 A. Boot to the Recovery Console in Windows XP and run fixmbr or fixboot to repair boot sector damage.

 B. Boot to the Windows Recovery Environment in Windows Vista/7 and run System Restore.

 C. Boot to a safe environment and run antivirus software.

 D. Remove a computer suspected of having a virus from the network, effectively quarantining the computer.

13. Which of the following are examples of grayware? (Select two.)

 A. Pop-up

 B. Spyware

 C. Trojan horse

 D. Virus

14. A user calls and complains that the technician who fixed his computer removed some software he used to listen to music on the Internet. A check of approved software does not include the LimeWire application, so what should the supervisor do?

 A. Applaud the technician for proper compliance.

 B. Educate the user about the legal issues involved with music downloads.

 C. Add the LimeWire application to the approved software list and make the technician apologize and reinstall the software.

 D. Check with the user's supervisor about adding LimeWire to the approved software list.

15. Cindy wants to put a policy in place at her company with regard to virus prevention or at least limitation. What policies would offer the best solution?

 A. Install antivirus software on every computer. Instruct users on how to run it.

 B. Install antivirus software on every computer. Set the software up to scan regularly.

 C. Install antivirus software on every computer. Set the software up to update the definitions and engine automatically. Set the software up to scan regularly.

 D. Install antivirus software on every computer. Set the software up to update the definitions and engine automatically. Set the software up to scan regularly. Educate the users about what sites and downloads to avoid.

■ Essay Quiz

1. Your boss is considering getting an Internet connection for the office so employees have access to e-mail, but she is concerned about hackers getting into the company server. What can you tell your boss about safeguards you will implement to keep the server safe?

2. A coworker complains that he is receiving a high amount of spam on his home computer through his personal e-mail account. What advice can you give him to alleviate his junk mail?

3. An intern in your IT department has asked for your help in understanding the differences between a virus, a worm, and a Trojan horse. What advice can you offer?

4. The boss's assistant has been asked to purchase a new coffee machine for the break room but is nervous about shopping online with the company credit card. What can you tell her about secure online purchases?

Lab Projects

• Lab Project 18.1

You have learned a little bit about the Local Security Policy in Windows. Fire up your Web browser and do a search for Local Security Policy. Make a list of at least five changes you might consider making to your personal computer by using the Local Security Policy tool. Be sure to include what the policy is, what it does, and where in the tool it can be configured.

• Lab Project 18.2

You know you must run antivirus and antispyware software on any computer connected to the Internet, and many companies will sell you good, bad, and indifferent software. Using the Internet, find free antivirus and free antispyware programs and make sure these are legitimate and reputable programs and not spyware masquerading as legitimate programs! What free antivirus did you find? What free antispyware did you find? How do you know these are reputable? Would you install these on your own personal computer? Why or why not?

Virtualization

chapter 19

On virtualization: "Once the world figures this stuff out, this is going to be a huge change to the corporate landscape."

—Jeff Birnbaum, Merrill Lynch

In this chapter, you will learn how to

- **Describe the concepts of virtualization**
- **Explain why PC and network administrators have widely adopted virtualization**
- **Describe how virtualization manifests in modern networks**

Virtualization takes your everyday notion of computing and turns it on its head. Left becomes right. Red becomes blue. Physical computers become virtual computers. It might sound complicated—properly configuring a real computer is hard enough—but once you see it in action, it makes perfect sense. In the simplest terms, *virtualization* is the process of using special software—a class of programs called *hypervisors* or *virtual machine managers*—to create a complete environment in which a guest operating system can function as though it were installed on its own computer. That guest environment is called a **virtual machine (VM)**. You learned about one very important virtual machine back in Chapter 10 called Windows XP Mode, which uses a program called Windows Virtual PC to run a virtual Windows XP operating system in Windows 7. Figure 19.1 shows another example: a system running Windows 7 using a program called VMware Workstation to host a virtual machine running Ubuntu Linux.

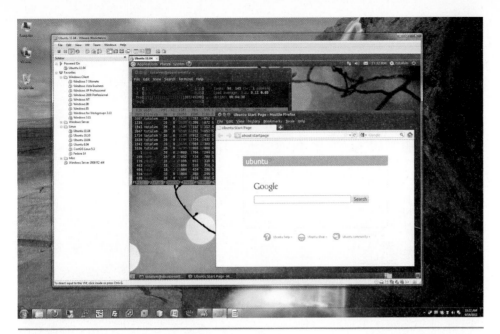

This chapter begins by explaining the ideas behind virtualization. The chapter then explores the motivating factors behind the widespread adoption of virtualization throughout the IT industry. The chapter concludes with an in-depth look at how modern networks implement virtualization. Some of the details presented here go beyond the CompTIA A+ 220-802 exam, but I include them to help you understand the scope and power of virtualization.

Historical/Conceptual

What Is Virtualization?

Ask 100 people what the term *virtual* means and you'll get a lot of different answers. Most people define *virtual* with words like "fake" or "pretend," but these terms only begin to describe it. Let's try to zero in on virtualization using a term that you've likely heard: *virtual reality*. For most of us, the idea of virtual reality starts with someone wearing headgear and gloves, as shown in Figure 19.2.

The headgear and the gloves work together to create a simulation of a world or environment that appears to be real, even though the person wearing them is located in a room that doesn't resemble the simulated space. Inside this virtual reality, you can see the world by turning your head, just as you do in the real world. Software works with the headset's inputs to emulate a physical world. At the same time, the gloves enable you to touch and move objects in the virtual world.

To make virtual reality effective, the hardware and software need to work together to create an environment convincing enough for a human

● **Figure 19.2** Virtual reality training (photo courtesy of NASA)

to work within it. Virtual reality doesn't have to be perfect—it has limitations—but it's pretty cool for teaching someone how to fly a plane or do a spacewalk, for example, without having to start with the real thing (see Figure 19.3).

Virtualization on a computer is virtually (sorry, can't pass up the pun) the same as virtual reality for humans. Just as virtual reality creates an environment that convinces humans they're in a real environment, virtualization convinces an operating system it's running on its own hardware.

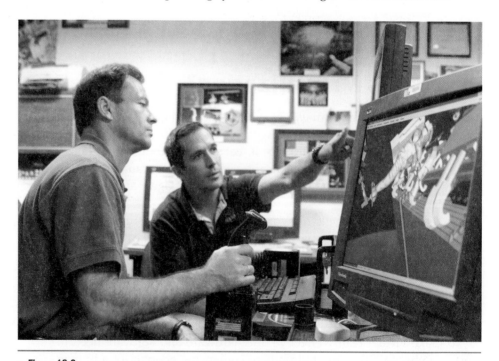

● **Figure 19.3** Using virtual reality to practice spacewalking (photo courtesy of NASA)

Meet the Hypervisor

A normal operating system uses programming called a *supervisor* to handle very low-level interaction among hardware and software, such as task scheduling, allotment of time and resources, and so on.

Because virtualization enables one machine—called the **host**—to run multiple operating systems simultaneously, full virtualization requires an extra layer of sophisticated programming to manage the vastly more complex interactions. One common method calls this extra programming a **hypervisor** or **virtual machine manager (VMM)**.

A hypervisor has to handle every input and output that the operating system would request of normal hardware. With a good hypervisor like VMware Workstation, you can easily add and remove virtual hard drives, virtual network cards, virtual RAM, and so on. Figure 19.4 shows the Hardware tab of the Virtual Machine Settings dialog box in VMware Workstation.

Virtualization even goes so far as to provide a virtualized BIOS and system setup utility for every virtual machine. Figure 19.5 shows VMware Workstation displaying the system setup utility, just like you'd see it on a regular computer.

• **Figure 19.4** Configuring virtual hardware in VMware Workstation

```
                    PhoenixBIOS Setup Utility
    Main    Advanced    Security    Boot    Exit

                                              Item Specific Help
   System Time:              [14:46:17]
   System Date:              [09/19/2011]
                                          <Tab>, <Shift-Tab>, or
   Legacy Diskette A:        [1.44/1.25 MB  3½"]  <Enter> selects field.
   Legacy Diskette B:        [Disabled]

 ▶ Primary Master           [None]
 ▶ Primary Slave            [None]
 ▶ Secondary Master         [VMware Virtual ID]
 ▶ Secondary Slave          [None]

 ▶ Keyboard Features

   System Memory:            640 KB
   Extended Memory:          785408 KB
   Boot-time Diagnostic Screen:  [Disabled]

 F1   Help    ↑↓  Select Item   -/+   Change Values    F9   Setup Defaults
 Esc  Exit    ↔   Select Menu   Enter Select ▶ Sub-Menu F10  Save and Exit
```

• **Figure 19.5** System setup utility in VMware Workstation

While the CompTIA A+ 220-802 exam objectives include emulation as a part of virtualization, the concepts are not the same. For the sake of completeness, however, know that emulating another platform (using a PC to run Sony PlayStation 2 games, for example) requires hardware several times more powerful than the platform being emulated.

Emulation Versus Virtualization

Virtualization takes the hardware of the host system and segments it into individual virtual machines. If you have an Intel system, a hypervisor creates a virtual machine that acts exactly like the host Intel system. It cannot act like any other type of computer. For example, you cannot create on an Intel system a virtual machine that acts like a Sony Play-Station 3. Hypervisors simply pass the code from the virtual machine to the actual CPU.

Emulation is very different from virtualization. An **emulator** is software or hardware that converts the commands to and from the host machine into an entirely different platform. Figure 19.6 shows a Super Nintendo Entertainment System emulator, Snes9X, running a game called *Donkey Kong Country* on a Windows system.

• **Figure 19.6** Super Nintendo emulator running on Windows

Sample Virtualization

You can perform virtualization in a number of ways; this chapter will show you several of them. Before I go any further, though, let's take the basic pieces you've learned about virtualization and put them together in one of its simpler forms. In this example, I'll use the popular VMware Workstation on a Windows 7 system and create a virtual machine running Ubuntu Linux.

Begin by obtaining a copy of VMware Workstation. This program isn't free, but VMware will give you a 30-day trial. Go to www.vmware.com to get a trial copy. A freshly installed copy of VMware Workstation looks like Figure 19.7.

Clicking New Virtual Machine prompts you for a Typical or Custom setup (see Figure 19.8). These settings are only for backward-compatibility with earlier versions of VMware, so just click Next.

The next dialog box is where the fun starts. Here, VMware Workstation asks for an operating system installation disc. Just because you're creating a virtual machine, don't think the operating system and applications aren't real. You need to install an operating system on that virtual machine. You do this just as you would on a machine without virtualization, using some form of optical media. Would you like to use Microsoft Windows in your virtual machine? No problem, but know that every virtual machine you create on which you install Windows requires a separate, legal copy of Windows.

Because virtual machines are so flexible on hardware, VMware Workstation enables you to use either the host machine's optical drive or an ISO file. I'm installing Ubuntu, so I downloaded the latest ISO image from the Ubuntu Web site (www.ubuntu.com), and as Figure 19.9 shows, I've pointed the dialog box to that image.

 Microsoft's Virtual PC is a free competitor to VMware Workstation. Virtual PC works well, but it lacks some of the more interesting features included in VMware Workstation.

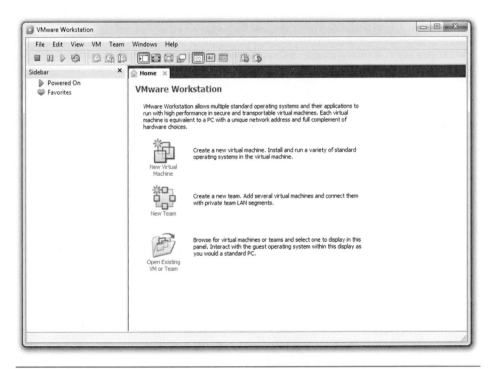

● **Figure 19.7** VMware Workstation

● **Figure 19.8** Selecting a Typical or Custom setup

● **Figure 19.9** Selecting the installation media

● **Figure 19.10** Setting the virtual drive size

● **Figure 19.11** Entering a VM name and location

Compared to some other virtualization programs, VMware Workstation is a powerful, easy-to-use program. If you look closely at Figure 19.9, you'll see that VMware reads the installation media (note the "Ubuntu 11.04 Detected"). Because VMware knows this operating system, it configures all of the virtual hardware settings automatically: amount of RAM, virtual hard drive size, and so on. You can change any of these settings, either before or after the virtual machine is created. Refer to Figure 19.4 to see these settings. Next, you need to accept the size of the virtual drive, as shown in Figure 19.10.

You also need to give the virtual machine a name (see Figure 19.11). By default, VMware Workstation uses a simple name. For this overview, accept

Use descriptive names for virtual machines. This will save you a lot of confusion when you have multiple VMs on a single hypervisor.

the default name: Ubuntu. This dialog box also lets you decide where you want to store the files that comprise the virtual machine. Note that VMware uses a folder in the user's Documents folder called Virtual Machines.

After you've gone through all the configuration screens, you can start using your virtual machine. You can start, stop, pause, add, or remove virtual hardware.

VMware is very convenient; it even configures the boot order in the virtual system setup to boot first from the installation media, making the Ubuntu installation automatic (see Figure 19.12).

After the virtual machine installs, you then treat the VM exactly as though it were a real machine. The only big difference is that VMware replaces CTRL-ALT-DELETE with CTRL-ALT-INSERT. Figure 19.13 shows VMware Workstation with the single VM installed but not running. A VM goes through a POST process just like any computer, as shown in Figure 19.14.

• **Figure 19.12** Ubuntu installing into the new virtual machine

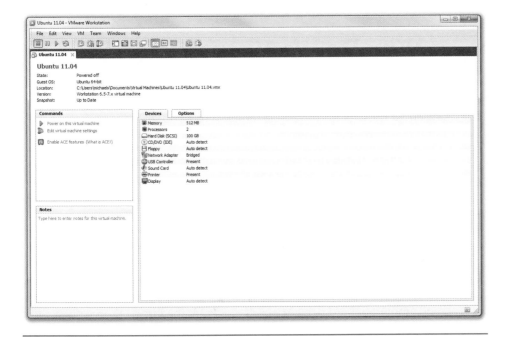

• **Figure 19.13** VMware Workstation with a single VM

• **Figure 19.14** POST in a virtual machine

If you wish, you can even access a complete virtual system setup utility by pressing the DELETE key just like on a real system.

Congratulations! You've just installed a *virtual desktop*. Virtual desktops were the first type of popular virtual machines seen in the PC world, championed by VMware and quickly copied by other virtualization programs.

There's a lot more to virtualization than just virtual desktops, however, but before I dive in too far, let's step back a moment and understand a very important question: Why do we virtualize?

Why Do We Virtualize?

Virtualization has taken the computing world by storm, but for those who have never seen virtualization, the big question has got to be: Why? Let's talk about the benefits of virtualization. While you read this section, keep in mind two important things:

- A single hypervisor on a single system will happily run as many virtual machines as its RAM, CPU, and drive space allow.

- A virtual machine that's shut down is little more than a file (or two) sitting on a hard drive.

Virtualized operating systems use the same security features as real operating systems. For each virtual machine user account, you'll need to keep track of user names, passwords, permissions, and so on, just like on a normal PC.

While you're reading about the benefits of virtualization, don't forget about the costs. To run one or more virtual machines, you'll need a powerful machine—fast processor, loads of RAM (this is usually the limiting factor in how many virtual machines you can run at the same time), and a good amount of hard drive space. If you want the virtual PC to connect to a network, your physical PC needs a NIC.

Power Saving

Before virtualization, each installed OS needed to be on a unique physical system. With virtualization, you can place multiple virtual PCs on a single physical system, reducing electrical power use substantially. Rather than one machine running Windows Server 2008 (or Server 2008 R2) and acting as a file server and DNS server, and a second machine running Linux for a DHCP server, for example, the same computer can handle both operating systems simultaneously. Expand this electricity savings over an enterprise network or on a data server farm and the savings—both in terms of dollars spent and electricity used—are tremendous.

Hardware Consolidation

Similar to power saving, why buy a high-end server, complete with multiple processors, RAID arrays, redundant power supplies, and so on, and only run a single server? With virtualization, you can easily beef up the RAM and run a number of servers on a single box.

System Recovery

Possibly the most popular reason for virtualizing is to keep uptime percentage as high as possible. Let's say you have a Web server installed on a single system. If that system goes down—due to hacking, malware, or so on—you need to restore the system from a backup, which may or may not be easily at hand. With virtualization, you merely need to shut down the virtual machine and reload an alternative copy of it.

Think of virtual machines like you would a word processing document. Virtual machines don't have a "File | Save" equivalent, but they do have something called a **snapshot** that enables you to save an extra copy of the virtual machine as it is exactly at the moment the snapshot is taken. Figure 19.15 shows VMware Workstation saving a snapshot.

Rebooting virtual machines is easy, but keep an eye on your physical machine. If your PC goes down, it brings all your virtual machines down with it! Be sure to back up mission-critical virtual machines to an external hard drive—remember that a virtual machine is just a file on your hard drive. You can always install the backed-up virtual machines on another physical machine if necessary.

System Duplication

Closely tied to system recovery, system duplication takes advantage of the fact that VMs are simply files, and like any file, they can be copied. Let's say you want to teach 20 students about Ubuntu Linux. Depending on the hypervisor you choose (VMware does this extremely well), you can simply install

• **Figure 19.15** Saving a snapshot

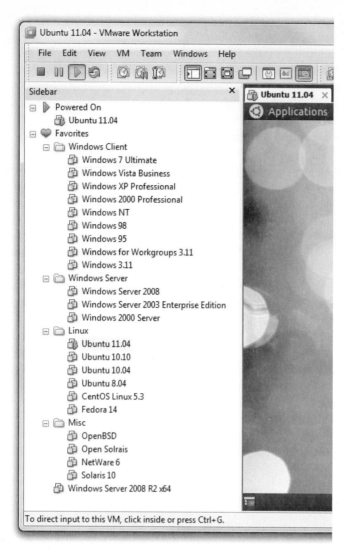

• Figure 19.16 Lots of VMs used for research

The system shown in Figure 19.16 could obviously never run all those VMs at the same time.

For all you abbreviation lovers, I have some good news and some bad news about "ESX." Officially, it means nothing. Unofficially, it stands for "Elastic Sky," which is probably why it officially means nothing.

a hypervisor on 20 machines and copy a single virtual machine to all the computers. Equally, if you have a virtualized Web server and need to add another Web server (assuming your physical box has the hardware to support it), why not just make a copy of the server and fire it up as well?

Research

Here's a great example that happens in my own company. I sell my popular Total Tester test banks: practice questions for you to test your skills on a broad number of certification topics. As with any distributed program, I tend to get a few support calls. Running a problem through the same OS, even down to the service pack, helps me solve the problem. In the days before virtualization, I commonly had seven to ten PCs, using dual-boot, each keeping copies of a particular Windows version. Today, a single hypervisor enables me to support a huge number of Windows versions on a single machine (see Figure 19.16).

Clearly there are a number of good reasons to virtualize some of the computers in a network. Let's look at implementation now.

■ Virtualization in Modern Networks

You've already seen virtualization in action with the example shown using VMware Workstation earlier in this chapter. Many networks use a few virtual machines to augment and refine a traditional network closet. VMware Workstation is how I first performed virtualization on PCs, but the technology and power have grown dramatically over the past few years.

VMware Workstation requires an underlying operating system (such as Windows), so it functions essentially like a very powerful desktop application. What if you could remove the OS altogether and create a bare-metal implementation of virtualization?

VMware introduced ESX in 2001 to accomplish this goal. ESX is a hypervisor that's powerful enough to replace the host operating system on a physical box, turning the physical machine into a machine that does nothing but support virtual machines; no Windows, no Ubuntu—just ESX.

ESX by itself isn't much to look at; it's a tiny operating system/hypervisor that's usually installed on something other than a hard drive. Figure 19.17 shows how I loaded my copy of ESX: via a small USB thumb drive. Power up the server; the server loads ESX off the thumb drive; and in short order, a very rudimentary interface appears where I can input

essential information, such as a master password and a static IP address.

Don't let ESX's small size fool you. It's small because it only has one job: to host virtual machines. ESX is an extremely powerful operating system/hypervisor.

Notice the built-in USB port shown in Figure 19.17. The popularity of hypervisors on dedicated servers makes these ports extremely common in a serious server box like the Dell system shown.

Powerful hypervisors like ESX are rarely administered directly at the box. Instead you use tools such as VMware's vSphere Client, so you can create, configure, and maintain virtual machines on the hypervisor server from the comfort of a client computer running this program. Once the VM is up and running, you can close the vSphere client, but the VM will continue to run happily on the server. For example, let's say you create a VM and install a Web server on that VM. As long as everything is running well on the Web server, you will find yourself using the vSphere client only to check on the Web server for occasional maintenance and administration.

• **Figure 19.17** USB drive on server system

So you now really have two different ways to virtualize: using virtual machine managers like VMware's Workstation to manage virtual desktops, and using powerful hypervisors like ESX to manage virtual servers. Granted, you could run a server like a Web browser in VMware Workstation, and you also could run a copy of Windows 7 Ultimate from an ESX system. Nothing is wrong with doing either of these.

Thus far, this chapter sounds like an advertisement for VMware. VMware really brought virtualization to the PC world and still holds a strong presence, but there are a number of alternatives to VMware products. Let's see what else is available.

Virtual Machine Managers

When it comes to the more basic virtual machine managers, you have a huge number of choices. The one you use is going to be determined by features and prices.

VMware Workstation

The granddaddy and front leader for virtualization, VMware Workstation, comes in both Windows and Linux versions. VMware Workstation runs virtually (pun!) on any operating system you'll ever need and is incredibly stable and proven. Too bad it's not free.

One of the more interesting features of VMware Workstation is VMTools. VMTools adds useful features such as copy/cut and paste between the virtual desktop and the real desktop.

A free version of ESX is available. Called ESXi, it lacks a number of ESX's features but is still quite powerful.

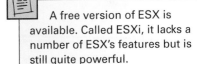

> **Tech Tip**
>
> **VMM Versus Hypervisor**
> *Some writers will use the term* virtual machine manager *to describe virtual machine software that runs on top of a host operating system. They'll use the term* hypervisor *to describe only software that does not need a host operating system. Using this terminology, VMware Workstation is a virtual machine manager and ESX is a hypervisor.*
>
> *Other writers call both the hosted and bare-metal—or native—virtualization software products* hypervisors, *but make a distinction in other descriptive words (such as* hosted *or* native*).*

Try This!

Creating a Virtual Machine

It's difficult to understand how virtual machines work (and how amazing they are) until you've made one yourself. VMware sells many different virtualization products, most of which are too powerful and too expensive for our experimentation purposes. Fortunately, they also offer VMware Player, a basic virtual machine manager that's easy enough for anyone to use, so Try This!

Go to VMware's Web site (www.vmware.com) and search for VMware Player. Follow the Download link and choose the version of VMware Player that matches your OS. (You'll need to sign up for an account before you can download the application.)

While that's downloading, go to the Ubuntu Linux Web site (www .ubuntu.com) and follow the links to download the latest version of Ubuntu. Don't use the Windows installer listed on the Ubuntu Download Web page. Instead, download the installation image using the Start download button.

When the downloads have finished, run the VMware Player executable file. Follow the instructions as you would with any other application. When finished, open VMware Player. Accept the End User License Agreement (EULA), then click on Create a New Virtual Machine.

Use the Easy Install method. VMware Player will build the virtual machine and install the Ubuntu operating system at the same time. You'll need to find where you saved the Ubuntu installation image. Use the default settings provided by the wizard, and create a user name and password when prompted.

After the virtual machine has been installed, you can launch it from the main VMware Player screen by selecting it from the list of machines and clicking *Play Virtual Machine*. Congratulations! You've just created a virtual machine on your PC.

Virtual PC

Microsoft has offered a few different virtual machine managers over the years, with the current mainstream product being Windows Virtual PC (see Figure 19.18). Windows Virtual PC is free, but has some serious limitations. First, it only works on Windows 7 Professional, Ultimate, and Enterprise. Second, it only officially supports Windows VMs, although a few intrepid souls have managed to get Linux working.

Remember Windows XP Mode from Chapter 10? It uses Virtual PC and a copy of Windows XP to create a virtual machine on your PC!

Cross Check

Compatibility

You learned about Windows XP Mode and other compatibility modes back in Chapter 10. Remember that Windows XP Mode is really just a virtual OS running inside Microsoft's Virtual PC. What other compatibility features does Windows 7 include? Which editions of Windows 7 include Windows XP Mode? Does Windows Vista include Windows XP Mode?

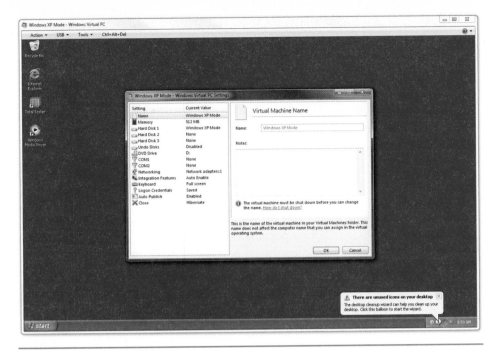

• **Figure 19.18** Windows Virtual PC

Parallels

Parallels is the most popular virtualization manager for Mac OS X (see Figure 19.19), although VMware Fusion is a close second. Parallels supports all popular operating systems, and even has a fair degree of 3-D graphics support; more so than even the mighty VMware. Parallels also offers Windows and Linux versions.

KVM

Of course, the open source world has its players too. While picking a single product to represent the Linux/Unix world is hard, no one who knows virtualization would disagree that KVM from Red Hat is a dominant player. Unlike the other virtual machine managers discussed, KVM also supports a few non-x86 processors.

Don't think for a moment that this list is complete! There are lots of other virtual machine options for your desktop, especially if your host machine runs Linux. The most fun you'll have learning about

• **Figure 19.19** Parallels for Mac

virtualization is the playtime involved experimenting with the many options available.

Hypervisors

While you have lots of choices when it comes to virtual machine managers, your choices for real embedded hypervisors are limited to the two biggies: VMware's ESX and Microsoft's HyperV. There are others, such as Oracle's VM Server, but nothing has the market share of ESX or HyperV.

ESX

I've already discussed a few aspects of ESX, so instead I'll delve into the features that make ESX so popular. When it comes to real server virtualization, VMware truly leads the pack with a host of innovations (some of which are add-on products) that make ESX almost unstoppable. Here are a few examples:

- **Interface with large storage** ESX virtual machines easily integrate with network attached storage (NAS) and storage area networks (SANs) to handle massive data storage.

- **Transparent fault tolerance** ESX can monitor and automatically recover failed VMs with little or no input.

- **Transparent server transfer** You can move a *running* VM from one machine to another. How cool is that?

- **High virtual CPUs** Most hypervisors support a limited number of virtual CPUs, usually two at most. ESX can support up to 32 CPUs, depending on the vSphere product version you purchase to support it.

HyperV

Although HyperV can't stand toe-to-toe with ESX, it has a few aces up its sleeve that give it some intrigue. First, it's free. This is important in that ESX, with only a few extra add-ons, can cost thousands of dollars. Second, it comes as a stand-alone product or as part of Windows Server 2008 and even on some versions of Windows 7, making it easy for those who like to play to access it. Third, its simplicity makes it easier to learn for those new to using hypervisors. Watch HyperV. If Microsoft does one thing well, it's taking market share away from arguably better, more powerful competitors, while slowly making its product better.

Chapter Summary

After reading this chapter and completing the exercises, you should understand the following about virtualization.

Describe the concepts of virtualization

- Virtual reality creates a simulation of a world or environment that appears to be real, even though the person wearing the headgear and gloves is located in a room that doesn't resemble the simulated space. Virtual computing follows a similar concept.

- In virtual computing, software called a hypervisor or virtual machine manager creates one or more environments, called virtual machines (VMs), on a single machine. You can install an OS into each VM and thus run several OSs simultaneously on a single machine.

- The hypervisor handles the communication between the OSs installed and the hardware. The hypervisor can easily add and remove hard drives, memory space, networking capabilities, and more.

- Emulation differs from virtualization: emulation software translates commands from an application into machine language the host computer can understand, whereas virtualization creates an environment that is native to the application—an operating system, in this case—requiring no translation.

Explain why PC and network administrators have widely adopted virtualization

- Going virtual enables companies to combine multiple servers onto fewer machines than in traditional computing. This offers tremendous savings in hardware purchases, electricity use, and the space used for computing.

- Because a VM is only a single file or two, a hacked or corrupted server can rapidly be replaced with a snapshot (a backup) taken of the properly working server. This provides better uptime than in a traditional server setup. Likewise, the minimal file numbers make it easy to duplicate a VM.

- The capability to run many operating systems on a single physical machine makes multiplatform testing and research much easier and less costly than with traditional setups.

Describe how virtualization manifests in modern networks

- The simplest way virtualization manifests in networks is through one or more VMs performing chores that would have taken multiple physical boxes previously. VMware Workstation is the most common VM implementation tool in these sorts of networks.

- More aggressive network needs can use bare-metal virtualization software that removes the need for an operating system on the VM-supporting machine. These hypervisors, such as VMware ESX, take up minuscule space. You manage them remotely through client software, rather than at the server box.

- The more popular virtual machine managers include the aforementioned VMware Workstation, plus Microsoft Virtual PC, Parallels for OS X, and KVM on the Linux side. The more popular native hypervisors include ESX and HyperV.

Key Terms

emulator *(680)*

host *(679)*

hypervisor *(679)*

snapshot *(685)*

virtual machine (VM) *(676)*

virtual machine manager (VMM) *(679)*

Key Term Quiz

Use the Key Terms list to complete the sentences that follow. Not all the terms will be used.

1. A(n) _____ is a complete environment for a guest operating system to function as though that operating system were installed on its own computer.

2. A machine that runs multiple operating systems simultaneously is called a(n) _____.

3. A bare-metal machine that supports virtualization software without needing a host operating system is commonly called a(n) _____.

4. A(n) _____ can convert the commands to and from a host machine to an entirely different platform.

5. You can create a(n) _____ as a backup for a virtual machine.

Multiple-Choice Quiz

1. Tom is installing a Windows 7 Ultimate virtual machine onto a copy of VMware Workstation. Which of the following does he need?

 A. A valid copy of Windows 7 Ultimate installation media

 B. The IP address for the virtual machine host

 C. A disk image of another computer's installed Windows 7 Ultimate

 D. A valid ESX key

2. The number of running virtual machines on a single host is limited by what factor?

 A. Physical RAM

 B. Virtual RAM

 C. Physical NICs

 D. Virtual NICs

3. When a virtual machine is not running, how is it stored?

 A. Firmware

 B. RAM drive

 C. Optical disc

 D. Files

4. VMware Workstation replaces CTRL-ALT-DELETE with which of the following?

 A. A mouse click

 B. CTRL-ALT-INSERT

 C. CTRL-ALT-TAB

 D. CTRL-ALT-SHIFT

5. Which of the following would *not* run on VMware Workstation for Windows?

 A. Windows XP

 B. Sony PlayStation 2

 C. Ubuntu Linux

 D. Windows Vista

6. Which of the following virtualization programs works well with Mac OS X? (Select the best answer.)

 A. ESX

 B. KVM

 C. Parallels

 D. Virtual PC

7. The boss flies into your office yelling that the virtualized Web server has been hacked and now displays only purple dinosaurs. Which of the following would be the fastest way to fix the problem?

 A. Restore from backup

 B. Run System Restore

 C. Reinstall Windows

 D. Load an earlier snapshot

8. Which of the following is *not* a good reason for virtualization?

 A. Power saving

 B. Hardware consolidation

 C. System recovery

 D. Reduced hardware costs

9. Powerful hypervisors like ESX are often booted from _____.

 A. Floppy diskettes

 B. USB thumb drives

 C. Firmware

 D. Windows

10. Which players dominate the entire hypervisor market? (Select two.)

 A. ESX

 B. HyperV

 C. Parallels

 D. KVM

■ Essay Quiz

1. A company has three discrete servers: a file server running Linux, a contact and e-mail server running Windows Server, and a DNS and DHCP server running an earlier version of Windows Server. Make a case for or against going virtual with this setup.

2. Write a comparative essay on VMware Workstation and ESX. What are the strengths of each type of virtualization setup? When would you use ESX over VMware Workstation?

Lab Projects

• Lab Project 19.1

Acquire a copy of VMware Workstation or another virtualization program and create some virtual machines. If you can add the VM host to a working network, then attempt to access the different VMs running and access other computers from any of the VMs. This should be a fun lab. Here are links to VM software:

www.vmware.com/products/workstation/overview.html

www.virtualbox.org/wiki/Downloads

www.microsoft.com/windows/virtual-pc/

• Lab Project 19.2

Analyze the current server setup at your school or office. Does it use virtualization? If so, which programs does it use for which purposes? If not, discuss how virtualization could be implemented to make the network more efficient.

The Complete PC Tech

"As no man is born an artist, so no man is born an angler."

—IZAAK WALTON, *THE COMPLEAT ANGLER* (1653)

In this chapter, you will learn how to

- **Describe how computers work**
- **Implement a troubleshooting methodology**
- **Describe a technician's toolkit**

When a mission-critical computer goes down, regardless of the industry, people get upset. Workers can't work, so they feel guilty. Employers can't get product out on time, so they feel anxious. Supervisors blame employees for fouling things up, or at least the employees fear such blame, even if they did not break the machine.

Into this charged atmosphere comes the tech, ready to fix the computer and move on to the next challenge. Accomplishing this task, though, requires three things: First, a good tech must know the broken machine inside and out—how it's *supposed* to work when working properly. Second, the tech has to calm the workers and supervisors, and get answers to questions to gain relevant information about the problem. Third, the tech must troubleshoot the problem and fix the machine.

This chapter starts with an overview of how computers work and then describes a proven troubleshooting methodology to help you figure out the source of problems and point you to the fix quickly. The chapter wraps up by discussing the tools every tech should have.

How Computers Work

You've spent a lot of time going through this book, reading about technologies and components in great detail. Each chapter contained troubleshooting information and methodologies for the components explained in that chapter. In Chapter 3, you learned how to troubleshoot just about every hardware issue you might encounter with a PC, from CPUs to power supplies. In Chapter 4, you dove into hard drives in gory detail. With each chapter, you added more and more information about the pieces that make up the personal computer today.

In this chapter, I want you to distill that knowledge, to think about the computer as a coherent machine. Each of the computer's components works together with all the other components to enable people to produce some amazing things.

To master the art of troubleshooting as a PC tech, you need to approach a technical problem and answer one question: "What can be causing this problem?" Because every process involves multiple components, you must understand the interconnectedness of those components. If Jane can't get the printer to print her document, for example, what could the problem be? Connectivity? Drivers? Paper jam? Slow network connection? Frozen application? Solar flares? Let's look at the process.

It's important to think of PCs in terms of the computing process: input, processing, output, and storage. Let's take a moment to go over the computing process, and you'll see how you can use it to help you fix computers.

When you run a program, your computer goes through three of the four stages of the **computing process**: input, processing, and output (see Figure 20.1). Input requires specific devices, such as the keyboard and mouse, which enable you to tell the computer to do something, such as open a program or type a word. The operating system (OS) provides an interface and tools so that the microprocessor and other chips can process your request. The image on the monitor or sound from the speakers effectively tells you that the computer has interpreted your command and spit out the result. The fourth stage, storage, comes into play when you want to save a document and when you first open programs and other files.

Making this process work, though, requires the complex interaction of many components, including multiple pieces of hardware and layers

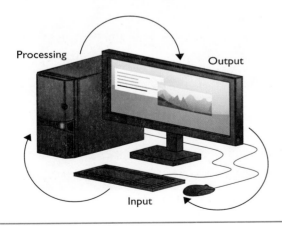

• **Figure 20.1** Input, processing, and output

Second Life is a massively multiplayer online role-playing game (MMORPG) that offers a unique twist on the genre. You can create just about anything you can imagine, as far as your time and talent can take you. *Second Life* has a functioning economy that spills out into the real world, meaning you can buy and sell things within the game and turn that into real U.S. dollars, although the more common scenario is to spend real money to get virtual possessions.

of software. As a tech, you need to understand all the components and how they work together so that when something doesn't work right, you can track down the source and fix it. A look at a modern program reveals that even a seemingly simple action or change on the screen requires many things to happen within the computer.

Games such as *Second Life* (see Figure 20.2) are huge, taking up multiple gigabytes of space on an Internet server. They simply won't fit into the RAM in most computers, so developers have figured out ways to minimize RAM usage.

In *Second Life*, for example, you move through the online world in a series of more or less seamlessly connected areas. Crossing a bridge from one island to another triggers the game to quickly update the information you're about to see on the new island, so you won't be out of the action and the illusion of being in the game world remains intact. Here's what happens when you press the w key on your keyboard and your character steps across the invisible zone line.

The keyboard controller reads the grid of your keyboard and, on discovering your input, sends the information to the CPU through the wires of the motherboard (see Figure 20.3). The CPU understands the keyboard controller because of a small program that was loaded into RAM from the ROM BIOS on the motherboard when the PC booted up.

The CPU and the application determine what should happen in the game, and on discovering that your character is about to cross the zone line, they trigger a whole series of actions. The application sends the signal to the OS that it needs a specific area loaded into RAM. The OS sends a signal to the CPU that it needs data stored on the hard drive plus information stored

• **Figure 20.2** The Second Life virtual world

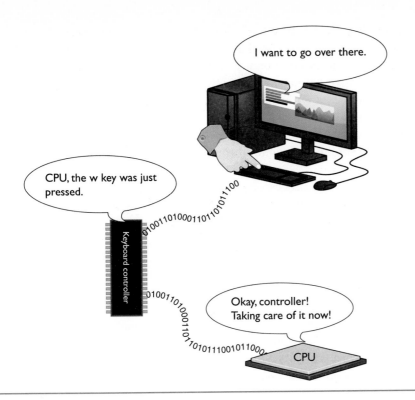

• **Figure 20.3** Keyboard to CPU

on the *Second Life* servers. The CPU then sends the commands to the hard drive controller for it to grab the proper stored data and send it to RAM, while at the same time sending a command to the NIC to download the updated information (see Figure 20.4).

• **Figure 20.4** CPU to hard drive and NIC

The hard drive controller tells the hard drive to cough up the data—megabytes worth—and then sends that data through the motherboard to the memory controller, which puts it into RAM and communicates with the CPU when it's finished. The network card and network operating system communicate with the *Second Life* servers and download the necessary updated information. The CPU then uses the application and OS to process the new data, sending video data to the video card and sound data to the sound card, again through the wires on the motherboard (see Figure 20.5).

The video card processor puts the incoming data into its RAM, processes the data, and then sends out commands to the monitor to update the screen. The sound card processor likewise processes the data and sends out commands to the speakers to play a new sound (see Figure 20.6).

For all of this to work, the PC has to have electricity, so the direct current (DC) provided by the power supply and the alternating current (AC) provided to the power supply must both be the proper voltage and amperage.

Finally, because *Second Life* is a network application, the OS has to send information through the NIC and onto the Internet to update everyone else's computer. That way, the other characters in the game world see you move forward a step (see Figure 20.7).

What do you see or hear with all these electrons zipping all over the place? Out of a seemingly blank vista (see Figure 20.8), a castle begins to appear, building itself piece by piece as your computer processes the new information and updates the video screen. You hear music begin to play from your speakers. Within a few seconds, with the data describing the new island fully downloaded and processed, the world on your monitor looks very different (see Figure 20.9). That's when all goes well. Many megabytes of data have flowed from your hard drive and across the Internet, been processed by multiple processors, and been sent to the monitor and the speakers.

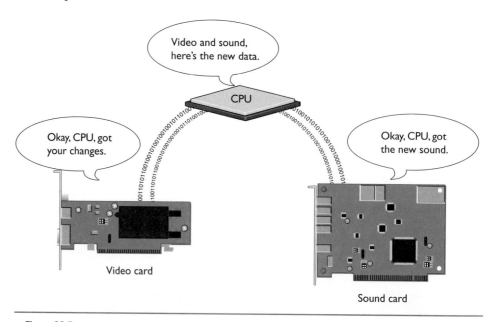

• **Figure 20.5**　CPU to video card and sound card

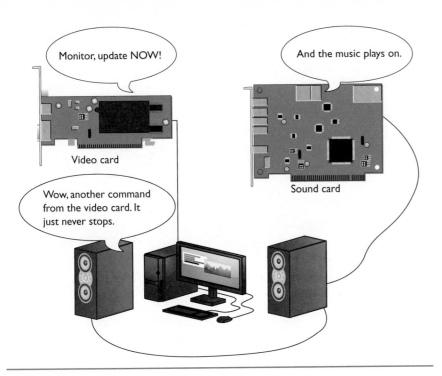

• **Figure 20.6** Updating the screen and speakers

To keep the action continuous and unbroken, *Second Life*, like many current online games, uses a process of continuous or **stream loading**: your computer constantly downloads updated information and data from the *Second Life* servers, so the world you see changes with every step you take. When done right, stream loading can do some amazing things. In the GameCube game *The Legend of Zelda: Wind Waker*, for example, the game anticipates where you will go next and loads that new area into RAM

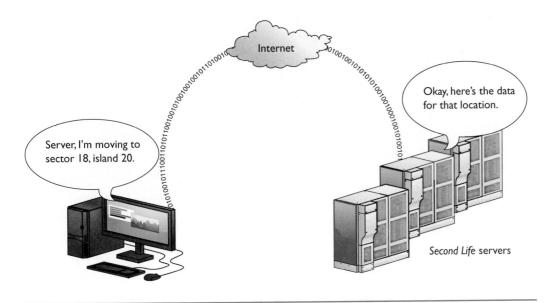

• **Figure 20.7** PC to Second Life servers

• **Figure 20.8** New area loading

• **Figure 20.9** Castle completed

Try This!

Analyze Your Apps

What applications do you use on your computer? What applications do your clients or potential clients use? Analyzing them in terms of the computing process can help elevate your troubleshooting game by a huge factor. Take for example Microsoft Excel, a program designed to let you take numbers and turn them into charts, among other things. When you sit down to work in Excel, you load it from the hard drive into memory and then input information via the keyboard and format things with the mouse. Every click requires the CPU to analyze and update RAM and the video card information.

before you take the step. You can be in one area and use a telescope to zoom in on another fully developed area (see Figure 20.10), making the experience amazingly seamless, just like real life.

Anytime a computer has a problem that's not immediately and clearly obvious (such as not powering up due to not having a power cord plugged in), you should use the computing process to help you zero in on the problem. But the computing process only defines the pieces and their interaction; good troubleshooting requires more than just rummaging around to find the problem. You need to combine the computing process with a troubleshooting theory to get the job done.

• **Figure 20.10** The Legend of Zelda: Wind Waker zoomed

Troubleshooting Theory

Troubleshooting theory is nothing more than a set of mental steps you use along with the computing process to diagnose and fix a computer. Troubleshooting theory includes talking to users to determine how and when the problem took place, determining a cause, testing, verification, and documentation. Techs use a number of good troubleshooting theories. Luckily for those taking the CompTIA A+ 220-802 certification exam, CompTIA clearly defines their vision of troubleshooting theory:

4.1 Given a scenario, explain the troubleshooting theory

- Identify the problem

 - Question the user and identify user changes to computer and perform backups before making changes

- Establish a theory of probable cause (question the obvious)

- Test the theory to determine cause

 - Once theory is confirmed, determine next steps to resolve problem

 - If theory is not confirmed, re-establish new theory or escalate

- Establish a plan of action to resolve the problem and implement the solution
- Verify full system functionality and if applicable implement preventative measures
- Document findings, actions and outcomes

Identify the Problem

There's a reason you're standing in front of a computer to repair it: something happened that the user of the computer has identified as "not good" and that's why you're here. First, you need to **identify the problem** by talking to the user. Get the user to show you what's not good. Is it an error code? Is something not accessible? Is a device not responding? Then ask the user that classic tech question (remember your communication skills here!): "Has anything recently changed on the computer that might have made this problem appear?" What you're really saying is: "Have you jacked with the computer? Did you install some evil program? Did you shove in a USB drive so hard you broke the connection?" Of course, you never say these things; simply ask nicely without accusing so the user can help you fix the problem (see Figure 20.11).

In most troubleshooting situations, it's important to back up critical files before making changes to a system. To some extent, this is a matter of proper ongoing maintenance, but if some important bit of data disappears and you don't have a backup, you know who the user will blame, don't you?

If you run into a partially functional system where you might have to reinstall the OS but can access the hard drive, you should definitely back up essential data, such as e-mail, browser favorites, important documents, and any data not stored on a regularly backed-up server. Because you can boot to a copy of Windows and go to the Recovery Console or System Recovery Options, you should never lose essential data, barring full-blown hard drive death.

 The CompTIA A+ 220-802 exam assumes that all techs should back up systems *every time* before working on them, even though that's not how it works in the real world.

Dead hard drives retain their data, so you can recover it—if you're willing to pay a lot of money. Having a good backup in place makes a lot more economic sense!

• **Figure 20.11** Tech asking nicely

Establish a Theory of Probable Cause (Question the Obvious)

Now it's time to analyze the issue and come up with a theory as to what is wrong, a **theory of probable cause**. Personally, I prefer the word "guess" at this point because very few errors are so obvious that you'll know what to do. Fall back on your knowledge of the computing process to localize the issue based on the symptoms. Keep your guesses...err...theories...simple. One of the great problems for techs is their desire to overlook the obvious problems in their desire to dig into the system (see Figure 20.12).

Outside the Case

Take a moment to look for clues before you open up the case. Most importantly, use all your senses in the process.

What do you see? Is a connector mangled or a plastic part clearly damaged? Even if that connector or part works fine, the physical abuse could provide extra information. If the user can't connect to a network, check the cable. Was something rolled over it that could have broken the thin internal wires? Is that a jelly smear near the jammed optical drive door? (No pun intended, really!) A visual examination of the external computer is important.

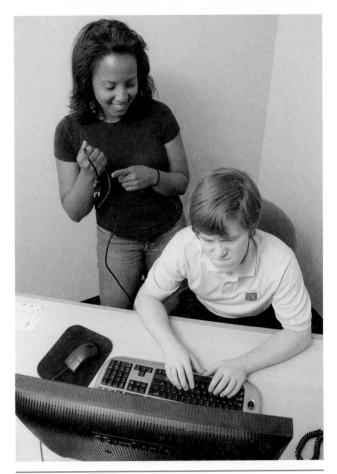

• Figure 20.12 Ford the Tech misses the obvious.

When you put your hand on the system unit, does it feel hot? Can you feel or hear the vibrations of the fans? If not, that would be a clue to an overheating or overheated computer. Modern computers can run when overly hot, but generally run very sluggishly. If you run through basic malware fixes and a computer still runs poorly, think about excessive heat as a potential problem.

If you spend a moment listening to the PC, you might get some clues to problem sources. A properly running hard drive (as you'll recall from Chapter 4) doesn't make a lot of sound, just a regular hum from the spinning platters. If you hear clicking or grinding sounds from a drive, that's a very bad sign and a very important clue! Excessive thrashing or disk access can likewise lead to some potential problem areas, like insufficient RAM or a badly fragmented drive.

Finally, don't forget your nose. If you smell the unmistakable odor of ozone, you know that's the smell electronic components give off when they cook or are simply running much too hot.

Inside the Case

Use all your senses when you go inside the system unit as well. Do you see any physical damage? Check the motherboard capacitors if you have a dead PC. Properly working capacitors should be nice and (usually) blue; they definitely shouldn't look like partly melted batteries or be bulging at the seams. Fans should be spinning. The power supply shouldn't be blistering

hot. You should be able to localize sounds better with the case off. And any smell of cooking components will definitely be stronger with the case off.

As you do your inspection, both outside and inside the case, don't jump to conclusions too quickly. When you see a problem that looks obvious, stop and give yourself an "Are you sure?" moment. Consider the possibility that a problem you've seen 50 times before might *not* be the problem this time. Of course, it probably *is* the same problem, but that quick rethink might save you trouble later.

Test the Theory to Determine Cause

Okay, so you've decided on a theory that makes sense. It's time to **test the theory** to see if it fixes the problem. The biggest challenge to fixing a computer is that the theory and the fix pretty much prove themselves at the same time. Let's go back to the situation where the power plug isn't plugged into the wall outlet. You observe that nothing happens when the PC power button is pressed. You check the back of the power supply and see that the power cable is plugged in. You then look at the wall outlet…not plugged in! So you quickly plug it in and *tada!* It works! You're a hero! In this simple case, your theory and your test are done in virtually the same move (see Figure 20.13).

Of course, most problems aren't that easy. In many cases, testing your theory does nothing more than verify that something is broken. Let's say you install an update for your video driver. You reboot, log on to Windows, and suddenly the screen freaks out. Ah, a bad video driver, right? To test, you reboot the computer and press F8 to get the boot options menu. You select VGA Mode (Windows XP) or Low Resolution Mode (Windows Vista/7) and reboot. Now the computer boots up just fine. You know what the problem is, but how do you fix it? Roll back the video driver? Reinstall an older driver? Try downloading another copy of the new driver and installing the video driver again? Any of these solutions may be the right one. Choose one and go for it (see Figure 20.14).

Uh oh, your first guess was wrong: the video is still messed up. No worries, just try another one of your theories. In most cases you'll just pick another theory and try again. But sometimes there's a point where the problem is bigger than you. It might be a problem on a server that you're not authorized to configure. It might be a problem with a user account, and techs in your company aren't allowed to change user accounts. It might be a problem with an in-house program and you don't have the skills to fix it. In these cases, you must **escalate** the problem.

Escalation is the process your company (or sometimes just you) goes through when you—the person assigned to repair a problem—are not able to get the job done. It's okay to escalate a problem because no one can fix

every problem. All companies should have some form of escalation policy. It might mean calling your boss. It might mean filling out and sending some in-house form to another department. Escalation is sometimes a more casual process. You might want to start researching the problem online; you might want to refer to in-house documentation to see if this problem has appeared in the past. (See "Document Findings, Actions, and Outcomes" later in this chapter.) You may want to call a coworker to come check it out (see Figure 20.15).

Verify and Prevent

Fantastic! Through either your careful work or escalation, you've solved the problem, or so you think. Remember two items here. First, even though *you* think the problem is fixed, the user/customer might not think it's fixed. Second, try to do something to prevent the problem from happening again in the future, if possible.

Verify Full System Functionality

You need to verify full system functionality to make sure the user is happy. Let's say a user can't print. You determine that the printer spool is stalled due to a locked-up laser printer. You reset the printer and the jobs all start printing. Job done, right? Well, during your theory testing, you switched the default printer to another laser printer on the third floor. The user doesn't know how to set the default printer back to the one you just fixed.

The best way to verify full system functionality is to have the user do whatever she needs to do on the repaired system for a few minutes while you watch. Any minor errors (such as incorrect default printers) will quickly become apparent, and you might learn some interesting aspects of how the user does her job. Knowing what your users do is critical for good techs to help them do their jobs better (see Figure 20.16).

If Applicable, Implement Preventive Measures

A very smart tech once told me, "A truly good support tech's work goal should be to never have to get out of his chair." That's a pretty tall order, but it makes sense to me. Do whatever you can to prevent this problem from repeating. For some problems, there are obvious actions to take, such as making sure anti-malware is installed so a computer doesn't get infected again. Sometimes there's no action to take at all: nothing can prevent

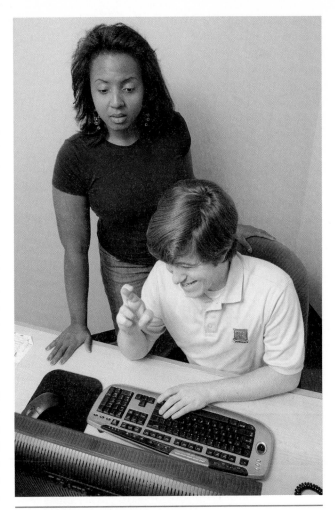

• **Figure 20.14** Ford the Tech takes a chance!

• **Figure 20.15** Ford the Tech asks for help from Scott.

• Figure 20.16 Ford the Tech sticks around and watches.

a hard drive that decides to die. But you can take one more critical action in almost every case: education. Take advantage of the time with the user to informally train him about the problem. Show him the dangers of malware or tell him that sometimes hard drives just die. The more your users know, the less time you'll spend out of your chair.

Document Findings, Actions, and Outcomes

Based on his famous quote, "Those who cannot remember the past are condemned to repeat it," I think the philosopher George Santayana would have made a great PC technician. As a tech, the last step of every troubleshooting job should be to **document** your findings, actions, and results. This documentation might be highly formalized in some organizations, or it might just be a few notes you jot down for your own use, but you must document! What was the problem? What did you do to fix it? What worked? What didn't? The best guide to use for documentation is: "What would I have liked to have known about this problem before I walked up to it?" Good documentation is the strongest sign of a good PC tech (see Figure 20.17).

Documenting problems helps you track the troubleshooting history of a machine over time, enabling you to make longer-term determinations about retiring it or changing out more parts. If you and fellow techs fix a specific problem with Mary's machine several times, for example, you might decide to swap out her whole system rather than fix it a fourth time.

Documenting helps fellow techs if they have to follow up on a task you didn't finish or troubleshoot a machine you've worked on previously. The reverse is also true. If you get a call about Frank's computer, for example, and check the records to find other service calls on his computer, you might find that the fix for a particular problem is already documented. This is especially true for user-generated problems. Having documentation of what you did also means you don't have to rely on your memory when your coworker asks what you did to fix the weird problem with Jane's computer a year ago!

Documenting also comes into play when you or a user has an accident onsite. If your colleague Joe drops a monitor on his foot and breaks both the monitor and his foot, for example, you need to fill out an *incident report*, just as you would with any kind of accident: electrical, chemical, or physical. An **incident report** should detail what happened and where it happened. This helps your supervisors take the appropriate actions quickly and efficiently.

• Figure 20.17 Ford documents a successful fix.

■ Tech Toolkit

Every tech should learn the basic parts of a **tech toolkit**—a Phillips-head screwdriver and a few other useful tools, such as a Torx wrench and a pair of tweezers. Any good tech makes a point to carry around at least these tools (see Figure 20.18). Over time, you'll add more tools as your experience grows. But your toolkit won't stop at Phillips screwdrivers and Torx wrenches. You should include two other types of tools in your tech toolkit: utilities and field replaceable units (FRUs).

• **Figure 20.18** Typical technician toolkit

Utilities

Windows comes with plenty of handy utilities, but there are times when you need to use stronger tools than these. The PC industry has thousands of third-party utilities that techs might use to diagnose and repair PCs. Sadly, there is no single selection of tools I can tell you to get: the tools one experienced tech uses differ from the tools I use based on experience, skills, and job functions. That doesn't mean you haven't been hearing my opinions! Throughout this book you've seen quite a few third-party utilities, and many of them are linked to on the media accompanying this book for you to use right away. Given that you already have my opinion on so many tools, let's instead talk about the types of third-party tools you'll find in most tech toolkits.

Many techs like to challenge me on the idea of carrying around tools. They say, "I know what I like; I'll just download them!" Well, sometimes you don't have Internet access and sometimes you need tools that are ready to go (see the next section). Granted, there are a number of tools that I would never carry on me. For example, device drivers change so often that keeping a copy on a thumb drive is a waste of time. The tools I'm listing here are the ones I promise you want with you, ready to go when you run into trouble.

Malware Cleaners

Ask any tech who works for Best Buy's Geek Squad, "What do you spend the most time doing on jobs?" and they will reply, "Cleaning malware." The first tech utilities you want in your toolkit are malware cleaners. To truly do it right, put your malware cleaners on a bootable optical disc because malware can sometimes attack a malware cleanup tool as you install. If you're not sure what to try first, grab a copy of the Ultimate Boot CD and try some of its fine cleanup tools.

Anti-Malware

After you clean the machine, make sure you have a copy of an anti-malware program that you can install so the user's machine doesn't get corrupted again. We talked about some of the popular freeware versions, but plenty of techs strongly prefer the pay versions and keep copies to sell to their customers.

Boot Tools

You need a tool that's better than the System Configuration utility at controlling what programs autostart on your Windows PC. OK, in this case, one tool stands out so strongly that you have to get it: Mark Russinovich's superb Autoruns. It's vastly superior to the built-in System Configuration utility and gives you incredible control of everything that's autostarting. Sure, there are others, but I love Autoruns. Get it at the Windows Sysinternals Web site, http://technet.microsoft.com/en-us/sysinternals.

Password Clearer

If you lose a Windows password, especially the Administrator password, and you can't log on to a system, you're in trouble. A number of tools let you reset any user's passwords. These programs don't let you *see* a password, only reset them, so if you have a user with encrypted folders, those won't be recoverable. None of these programs are easy to use, but when the alternative is not being able to log on, they will save you. Pretty much all of these programs run from bootable optical discs.

ZIP File Tool

Windows can read many compressed file formats (such as ZIP), but so many others are in use that it's often a good idea to have a third-party utility handy. I like 7-Zip (www.7-zip.org), but there are plenty of equally popular alternatives.

Backup

Odds are good that from time to time you'll need to do a backup for a system. I keep an external hard drive with a backup tool so I can go in fast and make backups of the most critical files.

Don't Forget Your Thumb Drives!

I guess I'm showing my age when I talk about putting all these tools on optical media. Sorry, I'm old. Almost all of these tools work equally well on USB thumb drives. I keep my tools on optical media because I still run into the occasional system that doesn't have CMOS settings for a bootable thumb drive.

Field Replaceable Units (FRUs)

The CompTIA A+ 220-802 exam expects you to know that FRUs are computer components such as cards, memory, hard drives, processors, or power supplies that can be easily replaced in the field.

Always carry several **field replaceable units (FRUs)**—a fancy way to say *spare parts*—when going to a job site or workstation. Having several known good components on hand enables you to swap out a potentially bad piece of hardware to see if that's the problem. Different technicians will have different FRUs. A printer specialist might carry a number of fusers, for example. Your employer will also have a big effect on what is an FRU and what is not. I generally carry a couple of RAM sticks (DDR, DDR2, and DDR3), a video card, a NIC, and a 300-watt power supply.

Chapter 20 Review

■ Chapter Summary

After reading this chapter and completing the exercises, you should understand the following about working as a tech.

Describe how computers work

- Good techs must know how their systems are supposed to work when working properly, must be able to calm workers and supervisors and get answers to relevant questions, and must be able to troubleshoot and fix computer problems. A question you must be able to answer is, "What can be causing this problem?"

- When you run a program, computers work through three stages of the four-stage computing process: input, processing, and output. Input requires special input devices such as a keyboard or mouse. The operating system provides the interface and tools so the CPU and other chips can process requests. The output devices, such as the monitor, speakers, and printer, tell you the computer has interpreted your commands. For all this to work, the PC must have electricity and proper AC/DC voltage and amperage.

- When you press a keyboard key, the keyboard controller reads the grid of your keyboard, discovers your input, and then sends the information to the CPU. The CPU understands the keyboard controller because of a small program that was loaded into RAM from the ROM BIOS on the motherboard when the PC booted up.

- Good techs understand the components involved in inputting, processing, and outputting, including the devices that store data, such as hard drives.

Implement a troubleshooting methodology

- The first step in fixing a computer problem is to identify the problem by talking to the client. To determine what the computer is doing or not doing, first allow the client to describe the situation; then ask leading questions to elicit answers, such as "Has anything recently changed on the computer that might have made this problem appear?"

- Once you have ascertained the problem the user is having with the computer, it is important to back up critical data. Unless the hard drive is dead, you should have no reason to lose any data that was accessible before.

- Once you have secured the user's data, you need to establish a theory of probable cause. In other words, look at the machine and determine why it's not working correctly. Don't overlook the obvious, such as a disconnected power or network cable. Use all of your senses: look for damaged components; feel for excessive heat or lack of vibration; listen for any unusual or telltale sounds; and sniff the air for the unmistakable smell of ozone.

- If you run into something more complex than a disconnected cord, don't be afraid to try multiple solutions. Take a chance and see if it works. If you have run out of ideas, escalate the problem; no one person can solve all problems.

- After you have successfully solved the user's problem, have the user sit down and perform the task. This enables you to verify full system functionality with the user.

- Once everything is verified and the customer is happy, make sure to document your findings thoroughly. Keeping records is important. If you or a colleague encounters a similar problem in the future, the answer will be readily available.

Describe a technician's toolkit

- Troubleshooting is more art than science, and as such, there is no step-by-step list of actions to follow. You need to be flexible.

- A well-stocked tech toolkit consists of a Phillips-head screwdriver, flat-head screwdriver, Torx wrench, nut driver, tweezers, grabber tool, flashlight, magnifying glass, and anti-static wrist strap. You should also carry several FRUs. Which FRUs you carry will depend on what kind of tech you are, but the FRUs most techs should carry include a few sticks each of DDR, DDR2, and DDR3 RAM, a video card, a NIC, and a 300-watt power supply.

- Malware is the most common source of consumer computer problems today. Make sure your toolkit is well stocked with anti-virus and other (preferably boot-time) malware removers.
- Lost logon passwords are a common problem, so your kit should include some form of password clearing utility. Remember, these just clear the existing password; they do not show it to you.
- Other handy tools to have are zip/archive extractors and backup utilities. Having these and the rest of your kit and a handy bootable thumb drive can make your job much easier onsite.

Key Terms

computing process *(695)*
document *(706)*
escalate *(704)*
field replaceable unit (FRU) *(708)*
identify the problem *(702)*
incident report *(706)*

stream loading *(699)*
tech toolkit *(707)*
test the theory *(704)*
theory of probable cause *(703)*
troubleshooting theory *(701)*
verify *(705)*

Key Term Quiz

Use the Key Terms list to complete the sentences that follow. Not all terms will be used.

1. A "spare part" you carry with you, such as an extra stick of RAM or a video card, is called a(n) _____.

2. A Phillips-head screwdriver and a few other useful tools should be in your _____.

3. Understanding the _____ enables you to troubleshoot problems more efficiently.

4. When asking questions to _____, remember to use a nonaccusatory tone.

5. Better online applications use _____ to download updated information and data constantly.

6. Once you have determined the problem with the machine and come up with probable causes, you should _____.

7. Once you have successfully repaired the machine, it is important to _____ with the user that everything is working correctly.

8. If you can't solve a troubleshooting problem, the next step is to _____ the problem to a higher-level tech.

9. A(n) _____ is your guess at what is wrong with the machine.

10. A(n) _____ gives the details about an accident on the job site.

Multiple-Choice Quiz

1. At what point during a repair should you escalate the problem?
 A. After the user describes the first problem
 B. As soon as you understand the problem
 C. As soon as you have a solution
 D. When you have tried all your theories and still can't resolve the problem

2. While working at the help desk, you get a call from a distraught user who says she has a blank screen. What would be useful follow-up questions? (Select two.)
 A. Is the computer turned on?
 B. Is the monitor turned on?
 C. Did you reboot?
 D. What did you do?

3. While working at the help desk, you get a call from Sharon in accounting. She's lost a file that she knows she saved to her hard drive. Which of the following statements would direct Sharon to open her My Documents folder in the most efficient and professional manner?

 A. Sharon, check My Documents.

 B. Sharon, a lot of programs save files to a default folder, often to a folder called My Documents. Let's look there first. Click on the Start button and move the mouse until the cursor hovers over My Documents. Then click the left mouse button and tell me what you see when My Documents opens.

 C. Probably just defaulted to My Docs. Why don't you open Excel or whatever program you used to make the file, and then open a document, and point it to My Documents.

 D. Look Sharon, I know you're a clueless noob when it comes to computers, but how could somebody lose a file? Just open up My Documents and look there for the file.

4. What tool should be in every technician's toolkit?

 A. Pliers

 B. Hammer

 C. Flat-head screwdriver

 D. Phillips-head screwdriver

5. Al in marketing calls in for tech support, complaining that he has a dead PC. What is a good first question or questions to begin troubleshooting the problem?

 A. Did the computer ever work?

 B. When did the computer last work?

 C. When you say "dead," what do you mean? What happens when you press the power button?

 D. What did you do?

6. While working at the help desk, you get a call from Bryce in sales complaining that he can't print and that every time he clicks on the network shared drive, his computer stops and freezes. He says he thinks it's his hard driver. What would be a good follow-up question or statement?

 A. Bryce, you're an idiot. Don't touch anything. I'll be there in five minutes.

 B. Okay, let's take this one step at a time. You seem to have two problems, one with printing and the second with the network shared drive, right?

 C. First, it's not a hard *driver*, but a hard *drive*. It doesn't have anything to do with the network share or printing, so that's just not right.

 D. When could you last print?

7. Phoebe's computer was recently updated during the companywide patch push. Now all Phoebe gets is a black screen. What should you check first?

 A. Take the monitor back to the maintenance room and check it with known good hardware.

 B. Check to make sure the monitor is properly plugged into the system unit and is getting power.

 C. Replace Phoebe's video card.

 D. Take Phoebe's computer back to the maintenance room and reimage it.

8. You've just installed new printer drivers into Roland's computer for the big networked laser printer. What should you do to complete the assignment?

 A. Document that you installed new printer drivers.

 B. Tell Roland to print a test page.

 C. Print a test page and go to the printer to verify the results. Assuming everything works, you're finished.

 D. Print a test page and go to the printer to verify the results. Document that you installed new printer drivers successfully.

9. After examining Paul's computer, you think the problem has something to do with his video card but you are not certain. Should you try your uncertain fix, escalate the problem, or do something else?

 A. Escalate; you need to be 100 percent correct before you attempt a fix.

 B. Stall for time and hope the problem fixes itself.

C. Calmly explain to Paul that his computer cannot be fixed.

D. Take a chance and try your first guess.

10. Upon responding to a coworker's request for help, you find her away from her desk and Microsoft Excel on the screen with a spreadsheet open. How do you proceed?

 A. Go find the coworker and ask her to exit her applications before you touch her computer.

 B. Exit Excel, save changes to the document, and begin troubleshooting the computer.

 C. Exit Excel without saving changes to the document and begin troubleshooting the computer.

 D. Use the Save As command to save the file with a new name, exit Excel, and begin troubleshooting the computer.

11. You have been working all afternoon on a user's workstation and you have finally fixed the user's problem. What should you do now?

 A. Tell the user the computer is fixed and leave.

 B. Invite the user to sit down and use the computer to make sure the problem is completely gone from the user's perspective.

 C. Tell the user the machine is fixed, go back to your office, and document the problem.

 D. As you leave for the tenth time, complain to the user that you are tired of always fixing his computer.

12. Which of the following makes a good field replaceable unit?

A. Video card

B. 20-inch CRT monitor

C. Set of 2.1 speakers

D. Printer

13. After replacing a keyboard a user has spilled coffee on for the fifth time, what should you say to the user?

 A. I can't guarantee the new keyboard will work if it gets dirty.

 B. I can't guarantee the new keyboard will work if you continue to spill coffee on it.

 C. These keyboards are expensive. Next time we replace one because you spilled coffee, it's coming out of your paycheck.

 D. You need to be more careful with your coffee.

14. When is it appropriate to yell at a user?

 A. When he screws up the second time

 B. When he interrupts your troubleshooting

 C. When he screws up the fifth time

 D. Never

15. Once you figure out what can be causing a computer to malfunction, what's your next step?

 A. Escalate the problem to a higher-level tech.

 B. Talk to the user about stream loading and other geeky things because your knowledge will put him or her at ease.

 C. Test your theory, starting with the obvious.

 D. Write an incident report to document the problem.

■ Essay Quiz

1. A friend is considering turning his computer hobby into a career and has asked your advice on outfitting himself as a freelance computer technician. What tools can you recommend to your friend?

2. A user phones you at your desk and reports that after pressing the power button on his computer and hearing the hard drive spin up, his screen remains blank. What questions can you ask to determine the problem? Remember, avoid an accusing tone.

3. Briefly explain the various steps in troubleshooting theory.

Lab Projects

• Lab Project 20.1

Think of items you would like to always have on hand as FRUs. Using the Internet, find prices for these items. Make a list of your items and their individual costs; then find the total cost for your equipment.

• Lab Project 20.2

Visit your local computer store or hardware store and purchase the items for a hardware tech toolkit. You may want to include a variety of screwdrivers, an anti-static wrist strap, tweezers, or other items.

• Lab Project 20.3

Create a software tech toolkit on an optical disc or USB flash drive loaded with a variety of drivers for NICs and video cards. Include free/open-source anti-virus software, anti-spyware software, and any other software tools you think might be useful.

Mapping to the CompTIA A+ 220-802 Exam Objectives

Competency	Chapter	Page(s)
1.0 Operating Systems		
1.1 Compare and contrast the features and requirements of various Microsoft operating systems.		
Windows XP Home, Windows XP Professional, Windows XP Media Center, Windows XP 64-bit Professional	2	24–26, 31
Windows Vista Home Basic, Windows Vista Home Premium, Windows Vista Business, Windows Vista Ultimate, Windows Vista Enterprise	2	27–28
Windows 7 Starter, Windows 7 Home Premium, Windows 7 Professional, Windows 7 Ultimate, Windows 7 Enterprise	2	29–30
Features		
32-bit vs. 64-bit	2	30–33
Aero, gadgets, user account control, bit-locker, shadow copy, system restore, ready boost, sidebar, compatibility mode, XP mode, easy transfer, administrative tools, defender, Windows firewall, security center, event viewer, file structure and paths, category view vs. classic view	2, 3, 5, 7, 10, 18	30, 32, 35, 48, 51, 56, 64, 68, 84, 200, 257, 272, 398, 414, 646, 657
Upgrade paths—differences between in-place upgrades, compatibility tools, Windows upgrade OS advisor	5	166
1.2 Given a scenario, install and configure the operating system using the most appropriate method.		
Boot methods	5	
USB	5	166
CD-ROM	5	166
DVD	5	166
PXE	5	192–193
Type of installations		
Creating image	5	190–191
Unattended installation	5	163
Upgrade	5	179
Clean install	5	179
Repair installation	10	378
Multiboot	5	163
Remote network installation	5	163
Image deployment	5	163
Partitioning	4	119–125
Dynamic	4	105
Basic	4	103

Competency	Chapter	Page(s)
Speed	12	452
Wake-on-LAN	14	513
PoE	13	484
QoS	14	527
1.7 Perform preventive maintenance procedures using appropriate tools.		
Best practices		
Scheduled backups	8	299
Scheduled check disks	8	301
Scheduled defragmentation	8	300
Windows updates	8	289
Patch management	8	289
Driver/firmware updates	10	393
Antivirus updates	18	650
Tools		
Backup	8	314–323
System restore	8	324–327
Check disk	8	301
Recovery image	10	384
Defrag	4, 8, 10	139, 300, 396
1.8 Explain the differences among basic OS security settings.		
User and groups	7	
Administrator	7	250
Power user	7	250
Guest	7	250
Standard user	7	251
NTFS vs. Share permissions	7	
Allow vs. deny	7	262–263
Moving vs. copying folders and files	7	264–265
File attributes	7	272
Shared files and folders	7	
Administrative shares vs. local shares	7	271
Permission propagation	7	264
Inheritance	7	264
System files and folders	6	217–218
User authentication	7	247
Single sign-on	14	506
1.9 Explain the basics of client-side virtualization.		
Purpose of virtual machines	19	684–686
Resource requirements	19	684
Emulator requirements	19	680
Security requirements	19	684

Competency	Chapter	Page(s)
Verify full system functionality and, if applicable, implement preventive measures	20	705
Document findings, actions, and outcomes	20	706
4.2 Given a scenario, troubleshoot common problems related to motherboards, RAM, CPU, and power with appropriate tools.		
Common symptoms		
Unexpected shutdowns	10	414
System lockups	10	384
POST code beeps	3	85
Blank screen on bootup	10	374
BIOS time and settings resets	10	408
Attempts to boot to incorrect device	10	374
Continuous reboots	10	384
No power	3	92
Overheating	3, 15	81, 562
Loud noise	3	82
Intermittent device failure	3	90–91
Fans spin—no power to other devices	3	90
Indicator lights	3	90
Smoke	3	82
Burning smell	3	82
BSOD	3	82
Tools		
Multimeter	3	92
Power supply tester	3	93
Loopback plugs	14	521
POST card	3	85–86
4.3 Given a scenario, troubleshoot hard drives and RAID arrays with appropriate tools.		
Common symptoms		
Read/write failure	4	145
Slow performance	4	146
Loud clicking noise	4	145
Failure to boot	4	146
Drive not recognized	4	145
OS not found	4	146
RAID not found	4	146
RAID stops working	4	146
BSOD	4	146
Tools		
Screwdriver	20	707
External enclosures	4	146
CHDKS	4	n/a
CHKDSK	4, 9	138, 359

Mike Meyer's CompTIA A+ Guide to 802: Managing and Troubleshooting PCs

Competency	Chapter	Page(s)
4.6 Given a scenario, troubleshoot operating system problems with appropriate tools.		
Common symptoms		
BSOD	10	393
Failure to boot	10	373
Improper shutdown	10	414
Spontaneous shutdown/restart	10	414
RAID not detected during installation	5	193
Device fails to start	10	374
Missing dll message	10	404
Services fails to start	10	403
Compatibility error	10	411
Slow system performance	10	407–408
Boots to safe mode	10	394–398
File fails to open	10	413
Missing NTLDR	10	373
Missing Boot.ini	10	374
Missing operating system	10	374–375
Missing Graphical Interface	10	392
Graphical Interface fails to load	10	392
Invalid boot disk	10	374
Tools		
Fixboot	10	377
Recovery console	10	375–378
Fixmbr	10	377
Sfc	9	360
Repair disks	10	379
Pre-installation environments	10	379
MSCONFIG	8	301
DEFRAG	10	396
REGSRV32	6	216
REGEDIT	6	211
Event viewer	10, 18	386, 640
Safe mode	10	394–398
Command prompt	10	404
Emergency repair disk	8	317
Automated system recovery	8, 10	316, 378
4.7 Given a scenario, troubleshoot common security issues with appropriate tools and best practices.		
Common symptoms		
Pop-ups	18	644
Browser redirection	18	649

appendix B

About the CD-ROM

The disc included with this book comes with:

- An introduction to CompTIA A+ video from the author, Mike Meyers
- Digital copy of the CompTIA A+ 220-802 exam objectives
- Total Tester practice exam software with hundreds of practice exam questions
- A link to hours of Mike Meyers video training
- Links to a collection of Mike's current favorite tools and utilities for PC troubleshooting
- A link to download the Adobe Digital Editions PDF copy of the book

The software can be installed on any Windows 98/NT/2000/XP/Vista/Windows 7 computer and must be installed to access the Total Tester practice exam software.

Playing the Mike Meyers Introduction Video

If your computer's optical drive is configured to auto-run, the menu will automatically start up upon inserting the disc. If the auto-run feature did not launch the disc, browse to the disc and double-click the Launch.exe icon.

From the opening screen you can launch the video message from Mike by clicking the **Mike Meyers Introduction Video** button. This launches the video file using your system's default video player.

Viewing the CompTIA Exam Objectives

To view the CompTIA A+ exam objectives, select the **CompTIA Exam Objectives** button from the main menu of the disc. On the next page, clicking the **CompTIA A+ (220-802) Objectives** button will open a PDF of the appropriate objectives. The objectives map is the official exam objective list from CompTIA as of the date of publication. Please visit the CompTIA Web site for the most up-to-date exam objectives. A PDF-viewing program must be installed to view the objectives list. Adobe Acrobat Reader is available from www.acrobat.com.

System Requirements

The software requires Windows XP or higher, Internet Explorer 7 or higher or Firefox with Flash Player, and 30 MB of hard disk space for full installation.

Installing and Running Total Tester

From the main screen you may install the Total Tester by clicking the **Software and Videos** button, then selecting the **Total Tester A+ Practice Exams** button. This will begin the installation process and place an icon on your desktop and in your Start menu. To run Total Tester, navigate to **Start | (All) Programs | Total Seminars** or double-click the icon on your desktop.

To uninstall the Total Tester software, go to **Start | Settings | Control Panel | Add/Remove Programs** (XP) or **Programs and Features** (Vista / 7), and then select the **A+ Total Tester** program. Select **Remove** and Windows will completely uninstall the software.

Total Tester

Total Tester provides you with a simulation of the CompTIA A+ 802 exam. You may select practice exams for CompTIA A+ Exam 802. The exams can be taken in either Practice mode or Exam Simulation mode. Practice mode provides an assistance window with hints, references to the book, an explanation of the answer, and the option to check your answer as you take the test. Both Practice mode and Exam Simulation mode provide an overall grade and a grade broken down by certification objective. To take a test, launch the program, select CompTIA A+ from the Installed Question Packs list, then select the 802 exam. You can then select either Practice Exam or Exam Simulation.

Mike's Cool Tools

Mike loves freeware/open source PC tools! Most of the utilities mentioned in the text can be downloaded from the Internet using URLs provided on the disc on the Mike's Cool Tools page. You can access the menu by clicking on the **Software and Videos** button on the main page of the disc and then selecting the **Access Mike's Cool Tools** link.

Please read the Cool Tools page for a description of the utilities.

> While all of the tools are "Mike Meyers Approved," there is no guarantee they will work for you. Read any and all documentation that comes with each utility before downloading and using that program.

Mike's Video Training

Your disc comes with a link to hours of free PC video training starring Mike Meyers. On the main page of the disc, click the **Software and Videos** link and then select **Access Mike Meyers Video Training**. You'll have access to several training segments, with an option to purchase even more of Mike's instructional videos.

Adobe Digital Editions Download

The contents of this book are available as a free download in the form of a secured Adobe Digital Editions PDF file.

The CD included with this book contains links to both Adobe Digital Editions and to the PDF book download Web page. First, download and install Adobe Digital Editions on your computer. Next, follow the link to the PDF download Web page listed below. You are required to provide your name, a valid e-mail address, and your unique access code in order to download the PDF.

Your unique access code can be found on the label that is adhered to the inside flap of the CD envelope. The CD envelope is inside the paper sleeve bound into the back of this book.

Upon submitting this information, an e-mail message will be sent to the e-mail address you provided. Follow the instructions included in the e-mail message to download your PDF.

To download your copy, please visit:

> http://books.mcgraw-hill.com/ebookdownloads/9780071795951

The unique access code entitles you to download one copy of the PDF to one personal computer. The unique access code can only be used once, and the PDF is only usable on the computer on which it was downloaded. Be sure to download the PDF to the computer you intend to use.

You need a copy of Adobe Digital Editions installed to open, view, and navigate the PDF. You can download the latest version of Adobe Digital Editions for free from Adobe's Web site, www.adobe.com, or use the version included on the CD. Remember, you must download and install Adobe Digital Editions before attempting to download the PDF.

Technical Support

For questions regarding the operation of the Adobe Digital Editions download, e-mail techsolutions@mhedu.com or visit http://mhp.software-assist.com.

For questions regarding the Total Tester software or operation of the CD, visit www.totalsem.com or e-mail support@totalsem.com.

For questions regarding book content, please e-mail customer .service@mcgraw-hill.com. For customers outside the United States, e-mail international_cs@mcgraw-hill.com.

%SystemRoot% The path where the operating system is installed.

10BaseT Ethernet LAN designed to run on twisted pair cabling. 10BaseT runs at 10 megabits per second. The maximum length for the cabling between the NIC and the switch (or hub, repeater, etc.) is 100 meters. It uses baseband signaling. No industry standard spelling exists, so sometimes it's written 10BASE-T or 10Base-T.

100BaseT Ethernet cabling system designed to run at 100 megabits per second on twisted pair cabling. It uses baseband signaling. No industry standard spelling exists, so sometimes it's written 100BASE-T or 100Base-T.

1000BaseT Gigabit Ethernet on UTP.

110 block The most common connection used with structured cabling, connecting horizontal cable runs with patch panels.

16-bit (PC Card) Type of PC Card that can have up to two distinct functions or devices, such as a modem/network card combination.

2.1 speaker system Speaker setup consisting of two stereo speakers combined with a subwoofer.

3.5-inch floppy drive Size of all modern floppy disk drives; the format was introduced in 1986 and is one of the longest surviving pieces of computer hardware.

34-pin ribbon cable Type of cable used by floppy disk drives.

3-D graphics Video technology that attempts to create images with the same depth and texture as objects seen in the real world.

40-pin ribbon cable PATA cable used to attach EIDE devices (such as hard drives) or ATAPI devices (such as optical drives) to a system. (*See* PATA.)

5.1 speaker system Speaker setup consisting of four satellite speakers plus a center speaker and a subwoofer.

64-bit processing A type of processing that can run a compatible 64-bit operating system, such as Windows 7, and 64-bit applications. 64-bit PCs have a 64-bit-wide address bus, enabling them to use more than 4 GB of RAM.

8.3 naming system File-naming convention that specified a maximum of eight characters for a filename, followed by

a three-character file extension. Has been replaced by LFN (long filename) support.

80-wire ribbon cable PATA cable used to attach fast EIDE devices (such as ATA/100 hard drives) or ATAPI devices (such as optical drives) to a system. (*See* PATA.)

802.11a Wireless networking standard that operates in the 5-GHz band with a theoretical maximum throughput of 54 Mbps.

802.11b Wireless networking standard that operates in the 2.4-GHz band with a theoretical maximum throughput of 11 Mbps.

802.11g Wireless networking standard that operates in the 2.4-GHz band with a theoretical maximum throughput of 54 Mbps and is backward compatible with 802.11b.

802.11n Wireless networking standard that can operate in both the 2.4-GHz and 5-GHz bands and uses multiple in/multiple out (MIMO) to achieve a theoretical maximum throughput of 100+ Mbps.

A/V sync Process of synchronizing audio and video.

AC (alternating current) Type of electricity in which the flow of electrons alternates direction, back and forth, in a circuit.

AC'97 Sound card standard for lower-end audio devices; created when most folks listened to stereo sound at best.

accelerometer Feature in smartphones and tablets that rotates the screen when the device is physically rotated.

access control Security concept using physical security, authentication, users and groups, and security policies.

ACPI (Advanced Configuration and Power Interface) Power management specification that far surpasses its predecessor, APM, by providing support for hot-swappable devices and better control of power modes.

Action Center A one-page aggregation of event messages, warnings, and maintenance messages in Windows 7.

activation Process of confirming that an installed copy of a Microsoft product (most commonly Windows or a Microsoft Office application) is legitimate. Usually done at the end of software installation.

active matrix Type of liquid crystal display (LCD) that replaced the passive matrix technology used in most portable computer displays. Also called TFT (thin film transistor).

active partition On a hard drive, primary partition that contains an operating system.

active PFC (power factor correction) Circuitry built into PC power supplies to reduce harmonics.

activity light An LED on a NIC, hub, or switch that blinks rapidly to show data transfers over the network.

ad hoc mode Decentralized wireless network mode, otherwise known as peer-to-peer mode, where each wireless node is in meshed contact with every other node.

Add or Remove Programs Applet allowing users to manually add or remove a program to or from the system.

address bus Set of wires leading from the CPU to the memory controller chip (traditionally the Northbridge) that enables the CPU to address RAM. Also used by the CPU for I/O addressing. On current CPUs with built-in memory controllers, the address bus refers to the internal electronic channel from the microprocessor to RAM, along which the addresses of memory storage locations are transmitted. Like a post office box, each memory location has a distinct number or address; the address bus provides the means by which the microprocessor can access every location in memory.

address space Total amount of memory addresses that an address bus can contain.

administrative shares Administrator tool to give local admins access to hard drives and system root folders.

Administrative Tools Group of Control Panel applets, including Computer Management, Event Viewer, and Reliability and Performance Monitor.

administrator account User account, created when the OS is first installed, that is allowed complete, unfettered access to the system without restriction.

Administrators group List of members with complete administrator privileges.

ADSL (asymmetric digital subscriber line) Fully digital, dedicated connection to the telephone system that provides average download speeds of 7 Mbps and upload speeds of 512 Kbps.

Advanced Encryption Standard (AES) A block cipher created in the late 1990s that uses a 128-bit block size and a 128-, 192-, or 256-bit key size. Practically uncrackable.

Advanced Startup Options menu Menu that can be reached during the boot process that offers advanced OS startup options, such as to boot to Safe Mode or boot into Last Known Good Configuration.

adware Type of malicious program that downloads ads to a user's computer, generating undesirable network traffic.

Aero The Windows Vista/7 desktop environment. Aero adds some interesting aesthetic effects such as window transparency and Flip 3D.

AGP (Accelerated Graphics Port) 32/64-bit expansion slot designed by Intel specifically for video that runs at 66 MHz and yields a throughput of at least 254 Mbps. Later versions (2×, 4×, 8×) give substantially higher throughput.

algorithm Set of rules for solving a problem in a given number of steps.

ALU (arithmetic logic unit) CPU logic circuits that perform basic arithmetic (add, subtract, multiply, and divide).

AMD (Advanced Micro Devices) CPU and chipset manufacturer that competes with Intel. Produces the popular Phenom, Athlon, Sempron, Turion, and Duron microprocessors; also produces video card processors under its ATI brand.

AMI (American Megatrends, Inc.) Major producer of BIOS software for motherboards, as well as many other computer-related components and software.

amperes (amps or A) Unit of measure for amperage, or electrical current.

amplitude Loudness of a sound card.

AMR (audio modem riser) Proprietary slot used on some motherboards to provide a sound interference–free connection for modems, sound cards, and NICs.

analog Device that uses a physical quantity, such as length or voltage, to represent the value of a number. By contrast, digital storage relies on a coding system of numeric units.

Android Smartphone and tablet OS created by Google.

anti-aliasing In computer imaging, blending effect that smoothes sharp contrasts between two regions—e.g., jagged lines or different colors. Reduces jagged edges of text or objects. In voice signal processing, process of removing or smoothing out spurious frequencies from waveforms produced by converting digital signals back to analog.

anti-static bag Bag made of anti-static plastic into which electronics are placed for temporary or long-term storage. Used to protect components from electrostatic discharge.

anti-static mat Special surface on which to lay electronics. These mats come with a grounding connection designed to equalize electrical potential between a workbench and

one or more electronic devices. Used to prevent electrostatic discharge.

anti-static wrist strap Special device worn around the wrist with a grounding connection designed to equalize electrical potential between a technician and an electronic device. Used to prevent electrostatic discharge.

antivirus program Software designed to combat viruses by either seeking out and destroying them or passively guarding against them.

API (application programming interface) Software definition that describes operating system calls for application software; conventions defining how a service is invoked.

APIPA (Automatic Private IP Addressing) Feature of Windows that automatically assigns an IP address to the system when the client cannot obtain an IP address automatically.

APM (Advanced Power Management) BIOS routines that enable the CPU to turn on and off selected peripherals.

app A program for a tablet or smartphone. Also, a program written for Windows 8 Metro interface.

applet Generic term for a program in the Windows Control Panel.

Applications Name of the tab in Task Manager that lists running applications.

archive To copy programs and data onto a relatively inexpensive storage medium (disk, tape, etc.) for long-term retention.

archive attribute Attribute of a file that shows whether the file has been backed up since the last change. Each time a file is opened, changed, or saved, the archive bit is turned on. Some types of backups turn off this archive bit to indicate that a good backup of the file exists on tape.

ARP (Address Resolution Protocol) Protocol in the TCP/IP suite used with the command-line utility of the same name (arp) to determine the MAC address that corresponds to a particular IP address.

ASCII (American Standard Code for Information Interchange) Industry-standard 8-bit characters used to define text characters, consisting of 96 upper- and lowercase letters, plus 32 nonprinting control characters, each of which is numbered. These numbers were designed to achieve uniformity among computer devices for printing and the exchange of simple text documents.

aspect ratio Ratio of width to height of an object. Standard television has a 4:3 aspect ratio.

ASR (Automated System Recovery) Windows XP tool designed to recover a badly corrupted Windows system; similar to the ERD in Windows 2000.

assertive communication Means of communication that is not pushy or bossy but is also not soft. Useful in dealing with upset customers as it both defuses their anger and gives them confidence that you know what you're doing.

AT (Advanced Technology) Model name of the second-generation, 80286-based IBM computer. Many aspects of the AT, such as the BIOS, CMOS, and expansion bus, have become de facto standards in the PC industry. The physical organization of the components on the motherboard is called the AT form factor.

ATA (AT Attachment) Type of hard drive and controller designed to replace the earlier ST506 and ESDI drives without requiring replacement of the AT BIOS—hence, AT attachment. These drives are more popularly known as IDE drives. (*See* IDE.) The ATA/33 standard has drive transfer speeds up to 33 MBps; the ATA/66 up to 66 MBps; the ATA/100 up to 100 MBps; and the ATA/133 up to 133 MBps. (*See* Ultra DMA.)

ATA/ATAPI-6 Also known as ATA-6 or "Big Drive." Replaced the INT13 extensions and allowed for hard drives as large as 144 petabytes (144 million GB).

ATAPI (ATA Packet Interface) Series of standards that enables mass storage devices other than hard drives to use the IDE/ATA controllers. Popular with optical drives. (*See* EIDE.)

ATAPI-compliant Devices that utilize the ATAPI standard. (*See* ATAPI.)

Athlon Name used for a popular series of CPUs manufactured by AMD.

attrib.exe Command used to view the specific properties of a file; can also be used to modify or remove file properties, such as read-only, system, or archive.

attributes Values in a file that determine the hidden, read-only, system, and archive status of the file.

ATX (Advanced Technology Extended) Popular motherboard form factor that generally replaced the AT form factor.

audio interface High-end external sound device used by audio engineers and recording artists.

authentication Any method a computer uses to determine who can access it.

authorization Any method a computer uses to determine what an authenticated user can do.

autodetection Process through which new disks are automatically recognized by the BIOS.

Automatic Private IP Addressing (APIPA) A networking feature of operating systems that enables DHCP clients to self-configure an IP address and subnet mask automatically when a DHCP server isn't available.

Automatic Updates Feature allowing updates to Windows to be retrieved automatically over the Internet.

AutoPlay Windows XP/Vista/7 setting, along with autorun.inf, enabling Windows to automatically detect media files and begin using them. (*See* autorun.inf.)

autorun.inf File included on some media that automatically launches a program or installation routine when the media is inserted/attached to a system.

autosensing Used by better-quality sound cards to detect a device plugged into a port and to adapt the features of that port.

auto-switching power supply Type of power supply able to detect the voltage of a particular outlet and adjust accordingly.

Award Software Major brand of BIOS software for motherboards. Owned by Phoenix Technologies.

backlight One of three main components used in LCDs to illuminate an image.

backside bus Set of wires that connects the CPU to Level 2 cache. First appearing in the Pentium Pro, all modern CPUs have a backside bus. Some buses run at the full speed of the CPU, whereas others run at a fraction. Earlier Pentium IIs, for example, had backside buses running at half the speed of the processor. (*See also* frontside bus and external data bus.)

Backup and Restore Center Windows Vista/7's backup utility (Windows 7 drops "Center" from the name). It offers two options: create a backup or restore from a backup.

Backup or Restore Wizard Utility contained within Windows that allows users to create system backups and set system restore points.

Backup Utility (ntbackup) Windows XP's tool for creating and restoring backups.

ball mouse Input device that enables users to manipulate a cursor on the screen by using a ball and sensors that detect the movement and direction of the ball.

bandwidth Piece of the spectrum occupied by some form of signal, such as television, voice, or fax data. Signals require a certain size and location of bandwidth to be transmitted. The higher the bandwidth, the faster the signal transmission, allowing for a more complex signal such as audio or video. Because bandwidth is a limited space, when one user is occupying it, others must wait their turn. Bandwidth is also the capacity of a network to transmit a given amount of data during a given period.

bank Total number of SIMMs or DIMMs that can be accessed simultaneously by the chipset. The "width" of the external data bus divided by the "width" of the SIMM or DIMM sticks. DIMM slots that must be populated to activate dual- or triple-channel memory.

bar code reader Tool to read Universal Product Code (UPC) bar codes.

basic disk Hard drive partitioned in the "classic" way with a master boot record (MBR) and partition table. (*See also* dynamic disks.)

baud One analog cycle on a telephone line. In the early days of telephone data transmission, the baud rate was often analogous to bits per second. Due to advanced modulation of baud cycles as well as data compression, this is no longer true.

bcdedit A command-line tool that enables you to view the BCD store, which lists the Windows boot options.

BD-R (Blu-ray Disc-Recordable) Blu-ray Disc format that enables writing data to blank discs.

BD-RE (Blu-ray Disc-REwritable) Blu-ray Disc equivalent of the rewritable DVD, allows writing and rewriting several times on the same BD. (*See* Blu-ray Disc.)

BD-ROM Blu-ray Disc equivalent of a DVD-ROM or CD-ROM. (*See* Blu-ray Disc.)

beep codes Series of audible tones produced by a motherboard during the POST. These tones identify whether the POST has completed successfully or whether some piece of system hardware is not working properly. Consult the manual for your particular motherboard for a specific list of beep codes.

binary numbers Number system with a base of 2, unlike the number systems most of us use that have bases of 10 (decimal numbers), 12 (measurement in feet and inches), and 60 (time). Binary numbers are preferred for computers for precision and economy. An electronic circuit that can detect the difference between two states (on–off, 0–1) is easier and more inexpensive to build than one that could detect the differences among ten states (0–9).

biometric device Hardware device used to support authentication; works by scanning and remembering a unique aspect of a user's various body parts (e.g., retina, iris, face, or fingerprint) by using some form of sensing device such as a retinal scanner.

BIOS (basic input/output services) Classically, software routines burned onto the system ROM of a PC. More commonly seen as any software that directly controls a particular piece of hardware. A set of programs encoded in read-only memory (ROM) on computers. These programs handle startup operations and low-level control of hardware such as disk drives, the keyboard, and monitor.

bit Single binary digit. Also, any device that can be in an on or off state.

bit depth Number of colors a video card is capable of producing. Common bit depths are 16-bit and 32-bit, representing 65,536 colors and 16.7 million colors (plus an 8-bit alpha channel for transparency levels), respectively.

BitLocker Drive Encryption Drive encryption software offered in Windows Vista/7 Ultimate and Enterprise editions. BitLocker requires a special chip to validate hardware status and to ensure that the computer hasn't been hacked.

Bluetooth Wireless technology designed to create small wireless networks preconfigured to do specific jobs, but not meant to replace full-function networks or Wi-Fi.

Blu-ray Disc (BD) Optical disc format that stores 25 or 50 GB of data, designed to be the replacement media for DVD. Competed with HD DVD.

boot To initiate an automatic routine that clears the memory, loads the operating system, and prepares the computer for use. Term is derived from "pull yourself up by your bootstraps." PCs must do that because RAM doesn't retain program instructions when power is turned off. A cold boot occurs when the PC is physically switched on. A warm boot loads a fresh OS without turning off the computer, lessening the strain on the electronic circuitry. To do a warm boot, press the CTRL-ALT-DELETE keys twice in rapid succession (the three-fingered salute).

Boot Configuration Data (BCD) file File that contains information about the various operating systems installed on the system as well as instructions for how to actually load (bootstrap) them.

boot sector First sector on a PC hard drive or floppy disk, track 0. The boot-up software in ROM tells the computer to load whatever program is found there. If a system disk is read, the program in the boot record directs the computer to the root directory to load the operating system.

boot.ini Text file used during the boot process that provides a list of all OSs currently installed and available for ntldr (NT Loader). Also tells where each OS is located on the system. Used in Windows XP and earlier Microsoft operating systems.

bootable disk Disk that contains a functional operating system; can also be a floppy disk, USB thumb drive, or optical disc.

bootmgr Windows Vista/7's Boot Manager.

bootrec A Windows Recovery Environment troubleshooting and repair tool that repairs the master boot record, boot sector, or BCD store. It replaces the fixboot and fixmbr Recovery Console commands used in Windows XP and earlier operating systems.

bootstrap loader Segment of code in a system's BIOS that scans for an operating system, looks specifically for a valid boot sector, and, when one is found, hands control over to the boot sector; then the bootstrap loader removes itself from memory.

bps (bits per second) Measurement of how fast data is moved from one place to another. A 56K modem can move ~56,000 bits per second.

bridge A device that connects two networks and passes traffic between them based only on the node address, so that traffic between nodes on one network does not appear on the other network. For example, an Ethernet bridge only looks at the MAC address. Bridges filter and forward packets based on MAC addresses and operate at Level 2 (Data Link layer) of the OSI seven-layer model.

broadband Commonly understood as a reference to high-speed, always-on communication links that can move large files much more quickly than a regular phone line.

broadcast A network transmission addressed for every node on the network.

browser Program specifically designed to retrieve, interpret, and display Web pages.

BSoD (Blue Screen of Death) Infamous error screen that appears when Windows encounters an unrecoverable error.

BTX (Balanced Technology eXtended) Motherboard form factor designed as an improvement over ATX.

buffer underrun Inability of a source device to provide a CD burner with a constant stream of data while burning a CD-R or CD-RW.

buffered/registered DRAM Usually seen in motherboards supporting more than four sticks of RAM, required to address interference issues caused by the additional sticks.

bug Programming error that causes a program or a computer system to perform erratically, produce incorrect results, or crash. The term was coined when a real bug was found in one of the circuits of one of the first ENIAC computers.

burn Process of writing data to a writable optical disc, such as a DVD-R.

burn-in failure Critical failure usually associated with manufacturing defects.

bus Series of wires connecting two or more separate electronic devices, enabling those devices to communicate. Also, a network topology where computers all connect to a main line called a bus cable.

bus mastering Circuitry allowing devices to avoid conflicts on the external data bus.

bus topology Network configuration wherein all computers connect to the network via a central bus cable.

byte Unit of 8 bits; fundamental data unit of personal computers. Storing the equivalent of one character, the byte is also the basic unit of measurement for computer storage.

CAB files Short for cabinet files. These files are compressed and most commonly used during OS installation to store many smaller files, such as device drivers.

cache (disk) Special area of RAM that stores the data most frequently accessed from the hard drive. Cache memory can optimize the use of your systems.

cache (L1, L2, L3, etc.) Special section of fast memory, usually built into the CPU, used by the onboard logic to store information most frequently accessed by the CPU.

calibration Process of matching the print output of a printer to the visual output of a monitor.

capacitive touchscreen Type of touchscreen that uses electrical current in your body to determine movement of your fingers across the screen.

card reader Device with which you can read data from one of several types of flash memory.

card services Uppermost level of PCMCIA services. The card services level recognizes the function of a particular PC Card and provides the specialized drivers necessary to make the card work. (*See also* socket services.)

CardBus 32-bit PC cards that can support up to eight devices on each card. Electrically incompatible with earlier PC cards (3.3 V versus 5 V).

CAT 5 Category 5 wire; a TIA/EIA standard for UTP wiring that can operate at up to 100 megabits per second.

CAT 5e Category 5e wire; TIA/EIA standard for UTP wiring that can operate at up to 1 gigabit per second.

CAT 6 Category 6 wire; TIA/EIA standard for UTP wiring that can operate at up to 10 gigabits per second.

CAT 6a Category 6a wire; augmented CAT 6 UTP wiring that supports 10GBaseT networks at the full 100 meter distance between a node and a switch.

catastrophic failure Describes a failure in which a component or whole system will not boot; usually related to a manufacturing defect of a component. Could also be caused by overheating and physical damage to computer components.

CCFL (cold cathode fluorescent lamp) Light technology used in LCDs and flatbed scanners. CCFLs use relatively little power for the amount of light they provide.

cd (chdir) Shorthand for "change directory." Allows you to change the focus of the command prompt from one directory to another.

CD (compact disc) Originally designed as the replacement for vinyl records, has become the primary method of long-term storage of music and data.

CD quality Audio quality that has a sample rate of 44.4 KHz and a bit rate of 128 bits.

CDDA (CD-Digital Audio) Special format used for early CD-ROMs and all audio CDs; divides data into variable-length tracks. A good format to use for audio tracks but terrible for data because of lack of error checking.

CD-R (CD-recordable) CD technology that accepts a single "burn" but cannot be erased after that one burn.

CD-ROM (compact disc/read-only memory) Read-only compact storage disc for audio or video data. CD-ROMs are read by using CD-ROM drives and optical drives with backward compatibility, such as DVD and Blu-ray Disc drives.

CD-RW (CD-rewritable) CD technology that accepts multiple reads/writes like a hard drive.

Celeron Lower-cost brand of Intel CPUs.

cellular wireless networks Networks that enable cell phones, smartphones, and other mobile devices to connect to the Internet.

Centrino Marketing name for an Intel laptop solution including the mobile processor, support chips, and wireless networking.

Centronics connector Connector used with older printers.

certification License that demonstrates competency in some specialized skill.

Certified Cisco Network Associate (CCNA) One of the certifications demonstrating a knowledge of Cisco networking products.

chain of custody A documented history of who has been in possession of a system.

CHAP (Challenge Handshake Authentication Protocol) Common remote access protocol; the serving system challenges the remote client, usually by means of asking for a password.

chassis intrusion detection Feature offered in some chassis that trips a switch when the chassis is opened.

chipset Electronic chips, specially designed to work together, that handle all of the low-level functions of a PC. In the original PC, the chipset consisted of close to 30 different chips; today, chipsets usually consist of one, two, or three separate chips embedded into a motherboard.

chkdsk (CheckDisk) Hard drive error detection and, to a certain extent, correction utility in Windows. Originally a DOS command (chkdsk.exe); also the executable for the graphical Error-checking tool.

clean installation Installing an operating system on a fresh drive, following a reformat of that drive. Often it's the only way to correct a problem with a system when many of the crucial operating system files have become corrupted.

cleaning kit Method for cleaning floppy or optical drives.

client Computer program that uses the services of another computer program. Also, software that extracts information from a server; your auto-dial phone is a client, and the phone company is its server. Also, a machine that accesses shared resources on a server.

client/server Relationship in which client software obtains services from a server on behalf of a person.

client/server network Network that has dedicated server machines and client machines.

clock cycle Single charge to the clock wire of a CPU.

clock-multiplying CPU CPU that takes the incoming clock signal and multiples it inside the CPU to let the internal circuitry of the CPU run faster.

clock speed Speed at which a CPU executes instructions, measured in MHz or GHz. In modern CPUs, the internal speed is a multiple of the external speed. (*See also* clock-multiplying CPU.)

clock (CLK) wire A special wire that, when charged, tells the CPU that another piece of information is waiting to be processed.

closed source Software that is solely controlled by its creator or distributor.

cluster Basic unit of storage on a floppy or hard disk. Multiple sectors are contained in a cluster. When Windows stores a file on a disk, it writes those files into dozens or even hundreds of contiguous clusters. If there aren't enough contiguous open clusters available, the operating system finds the next open cluster and writes there, continuing this process until the entire file is saved. The FAT or MFT tracks how the files are distributed among the clusters on the disk.

CMOS (complementary metal-oxide semiconductor) Originally, the type of nonvolatile RAM that held information about the most basic parts of your PC, such as hard drives, floppies, and amount of DRAM. Today, actual CMOS chips have been replaced by flash-type nonvolatile RAM. The information is the same, however, and is still called CMOS—even though it is now almost always stored on Flash RAM.

CMOS setup program Program enabling you to access and update CMOS data.

CNR (communications and networking riser) Proprietary slot used on some motherboards to provide a sound interference–free connection for modems, sound cards, and NICs.

coaxial cable Cabling in which an internal conductor is surrounded by another, outer conductor, thus sharing the same axis.

code Set of symbols representing characters (e.g., ASCII code) or instructions in a computer program (a programmer writes source code, which must be translated into executable or machine code for the computer to use).

code names Names that keep track of different variations within CPU models.

codec (compressor/decompressor) Software that compresses or decompresses media streams.

color depth Term to define a scanner's ability to produce color, hue, and shade.

COM port(s) Serial communications ports available on your computer.

command A request, typed from a terminal or embedded in a file, to perform an operation or to execute a particular program.

command-line interface User interface for an OS devoid of all graphical trappings.

command prompt Text prompt for entering commands.

CompactFlash (CF) One of the older but still popular flash media formats. Its interface uses a simplified PC Card bus, so it also supports I/O devices.

compatibility modes Feature of Windows 2000 and beyond to allow software written for previous versions of Windows to operate in newer operating systems.

compliance Concept that members of an organization must abide by the rules of that organization. For a technician, this often revolves around what software can or cannot be installed on an organization's computer.

component failure Occurs when a system device fails due to a manufacturing or some other type of defect.

Component Services Programming tools in Windows for the sharing of data objects between programs.

compression Process of squeezing data to eliminate redundancies, allowing files to use less space when stored or transmitted.

CompTIA A+ 220-801 One half of the CompTIA A+ certification for PC technicians. The 801 exam focuses primarily on hardware and networking.

CompTIA A+ 220-802 The second half of the CompTIA A+ certification for PC technicians. The 802 exam focuses primarily on software, security, and troubleshooting.

CompTIA A+ certification Industry-wide, vendor-neutral computer certification program that demonstrates competency as a computer technician.

CompTIA Network+ certification Industry-wide, vendor-neutral certification for network technicians, covering network hardware, installation, and troubleshooting.

Computer Default interface in Windows Vista and Windows 7 for Windows Explorer; displays hard drives and devices with removeable storage. (*See* My Computer.)

computer administrator One of three types of user accounts in Windows XP, has access to all resources on the computer. A member of the local Administrators group.

Computer Management Applet in Windows' Administrative Tools that contains several useful snap-ins, such as Device Manager and Disk Management.

computing process Four parts of a computer's operation: input, processing, output, and storage.

Computing Technology Industry Association (CompTIA) Nonprofit IT trade association that administers the CompTIA A+, CompTIA Network+ exams and many other vendor-neutral IT certification exams.

conditioning charger Battery charger that contains intelligent circuitry that prevents portable computer batteries from being overcharged and damaged.

connectors Small receptacles used to attach cables to a system. Common types of connectors include USB, PS/2, and DB-25.

consumables Materials used up by printers, including paper, ink, ribbons, and toner cartridges.

container file File containing two or more separate, compressed tracks, typically an audio track and a moving-picture track. Also known as a *wrapper*.

context menu Small menu brought up by right-clicking on objects in Windows.

Control Panel Collection of Windows applets, or small programs, that can be used to configure various pieces of hardware and software in a system.

controller card Card adapter that connects devices, such as a disk drive, to the main computer bus/motherboard.

convergence Measure of how sharply a single pixel appears on a CRT; a monitor with poor convergence produces images that are not sharply defined.

copy backup Type of backup similar to a normal or full backup, in that all selected files on a system are backed up. This type of backup does not change the archive bit of the files being backed up.

copy command Command in the command-line interface for making a copy of a file and pasting it in another location.

Core Name used for the family of Intel CPUs that succeeded the Pentium 4.

counter Used to track data about a particular object when using the Performance console in Windows XP.

CPU (central processing unit) "Brain" of the computer. Microprocessor that handles primary calculations for the computer. CPUs are known by names such as Core i5 and Phenom II.

CRC (cyclic redundancy check) Very accurate mathematical method used to check for errors in long streams of transmitted data. Before data is sent, the main computer uses the data to calculate a CRC value from the data's contents. If the receiver calculates from the received data a different CRC value, the data was corrupted during transmission and is re-sent. Ethernet packets use the CRC algorithm in the FCS portion of the frame.

C-RIMM or CRIMM (continuity RIMM) Passive device added to populate unused banks in a system that uses Rambus RIMMs.

crimper A specialized tool for connecting UTP wires to an RJ-45 connector. Also called a *crimping tool*.

CrossFire Technology that combines the power of multiple AMD graphics cards in a system.

crossover cable Special UTP cable used to connect hubs or to connect network cards without a hub. Crossover cables reverse the sending and receiving wire pairs from one end to the other.

CRT (cathode ray tube) Tube of a monitor in which rays of electrons are beamed onto a phosphorescent screen to produce images. Also, a shorthand way to describe a monitor that uses CRT rather than LCD technology.

CSMA/CA (carrier sense multiple access/collision avoidance) Networking scheme used by wireless devices to transmit data while avoiding data collisions, which wireless nodes have difficulty detecting.

CSMA/CD (carrier sense multiple access/collision detection) Networking scheme used by Ethernet devices to transmit data and resend data after detection of data collisions.

cylinder Single track on all the platters in a hard drive. Imagine a hard drive as a series of metal cans, nested one inside another; a single can would represent a cylinder.

daily backup Backup of all files that have been changed on that day without changing the archive bits of those files. Also called *daily copy backup*.

daisy-chaining Method of connecting several devices along a bus and managing the signals for each device.

data classification System of organizing data according to its sensitivity. Common classifications include public, highly confidential, and top secret.

data roaming A feature of cellular data systems that enables the signal to jump from cell tower to cell tower and from your provider to another provider without obvious notice.

data structure Scheme that directs how an OS stores and retrieves data on and off a drive. Used interchangeably with the term file system. (*See also* file system.)

DB connectors D-shaped connectors used for a variety of connections in the PC and networking world. Can be male (with prongs) or female (with holes) and have a varying number of pins or sockets. Also called D-sub, D-subminiature, or D-shell connectors.

DB-15 connector A two- or three-row D-sub connector (female) used for 10Base5 networks, MIDI/joysticks, and analog video.

DB-25 connector D-sub connector (female), commonly referred to as a parallel port connector.

DC (direct current) Type of electricity in which the flow of electrons is in a complete circle in one direction.

DDR SDRAM (double data rate SDRAM) Type of DRAM that makes two processes for every clock cycle. (*See also* DRAM.)

DDR2 SDRAM Type of SDRAM that sends 4 bits of data in every clock cycle. (*See also* DDR SDRAM.)

DDR3 SDRAM Type of SDRAM that transfers data at twice the rate of DDR2 SDRAM.

debug To detect, trace, and eliminate errors in computer programs.

decibels Unit of measurement typically associated with sound. The higher the number of decibels, the louder the sound.

dedicated server Machine that is not used for any client functions, only server functions.

default gateway In a TCP/IP network, the nearest router to a particular host. This router's IP address is part of the necessary TCP/IP configuration for communicating with multiple networks using IP.

definition file List of virus signatures that an antivirus program can recognize.

defragmentation (defrag) Procedure in which all the files on a hard disk are rewritten on disk so that all parts of each file reside in contiguous clusters. The result is an improvement in disk speed during retrieval operations.

degauss Procedure used to break up the electromagnetic fields that can build up on the cathode ray tube of a monitor; involves running a current through a wire loop. Most monitors feature a manual degaussing tool.

del (erase) command Command in the command-line interface used to delete/erase files.

desktop User's primary interface to the Windows operating system.

desktop extender Portable computer that offers some of the features of a full-fledged desktop computer but with a much smaller footprint and lower weight.

desktop replacement Portable computer that offers the same performance as a full-fledged desktop computer; these systems are normally very heavy to carry and often cost much more than the desktop systems they replace.

device driver Program used by the operating system to control communications between the computer and peripherals.

Device Manager Utility that enables techs to examine and configure all the hardware and drivers in a Windows PC.

DHCP (Dynamic Host Configuration Protocol) Protocol that enables a DHCP server to set TCP/IP settings automatically for a DHCP client.

differential backup Similar to an incremental backup. Backs up the files that have been changed since the last backup. This type of backup does not change the state of the archive bit.

digital camera Camera that simulates film technology electronically.

digital certificate Form in which a public key is sent from a Web server to a Web browser so that the browser can decrypt the data sent by the server.

Digital Living Network Alliance (DLNA) devices
Devices that connect to a home network, discover each other, and share media. In theory, DLNA devices should work with minimal setup or fuss, even if sourced from different manufacturers.

digital zoom Software tool to enhance the optical zoom capabilities of a digital camera.

digitally signed driver A driver designed specifically to work with Windows that has been tested and certified by Microsoft to work stably with Windows.

digitizer A tablet that enables users to paint, ink, pencil, or otherwise draw on a computer.

DIMM (dual inline memory module) 32- or 64-bit type of DRAM packaging, similar to SIMMs, with the distinction that each side of each tab inserted into the system performs a separate function. DIMMs come in a variety of sizes, with 184- and 240-pin being the most common on desktop computers.

dipole antennas Standard straight-wire antennas that provide the most omnidirectional function.

dir command Command used in the command-line interface to display the entire contents of the current working directory.

directory Another name for a folder.

directory service Centralized index that each PC accesses to locate resources in the domain.

DirectX Set of APIs enabling programs to control multimedia, such as sound, video, and graphics. Used in Windows Vista and Windows 7 to draw the Aero desktop.

Disk Cleanup Utility built into Windows that can help users clean up their disks by removing temporary Internet files, deleting unused program files, and more.

disk cloning Taking a PC and making a duplicate of the hard drive, including all data, software, and configuration files, and transferring it to another PC. (*See* image installation.)

disk duplexing Type of disk mirroring using two separate controllers rather than one; faster than traditional mirroring.

disk initialization A process that places special information on every hard drive installed in a Windows system.

Disk Management Snap-in available with the Microsoft Management Console that enables techs to configure the various disks installed in a system; available in the Computer Management Administrative Tool.

disk mirroring Process by which data is written simultaneously to two or more disk drives. Read and write speed is decreased but redundancy in case of catastrophe is increased.

disk quota Application allowing network administrators to limit hard drive space usage.

disk striping Process by which data is spread among multiple (at least two) drives. Increases speed for both reads and writes of data. Considered RAID level 0 because it does not provide fault tolerance.

disk striping with parity Method for providing fault tolerance by writing data across multiple drives and then including an additional drive, called a parity drive, that stores information to rebuild the data contained on the other drives. Requires at least three physical disks: two for the data and a third for the parity drive. This provides data redundancy at RAID levels 3–5 with different options.

disk thrashing Hard drive that is constantly being accessed due to lack of available system memory. When system memory runs low, a Windows system will utilize hard disk space as "virtual" memory, thus causing an unusual amount of hard drive access.

diskpart A fully functioning command-line partitioning tool.

display adapter Handles all the communication between the CPU and the monitor. Also known as a video card.

Display applet Tool in Windows XP and Windows 7 used to adjust display settings, including resolution, refresh rate, driver information, and color depth. (For the comparable tool in Windows Vista, *see* Personalization applet.)

DisplayPort Digital video connector used by Apple Mac desktop models and some PCs, notably from Dell. Designed by VESA as a royalty-free connector to replace VGA and DVI.

DMA (direct memory access) modes Technique that some PC hardware devices use to transfer data to and from the memory without using the CPU.

DMA controller Resides between the RAM and the devices and handles DMA requests.

DNS (domain name service) TCP/IP name resolution system that translates a host name into an IP address.

DNS domain Specific branch of the DNS name space. First-level DNS domains include .com, .gov, and .edu.

docking station Device that provides a portable computer extra features such as a DVD drive or PC Card, in addition to legacy and modern ports. Similar to a port replicator.

document findings, actions, and outcomes Recording each troubleshooting job: what the problem was, how it was fixed, and other helpful information. (One of the steps a technician uses to solve a problem.)

Documents folder Windows Vista/7 folder for storing user-created files. Replaces the My Documents folder previously used in Windows 2000/XP. (*See* My Documents.)

Dolby Digital Technology for sound reductions and channeling methods used for digital audio.

domain Groupings of users, computers, or networks. In Microsoft networking, a domain is a group of computers and users that share a common account database and a common security policy. On the Internet, a domain is a group of computers that share a common element in their hierarchical name. Other types of domains exist—e.g., broadcast domain, etc.

domain-based network Network that eliminates the need for logging on to multiple servers by using domain controllers to hold the security database for all systems.

DOS (Disk Operating System) First popular operating system available for PCs. A text-based, single-tasking operating system that was not completely replaced until the introduction of Windows 95.

dot-matrix printer Printer that creates each character from an array of dots. Pins striking a ribbon against the paper, one pin for each dot position, form the dots. May be a serial printer (printing one character at a time) or a line printer.

dot pitch Value relating to CRTs, showing the diagonal distance between phosphors measured in millimeters.

double-sided RAM RAM stick with RAM chips soldered to both sides of the stick. May only be used with motherboards designed to accept double-sided RAM. Very common.

dpi (dots per inch) Measure of printer resolution that counts the dots the device can produce per linear (horizontal) inch.

DPMS (display power-management signaling) Specification that can reduce CRT power consumption by 75 percent by reducing/eliminating video signals during idle periods.

DRAM (dynamic random access memory or dynamic RAM) Memory used to store data in most personal computers. DRAM stores each bit in a "cell" composed of a transistor and a capacitor. Because the capacitor in a DRAM cell can only hold a charge for a few milliseconds, DRAM must be continually refreshed, or rewritten, to retain its data.

DriveLock CMOS program enabling you to control the ATA security mode feature set. Also known as *drive lock*.

driver signing Digital signature for drivers used by Windows to protect against potentially bad drivers.

DS3D (DirectSound3D) Introduced with DirectX 3.0, DS3D is a command set used to create positional audio, or sounds that appear to come from in front, in back, or to the side of a user. Merged with DirectSound into DirectAudio in DirectX 8. (*See also* DirectX.)

DSL (digital subscriber line) High-speed Internet connection technology that uses a regular telephone line for connectivity. DSL comes in several varieties, including asynchronous (ADSL) and synchronous (SDSL), and many speeds. Typical home-user DSL connections are ADSL with a download speed of 7 Mbps and an upload speed of 512 Kbps.

D-subminiature *See* DB connectors.

DTS (Digital Theatre Systems) Technology for sound reductions and channeling methods, similar to Dolby Digital.

dual boot Refers to a computer with two operating systems installed, enabling users to choose which operating system to load on boot. Can also refer to kicking a device a second time just in case the first time didn't work.

dual-channel architecture Using two sticks of RAM (either RDRAM or DDR) to increase throughput.

dual-channel memory Form of DDR, DDR2, and DDR3 memory access used by many motherboards that requires two identical sticks of DDR, DDR2, or DDR3 RAM.

dual-core CPUs that have two execution units on the same physical chip but share caches and RAM.

dual-scan passive matrix Manufacturing technique for increasing display updates by refreshing two lines at a time.

DualView Microsoft feature enabling Windows to use two or more monitors simultaneously.

dumpster diving To go through someone's trash in search of information.

DUN (Dial-up Networking) Software used by Windows to govern the connection between the modem and the ISP.

duplexing Similar to mirroring in that data is written to and read from two physical drives, for fault tolerance. Separate controllers are used for each drive, both for additional fault tolerance and for additional speed. Considered RAID level 1. Also called *disk duplexing* or *drive duplexing*.

Duron Lower-cost version of AMD's Athlon series of CPUs.

DVD (digital versatile disc) Optical disc format that provides for 4–17 GB of video or data storage.

DVD-ROM DVD equivalent of the standard CD-ROM.

DVD-RW/DVD+RW Incompatible rewritable DVD media formats.

DVD-Video DVD format used exclusively to store digital video; capable of storing over 2 hours of high-quality video on a single DVD.

DVI (Digital Visual Interface) Special video connector designed for digital-to-digital connections; most commonly seen on PC video cards and LCD monitors. Some versions also support analog signals with a special adapter.

dxdiag (DirectX Diagnostics Tool) Diagnostic tool for getting information about and testing a computer's DirectX version.

dye-sublimation printer Printer that uses a roll of heat-sensitive plastic film embedded with dyes, which are vaporized and then solidified onto specially coated paper to create a high-quality image.

dynamic disks Special feature of Windows that enables users to span a single volume across two or more drives. Dynamic disks do not have partitions; they have volumes. Dynamic disks can be striped, mirrored, and striped or mirrored with parity.

EAX (Environment Audio eXtensions) 3-D sound technology developed by Creative Labs but now supported by most sound cards.

ECC (error correction code) Special software, embedded on hard drives, that constantly scans the drives for bad sectors.

ECC RAM/DRAM (error correction code DRAM) RAM that uses special chips to detect and fix memory errors.

Commonly used in high-end servers where data integrity is crucial.

effective permissions User's combined permissions granted by multiple groups.

EFI (Extensible Firmware Interface) Firmware created by Intel and HP that replaced traditional 16-bit BIOS and added several new enhancements.

EFS (encrypting file system) Encryption tool found in NTFS 5 and later.

EIA/TIA *See* TIA/EIA.

EIDE (Enhanced IDE) Marketing concept of hard drive–maker Western Digital, encompassing four improvements for IDE drives, including drives larger than 528 MB, four devices, increase in drive throughput, and non–hard drive devices. (*See* ATAPI, PIO mode.)

electric potential The voltage differential between any two objects, one of which is frequently ground or earth, resulting in a degree of attraction for the electrons to move from one of the objects to the other. A large difference between a person and a doorknob, for example, can lead to a shocking experience when the two touch. *See* electrostatic discharge (ESD).

electromagnetic interference (EMI) Electrical interference from one device to another, resulting in poor performance of the device being interfered with. Examples: Static on your TV while running a blow dryer, or placing two monitors too close together and getting a "shaky" screen.

electrostatic discharge (ESD) Uncontrolled rush of electrons from one object to another. A real menace to PCs, as it can cause permanent damage to semiconductors.

eliciting answers Communication strategy designed to help techs understand a user's problems better. Works by listening to a user's description of a problem and then asking cogent questions.

e-mail (electronic mail) Messages, usually text, sent from one person to another via computer. Can also be sent automatically to a group of addresses (mailing list).

emergency repair disk (ERD) Saves critical boot files and partition information and is the main tool for fixing boot problems in Windows 2000.

emulator Software or hardware that converts the commands to and from the host machine into an entirely different platform.

encryption Making data unreadable by those who do not possess a key or password.

equipment rack A metal structure used in equipment rooms to secure network hardware devices and patch panels. Most racks are 19 inches wide. Devices designed to fit in such a rack use a height measurement called *units*, or simply *U*.

erase lamp Component inside laser printers that uses light to make the coating of the photosensitive drum conductive.

Error-checking Windows graphical tool that scans and fixes hard drive problems. Often referred to by the name of the executable, chkdsk, or Check Disk.

eSATA Serial ATA-based connector for external hard drives and optical drives.

escalate Process used when person assigned to repair a problem is not able to get the job done, such as sending the problem to someone with more expertise.

Establish a plan of action and implement the solution
After establishing and testing a theory about a particular problem, techs solve the problem. (One of the steps a technician uses to solve a problem.)

Establish a theory of probable cause After identifying a problem, techs question the obvious to determine what might be the source of the problem. (One of the steps a technician uses to solve a problem.)

Ethernet Name coined by Xerox for the first standard of network cabling and protocols. Based on a bus topology.

Ethic of Reciprocity Golden Rule: Do unto others as you would have them do unto you.

EULA (End User License Agreement) Agreement that accompanies a piece of software, to which the user must agree before using the software. Outlines the terms of use for the software and also lists any actions on the part of the user that violate the agreement.

event auditing Feature of Event Viewer's Security section that creates an entry in the Security Log when certain events happen, such as a user logging on.

Event Viewer Utility made available as an MMC snap-in that enables users to monitor various system events, including network bandwidth usage and CPU utilization.

expand Command-line utility included with Windows used to access files within CAB files.

expansion bus Set of wires going to the CPU, governed by the expansion bus crystal, directly connected to expansion slots of varying types (PCI, AGP, PCIe, etc.).

expansion bus crystal Controls the speed of the expansion bus.

expansion slots Connectors on a motherboard that enable users to add optional components to a system. (*See also* AGP, PCI, and PCIe.)

ExpressCard The high-performance serial version of the PC Card that replaced PC Card slots on laptop PCs over the past decade. ExpressCard comes in two widths: 34 mm and 54 mm, called *ExpressCard/34* and *ExpressCard/54*.

extended partition Type of nonbootable hard disk partition. May only have one extended partition per disk. Purpose is to divide a large disk into smaller partitions, each with a separate drive letter.

Extensible Authentication Protocol (EAP) Authentication wrapper that EAP-compliant applications can use to accept one of many types of authentication. While EAP is a general-purpose authentication wrapper, its only substantial use is in wireless networks.

extension Two, three, four, five or more letters that follow a filename and identify the type of file. Common file extensions are .zip, .exe, .doc, .java, and .xhtml.

external data bus (EDB) Primary data highway of all computers. Everything in your computer is tied either directly or indirectly to the external data bus. (*See also* frontside bus and backside bus.)

Fast User Switching Account option that is useful when multiple users share a system; allows users to switch without logging off.

FAT (file allocation table) Hidden table that records how files on a hard disk are stored in distinct clusters; the only way DOS knows where to access files. Address of first cluster of a file is stored in the directory file. FAT entry for the first cluster is the address of the second cluster used to store that file. In the entry for the second cluster for that file is the address for the third cluster, and so on until the final cluster, which gets a special end-of-file code. There are two FATs, mirror images of each other, in case one is destroyed or damaged. Also refers to the 16-bit file allocation table when used by Windows 2000 and later NT-based operating systems.

FAT16 File allocation table that uses 16 bits for addressing clusters. Used as the primary hard drive format on DOS and early Windows 95 machines; currently used with smaller (2 GB or less) capacity flash media devices.

FAT32 File allocation table that uses 32 bits for addressing clusters. Commonly used with Windows 98 and Windows Me systems. Some Windows 2000 Professional and Windows XP systems also use FAT32, although most modern Windows systems use the more robust NTFS. Default format for flash media devices larger than 2 GB.

FAT64 (exFAT) A Microsoft-proprietary file system that breaks the 4-GB file-size barrier, supporting files up to 16 exabytes (EB) and a theoretical partition limit of 64 zettabytes (ZB). Envisioned for use with flash media devices with a capacity exceeding 2 TB.

FCS (Frame Check Sequence) Portion of an Ethernet frame used for error checking, most commonly with the CRC algorithm.

FDISK Disk-partitioning utility used in DOS and Windows 9*x* systems.

fiber-optic cable High-speed cable for transmitting data, made of high-purity glass sealed within an opaque tube. Much faster than conventional copper wire such as coaxial cable.

file Collection of any form of data that is stored beyond the time of execution of a single job. A file may contain program instructions or data, which may be numerical, textual, or graphical information.

file allocation unit Another term for cluster. (*See also* cluster.)

file association Windows term for the proper program to open a particular file; for example, the file association for opening .MP3 files might be Winamp.

file format How information is encoded in a file. Two primary types are binary (pictures) and ASCII (text), but within those are many formats, such as BMP and GIF for pictures. Commonly represented by a suffix at the end of the filename; for example, .txt for a text file or .exe for an executable.

file server Computer designated to store software, courseware, administrative tools, and other data on a LAN or WAN. It "serves" this information to other computers via the network when users enter their personal access codes.

file system Scheme that directs how an OS stores and retrieves data on and off a drive; FAT32 and NTFS are both file systems. Used interchangeably with the term "data structure." (*See also* data structure.)

filename Name assigned to a file when the file is first written on a disk. Every file on a disk within the same folder must have a unique name. Filenames can contain any character (including spaces), except the following: \ / : * ? " < > |

Files and Settings Transfer Wizard Windows XP's system for moving files and settings to a new PC.

firewall Device that restricts traffic between a local network and the Internet.

FireWire (IEEE 1394) Interconnection standard to send wide-band signals over a serialized, physically thin connector system. Serial bus developed by Apple and Texas Instruments; enables connection of 63 devices at speeds up to 800 megabits per second.

firmware Embedded programs or code stored on a ROM chip. Generally OS-independent, thus allowing devices to operate in a wide variety of circumstances without direct OS support. The system BIOS is firmware.

Flash ROM ROM technology that can be electrically reprogrammed while still in the PC. Overwhelmingly the most common storage medium of BIOS in PCs today, as it can be upgraded without a need to open the computer on most systems.

flatbed scanner Most popular form of consumer scanner; runs a bright light along the length of the tray to capture an image.

FlexATX Motherboard form factor. Motherboards built in accordance with the FlexATX form factor are very small, much smaller than microATX motherboards.

Flip 3D In the Aero desktop environment, a three-dimensional replacement for ALT-TAB. Accessed by pressing the WINDOWS KEY-TAB key combination.

floating point unit (FPU) Special CPU circuitry that handles complex numbers.

floppy disk Removable storage media that can hold between 720 KB and 1.44 MB of data.

floppy drive System hardware that uses removable 3.5-inch disks as storage media.

flux reversal Point at which a read/write head detects a change in magnetic polarity.

FM synthesis Producing sound by electronic emulation of various instruments to more-or-less produce music and other sound effects.

Folders list A tree menu in Windows Explorer for Windows 2000 and XP that displays the file structure on the left side of the window; toggled on with the Folders button. In Windows Vista and 7, the Folders list is active by default.

form factor Standard for the physical organization of motherboard components and motherboard size. Most common form factors are ATX and BTX.

format command Command in the command-line interface used to format a storage device.

formatting Magnetically mapping a disk to provide a structure for storing data; can be done to any type of disk,

including a floppy disk, hard disk, or other type of removable disk.

FPU (floating point unit) Formal term for math coprocessor (also called a numeric processor) circuitry inside a CPU. A math coprocessor calculates by using a floating point math (which allows for decimals). Before the Intel 80486, FPUs were separate chips from the CPU.

fragmentation Occurs when files and directories get jumbled on a fixed disk and are no longer contiguous. Can significantly slow down hard drive access times and can be repaired by using the defrag utility included with each version of Windows. (*See also* defragmentation.)

frame A data unit transferred across a network. Frames consist of several parts, such as the sending and receiving MAC addresses, the data being sent, and the frame check sequence.

freeware Software that is distributed for free, with no license fee.

frequency Measure of a sound's tone, either high or low.

frontside bus Wires that connect the CPU to the main system RAM. Generally running at speeds of 66–133 MHz. Distinct from the expansion bus and the backside bus, though it shares wires with the former.

front-view projector Shoots the image out the front and counts on you to put a screen in front at the proper distance.

FRU (field replaceable unit) Any part of a PC that is considered to be replaceable "in the field," i.e., a customer location. There is no official list of FRUs—it is usually a matter of policy by the repair center.

FTP (File Transfer Protocol) Rules that enable two computers to talk to one another during a file transfer. Protocol used when you transfer a file from one computer to another across the Internet. FTP uses port numbers 20 and 21.

fuel cells Power source that uses chemical reactions to produce electricity. Lightweight, compact, and stable devices expected to replace batteries as the primary power source for portable PCs.

full-duplex Any device that can send and receive data simultaneously.

Full-Speed USB USB standard that runs at 12 Mbps. Also known as USB 1.1.

Function (fn) key Special key on many laptops that enables some keys to perform a third duty.

fuser assembly Mechanism in laser printers that uses two rollers to fuse toner to paper during the print process.

future-proofing Configuring a PC so that it will run programs (especially games) released in the coming years.

gain Ratio of increase of radio frequency output provided by an antenna, measured in decibels (dB).

GDI (graphical device interface) Component of Windows that utilizes the CPU rather than the printer to process a print job as a bitmapped image of each page.

general protection fault (GPF) Error code usually seen when separate active programs conflict on resources or data.

geometry Numbers representing three values: heads, cylinders, and sectors per track; defines where a hard drive stores data.

geotracking Feature in cellular phones that enables the cell phone companies and government agencies to use the ID or MAC address to pinpoint where your phone is at any given time.

giga Prefix for the quantity 1,073,741,824 (2^{30}) or for 1 billion. One gigabyte would be 1,073,741,824 bytes, except with hard drive labeling, where it means 1 billion bytes. One gigahertz is 1 billion hertz.

Global Positioning System (GPS) Technology that enables a mobile device to determine where you are on a map.

globally unique identifier (GUID) partition table (GPT) Partitioning scheme that enables you to create more than four primary partitions without needing to use dynamic disks.

GPU (graphics processing unit) Specialized processor that helps the CPU by taking over all of the 3-D rendering duties.

grayscale depth Number that defines how many shades of gray the scanner can save per dot.

grayware Program that intrudes into a user's computer experience without damaging any systems or data.

group Collection of user accounts that share the same access capabilities.

Group Policy Means of easily controlling the settings of multiple network clients with policies such as setting minimum password length or preventing Registry edits.

guest account Very limited built-in account type for Windows; a member of the Guest group.

GUI (graphical user interface) Interface that enables user to interact with computer graphically, by using a mouse or other pointing device to manipulate icons that represent programs or documents, instead of using only text as in early interfaces. Pronounced "gooey."

gyroscope Device that can detect the position of the tablet or phone in 3-D space.

HAL (hardware abstraction layer) Part of the Windows OS that separates system-specific device drivers from the rest of the NT system.

handshaking Procedure performed by modems, terminals, and computers to verify that communication has been correctly established.

hang When a computer freezes and does not respond to keyboard commands, it is said to "hang" or to have "hung."

hang time Number of seconds a too-often-hung computer is airborne after you have thrown it out a second-story window.

hard drive Data-recording system using solid disks of magnetic material turning at high speeds to store and retrieve programs and data in a computer. Abbreviated HDD for *hard disk drive*.

hardware Physical computer equipment such as electrical, electronic, magnetic, and mechanical devices. Anything in the computer world that you can hold in your hand. A floppy drive is hardware; Microsoft Word is not.

hardware profile Feature in Windows XP that enables the user to switch several hardware configurations at once during the Windows boot process.

hardware protocol Defines many aspects of a network, from the packet type to the cabling and connectors used.

HBA (host bus adapter) Connects SATA devices to the expansion bus. Also known as the SATA controller.

HD (Hi-Definition) Multimedia transmission standard that defines high-resolution images and 5.1, 6.1, and 7.1 sound.

HDA (High Definition Audio) Intel-designed standard to support features such as true surround sound with many discrete speakers. Often referred to by its code name, Azalia.

HDD (hard disk drive) Data-recording system using solid disks of magnetic material turning at high speeds to store and retrieve programs and data in a computer.

HDMI (High Definition Multimedia Interface) Single multimedia connection that includes both high-definition video and audio. One of the best connections for outputting to television. Also contains copy protection features.

head actuator Mechanism for moving the arms inside a hard drive on which the read/write heads are mounted.

heads Short for read/write heads used by hard drives to store data.

heat dope *See* thermal compound.

hex (hexadecimal) Base-16 numbering system using ten digits (0 through 9) and six letters (A through F). In the computer world, shorthand way to write binary numbers by substituting one hex digit for a four-digit binary number (e.g., hex 9 = binary 1001).

hibernation Power management setting in which all data from RAM is written to the hard drive before going to sleep. Upon waking up, all information is retrieved from the hard drive and returned to RAM.

hidden attribute File attribute that, when used, does not allow the dir command to show a file.

hierarchical directory tree Method by which Windows organizes files into a series of folders, called directories, under the root directory. (*See also* root directory.)

high gloss Laptop screen finish that offers sharper contrast, richer colors, and wider viewing angles than a matte finish, but is also much more reflective.

high-level formatting Format that sets up a file system on a drive.

high-voltage anode Component in a CRT monitor that has very high voltages of electricity flowing through it.

Hi-Speed USB USB standard that runs at 480 Mbps. Also referred to as USB 2.0.

home screen The default "desktop" of a mobile device.

home server PC A computer built to store files on a small office/home office (SOHO) network.

HomeGroup A Windows 7 feature that connects a group of computers using a common password—no special user names required. Each computer can be a member of only one homegroup at a time. Homegroups enable simple sharing of documents and printers between computers.

honesty Telling the truth—a very important thing for a tech to do.

horizontal cabling Cabling that connects the equipment room to the work areas.

host On a TCP/IP network, single device that has an IP address—any device (usually a computer) that can be the source or destination of a data packet. In the mainframe world, computer that is made available for use by multiple people simultaneously. Also, in virtualization, a computer running one or more virtual operating systems.

hot-swappable Any hardware that may be attached to or removed from a PC without interrupting the PC's normal processing.

HRR (horizontal refresh rate) Amount of time it takes for a CRT to draw one horizontal line of pixels on a display.

HTML (Hypertext Markup Language) ASCII-based, script-like language for creating hypertext documents such as those on the World Wide Web.

HTPC A home theater PC designed to attach to a TV or projector for movie and TV viewing.

HTTP (Hypertext Transfer Protocol) Extremely fast protocol used for network file transfers in the WWW environment. Uses port 80.

HTTPS (HTTP over Secure Sockets Layer) Secure form of HTTP used commonly for Internet business transactions or any time when a secure connection is required. Uses port 443. (*See also* HTTP.)

hub Electronic device that sits at the center of a star topology network, providing a common point for the connection of network devices. Hubs repeat all information out to all ports and have been replaced by switches, although the term is still commonly used.

hybrid A network topology that combines features from multiple other topologies, such as the star-bus topology.

hyperthreading CPU feature that enables a single pipeline to run more than one thread at once.

hypervisor Software that enables a single computer to run multiple operating systems simultaneously.

I/O (input/output) General term for reading and writing data to a computer. "Input" includes data entered from a keyboard, identified by a pointing device (such as a mouse), or loaded from a disk. "Output" includes writing information to a disk, viewing it on a CRT, or printing it to a printer.

I/O addressing Using the address bus to talk to system devices.

I/O advanced programmable interrupt controller (IOAPIC) Typically located in the Southbridge, acts as the traffic cop for interrupt requests to the CPU.

I/O base address First value in an I/O address range.

ICH (I/O Controller Hub) Official name for Southbridge chip found in Intel's chipsets.

icon Small image or graphic, most commonly found on a system's desktop, that launches a program when selected.

ICS (Internet Connection Sharing) Windows feature that enables a single network connection to be shared among several machines. ICS was first introduced with Windows 98.

IDE (integrated drive electronics) PC specification for small- to medium-sized hard drives in which the controlling electronics for the drive are part of the drive itself, speeding up transfer rates and leaving only a simple adapter (or "paddle"). IDE only supported two drives per system of no more than 504 MB each, and has been completely supplanted by Enhanced IDE. EIDE supports four drives of over 8 GB each and more than doubles the transfer rate. The more common name for PATA drives. Also known as *intelligent drive electronics*. (*See* PATA.)

identify the problem To question the user and find out what has been changed recently or is no longer working properly. (One of the steps a technician uses to solve a problem.)

IEC-320 Connects the cable supplying AC power from a wall outlet into the power supply.

IEEE (Institute of Electronic and Electrical Engineers) Leading standards-setting group in the United States.

IEEE 1284 IEEE standard governing parallel communication.

IEEE 1394 IEEE standard governing FireWire communication. (*See also* FireWire.)

IEEE 1394a FireWire standard that runs at 400 Mbps.

IEEE 1394b FireWire standard that runs at 800 Mbps.

IEEE 802.11 Wireless Ethernet standard more commonly known as Wi-Fi.

image deployment Operating system installation that uses a complete image of a hard drive as an installation media. Helpful when installing an operating system on a large number of identical PCs.

image file Bit-by-bit image of data to be burned on CD or DVD—from one file to an entire disc—stored as a single file on a hard drive. Particularly handy when copying from CD to CD or DVD to DVD.

IMAP4 (Internet Message Access Protocol version 4) An alternative to POP3 that retrieves e-mail from an e-mail server, like POP3; IMAP uses TCP port 143.

impact printer Uses pins and inked ribbons to print text or images on a piece of paper.

impedance Amount of resistance to an electrical signal on a wire. Relative measure of the amount of data a cable can handle.

incident report Record of the details of an accident, including what happened and where it happened.

incremental backup Backs up all files that have their archive bits turned on, meaning that they have been changed since the last backup. Turns the archive bits off after the files have been backed up.

Information Technology (IT) Field of computers, their operation, and their maintenance.

infrastructure mode Wireless networking mode that uses one or more WAPs to connect the wireless network nodes to a wired network segment.

inheritance NTFS feature that passes on the same permissions in any subfolders/files resident in the original folder.

ink cartridge Small container of ink for inkjet printers.

inkjet printer Uses liquid ink, sprayed through a series of tiny jets, to print text or images on a piece of paper.

installation disc Typically a CD-ROM or DVD that holds all the necessary device drivers.

instruction set All of the machine-language commands that a particular CPU is designed to understand.

integrated memory controller (IMC) Memory controller circuitry built into the CPU. An IMC enables faster control over things like the large L3 cache shared among multiple cores.

integrity Always doing the right thing.

interface Means by which a user interacts with a piece of software.

Interrupt 13 (INT13) extensions Improved type of BIOS that accepts EIDE drives up to 137 GB.

interrupt/interruption Suspension of a process, such as the execution of a computer program, caused by an event external to the computer and performed in such a way that the process can be resumed. Events of this kind include sensors monitoring laboratory equipment or a user pressing an interrupt key.

inverter Device used to convert DC current into AC. Commonly used with CCFLs in laptops and flatbed scanners.

iOS The operating system of Apple mobile devices.

IP address Numeric address of a computer connected to the Internet. An IPv4 address is made up of four octets of 8-bit binary numbers translated into their shorthand numeric values. An IPv6 address is 128 bits long. The IP address can be broken down into a network ID and a host ID. Also called *Internet address.*

ipconfig Command-line utility for Windows servers and workstations that displays the current TCP/IP configuration of the machine. Similar to winipcfg and ifconfig.

IPsec (Internet Protocol security) Microsoft's encryption method of choice for networks consisting of multiple networks linked by a private connection, providing transparent encryption between the server and the client.

IPv4 (Internet Protocol version 4) Internet standard protocol that provides a common layer over dissimilar networks; used to move packets among host computers and through gateways if necessary. Part of the TCP/IP protocol suite. Uses the dotted-decimal format—xxx.xxx.xxx.xxx.

IPv6 (Internet Protocol version 6) Protocol in which addresses consist of eight sets of four hexadecimal numbers, each number being a value between 0000 and FFFF, using a colon to separate the numbers. Here's an example: FEDC:BA98:7654:3210:0800:200C:00CF:1234.

IrDA (Infrared Data Association) protocol Protocol that enables communication through infrared devices, with speeds of up to 4 Mbps.

IRQ (interrupt request) Signal from a hardware device, such as a modem or a mouse, indicating that it needs the CPU's attention. In PCs, IRQs are sent along specific IRQ channels associated with a particular device. IRQ conflicts were a common problem in the past when adding expansion boards, but the plug-and-play specification has removed this headache in most cases.

ISA (Industry Standard Architecture) Industry Standard Architecture design was found in the original IBM PC for the slots that allowed additional hardware to be connected to the computer's motherboard. An 8-bit, 8.33-MHz expansion bus was designed by IBM for its AT computer and released to the public domain. An improved 16-bit bus was also released to the public domain. Replaced by PCI in the mid-1990s.

ISDN (integrated services digital network) CCITT (Comité Consultatif Internationale de Télégraphie et Télé-phonie) standard that defines a digital method for communications to replace the current analog telephone system. ISDN is superior to POTS telephone lines because it supports a transfer rate of up to 128 Kbps for sending information from computer to computer. It also allows data and voice to share a common phone line. DSL reduced demand for ISDN substantially. (*See also* POTS.)

ISO-9660 CD format to support PC file systems on CD media. Supplanted by the Joliet format.

ISO file Complete copy (or image) of a storage media device, typically used for optical discs.

ISP (Internet service provider) Company that provides access to the Internet, usually for money.

jack (physical connection) Part of a connector into which a plug is inserted. Also referred to as ports.

Joliet Extension of the ISO 9660 format. Most popular CD format to support PC file systems on CD media.

joule Unit of energy describing (in this book) how much energy a surge suppressor can handle before it fails.

joystick Peripheral often used while playing computer games; originally intended as a multipurpose input device.

Jump List A Windows 7 menu that shows context-sensitive information about whatever is on the taskbar.

jumper Pair of small pins that can be shorted with a shunt to configure many aspects of PCs. Often used in configurations that are rarely changed, such as master/slave settings on IDE drives.

Kerberos Authentication encryption developed by MIT to enable multiple brands of servers to authenticate multiple brands of clients.

kernel Core portion of program that resides in memory and performs the most essential operating system tasks.

keyboard Input device. Three common types of keyboards exist: those that use a mini-DIN (PS/2) connection, those that use a USB connection, and those that use wireless technology.

Knowledge Base Large collection of documents and FAQs that is maintained by Microsoft. Found on Microsoft's Web site, the Knowledge Base is an excellent place to search for assistance on most operating system problems.

KVM (keyboard, video, mouse) switch Hardware device that enables multiple computers to be viewed and controlled by a single mouse, keyboard, and screen.

LAN (local area network) Group of PCs connected via cabling, radio, or infrared that use this connectivity to share resources such as printers and mass storage.

laptop Traditional clamshell portable computing device with built-in LCD monitor, keyboard, and trackpad.

laser Single-wavelength, in-phase light source that is sometimes strapped to the head of sharks by bad guys. Note to henchmen: Lasers should never be used with sea bass, no matter how ill-tempered they might be.

laser printer Electro-photographic printer in which a laser is used as the light source.

Last Known Good Configuration Option on the Advanced Startup Options menu that enables your system to revert to a previous configuration to troubleshoot and repair any major system problems.

latency Amount of delay before a device may respond to a request; most commonly used in reference to RAM.

LBA (logical block addressing) Translation (algorithm) of IDE drives promoted by Western Digital as a standardized method for breaking the 504-MB limit in IDE drives. Subsequently universally adopted by the PC industry and now standard on all EIDE drives.

LCD (liquid crystal display) Type of display commonly used on portable PCs. Also have mostly replaced CRTs as the display of choice for most desktop computer users, due in large part to rapidly falling prices and increasing quality. LCDs use liquid crystals and electricity to produce images on the screen.

LED (light-emitting diode) Solid-state device that vibrates at luminous frequencies when current is applied.

LED monitor LCD monitor that uses LEDs instead of CCFL tubes for backlighting, creating much higher contrast ratios and image quality.

Level 1 (L1) cache First RAM cache accessed by the CPU, which stores only the absolute most-accessed programming and data used by currently running threads. Always the smallest and fastest cache on the CPU.

Level 2 (L2) cache Second RAM cache accessed by the CPU. Much larger and often slower than the L1 cache, and accessed only if the requested program/data is not in the L1 cache.

Level 3 (L3) cache Third RAM cache accessed by the CPU. Much larger and slower than the L1 and L2 caches, and accessed only if the requested program/data is not in the L2 cache. Seen only on high-end CPUs.

Li-Ion (Lithium-Ion) Battery commonly used in portable PCs. Li-Ion batteries don't suffer from the memory effects of Nickel-Cadmium (Ni-Cd) batteries and provide much more power for a greater length of time.

Library Feature in Windows 7 that aggregates folders from multiple locations and places them in a single, easy-to-find spot in Windows Explorer.

Lightweight Directory Access Protocol (LDAP) Protocol used by many operating systems and applications to access directories.

limited user account User account in Windows XP that has limited access to a system. Accounts of this type cannot alter system files, cannot install new programs, and cannot edit settings by using the Control Panel.

link light An LED on NICs, hubs, and switches that lights up to show good connection between the devices.

Linux Open-source UNIX-clone operating system.

liquid cooling A method of cooling a PC that works by running some liquid—usually water—through a metal block that sits on top of the CPU, absorbing heat. The liquid gets heated by the block, runs out of the block and into something that cools the liquid, and is then pumped through the block again.

Live DVD The Windows installation media, which loads the Windows Preinstallation Environment (WinPE) directly from disc into memory and doesn't access or modify the hard drive.

Local Security Policy Windows tool used to set local security policies on an individual system.

local user account List of user names and their associated passwords with access to a system, contained in an encrypted database.

Local Users and Groups Tool enabling creation and changing of group memberships and accounts for users.

log files Files created in Windows to track the progress of certain processes.

logical drives Sections of an extended partition on a hard drive that are formatted and (usually) assigned a drive letter, each of which is presented to the user as if it were a separate drive.

logon screen First screen of the Windows interface, used to log on to the computer system.

loopback plug Device used during loopback tests to check the female connector on a NIC.

Low-Speed USB USB standard that runs at 1.5 Mbps. Also called USB 1.1.

LPT port Commonly referred to as a printer port; usually associated with a local parallel port.

LPX First slimline form factor; replaced by NLX form factor.

lumens Unit of measure for amount of brightness on a projector or other light source.

Mac (Also **Macintosh**.) Apple Computers' flagship operating system, currently up to OS Xv10.8 "Mountain Lion" and running on Intel-based hardware.

MAC (media access control) address Unique 48-bit address assigned to each network card. IEEE assigns blocks of possible addresses to various NIC manufacturers to help ensure that the address is always unique. The Data Link layer of the OSI model uses MAC addresses for locating machines.

MAC address filtering Method of limiting wireless network access based on the physical, hard-wired address of the units' wireless NIC.

machine language Binary instruction code that is understood by the CPU.

maintenance kits Set of commonly replaced printer components provided by many manufacturers.

mass storage Hard drives, CD-ROMs, removable media drives, etc.

matte Laptop screen finish that offers a good balance between richness of colors and reflections, but washes out in bright light.

MBR (master boot record) Tiny bit of code that takes control of the boot process from the system BIOS.

MCC (memory controller chip) Chip that handles memory requests from the CPU. Although once a special chip, it has been integrated into the chipset or CPU on modern PCs.

MCH (Memory Controller Hub) Intel-coined name for what is now commonly called the Northbridge.

md (mkdir) command Command in the command-line interface used to create directories.

mega- Prefix that stands for the binary quantity 1,048,576 (2^{20}) or the decimal quantity of 1,000,000. One megabyte is 1,048,576 bytes. One megahertz, however, is a million hertz. Sometimes shortened to *Meg*, as in "a 286 has an address space of 16 Megs."

megapixel Term used typically in reference to digital cameras and their ability to capture data.

memory Device or medium for temporary storage of programs and data during program execution. Synonymous with storage, although it most frequently refers to the internal storage of a computer that can be directly addressed by operating instructions. A computer's temporary storage capacity is measured in kilobytes (KB), megabytes (MB), or gigabytes (GB) of RAM (random-access memory). Long-term data storage on disks is also measured in kilobytes, megabytes, gigabytes, and terabytes.

memory addressing Taking memory address from system RAM and using it to address nonsystem RAM or ROM so the CPU can access it.

Memory Stick Sony's flash memory card format; rarely seen outside of Sony devices.

mesh topology Network topology where each computer has a dedicated line to every other computer, most often used in wireless networks.

MFT (master file table) Enhanced file allocation table used by NTFS. (*See also* FAT.)

microATX (μATX) Variation of the ATX form factor, which uses the ATX power supply. MicroATX motherboards are generally smaller than their ATX counterparts but retain all the same functionality.

microBTX Variation of the BTX form factor. MicroBTX motherboards are generally smaller than their BTX counterparts but retain all the same functionality.

microdrive Tiny hard drives using the CompactFlash form factor. (*See also* CompactFlash (CF).)

microprocessor "Brain" of a computer. Primary computer chip that determines relative speed and capabilities of the computer. Also called CPU.

Microsoft Certified IT Professional (MCITP) An advanced IT certification specifically covering Microsoft products.

MIDI (musical instrument digital interface) Interface between a computer and a device for simulating musical instruments. Rather than sending large sound samples, a computer can simply send "instructions" to the instrument describing pitch, tone, and duration of a sound. MIDI files are therefore very efficient. Because a MIDI file is made up of a set of instructions rather than a copy of the sound, modifying each component of the file is easy. Additionally, it is possible to program many channels, or "voices," of music to be played simultaneously, creating symphonic sound.

MIDI-enabled device External device that enables you to input digital sound information in the MIDI format; for example, a MIDI keyboard (the piano kind).

migration Moving users from one operating system or hard drive to another.

MIMO (multiple in/multiple out) Feature of 802.11n devices that enables the simultaneous connection of up to four antennas, greatly increasing throughput.

mini-audio connector Very popular, 1/8-inch diameter connector used to transmit two audio signals; perfect for stereo sound.

mini connector One type of power connector from a PC power supply unit. Supplies 5 and 12 volts to peripherals. Also known as a floppy connector.

mini-DIN Small connection most commonly used for keyboards and mice. Many modern systems implement USB in place of mini-DIN connections. Also called *PS/2*.

Mini-ITX The largest and the most popular of the three ITX form factors. At a miniscule 6.7 by 6.7 inches, Mini-ITX competes with microATX and proprietary small form factor (SFF) motherboards.

Mini-PCI Specialized form of PCI designed for use in laptops.

Mini-PCIe Specialized form of PCIe designed for use in laptops.

mini power connector Connector used to provide power to floppy disk drives.

mirror set A type of mirrored volume created by Windows 7 Professional, Enterprise, and Ultimate editions. (*See also* mirroring.)

mirrored volume Volume that is mirrored on another volume. (*See also* mirroring.)

mirroring Reading and writing data at the same time to two drives for fault tolerance purposes. Considered RAID level 1. Also called *drive mirroring*.

MMC (Microsoft Management Console) Means of managing a system, introduced by Microsoft with Windows 2000. The MMC allows an administrator to customize management tools by picking and choosing from a list of snap-ins. Available snap-ins include Device Manager, Users and Groups, and Computer Management.

MMX (multimedia extensions) Specific CPU instructions that enable a CPU to handle many multimedia functions, such as digital signal processing. Introduced with the Pentium CPU, these instructions are used on all ×86 CPUs.

mode Any single combination of resolution and color depth set for a system.

modem (modulator/demodulator) Device that converts a digital bit stream into an analog signal (modulation) and converts incoming analog signals back into digital signals (demodulation). Analog communications channel is typically a telephone line, and analog signals are typically sounds.

module Small circuit board that DRAM chips are attached to. Also known as a "stick."

Molex connector Computer power connector used by optical drives, hard drives, and case fans. Keyed to prevent it from being inserted into a power port improperly.

monaural Describes recording tracks from one source (microphone) as opposed to stereo, which uses two sources.

monitor Screen that displays data from a PC. Can use either a cathode ray tube (CRT) or a liquid crystal display (LCD) to display images.

motherboard Flat piece of circuit board that resides inside your computer case and has a number of connectors on it. Every device in a PC connects directly or indirectly to the motherboard, including CPU, RAM, hard drives, optical drives, keyboard, mouse, and video cards.

motherboard book Valuable resource when installing a new motherboard. Normally lists all the specifications about a motherboard, including the type of memory and type of CPU usable with the motherboard.

mount point Drive that functions like a folder mounted into another drive.

mouse Input device that enables users to manipulate a cursor on the screen to select items.

move command Command in the command-line interface used to move a file from one location to another.

MP3 Short for MPEG Audio Layer 3. A type of compression used specifically for turning high-quality digital audio files into much smaller, yet similar sounding, files.

MPA (Microsoft Product Activation) Introduced by Microsoft with the release of Windows XP, prevents unauthorized use of Microsoft's software by requiring users to activate the software.

MPEG-2 (Moving Pictures Experts Group) Standard of video and audio compression offering resolutions up to 1280 × 720 at 60 frames per second.

MPEG-4 (Moving Pictures Experts Group) Standard of video and audio compression offering improved compression over MPEG-2.

MS-CHAP Microsoft's variation of the CHAP protocol, which uses a slightly more advanced encryption protocol. Windows Vista uses MS-CHAP v2 (version 2), and does not support MS-CHAP v1 (version 1).

msconfig (System Configuration Utility) Executable file that runs the Windows System Configuration utility, which enables users to configure a system's boot files and critical system files. Often used for the name of the utility, as in "just run msconfig."

MSDS (material safety data sheet) Standardized form that provides detailed information about potential environmental hazards and proper disposal methods associated with various PC components.

msinfo32 Provides information about hardware resources, components, and the software environment. Also known as System Information.

multiboot installation OS installation in which multiple operating systems are installed on a single machine. Can also refer to kicking a device several times in frustration.

multicore processing Using two or more execution cores on one CPU die to divide up work independently of the OS.

multimedia extensions (MMX) Originally an Intel CPU enhancement designed for graphics-intensive applications (such as games). It was never embraced but eventually led to improvements in how CPUs handle graphics.

multimeter Device used to measure voltage, amperage, and resistance.

multisession drive Recordable CD drive capable of burning multiple sessions onto a single recordable disc. A multisession drive also can close a CD-R so that no further tracks can be written to it.

multitasking Process of running multiple programs or tasks on the same computer at the same time.

multitouch Input method on many smartphones and tablets that enables you to use multiple fingers to do all sorts of fun things, such as using two fingers to scroll or swipe to another screen or desktop.

music CD-R CD using a special format for home recorders. Music CD-R makers pay a small royalty to avoid illegal music duplication.

My Computer Default interface in Windows XP for Windows Explorer; displays hard drives and devices with removeable storage. (*See* Computer.).

My Documents Introduced with Windows 98 and used in Windows 2000 and Windows XP; folder that provides a convenient place for users to store their documents, log files, and any other type of files.

My Network Places Folder in Windows XP that enables users to view other computers on their network or workgroup.

Nano-ITX A 4.7 inch by 4.7 inch variation of the ITX form factor.

NAT (Network Address Translation) A means of translating a system's IP address into another IP address before sending it out to a larger network. NAT manifests itself by a

NAT program that runs on a system or a router. A network using NAT provides the systems on the network with private IP addresses. The system running the NAT software has two interfaces: one connected to the network and the other connected to the larger network.

The NAT program takes packets from the client systems bound for the larger network and translates their internal private IP addresses to its own public IP address, enabling many systems to share a single IP address.

native resolution Resolution on an LCD monitor that matches the physical pixels on the screen. CRTs do not have fixed pixels and therefore do not have a native resolution.

navigation pane Windows 7's name for the Folders list in Windows Explorer.

net command Command in Windows that enables users to view a network without knowing the names of the other computers on that network.

NetBIOS (Network Basic Input/Output System) Protocol that operates at the Session layer of the OSI seven-layer model. This protocol creates and manages connections based on the names of the computers involved.

NetBIOS Extended User Interface (NetBEUI) The default networking protocol for early versions of Windows.

netbook Small, low-power laptop used primarily for Web browsing.

network Collection of two or more computers interconnected by telephone lines, coaxial cables, satellite links, radio, and/or some other communication technique. Group of computers that are connected and that communicate with one another for a common purpose.

Network Interface in Windows Vista and Windows 7 for Windows Explorer; displays networked computers and other devices, such as network printers.

network attached storage (NAS) A device that attaches to a network for the sole purpose of storing and sharing files.

network ID Number that identifies the network on which a device or machine exists. This number exists in both IP and IPX protocol suites.

network printer Printer that connects directly to a network.

network protocol Software that takes the incoming data received by the network card, keeps it organized, sends it to the application that needs it, and then takes outgoing data from the application and hands it to the NIC to be sent out over the network.

network technology A practical application of a topology and other critical standards to provide a method to get data from one computer to another on a network. It defines many aspects of a network, from the topology, to the frame type, to the cabling and connectors used.

NIC (network interface card or controller) Expansion card or motherboard interface that enables a PC to connect to a network via a network cable. A *wireless NIC* enables connection via radio waves rather than a physical cable.

Ni-Cd (Nickel-Cadmium) Battery used in the first portable PCs. Heavy and inefficient, these batteries also suffered from a memory effect that could drastically shorten the overall life of the battery. (*See also* Ni-MH, Li-Ion.)

Ni-MH (Nickel-Metal Hydride) Battery used in early portable PCs. Ni-MH batteries had fewer issues with the memory effect than Ni-Cd batteries. Ni-MH batteries have been replaced by Lithium-Ion batteries. (*See also* Ni-Cd, Li-Ion.)

nit Value used to measure the brightness of an LCD display. A typical LCD display has a brightness of between 100 and 400 nits.

NLQ (near-letter quality) Designation for dot-matrix printers that use 24-pin printheads.

NLX Second form factor for slimline systems. Replaced the earlier LPX form factor. (NLX apparently stands for nothing; it's just a cool grouping of letters.)

NMI (non-maskable interrupt) Interrupt code sent to the processor that cannot be ignored. Typically manifested as a BSoD.

NNTP (Network News Transfer Protocol) Protocol run by news servers that enable newsgroups.

non-system disk or disk error Error that occurs during the boot process. Common causes for this error are leaving a nonbootable floppy disk, CD, or other media in the drive while the computer is booting.

nonvolatile memory Storage device that retains data even if power is removed; typically refers to a ROM or flash ROM chip, but also could be applied to hard drives, optical media, and other storage devices.

normal backup Full backup of every selected file on a system. Turns off the archive bit after the backup.

Northbridge Chip that connects a CPU to memory, the PCI bus, Level 2 cache, and AGP activities. Communicates with the CPU through the frontside bus. Newer CPUs feature an integrated Northbridge.

notebook *See* laptop.

notification area Contains icons representing background processes, the system clock, and volume control. Located by default at the right edge of the Windows taskbar. Most users call this area the system tray.

nslookup Command-line program in Windows used to determine exactly what information the DNS server is providing about a specific host name.

ntdetect.com One of the critical Windows NT/2000/XP startup files.

NTFS (NT file system) Robust and secure file system introduced by Microsoft with Windows NT. NTFS provides an amazing array of configuration options for user access and security. Users can be granted access to data on a file-by-file basis. NTFS enables object-level security, long filename support, compression, and encryption.

NTFS permissions Restrictions that determine the amount of access given to a particular user on a system using NTFS.

ntldr (NT Loader) Windows NT/2000/XP boot file. Launched by the MBR or MFT, ntldr looks at the boot.ini configuration file for any installed operating systems.

NVIDIA Corporation One of the foremost manufacturers of graphics cards and chipsets.

object System component that is given a set of characteristics and can be managed by the operating system as a single entity.

object access auditing Feature of Event Viewer's Security section that creates an entry in the Security Log when certain objects are accessed, such as a file or folder.

ODBC Data Source Administrator Programming tool for configuring the Open Database Connectivity (ODBC) coding standard. Data Source Administrator enables you to create and manage entries called Data Source Names (DSNs) that point OBDC to a database. DSNs are used by ODBC-aware applications to query ODBC to find their databases.

offline files Windows 7 feature that enables storing a local, duplicate copy of files and folders on a hard drive. When the laptop connects to a network, Windows automatically syncs those offline files with the files and folders on a file server or other PC.

ohm(s) Electronic measurement of a cable's impedance.

open source Software environment that is not controlled by a central creator or distributer.

OLED (organic light-emitting diode) Display technology where an organic compound provides the light for the screen, thus eliminating the need for a backlight or inverter.

OpenGL One of two popular APIs used today for video cards. Originally written for UNIX systems but now ported to Windows and Apple systems. (*See also* DirectX.)

optical disc/media Types of data discs (such as DVDs, CDs, BDs, etc.) that are read by a laser.

optical drive Drive used to read/write to optical discs, such as CDs or DVDs.

optical mouse Pointing device that uses light rather than electronic sensors to determine movement and direction the mouse is being moved.

optical resolution Resolution a scanner can achieve mechanically. Most scanners use software to enhance this ability.

optical zoom Mechanical ability of most cameras to "zoom" in as opposed to the digital ability.

option ROM Alternative way of telling the system how to talk to a piece of hardware. Option ROM stores BIOS for the card in a chip on the card itself.

OS (operating system) Series of programs and code that creates an interface so users can interact with a system's hardware; for example, DOS, Windows, and Linux.

OS X Current operating system on Apple Macintosh computers. Based on a UNIX core, early versions of OS X ran on Motorola-based hardware; current versions run on Intel-based hardware. Pronounced "ten" rather than "ex."

OSI seven-layer model Architecture model based on the OSI protocol suite that defines and standardizes the flow of data between computers. The seven layers are:

Layer 1 The Physical layer Defines hardware connections and turns binary into physical pulses (electrical or light). Repeaters and hubs operate at the Physical layer.

Layer 2 The Data Link layer Identifies devices on the Physical layer. MAC addresses are part of the Data Link layer. Bridges operate at the Data Link layer.

Layer 3 The Network layer Moves packets between computers on different networks. Routers operate at the Network layer. IP and IPX operate at the Network layer.

Layer 4 The Transport layer Breaks data down into manageable chunks. TCP, UDP, SPX, and NetBEUI operate at the Transport layer.

Layer 5 The Session layer Manages connections between machines. NetBIOS and Sockets operate at the Session layer.

Layer 6 The Presentation layer Can also manage data encryption; hides the differences between various types of computer systems.

Layer 7 The Application layer Provides tools for programs to use to access the network (and the lower layers). HTTP, FTP, SMTP, and POP3 are all examples of protocols that operate at the Application layer.

overclocking To run a CPU or video processor faster than its rated speed.

P1 power connector Provides power to ATX motherboards; 20-pin with original ATX motherboards, 24-pin on current units.

P4 12V connector Provides additional 12-volt power to motherboards that support Pentium 4 and later processors.

P8 and P9 connectors Provide power to AT-style motherboards.

packet Basic component of communication over a network. Group of bits of fixed maximum size and well-defined format that is switched and transmitted as a single entity through a network. Contains source and destination address, data, and control information.

page fault Minor memory-addressing error.

page file Portion of the hard drive set aside by Windows to act like RAM. Also known as *virtual memory* or *swap file*.

PAN (personal area network) Small wireless network created with Bluetooth technology and intended to link PCs and other peripheral devices.

parallel execution When a multicore CPU processes more than one thread.

parallel port Connection for the synchronous, high-speed flow of data along parallel lines to a device, usually a printer.

Parental Controls Tool to allow monitoring and limiting of user activities; designed for parents to control the content their children can access.

parity Method of error detection where a small group of bits being transferred is compared to a single parity bit set to make the total bits odd or even. Receiving device reads the parity bit and determines if the data is valid, based on the oddness or evenness of the parity bit.

parity RAM Earliest form of error-detecting RAM; stored an extra bit (called the parity bit) to verify the data.

partition Section of the storage area of a hard disk. Created during initial preparation of the hard disk, before the disk is formatted.

partition boot table Sector of a partition that stores information important to its partition, such as the location of the OS boot files. Responsible for loading the OS on a partition.

partition table Table located in the boot sector of a hard drive that lists every partition on the disk that contains a valid operating system.

partitioning Electronically subdividing a physical hard drive into groups called partitions (or volumes).

passcode lock Mobile device security feature that requires you to type in a series of letters, numbers, or motion patterns to unlock the mobile device each time you press the power button.

passive matrix Technology for producing colors in LCD monitors by varying voltages across wire matrices to produce red, green, or blue dots.

password Key used to verify a user's identity on a secure computer or network.

Password Authentication Protocol (PAP) Oldest and most basic form of authentication. Also the least safe, because it sends all passwords in clear text.

password reset disk Special type of floppy disk with which users can recover a lost password without losing access to any encrypted, or password-protected, data.

PATA (parallel ATA) Implementation that integrates the controller on the disk drive itself. (*See also* ATA, IDE, SATA.)

patch Small piece of software released by a software manufacturer to correct a flaw or problem with a particular piece of software.

patch cables Short (2 to 5 feet) UTP cables that connect patch panels to the hubs.

patch panel A panel containing a row of female connectors (ports) that terminate the horizontal cabling in the equipment room. Patch panels facilitate cabling organization and provide protection to horizontal cabling.

path Route the operating system must follow to find an executable program stored in a subfolder.

PC bus Original 8-bit expansion bus developed by IBM for PCs; ran at a top speed of 4.77 MHz. Also known as the XT bus.

PC Card Credit card–sized adapter card that adds functionality in many notebook computers, PDAs, and other computer devices. PC Cards come in 16-bit and CardBus parallel format and ExpressCard serial format. (*See also* PCMCIA.)

PC tech Someone with computer skills who works on computers.

PCI (Peripheral Component Interconnect) Design architecture for the expansion bus on the computer motherboard that enables system components to be added to the computer. Local bus standard, meaning that devices added to a computer through this port will use the processor at the motherboard's full speed (up to 33 MHz) rather than at the slower 8-MHz speed of the regular bus. Moves data 32 or 64 bits at a time rather than the 8 or 16 bits the older ISA buses supported.

PCIe (PCI Express) Serialized successor to PCI and AGP that uses the concept of individual data paths called lanes. May use any number of lanes, although a single lane (×1) and 16 lanes (×16) are the most common on motherboards.

PCI-X (PCI Extended) Enhanced version of PCI, 64 bits wide. Typically seen in servers and high-end systems.

PCL (printer control language) Printer control language created by Hewlett-Packard and used on a broad cross-section of printers.

PCM (pulse code modulation) Sound format developed in the 1960s to carry telephone calls over the first digital lines.

PCMCIA (Personal Computer Memory Card International Association) Consortium of computer manufacturers who devised the PC Card standard for credit card–sized adapter cards that add functionality in many notebook computers, PDAs, and other computer devices. (*See also* PC Card.)

PDA (personal digital assistant) Handheld computer that blurred the line between calculators and computers. Early PDAs were calculators that enabled users to program in such information as addresses and appointments. Later PDAs, such as the Palm and PocketPC, were fully programmable computers. Most PDAs used a pen/stylus for input rather than a keyboard. A few of the larger PDAs had a tiny keyboard in addition to the stylus. Smartphones and tablets have supplanted PDAs for almost all uses.

Pearson VUE The company that administers the CompTIA A+ exams.

peer-to-peer network Network in which each machine can act as both a client and a server.

pen-based computing Input method used by many PDAs that combines handwriting recognition with modified mouse functions, usually in the form of a pen-like stylus.

Pentium Name given to the fifth and later generations of Intel microprocessors; has a 32-bit address bus, 64-bit external data bus, and dual pipelining. Also used for subsequent generations of Intel processors—the Pentium Pro, Pentium II, Pentium III, and Pentium 4. Pentium name was retired after the introduction of the Intel Core CPUs.

Performance Tab in Task Manager that tracks PC performance.

Performance console Windows XP tool used to log resource usage over time.

Performance Information and Tools Applet that provides a relative feel for how your computer stacks up against other systems using the Windows Experience Index.

Performance Logs and Alerts Snap-in enabling the creation of a written record of most everything that happens on the system.

Performance Monitor Windows 7's tool for observing a computer's performance.

Performance Options Tool enabling users to configure CPU, RAM, and virtual memory settings.

peripheral Any device that connects to the system unit.

permission propagation Term to describe what happens to permissions on an object when you move or copy it.

persistence Phosphors used in CRT screens continuing to glow after being struck by electrons, long enough for the human eye to register the glowing effect. Glowing too long makes the images smeary, and too little makes them flicker.

Personalization applet Windows Vista applet with which users can change display settings such as resolution, refresh rate, color depth, and desktop features. The Windows 7 version focuses on managing themes, desktop icons, mouse pointers, and account pictures. For other options, *see* Display.

PGA (pin grid array) Arrangement of a large number of pins extending from the bottom of the CPU package. There are many variations on PGA.

Phillips-head screwdriver Most important part of a PC tech's toolkit.

phishing The act of trying to get people to give their usernames, passwords, or other security information by pretending to be someone else electronically.

Phoenix Technologies Major producer of BIOS software for motherboards.

phosphor Electro-fluorescent material that coats the inside face of a cathode ray tube (CRT). After being hit with an electron, it glows for a fraction of a second.

photosensitive drum Aluminum cylinder coated with particles of photosensitive compounds. Used in a laser printer and often contained within the toner cartridge.

picoBTX Variation of the BTX form factor. picoBTX motherboards are generally smaller than their BTX or microBTX counterparts but retain the same functionality.

Pico-ITX A 3.8 by 2.8 inch version of the ITX form factor.

pin 1 Designator used to ensure proper alignment of floppy drive and hard drive connectors.

pinch Multitouch gesture that enables you to make an image bigger or smaller.

pinned application Windows 7's method of attaching programs to the taskbar. A pinned application gets a permanent icon displayed on the taskbar.

ping (packet Internet groper) Slang term for a small network message (ICMP ECHO) sent by a computer to check for the presence and aliveness of another. Used to verify the presence of another system. Also, the command used at a prompt to ping a computer.

PIO (programmed I/O) mode Series of speed standards created by the Small Form Factor Committee for the use of PIO by hard drives. Modes range from PIO mode 0 to PIO mode 4.

pipeline Processing methodology where multiple calculations take place simultaneously by being broken into a series of steps. Often used in CPUs and video processors.

pixel (picture element) In computer graphics, smallest element of a display space that can be independently assigned color or intensity.

plug Hardware connection with some sort of projection that connects to a port.

plug and play (PnP) Combination of smart PCs, smart devices, and smart operating systems that automatically configure all necessary system resources and ports when you install a new peripheral device.

polygons Multisided shapes used in 3-D rendering of objects. In computers, video cards draw large numbers of triangles and connect them to form polygons.

polymorph virus Virus that attempts to change its signature to prevent detection by antivirus programs, usually by continually scrambling a bit of useless code.

polyphony Number of instruments a sound card can play simultaneously.

POP3 (Post Office Protocol) Refers to the way e-mail software such as Eudora gets mail from a mail server. When you obtain a SLIP, PPP, or shell account, you almost always get a POP account with it. It is this POP account that you tell your e-mail software to use to get your mail. Uses port 110.

pop-up Irritating browser window that appears automatically when you visit a Web site.

port (networking) In networking, the number used to identify the requested service (such as SMTP or FTP) when connecting to a TCP/IP host. Examples: 80 (HTTP), 20 (FTP), 69 (TFTP), 25 (SMTP), and 110 (POP3).

port (physical connection) Part of a connector into which a plug is inserted. Physical ports are also referred to as jacks.

port forwarding Preventing the passage of any IP packets through any ports other than the ones prescribed by the system administrator.

port replicator Device that plugs into a USB port or other specialized port and offers common PC ports, such as serial, parallel, USB, network, and PS/2. By plugging your notebook computer into the port replicator, you can instantly connect the computer to non-portable components such as a printer, scanner, monitor, or full-sized keyboard. Port replicators are typically used at home or in the office with the non-portable equipment already connected.

port triggering Router function that enables you to automatically open an incoming connection to one computer based on a specific outgoing connection.

positional audio Range of commands for a sound card to place a sound anywhere in 3-D space.

POST (power-on self test) Basic diagnostic routine completed by a system at the beginning of the boot process to make sure a display adapter and the system's memory are installed; it then searches for an operating system. If it finds one, it hands over control of the machine to the OS.

PostScript Language defined by Adobe Systems, Inc. for describing how to create an image on a page. The description is independent of the resolution of the device that will actually create the image. It includes a technology for defining the shape of a font and creating a raster image at many different resolutions and sizes.

power conditioning Ensuring and adjusting incoming AC wall power to as close to standard as possible. Most UPS devices provide power conditioning.

power good wire Used to wake up the CPU after the power supply has tested for proper voltage.

Power over Ethernet Technology that provides power and data transmission through a single network cable.

power plans Windows Vista/7 feature that enables better control over power use by customizing a balanced, power saver, or high performance power plan.

PowerShell *See* Windows PowerShell.

power supply fan Small fan located in a system power supply that draws warm air from inside the power supply and exhausts it to the outside.

power supply unit Provides the electrical power for a PC. Converts standard AC power into various voltages of DC electricity in a PC.

Power Users group Second most powerful account and group type in Windows after Administrators.

ppm (pages per minute) Speed of a printer.

PPP (Point-to-Point Protocol) Enables a computer to connect to the Internet through a dial-in connection and enjoy most of the benefits of a direct connection.

preboot execution environment (PXE) Technology that enables a PC to boot without any local storage by retrieving an OS from a server over a network.

primary corona Wire that is located near the photosensitive drum in a laser printer and is charged with extremely high voltage to form an electric field, enabling voltage to pass to the photosensitive drum, thus charging the photosensitive particles on the surface of the drum. Also called the *primary charge roller*.

primary partition Partition on a Windows hard drive that can store a bootable operating system.

print resolution Quality of a print image.

print spooler Area of memory that queues up print jobs that the printer will handle sequentially.

printed circuit board (PCB) Copper etched onto a nonconductive material and then coated with some sort of epoxy for strength.

printer Output device that can print text or illustrations on paper. Microsoft uses the term to refer to the software that controls the physical print device.

printhead Case that holds the printwires in a dot-matrix printer.

printwires Grid of tiny pins in a dot-matrix printer that strike an inked printer ribbon to produce images on paper.

PRML (Partial Response Maximum Likelihood) Advanced method of RLL that uses powerful, intelligent circuitry to analyze each flux reversal on a hard drive and to make a best guess as to what type of flux reversal it just read. This allows a dramatic increase in the amount of data a hard drive can store.

Problem Reports and Solutions Control Panel applet in Windows Vista that lists all Windows Error Reporting issues (plus a few easy-to-check items like firewall and antimalware status).

Processes Tab in Task Manager that lists all running processes on a system. Frequently a handy tool for ending buggy or unresponsive processes.

product key Code used during installation to verify legitimacy of the software.

profile A list of settings that a calibration device creates when calibrating monitors and printers.

program/programming Series of binary electronic commands sent to a CPU to get work done.

Programs and Features Windows Vista/7 replacement for the Add or Remove Programs applet; enables uninstalling programs and altering Windows features.

projector Device for projecting video images from PCs or other video sources, usually for audience presentations. Available in front- and rearview displays.

prompt A character or message provided by an operating system or program to indicate that it is ready to accept input.

proprietary Technology unique to a particular vendor.

protocol Agreement that governs the procedures used to exchange information between cooperating entities. Usually includes how much information is to be sent, how often it is sent, how to recover from transmission errors, and who is to receive the information.

proxy server Device that fetches Internet resources for a client without exposing that client directly to the Internet. Usually accepts requests for HTTP, FTP, POP3, and SMTP resources. Often caches, or stores, a copy of the requested resource for later use. Common security feature in the corporate world.

Public folder Folder that all users can access and share with all other users on the system or network.

punchdown tool A specialized tool for connecting UTP wires to an punchdown block.

Quality of Service (QoS) Policies that control how much bandwidth a protocol, PC, user, VLAN, or IP address may use.

queue Area where objects wait their turn to be processed. Example: the printer queue, where print jobs wait until it is their turn to be printed.

Quick Launch toolbar Enables you to launch commonly used programs with a single click.

QVGA Video display mode of 320 × 240.

RAID (redundant array of independent disks) Seven-level (0–6) way of creating a fault-tolerant storage system:

Level 0 Uses byte-level striping and provides no fault tolerance.

Level 1 Uses mirroring or duplexing.

Level 2 Uses bit-level striping.

Level 3 Stores error-correcting information (such as parity) on a separate disk, and uses data striping on the remaining drives.

Level 4 Level 3 with block-level striping.

Level 5 Uses block-level and parity data striping.

Level 6 Same as RAID 5 but with double distributed parity.

Also known as *redundant array of inexpensive disks*.

RAID 5 volume Striped set with parity. (*See also* RAID).

rails Separate DC voltage paths within an ATX power supply.

RAM (random access memory) Memory that can be accessed at random; that is, memory which you can write to or read from without touching the preceding address. This term is often used to mean a computer's main memory.

RAMDAC (random access memory digital-to-analog converter) Circuitry used on video cards that support analog monitors to convert the digital video data to analog.

raster image Pattern of dots representing what the final product should look like.

raster line Horizontal pattern of lines that forms an image on the monitor screen.

RDRAM (Rambus DRAM) Patented RAM technology that uses accelerated clocks to provide very high-speed memory.

read-only attribute File attribute that does not allow a file to be altered or modified. Helpful when protecting system files that should not be edited.

rd (rmdir) command Command in the command-line interface used to remove directories.

rearview projector Projector that shoots an image onto a screen from the rear. Rearview projectors are usually self-enclosed and very popular for TVs, but are virtually unheard of in the PC world.

Recovery Console Command-line interface boot mode for Windows that is used to repair a Windows XP system suffering from massive OS corruption or other problems.

Recycle Bin Location to which files are moved when they are deleted from a modern Windows system. To permanently remove files from a system, they must be emptied from the Recycle Bin.

regedit.exe Program used to edit the Windows Registry.

region code Encoding that restricts you from playing DVD or Blu-ray Disc movies on a player that doesn't share the same region code.

register Storage area inside the CPU used by the onboard logic to perform calculations. CPUs have many registers to perform different functions.

registration Usually optional process that identifies the legal owner/user of the product to the supplier.

Registry Complex binary file used to store configuration data about a particular system. To edit the Registry, users can use the applets found in the Control Panel or regedit.exe or regedt32.exe.

Reliability and Performance Monitor Windows Vista's extended Performance applet.

remediation Repairing damage caused by a virus.

remnant Potentially recoverable data on a hard drive that remains despite formatting or deleting.

Remote Assistance Feature of Windows that enables users to give anyone control of his or her desktop over the Internet.

Remote Desktop Windows tool used to enable a local system to graphically access the desktop of a remote system.

Remote Desktop Protocol Protocol used for Microsoft's Remote Desktop tool. Uses port 3389.

remote network installation A common method of OS installation where the source files are placed in a shared directory on a network server. Then, whenever a tech needs to install a new OS, he can boot the computer, connect to the source location on the network, and start the installation from there.

removable media Any storage on a computer that can be easily removed. For example, CD-ROM discs, flash drives, or memory cards.

ren (rename) command Command in the command-line interface used to rename files and folders.

resistance Difficulty in making electricity flow through a material, measured in ohms.

resistive touchscreen Type of touchscreen that responds to the pressure applied to the screen.

resistor Any material or device that impedes the flow of electrons. Electronic resistors measure their resistance (impedance) in ohms. (*See* ohm(s).)

resolution Measurement for CRTs and printers expressed in horizontal and vertical dots or pixels. Higher resolutions provide sharper details and thus display better-looking images.

resources Data and services of a PC.

respect How all techs should treat their customers.

response rate Time it takes for all of the sub-pixels on the panel to go from pure black to pure white and back again.

restore point System snapshot created by the System Restore utility that is used to restore a malfunctioning system. (*See also* System Restore.)

RET (resolution enhancement technology) Technology that uses small dots to smooth out jagged edges that are typical of printers without RET, producing a higher-quality print job.

RFI (radio frequency interference) Another form of electrical interference caused by radio-wave emitting devices, such as cell phones, wireless network cards, and microwave ovens.

RG-58 Coaxial cabling used for 10Base2 networks.

RIMM Individual stick of Rambus RAM. The letters don't actually stand for anything; they just rhyme with SIMM and DIMM.

ring Network topology where the computers form a circle and all data flows in one direction only.

RIP (raster image processor) Component in a printer that translates the raster image into commands for the printer.

riser card Special adapter card, usually inserted into a special slot on a motherboard, that changes the orientation of expansion cards relative to the motherboard. Riser cards are used extensively in slimline computers to keep total depth

and height of the system to a minimum. Sometimes called a daughterboard.

RJ (registered jack) connector UTP cable connector, used for both telephone and network connections. RJ-11 is a connector for four-wire UTP; usually found in telephone connections. RJ-45 is a connector for eight-wire UTP; usually found in network connections.

RJ-11 *See* RJ (registered jack) connector.

RJ-45 *See* RJ (registered jack) connector.

robocopy command Powerful command-line utility for copying files and directories, even over a network.

ROM (read-only memory) Generic term for nonvolatile memory that can be read from but not written to. This means that code and data stored in ROM cannot be corrupted by accidental erasure. Additionally, ROM retains its data when power is removed, which makes it the perfect medium for storing BIOS data or information such as scientific constants.

root directory Directory that contains all other directories.

root keys Five main categories in the Windows Registry:
HKEY_CLASSES_ROOT
HKEY_CURRENT_USER
HKEY_USERS
HKEY_LOCAL_MACHINE
HKEY_CURRENT_CONFIG

router Device connecting separate networks; forwards a packet from one network to another based on the network address for the protocol being used. For example, an IP router looks only at the IP network number. Routers operate at Layer 3 (Network) of the OSI seven-layer model.

RS-232 Standard port recommended by the Electronics Industry Association for serial devices.

run A single piece of installed horizontal cabling.

Run dialog box Command box in which users can enter the name of a particular program to run; an alternative to locating the icon in Windows.

S.M.A.R.T. (Self-Monitoring, Analysis, and Reporting Technology) Monitoring system built into hard drives.

S/PDIF (Sony/Philips Digital Interface Format) Digital audio connector found on many sound cards. Users can connect their computers directly to a 5.1 speaker system or receiver. S/PDIF comes in both a coaxial and an optical version.

Safe Mode Important diagnostic boot mode for Windows that only runs very basic drivers and turns off virtual memory.

sampling Capturing sound waves in electronic format.

SATA (serial ATA) Serialized version of the ATA standard that offers many advantages over PATA (parallel ATA) technology, including thinner cabling, keyed connectors, and lower power requirements.

SATA bridge Adapter that allows PATA devices to be connected to a SATA controller.

SATA power connector 15-pin, L-shaped connector used by SATA devices that support the hot-swappable feature.

satellites Two or more standard stereo speakers to be combined with a subwoofer for a speaker system (i.e., 2.1, 5.1, etc.).

Scalable Link Interface (SLI) Technology for connecting two or more NVIDIA GPUs together in a system.

scan code Unique code corresponding to each key on the keyboard, sent from the keyboard controller to the CPU.

Scheduled Tasks Windows XP's utility enabling users to set tasks to run automatically at certain times.

SCSI (small computer system interface) Powerful and flexible peripheral interface popularized on the Macintosh and used to connect hard drives, CD-ROM drives, tape drives, scanners, and other devices to PCs of all kinds. Normal SCSI enables up to seven devices to be connected through a single bus connection, whereas Wide SCSI can handle 15 devices attached to a single controller.

SCSI chain Series of SCSI devices working together through a host adapter.

SCSI ID Unique identifier used by SCSI devices. No two SCSI devices may have the same SCSI ID.

SD (Secure Digital) Very popular format for flash media cards; also supports I/O devices.

SDRAM (synchronous DRAM) DRAM that is synchronous, or tied to the system clock and thus runs much faster than traditional FPM and EDO RAM. This type of RAM is used in all modern systems.

SEC (single-edge cartridge) CPU package where the CPU was contained in a cartridge that snapped into a special slot on the motherboard called Slot 1.

sector Segment of one of the concentric tracks encoded on the disk during a low-level format. A sector holds 512 bytes of data.

sector translation Translation of logical geometry into physical geometry by the onboard circuitry of a hard drive.

sectors per track (sectors/track) Combined with the number of cylinders and heads, defines the disk geometry.

segment The connection between a computer and a switch.

serial port Common connector on a PC. Connects input devices (such as a mouse) or communications devices (such as a modem).

server Computer that shares its resources, such as printers and files, with other computers on a network. Example: network file system server that shares its disk space with a workstation that does not have a disk drive of its own.

service A program that runs in the background of a PC but displays no icons anywhere. You can view a list of services in the Task Manager Windows Vista and Windows 7. Also, a program stored in a ROM chip.

service pack Collection of software patches released at one time by a software manufacturer.

Services Tab in Windows Vista/7's Task Manager that lists all running services on a system.

setupapi.log Log file that tracks the installation of all hardware on a system.

setuplog.txt Log file that tracks the complete installation process, logging the success or failure of file copying, Registry updates, and reboots.

sfc (System File Checker) Command-prompt program (sfc.exe) that scans, detects, and restores Windows system files, folders, and paths.

shadow mask CRT screen that allows only the proper electron gun to light the proper phosphors.

share-level security Security system in which each resource has a password assigned to it; access to the resource is based on knowing the password.

Shared Documents Windows pre-made folder that is accessible by all user accounts on the computer.

shared memory Means of reducing the amount of memory needed on a video card by borrowing from the regular system RAM, which reduces costs but also decreases performance.

shareware Program protected by copyright; holder allows (encourages!) you to make and distribute copies under the condition that those who adopt the software after preview pay a fee to the holder of the copyright. Derivative works are not allowed, although you may make an archival copy.

shunt Tiny connector of metal enclosed in plastic that creates an electrical connection between two posts of a jumper.

SID (security identifier) Unique identifier for every PC that most techs change when cloning.

sidebanding Second data bus for AGP video cards; enables the video card to send more commands to the Northbridge while receiving other commands at the same time.

signal-to-noise ratio Measure that describes the relative quality of an input port.

signature Code pattern of a known virus; used by antivirus software to detect viruses.

SIMM (single in-line memory module) DRAM packaging distinguished by having a number of small tabs that install into a special connector. Each side of each tab is the same signal. SIMMs come in two common sizes: 30-pin and 72-pin.

simple file sharing Allows users to share locally or across the network but gives no control over what others do with shared files.

simple volume Volume created when setting up dynamic disks. Acts like a primary partition on a dynamic disk.

single-sided RAM Has chips on only one side as opposed to double-sided RAM.

single source *See* closed source.

sleep timers A feature that enables you to put the computer into Standby after a set period of time, or to turn off the monitor or hard drive after a time, thus creating your own custom power scheme.

slimline Motherboard form factor used to create PCs that were very thin. NLX and LPX were two examples of this form factor.

slot covers Metal plates that cover up unused expansion slots on the back of a PC. Useful in maintaining proper airflow through a computer case.

smart battery Portable PC battery that tells the computer when it needs to be charged, conditioned, or replaced.

smart card Hardware authentication involving a credit card–sized card with circuitry that can be used to identify the bearer of that card.

SmartMedia Format for flash media cards; no longer used with new devices.

smartphone A cell phone enhanced to do things formerly reserved for fully grown PCs, such as Web browsing, document viewing, and media consumption.

SMM (System Management Mode) Special CPU mode that enables the CPU to reduce power consumption by selectively shutting down peripherals.

SMTP (Simple Mail Transport Protocol) Main protocol used to send electronic mail on the Internet. Uses port 25.

snap-ins Small utilities that can be used with the Microsoft Management Console.

snapshot Virtualization feature that enables you to save an extra copy of the virtual machine as it is exactly at the moment the snapshot is taken.

SNMP (Simple Network Management Protocol) A set of standards for communication with devices connected to a TCP/IP network. Examples of these devices include routers, hubs, and switches. Uses port 161.

social engineering Using or manipulating people inside the networking environment to gain access to that network from the outside.

socket services Device drivers that support the PC Card socket, enabling the system to detect when a PC Card has been inserted or removed, and providing the necessary I/O to the device.

SO-DIMM (small-outline DIMM) Memory used in portable PCs because of its small size.

soft power Characteristic of ATX motherboards, which can use software to turn the PC on and off. The physical manifestation of soft power is the power switch. Instead of the thick power cord used in AT systems, an ATX power switch is little more than a pair of small wires leading to the motherboard.

software Single group of programs designed to do a particular job; always stored on mass storage devices.

solid core A cable that uses a single solid wire to transmit signals.

solid ink printers Printer that uses solid sticks of nontoxic "ink" that produce vibrant color documents with much less waste than color laser printers.

sound card Expansion card that can produce audible tones when connected to a set of speakers.

Southbridge Part of a motherboard chipset; handles all the inputs and outputs to the many devices in the PC.

spam Unsolicited e-mails from both legitimate businesses and scammers that account for a huge percentage of traffic on the Internet.

spanned volume Volume that uses space on multiple dynamic disks.

SPD (serial presence detect) Information stored on a RAM chip that describes the speed, capacity, and other aspects of the RAM chip.

speaker Device that outputs sound by using magnetically driven diaphragm.

sprite Bitmapped graphic such as a BMP file used by early 3-D games to create the 3-D world.

spyware Software that runs in the background of a user's PC, sending information about browsing habits back to the company that installed it onto the system.

SRAM (static RAM) RAM that uses a flip-flop circuit rather than the typical transistor/capacitor of DRAM to hold a bit of information. SRAM does not need to be refreshed and is faster than regular DRAM. Used primarily for cache.

SSD (solid-state drive) Data storage device that uses flash memory to store data.

SSH (Secure Shell) Terminal emulation program similar to Telnet, except that the entire connection is encrypted. Uses port 22.

SSID (service set identifier) Parameter used to define a wireless network; otherwise known as the network name.

SSL (Secure Sockets Layer) Security protocol used by a browser to connect to secure Web sites.

standard user account User account in Windows Vista that has limited access to a system. Accounts of this type cannot alter system files, cannot install new programs, and cannot edit some settings by using the Control Panel without supplying an administrator password. Replaces the Limited accounts in Windows XP.

standouts Small connectors that screw into a computer case. A motherboard is then placed on top of the standouts, and small screws are used to secure it to the standouts.

star bus A hybrid network topology where the computers all connect to a central bus—a switch—but otherwise take the form of a star topology.

star topology Network topology where the computers on the network connect to a central wiring point, usually called a hub.

Start button Button on the Windows taskbar that enables access to the Start menu.

Start menu Menu that can be accessed by clicking the Start button on the Windows taskbar. Enables you to see all programs loaded on the system and to start them.

Startup Repair A one-stop, do-it-all troubleshooting option that performs a number of boot repairs automatically.

static charge eliminator Device used to remove a static charge.

static IP address Manually set IP address that will not change.

stealth virus Virus that uses various methods to hide from antivirus software.

stepper motor One of two methods used to move actuator arms in a hard drive. (*See also* voice coil motor.)

stereo Describes recording tracks from two sources (microphones) as opposed to monaural, which uses one source.

stick Generic name for a single physical SIMM, RIMM, or DIMM.

STP (shielded twisted pair) Cabling for networks, composed of pairs of wires twisted around each other at specific intervals. Twists serve to reduce interference (also called crosstalk)—the more twists, the less interference. Cable has metallic shielding to protect the wires from external interference.

stranded core A cable that uses a bundle of tiny wire strands to transmit signals. Stranded core is not quite as good a conductor as solid core, but it will stand up to substantial handling without breaking.

stream loading Process a program uses to constantly download updated information.

streaming media Broadcast of data that is played on your computer and immediately discarded.

stripe set Two or more drives in a group that are used for a striped volume.

striped volume RAID 0 volumes. Data is spread across two drives for increased speed.

strong password Password containing at least eight characters, including letters, numbers, and punctuation symbols.

structured cabling Standards defined by TIA/EIA that define methods of organizing the cables in a network for ease of repair and replacement.

stylus Pen-like input device used for pen-based computing.

subnet mask Value used in TCP/IP settings to divide the IP address of a host into its component parts: network ID and host ID.

sub-pixels Tiny liquid crystal molecules arranged in rows and columns between polarizing filters used in LCDs.

subwoofer Powerful speaker capable of producing extremely low-frequency sounds.

Super I/O chip Chip specially designed to control low-speed, legacy devices such as the keyboard, mouse, and serial and parallel ports.

SuperSpeed USB A fast form of USB, with speeds up to 5 Gbps. Also called USB 3.0.

surge suppressor Inexpensive device that protects your computer from voltage spikes.

SVGA (super video graphics array) Video display mode of 800 × 600.

swap file *See* page file.

swipe Gesture for mobile devices where you hold your finger on the screen and slide it across the screen, either right to left or top to bottom, depending on the type of application.

switch Device that filters and forwards traffic based on some criteria. A bridge and a router are both examples of switches.

SXGA Video display mode of 1280 × 1024.

SXGA+ Video display mode of 1400 × 1050.

sync The process of keeping files on mobile devices up to date with the versions on desktop PCs or over the Internet.

synchronize *See* sync.

syntax The proper way to write a command-line command so that it functions and does what it's supposed to do.

Sysprep (System Preparation Tool) Windows tool that makes cloning of systems easier by making it possible to undo portions of the installation.

system BIOS Primary set of BIOS stored on an EPROM or flash ROM chip on the motherboard. Defines the BIOS for all the assumed hardware on the motherboard, such as keyboard controller, floppy drive, basic video, and RAM.

system bus speed Speed at which the CPU and the rest of the PC operates; set by the system crystal.

system crystal Crystal that provides the speed signals for the CPU and the rest of the system.

system disk Any device with a functional operating system.

system fan Any fan controlled by the motherboard but not directly attached to the CPU.

System File Checker *See* sfc.

System Monitor Utility that can evaluate and monitor system resources, such as CPU usage and memory usage.

System Protection Feature in Windows Vista/7 that enables you to restore any previous version of a file or folder.

system resources In classic terms, the I/O addresses, IRQs, DMA channels, and memory addresses. Also refers to other computer essentials such as hard drive space, system RAM, and processor speed.

System Restore Utility in Windows that enables you to return your PC to a recent working configuration when something goes wrong. System Restore enables you to select a restore point and then returns the computer's system settings to the way they were at that restore point—all without affecting your personal files or e-mail.

system ROM ROM chip that stores the system BIOS.

system setup utility *See* CMOS setup program.

System Tools Menu containing tools such as System Information and Disk Defragmenter, accessed by selecting Start | Programs or All Programs | Accessories | System Tools.

system tray Contains icons representing background processes and the system clock. Located by default at the right edge of the Windows taskbar. Accurately called the notification area.

system unit Main component of the PC, in which the CPU, RAM, CD-ROM, and hard drive reside. All other devices—the keyboard, mouse, and monitor—connect to the system unit.

T568A Wiring standard for Ethernet cable.

T568B Wiring standard for Ethernet cable.

tablet A mobile device consisting of a large touchscreen, enabling the user to browse the Web, view media, or even play games.

Tablet PC Small portable computer distinguished by the use of a touchscreen with stylus and handwriting recognition as the primary modes of input. Also the name of the Windows XP–based operating system designed to run on such systems.

tailgating Form of infiltration and social engineering that involves following someone else through a door as if you belong in the building.

Take Ownership Special permission allowing users to seize control of a file or folder and potentially prevent others from accessing the file/folder.

tap Touchscreen gesture where you press a spot on the screen to start an app or interact with a running app.

Task Manager Shows all running programs, including hidden ones, and is accessed by pressing CTRL-SHIFT-ESC. Able to

shut down an unresponsive application that refuses to close normally.

Task Scheduler Windows Vista/7's utility enabling users to set tasks to run automatically at certain times.

taskbar Contains the Start button, the system tray, the Quick Launch toolbar, and buttons for running applications. Located by default at the bottom of the desktop.

tasklist A command-line version of the Task Manager.

TCP/IP (Transmission Control Protocol/Internet Protocol) Communication protocols developed by the U.S. Department of Defense to enable dissimilar computers to share information over a network.

tech toolkit Tools a PC tech should never be without, including a Phillips-head screwdriver, a pair of tweezers, a flat-head screwdriver, a hemostat, a Torx wrench, a parts retriever, and a nut driver or two.

telecommunications room Area where all the cabling from individual PCs in a network runs to.

telephone scams Social engineering attack in which the attacker makes a phone call to someone in an organization to gain information.

Telnet Terminal emulation program for TCP/IP networks that allows one machine to control another as if the user were sitting in front of it. Uses port 23.

Temporal Key Integrity Protocol (TKIP) Deprecated encryption standard that provided a new encryption key for every sent packet.

tera- Prefix that usually stands for the binary number 1,099,511,627,776 (2^{40}). When used for mass storage, it's often shorthand for 1 trillion bytes.

terminal Dumb device connected to a mainframe or computer network that acts as a point for entry or retrieval of information.

terminal emulation Software that enables a PC to communicate with another computer or network as if the PC were a specific type of hardware terminal.

termination Using terminating resistors to prevent packet reflection on a network cable.

terminator Resistor that is plugged into the end of a bus cable to absorb the excess electrical signal, preventing it from bouncing back when it reaches the end of the wire. Terminators are used with coaxial cable and on the ends of SCSI chains. RG-58 coaxial cable requires resistors with a 50-ohm

impedance. Also, a humanoid robot from the future designed by Skynet to destroy all human life. He'll be back.

test the theory Attempt to resolve the issue by either confirming the theory and learning what needs to be done to fix the problem, or by not confirming the theory and forming a new one or escalating. (One of the steps a technician uses to solve a problem.)

texture Small picture that is tiled over and over again on walls, floors, and other surfaces to create the 3-D world.

TFT (thin film transistor) Type of LCD screen. (*See also* active matrix.)

theory of probable cause One possible reason why something is not working; a guess.

thermal compound Paste-like material with very high heat-transfer properties. Applied between the CPU and the cooling device, it ensures the best possible dispersal of heat from the CPU. Also called heat dope.

thermal printer Printers that use heated printheads to create high-quality images on special or plain paper.

thermal unit Combination heat sink and fan designed for BTX motherboards; blows hot air out the back of the case instead of just into the case.

thick client CompTIA's name for a standard desktop computer.

thin client A system designed to handle only very basic applications with an absolute minimum amount of hardware required by the operating system.

thread Smallest logical division of a single program.

throttling Power reduction/thermal control capability allowing CPUs to slow down during low activity or high heat build-up situations. Intel's version is known as SpeedStep, AMD's as PowerNow!.

throw Size of the image a projector displays at a certain distance from the screen.

TIA/EIA (Telecommunications Industry Association/Electronic Industries Alliance) Trade organization that provides standards for network cabling and other electronics.

tiers Levels of Internet providers, ranging from the Tier 1 backbones to Tier 3 regional networks.

timbre Qualities that differentiate the same note played on different instruments.

tone generator *See* toner.

tone probe *See* toner.

toner A fine powder made up of plastic particles bonded to iron particles, used to create the text and images on a laser printer. Also, generic term for two devices used together—a tone generator and a tone locator (probe)—to trace cables by sending an electrical signal along a wire at a particular frequency. The tone locator then emits a sound when it distinguishes that frequency.

toner cartridge Object used to store the toner in a laser printer. (*See also* laser printer, toner.)

topology The way computers connect to each other in a network.

touch interface The primary user interface on modern mobile devices where keys are replaced with tactile interaction.

touchpad Flat, touch-sensitive pad that serves as a pointing device for most laptops.

touchscreen Monitor with a type of sensing device across its face that detects the location and duration of contact, usually by a finger or stylus.

tracert Command-line utility used to follow the path a packet takes between two hosts. Also called traceroute.

traces Small electrical connections embedded in a circuit board.

track Area on a hard drive platter where data is stored. A group of tracks with the same diameter is called a cylinder.

trackball Pointing device distinguished by a ball that is rolled with the fingers.

TrackPoint IBM's pencil eraser–sized joystick used in place of a mouse on laptops.

transfer corona Thin wire, usually protected by other thin wires, that applies a positive charge to the paper during the laser printing process, drawing the negatively charged toner particles off of the drum and onto the paper. Newer printers accomplish the same feat using a *transfer roller* that draws the toner onto the paper.

transparency Effect in the Aero desktop environment (Windows Vista/7) that makes the edges of windows transparent.

triad Group of three phosphors—red, green, blue—in a CRT.

Trojan horse Program that does something other than what the user who runs the program thinks it will do. Used to disguise malicious code.

troubleshooting theory Steps a technician uses to solve a problem: identify the problem, establish a theory of probable cause, test the theory, establish and implement a plan of action, verify functionality, and document findings.

Trusted Platform Module A hardware platform for the acceleration of cryptographic functions and the secure storage of associated information.

tunneling Creating an encrypted link between two programs on two separate computers.

TV tuner Typically an add-on device that allows users to watch television on a computer.

TWAIN (technology without an interesting name) Programming interface that enables a graphics application, such as a desktop publishing program, to activate a scanner, frame grabber, or other image-capturing device.

U (Units) The unique height measurement used with equipment racks; 1 U equals 1.75 inches.

UAC (User Account Control) Windows Vista and Windows 7 feature that enables standard accounts to do common tasks and provides a permissions dialog box when standard and administrator accounts do certain things that could potentially harm the computer (such as attempt to install a program).

UART (universal asynchronous receiver/transmitter) Device that turns serial data into parallel data. The cornerstone of serial ports and modems.

UDF (universal data format) Replaced the ISO-9660 formats, enabling any operating system and optical drive to read UDF formatted disks.

UEFI (Unified Extensible Firmware Interface) Consortium of companies that established the UEFI standard that replaced the original EFI standard.

Ultra DMA Hard drive technology that enables drives to use direct memory addressing. Ultra DMA mode 3 drives—called ATA/33—have data transfer speeds up to 33 MBps. Mode 4 and 5 drives—called ATA/66 and ATA/100, respectively—transfer data at up to 66 MBps for mode 4 and 100 MBps for mode 5. Mode 6 pushed the transfer rate to 133 MBps. Modes 4, 5, and 6 require an 80-wire cable and a compatible controller to achieve these data transfer rates.

Ultrabook Thin, powerful laptop powered by Intel processors and built according to the Intel design specification. Competes directly with the Apple Mac Air.

unattended installation A type of OS installation where special scripts perform all the OS setup duties without human intervention.

unauthorized access Anytime a person accesses resources in an unauthorized way. This access may or may not be malicious.

UNC (Universal Naming Convention) Describes any shared resource in a network using the convention \\<*server name*>\<*name of shared resource*>.

Unicode 16-bit code that covers every character of the most common languages, plus several thousand symbols.

unsigned driver Driver that has not gone through the Windows Certification Program to ensure compatibility. The Windows Certification Program was formerly know as the Windows Hardware Quality Labs and the Microsoft Windows Logo Program.

UPC (Universal Product Code) Bar code used to track inventory.

update Individual fixes for Windows that come out fairly often, on the order of once a week or so.

Upgrade Advisor The first process that runs on the Windows XP installation CD. It examines your hardware and installed software (in the case of an upgrade) and provides a list of devices and software that are known to have issues with XP. It can also be run separately from the Windows XP installation, from the Windows XP CD. The Upgrade Advisor is also available for Windows Vista and Windows 7.

upgrade installation Installation of Windows on top of an earlier installed version, thus inheriting all previous hardware and software settings.

UPS (uninterruptible power supply) Device that supplies continuous clean power to a computer system the whole time the computer is on. Protects against power outages and sags.

URL (uniform resource locator) An address that defines the location of a resource on the Internet. URLs are used most often in conjunction with HTML and the World Wide Web.

USB (universal serial bus) General-purpose serial interconnect for keyboards, printers, joysticks, and many other devices. Enables hot-swapping of devices.

USB host controller Integrated circuit that is usually built into the chipset and controls every USB device that connects to it.

USB hub Device that extends a single USB connection to two or more USB ports, almost always directly from one of the USB ports connected to the root hub.

USB root hub Part of the host controller that makes the physical connection to the USB ports.

USB thumb drive Flash memory device that uses the standard USB connection.

user account Container that identifies a user to an application, operating system, or network, including name, password, user name, groups to which the user belongs, and other information based on the user and the OS being used. Usually defines the rights and roles a user plays on a system.

User Accounts applet Windows XP (and later versions) applet for creating and modifying user accounts.

user interface Visual representation of the computer on the monitor that makes sense to the people using the computer, through which the user can interact with the computer. This can be a graphical user interface (GUI) like Windows 7 or a command-line interface like the Windows PowerShell or the Recovery Console.

user profiles Settings that correspond to a specific user account and may follow users regardless of the computers where they log on. These settings enable the user to have customized environment and security settings.

User's Files Windows Vista and Windows 7 default location for content specific to each user account on a computer. It is divided into several folders such as Documents, Pictures, Music, and Video. Similar to My Documents folder structure in Windows XP.

Users and Passwords applet Windows 2000 application that allowed management of user accounts and passwords.

Users group List of local users not allowed, among other things, to edit the Registry or access critical system files. They can create groups, but can only manage the groups they create.

USMT (User State Migration Tool) Advanced application for file and settings transfer of multiple users.

UTP (unshielded twisted pair) Popular type of cabling for telephone and networks, composed of pairs of wires twisted around each other at specific intervals. The twists serve to reduce interference (also called crosstalk). The more twists, the less interference. Unlike its cousin, STP, UTP cable has no metallic shielding to protect the wires from external interference. 1000BaseT uses UTP, as do many other networking technologies. UTP is available in a variety of grades, called categories, as follows:

CAT 1 UTP Regular analog phone lines—not used for data communications.
CAT 2 UTP Supports speeds up to 4 megabits per second.
CAT 3 UTP Supports speeds up to 16 megabits per second.
CAT 4 UTP Supports speeds up to 20 megabits per second.
CAT 5 UTP Supports speeds up to 100 megabits per second.
CAT 5e UTP Supports speeds up to 1000 megabits per second.
CAT 6 UTP Supports speeds up to 10 gigabits per second.
CAT 6a UTP Supports speeds up to 10 gigabits per second.

V standards Standards established by CCITT for modem manufacturers to follow (voluntarily) to ensure compatible speeds, compression, and error correction.

vendor specific Stores that only sell products from one manufacturer, like the Apple store.

verify full system functionality Making sure that a problem has been resolved and will not return. (One of the steps a technician uses to solve a problem.)

vertices Used in the second generation of 3-D rendering; have a defined X, Y, and Z position in a 3-D world.

VESA (Video Electronics Standards Association) Consortium of computer manufacturers that standardize improvements to common IBM PC components. VESA is responsible for the Super VGA video standard and the VLB bus architecture.

VGA (video graphics array) Standard for the video graphics adapter that was built into IBM's PS/2 computer. It supports 16 colors in a 640 × 480 pixel video display.

video capture Computer jargon for the recording of video information, such as TV shows or movies.

video card Expansion card that works with the CPU to produce the images displayed on your computer's display.

video display *See* monitor.

virtual machine (VM) A complete environment for a guest operating system to function as though that operating system were installed on its own computer.

virtual machine manager (VMM) *See* hypervisor.

virus Program that can make a copy of itself without your necessarily being aware of it. Some viruses can destroy or damage files. The best protection is to back up files regularly.

virus definition or data file Files that enable the virus protection software to recognize the viruses on your system and clean them. These files should be updated often. They are also called signature files, depending on the virus protection software in use.

virus shield Passive monitoring of a computer's activity, checking for viruses only when certain events occur.

VIS (viewable image size) Measurement of the viewable image that is displayed by a CRT rather than a measurement of the CRT itself.

voice coil motor One of two methods used to move actuator arms in a hard drive. (*See also* stepper motor.)

VoIP (Voice over Internet Protocol) Collection of protocols that make voice calls over a data network possible.

volatile Memory that must have constant electricity to retain data. Alternatively, any programmer six hours before deadline after a nonstop, 48-hour coding session, running on nothing but caffeine and sugar.

volts (V) Measurement of the pressure of the electrons passing through a wire, or voltage.

volume Physical unit of a storage medium, such as tape reel or disk pack, that is capable of having data recorded on it and subsequently read. Also, a contiguous collection of cylinders or blocks on a disk that are treated as a separate unit.

volume boot sector First sector of the first cylinder of each partition; stores information important to its partition, such as the location of the operating system boot files.

voucher Means of getting a discount on the CompTIA A+ exams.

VPN (Virtual Private Network) Encrypted connection over the Internet between a computer or remote network and a private network.

VRM (voltage regulator module) Small card supplied with some CPUs to ensure that the CPU gets correct voltage. This type of card, which must be used with a motherboard specially designed to accept it, is not commonly seen today.

VRR (vertical refresh rate) The amount of time it takes for a CRT to draw a complete screen. This value is measured in hertz, or cycles per second. Most modern CRTs have a VRR of 60 Hz or better.

wait state Occurs when the CPU has to wait for RAM to provide code. Also known as pipeline stall.

WAP (wireless access point) Device that centrally connects wireless network nodes.

wattage (watts or W) Measurement of the amps and volts needed for a particular device to function.

wave table synthesis Technique that supplanted FM synthesis, wherein recordings of actual instruments or other sounds are embedded in the sound card as WAV files. When a particular note from a particular instrument or voice is requested, the sound processor grabs the appropriate prerecorded WAV file from its memory and adjusts it to match the specific sound and timing requested.

Web browser Program designed to retrieve, interpret, and display Web pages.

Web server A computer that stores and shares the files that make up Web sites.

webcam PC camera most commonly used for Internet video.

Welcome screen Logon screen for Windows XP. Enables users to select their particular user account by clicking on their user picture.

WEP (Wired Equivalent Privacy) Wireless security protocol that uses a standard 40-bit encryption to scramble data packets. Does not provide complete end-to-end encryption and is vulnerable to attack.

Wi-Fi Common name for the IEEE 802.11 wireless Ethernet standard.

Wi-Fi Protected Setup (WPS) A standard included on many WAPs and clients to make secure connections easier to configure.

wide area network (WAN) A widespread group of computers connected using long-distance technologies.

wildcard Character used during a search to represent search criteria. For instance, searching for *.doc will return a list of all files with a .doc extension, regardless of the filename. The * is the wildcard in that search.

WiMAX (Worldwide Interoperability for Microwave Access) An updated wireless standard (also known as 802.16) with a range of up to 30 miles.

Windows 2000 Windows version that succeeded Windows NT; it came in both Professional and Server versions.

Windows 7 Version of Windows; comes in many different editions for home and office use, but does not have a Server edition.

Windows 7 Compatibility Center Microsoft's current Web site that lists the hardware and software that work with Windows 7.

Windows 8 Version of Windows noted for the Metro interface. Used for desktop and portable PCs and for mobile devices.

Windows 9*x* Term used collectively for Windows 95, Windows 98, Windows 98 SE, and Windows Me.

Windows Certification Program A rigorous testing program for hardware manufacturers. Hardware and drivers that survive the testing get to wear the *Designed for Windows* logo. The drivers get a digital signature that says Microsoft tested them and found all was well.

Windows Easy Transfer Windows Vista/7's method of transferring files and settings to a new PC.

Windows Explorer Windows utility that enables you to manipulate files and folders stored on the drives in your computer.

Windows Logo'd Products List List of products that have passed the Microsoft Windows Logo Program and are compatible with Windows operating system. Formerly called the Hardware Compatibility List (or HCL).

Windows NT Precursor to Windows 2000, XP, Vista, and 7, which introduced many important features (such as HAL and NTFS) used in all later versions of Windows.

Windows PowerShell Command-line tool included with Windows 7 and available for earlier versions from Microsoft. Offers a number of powerful scripting tools for automating changes both on local machines and over networks.

Windows Preinstallation Environment (WinPE) The installation program for Windows Vista and 7.

Windows Recovery Environment (WinRE) An special set of tools in the Windows Vista/7 setup that enables you to access troubleshooting and repair features.

Windows Sidebar User interface feature in Windows Vista that enables users to place various gadgets, such as clocks, calendars, and other utilities, on the right side of their desktop.

Windows Update Microsoft application used to keep Windows operating systems up to date with the latest patches or enhancements. (*See* Automatic Updates.)

Windows Vista Version of Windows; comes in many different editions for home and office use, but does not have a Server edition.

Windows XP Version of Windows that replaced both the entire Windows 9*x* line and Windows 2000; does not have a Server version.

Windows XP Mode A Windows XP virtual machine that ships with Professional, Enterprise, and Ultimate editions of Windows 7 to enable users to run programs that don't work on Windows 7.

work area In a basic structured cabling network, often simply an office or cubicle that potentially contains a PC attached to the network.

workgroup A simple, decentralized network that Windows PCs are configured to use by default.

worm Very special form of virus. Unlike other viruses, a worm does not infect other files on the computer. Instead, it replicates by making copies of itself on other systems on a network by taking advantage of security weaknesses in networking protocols.

WPA (Wi-Fi Protected Access) Wireless security protocol that uses encryption key integrity-checking and EAP and is designed to improve on WEP's weaknesses.

WPA 2 (Wi-Fi Protected Access 2) Wireless security protocol, also known as IEEE 802.11i. Uses the Advanced Encryption Standard (AES) and replaces WPA.

WQUXGA Video display mode of 2560 × 1600.

wrapper *See* container file.

WSXGA Video display mode of 1440 × 900.

WSXGA+ Video display mode of 1680 × 1050.

WUXGA Video display mode of 1920 × 1200.

WVGA Video display mode of 800 × 480.

WWW (World Wide Web) System of Internet servers that supports documents formatted in HTML and related protocols. Can be accessed by applications that use HTTP and HTTPS, such as Web browsers.

www.comptia.org CompTIA's Web site.

WXGA Video display mode of 1280 × 800.

x64 Describes 64-bit operating systems and software.

x86 Describes 32-bit operating systems and software.

xcopy command Command in the command-line interface used to copy multiple directories at once, which the copy command could not do.

xD (Extreme Digital) picture card Very small flash media card format.

Xeon Line of Intel CPUs designed for servers.

XGA (extended graphics array) Video display mode of 1024 × 768.

XPS (XML Paper Specification) print path Improved printing subsystem included in Windows Vista. Has enhanced color management and better print layout fidelity.

XT bus *See* PC bus.

ZIF (zero insertion force) socket Socket for CPUs that enables insertion of a chip without the need to apply pressure. Intel promoted this socket with its overdrive upgrades. The chip drops effortlessly into the socket's holes, and a small lever locks it in.

how to take, 8–9

mapping to exam objectives, 714–727

exFAT, 118

expansion cards, replacing in portable computers, 571–572

expansion slots, portable computers

overview of, 549

PC cards, 549–551

ExpressCard, 550–551

extended partitions, 103–104

Extended Unique Identifier, 64-bit (EUI-64), IPv6 addresses, 476

extensions, file, 42, 340–341

F

F-type connectors, for coaxial cable, 453

factory recovery partitions, 107

fans, managing heat in portable computers, 562

Fast User Switching, 254

FAT (file allocation table)

bad-sector marker and, 112

clustering and, 111

creating partitions and volumes, 128

data structures, 110

end-of-file marker (FFFF) and, 111–112

FAT 32, 115

FAT 64, 118–119

fragmentation and, 113–115

history of Windows OSs and, 22

NTFS preferred in terms of security, 636–637

FDISK (Linux OSs), as partitioning utility, 107

FDISK (Windows OSs), as partitioning utility, 107

FFFF (end-of-file marker), FAT (file allocation table) and, 111–112

fiber optic cable, 451–452

field replaceable units (FRUs), 570–573, 708

file allocation table. *See* FAT (file allocation table)

file allocation units, 111

file associations, 212–213

file extensions, 42, 340–341

file formats

ASCII, 341–342

Unicode, 342

file permissions, NTFS, 262–263

file recovery software, 415

file sharing

networking and, 530

simple file sharing, 267–268

in Windows Vista/7, 269–270

in Windows XP, 266–267

file systems

FAT 16, 111–115

FAT 32, 115

FAT 64, 118–119

FAT (file allocation table), 110–111

formatting hard drives, 101, 110

NTFS, 116–118

filenames

in DOS and Windows OSs, 340–341

renaming files, 354

using wildcards with, 354

files

associations, 212–213

attributes, 317–318, 351–353

backing up, 61

compressing directory files (compact command), 362–363

copying and moving, 42–43, 355–357

copying in multi-directory jobs (xcopy command), 357–358

copying with robocopy command, 358

deleting (del command), 355

encrypting, 271–272

encrypting with cipher command, 363–364

formats, 341–342

manipulating from command-line, 350–351

missing files or file versions, 413

naming, 340–341, 354

NTFS permissions, 262–263

organizing, 44–45, 343

path for, 343

scanning and repairing system files, 360–361

sharing, 266–270, 530

showing/hiding, 43–44

transferring to new computer, 63

Files and Settings Transfer Wizard (Windows XP)

backing up existing data prior to new install or upgrade, 164

migration of data and users to new system, 197–200

System Tools menu, 63

fingerprints, as access control technique, 635

fire extinguishers, classes of, 94

firewalls

hardware firewalls, 657–660

overview of, 657

software firewalls, 660–665

FireWire (IEEE 1394), 551–552

firmware upgrade, 89–90

first-person shooters (FPSs), 3-D games, 434

flash-memory, storage slots on portable computers, 551

Flash ROM, for updating system BIOS, 89–90

Flip 3D, Aero desktop and, 36

floppy disks, boot sectors on, 87

Fluke MicroScanner, for troubleshooting cable, 522

FN (Function) key

for cycling through display options, 547

on keyboards, 537

folder permissions, NTFS, 262

folders

backing up, 61

copying and moving files to/from, 42–44

copying with robocopy command, 358